MO

GROU

# MODELS OF INPATIENT
# GROUP PSYCHOTHERAPY

VIRGINIA BRABENDER

AND

APRIL FALLON

AMERICAN PSYCHOLOGICAL ASSOCIATION

WASHINGTON, DC

Published by the
American Psychological Association
750 First Street, NE
Washington, DC 20002

Copies may be ordered from
APA Order Department
P.O. Box 2710
Hyattsville, MD 20784

This book was typeset in Palatino by Impressions, A Division of Edwards Brothers, Inc., Madison, WI.

Printer: BookCrafters, Chelsea, MI
Cover designer: Grafik Communications, Alexandria, VA
Technical/Production Editor: Cynthia L. Fulton

**Library of Congress Cataloging-in-Publication Data**

Brabender, Virginia.
    Models of Inpatient Group Psychotherapy / Virginia Brabender
and April Fallon
        p. cm.
    Includes bibliographic references and index.
    ISBN 1-55798-174-4 (acid-free paper)
    1. Group psychotherapy. 2. Psychiatric hospital care.
I. Brabender, Virginia. II. Fallon, April.
[DNLM: 1. Psychotherapy, Group—methods. VM430 M689]
RC488.M63 1992
616.89'152—dc20
DNLM/DLC
for Library of Congress                                    92-17871
                                                                CIP

*Printed in the United States of America*
*First edition*

Dedicated with love
To our husbands, Arthur and Rao
and
To our sons, Jacob and Emile

# Contents

Rx Use Interlocking Comparison
6/9/93    3-4
          4-5
          5-6
          6-7
          7-8
          8-9
          (><)
          Cut

# Foreword

I n the late 1960s, a number of colleagues and I dreamed of developing a training program that would integrate the major theories and modes of psychotherapy. Experience and age have taught us how impossible, even undesirable, that goal was, especially within the confines of a training program. Wisely, Brabender and Fallon set and achieve a more pragmatic, but nonetheless formidable, goal in this text. In their presentation of the major models of group psychotherapy, they acknowledge and analyze the many differences among the models, including areas of incompatibility of theory, goals, and therapist technique, noting how and under what circumstances each model may be effective. This approach leaves therapists free to choose which model to use or what aspects of another model to incorporate within their primary model to make it more effective. Although the authors do not attempt to integrate the models, they do note a number of important areas of similarity, including the therapeutic value of firm internal and external group boundaries; clear group and individual goals; cognitive frameworks within which patients can organize and understand their emotional experiences; "warmth, responsivity, and a moderate degree of transparency" in the therapist; and a primary focus on the here-and-now. In brief, despite considerable diversity and, even, incompatibility of method and theory, important commonalities emerge.

The authors show outstanding sensitivity to the effects of the current ethos created by limited resources, managed care, and rapid patient turnover on the practice of inpatient group psychotherapy and on the selection of a group therapy model. Not surprisingly, they also pay special attention to the interactions between and among therapy groups and the various contexts in which they exist: the hospital, the units on which the groups meet and the patients live, the primary theory and practice orientations of the hospital, and so on. Clearly, they have worked and lived with the units, groups, and theories about which they write.

One of the most striking things about this book is the fair and even-handed manner in which the authors describe, demonstrate, and assess the various models of group therapy. Given the diversity of the models examined and the fact that the authors presumably have particular perspectives of their own, this is a major achievement. Each model is described in satisfying detail: Theoretical underpinnings are discussed, including their antecedents and their relations to other models; research related to each model is reviewed; and extensive, rich, and varied clinical examples demonstrate how each model works. The dispassionate critiques of each model, outlining what each can and cannot offer to which patients and in what contexts, will not only assist the practitioner but will help proponents of the various models better understand and respect each other.

Brabender and Fallon have written the most thorough overview of the theory and practice of inpatient group psychotherapy to date. Most of what they discuss is also relevant to outpatient group therapists, and nongroup therapists will find much that is helpful in the reviews of the major psychological theories of psychopathology and treatment. Teachers and supervisors of residents and interns will find this an exceptional and much needed book.

This work signals the beginning of the end of a strange enigma. Inpatient group psychotherapy is arguably the longest standing form of group psychotherapy. Yet, despite its relatively long history, it has been written about, researched, and understood less than have most other forms of therapy. As Brabender and Fallon note, most research and technical writing about inpatient group psychotherapy has taken place in the past 15 years. Additionally, although inpatient group psychotherapy is one of the most complex and difficult forms of treatment practiced, it is frequently practiced by the least experienced clinicians. In so effectively pulling together the major perspectives and practices in the field, this text will do much to improve mental health professionals' knowledge and appreciation of inpatient group psychotherapy. It should do much to encourage further research and a willingness among senior clinicians to practice this mode of treatment and to train others in its art and science.

CECIL RICE, PHD
EXECUTIVE DIRECTOR
BOSTON INSITUTE FOR PSYCHOTHERAPY
BOSTON, MA

# Preface

For many years we have been involved with conducting inpatient group psychotherapy and training inpatient group psychotherapists. From leading group psychotherapy in a variety of inpatient settings, we became convinced that there exists no model that is applicable to all inpatient situations. The group exists within a context that can either compromise or enhance any particular model's efficacy. For example, we had the opportunity to do co-therapy in an eight-session closed-ended group at Friends Hospital, a private psychiatric hospital in Philadelphia. The group was composed of members from eight different units. Initially, we attempted to use an interpersonal approach in which members were encouraged to provide each other with feedback on their behavior in the group. We found that the closed-ended aspect of the group enabled the group to undergo a developmental process, which is unusual in the typical inpatient group because of its high level of membership flux. We also discovered that when these developmental phenomena were ignored, the efficacy of the group was compromised. This experience led to our construction of a developmental model that integrates developmental, systems, and interpersonal perspectives.

In every inpatient setting, there are certain fixed features of the setting that will render some models more effective than others. If practitioners are aware of the range of models currently available in the field and are cognizant of the enhancing or limiting features of the setting, they are more likely to find a group therapy model that fits well with their setting. The goal of our text is to develop such an awareness.

We have noted that there are few comparative analyses of the different approaches. Within the existing literature, practitioners have been given little assistance in recognizing the important ways in which these approaches differ from one another, particularly ways that may relate to the approaches' relative degrees of appropriateness for different settings. Exacerbating this problem is that model designers themselves, although sometimes describing inclusionary and exclusionary criteria for group members, do not elucidate the contextual features (e.g., philosophy of the unit) that are necessary for successful application of the model. In fact, sometimes model builders write in a monotheistic tone; they assume that, rather than selecting a model to fit the setting, the practitioner can somehow alter the setting to conform to the demands of the model. Throughout this text, we attempt to differentiate the models from one another particularly on variables relevant to the selection of a model.

We feel that not only would the practitioner be assisted by a book presenting and comparing models of inpatient psychotherapy groups but so, too, would students seeking to familiarize themselves with the basics of this modality. Both of us have been involved with training nursing and social work students, psychology interns, and psychiatry residents in group therapy. In conducting seminars in group psychotherapy for psychology interns and psychiatry residents, we found that they frequently complained that many of the seminal articles on particular approaches assumed a specialized background on the part of the reader that they had not yet acquired. The trainees also routinely lamented that many articles on different approaches lacked clinical illustrations that would enable them to understand both at a theoretical and at a "hands-on" level how to conduct group psychotherapy with specific interventions.

We have undertaken this text to assist both the inpatient therapist in discovering an appropriate model for his or her setting and the student in seeking an exposure to a range of models. In this book, we present the major models we believe are frequently used in inpatient group psychotherapy today. (More specific criteria for our selection of models are presented in chapter 1.) To facilitate the reader's comparison of the models with one another, we have followed a consistent outline for all of the models. Particularly for the beginning-level inpatient group psychotherapist, we have included an extended clinical example of each model. We have also attempted to characterize the context in which each model is likely to flourish.

As psychologists who "grew up" with the Boulder practitioner–scientist model, we feel that no clinical presentation could be complete without attention to the empirical viability of the models we describe. Hence, we have included a description of the research on each model (or elements of the model) and have attempted to suggest some of the major questions that could be elucidated through empirical inquiry. Given the paucity of comparative research on the models, any systematic efforts in this area would be of immense benefit to increasing the credibility of group therapy as a valuable component of inpatient treatment. We hope that our presentation will engender in the researcher a sensitivity to the systems factors that may differentially influence each model's efficacy.

VIRGINIA BRABENDER
APRIL FALLON

# Acknowledgments

T here are many people who assisted us on our long journey to the completion of this book. During the past year and a half, barely a day went by when we did not consult someone on some aspect or point that we were pursuing at the moment. Our family, friends, and colleagues were amazingly tolerant of our singular focus in life. For that we are very grateful.

A number of individuals deserve special mention. First, we thank the editorial staff of the American Psychological Association for their tremendous expertise in helping us to develop this text. Specifically, we thank Julia Frank-McNeil, Mary Lynn Skutley, Theodore J. Baroody, and Cynthia L. Fulton. We also thank our reviewers and consultants, who gave us invaluable suggestions on individual chapters. For their help on the object relations model and the developmental model, we thank Anne Alonso and Howard Kibel; on the interpersonal model, Cecil Rice; on the cognitive–behavioral model, Rick E. Ingram, Ronald Coleman, Kenneth Barber, Arthur Freeman, James Herbert; on the problem-solving model, Roy MacKenzie and George Spivack; and on the behavioral model, Kim Mueser. Of course, any remaining shortcomings of our text are our responsibility alone.

For their comments on a variety of chapters and in a variety of ways, we thank Joan Cooper, Elizabeth Fallon, Rachel Ginzberg, Mark Lowenthal, Dara Simenhoff, and LaVerne Zeigenfuss. We also thank our students and participants in our workshops who have allowed us to "try out" our material on them and have offered useful reactions. The secretarial assistance of Carol Bricklin and Lori Herman is also much appreciated.

Our respective institutions, Widener University and Eastern Pennsylvania Psychiatric Institute (EPPI) of the Medical College Hospitals, were very supportive of this project through grant money and otherwise. We also thank our supervisors, Jules Abrams, Director of the Institute for Graduate Clinical Psychology at Widener University, and Emil Coccaro, Director of Outpatient Services at EPPI, for their encouragement and many considerations along the way.

Finally, we express the deepest gratitude to our husbands and parents for their love and support during this project and always.

# I

# Theoretical and Practical Perspectives

# Introduction to Inpatient Group Psychotherapy

The field of group psychotherapy in its evolutionary process toward further differentiation has come to recognize the inpatient group as a special arena of treatment. In the early days of group psychotherapy, writings were characterized by an interest in differentiating group therapy from individual therapy. Early contributors to the inpatient literature such as Lazell (1921) and Marsh (1935) frequently provided a list of benefits conferred by group participation that were absent in individual treatment. Rather than focusing on the unique features of inpatients or certain populations, they seemed to be primarily interested in exploring the wonders of this new modality. During the second World War, Bion (1959), Foulkes (1948), and others invested considerable intellectual energy in the identification of those processes that are unique to groups. Although Bion studied both inpatient groups and training groups, he did not critically distinguish between them. The psychoanalytically oriented approaches to group psychotherapy that developed in the 1950s, which were originally developed for outpatient groups, were often applied to inpatients with little adaptation. Increasingly, there was a recognition in the field that the inpatient situation is radically different from the outpatient situation and warrants its own methodology (Frank, 1963). This recognition gave rise to the development of principles and techniques specifically designed for the inpatient setting. However, not until the 1980s were these principles and techniques organized into more formal categories that offered a fairly systematized integration of goals, intervention strategies, and the like. Some even referred to their contributions as *models* (e.g., Maxmen, 1984).

From the standpoint of this book, a model is a theoretical construct used as a shorthand to connote a guiding conceptual framework. Such a framework includes a set of assumptions about psychopathology and the processes effecting its alteration, a specification of goals for the psychotherapy group, and interventions that purportedly accomplish these goals. It may or may not include a theory of group process.

It is only recently that the field has acknowledged that special approaches must be designed for the inpatient setting. However, even now there are other reasons why the inpatient therapist is hindered from model use. One factor is the tendency of training opportunities to lag behind theoretical developments. Currently, many inpatient group psychotherapists receive their training in group therapy using the long-term outpatient group as the prototype of group work. They often apply these long-term approaches to their inpatient groups with only minor adaptations. An equally important factor is that the literature on the inpatient models that did develop in the 1980s is extremely scattered. The fact that these models have been neither presented in detail in one place nor compared on a set of common dimensions has hindered therapists in considering their relative merits. Finally, some of the characteristics of inpatients themselves may discourage the practitioner from applying a model. The needs of most inpatients are multifaceted. The typical inpatient could benefit from symptom alleviation, improvement in interpersonal relations, help in formulating discharge plans, and so on. Embracing a model invariably entails a delimitation of the objectives of the treatment. The therapist may see himself or herself as neglecting group members in some areas in which they undoubtedly and often direly need help.

## The Importance of Models

Although models have not played a prominent role in the history of inpatient group psychotherapy until recently, we believe that they are of utmost importance for the further development of this modality within the inpatient environment. Since the mid-1960s, outcome studies have compared the efficacy of essentially psychoanalytic groups, used with little modification from outpatient group psychotherapy, with that of highly structured groups that take into account the special needs of inpatient group members (Beutler, Frank, Schieber, Calvert, & Gaines, 1984; Kanas, Rogers, Kreth, Patterson, & Campbell, 1980; Pattison, Brissenden, & Wohl, 1967). Subjects in the structured groups did better than did those in psychoanalytically oriented groups that emphasized the expression of intense affect. Although these studies have been used primarily to demonstrate the inefficacy of a psychoanalytic approach, they also demonstrate that for a theoretical base to be useful, it must be applied with a recognition of the special features of the inpatient situation.

Of what advantage is the use of a model in an inpatient psychotherapy group? Why is it insufficient for the treatment to be guided by a few broad theoretical principles? There are a number of benefits that model use confers on the therapist and the group, particularly when the model has been specifically developed for the inpatient situation.

A first benefit of model use is its contribution of a system of meaning by which events in the group can be understood. Certainly, any group behavior can be understood from a plenitude of perspectives. A member's harsh criticism of another may be seen as a self-defeating social behavior, a projection of the criticizing member's unwanted parts, an avoidance of intimacy, a harbinger of the group's move into the fight/flight mode, and so on. The therapist's choice of a particular system of meaning determines behaviors and events attended to and enables the therapist to intervene systematically rather than haphazardly. That is, the therapist can plan an intervention that is consistent with the chosen system and test the success of the intervention on the basis of what that system would see as the sequelae of a successful intervention. Moreover, the adoption of an interpretive framework facilitates the formulation of timely interventions. The inexperienced therapist, in particular, is handicapped if before devising an intervention, he or she must first settle on an appropriate theoretical framework.

A consistent framework by which events in the group are understood is also beneficial because through it, members are able to see a thread of continuity in all of the therapist's interventions. The perception of a clear direction to the therapist's comments enhances members' sense that the group has a purpose. Moreover, when the therapist makes a commitment to a particular framework, he or she is able to make interventions with a greater sense of confidence and conviction than when he or she vacillates among different frames of reference. Emphasizing this point, Yalom (1983) wrote,

> By developing a cognitive framework that permits an ordering of all the inchoate events of therapy, the therapist experiences a sense of inner order and mastery — a sense that, if deeply felt, is automatically conveyed to patients and generates in them a corresponding sense of mastery and clarity. (p. 122)

A second benefit of model use is that it leads the therapist to limit and make more specific the goals he or she is pursuing. Both the reduction in the range of goals and their higher level of specificity makes their achievement more likely than if the goals are broad and vague. This function of models is of special importance given that the length of hospitalization has diminished considerably over the past two decades (Erickson, 1984; Kiesler & Simpkins, 1991), with patients' tenure in groups decreasing concomitantly. Generally, the therapist does not have time to pursue an ambitious set of goals. Although embracing a model means that some objectives that have great importance for inpatients may have to be abandoned, the therapist must keep in mind that group psychotherapy is only one of many modalities in which a patient participates during hospitalization. What is essential is that the treatment package as a totality addresses all of the patients' critical needs; it is not necessary (or possible) for one modality to do so.

A third benefit of model use is the provision of a ready set of interventions that are compatible with both the goals of the model and the meaning ascribed to events in the group by the model. Because the featured models of this text have been developed specifically for inpatient groups, they anticipate likely events that occur within this type of group and provide the therapist with strategies for approaching them. For example, almost all models included in this text recognize that psychotic material may enter the inpatient group whether the therapist has excluded psychotic persons from the group or not. Some models provide tactics for helping the therapist to intervene in relation to these manifestations in a way that is consistent with the goals of the group.

A model also confers benefits beyond the immediate effects of its application during the group sessions. The therapist's use of a model is likely to increase the therapist's ability to develop a "pro-group climate" on the unit (Rice & Rutan, 1981). A pro-group climate is one wherein the treatment is seen as a valuable component of the patient's treatment package and wherein all members of the treatment team strive to safeguard its successful operation. The therapist can much more readily engender support for the group when the goals and methods are sufficiently defined so that other staff can see where the group fits into the overall therapeutic strategy for a patient. Moreover, when the therapist can be highly specific about what the group can and cannot do, the treatment team is helped in understanding patients' reactions to the group and are less likely to be disappointed by the results of a patient's involvement in the group (e.g., a patient fails to show a diminution in symptoms when this, in fact, is not a goal of the group).

In this age of financial accountability and quality assurance monitoring, practitioners need to specify with a high level of precision what they are endeavoring to achieve with a patient at various points and to what extent they have achieved it. The concrete and articulated set of goals associated with each model provides the therapist with a framework for defining each member's work and thereby assists the therapist in this task.

Finally, the use of a well-delineated model facilitates research and training activities. With respect to research, the therapist's pursuit of a delimited set of goals and use of a specifiable set of techniques enable the evaluation of the comparative efficacy of that model in relation to other models not only by the primary exponent of the model but by other practitioner–scientists in other settings who, with a model in hand, are able to replicate the methodology. Moreover, the concrete description of goals permits the selection of outcome measures that are congruent with the kind of change that the interventions of the model are designed to effect. The use of a model is also helpful for training interns, residents, and others students. In the face of the complexity of events of an inpatient group, students are in particular need of a system of meaning with clear goals, methods of intervening, and means for determining whether their interventions are successful. The intense affect that often characterizes an inpatient group can be confusing and anxiety arousing to students. However, these disturbing feelings are kept in better moderation by students' possession of a cognitive frame to organize their reactions to the affect in the group.

## Factors to Consider in Model Selection

In the past 15 years, possibly in response to some of the factors we have mentioned—such as the reduced length of stay and the discovery from outcome studies that unstructured inpatient groups do not appear to aid inpatients—a number of inpatient models from a variety of theoretical viewpoints have been proposed. Existing models differ from one another in a variety of ways. They differ from one another in their underlying assumptions about psychopathology and change. For example, whereas some models assume that psychopathology is due to the presence of a deficit, others assume that intrapsychic conflict underlies psychological disorders (Kibel, 1992). However, a model is defined not only by its theoretical underpinnings but by the treatment context in which it is most effectively applied. In the past, how different treatment environments affect the relative efficacy of competitive models has been given little consideration. We will consider various aspects of the treatment environment to show that such consideration is amply warranted.

One important aspect of any treatment environment is the nature of the population served within the setting. The research literature gives strong indication that whether one model is more effective than another depends greatly on the population with which the model is applied. We consider two examples of this point. Coché, Cooper, and Petermann (1984) examined the relation between gender and type of group therapy model using a variety of dependent measures. They found that whereas male group members made greater gains in a problem-solving therapy, female group members derived more from an interpersonally oriented group (chapter 2 presents a more in-depth look at this study).

In a second study, Greene and Cole (1991) explored the potential interaction between level of personality organization, nature of the psychopathology, and the type of inpatient model used. Level of organization was varied through the inclusion of patients diagnosed with borderline personality disorder versus psychosis. The nature of the psychopathology was manipulated through the presence of group members with anaclitic versus introjective pathology. Anaclitic pathology is seen in difficulties in maintaining close, stable relationships with others. Introjective pathology manifests itself in the failure to enjoy an enduringly positive and cohesive sense of self. The group model was varied through the assignment of members to an unstructured, psychodynamic group versus a structured, task-oriented activity group. The investigators found that members' perceptions of themselves and the group were determined both by their level of organization and by the nature of their psychopathology. Whereas the borderline patients exhibited more favorable self-perceptions in the psychodynamic group, the psychotic patients exhibited greater self-regard in the task-oriented group. Moreover, whereas the anaclitic patients were sensitive to the structure of the group in that they viewed themselves more positively in the psychodynamic than they did in the task-oriented group, the introjective patients performed comparably in both models.

These studies by Coché et al. (1984) and Greene and Cole (1991), as well as other studies (e.g., Gould & Glick, 1976; Johnson, Sandel, & Bruno, 1984; Kanas et al., 1980) show that the characteristics of group members, their level of organization, typical dynamics, gender, and other factors make a difference in how effective a given model can be. In fact, we assert that the efficacy of a model cannot be judged apart from its context.

Although the moderating effects of subject variables on the efficacy of models have been subjected to some empirical scrutiny, the effect of setting variables, particularly those variables that define the hospital system itself (apart from the population it serves), such as its philosophy or mission, have been largely ignored. Yet, there is reason to believe that they are no less important than subject variables. In the late 1960s, a series of studies on therapeutic communities showed that many aspects of life on a unit (e.g., values, norms, and staff attitudes) had a significant effect on the emotional atmosphere of the psychotherapy group (e.g., Astrachan, Harrow, & Flynn, 1968). These studies revealed that all of the features that define the unit affect the transpirings of the psychotherapy group. Therefore, in the selection of the model, the attributes of the unit, and even those of the broader system of the institution (of which the unit is a subsystem), must be taken into account. One might expect that if a therapist attempted to use a model that was distinctly at odds with ethos of the unit, the therapist would be hindered in applying that model successfully. A recent study by Karterud (1988) showed that the emotional tenor of the unit affected highly specific aspects of the inpatient group such as the extent to which members made emotionally charged comments, focused on the here-and-now, or dwelled on practical, extragroup concerns. Like the earlier investigations of Astrachan et al. (1968) and others, Karterud's study suggests that certain treatment environments would be congenial to some models and not to others.

The necessity of considering the nature of the setting in selecting a model also becomes apparent with the recognition of the rootedness of each of the major models in the clinical situations in which they were constructed. Consider the problem-solving model, devised largely by Coché based on the work of Spivack, Shure, and others. Coché developed his approach at a private psychiatric hospital in which the psychotherapy group was composed of members from various units of the hospital. This arrangement was not idiosyncratic to the psychotherapy group but reflected how all treatment was organized at that institution. In Coché's setting, the therapist had considerable latitude in deciding who would be accepted for a certain group. The therapist determined when a new group would begin and how many times a week the group would meet. Finally, the therapist had some influence over the date that members would be discharged from the hospital and could even invite patients to return to complete any remaining steps of the treatment on an outpatient basis. The therapist's unusual degree of control over compositional and temporal variables enabled Coché to create a time-limited format of eight sessions in which members could work progressively on acquiring problem-solving skills. Had the therapist been working in a setting in which there was limited control over who was admitted to the group, when members were admitted, or how long they stayed, this model would have been impossible to implement (save some radical modification of it). If the group had changed membership on a near-daily basis and if members remained in the group for only several sessions, they might have gained some exposure to the five-step process, but they would not have time to practice, master, and apply it to their own situations.

The example of the problem-solving model emphasizes the importance that in selecting a model a therapist must give not only to broad institutional variables, such as the philosophy of the hospital, but also to those variables that will define the frame of the treatment such as likely number of sessions per week, length of session, patient turnover, and so on. These variables become especially important if they are not subject to the therapist's control or modification. In addition to the population and setting variables described earlier, there is an array of therapist variables that limit the potential efficacy of different models. Models vary in terms of the demands they place on the therapist's clinical training, personality style, need for stimulation, and the like.

In conclusion, then, the choice of a model is an act requiring the consideration of many factors. Certainly, an important starting point is the therapist's own theoretical orientation. As indicated earlier, models make different assumptions about the nature of psychopathology and the processes of change. A therapist could not practice with conviction a model that was philosophically at odds with his or her view of treatment. However, this step is not sufficient. In addition, the therapist must consider the treatment context in which he or she exists—the setting, patient, and other therapist variables. Each model makes a different pattern of demands in these various areas. To select a potentially viable and effective model, it is important for the therapist to see if there is an at-least-approximate match between the demands of the model and the features of the population, setting, and therapist (Beutler & Clarkin, 1990; Dies, 1992a).

# How To Use This Book

This text describes various models of inpatient group psychotherapy. By presenting an array of models, we hope that the reader will see that tremendous variety does exist and will find one that fits his or her setting, the population, and theoretical and technical proclivities. The models that we feature were chosen on several bases. The first was that a particular approach described in the literature had to have the features of a model we outlined earlier. That is, it had to incorporate a model of psychopathology, a statement of goals, and a specification of interventions. This requirement resulted in the exclusion of many contributions that simply proposed techniques or principles to be used in the inpatient group. The second basis was the presence of some reasonable level of clinical interest in the model as reflected by the literature on inpatient groups over the past 20 years. There were some approaches emerging in the literature (e.g., self psychology), the literature base of which specifically for inpatient groups was too scant to warrant inclusion. The third basis was the power of the model to be used in a range of inpatient conditions. For example, because of space considerations, we excluded from the text some very interesting models that were designed to be applied to specific diagnostic groups such as inpatients with depression (e.g., Betcher, 1983) or anorexia nervosa (e.g., Hendren, Atkins, Sumner, & Barber, 1987). However, those familiar with some of these models may notice that they have important conceptual links with one or more models presented in the text. The fourth consideration pertained to the overall distribution of models. We have sought to include models that are highly varied in terms of theoretical orientation, goals, techniques, and the demands they place on clinical settings. Once again, our intent here was to maximize the likelihood that each reader—given the specificities of his or her setting, population, and person—could find an appropriate model.

We would be remiss if we did not acknowledge that our taxonomy of models, like all other taxonomies, has some element of arbitrariness. We encourage the reader to recognize that if some other team were attempting to organize the theoretical and technical contributions that have been made in the field of inpatient group psychotherapy, they may have done it in a substantially different but equally descriptive way. This same point applies to our placement of the contributions of various writers in one model category or another. Some writers have ties to a variety of models, and we have endeavored to distill the major emphases of their writings.

Applying the stated criteria, we have selected seven models for inclusion in the text. The first model we present is the educative model, proposed by Jerrold Maxman in 1978. Our survey of the literature reveals that this was, if not the first, certainly one of the first models that took into account the characteristic features of the inpatient situation. Although this model offers practitioners somewhat less direction than do most of the other models, particularly in regard to methodology, it accords therapists great flexibility in tailoring their interventions to the particularities of the their settings. The next model we describe is the popular interpersonal model, to which most practitioners gain exposure through the writings of Irvin Yalom (Dies, 1992b). Even neophyte practitioners are probably at least somewhat familiar with Yalom's (1983) highly structured versions of an interpersonal approach that have been applied in many inpatient sites. However, in other sites, a more unstructured version, similar to Yalom's (1970) original writings, is possible and continues to be used. Our chapter aims to capture the richness of all of these contemporary interpersonal applications.

The next two models we present are psychodynamically oriented. Within the past decade or so, there has been an interest in applying psychodynamic concepts to the inpatient setting in a way that takes into account the realities of the inpatient setting (e.g., the short-term time frame, the severity of the pathology of members). The object relations/systems model, developed by

Kibel and others, integrates concepts from object relations and general systems theory. More than any extant approach, this model acknowledges the importance of the group's embeddedness in a larger treatment context, typically a psychiatric unit. Rather than regarding the unit as a potential intruder on the sanctity of the group, this model uses the relation between the unit and the group to effect positive intrapsychic change in members. The developmental model, which examines the vicissitudes of the group process over time, is distinguished from many of the other models we present by the demands it places on the group for some stability of membership. Although this demand may preclude many practitioners from adopting this model in a wholesale way, this conceptual framework is useful in that it can be integrated with other theoretical motifs. For example, the developmental model can be used to understand group-level resistances that emerge in the application of a cognitive–behavioral model.

The next model reviewed, the cognitive–behavioral model, offers a methodology by which maladaptive cognitions can be altered. Although this model has been applied for many years to individual outpatient psychotherapy, its extension to the inpatient group setting by Freeman, Coleman, and others is very recent. The problem-solving model develops members' skills in arriving at and selecting appropriate solutions to adaptive challenges. This model has probably received less attention in the mainstream group therapy literature than it deserves given the rather substantial research base supporting its efficacy with an inpatient population. Our last chapter features the highly varied behavioral approaches. Many of the techniques presented in this chapter can be adopted by the practitioner using nonbehavioral models. In this chapter, the focus is most intensively on social skills training given that this approach complements the other models that are presented in this text.

To enhance the reader's ease in making comparisons among the models, we have followed a repetitive outline from chapter to chapter. In the presentation of each model, we begin with a brief historical and theoretical exposition. Because the type of change the model targets is inextricably entwined with its view of psychopathology and the change process, we also describe the goals of the group in this section. Following the theoretical section is a technical section in which we describe the role of the leader, the major interventions of the model, and the type of material that emerges from the application of the model's interventions. We then provide a clinical illustration of the model. The reader more experienced in conducting inpatient groups might notice that in our vignettes, events move along quickly and there is considerably less resistance than is commonly observed in inpatient groups. Our recognition of the lack of realism was balanced by our wish to demonstrate a variety of characteristic techniques and processes in a relatively small amount of space. The next section is a presentation of the empirical research to date that would speak to the efficacy of the model. Our presentation of the research is highly variable depending on the model. Some models such as the problem-solving and interpersonal models have been compared with other models. Others such as the object relations/systems model have not. In the absence of any outcome data, we chose to review the efficacy of various unique components of the model. For example, when reviewing the educative model, we consider the empirical literature on leaderless groups. For others (e.g., the cognitive–behavioral model), we review the model's efficacy in an outpatient setting with patients of similar diagnostic categories in an inpatient setting. We then provide a critique of each model. Finally, we return to the treatment environment itself and consider what the model requires of that environment for its successful application.

Our text culminates in a comparative analysis of all of the models. We attempt to assist the reader in the selection of an appropriate model for his or her treatment environment by considering, once again, the dimensions of the setting. We show how certain classes of models are more compatible than others with particular types of settings.

We warn the reader in advance that the selection of a model will never be the final step. It is highly unlikely that any model the reader encounters will be perfectly compatible with his or her setting. Any chosen model will require adaptation to the particular setting. Just as models place demands on the setting, so too do both the setting and the model place demands on the therapist's ingenuity for the creation of a goodness-of-fit between them.

# References

Astrachan, B. M., Harrow, M., & Flynn, H. R. (1968). Influence of a psychiatric setting on behavior in group therapy meetings. *Social Psychiatry, 3*(4), 165–172.

Betcher, R. W. (1983). The treatment of depression in brief inpatient group psychotherapy. *International Journal of Group Psychotherapy, 33*(3), 365–385.

Beutler, L. E., & Clarkin, J. F. (1990). *Systematic treatment selection: Toward targeted therapeutic interventions.* New York: Brunner/Mazel.

Beutler, L. E., Frank, M., Schieber, S. C., Calvert, S., & Gaines, J. (1984). Comparative effects of group psychotherapies in a short-term inpatient setting: An experience with deteriorating effects. *Psychiatry, 47,* 66–76.

Bion, W. R. (1959). *Experiences in groups.* London: Tavistock.

Coché, E., Cooper, J. B., & Petermann, K. J. (1984). Differential outcomes of cognitive and interactional group therapies. *Small Group Behavior, 15*(4), 497–509.

Dies, R. R. (1992a). Models of group psychotherapy : Sifting through the confusion. *International Journal of Group Psychotherapy, 42*(1), 1–17.

Dies, R. R. (1992b). The future of group therapy. *Psychotherapy, 29*(1), 58–64.

Erickson, R. C. (1984). *Inpatient small group psychotherapy: A pragmatic approach.* Springfield, IL: Charles C Thomas.

Foulkes, S. H. (1948). *Introduction to group-analytic psychotherapy.* London: Heinemann.

Frank, J. D. (1963). Group therapy in the mental hospital. In M. Rosenbaum & M. Berger (Eds.), *Group psychotherapy and group function* (pp. 453–468). New York: Basic Books.

Gould, E., & Glick, I. (1976). Patient–staff judgments of treatment program helpfulness on a psychiatric ward. *British Journal of Medical Psychology, 49,* 23–33.

Greene, L. R., & Cole, M. B. (1991). Level and form of psychopathology and the structure of group therapy. *International Journal of Group Psychotherapy, 41*(4), 499–521.

Hendren, R. L., Atkins, D. M., Sumner, C. R., & Barber, J. K. (1987). Model for the group treatment of eating disorders. *International Journal of Group Psychotherapy, 37*(4), 589–602.

Johnson, D., Sandel, S., & Bruno, C. (1984). Effectiveness of different group structures for schizophrenic, character disordered and normal groups. *International Journal of Group Psychotherapy, 34,* 415n–429.

Lazell, E. W. (1921). The group treatment of dementia praecox. *Psychoanalytic Review*, *8*, 168–179.

Kanas, N., Rogers, M., Kreth, E., Patterson, L., & Campbell, R. (1980). The effectiveness of group psychotherapy during the first three weeks of hospitalization: A controlled study. *Journal of Nervous and Mental Disorder*, *168*, 487–492.

Karterud, S. (1988). The influence of task definition, leadership and therapeutic style on inpatient group cultures. *International Journal of Therapeutic Communities*, *9*(4), 231–247.

Kibel, H. (1992). Inpatient group psychotherapy. In A. Alonso & H. Swiller (Eds.), *Group therapy in clinical practice* (pp. 93–112). Washington, DC: American Psychiatric Press.

Kiesler, C. A., & Simpkins, C. (1991). The de facto national system of psychiatric inpatient care: Piecing together the national puzzle. *American Psychologist*, *46*(6), 1–6.

Marsh, L. C. (1935). Group therapy in the psychiatric clinic. *Journal of Nervous and Mental Diseases*, *82*, 381–392.

Maxmen, J. S. (1978). An educative model for inpatient group psychotherapy. *International Journal of Group Psychotherapy*, *28*, 321–337.

Maxmen, J.S. (1984). Helping patients survive theories: The practice of an educative model. *International Journal of Group Psychotherapy*, *34*(3), 355–368.

Pattison, E. M., Brissenden, E., & Wohl, T. (1967). Assessing special effects of inpatient group psychotherapy. *International Journal of Group Psychotherapy*, *17*, 283–297.

Rice, C., & Rutan, J. (1981). Boundary maintenance in inpatient therapy groups. *International Journal of Group Psychotherapy*, *31*(3), 297–309.

Yalom, I. D. (1970). *The theory and practice of group psychotherapy*. New York: Basic Books.

Yalom, I. D. (1983). *Inpatient group psychotherapy*. New York: Basic Books.

Chapter

# 2

# The Dimensions of the Setting

A specific hospital inpatient setting can be contrasted with other settings along a seemingly infinite number of variables. For example, a particular setting may differ from others in the level of staff training, the horticultural splendor of the grounds, the socioeconomic status of the typical patient, or the calibre of the recreational facilities. As some of these examples suggest, not all features that characterize a setting crucially affect what kinds of group models will be viable within that setting. The practitioner designing a psychotherapy group for a given system must isolate those aspects of the system that are likely to have the most significant influence on the functioning of the group. The purpose of this chapter is to describe a set of six dimensions or classes of variables.[1] From our survey of the literature, the variables within these classes appear to bear significantly on the potential of different models to be effective in a setting. These dimensions are clinical mission of the care setting, context of the group in the system, temporal variables, size of the group, composition of members, and therapist variables. In this chapter, we describe how settings differ from one another on the variables within these categories and how this variability

---

[1] The term *dimension* is not intended as having any statistical meaning in this context.

19

creates constraints in what models are likely to be viable within a given setting.

In considering the variables to be discussed, the clinician should determine the degree of alterability of a given variable within the setting. Some variables within a setting are absolute. Frequently, these variables define the organization or institution in which the inpatient group takes place. For example, the hospital may have a particular patient population that it seeks to serve. It is unlikely that the group psychotherapist can alter this feature unless the system has a readiness to change and the therapist has an extraordinary degree of power within the system (Erickson, 1984). Other features of the setting are moderately alterable. That is, they are alterable if the therapist is able to use effective strategies for and commit sufficient energy to their modification. Many of the features in this category represent administrative conveniences to other staff. For instance, the psychotherapy group may meet only twice a week so that other activities can be scheduled. Still other features are more or less accidental and are readily subject to modification. For example, it may be the case that in a particular institution, group psychotherapy takes place at the end of the treatment day, when members have little energy to involve themselves intensively. A mere change in scheduling might do much to affect what work is possible in group.

The importance of a feature and its amenability to change can be grasped only through an understanding of the broader system in which it is embedded. A particular feature may appear inconsequential but in fact may be woven into the structure of the hospital system and the patients it seeks to serve. For example, if group psychotherapy is scheduled at the end of the patient's day, a time that the group therapist does not see as optimal, the therapist may assume that a time change is a relatively easy matter. On seeking to implement a change, however, the therapist may learn that if the group is scheduled at another time, it would be necessary to move patient visiting hours to the end of the day, an undesirable circumstance given that the hospital is in a crime-ridden neighborhood. A change in time would discourage visitations.

A variable's position on the continuum of modifiability is relevant in determining whether a model must be chosen to accommodate the variable or vice versa. Unmodifiable variables have the most limiting effects on whether a particular group model can be effective. Suppose, for instance, that the hospital has a mission to serve disadvantaged populations and that the therapist has an interest in conducting groups for people who have considerable sophistication with respect to the purposes and processes of psychotherapy. The failure of the therapist to heed the institutional mission will serve neither the patients' needs to have a group geared to their particular set of resources and resistances nor the therapist's professional need to be competent and helpful. The features that are modifiable are important because their consideration enables the therapist to use a model under the most optimal conditions possible in that setting. For example, a number of models demand that the group take place in a setting that is strongly supportive of its goals and methods. With some effort, the therapist can effect a significant change in staff members' attitudes toward the group. However, failure of the group therapist to attend to the setting's view of the group has rendered many inpatient groups ineffective.

In this chapter, we acquaint the reader with the six dimensions that we use in all subsequent chapters to relate models to the various kinds of settings in which they are used. We attempt to show in a general way how a setting's status with respect to the variables associated with each of the six dimensions can hinder or facilitate group effectiveness across the different types of group models. In chapter 10, we return to these dimensions and address in a much more specific way the relations of these classes of variables to the seven models that we feature in this book.

Two important caveats must be made prior to the introduction of the six dimensions. First, this list should be regarded as neither comprehensive nor revealing of the categories that are most crucial in any individual practitioner's setting. We have selected for exploration those variables that have received significant attention in the literature. There are probably other equally important variables that await investigation as well. Examples of such variables are race and cultural background. Although there is emerging literature on these areas, much of it pertains to outpatient treatment and is not sufficient to enable our commentary or speculation in relation to inpatient models. Second, our discussion assumes that the institutional environment is reasonably hospitable to the creation and conduct of psychotherapy groups. That is, our point of departure is that group psychotherapy of some form is a feasible enterprise within a setting. There may be some settings in which this is not the case. The reader is urged to consult two excellent, thorough discussions of this issue, one by Borriello (1976), who analyzed the relevant features of the suprasystem of the hospital, and the other by Klein and Kugel (1981), who focused on the characteristics of the unit in relation to the viability of group psychotherapy in the setting.

## Clinical Mission of the Care Setting

### Values, Goals, and Philosophy

Institutions differ from one another in the particular values that they establish for the institution itself, how these values are operationalized, and the breadth and content of goals that are pursued for the individual patient. We consider each of these aspects in turn.

The extent to which a setting places emphases on clinical care, teaching, research, the satisfaction of external accrediting groups, the cultivation of national reputation, and the generation of revenue will affect a given model's viability within the setting. For example, in an institution that embraces the goal of training, funds will be allocated for staff development. If group psychotherapy is perceived to be an important area of training, those staff who perform group therapy will be provided with the necessary resources (e.g., outside consultants, speakers, monies for extrainstitutional continuing education) to improve their work. In such a setting (relative to a setting that does not highly value training), staff not only get exposure to a greater diversity of models but are better equipped to use those models that place greater demands on their training. The setting's resources for training in group therapy are of particular importance given that "few, if any, of the professional disciplines receive any instruction in group therapy during their training, and virtually none of them receive any instruction in inpatient group psychotherapy" (Yalom, 1983, p. 15).

Another example of the effect of institutional values on model selection is when a hospital places minimal emphasis on coordinating treatment among professionals representing various modalities. In such settings, the time spent in interdisciplinary coordination may be perceived to be cost-ineffective. There are a number of models in this book that demand a high level of coordination between the group psychotherapist and other members of the treatment team. The use of these models would be at best hampered and at worst precluded in such a setting.

A complicating factor in this analysis is that a given hospital system may have subsystems that have competing values and priorities. For example, one faction within the hospital may support the institution's development of its reputation as a training hospital. Another faction may be concerned with the maintenance of solvency. These subsystems may reflect a conflict within the institution-at-large about what the institutional values should be. Institutions resolve conflicts in various ways. One way may be to allow one powerful subsystem with a particular set of values to dictate policy. When this occurs, group therapists must concern themselves not only with a model's compatibility with the values of the institution but with its compatibility with those of the powerful subsystem.

How an institution operationalizes its values is also important in model selection. For example, two inpatient settings may each emphasize the pursuit of humanistic ideals and high responsivity to social problems. However, one institution may define this pursuit as an engagement in community outreach to disadvantaged populations. Another may fulfill its perceived social responsibility by ensuring that those patients who are admitted to the hospital are able to receive treatment for the necessary duration regardless of the limits of their insurance coverage. In these examples, the two different ways of defining social responsibility will affect the composition of the group and, consequently, the approach that will be most effective. The institution reaching out to disadvantaged groups may attract patients for whom the notion of "talk therapy" (let alone talking within a group of strangers!) is quite foreign. Hollingshead and Redlich (1958) found that individuals of a low socioeconomic status (SES) are more likely to expect to receive medication as the primary aspect of their treatment than are individuals of higher SES. Erickson (1984) described the expectation of low-income patients that their participation in any therapeutic modality will yield concrete solutions to their problems. A major consideration of the group psychotherapist working with this population is how to facilitate members adapting to the group and seeing it as a beneficial modality. The group therapist who treats higher SES patients is likely to confront a different set of resistances. For instance, one of us ran a cognitive–behavioral group at a private psychiatric hospital treating middle-class patients. Many of the members had been through individual psychodynamic therapy at some point prior to their admission. They were quick to argue with the therapist that unless group therapy provided them with an opportunity to explore the early familial roots of their symptoms (an exploration outside the parameters of the model), any positive effects from their participation in the group would be "superficial."

Finally, settings differ in their expectations of what kinds of change should occur in the patient as a function of hospitalization. Some institutions define themselves as treating patients in a holistic fashion. Although the patient will present with specific psychological complaints, the hospital views its mission as assisting the individual with any interpersonal, financial, or physical problem that emerges during the course of the his or her hospitalization. In contrast, some settings define their tasks in narrower terms, focusing on only the target complaints themselves. Of course, the extent to which an institution has a global versus a narrow focus ranges in degree. The more holistic a setting, the greater the range of models that can be successfully applied. Conversely, when an institution's treatment goals are more focal, fewer models are likely to be seen as effective by the staff given that only a small subset of existing models aim to modify target complaints.

## Theoretical Orientation

Institutions vary from one another not only in terms of values but also with respect to theoretical orientation. For example, there are some hospitals in the United States that have outstanding reputations for being bastions of psychoanalytic thought. As social psychological studies have repeatedly shown, violation of a group norm can lead to ostracism (Shaw, 1981). For the group therapist who attempts to use behavioral techniques in such places, there is a risk of having one's group work perceived as on a psychotherapeutic par with the Tuesday evening social. Although there may be many other factors within the system that would compel the therapist to use a behavioral approach, the institutional image of what constitutes psychotherapy must be addressed.

For example, in one institution, a group psychotherapist wished to use a Gestalt model in a primarily psychodynamically oriented institution. She provided regular in-services to unit staff in which she translated Gestalt concepts into psychoanalytic terms. Although her approach required more effort than if she had used an approach that was more familiar and coherent to the staff, she was successful in creating a pro-group climate (Rice & Rutan, 1981) as defined in chapter 1. Hence, the therapist who is willing to go against the theoretical grain of an institution must be committed to investing energy into the creation of a friendly "home" for the group within the institution.

## Discerning Values, Philosophies, and Theoretical Orientations

We caution the reader that the process of determining a model's fit with an institution's values, mission, and so on is not as simple as reading the institution's official statement of purpose. Institutions frequently have unarticulated agendas and goals that affect any model's ability to thrive within that setting. Consider the following example:

A nonprofit psychiatric hospital generally known for serving affluent patients was under pressure by the surrounding community to increase the number of public assistance patients that it admitted. Eventually, in the interest of preserving its public relations, the institution not only agreed to expand its number of federally funded beds but also, with great fanfare, announced the creation of special programs that would be tailored to the needs of this population—needs that hospital administrators saw as clearly different from those of its more longstanding population. Many specialists were hired, one of whom was a group psychotherapist who had run groups in institutions that primarily served relatively disadvantaged populations. The therapist designed a group with an interpersonal focus that was in many ways similar to the groups that already existed within the setting. This similarity led the therapist to believe that his group would be compatible with the theoretical orientation of many staff members and would therefore be accepted. However, the therapist found that he encountered various types of staff resistance to the existence of the group. For example, patients were often unable to attend group because of conflicting appointments with medical specialists. He frequently had an insufficient number of patients to run the group. When the group was held, staff would intervene in various ways to make difficult his establishment of an interpersonal focus. For example, staff would urge patients to bring somatic problems to group and to discuss there the unpleasant side effects of medication. When staff heard certain types of feedback that members expressed in the group, they would often express a concern that a given patient was too fragile to handle it.

What the puzzled and dismayed group therapist failed to recognize was that the institution's stated mission was not at one with its real mission. The institution regarded the community's demand as a threat to its integrity as an organization. The effort of the organization was to place the threat within the organization where it could be managed (and subdued) more easily (Hirschhorn, 1988). By identifying this new population as having radically different needs and resources than their more affluent patients and by seeing the new population as being treatable by biological interventions only, the institution compartmentalized that population. Through this compartmentalizing, the institution continued to keep individuals in the warded-off group on the periphery of the organization in a way that would be less apparent to the community. The group therapist's approach to conducting the group was at odds with the institution's effort to maintain the status quo. Although the therapist's theoretical orientation was similar to that of staff working with the more long-standing patient population, this similarity was in fact a detriment. It implied some commonality between the old and new populations. Had the group therapist been cognizant of the institutional dynamics, he might have decided to either adopt an alternative model, use an interpersonal approach in a way that would take into account the staff's resistance to it, or not accept the position altogether.

In the example just discussed, the psychotherapy group was affected by the institution's effort to contain an external pressure. In some instances, external pressures are effective in getting institutions to operate in ways that may be at odds with their long-held values. For example, Gabbard (1992) commented on how the demand on hospitals to satisfy regulatory agencies has diminished the opportunities of treatment team members to have meaningful discussions with one another. He wrote,

> the required documentation of treatment plans and justification for treatment being delivered has shifted the focus of staff meetings from the processing of transference–countertransference developments to the tedious writing of accounts that will satisfy surveyors and lead to accreditation. (p. 16)

Here, too, the psychotherapy group will be affected. Even if staff philosophically have a recognition of the value of communication and treatment coordination, their efforts to satisfy external bodies will hinder the application of those models that are especially dependent on such interaction.

The task of the group therapist who is interested in designing an appropriate group is to determine how the tensions between both an institution's actual and stated goals and the institutional and sociocultural systems in which it is embedded affect the viability of different models in that setting.

# The Context of the Group

## The Locus of the Group in the System

The immediate context in which the group takes place has a limiting effect on the goals and methods that can be embraced by the group therapist. In the most typical inpatient situation, group sessions are held on a residential-treatment unit: Group members all live and work in the same place. In this circumstance, group members have a multiplicity of roles both in relation to one another and in relation to the staff. Inside the group, members may be rivals for the therapist's attention. Outside the group, they may be confidantes and co-members of a unit entertainment committee. An example of multiplicity of roles in relation to staff is when the nurse who dispenses the medication at 1:00 p.m. is the same individual who leads the group at 2:00 p.m. An alternate situation is that in which patients from different units are included in the same psychotherapy group. This arrangement occurs when an institution has more than one psychiatric unit. The intent of organizing mixed-unit groups is usually to achieve more homogeneity among the members of the group in, for example, level of functioning or symptomatology.

The context in which a group takes place (i.e., a unit-based versus an extraunit group) is important because when group therapy takes place on a unit, the group is part of a therapeutic milieu or treatment environment. Events occurring on the unit are likely to affect members' responses within the group profoundly (Astrachan, Harrow, & Flynn, 1968). As will be seen, models differ in the degree to which they take account of group–milieu relations. To the extent that members are affected within the group by life on the unit, models that actively make use of the connection between group–unit responses are more likely to be effective than are those that pay little attention to the influence of the unit.

When members from different units are combined into a group, the extent to which any one unit can determine the goals, themes, and norms of the group will be diminished relative to the circumstance in which the members of the group would be drawn exclusively from that unit. Ghuman and Sarles (1989) found that when the themes of a unit-based adolescent group were compared with those of an extraunit group, the former group was more likely to gravitate toward the discussion of events and concerns that emerged on the unit. On the other hand, when the group was composed of patients from different units, members were better able to offer one another specific feedback in the manner of an outpatient group. The observations of these investigators suggest that when members of the group live on different units, those models that focus on issues stimulated by the experience of living on a unit may be less appropriate than those models that focus on intragroup experience.

## The System Perception of the Group

In defining "the context of the group," emphasis has been on where, organizationally, the group is located within the hospital system. The notion of context may be broadened to account for the status accorded the group in whatever context it resides. At one extreme, the group may be regarded as the patient's most important daily activity. At another extreme, it may be seen as a mere adjunct to other putatively more important interventions such as individual therapy or the patient's medical regimen. When a pro-group culture is absent, patients pick up the staff's negative attitude toward the group (Leonard, 1973). In such an environment, the group's integrity may be challenged repeatedly by various elements of the system. Among the challenges that the group receives are two particularly common ones. One type of challenge is that which disrupts the stability of the group boundaries. For example, other appointments may be scheduled for members concurrently with the time at which the group is in session. Members may be discharged from the hospital with no concern for their status in terms of their psychotherapeutic group progress. Dacey (1989) pointed out that these kinds of challenges to the integrity of the group make the establishment of cohesiveness practically impossible. If constant challenge to the group's integrity is an unchangeable feature, then it would behoove the therapist to choose a model that is less reliant on the development of cohesiveness.

Another type of challenge occurs when a staff member acts as if a group is pursuing a goal that is different from that which the therapist has established for the group. A case in point was the plight of a patient who was hospitalized at a private psychiatric hospital:

> Evelyn, 40-year-old woman, had recently entered a group. She had proceeded through a reasonably elaborate orientation to group therapy and appeared to understand the goals, norms, rules, and operating procedures. The group had begun to approach their feelings toward the therapist, particularly some of the disappointment they felt that the therapist was not going to offer members concrete suggestions in the solution of their problems.
>
> Evelyn came to the session with a letter. She indicated to the group that she had attempted to read it to her psychiatrist. However, her psychiatrist hastily instructed her to read it to the group and to receive their feedback. She indicated that she would follow his instructions despite the fact that originally she had not planned to share the letter with the group. She proceeded to read the letter, which was from her sister. The letter documented instances of child abuse inflicted on both her sister and herself. In the letter, the sister advised Evelyn to discontinue her relationship with their father, the abuser. After reading the letter, Evelyn asked the group to assist her in resolving the conflict of whether to follow the advice of the sister. Although the group made a few general comments, they quickly used the topic of an abusing parent as a segue to discussing their feelings of dissatisfaction toward the therapist—a depriving if not abusing "parent." Evelyn was humiliated that she had revealed this sensitive material to the group despite her wish not to do so. After the group, she stated her resolve not to return.

There may have been many ways in which the therapist could have intervened to spare Evelyn a traumatic reaction in the group. However, the therapist's task was certainly made more difficult by the cavalier assignment given to Evelyn by her psychiatrist, an assignment that circumvented Evelyn's own good intuitive grasp of what disclosures were appropriate at that point in the group's life. Moreover, the assignment was made with the implied promise that Evelyn would receive some very concrete advice from the group. Because the entire group was dealing with frustration concerning this very expectation, its endorsement by a staff member outside the group only led members to feel more exasperated and less willing to examine the expectation in a spirit of exploration.

This example highlights an extremely important aspect of the psychological context in which the group takes place: the system's definition of what the group ought to do. Frequently, the group is perceived as existing to do whatever cannot be done easily elsewhere in the system. In the preceding example, the psychiatrist in a hurry may have perceived group psychotherapy as an opportunity for his patients to get more prolonged individual attention than he could provide. In fact, there are some models that can easily accommodate this expectation. Alternatively, the group may be seen as a place in which limits are imposed so that the "troublemakers" on the unit are rendered more tractable. The group may be regarded as an arena in which tension on the unit can get "siphoned off." In some cases, these perceptions may be congruent with the therapist's perception of the group; in some cases, they may not. Nonetheless, unless the therapist is willing to reckon with the system perception in some manner, he or she will constantly be contending with the dissatisfaction of members such as Evelyn who are caught between two opposing sets of staff perceptions about the group.

# Temporal Variables

## Duration of Participation in the Group

Temporal variables are highly important in determining what models are likely to be effective in a setting. The most obvious temporal variable relating to the inpatient group is length of hospitalization. Because duration of hospitalization is generally brief (typically less than a month), the nature of group participation is usually short term. However, within the literature, participation in inpatient groups is almost invariably significantly briefer than in outpatient groups; this has led writers in the area to ignore the reality that not all brief durations are equivalently brief. In one clinical setting, a group member may have the opportunity to participate in only a single session. In another setting, a member may be present for 16 sessions. Certainly, the goals and methods that would be useful in each case would be different.

The variable of length of time of group participation is important in at least two respects, one of which pertains to the individual, the other to the group-as-a-whole. What the individual can achieve in the group is critical to how long he or she remains in the group. Whereas the goals of some models can be accomplished in a single session, those of others require a longer term involvement. For example, if the goal of a model is to elicit a positive attitude toward therapy, then that goal may be accomplished in a single session in which the member has a satisfying experience with the other group members. If the goal is to modify depressive cognitions that have been present with the person for many years, then it is unlikely that a single session will suffice.

With respect to the effect of member's length of participation in the group as a social system, it may be noted that the longer members remain in the hospital and, consequently, in the group, the more consistent will be the membership of the group. The degree of membership stability will determine the relative feasibility of approaches that are cross-sectional versus longitudinal. In a group in which membership changes on a daily basis, a cross-sectional approach is appropriate. With a cross-sectional approach, a single session is regarded as the entire life of the group. The essential learning that occurs within a session is in no way dependent on participation in prior sessions. In contrast, with a longitudinal approach, the group's experience in past sessions provides a backdrop against which events in the present session are understood. For example, within a longitudinal approach, if Mary comes into a session angry, one might question what had happened in the prior session that angered Mary. However, if the membership has changed significantly, the discussion of the previous session's events would dilute the intensity of the group's experience because the material would be mere hearsay to most members.

In the preceding discussion, it was assumed that the individual's participation in group psychotherapy was relatively brief (i.e., a month or less). Although they are less common today than they were 10 and certainly 20 years ago, there are settings, especially some state facilities and long-term units of private hospitals, in which the length of stay can be as long as 2 years (Beutler & Clarkin, 1990). Most existing models have been developed for a short-term time frame, although there are exceptions (e.g., Klein, Hunter, & Brown, 1986). This book features several models with sufficiently flexible goals to enable their application to the long-term situation.

## Closed-Ended Versus Open-Ended Groups

Most inpatient groups are open-ended. That is, members enter and leave the group on an ongoing basis. An alternate format is one in which the group membership is constant (Brabender, 1985; Rawlings & Gauron, 1973). The group is closed-ended in that once the group begins, no new members are added; all members end the group at the same time. Relative to open-ended groups, closed-ended groups, not having to withstand the disruptive effects of membership turnover, are likely to achieve a higher level of cohesiveness, which promotes the group's development. Schopler and Galinsky (1990) found that the longer a group's membership remained constant, the further it advanced developmentally as exhibited by the group's achievement of certain formative tasks such as bonding among members, the acceptance of norms, and so on. Therefore, closed-ended groups are better able to use those models that either focus on the group's development specifically or that require the group's access to those processes characteristic of a mature group. For example, relative to an open-ended group, a closed-ended group is better able to use the ability of a group to process differences among members, which is generally seen as emerging later in a group's life than is the ability to recognize similarities (e.g., Agazarian & Peters, 1981; Brabender, 1985; MacKenzie & Livesley, 1983). As the reader will see, some models focus much more than others on members' explorations of the ways in which they are different from one another.

## Number of Sessions per Week

Another temporal variable of great importance is the number of sessions that occur per week. When groups meet infrequently (e.g., twice a week), the therapist is handicapped in using any model that demands that the group either achieve a high level of cohesiveness or have a capacity to connect present with past group events. Fortunately, some models require only that degree of cohesiveness that can develop in a single session. They do not entail the group's consideration of its own history across sessions. However, other models require that fairly complex learning be carried from one session to the next; these models may be difficult to apply if the therapist is not be able to reinforce a given session's learning in a temporally proximate session.

# Size of the Group

Size of the group is an important consideration for at least two reasons. The first is that size affects the extent to which each member can actively participate. All else being equal, the larger the group, the less time each member has to respond and to obtain a response. Some models emphasize the importance of individually centered interventions as when, for example, a model requires that the session begin with a go-around in which each member reviews his or her homework from the past session. In a group of 12 members meeting for 60 minutes, it would be nearly impossible for the group to complete the specified steps for a session in which each member formulated an individual agenda. There are other models, however, that place less emphasis on individually centered interventions and consequently are less sensitive to group size. For example, one model that we describe uses of range of interventions but concentrates on group-as-a-whole interpretations and is amenable to use with a relatively large group (e.g., 12 members). It does not require that the member be the direct object of the group's (or therapist's) attention to benefit from the group.

The second important consideration in terms of group size is the requirement of some models that a diversity of interpersonal styles be present in the group. If the group is too small, the range of styles may not be adequate. Hence, a small group using a model that requires members to resolve a series of conflicts may be too limited in interpersonal resources to function effectively. The limited range of styles may excessively constrict the aspects of the conflicts that emerge and the range of solutions to the conflicts that are offered.

The variable of group size is likely to interact with other structural features such as the length and frequency of sessions (temporal variables). For example, a group that is larger than what is seen as ideal for application of the model may provide ample opportunity for individual involvement depending on the frequency with which the group meets and length of each session.

# Group Composition

As discussed in chapter 1, compositional variables have received much more consideration in the literature than have setting variables in terms of the extent to which they interact with different models' effectiveness. This section explores some of the compositional variables that have received particular attention in the literature.

## Level of Ego Functioning

The compositional variable that probably has received the greatest degree of attention is level of ego functioning. Leopold (1977) suggested that the kind of approach that would be appropriate for an inpatient who is severely regressed (i.e., impaired in most major areas of ego functioning such as the ability to see reality veridically, to control impulses, to tolerate frustration, etc.) is different from that which would be appropriate for the patient whose reality testing is impaired in only moderate or minor ways. Specifically, Leopold argued that for the highly regressed (typically psychotic) patient, those approaches that emphasize a high level of support, warmth, and individual attention from the therapist are most likely to be effective. He saw it as important to provide the patient with a highly positive emotional experience to help the patient be less anxious and more trusting of others. For the less regressed inpatient, he advocated those approaches that require the members' tolerance of some anxiety in the group as they learn about their dysfunctional interpersonal patterns. Such an approach is more exploratory than that recommended for the regressed patient.

Generally, the research has provided confirmation for Leopold's (1977) view that those approaches and techniques that emphasize emotional support are likely to be more effective with a highly regressed population than are those that involve personal exploration and some anxiety arousal. For example, whereas Kanas, Rogers, Kreth, Patterson, and Campbell (1980) found that acutely psychotic patients either were not helped or were hurt by an insight-oriented therapy, Kanas (1988) reported favorable results with a reality-based supportive approach with a group of schizophrenic patients. Coché and Polikoff (1979) discovered that a high level of self-disclosure was associated with good outcomes in high-functioning inpatients and with poor outcomes in low-functioning inpatients. Leszcz, Yalom, and Norden (1985) found that lower functioning inpatients were more likely than were higher functioning inpatients to see as helpful those therapeutic processes that were supportive rather than exploratory. In particular, lower functioning group members saw the instillation of hope and the obtaining of advice as important to their progress in the group. The research has also suggested that the lower the ego functioning of the group members, the more they are helped by a high level of structure. For example, chapter 1 cited a study by Greene and Cole (1991) in which psychotic patients had better outcomes in a highly structured task group, whereas borderline patients (operating at a higher ego-functioning level) had better outcomes in a less structured interactional group.

In summary, then, lower functioning patients are likely to benefit from models that (a) are highly supportive, (b) encourage a low or moderate but never high level of disclosure or exploration of private experience, (c) do not require the tolerance of anxiety in the sessions, and (d) provide a structured session in which members can anticipate the flow of events. As the reader will see, there are a number of existing models that have these characteristics.

For the higher functioning inpatient (i.e., that patient at the borderline level who has some capacity to test reality, is free of hallucinations and delusions, and can at least minimally modulate affects and impulses), there is somewhat less consistency in the literature as to the features of any adequate model of group treatment. What distinguishes those models that have been proposed for higher functioning inpatients is the use of processes requiring that the group members withstand some minimal level of anxiety during the sessions. For example, some models require members' tolerance of the anxiety associated with hearing negative observations about themselves. Other models entail that members accept the expression of anger in the sessions. However, all proponents of these and other models that have been constructed for the treatment of higher functioning inpatients emphasize the necessity of both titrating the amount of anxiety to which group members are subjected and providing a good measure of emotional support.

The preceding discussion of levels of ego functioning assumes that the setting allows for patient groups that are homogeneous on this variable. In some settings, particularly those in which there are not a large number of patients from which to draw, it is necessary to include members at all levels of ego functioning in the same group; this situation frequently occurs on small psychiatric units of general hospitals. In such instances, the therapist may consider using a model that, although designed for the lower functioning patient, can include individually directed interventions tailored to the resources of higher functioning patients.

## Diagnostic Category

Related to level of ego functioning is the diagnostic composition of the group. There are two major questions that might be posed in relation to diagnosis. First, are the groups homogenous or heterogeneous with respect to diagnosis? Second, what are the particular diagnoses that characterize the group?

In most inpatient settings, practical considerations frequently dictate that patients with various diagnoses are placed in the same group (Erickson, 1986). Heterogeneity of diagnosis is a far less limiting factor in model selection than is heterogeneity of ego functioning. In fact, most of the models presented in this text were constructed with the diagnostically heterogeneous group in mind. There are, however, some important exceptions. One exception exists in relation to those models that are specifically geared toward the reduction of a particular symptom or problem. If the patient does not have the symptom, those models have little to offer him or her. A second exception is the type of model that can theoretically accommodate a range of diagnoses and symptom patterns but that practically must be used with a particular problem so to be applied parsimoniously (i.e., most interventions are applicable to most members). A third exception pertains to those models that, although they accommodate a range of diagnoses, exclude specific diagnostic categories. The reader will notice, for example, that many models presented in this book exclude patients with acute mania or psychosis. In such cases, the exclusion pertains not simply to the diagnosis but also to the level of ego functioning. That is, the patient's lack of access to ego resources leads to disorganized behavior in the sessions that sabotages the therapist's efforts to create a sense of safety for all group members.

In inpatient settings, it is increasingly common for patients with particular diagnoses or problem areas to be treated on the same unit (Beutler & Clarkin, 1990). If the unit is homogeneous with respect to diagnosis, the group taking place on the unit is also diagnostically homogeneous. Indeed, there has been an increasing number of reports of such diagnostically homogeneous groups in both inpatient and outpatient hospital settings. For example, models have been developed for depression (Betcher, 1983; Whitaker & Deikman, 1980), eating disorders (Duncan & Kennedy, 1992; Hendren, Atkins, Sumner, & Barber, 1987; Kaplan, Kerr, & Maddocks, 1992), and schizophrenia (Kanas, 1988).

Although the therapist may create a model that is tailored to the special needs of a diagnostically homogeneous group, the therapist who seeks to use a model originally developed for a more heterogenous group may encounter certain problems. A patient's diagnosis is predictive of the kind of resource that he or she is likely to bring to the group. Thus, diagnostic homogeneity may be a hindrance if a model requires a resource that a particular diagnostic group is not likely to possess in abundance. For example, Slife, Sasscer-Burgos, Froberg, and Ellington (1989) found that depressed patients exhibited difficulty in processing interactions with others. Relative to a diagnostically mixed group of nondepressed inpatients, depressed inpatients showed a lesser ability to observe videotapes of group sessions and correctly decipher the feelings that members were having toward one another. Also, depressed individuals showed a relative weakness in giving and receiving feedback. Certainly, a group capitalizing on these processes would risk being unduly sluggish and hence fail to hold members' interest if the group were exclusively composed of depressed individuals.

As the earlier discussion of diagnostically heterogeneous groups suggested, there are certain models that are best applied with diagnostically homogeneous groups. Diagnostically homogeneous groups are generally viewed as working well with models that establish symptom reduction as a primary goal (Beutler & Clarkin, 1990; Weiner, 1986). Frequently, these symptomatically targeted models have a major didactic component that can be introduced efficiently because the instruction pertains to all group members. Those models that emphasize similarities among members rather than differences are also useful with diagnostically homogeneous groups because the similarities will inevitably be more obvious in the diagnostically homogeneous group (Weiner, 1986).

If a group is diagnostically homogenous, the particular diagnosis itself will play a role in establishing which model is likely to be effective. For example, according to Barr (1986), a viable model for a group of schizophrenics would be one that takes into account members' terror of human contact; emphasizes issues related to reality testing, affect modulation, and problem solving; and makes allowances for the occurrence of behaviors that would be seen as disruptive in a mixed group. In a group of depressed individuals, these considerations would be less relevant.

## Psychological Sophistication

Psychological sophistication refers to the extent to which an individual is willing to take responsibility for his or her symptoms or difficulties—a willingness based on a recognition that feelings, impulses, and fantasies that are not immediately evident may have a determining role in their experiences or behaviors. A fascinating if not often disarming reality is that this factor is not necessarily associated with level of functioning or diagnosis. Therapists working in every modality have encountered the schizophrenic individual who is utterly incapable of functioning outside the confines of the institution but who is an Artesian well of trenchant observations about himself and other people in his life. Occasionally, the high level of psychological mindedness that such ego-disturbed individuals are able to achieve is a function of their many years of involvement in psychotherapy. These individuals become experts at self-analysis. Conversely, it is not unusual to encounter a patient who has a less malignant diagnosis than many and a relatively good capacity to negotiate life's ordinary stressors but who is able to comprehend reality in only the most concrete, superficial terms. Self-reflection to such persons is anathema.

As we show, the models in this book place very different demands on the psychological sophistication of the group member. For example, some models entail members' acceptance of the notion that factors lying outside of their awareness can produce symptoms. Others require only that a patient be able to focus on symptoms and their relations to the environmental stimuli that may intensify or ameliorate them.

When there is a large disparity between the demands of a model and the level of psychological sophistication of a given member, predictable negative consequences ensue. If the member's level of psychological awareness greatly exceeds the demands of the model, then the member is likely to have a devaluing attitude toward the therapy, the therapist, and, not infrequently, the other group members. Although the member may cling to his or her attitude because it serves as an effective vehicle for resistance, it may be difficult within the confines of the model for the therapist to interpret it as such. When a member's level of psychological awareness is markedly below the demands of the model, the member tends to experience the sessions as a series of narcissistic insults; sessions may induce confusion, anxiety, and a wish to leave the group. A member is most likely to act on the wish to leave if he or she perceives other members as better able to satisfy the demands of the model.

A consistent discrepancy between the demands of a model and the resources of the entire group generally will be detected by the therapist who recognizes the inefficacy of the model and its inappropriateness for that patient population. The model can then be altered or discarded in favor of an alternate model. A more subtle and more commonplace problem is one wherein the range of positions that members occupy on this dimension of psychological sophistication is so variable that the therapist is unable to tailor his or her interventions in a way that will effectively reach each member. What this sort of variability necessitates is the adoption of a wide-band model with interventions that can be aimed at various levels. As indicated earlier, some models lend themselves to application in groups of varying levels of psychological sophistication.

## Gender

The typical inpatient group is composed of a mix of men and women, with a greater number of women. The greater number of women in inpatient groups reflects the fact that women are admitted in significantly greater numbers than are men to private and public psychiatric facilities (Bachrach & Nadelson, 1988; Russo, 1990). In some facilities, however, it is the practice to create separate groups for male and female patients either because it is perceived that men and women have different treatment needs or because it is assumed that each gender experiences greater comfort in same-gender groups. For example, Golden and Dominiak (1986) described a women's group that was established on a long-term coed adolescent inpatient unit. They argued that in a same-gender group, female adolescents were able to explore separation and individuation processes that are pertinent only to their sex. Moreover, a same-gender group provides female adolescents with a more comfortable forum to talk about "struggles to attain intimacy in relations with males, birth control, concerns with menstruation and body image" (Golden & Dominiak, 1986, p. 219). In addition, there are some same-gender programs for the treatment of disorders that are characteristically those of women (e.g., eating disorders).

A question might be raised as to whether the use of a same-gender or mixed-gender group makes a difference in how male and female members perceive and behave in the group. Do women respond differently if men are present than if they are with members of their own sex? How are men affected by the presence or absence of women? If, indeed, men and women respond differentially depending on whether they are placed in a same-gender or a mixed-gender group, then this variability might have implications for what models might be most useful with each. For example, suppose women and men became more expansive in the feelings that they were willing to express in a mixed-gender group. If so, the mixed-gender group would be conducive to the use of those models that use and assume a wide range of expression.

The issue of same-gender versus mixed-gender groups is one that has evoked a great deal of speculation but very little systematic attention in the literature. The few studies in which mixed-gender and same-gender groups have been examined empirically suggest that this variable is a powerful one. Aries (1976) found that men perceived themselves to be more engaged by the group experience and were able to address a greater diversity of themes when the group was composed of men and women rather than exclusively men. In a same-gender group, the male members focused almost entirely on themes related to competition and aggression. Unlike male members, female members were more inclined to feel an increasingly high level of emotional involvement and were less likely to take a passive role in same-gender groups. In contrast to Aries's finding, the male and female subjects in a study by Carlock and Martin (1977) found same-gender groups to be much less exciting than mixed-gender groups. Moreover, subjects in mixed-gender groups were more interested in attending to the here-and-now than to relationships outside of the group. They were also more focused on issues related to heterosexual relationships than were members in same-gender groups. As in the Aries study, Carlock and Martin found that women were more inclined to take a passive role in relation to men in mixed-gender groups.

The obstacle to regarding the results of these studies as anything more than suggestive lies in the fact that the groups studied were not inpatient groups. The participants in the groups were not even psychotherapy patients: They were students seeking an enrichment experience. Moreover, these groups deviated in significant ways from a typical inpatient psychotherapy group. For example, in the Carlock and Martin (1977) study, the number of men exceeded the number of women in the mixed-gender groups. This arrangement would be very unusual in an inpatient group in which the number of women typically surpasses the number of men. Would men be able to achieve the same level of dominance as they did and would women be as passive as they were in the cited studies if women were in the majority? Clearly, it would be of greater benefit to examine this variable in an inpatient setting.

With these significant caveats in mind, the implications of each group format as suggested by the prior studies might be considered. For men, the same-gender group appears to provide a narrower experience and invokes highly stereotypic sex role behaviors. For example, male members might be disinclined to respond in a nurturing way toward one another because nurturant behavior is at odds with the masculine sex role stereotype. The limited range of interpersonal behaviors in all-male groups may hinder the applications of those models that emphasize interpersonal exploration within the immediate setting of the group (e.g., developmental, interpersonal, object relations/systems models). As indicated earlier, these models frequently assume that there is some degree of variability in interpersonal styles in the group. Members in an all-male group may have difficulty seeing other members' behavior in a sufficiently objective way to render meaningful feedback given that other members' behavior is likely to be similar to their own. Also, if their limited range of behaviors is not representative of their typical repertoire of social responses, the feedback may have restricted relevance and resonance. The all-female group shows the high level of variability in interpersonal style and range of affective expression conducive to the use of models emphasizing interpersonal exploration. However, individuals in both all-male and all-female groups seem less inclined than those in mixed-gender groups to focus on the here-and-now, a focus that is central to the interpersonally oriented models.

Within the mixed-gender group, the fact that women's social behaviors are stereotypic is not a deterrent to the application of a model emphasizing interpersonal exploration given that male members typically engage in behavior that female members avoid. For example, suppose that a model requires that at a certain point in the life of the group, members take an active role in expressing aggression. Although women will generally avoid taking initiative in this area, men will not. The dialectic between men's willingness to express anger and women's inhibition to do so may in itself serve as a focal point for the group's interpersonal exploration.

Although women's engagement in stereotypic sex role behavior may not be a deterrent to the application of a particular model from the standpoint of the group-as-a-whole, it may be a deterrent to the women themselves if the passivity reveals a lack of engagement in the group. As suggested by Coché, Cooper, and Petermann (1984), however, this interpretation does not appear to be the case . Male and female inpatients were randomly assigned to groups run according to either a problem-solving model or an interpersonal model. Both of these models are described in subsequent chapters. All groups were composed of both men and women, with an approximately equal number of each. Before and after the group, measures were taken on each patient's self-concept and degree of psychopathology as viewed by the patient himself or herself. The investigators also had a nurse on the patient's hall rate the patient's degree of improvement or deterioration in relation to the patient's key complaints. Coché et al. found neither interpersonal nor problem-solving therapy was more effective across both male and female subjects. However, they found that the relative degree of efficacy of a particular model of therapy depended on the gender of the subject: Women made greater gains in the interpersonal groups (suggesting their adequate level of engagement), whereas men made greater gains in the problem-solving group. This interaction between subject gender and therapy model was observed in both the patient's own ratings and in the ratings of the staff person.

The Coché et al. (1984) study suggests that in the same-gender group, one is likely to observe greater progress for men if the therapy emphasizes cognitive elements. Women are more likely to respond to groups stressing affective and interpersonal elements.

The Coché et al. (1984) study also has implications for the mixed-gender group. The results suggest that to engage fully the member of a mixed-gender group, a model needs prominent affective and cognitive features. Any model that requires a high level of affective exchange in the absence of a cognitive framework to organize the affect is likely to discourage men's involvement in the group. Conversely, too emphatic of a cognitive element prior to the time the group has achieved cohesiveness is likely to disenchant female members. Alonso and Rutan (1979) pointed out that early in the life of the group, it is important for female members to have opportunities to nurture other members because these nurturing skills are an area of major strength for women. The recognition of this strength enables women to feel "at home" in the group (Brabender, 1992). Most of the models in this book have at least the potential for the integration of cognitive and affective elements. However, it is incumbent on the therapist to make each sufficiently salient, particularly in a member's early participation, so that the group is a safe and attractive arena of work for both men and women.

## Age

The models that we consider in this book will be those that were primarily developed for a mixed-age group ranging from late adolescence through senescence. Although some observations are made about children's inpatient groups, we do not focus on these groups in any comprehensive or systematic way.

The creation of age-specific treatment units is a relatively new development (Stein & Kymissis, 1989), and with it has come the creation of age-specific psychotherapy groups, particularly for adolescents and the elderly. In the literature, a wide variety of models have been proposed to guide the operation of these groups. For example, Klein et al. (1986) and Ramos and Richmond (1991) described approaches for the long-term treatment of adolescent inpatients. Beitel et al. (1983) described an inpatient adolescent group on a short-term unit. Siegel (1987) described an approach to group psychotherapy with adolescents in a residential setting. On the other end of the age continuum, Moran and Gatz (1987) described methods for treating the elderly in nursing homes. Bienenfeld (1988) outlined an approach for treating elderly patients in state hospitals. Gilewski (1986), Saul (1988), and Shoham and Neuschatz (1985) described models developed for treating elderly inpatients suffering from confusion and disorientation. In this book, we do not cover models developed and used exclusively for one age group, although we mention when the models that we do cover have specific applicability to an age group.

Despite the increased popularity of same-age groups, there are many settings in which adolescents or the elderly are included in general adult groups. Sometimes their inclusion is determined by convenience. For example, an adolescent unit may have a policy that unless an adolescent actually lives on the unit, he or she is not eligible to be in a group on the unit. If a patient is placed on a general adult unit simply because there are no more beds on the adolescent unit or because of judgment on the part of the staff that intensive peer involvement may be too stressful for that individual, a general adult group may be the patient's only opportunity to participate in a psychotherapy group. In some settings such as acute-care psychiatric units of a general hospital, there may be not be a sufficient number of adolescent or elderly patients to form a separate group.

In some instances, age homogeneity or heterogeneity may be more desirable for the application of a given model. For example, a model that is geared toward the cognitive capabilities of the members of the group works best with a group that is relatively homogeneous for age. Such a model is optimal if adolescents are treated separately from latency-age children and if adults are treated separately from adolescents. Models that capitalize on differences in the resources, issues, and interpersonal styles that members bring to the group often profit from some age heterogeneity.

Typically, however, the therapist does not control whether the psychotherapy group is heterogeneous or homogeneous in terms of age. This factor is typically determined on the basis of how treatment is generally organized within an institution. If there are same-age units, there will be same-age groups. How does the therapist proceed if age heterogeneity versus homogeneity is a constraint of the setting? If the group is heterogeneous, the therapist faces very little restriction in terms of model use. Most of the models that we cover in this book were designed with a reasonably heterogeneous age group in mind. If the group is homogeneous, the therapist must come to know the special characteristics of his or her population. Age homogeneity provides the therapist with a special opportunity to tailor the model to the special needs and challenges of that age group.

For example, a therapist designing a group for an adolescent population might take into account the rapidity and intensity by which group-as-a-whole resistances develop in this age group (Stein & Kymissis, 1989). This phenomenon might warrant particular consideration of those models that are geared to the understanding and handling of group-level resistances and, in particular, the negative feelings toward authority that are endemic to adolescence (Kraft, 1983). The peer orientation of adolescents (Kraft, 1961) might lead the therapist to consider models that involve a great deal of member-to-member interaction.

A group of elderly patients presents a different set of needs. Writers on residential or inpatient groups for the elderly have emphasized the readiness by which elderly members focus on existential themes of loss, disability, and death (e.g., Berland & Poggi, 1979; Goodman, 1988; Johnson, 1985; Leszcz, Feigenbaum, Sadavoy, & Robinson, 1985; Sorensen, 1986). The use of reminiscence techniques wherein members can delve into their past and integrate past events with present experiences has been found to diminish the fear of death (Butler, 1963). The demand of some models for members to remain within the here-and-now may be inappropriate for this age group, which might be better served by models that have a more flexible focus. Lakin (1988) found that in a same-age group for the elderly, members manifested an unwillingness to confront the differences among themselves, which would also bode poorly for those models that emphasize the process of feedback. Writers on inpatient group psychotherapy for the elderly have noted that in a same-age group, the therapist must prepare to see members who are highly varied in their level of functioning. In an inpatient group, there may be members who are neurologically intact and cognitively fit and others who suffer from varying degrees of cerebral dysfunction (Sorensen, 1986). An effective model for this age group must have the flexibility to enable the therapist to cater to these different levels.

In sum, then, certain models work for particular age groups, whereas others do not. In a same-age group, the therapist must attend closely to the fit between the characteristics of that age group and the provisions and requirements of the model.

## Therapist Variables

The therapist, too, is an extremely important part of the treatment. The therapist's personality style (including predilection for certain types of leadership behaviors), resistances, need for intellectual stimulation, and other personal factors will play a role in determining what model can work within a setting. Many of these factors are difficult to operationalize, particularly in view of the almost negligible investigation to which they have been subjected in the realm of group psychotherapy. We focus on several therapist variables that have been addressed in terms of models of inpatient group psychotherapy: the theoretical leaning of the group therapist, his or her training in group psychotherapy, and the structure of the group leadership (co-therapy or single leader).

Some models require that the therapist accept a very specific view of psychopathology such as a psychoanalytic view. There are many practitioners who would not be able to use these models because they do not endorse the assumptions underlying the model. Other models are compatible with a diversity of theoretical orientations. Often, these are models that have roots in different schools of thought of psychotherapy. They are capable of being used by therapists with widely diverging views on the nature and origins of psychological problems.

Existing models also place different demands on the training of the therapist. On one end of the continuum are models that demand that the therapist have an understanding of a particular, often complicated, theoretical approach to human psychology, psychopathology, and group process. On the other end of the continuum are those models that entail the mastery of a set of techniques to effect change in a few highly circumscribed target behaviors. Although the therapist's understanding of the subtleties of group dynamics and psychopathology would facilitate the application of any model, for some models, such understanding is not essential.

Although the models that we review in this book are highly variable in terms of the demands they place on the therapist, they are less variable in terms of their recommendations about co-therapy. Whereas certain models could be performed by a single therapist, co-therapy is the arrangement of choice for all the models. All inpatient models require a high level of activity from the therapist, and some models require that the therapist perform a complex set of tasks. The presence of a co-therapy team renders each leader's fund of responsibilities more manageable. In addition, the co-therapy arrangement is helpful when one therapist must respond to the inevitable emergencies that arise with individual patients (e.g., a patient declares a suicidal intent and runs out of the room). Most important, the co-therapy structure is an antidote to the high level of stress that accompanies leading an inpatient group.[2] Therapists usually value the opportunity to clarify their perceptions about the group and to obtain support for the difficult events and personalities that they encounter in sessions. Although for all models the co-therapy arrangement is most desirable, for some models, the presence of a team rather than a single leader is almost mandatory. Certain models, by virtue of the number and variety of tasks required, would be nearly impossible to apply with only a single therapist.

---

[2] There are other antidotes such as the presence of regular supervision or the use of the treatment team.

# Summary and Comment

This chapter reviewed those dimensions that distinguish clinical settings from one another and that bear on the clinician's choice of an appropriate model for psychotherapy groups within that setting. The six areas discussed were clinical mission of the care setting, group context, temporal variables, group size, compositional variables, and therapist variables. Although there are many other dimensions that we might have discussed (given that settings can differ from one another in an infinite number of ways), we selected those dimensions that, in our opinion, are generally most determining of the level of effectiveness of a particular model in any given setting. Certainly, however, within the reader's setting, there may be other sets of variables that have great significance. It is important that the reader consider these variables in model selection.

It is unlikely that the requirements of any model presented in this book are perfectly congruent with the features of a given setting. Rather than making an easy and obvious match between a model and a setting, the practitioner will most typically face the challenge of deciding which model is more congruent with the setting than others. Usually the selection process will entail a determination of which incongruities between the setting and a model can be minimized through either a change in the model or a change in the setting. For example, Froberg and Slife (1987) in discussing the limitations of the interactional agenda version of the interpersonal model, pointed out that whereas Yalom (1983) designed a format for a 75-minute session, many inpatient groups meet for significantly briefer durations. If, in other important respects, this model appears to be a good fit for the setting, then the practitioner may attempt to lobby for expanded group sessions. However, if the lengthened sessions are not possible, then the group therapist may make an adaptation in the model, as suggested by Froberg and Slife, that would entail that the therapist prioritize members' agendas in a more active way than that suggested by Yalom.

Ultimately, the inpatient group psychotherapist must reckon with the reality that his or her clinical setting is unique. Although any one of the models presented in this book may be an excellent point of departure for the construction of a model, it is only that, a point of departure. It is important for the clinician to keep in mind that all of these models were developed for some setting other than that in which the clinician is practicing. The most effective model will invariably be that model that is tailored to all of the features of a setting, both those features that a setting shares with others and those that set it apart.

# References

Agazarian, Y., & Peters, R. (1981). *The visible and invisible group: Perspectives on group psychotherapy and group process.* London: Routledge & Kegan Paul.

Alonso, A., & Rutan, J. S. (1979). Women in group therapy. *International Journal of Group Psychotherapy, 29*(4), 481–491.

Aries, E. (1976). Interaction patterns and themes of male, female, and mixed groups. *Small Group Behavior, 7*(1), 7–18.

Astrachan, B. M., Harrow, M., & Flynn, H. (1968). Influence of the value system of a psychiatric setting on behavior in group therapy meetings. *Social Psychiatry, 3*, 165–172.

Bachrach, L., & Nadelson, C. (1988). *Treating chronically mentally ill women.* Washington, DC: American Psychiatric Association.

Barr, M. A. (1986). Homogeneous groups with acutely psychotic schizophrenics. *Group, 10*(1), 7–12.

Beitel, A., Everts, P., Boile, B., Nagel, E., Bragdon, C, & MacKesson, B. (1983). Hub group: An innovative approach to group therapy in a short-term inpatient adolescent unit. *Adolescence, 18,* 1–15.

Berland, D. I., & Poggi, R. (1979). Expressive group psychotherapy with the aging. *International Journal of Group Psychotherapy, 29*(1), 87–108.

Betcher, R. W. (1983). The treatment of depression in brief inpatient group psychotherapy. *International Journal of Group Psychotherapy, 33,* 365–385.

Beutler, L. E., & Clarkin, J. F. (1990). *Systematic treatment selection: Toward targeted therapeutic intervention.* New York: Brunner/Mazel.

Bienenfeld, D. (1988). Group psychotherapy with the elderly in the state hospital. In B. W. Maclennan, S. Saul, & M. B. Weiner (Eds.), *Group psychotherapies for the elderly* (pp. 177–187). Madison, CT: International Universities Press.

Borriello, J. F. (1976). Group therapy in hospital systems. In L. R. Wolberg & M. L. Aronson (Eds.), *Group therapy* (pp. 99–108). New York: Stratton.

Brabender, V. (1985). Time-limited inpatient group therapy: A developmental model. *International Journal of Group Psychotherapy, 35*(3), 373–390.

Brabender, V. (1992). The growth of women in a short-term inpatient group. *Group, 16* (3), 131–146.

Butler, R. N. (1963). The life review: An interpretation of reminiscence in the aged. *Psychiatry, 26*, 65–76.

Carlock, C. H., & Martin, P. Y. (1977). Sex composition and the intensive group experience. *Social Work, 22*, 27–32.

Coché, E., Cooper, J. B. Petermann, K. J. (1984). Differential outcomes of cognitive and interactional group therapies. *Small Group Behavior, 15*(4), 497–509.

Coché, E., & Polikoff, B. (1979). Self-disclosure in short-term group psychotherapy. *Group, 3*, 35–41.

Dacey, C. (1989). Inpatient group psychotherapy: Cohesion facilitates separation. *Group, 13*(l), 23–30.

Duncan, J., & Kennedy, S. H. (1992). Inpatient group treatment. In H. Harper-Giuffre & R. R. MacKenzie (Eds.), *Group therapy for eating disorders* (pp. 149–160). Washington, DC: American Psychiatric Association.

Erickson, R. C. (1984). *Inpatient small group psychotherapy: A pragmatic approach.* Springfield, IL: Charles C Thomas.

Erickson, R. C. (1986). Heterogeneous groups: A legitimate alternative. *Group, 10*(1), 21–33.

Froberg, W., & Slife, B. D. (1987). Overcoming obstacles to the implementation of Yalom's model of inpatient group psychotherapy. *International Journal of Group Psychotherapy, 37*(3), 371–388.

Gabbard, G. (1992). The therapeutic relationship in psychiatric hospital treatment. *Bulletin of the Menninger Clinic, 56*(1), 4–19.

Ghuman, H. S., & Sarles, R. M. (1989). Three group psychotherapy settings with long-term adolescent inpatients: Advantages and disadvantages. *Psychiatric Hospital, 19*(4), 161–164.

Gilewski, M. J. (1986). Group therapy with cognitively impaired older adults. *Clinical Gerontology, 5*, 281–296.

Golden, D. L., & Dominiak, G. M. (1986). Single-gender group psychotherapy: A "women's group" for adolescent inpatients. *Group, 10*(4), 217–227.

Goodman, R. K. (1988). A geriatric group in an acute care psychiatric teaching hospital: Pride or prejudice? In B. W. Maclennan, S. Saul, & M. B. Weiner (Eds.), *Group psychotherapies for the elderly* (pp. 151–164). Madison, CT: International Universities Press.

Greene, L. R., & Cole, M. B. (1991). Level and form of psychopathology and the structure of group therapy. *International Journal of Group Psychotherapy, 41*(4), 499–521.

Hendren, R. L., Atkins, D. M., Sumner, C. R., & Barber, J. K. (1987). Model for the group treatment of eating disorder. *International Journal of Group Psychotherapy, 37*(4), 589–602.

Hirschhorn, L. (1988). *The workplace within: The psychodynamics of organizational life.* Cambridge, MA: MIT Press.

Hollingshead, A. B., & Redlich, S. C. (1958). *Social class and mental illness.* New York: Wiley.

Johnson, D. R. (1985). Expressive group psychotherapy with the elderly: A drama therapy approach. *International Journal of Group Psychotherapy, 35*(1), 109–127.

Kanas, N. (1988). Therapy groups for schizophrenic patients on acute care units. *Hospital and Community Psychiatry, 39*(5), 546–549.

Kanas, N., Rogers, M., Kreth, E., Patterson, L., & Campbell, R. (1980). The effectiveness of group psychotherapy during the first three weeks of hospitalization: A controlled study. *Journal of Nervous and Mental Disease, 168,* 487–492.

Kaplan, A. S., Kerr, A., & Maddocks, S. E. (1992). Day hospital group treatment. In H. Harper-Giuffre & K. R. MacKenzie (Eds.), *Group psychotherapy for eating disorders* (pp. 161–179). Washington, DC: American Psychiatric Association.

Klein, R. H., Hunter, D. E., & Brown, S. L. (1986). Long-term inpatient group psychotherapy: The ward group. *International Journal of Group Psychotherapy, 36*(3), 361–380.

Klein, R. H., & Kugel, B. (1981). Inpatient group psychotherapy from a systems perspective: Reflections through a glass darkly. *International Journal of Group Psychotherapy, 31*(3), 311–328.

Kraft, I. A. (1961). Some special considerations in adolescent group psychotherapy. *International Journal of Group Psychotherapy, 11,* 196–203.

Kraft, I. A. (1983). Child and adolescent group psychotherapy. In H. I. Kaplan & B. J. Sadock (Eds.), *Comprehensive group psychotherapy* (pp. 223–234). Baltimore, MD: Wallace & Wilkins.

Lakin, M. (1988). Group therapies with the elderly: Issues and prospects. In B. W. Maclennan, S. Saul, & M. B. Weiner (Eds.), *Group psychotherapies for the elderly* (pp. 43–55). Madison, CT: International Universities Press.

Leonard, C. V. (1973). What helps most about hospitalization. *Comprehensive Psychiatry, 14,* 365–369.

Leopold, H. S. (1977). Selective group approaches with psychotic patients in hospital settings. *Journal of Psychotherapy, 30,* 95–105.

Leszcz, M., Feigenbaum, E., Sadavoy, J., & Robinson, A. (1985). A men's group: Psychotherapy of elderly men. *International Journal of Group Psychotherapy, 35*(2), 177–196.

Leszcz, M., Yalom, I. D., & Norden, M. (1985). The value of inpatient group psychotherapy: Patients' perceptions. *International Journal of Group Psychotherapy, 35*(3), 411–433.

MacKenzie, K. R., & Livesley, W. J. (1983). A developmental model for brief group therapy. In R. R. Dies & K. R. MacKenzie (Eds.), *Advances in group psychotherapy: Integrating research and practice.* Madison, CT: International Universities Press.

Moran, J. A., & Gatz, M. (1987). Group therapies for nursing home adults: An evaluation of two treatment approaches. *Gerontologist, 27,* 558–591.

Ramos, N., & Richmond, A. H. (1991). Adolescent group therapy in an inpatient facility. *Group, 15*(2), 81–88.

Rawlings, E. I., & Gauron, E. F. (1973). Responders and non-responders to an accelerated time-limited group. *Perspectives in Psychiatric Care, 11*(2), 65–69.

Rice, C., & Rutan, J. (1981). Boundary maintenance in inpatient therapy groups. *International Journal of Group Psychotherapy, 31,* 297–309.

Russo, N. F. (1990). Overview: Forging research priorities in women's mental health. *American Psychologist, 45*(3), 368–373.

Saul, S. (1988). Group therapy with confused and disoriented elderly people. In B. W. Maclennan, S. Saul, & M. B. Weiner (Eds.), *Group psychotherapies for the elderly* (pp. 199–208). Madison, CT: International Universities Press.

Schopler, J. H., & Galinsky, M. J. (1990) Can open-ended groups move beyond beginnings? *Small Group Research, 21*(4), 435–449.

Shaw, M. (1981). *Group dynamics: The psychology of small group behavior.* New York: McGraw-Hill.

Shoham, H., & Neuschatz, S. (1985). Group therapy with senile patients. *National Association of Social Workers, 30*(1), 69–73.

Siegel, L. I. (1987). Confrontation and support in group therapy in the residential treatment of severely disturbed adolescents. *Adolescence, 12*(87), 681–690.

Slife, B. D., Sasscer-Burgos, J., Froberg, W., & Ellington, S. (1989). Effect of depression on processing interactions in group psychotherapy. *International Journal of Group Psychotherapy, 39*(1), 79–104.

Sorensen, M. (1986). Narcissism and loss in the elderly: Strategies for an inpatient older adults group. *International Journal of Group Psychotherapy, 36*(4), 533–547.

Stein, M. D., & Kymissis, P. (1989). Adolescent inpatient group psychotherapy. In F. J. C. Azima & L. H. Richmond (Eds.), *Adolescent group psychotherapy* (pp. 69–84). Madison, CT: International Universities Press.

Weiner, M. F. (1986). Homogeneous groups. In A. J. Frances & R. E. Hales (Eds.), *American Psychiatric Association annual review* (pp. 714–727). Washington, DC: American Psychiatric Association.

Whitaker, L., & Deikman, A. (1980). Psychotherapy of severe depression. *Psychotherapy: Theory, Research and Practice, 17*(1), 85–93.

Yalom, I. D. (1983). *Inpatient group psychotherapy.* New York: Basic Books.

# II

# The Models

# 3

# The Educative Model

The education of patients about aspects of their personality or character, the origins or precipitants of their psychopathology, and the role that these aspects contribute to problems in living is an important goal of many group therapy models. Models vary in the extent to which education is a primary function of the group. When education is a significant focus, models also differ in their methods of accomplishing this goal; that is, models vary in their requirement that patients discover problems and solutions on their own. At one end of the spectrum are the psychoeducational groups in which the leader is active in didactically disseminating specific information. These groups are specifically designed to impart knowledge to patients and their families about their illnesses and to teach techniques by which they can cope more effectively with the symptoms (Clarke & Lewinsohn, 1989; Ettin, Heiman, & Kopel, 1988; Hoberman, Lewinsohn, & Tilson, 1988; Plante, Pinder, & Howe, 1988). At the other end of the spectrum are those models in which members actively discover for themselves (with other members' input) either how to understand their emotional reactions (e.g., the object relations/systems model and the interpersonal model) or how to manage more effectively an existing disease (e.g., Alcoholics Anonymous groups). In this chapter, we present an inpatient model that, like those at the latter end of the spectrum, actively focuses on educating patients to think "clinically" so that they may more effectively cope with their illnesses.

# Theoretical Underpinnings

The educative model has been most clearly articulated by Maxmen (1978, 1984), who formalized this model while at the short-term inpatient service of Dartmouth-Hitchcock Medical Center.[1] This model was one of the first systematic efforts to design a group psychotherapy approach specifically for inpatients. Unlike earlier contributions, it was not fashioned after approaches of long-term outpatient group therapy but entailed a recognition that the inpatient group in a short-term setting has many unique features. The model was developed to aid patients who display more disturbed behavioral symptomatology, greater psychological disorganization, intensely primitive and numerous dependency demands, greater denial of difficulties, and more hopelessness and ineffectualness than do outpatients (Maxmen, 1978).

In constructing this model, Maxmen took into account a number of factors. The first pertained to a prior research finding concerning patients' interests in discussing their symptomatology (Talland & Clark, 1954). Maxmen believed that the inpatient group psychotherapist should capitalize on this interest: Symptoms that precipitated hospitalization became a focus of the group. The second factor related to the brief time that patients would attend group; Maxmen recognized that it was unrealistic to expect that the group experience would resolve even a major portion of an individual's problems. Thus, a focused criterion group was adapted to an inpatient population (Maxmen, 1978). A *focused criterion group* is a group that is designed to eliminate undesirable or self-destructive target behaviors (e.g., overeating, drug abuse). Leader-fostered group support and sanctions, rather than interpretation or transference, help members not to engage in target behaviors, and "group process" is what primarily produces change (Singer, Astrachan, Gould, & Klein, 1975). The "target behaviors" chosen for this inpatient model were the

---

[1] In writing about short-term groups, others such as Waxer (1977), have promoted ideas similar to Maxmen's but have done so in a less developed fashion.

symptoms that precipitated hospitalization. The third factor pertained to an important reality of inpatient group life: the extragroup contact (i.e., shared experiences on the residential unit)
that both therapists and patients have with each other. Rather
than regarding this contact as sullying the treatment (as would
an outpatient therapist), the inpatient therapist uses it as a resource for augmenting the group experience. Finally, Maxmen
was influenced by an evolving literature on therapeutic factors
(to which he was a major contributor). The model highlights
certain therapeutic factors:[2] group cohesiveness (the individual's
attraction to the group and members in it and the "we-ness"
that members experience being part of the group), instillation of
hope (the belief or hope that treatment can be effective), and
universality (the discovery that problems are not unique and that
members have similar concerns). This model deemphasizes the
use of catharsis (the expression of emotion or affect), insight (the
discovery of something about one's behavior, one's motivational
system, or one's unconscious), and identification (imitating positive attributes of either the therapist or other group members).
The strategies it uses are based on Maxmen's own research findings that when asked, patients reported that cohesiveness, instillation of hope, altruism, and universality were the most valuable factors in a group setting, whereas catharsis, insight, and
identification were less important (Maxmen, 1973).

The educative model is atheoretical with respect to the etiology
of psychopathology (Maxmen, 1984). Thus, the utility of this
model is not constrained by the theoretical orientation of the
treating practitioners in charge of the unit or even the theoretical
orientation of the group therapist. This model does not imply
that, patients, their biology, their families, or society causes the
illness, although it acknowledges that each may aggravate it.

---

[2] It is a standard practice among group psychotherapists to conceptualize
therapeutic change to occur through an interplay of various human experiences,
which Yalom (1975) referred to as the *11 curative factors* or more recently as
*therapeutic factors* (Yalom, 1985). These are instillation of hope, universality,
imparting of information, altruism, recapitulation of the primary family group,
development of socializing techniques, imitative behavior (identification) interpersonal learning, group cohesiveness, catharsis, and existential factors.

The patient is seen as a "normal" person who also has an illness (i.e., psychopathology; Maxmen, 1984). Psychiatric patients (and their mental illness) are likened to medical patients (and their medical illness). For example, with a medical illness such as glaucoma, the patient's glaucoma and personality are separate issues. Similarly, this model sees the patient's psychopathology (e.g., schizophrenia) as not necessarily part of the personality. That is, the patients' "crazy" symptoms are distinct from the patients themselves and their coping responses (even if the coping responses are ineffective). As Kibel (1984) commented in describing the educative model, "It is as if the personality has been invaded by an illness that it is unable to temper" (p. 337). Viewing it in this way, an otherwise "normal" individual must conduct his or her life with the additional burdens of psychopathology (Maxmen, 1984). The basic assumption of this model about the essential nature of people reflects the belief that people are basically good and capable. As Kibel said about the educative model in contrasting it with the object relations model, a fundamentally healthy core self is threatened and merely needs assistance to be "shored up" (Kibel, 1984). This notion is different from one that would be endemic to the object relations/ systems model wherein everything patients feel, think, and do is a product of their psychodynamics (and perhaps the system in which they operate). For the educative model, the self is autonomous from, and yet affected by, psychopathology; conversely, for the object relations/systems model or the developmental model, psychopathology is integral to and inseparable from the self.

This model uses the evidence that short-term group therapy has not been shown to be effective in alleviating the symptomatology of major psychopathology (e.g., hallucinations and delusions; American Psychiatric Association, 1982; Pattison, Brissenden, & Wohl, 1967). The educative model is not aimed at ameliorating or eliminating symptoms; no psychiatric "cure" is intended. Rather, the group's mission is to aid patients to develop more healthy or adaptive thinking so they can deal with or manage the psychiatric crises that precipitated their hospitalization (Waxer, 1977). The educative model is directed toward teaching the patient to cope with the illness and leaves the task of "curing" it to other types of treatment (Maxmen, 1984). Thus, in this model, the group therapist deaccenuates the issues of causality. At first glance, it might seem that it is similar to a support group for people with medical problems (e.g., diabetes). However, unlike such a support group, an educative group is designed to be more than "mere support" given that the quality of interpersonal relationships, although perhaps not causal, is a more important moderating factor in mental illness than it is in, for example, diabetes.

Behavior is a primary focus because it is the development or exacerbation of behavioral symptoms that leads to a patient's hospitalization. It is the adequate attenuation of this symptomatic behavior that is required for hospital discharge, and it is the patient's ability to respond adaptively to intensifications of disturbed behavior that will avert future hospitalization. A behavioral focus is encouraged by the group leader also because it is easier for patients to identify and discuss concrete issues and events than it is for them to understand intrapsychic conflict or articulate other unconscious activity.[3] If patients are asked to examine behavior, they will participate more readily and act more therapeutically at an earlier point in their group involvement. The educative model's emphasis on behavior does not exclude the exploration of subjective experiences; however, the discussion of feelings and attitudes should concentrate on those emotions that are proximally related to (precede, accompany, and follow) those manifest symptoms related to the patients' requirements of hospitalization (Maxmen, 1978).

The nexus of this group is to learn to "think clinically" and "behave therapeutically" toward one another. Group members are said to be behaving therapeutically when they focus on those behaviors (and related feelings) that directly precipitated and continue to sustain hospitalization (Maxmen, 1978). Working therapeutically is considered more important than is resolving problems or ameliorating symptoms. Group cohesiveness, a highly valued aspect of group by inpatients, can be facilitated if

---

[3] This is not to be confused with behavioral therapy wherein specific behaviors are taught, modified, practiced, and reinforced.

patients share the common task of behaving therapeutically (Maxmen, 1978). The assumption is that if patients learn to act therapeutically toward one another, they will then be able to apply what they have learned toward their own difficulties.

## Goals of Treatment

The goal of the educative model is the development of the patients' abilities to help themselves and others by learning to think clinically and to behave therapeutically toward others. Patients learn to think clinically so that they can more effectively manage the sequelae of their mental illnesses. Specifically, this is done by teaching group members to identify their own maladaptive behaviors and to recognize and avoid potentially problematic situations that could then lead to an exacerbation of symptomatology (Maxmen, 1978). The expectation is that when symptoms intensify, patients will be able to engage in a self-examination process to minimize the dysfunctional impact of the symptoms. An analytically oriented practitioner might refer to this process as the *strengthening of the observing ego*. In behaving therapeutically toward others, participants realize that they have altruistic capabilities, recognize that their difficulties are not unique, and in the process learn to accept aid from others. Note that this model of group therapy has different goals than other inpatient hospital treatments such as pharmacotherapy. To contrast the relative success of group psychotherapy with that of pharmacotherapy is as meaningless as comparing the efficacy of a group experience for diabetics with insulin for treating them. In this way, it is more similar to a group therapy on a medical ward. For example, with a group for cancer patients, the group experience will not "cure" the cancer. Yet, such a group could still aid patients in coping with their illnesses (e.g., instilling hope, recognizing reoccurrences sooner, learning to use community resources) and in that indirect manner increase an individual's longevity (Spiegel, 1990). Similarly, with the educative model, it is proposed that the goals are to help patients cope with their mental illnesses.

# Technical Considerations

## The Role of the Leader

The therapist is instructive: He or she advises patients how to think clinically and act therapeutically. Unlike other educational models and contrary to what the term *educative* might connote, therapists are not didactic; they do not give lectures or instructions (Maxmen, 1984). In an educative model, leaders do not make their relationships to the patients a central group focus (as is more likely to happen in the object relations/systems or developmental models). When the inevitably strong feelings toward the group therapist surface, they are dealt with like any other significant here-and-now issue: The feelings or events are acknowledged. However, if these reactions do not relate to the patients' target symptoms, the group energies are refocused on the target behaviors (Maxmen, 1978).

The group's effectiveness is ultimately the responsibility of the therapist. The therapist discharges this responsibility by performing three tasks: maintaining group boundaries, facilitating the development of norms, and teaching patients to help one another. The boundaries set are both compositional, such as who should be in the group, and temporal, such as when and for how long group sessions should last (Maxmen, Tucker, & LeBow, 1974). Group norms should include emphasizing behavior in the here-and-now, encouraging expedient discussion of target problems (e.g., reinforcing that group is not one-to-one treatment with an audience), discouraging inappropriate activity, (e.g., long soliloquies of tragic life histories) and encouraging participation of all members (Maxmen et al., 1974; Waxer, 1977). The responsibility to behave therapeutically is deliberately and persistently delegated to patients, not to the leaders. The rationale for this position is that if therapists directly or indirectly give the message that only they have the "answers," dependent behavior is reinforced and patients experience decreased self-esteem and diminished effectiveness (Maxmen, 1978). Conversely, encouraging patients to take responsibility for comments enhances their self-regard and decreases their sense of alienation. The task of the leader is to motivate patients and to actively foster patients behaving clinically by avoiding the search for "elusive dynamic issues" and redirecting patients to focus on their specific target symptoms (Maxmen, 1978). This delimitation of scope sometimes requires that the therapist continues to refocus members on what each of them intends to do with problems currently facing them (Waxer, 1977). In this way, patients are encouraged to take responsibility for their lives and for the rate of their therapeutic gain. Occasionally, the educative model allows the therapist to comment directly on an individual's behavior or the group dynamics. This intervention is suggested when members have failed to behave therapeutically, despite the therapist's efforts to help them do so (Maxmen, 1978). Further delineation of its appropriate use has not yet been articulated. Group process has been explored in an inpatient setting only when it interferes with group work.

In this model, the therapist responds to the manifest rather than latent content of members' communication. For example, if after a difficult session a patient says that he feels better and is ready to leave the hospital, the therapist may congratulate him and the group and concentrate on the positive aspects. Therapists also reinforce behaviors by praising patients when they make useful comments. If the patients avoid issues or behave countertherapeutically, the leader labels the avoidance and recommends alternative approaches (Maxmen, 1978). For example, sometimes patients rally around the fantasy that they could make more gains if the therapists never attended. Here, the therapist may advise patients that, given the brief time they will be in the hospital, it would be valuable for them to engage with enthusiasm in leaderless groups in addition to what they might accomplish in the group with the therapist present (Waxer, 1977). Another type of resistance with which the therapist may deal occurs when a patient fails to mention what precipitated his or her hospitalization. The therapist may say,

> You have been very helpful to others in their struggles of examining what brought them here. However, I am concerned because you have not permitted other members to help you focus on your issues that brought you into the hospital. In about a week, you will be facing the same

stresses. If you are to make use of what we have to offer, it would be in your best interests to tell us the details of what brought you here.

This model advocates a moderate level of therapist self-disclosure or transparency. That is, the therapist may disclose personal information (e.g., "We're all uncomfortable now") as long as the disclosure is limited to directly facilitating the group task. Therapists are encouraged to use a wide range of persuasive techniques—"to joke, swear, charm, or even cajole patients in order to motivate them to behave therapeutically" (Maxmen, 1978, p. 331). Therapists are free to provide encouragement, praise, and suggestion as long as the intent is to delegate the responsibility of making therapeutic comments to the group members. Actively and directly, the therapist attempts to do for patients only what they are not able to do for themselves and does not perform for them what they have already mastered (Maxmen, 1978).

## Content of the Session

As previously stated, the primary goal of the educative model is to increase patients' abilities to think clinically so that they can learn to respond appropriately and effectively to the consequences of their mental illnesses. An atmosphere of mutual support is the focus (Mushet, Whalan, & Power, 1989). The opportunity for patients to make therapeutic comments to others encourages hope, increases group cohesiveness, illustrates the universality of problems, and facilitates altruistic behavior—all factors that group inpatients have judged to be the most therapeutic (Maxmen, 1973). These four factors should be stressed frequently if the setting is a short-term acute care facility in which patient turnover is frequent (Maxmen et al., 1974). For example, when a patient spontaneously states that he or she is feeling better, whether or not the gains are real, the therapist should positively acknowledge the statement and encourage others to identify what the patient did to feel better. For example, in response to a member's declaration of marked improvement, the therapist might say, "I am glad to hear that. Does the group know how Mr. A accomplished this?" (Maxmen et al., 1974, p.

183). Praising the patient encourages hope in all. Engaging the group in the exploration of how this positive change was accomplished facilitates altruistic behavior and increases cohesiveness. This tact is similar to what is done in the interpersonal model (chapter 4), wherein an effort is made to focus on what led to changes in the patients' behaviors that are associated with positive outcomes (Yalom, 1983).

This model attempts to provide an experience that is not offered by the other hospital treatments the patient receives. The uniqueness of the group lies in its interpersonal nature, with the opportunity for patients to experience and clarify their contributions to their dysfunctional relationships with people as they relate to the target symptoms. The expectations of patients' conduct in the group follows the same general rules of conduct that society prescribes for social exchanges. For example, a patient needlessly insulting another patient is as inappropriate in the group setting as it would be in any other social encounter outside the hospital. As Maxmen (1984) incisively said, "Mental illness is no excuse for bad manners" (p. 358).

A here-and-now focus (a focus on what is happening in the immediate present as opposed to a historical investigation) is of utmost importance in this model. Although many of the group models in this book focus on immediate experience as their cornerstone, the educative model is distinguished by the manner in which it uses the here-and-now. (See Ferencik, 1991, and Slife & Lanyon, 1991, for a discussion of the here-and-now focus.) In this model, the here-and-now focus is a guided one that must relate to the target symptoms. This guided here-and-now focus is contrasted with the interactional agenda of the interpersonal model (see chapter 4), wherein patients are permitted to establish any agenda that relates to an immediate interpersonal concern. Of course, much of the time these concerns will relate to the patients' target symptoms. The difference between a guided and an unguided focus is likely to affect differentially the behavior of certain categories of patients. For example, individuals with borderline personality disorder often do not talk spontaneously about the factors or situations that have precipitated their hospitalization. Rather, they often remain fixed in the helper role unless a crisis occurs (Slavinska-Holy, 1983). Consequently, these individuals, although enticed by the model's injunction to members to behave therapeutically, would at the same time be aided by the educative model's insistence that members be directed toward target symptoms. Also, for some depressed patients who recoil from here-and-now exploration, the anchoring of the group in a focus on target symptoms may be reassuring. Another respect in which these foci are different is that the interpersonal approach allows for the emergence of interpersonal concerns that although important, were not apparent at the time of admission. For example, the patient may have been hospitalized because of intrusive behavior in public places. However, preceding the intrusiveness may have been a prolonged period of isolation that propelled the patient to take desperate measures to relieve loneliness. The educative model may provide a strong focus on the patient's intrusiveness. In contrast, the interpersonal model may be of greater assistance to that patient in enabling him or her to identify, say, his or her proclivity to imagine rejections, a tendency that originally drove the patient to self-isolation.

In the educative model, the therapist uses situations that arise in the group to illustrate how patients can more effectively aid one another. The educative model expands the here-and-now focus to include the hospital, unit events, and interactions that occur outside the group (patients are encouraged to continue discussing the issues raised in group between sessions). Behaviors seen by any and all group participants are considered eligible and valuable for group scrutiny. This widening of the group context has the advantage of enriching the myriad events available for group exploration and facilitates members' integration of the total hospital experience. Practically, however, this feature requires that group members be from the same unit given that the events referred to must be witnessed by others in the hospital. It therefore limits the use of the model to those settings in which same-unit living arrangements are possible. However, we think that this model can be adapted to the circumstances in which members do not reside on the same unit, although if members are not from the same living area, the group leaders must sharply limit the use of extragroup events in the session; otherwise, such events would be similar to the presentation of historical events or events that occur outside the hospital. Often, the multitude of here-and-now events requires that group leaders need to help patients to prioritize. Proponents of both the interpersonal model (Yalom, 1983) and the educative model (Maxmen, 1978, 1984) agree that patients need to be trained to give top priority to the here-and-now issues that most directly relate to the target symptoms of the greatest number of group members.

Sometimes, fascinating issues unfold in a group session that are not seminal to the patients' target symptoms. The examination of important topics that do not relate directly to target symptoms is considered a resistance to exploration of the more immediate issues that precipitated or perpetuate the patient's need to be hospitalized (see Clinical Illustration for an example). Historical material is considered useful only if it directly relates to symptoms that precipitated hospitalization. Similarly, expanding consciousness, increasing sensitivity, and expressing hostility are important only if they facilitate the development or improvement of adaptive behaviors (Maxmen et al., 1974). In this regard, exploration of group process is done only to overcome obstacles that interfere with group work. The group therapist uses his or her understanding of group dynamics to refocus members on the group's main task. Thus, an appreciation of the extensive literature on group dynamics and clinical experience in the model's use is helpful but is not essential.

For the participants to aid one another, it is essential that they know what led each patient to be hospitalized. If, after a number of attempts, the patients are not able to elicit another patient's behaviors that precipitated hospitalization, the leader must do so; the therapist reveals why the patient needed hospitalization (Maxmen, 1978). Such disclosures occur only after (a) the patient has been given ample opportunity to become accustomed to the workings of the group, (b) members have made repeated efforts to elicit this information and have not succeeded, and (c) the patient continues to desire to attend the group. It is felt that to allow a patient to remain silent about his or her reasons for hospitalization is to suggest that he or she is too fragile to handle reality (Maxmen, 1978, 1984).

## Leaderless Meetings

One of the unique features of the educative model is its proviso and advocacy for the establishment of regular meetings without staff. Although the leaderless meeting as a technique has been in use since the early part of this century, particularly in the context of therapeutic communities (Ansbacher, 1951), the educative model is the only model in this book that uses it. Leaderless meetings can be structurally of two types. In the first type, they are built into the group program, occur with some regularity, and alternate with leader-led sessions. These leaderless sessions have traditionally been referred to as *alternate meetings*, and there is some literature to support their efficacy at least in an outpatient setting (Desmond & Seligman, 1977). The second type of leaderless meetings are of an impromptu nature and arise when unresolved issues cannot be addressed or accommodated in a leader-led session (e.g., when the group is out of time or an event or issue on the unit arises prior to the next leader-led session). An impromptu session also can occur when the leader assigns a task to be completed by the entire group or subgroup before the next session. In each of these cases, members of the group can officially gather and hold sessions without the leader but with the staff's and leader's endorsement. In the impromptu type of group, members almost without exception need a setting in which they are lodged on the same unit, whereas with the scheduled alternate meeting, living on different units is possible. The educative model specifically endorses the alternate session. However, all shared group activities, whether they be community meeting or occupational therapy, are valued as places for patients to discuss issues given that they can facilitate the development of cohesiveness and increase patients' sense of continuity (Waxer, 1977).

One particular feature of alternative meetings is consistent with a central tenet of the educative model: The group's value is derived from patients' experiencing themselves, rather than the leader, as the primary therapeutic agents (Maxmen, 1978). Indeed, there is some evidence that the emotional climate of leaderless sessions is less depressed and less tense than are leader-led sessions (Harrow, Astrachan, Becker, Miller, &

Schwartz, 1967) and that they have a significantly higher level of verbal interaction and problem-solving attempts than do leader-led sessions (Astrachan, Harrow, Becker, Schwartz, & Miller, 1967; Becker, Harrow, Astrachan, Detre, & Miller, 1968). An additional advantage of the leaderless group session is the increase in the frequency of sessions without the requirement of additional staffing. Increased frequency of meetings, like other shared activities, can enhance the development of cohesiveness as well as give a headstart toward clarification and consolidation of the target symptoms to be addressed in groups (Waxer, 1977).

Leaderless sessions are indirectly affected by the milieu. Thus, these groups are likely to have the greatest utility in settings that encourage patients to assume major roles as change agents. Unless the unit is structured so that there is an adequate forum for patients to learn what topics to discuss and how this can be done, "staffless groups can readily flounder into meaningless chit chat" (Maxmen et al., 1974, p. 187).

## Selection and Preparation

Groups consist of 4 to 12 patients and 1 to 2 therapists (Maxmen et al., 1974). Staff selectively refer patients to group therapy. Although the therapist solicits input from the treatment team and even from the group members on the appropriateness of a patient for group, the therapist makes the final decision (Maxmen, 1984). Admission should be based more on the therapist's appraisal of the patient's potential to behave therapeutically and less on diagnosis. Patients who are persistently mute, physically disruptive, hyperactive, unable to concentrate, very severely regressed, considerably brain-damaged, or slated to be discharged within a few days should not join the group (Maxmen, 1978; Maxmen et al., 1974). This latter feature provides for the creation of a somewhat more stable group than do other models that place no such demands for a required length of tenure of a member. In addition, although group patients may have been involuntarily admitted into the hospital, group attendance should be voluntary. The "admission-as-privilege"[4] avoids power struggles

---

[4] The educative model encourages leaders to reward patients who function

with patients (Maxmen, 1984). Even more important, patients who do not wish to be in a group have the potential to affect cohesiveness detrimentally. Because cohesiveness is important to the successful functioning of these groups, any factor that adversely affects cohesiveness should be eliminated or at least minimized. Revealing confidential admission data requires "voluntary" attendance so as not to create ethical dilemmas. Thus, the model is limited to those settings that permit voluntary group attendance. At the same time, much time can be "wasted" with discussion of voluntary status. In many instances, voluntary participation is a pseudo-issue because it masks the reality that all patients bring resistance to groups. It also obscures important considerations such as the achievement of beneficial participation (Silverman & Powers, 1985). An argument can be made that voluntary patients in effect agree and submit to a composite treatment program (Erickson, 1981).

An individual pre-group session has been suggested for the purpose of screening and orienting prospective group members (Maxmen et al., 1974). However, there is some disagreement about the necessity of the screening process. In some settings, referral agents are extraordinarily accurate and appropriate in their recommendations for the educative group; in this case, the screening portion of the pre-group orientation can be eliminated without disruption to the group census or group process (Silverman & Powers, 1985).

A pre-group orientation still remains essential because it also functions to educate patients about the particulars of the frame (e.g., time, place, number of patients in group), the purpose, and personal conduct in the group setting. Prospective patients' preconceived notions and fantasies about the group should be explored. The pre-group session is particularly essential to help patients understand that they are expected to reveal their reasons for hospitalization so that they can begin to learn to think clinically with the eventual goal of being able to respond effectively to the consequences of their illnesses. They are made aware that

---

as valuable group members, either by offering them "tokens" (or an equivalent) or increased hospital privileges (Maxmen et al., 1974).

the goals are not to reduce symptoms or necessarily solve problems. Consonant with the model is the view that patients as well as staff can effectively orient a prospective member (Maxmen et al., 1974). However, care must be taken when allowing other members to orient new members because there is some evidence that inpatients may not be the most effective agents in this task (Verinis, 1970). To aid in this process of education, the dissemination of a group therapy information sheet such as that in Appendix A is encouraged to reinforce the verbal orientation (Maxmen et al., 1974). This sheet focuses on the connection between interpersonal style and target symptoms and gives many examples on how members "help each other" and "don't help each other." We also believe that consent to reveal admission data should also be obtained from patients at this pre-group session and, in addition, be explained on the information sheet.

## Therapeutic Frame

Each session is 45–60 minutes in length because of inpatients' relatively short attention spans (Maxmen, 1978). When a patient enters group, he or she can be encouraged to help others with their problems. If the leaders initially accept and even legitimize the new member's role as a helper rather than accentuate his or her need for help, the patient's resistance to group is likely to be diminished, and it will be easier for the patient to assimilate the group's norms (Maxmen, 1978). As acculturation to the group develops, the member may be more able to acknowledge and accept therapeutic aid. Thus, this model may be a particularly good one for those patients who are superficial in their interactions or are frightened of the group experience and thus defend against their fears by remaining silent or by functioning in the helping role. Three to five sessions per week are seen as desirable (Maxmen, 1978).

# Clinical Illustration

The following is a vignette of an educative group in an acute short-term care facility. On this day, the group consisted of 6 members and a therapist.

## Group Members

Nancy, a married woman in her forties, had marital difficulties that led to a suicidal gesture and admittance to the hospital from the emergency room. She had been attending group for 2 weeks. The situation at home was indeed volatile, with past physical violence between her husband and her. Nancy's mood vacillated between being depressed and sulking to being irritable and critical, with complaints that the nurses on the unit, her doctors, her two children, and her husband were not interested in her, not doing enough to help her, and were the causes of all her difficulties.

Nick, a lawyer in his midthirties, had also been in the group for 2 weeks. Nick was admitted because of major depression with psychotic features. This was precipitated by his wife leaving after her discovery of his affair with another woman. Nick had been fairly successful at the technical aspects of his profession of law, but his relationships with colleagues and management of associates had caused considerable subordinate dissatisfaction. Initially, he had been very quiet in group. Eventually, he managed to make an occasional comment to another member but had not yet revealed what brought him into the hospital. Until this point, there was little evidence in the group setting of the essence of his interpersonal problems on the job.

Fanny was an attractive 18-year-old with a history of drug abuse, running away, promiscuity, and truancy from school. She was admitted to the hospital after a drug overdose that was precipitated by her parents' refusal to allow her to return home after she had been rejected by a boyfriend. She had been hospitalized many times previously, although this was her second session in her first group experience.

Ike, a plumber in his midfifties, had been a bachelor for 25 years. Prior to that, he had been married for 5 years. The details of why and how the relationship ended were unclear. Since the end of the relationship, he had led a solitary existence except for his involvement with his church. He had held the same job for 35 years. He was admitted to the hospital after a suicide attempt, which seems to have been precipitated by a severe anxiety attack. Psychological testing revealed no evidence of psychosis.

Sara was an attractive 28-year-old married mother of an 8-month-old boy. She was admitted to intensive care unit after a very serious suicide attempt. She had recently been transferred to the psychiatric unit 2 days prior and had attended one group meeting. Little information was available as to what precipitated the suicide attempt. Psychological testing was ordered to rule out brain damage and an underlying psychosis but was still in progress.

Mark, a college graduate of a very prestigious school, was in his midtwenties and living at home with his two parents; he was admitted to the hospital after a suicide attempt. This attempt was the result of auditory hallucinations instructing him to kill himself to save the world. He had several previous admissions after stopping his neuroleptic drug and Lithium. This was his third group session.

## The Session

The group had already begun before the leader was seated. As the leader sat down, the group was involved in a discussion about an event that took place shortly before the group began. Apparently, Fanny had asked Ike if he could help her put on a necklace that had a small clasp. After he had done so, they walked into the group room and sat across from each other. Ike looked at the floor. When the therapist entered the group room, Nick was speaking.

> Nick: Hey, I saw what happened out there . . . didn't know you had it in you old man! How come no one asks me to do anything like that? Tell me your secret!
>
> Mark: Maybe it's his deodorant.

(The group is silent for a few minutes.)

> Ike: (Abashedly) I . . . I don't know what you're talking about.
>
> Nick: Don't tell me you don't know . . . she was coming on to you!

Fanny:  (slightly shocked) I just asked him to put on my necklace (to Nick with feigned annoyance). You have a sick mind.

Nick:  Back off . . . I was just kidding . . . that's what's wrong with this place . . . no one has a sense of humor.

Nancy:  Well, I do think that Fanny puts herself in compromising positions . . . and ends up with the wrong type.

Fanny:  What do you mean "compromising" . . . I give in too much?

Nancy:  No, I mean you just ask for trouble. You could have asked *me* to help you instead of a man that you hardly know (shaking her head). You young people just ask for trouble!

Ike:  (softly with incredulity) *I* wouldn't bother her.

Nancy:  I didn't mean that you *would* . . . I just meant that other men . . .

Nick:  (interrupts Nancy) Don't worry about her Ike, she's just jealous . . . No one to pant after her.

Nancy:  (with some indignation) I beg your pardon?

Mark:  This sounds like the Senate hearing debate on the appointment to the Supreme Court. Some witnesses from my alma mater. The real question of whether he is competent is obscured by these controversial issues of pseudo-morality.

At this point, the group engages in an animated debate about a controversial current event involving issues of sexuality in the workplace and the innocence or guilt of the various parties. The discussion goes on for several minutes.

(One might wonder why the therapist did not intervene sooner. This is a judgment call. The therapist's rationale was that he wanted to give the group the opportunity to focus on target symptoms themselves. Because they did not, he then took the lead. In this model, the therapist does not assume that because patients have been previously told how to focus on the target symptoms, that they necessarily resist this direction for "unconscious reasons." Although the group seemed to be preoccupied with the expression of sexuality inside and outside the group, the therapist refrained from exploring the group process or other dynamic issues as such. Rather, the therapist took the lead in helping members to adopt a focus consistent with the primary goal of the model: to teach members to think clinically by isolating and focusing on those behaviors that are pertinent to each member's presenting problems. When such an interesting and charged issue is brought up and it does not appear to be related directly to the target symptoms or their associated feelings, the therapist acknowledges the importance and interest in the issue but then shifts the group's focus to the target symptoms.)

> Therapist: Perhaps our discussion of sexuality is making everyone a bit tense and that's understandable. But I think we're also talking about how we communicate to each other here and on the unit. (The leader directly and indirectly encourages discussion of current and extragroup behaviors provided that they are related to the issues that brought members into the hospital.) Fanny, you didn't see what you did with Ike as a sexual invitation but some other members did. You told us yesterday that you end up getting involved with men before you even realize that you are. In fact, you said that's part of the reason you're here. Maybe what happened here is something you do on the outside.

(With this intervention, the therapist intentionally bypasses the likelihood that Fanny is communicating her unconscious intent accurately—to elicit sexual interest. Instead, the therapist takes Fanny's explanation at face value. The therapist connects the here-and-now of group behavior with the target behaviors that brought Fanny into the hospital.)

> Fanny: So why do I do this?
> Therapist: Perhaps we could change your question a little bit to: What leads up to your doing this?

(The therapist here is working toward the primary goal of the group to help members to think clinically. The therapist refrains, however, from engaging with the member in the task of discovering causality.)

| Fanny: | I don't know . . . I see a man sitting by himself at a bar and I . . . I don't know . . . sometimes I feel sorry for these men who are by themselves so I go up and . . . we have some drinks and . . . the next thing is I'm in their apartment and it's the next day. |
| Nick: | (dramatically) Yes, you just sacrifice yourself for all the lonely men! |
| Sara: | (gives Nick a disdainful glance and then speaks to Fanny) Maybe Ike looked lonely to you just like the men in the bar. |
| Fanny: | (softly) Yeah, Ike, you do. You look lonely. |
| Ike: | (slowly) I don't mean to give you that impression. I don't want anyone to feel sorry for me. |
| Therapist: | I think that Fanny has pointed to a problem that we haven't yet really explored . . . Ike mentioned his suicide attempt having something to do with feeling he has no one in the world and that he's doomed to be alone. But we don't know much more than that. |

(When the patient fails to take the initiative in talking about the circumstances precipitating his or her hospitalization, the therapist does so.)

For the next several minutes, the group asks Ike about his life. He describes his terror of violating his seclusion and reveals that his suicide attempt occurred on an evening when he failed to appear for a blind date that had been arranged by someone at his church. He indicated that the anxiety was intolerable and suicide seemed like his only recourse.

| Sara: | So what is he supposed to do when he starts feeling so panicky? What am I supposed to do when I feel depressed? I don't know what to do. |
| Nick: | Yeah, I'm not hearing any direction here. None of us are going to be in the hospital that long and I'd sure like some answers before I leave. |

The nodding heads as Sara and Nick speak reveal that they are articulating what other members feel.

Therapist:   It's true that all of you will be getting out and facing many of the same situations. That's why it wouldn't help for me to give you answers. But you will have yourselves. Each one of you has resources for helping yourselves. Your job in here is to work with one another to find them.

Nick:   Yeah, you mean we do all the work while you take a snooze, ha ha. (Mark and Fanny snicker) Why are you here? What *is* your job anyway?

Sara:   (with sincerity) So how can you help us?

Therapist:   My job is to help you to work with one another, sort of like a coach does with a team, and learn from one another. Like right now . . . Ike said he felt that he wanted to jump out of his skin? I suspect group members could give him some good ideas on some other ways he might have coped with his anxiety besides trying to take his life.

(The therapist, through his role clarification, performs an important function: establishing the norm that members take responsibility for their work in the group. The therapist does not avoid negative transference but defuses it by providing members with an explanation for why the group works as it does. In this exchange, the therapist fosters the group's use of two of the most important curative factors: altruism and the instillation of hope. The therapist's expression of confidence that the group did have resources to help Ike catalyzed members to give him a list of suggestions.)

For the next several minutes, the group offered suggestions—some sensible, some not. Ike interjected some of his own, such as calling a priest at his local parish.

Therapist:   The group has given Ike a lot to think about.

(The therapist here reinforces not a particular solution but the fact that the group has been engaging in the activity of thinking clinically.)

Fanny:   I think I know what Ike is feeling . . . I've been feeling the same way too . . . I just stayed in my apartment drinking and doing drugs by myself. But I'm sick of it. I'm sick of being alone. I'm going to try to get out a little more.

Nick: Oh yeah, I saw that guy you were hanging out with in the cafeteria. I'm sorry I'm not going to be there to see what "cosmically cool dude" you pick up when you leave the hospital. (to other members) Did you see the guy? He had a mohawk! Tell me, is your preference a guy like that, I mean with a mohawk and chains?

Sara: He did?

Fanny: I was just talking . . .

Mark: I saw this picture "Beauty and the Beast" . . .

Nancy: (to Nick acerbically) You know, you're getting on my nerves. You like to be the buffoon, don't you? People in here have serious problems, and you sit there and make jokes . . . no wonder your wife left you. The way you act, no one is going to hang around *you* for long.

Mark starts rocking in his chair.

Fanny: I can't stand this! This (expletive) group isn't help-ing anyone.

Nick: (Plaintively) Hey, I said what I did because I think she's going to make the same mistakes over and over . . . I don't think she's learned her lesson yet and I was just trying to let her know that with a little bit of humor . . . but as I said before, a sense of humor is something this group doesn't have so maybe you're all better off if I just . . . (stands up to leave)

Therapist: Wait, Nick, I don't blame you for wanting to leave . . . in the last few seconds, the group has gotten uncomfortable for everyone . . . me included. I think you, and Fanny, and others are feeling criti-cized. And let's admit it, even if there's some truth in the criticism . . . who likes to be criticized? But maybe each member can let us know, as we go along, how it is easiest for them to hear critical com-ments about themselves.

> Fanny:     Well, I see Nick around on the unit. Well, I know
>            that guy I was with is no good. I know Nick cares
>            . . . but . . . I just feel he's like trying to embarrass
>            me. He sounds like the guys that are my age instead
>            of a man.
> Therapist: If Nick has something to say that may be a little
>            painful, how do you want him to say it to you?

(Here, the therapist takes the focus off of Nick's offensive behaviors by providing him with an alternate behavior that will be less alienating to members.)

> Fanny:     Well, I would like him to just give it to me straight
>            . . . without a lot of horsing around.
> Sara:      Every time things get serious in here, Nick has to
>            cut a joke.
> Therapist: Sounds like an important connection.
> Sara:      And I still want to hear about your situation, Nick.

Nick talked about how he responded to his wife's leaving by alternating between smoldering jocularity, which made it easy for her to dismiss his feelings, and very aggressive legal action, which further alienated her. Nancy, Sara, and Fanny were highly active in this discussion, helping Nick recognize other ways in which he could communicate his pain to his wife other than biting sarcasm or vindictive legal action.

> Therapist: (mindful that there were 10 minutes left in the session) Sara, you have been very helpful to Nick and others, but I'm concerned that even though you alluded in the last session to what caused your hospitalization, you haven't mentioned the details. Soon, you'll be facing the same stresses.

(Sara was the newest group member and in the prior session was allowed to take the role of helper vis-à-vis other members because this role is less threatening. The therapist observed that Sara was sufficiently comfortable in the group to not only help but be helped. However, to be assisted by members, Sara must disclose some of the details surrounding her hospitalization. Because Sara failed to do so, the therapist assumed this responsibility.)

> Sara: I felt I was depressed. But I don't feel that way now.
> Nancy: Why, dear? You are so attractive. You have a beautiful baby. Your husband is so handsome and *so* solicitous.
> Fanny: Nancy, those things don't always matter. One time I was with a guy who was gorgeous and had a sports car and spent lots of money on me and was a crack addict who hit me, but that's another story. Sara, why *did* you feel depressed?
> Sara: I read somewhere that it may be a biological illness, postpartum depression.
> Nancy: My doctor tells me that I have a biological illness too. But I know that when my husband and I weren't getting along, I felt even worse. I feel down, and that certainly is no biological disease causing our fighting. There must have been some specific things that you thought about. I mean was there anything that tipped you over the edge?
> Sara: I don't know. I felt overwhelmed. I couldn't do a good job with my child, and I went back to work a few weeks ago, and I felt like I couldn't continue to work as much as I did before. . . .

The group finishes the session with Sara offering some of the details of her dual roles as mother and career woman. The group focuses Sara on the relief she is experiencing being away from her dilemma and how those stresses have not changed because she has not focused on them while she is in the group. In the final few minutes, the group offers specific suggestions for how to manage both.

## Comment on the Session

During this session, Mark was the only member who was allowed not to reveal much about himself. The therapist felt that Mark was not yet able to make use of what the group might offer him. Although Mark's comments on the surface appeared somewhat psychotic or at best inappropriate, they nonetheless were derivatively in tune with the emotional tenor of the group. The immediate goal for Mark was to continue to experience the group as a positive experience. It was unclear from his presentation how much of his psychotic thinking was still present.

When Mark is more comfortable in group, the therapist will need to help him reveal more about his target symptoms. The major goals for Mark in group would be to (a) provide him with an opportunity to talk about his concerns; (b) help him to realize that people in the group and, by implication, others in his life could accept his thoughts so that he did not have the burden of managing them by himself; (c) learn to attend to what environmental situations might exacerbate his psychotic symptoms; and (d) foster the realization that informing the important people in his life about these hallucinations could help him resist acting destructively toward himself and others (Maxmen, 1978). Treating the hallucinations is not the principal objective of an educative group; that is the province of psychopharmacology.

It is important to note that the therapist can vary the level of interventions depending on the patients' tenure in the group and their levels of psychological functioning. For example, in response to Ike's silence, the therapist attempted to get him to narrate his story and allowed the group to give him suggestions. Later, in response to Nick's increasing jocularity, the therapist attempted to foster a more sophisticated understanding of the connection between environmental events (e.g., his wife leaving) and his maladaptive responses (sarcasm and jocularity). This switching of levels gives the therapist considerably more flexibility and allows for an increased heterogeneity of level of functioning among members.

## Status of the Research

Although there have been many references to the utility of the educative model, few have subjected it to systematic analysis. To date, there are no empirical studies comparing the efficacy of this model either with other types of therapies with the same goals (i.e., those that teach patients to think clinically) or to other models of inpatient group therapy. Because the goals of this type of group are not reduction of symptomatology, the use of a symptom-reduction outcome measure would not be appropriate. Thus, the benefits of therapies such as pharmacotherapy, the goal of which is to ameliorate symptoms, are not directly comparable to this model of group therapy because their goals are different.

Thus, to validate the efficacy of such a model, two separate aspects need to be addressed. First, it must be shown that a "treatment course" of the educative group does teach patients to think clinically. Ideally, it should also be shown that the educative group performs this function better than no treatment at all, preferably better than other interventions such as pharmacotherapy, milieu therapy, and activities therapy and at least as well as other types of group therapies. Second, it must be shown that being able to think therapeutically improves the patient's ability to cope with his or her illness. That is, this new learned skill (thinking clinically) should be demonstrated to improve the quality of the patient's life after hospitalization (e.g., by decreasing subjective distress, ameliorating complaints or symptoms, improving level of functioning by managing symptoms better, or increasing the length of stay in the community) more than no intervention at all.

Although studies that compare the educative model with other models or other types of therapies would be most helpful for examining the former's efficacy, a case could be made that some attempt to translate the more subjective therapeutic features of the former (e.g., therapeutic factors) into measurable objective phenomena (i.e., empirical research) may also provide some information about its utility. Also, the model has a number of different assumptions about what is and is not helpful; the research for each of these could be examined separately as well. Such an approach could be viewed as reductionistic in the sense that it is assumed that with such an approach, the single feature or procedure shown to be efficacious will not be obscured or negatively interact with other features. Indeed, the sum of the parts may be more or less than the whole. Therefore, this type of features analysis (which we present for almost all of the models in this text) is only suggestive, should be viewed with caution, and must await further empirical investigation.

We discuss four types of features: patient-perceived therapeutic factors; characteristics and interventions of the leader, including democratic leadership style and advice giving; member-to-member interaction, including the here-and-now focus and patient's level of activity; and auxiliary features of the group that enhance group experience, such as leaderless groups and pre-group preparation.

## Patient-Perceived Therapeutic Factors

The concept of curative or therapeutic factors was proposed by Corsini and Rosenberg (1955), who attempted to provide a taxonomy of potentially therapeutic processes in a psychotherapy group. Yalom (1970) later extended their work by devising a system of 12 factors. The early work on therapeutic factors was particularly important for the educative model because in 1973, Maxmen conducted a study on Yalom's scheme of therapeutic factors and used the results to design the educative model. Maxmen had inpatient group members in an interpersonally oriented group rank the 12 factors from most helpful to least helpful. He found that patients rated instillation of hope, group cohesiveness, altruism, and universality as most helpful. Catharsis and insight were rated as less helpful, and guidance, family reenactment, and identification were rated as least helpful. Maxmen concluded that if a particular set of factors is viewed by patients as important, then it should be given a prominent role in any adequate model of inpatient group psychotherapy. He therefore built into the design of the educative model means by which to facilitate members' development of hopefulness, group cohesiveness, an altruistic style of relating to one another, and the awareness of the universal nature of problems.

Subsequent research using various techniques for investigating therapeutic factors has generally supported Maxmen's findings about what factors patients see as important. For example, other investigators have found the instillation of hope (Goldberg, McNeil, & Binder, 1988), altruism (Macaskill, 1982; Marcovitz & Smith, 1983; Whalan & Mushet, 1986), universality (Brabender, Albrecht, Silliti, Cooper, & Kramer, 1983), and cohesiveness (Butler & Fuhriman, 1980, 1983; Kahn, Webster, & Storck, 1986; Whalan & Mushet, 1986) to be important to group members. To some extent, the endorsement of these factors runs across types of therapy group. Although one study (Whalan & Mushet, 1986) was conducted with educative groups, other studies were done on other types of groups such as the interpersonal model.

In contrast to Maxmen's findings, some studies (e.g., Kanas & Barr, 1982; Leszcz, Yalom, & Norden, 1985; Marcovitz & Smith, 1983) have found that members find the expression of affect (formerly labeled *catharsis* but with less of an emphasis on the unbridled nature of the manifestation of affect) to be of benefit. The educative model, on the basis of the earlier finding, places little emphasis on affective expressivity. It is possible, in light of the recent findings, that at least some members may find this group to be too repressive (i.e., involving too much weighing of cognitive understanding over affect). Subsequent studies have also found that some members value insight (Brabender et al., 1983; Marcovitz & Smith, 1983; Schaffer & Dreyer, 1982). However, a distinction must be made between genetic insight and self-understanding (Rohrbaugh & Bartels, 1975). Genetic insight (i.e., the development of an awareness of the early childhood– familial underpinnings of psychopathology) has generally been observed to be of little benefit to inpatient group members (Kibel, 1981). However, some interpersonal researchers (e.g., Rosegrant, 1988) have argued that self-understanding may be of benefit. This factor describes the process wherein the individual gains access to warded-off feelings and impulses that motivate present dysfunctional interpersonal behaviors.

If these differences in findings are real and not due solely to diversity of measurement or methodology, one explanation is that patient populations may be diverse in terms of level of functioning and psychopathology. This diversity may then systematically affect patient perceptions of what is important about the group. This is discussed further in chapter 4 (The Interpersonal Model).

In considering the results of the aforementioned investigations, it must be recognized that the study of therapeutic factors does not exist in a vacuum. Patients' perceptions of what is therapeutic are likely to be highly reflective of the particular model or type of group; the expectations, values, or beliefs of the therapist; the style and competence of the therapist; and the levels of functioning, types of psychopathologies, and life circumstances of other patients in the group.[5] For example, in the Marcovitz and Smith (1983) study, the patient population and type of inpatient unit were more similar to those in the Maxmen (1973) study; however, the results of the relative importance of various therapeutic factors to patients in the Marcovitz and Smith study were more similar to those in Yalom's (1970) original outpatient study. Marcovitz and Smith attributed this to the difference in the way they ran the group—with less of a behavioral focus and more emphasis on self-understanding than Maxmen (1978, 1984). An even clearer example of the differential impact of the therapist's style on therapeutic factors is when Whalan and Mushet (1986) ran an inpatient group using the educative model guidelines (Maxmen, 1978). They found that patients perceived altruism, universality, self-disclosure, and guidance from other patients as important. When the same clinicians ran the group using an interpersonal model (Yalom, 1983), patients perceived interpersonal learning to be the most salient factor in the inpatient's group experience (Mushet et al., 1989). Thus, patients' perceptions of what is therapeutic may reflect some of the therapist's emphasis of certain techniques.

Also, relevant to the interpretation of the therapeutic factors investigations is the recognition that patients' perceptions of perceived importance of various therapeutic factors often differ from those of their therapists (Bloch & Reibstein, 1980; Yalom & Elkin, 1974). In a study that evaluated both patient and staff perceptions, inpatients perceived self-responsibility and self-understanding as being most helpful in inpatient groups, whereas staff felt that expressing feelings toward others, modeling after other group members, and engaging in behavioral experimentation (e.g., interpersonal learning) were most useful (Schaffer & Dreyer, 1982).

Perceived importance may influence outcome in two ways. First, if members perceive particular aspects of group to be important, even if they are not, the presence of these aspects will enhance members' motivation to be in the group. Second, after

---

[5] To some extent, increasing the number and variety of subjects and groups in any study will decrease the influence of the latter.

patients leave the hospital, their perception of what was helpful is likely to influence their compliance with and follow-up of the recommended treatment. Despite improvement with the various therapies (Christenson, 1974; Hogarty & Goldberg, 1973) and the deleterious effects of noncompliance (Geller, 1986), patients often do not follow through on treatment because of some belief about the treatment and its meanings for them (Serban & Thomas, 1974; Smith, 1989). Even when two treatments are equally efficacious, individuals often express a preference for one (Budman et al., 1988; Green, 1988).

In conclusion, although the therapeutic factor studies cannot reveal what processes within a group mediate outcome, they can show what processes members believe to have therapeutic value. In general, the educative model is likely to have greater credibility to patients than some of the other models because it appears to emphasize what patients view as important.

## Member-to-Member Interaction

**Level of activity.** The educative model relies heavily on members' interactions with each other in the here-and-now. Thus, showing that increased patient interaction is associated with the accomplishment of therapeutic goals would provide evidence for the importance of this feature. There is some evidence, at least with time-limited outpatient groups, that both patients and therapists feel that the main therapeutic mechanisms reside in member-to-member interaction (Berzon, Pious, & Farson, 1963). Some researchers have found positive relations between verbal activity and patient improvement or outcome (McDaniel, Stiles, & McGaughey, 1981; Sloane, Staples, Cristol, & Yorkston, 1975; Yalom, 1985). Recent research suggests that a higher level of patient activity is associated with patients' subjective satisfaction and benefit as well as therapists' evaluations of benefit; however, patient activity was not related to reduction in symptomatology, improved self-esteem, or better social functioning (Soldz, Budman, Demby, & Feldstein, 1990). In fact, the more troubled patients appeared at the start of the group, the more likely they were to be active during the course of the group. Thus, level of activity per se did not seem to influence objective measures of symptomatology. The educative model does not, of course, directly aim at reducing symptomatology. These findings, however, do call into question whether patients must actively do the "work." Perhaps further delineation of types of patient verbalizations may reveal that there are certain kinds of verbal activity that directly further the goals of treatment. For instance, indiscriminant self-disclosure by patients is associated with a poorer outcome than is an intermediate level of self-disclosure (Coché & Polikoff, 1979). Similarly, perhaps only specific kinds of patient verbalizations further therapeutic goals. It must be cautioned, however, that the positive associations of activity and disclosure level with good outcome do not suggest a causal linkage; the level of activity or kind of disclosure may merely be an indication of a good prognosis or positive outcome rather than of verbal productions actually furthering the therapeutic goals.

**Cohesiveness.** Cohesiveness is the individual's attraction to the group and other members, including the we-ness or feeling of belonging and acceptance that patients feel about a group. As was discussed in chapter 2, there is considerable research literature demonstrating the salubrious effect of cohesiveness on group process and outcome.

The educative model emphasizes the importance of group cohesiveness. Although inpatients report that cohesiveness is important to them (Butler & Fuhriman, 1980, 1983; Cabral, Best, & Paton, 1975; Cabral & Paton, 1975; Kahn et al., 1986; Marcovitz & Smith, 1983), there are no empirical studies that have examined the connection between cohesiveness and outcome in inpatient groups. At the extreme, an individual's lack of attraction to the group may prevent him or her from attending the sessions; empirically, attraction to the group is inversely correlated with group drop-out rate (Falloon, 1981; Yalom, Houts, Newell, & Rand, 1967a). Certainly, with outpatient groups there is evidence that if an individual experiences little attraction to the group, they are more likely to have a negative outcome (Lieberman, Miles, & Yalom, 1973). There is no obvious reason why these results would be inapplicable to an inpatient group.

The quality of member-to-member interactions, a feature that is both greatly emphasized by the educative model and related to cohesiveness, seems to be more important in determining individual change than does the relationship to the therapist (Clark & Culber, 1965). Groups that are high in cohesion are more likely to have more improved members than are groups that are low in cohesion (Falloon, 1981; Flowers, Booraem, & Hartman, 1981). Thus, cohesiveness enhances the probability of a good outcome. However, inpatient groups often consist of patients who have considerably more interpersonal difficulties than do those in outpatient groups; it is unclear how the severity of interpersonal deficits affects the development of cohesion and subsequent outcome. It is also likely that time and patient turnover, the bane of short-term inpatient settings, affect the group's ability to develop cohesion.

Empirical evidence about the relation of cohesiveness to the accomplishment of the goals in the group is needed. Also important would be an understanding of the effect that patient turnover and limited time (factors unique to inpatient groups) have on cohesiveness. In addition, the effects, if any, that such factors as level and diversity of functioning, age, diagnostic differences, and where patients reside have on the development of cohesion in groups is an important empirical issue.

## Characteristics and Interventions of the Leader

The leadership style presented in the educative model seems reminiscent of that style presented in some of the classic research on leadership styles and small group (White & Lippitt, 1968). This classic research suggests that long-term positive changes are associated with a democratic leadership style. The educative model endorses a leadership style that resembles the democratic style in this classic research; this research then provides indirect support for the model's efficacy.

**The here-and-now intervention.** Essential to the educative model is the focus on the here-and-now. Although others (Yalom, 1983, 1985) have strongly advocated this emphasis, the educative focus is more specific in this regard than are the other models. The educative model focuses on the here-and-now as it relates to target symptoms. Although there has been some controversy about the effectiveness of the here-and-now approach as opposed to the there-and-then approach (Abramowitz

& Jackson, 1974; Kanas, 1986; Lomont, Gilner, Spector, & Skinner, 1969; see Yalom, 1985, for a critique), a recent empirical effort suggests that therapists' interpretations that illuminate a patient's pattern of behavior, the impact of the behavior on the patient's environment, or to some extent the historical cause of the behavior showed a significant positive effect on patient improvement over the course of therapy (Flowers & Booraem, 1990). Moreover, those patients receiving comments linking present patterns of behavior within the group to outside behavior showed the most improvement. This finding would seem to support the educative model's central focus on target symptoms over the interpersonal model's acceptance of any here-and-now issue that members might introduce. The investigators also found that interpretations of motive of behavior not only caused anxiety but appeared to increase symptoms over the course of treatment (Flowers & Booraem, 1990). Motives, of course, are not interpreted within the educative model. These findings further support the educative model's technique of linking present patterns within the group to target symptoms while not interpreting motives.

**Advice.** Although the educative model (Maxmen, 1978, 1984) encourages patients to do the work themselves, it does not oppose advice giving. Although not extensive, the evidence available suggests that advice is less helpful to patients than are other therapeutic responses (Frank, 1964; Lazarus, 1966; Samaan & Parker, 1973; Troth, Hall, & Seals, 1971). Furthermore, advice giving is an intervention that is rarely used by experienced therapists (Strupp & Wallach, 1965). Therapeutic responses such as reflection, disclosure, and interpretation have been more extensively researched than has advice giving (Flowers, 1979). However, there are different types of advice: simple advice without instructions (e.g., "You should not kick the door when you get angry"); advice with alternatives (e.g., "You could do this or that"); advice with specific instructions on how to do something; and group-process advice (e.g., "I think you should direct your comments to the other group members and not always to me"). Alternatives, instructions, and process advice produce more improvement in patients than does simple advice (Flowers, 1979). Thus, this research finding is consonant with the educative model technique that endorses the use of alternatives, instructions, and process advice. It is hypothesized that if an educative group session were evaluated for the presence of advice statements by the therapists, process advice would most likely be the most frequent advice intervention, followed by instruction and alternatives, and that few simple advice statements would be given.

## Pre-Group Preparation

A feature of the educative model is the importance it places on pre-group preparation. The procedure suggested is both an interview involving a verbal orientation and the distribution of a written handout (Maxmen et al., 1974). Several studies have attempted to evaluate the effects of pre-group evaluation on inpatients (Heitler, 1973; Jacobs, Trick, & Withersty, 1976; Truax, Shapiro, & Wargo, 1968; Truax, Wargo, Carkhuff, Kodman, & Moles, 1966). Despite various methods of preparation (interview, lectures, audiotape, videotape), the influence of preparation on group performance was equivocal (for reviews of this literature, see Mayerson, 1984, and Piper & Perrault, 1989). The findings suggest that there may be some positive effects in terms of patient expectations about group; patients reported themselves more ready to begin group (Hilkey, Wilhelm, & Horne, 1982) and more knowledgeable about how groups work (Jacobs et al., 1976) than when there was no preparation. In addition, pre-group training appears to elicit more ideal patient behavior in inpatient groups: Training improves the working alliance (Heitler, 1973), interpersonal openness (Pastushak, 1978), appropriate expression of emotion (Hilkey et al., 1982), and activity level and self-exploration (Heitler, 1973). However, preparation of any type did not increase patient satisfaction with the group experience (Heitler, 1973; Jacobs et al., 1976) or patients' perception of improvement (Truax et al., 1966, 1968).

Few inpatient studies have attempted to evaluate the effects of preparation on treatment outcome (Mayerson, 1984; Piper & Perrault, 1989). Those few studies on outcome in inpatient populations found that pretraining improves patients' concepts of their ideal self (Truax et al., 1966, 1968) but not their perception of any self-improvement. There is some evidence that pretraining facilitates increased movement toward target goals (Hilkey et al., 1982). There is also evidence that pretraining does improve the group experience for populations that are considered more resistant (e.g., prison inmates; Hilkey et al., 1982) or are considered unsophisticated with regard to psychotherapy (Heitler, 1973).

Modality and type of pre-group preparation have been systematically explored but only with outpatient populations. This research found that a fixed preparation (video, lecture) is less effective than is an interview with the opportunity to ask questions (Mayerson, 1984), and that modeling (in the form of examples and video) may be more effective than abstract verbalizations (Mayerson, 1984). These findings suggest that the educative model pre-group preparation (Maxmen et al., 1974) is likely to enhance a group experience and further treatment goals. Other demonstrated effects of pre-group preparation for outpatient groups are an increase in attendance (France & Dugo, 1985; Piper, Debbane, Bienvenu, & Garant, 1982; Piper, Debbane, Garant, & Bienvenu, 1979), a decrease in dropouts (Yalom, Houts, Newell, & Rand, 1967b), an increase in cohesiveness, and an acceleration of the work of therapy (Piper et al., 1979; Yalom, 1985). Although these findings are generally positive, their applicability to an inpatient setting remains for future empirical studies. This research should focus on whether and under what conditions pre-group preparation for the educative model can improve the patients' understanding about what is expected of them in group, increase their hope that they can accomplish this, and decrease their level of discomfort while in the group.

## Leaderless Groups

There are two types of leaderless groups: One is a leaderless session alternated with a leader-led session; the other is a group in which there are no leader-led sessions, and instruction is presented by means of written instruction, audiotape, or videotape. The educative model makes use of the former alternate-session format; the majority of the research presented here is related to the effectiveness of this format. Hence, unless otherwise specified, the use of the term *leaderless group* refers to practice of leader-led sessions alternated with leaderless sessions. In general, the research literature on leaderless groups is equivocal. Leaderless groups have been observed to be beneficial in some instances and detrimental in others (Astrachan et al., 1967; Truax & Wargo, 1969; Truax et al., 1966). Whether leaderless group are a positive addition to the group treatment depends on the patients' levels of intelligence, the severity and chronicity of the psychopathology, the degree of structure provided in the session, and the patients' environment outside the unled sessions including the type of leader-led session (Desmond & Seligman, 1977). These variables are discussed below.

In general, the utility of leaderless groups has been demonstrated with young educated patients who have acute psychiatric problems (Desmond & Seligman, 1977). One study with representative findings took place on an intermediate-term care inpatient unit using 3 groups of 8 patients, each which met in a leader-led group, a leaderless group, and a large group that included staff, patients, and relatives (Astrachan et al., 1967). They found that leader-led groups were not superior to leaderless groups in degree of interaction, amount of feedback given about patient behaviors, and frequency with which patients related content to feeling (Astrachan et al., 1967). They also found that in leaderless groups, there was a greater degree of problem-solving activity than in leader-led groups. Using the same format and population, Harrow et al. (1967) found that the emotional climate of the leaderless group was less depressed and less tense than that of the leader-led group. Becker et al. (1968) similarly reported that leaderless sessions had a significantly higher level of verbal interaction than did leader-led sessions. However, a larger follow-up study using similar methodology found that although there were a greater number of comments in the leaderless session, the interchanges were brief and shorter in duration compared with the less frequent but longer remarks when the therapist was present (Holmes & Cureton, 1970). Holmes and Cureton attributed these results to the difference in control that therapists had over other aspects of the patients' lives and privileges; in their study, therapists had no other control over other aspects of ward life.

Another feature that appears important in the success of the leaderless group is the support of the surrounding system. The importance that the setting places on the value of the leaderless meetings affects their effectiveness. In a study in which the leaderless session was effective, staff members (other than the group therapist) positively supported the group and emphasized on the unit norms of facing reality and problem solving (Astrachan et al., 1967; Becker, Harrow, & Astrachan, 1970). An analysis of the alternate session (both content and process) makes apparent the extent to which the influence of the group therapists and other staff members outside the group (line staff and individual therapists) extends into the alternate session (Astrachan, Harrow, & Flynn, 1968; Harrow et al., 1967). In effect, the leaderless session is not completely leaderless.[6]

However, there is evidence that under certain circumstances, the leaderless session produces negative results. Truax and colleagues (Truax & Carkhuff, 1965; Truax et al., 1966; Truax et al., 1968), in a set of studies with chronic hospitalized psychiatric patients, found that leaderless sessions led to a deterioration in self-concept (as measured by a self-report Q-sort). Stern and Seligman (1971) found similar results with a chronic Veterans Administration population: Leader-led sessions dealt more with group relationships and were more focused, task oriented, and active. In results similar to those of Holmes and Cureton (1970), Salzberg (1967) reported that patients were less verbal when the leader was present but that a greater percentage of the participants' responses focused on personal problems when the leader was there. In addition to the chronic, uneducated psychiatric patient, juvenile delinquents do not fare well in groups with leaderless sessions. For instance, with male and female institutionalized juvenile delinquents, the leaderless session was associated with poorer outcomes on personality measures (Truax et al., 1968; Truax & Wargo, 1966). Thus, it seems that the lead-

---

[6] One potential problem of this research is that the implementation and design may have affected the results given that the study was developed by the same individuals who sampled recordings of the session (Desmond & Seligman, 1977).

erless session may have limited utility for populations who are chronic, uneducated, and prone to acting out their impulses rather than verbally articulating them.

The lack of structure may also affect the efficacy of the leaderless session. Desmond and Seligman (1977) reported that of all the studies reporting positive results, 84% of the leaderless groups were structured by a particular set of procedures (e.g., Encountertapes, PEER program). In the few studies that reported positive results in groups that were not highly structured, the patients were all college educated. Conversely, in all the studies that reported negative results, no planned structure or feedback was provided for the leaderless sessions.

# Critique of the Model

## Strengths

Historically, the educative model was one of the first models to recognize that the inpatient group differs in important ways from the outpatient group. In fact, it seems to have served as an inspiration for later model development. Many of the strengths of the educative model derive from the recognition that outpatients are different from inpatients. One such strength is the appropriateness of the goals of the model for the typically short duration of members' participation in the group. Although it has not yet been demonstrated that members can be taught to think clinically during the course of their participation, this goal is far less ambitious than goals that are commonly pursued in outpatient groups such as intrapsychic conflict resolution. Similarly, the educative model is also based on an awareness of some of the limitations that inpatients often bring to the group. For example, the model does not require that patients have a good deal of psychological sophistication. This model is likely to appeal to patients because it has much face validity; it has reasonably succinct and clear goals that patients can understand. That is, members are not called on to work in the group in such a way that is at odds with their expectations for how a group should work. Although it introduces the examination of the here-and-now, the anxiety of this type of exploration is mitigated by the parameters that are set on it: The exploration only concerns the problems that brought the patient into the hospital.

Another major area of strength of this model is its acknowledgment of the importance and impact of the treatment team on patient care. The model accepts the inpatient group as one of many modalities to which the patient is exposed. By teaching patients to think clinically rather than focusing on symptom reduction as the goal of the group, the model assigns to the group a role that is distinctive in relation to other modalities. It uses those resources that are unique to a group such as peer pressure, support and feedback, as well as confrontation of those dysfunctional behavior patterns as they manifest themselves in group. Moreover, by not competing with other modalities, the educative model promotes a "pro-group" climate within the hospital.

The educative model is capable of being adopted by a wide variety of therapists. It does not presume the presence of an extensive background in group dynamics or personality theory for leaders. This feature is important because frequently individuals who lead inpatient groups have little prior training in group therapy. The model has enormous flexibility in terms of the therapist's theoretical orientation; as Kibel (1984) noted, the model itself is atheoretical.

Another strength is the model's recognition that patients are differentially able to use the group modality. Thus, within the model, there is allowance for interventions by both other patients and therapists to be "pitched" to patients at different levels. This was illustrated in the clinical example with Ike and Nick. For Ike, who appeared somewhat fragile, it was sufficient for him to tell his "story" and be given alternative responses by the group members. For Nick, however, in addition to telling his story, the relation between his interpersonal style in group and his current predicament could be addressed. The implication, then, is that patients of different levels of ego functioning and points of recovery can nicely coexist within the same group.

Finally, from a technical standpoint, this model is better developed than are the models presented in this book in terms of offering a rationale and a detailed approach to the preparation of patients for inpatient group therapy. This information sheet, which was developed for this model, could easily be adapted to a number of other models (e.g., interpersonal, object relations/systems).

## Weaknesses

A major weakness concerns the way in which this model handles negative affect—particularly aggression. In this model, aggressive feelings are handled like any other feelings—acknowledged but focused on in a rational manner only if the feelings relate to the target symptoms (i.e., if patients' mishandling of aggression gets them into trouble either inside or outside the hospital). Even when aggression is seen as relevant to patients' target symptoms, the effort is to get them to express it in ways that will be less destructive. However, frequently inpatients find their own anger to be intolerable (Hannah, 1984; Kibel, 1981). The request for cooperation among patients may implicitly convey to members that their aggressive feelings are negative and therefore should be overcome or subdued (Hannah, 1984). Although patients initially may feel relieved that aggression can be dismissed easily and that anxiety in the group can be overcome by working on a concrete problem, the group therapist may lose the opportunity to help the group work with their fears about aggression directly (Brabender, 1987; Hannah, 1984). Although such a message may evoke short-term good behavior, it is likely to exacerbate members' nonacceptance of aspects of their emotional life and may even produce an increase in these fears. There are other patients who respond to hostile feelings with overcompliance. This pattern is particularly likely in female inpatients (Bernandez, 1984; Brabender, 1992). For members whose behavioral repertoire is organized around the suppression of hostile feelings, problems with aggression may never come to the surface in the group because they are not likely to be seen as relevant to the members' target complaints.

Another weakness is that although this model takes into account the fact that the inpatient treatment is part of a treatment package, it does not provide an adequately articulated method for dealing with another important reality of inpatient group psychotherapy: the effect of the milieu on the group. The educative model recognizes the need for the inpatient therapist to maintain the boundaries of the group but gives insufficient attention to the observation of many that the boundaries between the inpatient group and hospital setting are highly permeable. As demonstrated by Astrachan and others, in large part, the tenor and issues in the group are stimulated by aspects and events of life on the unit. These influences exist on a group level. Although Maxmen (1984) attested to the existence of group-level resistances stimulated perhaps by events in the milieu, he saw it as sufficient to label these *resistances*. Such labeling, he believed, diminishes the intensity of the resistances, thereby enabling individuals within the group to work on their target complaints. We doubt whether labeling alone, in the absence of any real exploration of the group's responsibility to the milieu, will diminish the strength of the group-level issues.

The model is best used in a pro-group hospital culture wherein patients' abilities to think clinically are reinforced by other activities. There are some suggestions provided to reinforce patients' learning to think clinically, such as the patient advisory board (Maxmen et al., 1974). However, the conduct of the group when patients appear unable to learn to think clinically or when the number of these patients are not at a critical mass is not sufficiently addressed.

From a technical standpoint, this model could profit from further articulation. A criticism of this model, as well as of most other inpatient models, involves the multiplicity of relationships that staff and patients have in the hospital. This model does not address how and whether the group therapist should have multiple roles with the rest of the treatment team and patients; the model also does not address the potential impact that the multiple role relationships might have on the success of the group. Similarly, Maxmen identified a variety of interventions that should not be made by the therapist (e.g., genetic interpretations, exploratory comments about group process). However, he provided only vague counsel on how the therapist should use the "here-and-now" and how it should be connected to the exploration of the patterns of behavior precipitating hospitalization. There is a certain unfairness to this criticism given that the educative model was one of the first proposed inpatient models. Over the years, inpatient models have been characterized by increasingly greater methodological specificity.

A criticism related to the prior one is the failure of this model to consider countertransferential factors. As indicated previously, this model provides the therapist with only a general direction for intervention. As such, it permits and even requires a fair degree of improvisation. Thus, a therapist can give advice, joke, confront, interpret, and so on without much guidance as to when to use one kind of intervention rather than any other or what factors would contraindicate a certain intervention. For example, when appropriate, the therapist is urged to give advice based on the patient's need for it. However, there is no mechanism for distinguishing between the patient's need for advice and the therapist's own need to avoid the feelings of helplessness and hopelessness that are frequently stimulated by an inpatient group (Hannah, 1984). Furthermore, there is no encouragement for this kind of self-analysis within this model. This lack of instruction might invite acting-out responses from the therapist that are not congruent with the true (rather than expressed) needs of the patient.

Our final criticisms have to do with more specific features of the model. As indicated earlier, central to this model is the explicit acknowledgment of and focus on, by either patient or therapist, of what precipitated the hospitalization. This requirement is problematic for a number of reasons. First, some feel that requiring the reticent patient to reveal such information can be injurious to the patient's self-esteem because "these facets of the patient's life are associated with feelings of demoralization" (Kibel, 1978, p. 352). Moreover, because research has shown that patients with better prognoses withhold this information, demanding such disclosures undermines the patient's use of healthy defenses (Hannah, 1984). Second, there may be traumatic events (or remembrance of them) that have contributed to or precipitated the hospitalization, such as rape, childhood sexual abuse, or physical abuse. To require individuals to reveal such trauma before they are intrapsychically equipped to manage the consequences may be inadvertently reenacting another trauma. To make these problem areas an exception to the rule of revelation implicitly suggests fragility, which encourages patients to perceive these events as overwhelming, leading to further demoralization. Third, even if membership in the group is voluntary, the potential breach of confidentiality if patients do not themselves reveal this information or distort its content, places the therapist on the horns of an ethical dilemma. Although issues of confidentiality in group in general have been inadequately explored from a legal standpoint (Roback, Ochoa, Bloch, & Purdon, 1990), the legal complications of this potential breach in confidentiality are multiplied.

A final point is also ethically related. Despite the evidence of the value of the leaderless group (Astrachan et al., 1967), the educative model does not caution on the potential dangers of it. Most agree that a valuable function performed by the therapist is the modulation of aggression (Klein, 1985). Some think that the emergence of some aggression can be therapeutic (Brabender, 1987; Hannah, 1984; Kibel, 1978, 1981), whereas others believe that little aggression should be permitted in group (Yalom, 1983). If a therapist is not present, there is no guarantee that aggression will be regulated. Undue manifestation of the aggression affects individuals and has the potential to disrupt cohesiveness. There may be certain populations of patients for which this is more likely to occur, such as chronic schizophrenics and juvenile delinquents (Truax et al., 1968; Truax & Wargo, 1966).

# Demands of the Model

## Clinical Mission

The educative model can be effectively implemented in a wide range of settings. It is compatible with a setting that has as a primary focus teaching, clinical care, or research. Effective use of the model does not require that the institution within which it functions or the people in charge of the clinical activities espouse any particular theoretical orientation; it is compatible with a symptom-oriented or holistic approach to treatment. Therefore, individuals who understand the model but do not have formalized training in group psychotherapy could function as effective leaders. In fact, several researchers (Houpt, Astrachan, Lipsitch, & Anderson, 1972; Maxmen et al., 1974) have suggested that patients also could and perhaps should play a significant role in the orientation and preparation for group.

## Context of the Group

Although the model makes no demands on either the institution or the group therapist in terms of theoretical orientation, it does require a certain place or perspective within the system of which it is a part. Namely, the milieu must be one that has the potential to reinforce the sort of thing that is "taught" in group. Maxmen et al. (1974) had some suggestions in terms of patient governing bodies and the way in which privileges are given that could aid in this regard. However, we feel that the reinforcement also needs to come not only from the structural aspects of the treatment program but the other staff as well. Treating practitioners must not make demands that patients discuss certain things in group if they are unrelated to the target symptoms. The example given in chapter 2 wherein the patient was encouraged by the doctor to bring a letter to the group for discussion would have been appropriate only if it had been enlightening with regard to the dysfunctional aspects of the patient's interpersonal style as they related to the target symptoms.

The educative model functions best if it is an integral part of the program, with both staff and patients being part of the same community. This integrality is useful because some of the secondary features of the group (e.g., impromptu leaderless groups, extended here-and-now focus) constrain the locus of the group to the unit. The model was originally conceived as a group for patients who lived on the same unit. However, it is our belief that the model can be effective even if the structure of the setting demands a mixed-unit group. Some accommodations might be made so that leaderless groups can actually have a time slot and take place off the unit. The impromptu leaderless meeting, of course, would be precluded by a group that draws from more than one unit. The extended here-and-now focus is a bit more problematic. This focus limits two aspects of the setting: The leader must have access to the ward life that has transpired, and members must have ongoing contact with each other. For patients, the use of ward life (extended here-and-now focus) may need to be somewhat limited. Does the group leader have to be a member of the unit staff? Although Maxmen and others have not commented on this aspect of role relationship, it seems the educative model functions best if the therapist is also aware of the important interpersonal exchanges that occur in the course of daily activities. Some mechanism for obtaining this information about ward life would be necessary if the therapist is going to be an outside consultant.

## Temporal Variables

This model was originally designed to use with a group that is open-ended. It is not, however, a model that would favor radical, continuous change in membership. Patients who are able to attend for only a few sessions are excluded from the group. To foster cohesiveness and an understanding of what is to transpire in the group, the educative model favors excluding potential members rather than having chaos. There also must be time prior to group entrance for screening and preparation. This model could also be used with a closed-ended format, and in fact, this feature would probably enhance cohesiveness.

## Size

Although the educative model can accommodate 4 to 12 patients, we believe the model works best if the size of the group is somewhat less (4 to 9). Too few members would not allow a range of interpersonal exchange. Too many members would not permit adequate time to help every member relate target symptoms to life circumstances in a productive way.

## Composition

Perhaps the most important demand of the model in terms of composition is that participation be voluntary. Cohesiveness is an extremely important variable to the successful use of the model, and cohesiveness is markedly affected by whether patients have a choice about their participation. Given the research on pre-group preparation (i.e., that it is helpful to those patients who may be resistant or lack in understanding), all eligible patients should be given the initial interview and preparation, but the decision to join group should be voluntary.

The model can be used in a setting that has patients with a wide variety of ego functioning. The group can be either homogeneous or heterogeneous in this regard. It can tolerate patients with limited psychological sophistication given that there is no presumption that one needs to understand issues of conscious and unconscious motivation; comments are responded to at face value. It has been used in adolescent settings (R. R. Gogineni, personal communication, July 20, 1990) and mixed-aged (17 to 70 years) adult groups (Maxmen, 1973). It seems that it could be adapted to a geriatric population (Riley & Carr, 1989). Heterogeneous and homogenous age groups could effectively function with this model. The model could also accommodate a group that has a wide variety of symptoms (Maxmen, 1973). It could not, however, as easily accommodate patients that have a homogeneous set of symptoms. The reason for this is that if patients share a pool of maladaptive behaviors, they would not, in the short period that they are hospitalized, have the necessary detachment to recognize in others those behaviors that are maladaptive. The group members would not have the range of experience or coping skills to draw from, unlike a mixed-symptom group would. The potential exception to this rule could be a group that is part of a long-term residential treatment facility (e.g., state hospitals, long-term care facilities, etc.).

## Therapist Variables

The educative model is more vague than are many of the other models in terms of the methodology for conducting the group. Thus, it leaves the therapist to his or her own devices more than other models do. In terms of the way the group is conducted, it does not follow a format and leaves a fair degree of improvisation to the therapist. Thus, a more highly experienced therapist is likely to fare better than is a more inexperienced one. The educative model is atheoretical with respect to the etiology of psychopathology and does not require an extensive background in personality theory or psychopathology or an understanding of a highly technical theory of therapist intervention. A knowledge of, and experience with, group dynamics and its impact on the functioning of psychiatric patients is helpful but may not be as essential as it is for other models such as the developmental or object relations/systems models. In this regard, the educative model allows considerable flexibility in terms of who conducts the group. Certainly it requires a knowledge of the therapeutic factors and the relation of the patient-perceived factors to a method of implementation. To use this model effectively, therapists' expertise should be weighted on the side of experience rather than of theoretical knowledge.

A highly experienced therapist in this model is important for another reason. This model allows the therapist a fair degree of latitude and improvisation. The therapist can give advice, joke, confront, support, and so forth. However, the model itself provides little guidance about how to orchestrate these interventions. The only guidance the therapist is offered is not to do for the patients what they can do for themselves. Making this discrimination is not an easy task even for an intermediate-level therapist. Without a good experience base and the skills for self-analysis, this model may encourage acting out on the part of the therapist.

Co-therapy, as mentioned in chapter 2, is almost always advantageous, and the educative model is no exception in that regard. However, within the framework of this model, neither technical nor theoretical reasons mandate the presence of two therapists. Thus, co-therapy is a nice amenity but is not an essential requirement of this model.

## Summary

The educative model teaches patients to think clinically so that they can learn to cope effectively with their symptomatology. This goal is accomplished by having patients participate in a guided here-and-now focus on those behaviors and associated feelings that directly precipitated or sustain their hospitalization.

The model is atheoretical with respect to the etiology of psychopathology. It is effectively used by staff with a wide variety of theoretical orientations and by institutions that have a variety of clinical missions. The strength of this model lies in its realistic appraisal of the short-term frame of the treatment and patients' characteristic lack of psychological sophistication. Evidence for the efficacy of the model lies solely in the therapeutic factors research, and there is some evidence that the various components of the model are useful in other settings (e.g., pre-group preparation, alternate sessions). The model shows great promise but needs empirical work to support its efficacy and provide parameters for its use.

# References

Abramowitz, S. I., & Jackson, C. (1974). Comparative effectiveness of there-and-then versus here-and-now therapist interpretations in group psychotherapy. *Journal of Counseling Psychology, 21*(4), 288–293.

Ansbacher, H. L. (1951). The history of the leaderless group discussion technique. *Psychological Bulletin, 48*, 383–390.

American Psychiatric Association. (1982). *Psychotherapy research: Methodological and efficacy issues.* Washington, DC: American Psychiatric Association.

Astrachan, B. M., Harrow, M., Becker, R. E., Schwartz, A. H., & Miller, J. C. (1967). The unled patient group as a therapeutic tool. *International Journal of Group Psychotherapy, 17*, 178–191.

Astrachan, B. M., Harrow, M., & Flynn, H. R. (1968). Influence of the value-system of a psychiatric setting on behavior in group therapy meetings. *Social Psychiatry, 3*(4), 165–172.

Becker, R. E., Harrow, M., & Astrachan, B. (1970). Leadership and content in group psychotherapy. *Journal of Nervous and Mental Disease, 150*, 346–353.

Becker, R. E., Harrow, M., Astrachan, B. M., Detre, T., & Miller, G. C. (1968). Influence of the leader on the activity level of therapy groups. *Journal of Social Psychology, 74*, 39–51.

Bernandez, T. (1984). Women and anger: Conflicts with aggression in contemporary women. *Journal of the American Medical Association, 33*, 215–219.

Berzon, B., Pious, C., & Farson, R. E. (1963). The therapeutic event in group psychotherapy: A study of subjective reports by group members. *Journal of Individual Psychology, 19*, 204–212.

Bloch, S., & Reibstein, J. (1980). Perceptions by patients and therapists of therapeutic factors in group psychotherapy. *British Journal of Psychiatry, 137*, 274–278.

Brabender, V. M. (1987). Vicissitudes of countertransference in inpatient group psychotherapy. *International Journal of Group Psychotherapy, 37*(4), 549–567.

Brabender, V. (1992). The psychological growth of women in short-term inpatient groups. *Group, 16*(3), 131–146.

Brabender, V., Albrecht, B., Silliti, J., Cooper, J., & Kramer, E. (1983). A study of curative factors in short-term group psychotherapy. *Hospital and Community Psychiatry, 34*, 643–644.

Budman, S. H., Demby, A., Redondo, J. P., Hannan, M., Felstein, M., Ring, J., & Stringer, T. (1988). Comparative outcome in time-limited individual and group psychotherapy. *International Journal of Group Psychotherapy, 38*(1), 63–86.

Butler, T., & Fuhriman, A. (1980). Patient perspective on the curative process: A comparison of day treatment and outpatient psychotherapy groups. *Small Group Behavior, 11*(4), 371–388.

Butler, T., & Fuhriman, A. (1983). Curative factors in group therapy: A review of the recent literature. *Small Group Behavior, 14*(2), 131–142.

Cabral, R. J., Best, J., & Paton, A. (1975). Patients' and observers' assessments of process and outcome in group therapy: A follow-up study. *American Journal of Psychiatry, 132*, 1052–1054.

Cabral, R., & Paton, A. (1975). Evaluation of group therapy: Correlations between clients' and observers' assessments. *British Journal of Psychiatry, 126*, 475–477.

Christenson, J. (1974). A 5 year follow-up study of male schizophrenics: Evaluation of factors influencing success and failure in the community. *Acta Psychiatrica Scandinavica, 50*, 60–72.

Clark, J. B., & Culber, S. A. (1965). Mutually therapeutic perception and self-awareness in a t-group. *Journal of Applied Behavioral Science, 1*, 180–194.

Clarke, G., & Lewinsohn, P. M. (1989). The coping with depression course: A group psychoeducational intervention for unipolar depression. *Behavior Change, 6*(2), 54–69.

Coché, E., & Polikoff, B. (1979). Self-disclosure and outcome in short-term psychotherapy. *Group, 3*, 35–47.

Corsini, R., & Rosenberg, B. (1955). Mechanisms of group psychotherapy. *Journal of Abnormal and Social Psychology, 51*, 406–411.

Desmond, R. E., & Seligman, M. (1977). A review of research on leaderless groups. *Small Group Behavior, 8*(1), 3–24.

Erickson, R. (1981). Small group psychotherapy with patients on a short stay ward: An opportunity for innovation. *Hospital and Community Psychiatry, 32*, 269–272.

Ettin, M. F., Heiman, M. L., & Kopel, S. A. (1988). Group building: Developing protocols for psychoeducational groups. *Group, 12*(4), 205–225.

Falloon, I. (1981). Interpersonal variables in behavioral group therapy. *British Journal of Medical Psychology, 54*, 133–141.

Ferencik, M. (1991). A typology of the here-and-now: Issues in group therapy. *International Journal of Group Psychotherapy, 41*(2), 169–183.

Flowers, J. V. (1979). The differential outcome effects of simple advice, alternatives and instructions in group psychotherapy. *International Journal of Group Psychotherapy, 29*, 305–316.

Flowers, J. V., & Booraem, C. D. (1990). The effects of different types of interpretation on outcome in group psychotherapy. *Group, 14*(2), 81–88.

Flowers, J., Booraem, C., & Hartman, K. (1981). Client improvement on higher and lower intensity problems as a function of group cohesiveness. *Psychotherapy: Theory, Research and Practice, 18*, 246–251.

France, D. G., & Dugo, J. M. (1985). Pretherapy orientation as preparation for open psychotherapy groups. *Psychotherapy, 22*(2), 256–261.

Frank, G. H. (1964). The effect of directive and non-directive statements by therapists on the content of patient verbalizations. *Journal of General Psychology, 71*, 323–328.

Geller, J. L. (1986). In again, out again: Preliminary evaluation of a state hospital's worst recidivists. *Hospital and Community Psychiatry, 37*, 386–390.

Goldberg, F. S., McNeil, D. E., & Binder, R. L. (1988). Therapeutic factors in two forms of inpatient group psychotherapy: Music therapy and verbal therapy. *Group, 12*(3), 145–156.

Green, J. H. (1988). Frequent rehospitalization and noncompliance with treatment. *Hospital and Community Psychiatry, 39*, 963–966.

Hannah, S. (1984). The words of the therapist: Errors of commission and omission. *International Journal of Group Psychotherapy, 34*(3), 369–377.

Harrow, M., Astrachan, B. M., Becker, R. E., Miller, J. C., & Schwartz, A. H. (1967). Influence of the psychotherapist on the emotional climate in group therapy. *Human Relations, 20*(1), 49–64.

Heitler, J. B. (1973). Preparation of lower-class patients for expressive group psychotherapy. *Journal of Consulting and Clinical Psychology, 41*(2), 251–260.

Hilkey, J. H., Wilhelm, C. L., & Horne, A. M. (1982). Comparative effectiveness of videotape pretraining versus no pretraining on selected process and outcome variables in group therapy. *Psychological Reports, 50*, 1151–1159.

Hoberman, H. M., Lewinsohn, P. M., & Tilson, M. (1988). Group treatment of depression: Individual predictors of outcome. *Journal of Consulting and Clinical Psychology, 56*(3), 393–398.

Hogarty, G. B., Goldberg, S. C. (1973). Drug and sociotherapy in the aftercare of schizophrenic patients. *Archives of General Psychiatry, 28*, 54–64.

Holmes, J. S., & Cureton, E. E. (1970). Group therapy interaction with and without the leader. *Journal of Social Psychology, 81*, 127–128.

Houpt, J. L., Astrachan, B., Lipsitch, I., & Anderson, C. (1972). Re-entry groups: Bridging the hospital-community gap. *Social Psychiatry, 7*, 144–149.

Jacobs, M. K., Trick, O. L., & Withersty, D. (1976). Pretraining psychiatric inpatients for participation in group psychotherapy. *Psychotherapy: Theory, Research and Practice, 13*(4), 361–367.

Kahn, E. M., Webster, P. B., Storck, M. J. (1986). Brief reports: Curative factors in two types of inpatient psychotherapy groups. *International Journal of Group Psychotherapy, 36*(4), 579–585.

Kanas, N. (1986). Group therapy with schizophrenics: A review of controlled studies. *International Journal of Group Psychotherapy, 36*(3), 339–351.

Kanas, N., & Barr, M. A. (1982). Short-term homogeneous group therapy for schizophrenic inpatients: A questionnaire evaluation. *Group, 6*(4), 32–38.

Kibel, H. D. (1978). The rationale for the use of group psychotherapy for borderline patients on a short term unit. *International Journal of Group Psychotherapy, 28*(3), 339–358.

Kibel, H. D. (1981). A conceptual model for short-term inpatient group psychotherapy. *American Journal of Psychiatry, 138*(1), 74–80.

Kibel, H. D. (1984). Symposium: Contrasting techniques of short-term inpatient group psychotherapy. *International Journal of Group Psychotherapy, 34*(3), 335–338.

Klein, R. H. (1985). Some principals of short-term group therapy. *International Journal of Group Psychotherapy, 35*(3), 309–330.

Lazarus, A. A. (1966). Behavior rehearsal versus non-directive therapy versus advice in effecting behavior change. *Behavior, Research and Therapy, 4,* 209–212.

Leszcz, M., Yalom, I. D., & Norden, M. (1985). The value of inpatient group psychotherapy: Patients' perceptions. *International Journal of Group Psychotherapy, 35*(3), 411–433.

Lieberman, M., Miles, M., & Yalom, I. (1973). *Encounter group: First facts.* New York: Basic Books.

Lomont, J. F., Gilner, F. N., Spector, N. J., & Skinner, K. K. (1969). Group assertion training and group insight therapies. *Psychological Reports, 25,* 463–470.

Macaskill, N. D. (1982). Therapeutic factors in group therapy. *International Journal of Group Psychotherapy, 32*(1), 61–73.

Marcovitz, R. J., & Smith, J. E. (1983). Patients' perceptions of curative factors in short-term group psychotherapy. *International Journal of Group Psychotherapy, 33*(1), 21–39.

Maxmen, J. (1973). Group therapy as viewed by hospitalized patients. *Archives of General Psychiatry, 28,* 404–408.

Maxmen, J. S. (1978). An educative model for inpatient group therapy. *International Journal of Group Psychotherapy, 28,* 321–337.

Maxmen, J. S. (1984). Helping patients survive theories: The practice of an educative model. *International Journal of Group Psychotherapy, 34*(3), 355–368.

Maxmen, J. S., Tucker, G. J., & LeBow, M. D. (1974). *Rational hospital psychiatry: The reactive environment.* New York: Brunner/Mazel.

Mayerson, N. H. (1984). Preparing clients for group therapy: A critical review and theoretical formulation. *Clinical Psychology Review, 4,* 191–213.

McDaniel, S. H., Stiles, W. B., & McGaughey, K. J. (1981). Correlations of male college students' verbal response mode use in psychotherapy with measures of psychological disturbance and psychotherapy outcome. *Journal of Consulting and Clinical Psychology, 49,* 571–582.

Mushet, G. L., Whalan, G. S., & Power, R. (1989). In-patients' views of the helpful aspects of group psychotherapy: Impact of therapeutic style and treatment setting. *British Journal of Medical Psychology, 62*, 135–141.

Pastushak, R. (1978). The effects of videotaped pretherapy training on interpersonal openness, self-disclosure and group psychotherapy outcome (Doctoral dissertation, Temple University). *Dissertation Abstract International, 39*, 2.

Pattison, E. M., Brissenden, A., & Wohl, T. (1967). Assessing specific effects of inpatient group psychotherapy. *International Journal of Group Psychotherapy, 17*, 283–297.

Piper, W. E., Debbane, E., Bienvenu, J., & Garant, J. (1982). A study of group pretraining for group psychotherapy. *International Journal of Group Psychotherapy, 32*, 309–325.

Piper, W. E., Debbane, E., Garant, J., & Bienvenu, J. (1979). Pretraining for group psychotherapy: A cognitive-experimental approach. *Archives of General Psychiatry, 36*, 1250–1256.

Piper, W. E., & Perrault, E. L. (1989). Pretherapy preparation for group members. *International Journal of Group Psychotherapy, 39*(1), 17–34.

Plante, T. G., Pinder, S. L., & Howe, D. (1988). Introducing the living with illness group: A specialized treatment for patients with chronic schizophrenic conditions. *Group, 12*(4), 198–204.

Riley, K. P., & Carr, M. (1989). Group psychotherapy with older adults: The value of an expressive approach. *Psychotherapy, 26*, 366–371.

Roback, H. B., Ochoa, E., Bloch, E., & Purdon, S. (1992). Guarding confidentiality in clinical groups: The therapist's dilemma. *International Journal of Group Psychotherapy, 42*(1), 81–103.

Rohrbaugh, M., & Bartels, B. D. (1975). Participants' perceptions of "curative factors" in therapy and growth groups. *Small Group Behavior, 6*(4), 430–456.

Rosegrant, J. (1988). A dynamic/expressive approach to brief inpatient group psychotherapy. *Group, 12*(2), 103–112.

Salzberg, H. C. (1967). Verbal behavior in group psychotherapy with and without a therapist. *Journal of Counseling Psychology, 14*(1), 24–27.

Samaan, M. D., & Parker, C. E. (1973). Effects of behavioral reinforcement and advice-giving counseling on information seeking behavior. *Journal of Counseling Psychology, 20*, 193–201.

Schaffer, J. B., & Dreyer, S. F. (1982). Staff and inpatient perceptions of change mechanisms in group psychotherapy. *Clinical and Research Reports, 139*, 127–128.

Seligman, M., & Sterne, D. M. (1969). Verbal behavior in therapist-led, leadership, and alternating group psychotherapy sessions. *Journal of Counseling Psychology, 16*(4), 325–328.

Serban, G., & Thomas, A. (1974). Attitudes and behaviors of acute and chronic schizophrenic patients regarding ambulatory treatment. *American Journal of Psychiatry, 131*, 991–995.

Silverman, W. H., & Powers, L. (1985). Major themes in brief inpatient group psychotherapy. *Journal of Group Psychotherapy, Psychodrama, and Sociometry, 38*, 115–121.

Singer, D. L., Astrachan, B. M., Gould, L. J., & Klein, E. B. (1975). Boundary management in psychological work with groups. *Journal of Applied and Behavioral Science, 11*, 137–176.

Slavinska-Holy, N. (1983). Combining individual and homogeneous group psychotherapies for borderline conditions. *International Journal of Group Psychotherapy, 33*(3), 297–312.

Slife, B. D., Sasscer-Burgos, J., Froberg, W., & Ellington, S. (1989). Effect of depression on processing interactions in group psychotherapy. *International Journal of Group Psychotherapy, 39*(1), 79–104.

Sloane, R. B., Staples, F. R., Cristol, A. H., & Yorkston, L. (1975). *Psychotherapy versus behavior therapy.* Cambridge, MA: Harvard University Press.

Smith, L. D. (1989). Medication refusal and the rehospitalized mentally ill inmate. *Hospital and Community Psychiatry, 40*(5), 491–496.

Soldz, S., Budman, S., Demby, A., & Feldstein, M. (1990). Patient activity and outcome in group psychotherapy: New findings. *International Journal of Group Psychotherapy, 40*(1), 53–62.

Spiegel, D. (1990). Can psychotherapy prolong cancer survival? *Psychosomatics, 31*(4), 361–366.

Stern, D. M., & Seligman, M. (1971). Further comparisons of verbal behavior in therapist-led, leaderless, and altenating group psychotherapy sessions. *Journal of Consulting Psychology, 18*(5), 472–477.

Strupp, H. H., & Wallach, M. S. (1965). A further study of psychiatrist's responses in quasi-therapeutic situations. *Behavioral Science, 10*, 113–134.

Talland, G. A., & Clark, D. H. (1954). Evaluation of topics in therapy group discussion. *Journal Clinical Psychology, 10*, 131–137.

Troth, W. A., Hall, G. L., & Seals, J. M. (1971). Counselor–counselee interaction. *Journal or Counseling Psychology, 18*, 77–80.

Truax, C. B., & Carkhuff, R. R. (1965). Personality change in hospitalized mental patients during group psychotherapy as a function of the use of alternate sessions and various therapy pretraining. *Journal of Clinical Psychology, 21*, 225–228.

Truax, C. B., Shapiro, J. G., & Wargo, D. G. (1968). The effects of alternate sessions and vicarious therapy pretraining on group psychotherapy. *International Journal of Group Psychotherapy, 18*, 186–198.

Truax, C. B., & Wargo, D. G. (1966). Psychotherapeutic encounters that change behaviors for better or worse. *American Journal of Psychotherapy, 20*, 499–520.

Truax, C. B., & Wargo, D. G. (1969). Effects of vicarious therapy pretraining and alternative sessions on outcome in group psychotherapy with outpatients. *Journal of Consulting and Clinical Psychology, 33*(4), 440–447.

Truax, C. B., Wargo, D. G., Carkhuff, R. R., Kodman, J., & Moles, E. A. (1966). Changes in self-concepts during group psychotherapy as a function of alternate sessions and vicarious therapy pretraining in institutional mental patients and juvenile delinquents. *Journal of Consulting Psychology, 30,* 309–314.

Verinis, J. S. (1970). The ex-patient as a lay therapist: Attitudes of group members toward him. *Psychotherapy: Theory, Research and Practice, 7*(3), 161–163.

Waxer, P. H. (1977). Short-term group psychotherapy: Some principles and techniques. *International Journal of Group Psychotherpy, 27,* 33–42.

Whalan, G. S., & Mushet, G. L. (1986). Consumers' views of the helpful aspects of an in-patient psychotherapy group: A preliminary communication. *British Journal of Medical Psychology, 59,* 337–339.

White, R., & Lippitt, R. (1968). Leader behavior and member reaction in three "social climates." In D. Cartwright & A. Zander (Eds.), *Group dynamics* (pp. 318–335). New York: Harper & Row.

Yalom, I. D. (1970). *The theory and practice of group psychotherapy.* New York: Basic Books.

Yalom, I. D. (1983). *Inpatient group psychotherapy.* New York: Basic Books.

Yalom, I. D. (1985). *The theory and practice of group psychotherapy* (3rd ed.). New York: Basic Books.

Yalom, I. D., & Elkin, G. (1974). *Everyday gets a little closer: A twice told therapy.* New York: Basic Books.

Yalom, I. D., Houts, P. S., Newell, G., & Rand, K. H. (1967a). Prediction of improvement in group therapy. *Archives of General Psychiatry, 17,* 159–168.

Yalom, I. D., Houts, P., Newell, G., & Rand, K. (1967b). Preparation of patients for group therapy: A controlled study. *Archives of General Psychiatry, 17,* 416–427.

# Appendix A
## Group Therapy Information[7]

People often feel uncomfortable their first time in group and don't know what is expected of them. This sheet is intended to give new members an introduction to what they should do in group therapy.

Group therapy is an important therapy for many people with emotional problems. It is prescribed for some and not for others, just as medications may or may not be prescribed. Groups are of different sizes and may include patients with varying ages and problems.

The task of the group is to help members learn more helpful ways to deal with their problems and feelings. People tend to use the same ways of dealing with other people in group that they use in their private lives. For instance, if the way someone behaves in the group makes you feel uncomfortable, it probably makes people in his private life also feel uncomfortable.

For example, Jack, a businessman, looked angrily at any group member who did not agree with him. He used the same method outside the group with his wife and boss. Also, a person who has difficulty speaking up in the group probably has difficulty speaking up in his [or her] private life.

For instance, JoAnn had difficulty talking with members of the group. At home she also had difficulty talking. Her friends felt uncomfortable about this and stopped visiting her. As a result, JoAnn was increasingly alone, which made her problems worse.

In both cases, the person was unaware of the effect he had on others and how his behavior affected them. These people were helped when other people in the group told them how they were behaving.

Members also help each other by asking questions to find out more about each other, pointing out to others how they look or seem and sharing their own emotional reactions.

---

[7] From Maxmen et al. (1974, pp. 257–259). Copyright 1974 by Brunner/Mazel. Reprinted by permission.

Because you have problems does not mean that you can't help others.

Members don't help each others when they:

1. avoid tense subjects or change the issue when people become uncomfortable. Often, it is necessary to talk about painful issues, if one wants to get better;
2. argue without trying to see what the other person is saying;
3. depend on the staff to tell them what to do;
4. talk to just one or a few of the patients in a group, shutting off the rest of the group;
5. talk about events that occurred outside the group and therefore can't be dealt with by the group.

For example, the group was talking about loneliness and Mary began to cry. They continued their discussion and ignored Mary. This was an unfortunate way to deal with the problem. Mary felt frustrated because she wanted to tell the group of her loneliness since the death of her mother. The group lost a chance to offer her support and advice on how to cope with her grief.

Another illustration was Bill, who liked to talk about his childhood and rambled on for a long time about this during group. This was not helpful to Bill or to the other members of the group, and in doing so Bill lost a valuable opportunity to talk about his alcoholism, which was the reason for his admission.

Therapists are there to help keep the group focused on the task.

Groups are frequently observed by other members of the staff involved in patient care, and these observers give the therapists information and advice on how they have conducted their job. You will be notified if your doctor feels group therapy will be beneficial for you.

# 4

# The Interpersonal Model

Our survey of articles published between 1970 and 1990 on inpatient groups suggested that those writers on inpatient groups who paid allegiance to some specific model of group psychotherapy often claimed to use an interpersonal or interactional model (Fallon & Brabender, 1992). Although the interpersonal model appears to take many different forms depending on the patient population and setting in which it is applied, all applications emphasize the usefulness of interpersonal learning within the group. In the interpersonal approach, the group is seen as a social microcosm in which an individual's typical style of relating inevitably emerges (Leszcz, 1986a, 1992; Yalom, 1970/1985). Members have an opportunity in the here-and-now context of the group to observe themselves and to learn about others' reactions to their behavior. Increasingly, members have a realization of both their responsibility for their interactions with others and their power to alter them. This realization, when accompanied by a greater knowledge of their maladaptive patterns of behavior, creates an impetus to attempt new and more positive behaviors within the group and eventually in their lives outside of therapy. Common to all versions of the interpersonal model is the notion that for the model to be effective, members must be both affectively and cognitively engaged in this process of interpersonal learning.

This chapter focuses on three versions of the interpersonal model. The first version involves the application of the Sullivanian principles of social learning in a group session with a relatively unstructured format. The second and third were developed by Yalom (1983). The interactional agenda model was devised for group members who have a capacity to use exploratory and supportive interventions. The focus group model was created for group members who require exclusively supportive techniques. This chapter contrasts these three types of interpersonal group therapy.

# Theoretical Underpinnings

## Historical Background and Basic Concepts

The interpersonal approach to group psychotherapy was greatly influenced by the interpersonal approach to psychopathology developed by Harry Stack Sullivan (1940, 1953). According to Sullivan, a conflict theorist, personality development proceeds through the interplay of two opposing forces: the pursuit of satisfaction and the avoidance of insecurity. Psychopathology is the result of *parataxic distortion,* a particularly maladaptive means of negotiating this conflict. Parataxic distortion is an unconscious misperception of another's response, a misperception based on early life experience and current need states. The parataxic distortion becomes embedded in the complex network of perceptions, images, and fantasies about the self (which Sullivan referred to as the *self-system*) so as to secure a particular satisfaction and enable the avoidance or minimization of anxiety. However, the distortion has little adaptive value because it is not tailored to contemporary reality and often begets the very reaction it is designed to avoid.

For example, a man may envision himself to be a great entertainer. He jests continually and imagines that others respond to him with adulation. Indeed, they do not. This distortion of others' reactions may be the result of the man's need to disguise from himself the indifference of his parents in his early years of development. As a child, through his lavish displays of jocularity, he could secure from his parents moments of attention and, at the same time, hide from himself his own deprivation. Although his contemporary peers respond to his forced jesting with disdain and boredom rather than delight, he fails to see these reactions clearly. The therapeutic process involves the correction of such distortions. By recognizing the distortion as such, by understanding its origins in his early development, and by seeing its untoward effects on his everyday social relations, the individual is able to abandon behaviors attached to the distortion. The individual is thus freed to develop more flexible and less defensive modes of interaction. These new modes of interaction, tailored to contemporary rather than historical realities, are more likely to enable the achievement of satisfaction in present relationships.

Other important contributors to the interpersonal approach to group psychotherapy were those theoreticians who provided a recognition of the power of the here-and-now (i.e., the focus on members' contemporaneous interactions with one another). Prominent among these theoreticians are Moreno and Lewin. Moreno (1934) had group members bring family conflicts into the present through the enactment of psychodramas. Lewin and his co-workers (Benne, Bradford, and Lippitt) observed T-groups that were designed to effect positive change among co-workers in an organization. Their observations led them to appreciate the change that individuals can undergo if they are provided with an opportunity to learn how others see them within the immediate context of the group (see Benne, 1964).

Irvin Yalom, perhaps this country's best known writer and thinker on group psychotherapy, is the originator and primary expostulator of the interpersonal approach to group psychotherapy. Yalom's approach is based on Sullivan's interpersonal theory and a here-and-now methodology. Yalom (1985) first proposed an interpersonal approach to group psychotherapy in his classic text *The Theory and Practice of Group Psychotherapy*, first published in 1970. Yalom (1985, 1986) made the point that within the group forum, the exploration of genetic or early familial factors that produce psychopathology may not be as important, powerful, or effective as is interpersonal learning within the group. Although Yalom outlined a variety of mechanisms that can be used in the group to further the well-being of its members, the primary mutative process is interpersonal learning within the here-and-now.

Interpersonal learning consists of a two-stage process. In the first stage, members are plunged into a richly affective expression of their immediate reactions to one another. To achieve such an exploration, the therapist must possess a facility in "activating" the here-and-now. That is, the therapist must redirect members' focus from events that may be historical and out-of-the-room to their present transactions with one another. For example, in an outpatient group, Fred, who had been describing to the group his rage at his neighbors' loud playing of their stereo was queried by the therapist as to whether any members were playing their music too loudly in the group. Fred then spoke of his irritation toward another member, Sue, who had dominated the prior week's session. At this point, other members also expressed annoyance toward Sue. Sue then reciprocated the expression of hostility. If members were permitted to remain in this stage of affective expression, they might have obtained some temporary catharsis from the session but would have achieved little that could be transferred to interpersonal situations in their lives outside of group.

The second stage involves the analysis of the affective expressions. In this example, Sue was asked to share perceptions that she had of Fred during the prior week. She said that he appeared bored and indifferent. She noticed that he was the only member of the group who had nothing to say in response to her disclosures. Fred then offered that he was waiting for her to finish because he, too, had something important to share with the group. The therapist posed to the group whether anyone was able to detect that Fred had something to share. Other members responded that Fred seemed somewhat uninterested, as if nothing was or even could be of importance in the group. The therapist went on to help Fred explore and test out some of his fantasies about what would have happened had he spoken up. The therapist also pointed out that Fred was being much more active and direct during the present session and encouraged him to note members' reactions to this altered mode of relating.

How had the group enabled Fred to become more interpersonally effective? Fred learned that when he wants attention that others are receiving, he responds in a behaviorally passive way (i.e., by withdrawing). He saw the negative effect that his withdrawal had on others (they saw him as uncaring) and himself (he continued to be frustrated). He also experimented with a new mode of communication and tested in reality any fears that he attached to its adoption.

The interpersonal approach has been used in inpatient settings over the past 30 years. However, rarely has it been labeled as such. In the early 1960s, Frank (1963) described inpatient groups in a state hospital setting. He anticipated some of the elements (e.g., working within the here-and-now) that ultimately became central to the interpersonal approach. In the 1970s and the early 1980s, some inpatient group therapists (e.g., Bailine, Katch, & Golden, 1977; Beard & Scott, 1975; Beutler, Frank, Schieber, Calvert, & Gaines, 1984), influenced by Yalom's (1970/1985) *The Theory and Practice of Group Psychotherapy*, conducted groups in pursuit of the interpersonal goal of helping members develop more effective ways of relating to others. These practitioners used the interpersonal methodology of focusing on members' here-and-now experiences in the context of a relatively unstructured session in which they could reveal spontaneously their characteristic ways of interacting with others. Elements of insight were often incorporated into the treatment. Such incorporation was consonant with the Sullivanian conflict-based premise that the perceptual distortions that give rise to maladaptive social behaviors are unconscious and are associated with hidden affects, impulses, and fantasies.

In 1983, Yalom published *Inpatient Group Psychotherapy*, a text that describes two models for using the interpersonal approach in an inpatient setting. One model, the interactional agenda model, was developed for relatively high-functioning inpatients, and the other, the focus group model, for low-functioning inpatients. These models are interpersonally oriented in that they embrace interpersonal goals and methods. However, they are modified in relation to the interpersonal approach that Yalom described in his 1970 text in consideration of the special features of the inpatient environment. Such features include the brevity of members' tenures in the group, members' degrees of pathology, and the fact that the group takes place on a treatment unit.

The agenda and focus group formats were based on Yalom's own experience in leading daily inpatient groups, his observation of groups in 25 inpatient settings;[1] and his own research studies and knowledge of the literature.

These two formats differ from the earlier applications of the interpersonal model in three ways that are particularly important for our later discussion. First, the agenda and focus group models differ from earlier applications in terms of degree of structure. Whereas the earlier forms of this model generally involved relatively unstructured sessions in which members spontaneously produced material, the agenda and focus group models both have a highly articulated format. Second, the goals of the unstructured and structured applications are somewhat different. Although all versions of the interpersonal approach endorse the goal of helping members acquire more interpersonally effective behaviors, the unstructured versions appear to have remained truer to their Sullivanian origins. That is, they are consistent with Sullivan's conflict model of psychopathology wherein maladaptive social behavior is seen as serving a defensive function for the person. The modification of behavior does not entail simply the recognition of problematic behaviors and their impact on others but also the development of insight into the impulses and feelings that have sustained the maladaptive behaviors. As we discuss later, Yalom (1983) saw the fostering of insight as having limited utility in the inpatient group. Third, the leader in the later models is more active than in the prior applications of the interpersonal approach. Of course, the more that members interact with the leader, the less they interact with one another. Hence, whereas unstructured versions are more member centered (i.e., emphasize member-to-member interaction), the later models are more leader centered.

In contemporary inpatient group psychotherapy, there are at least two ways in which the interpersonal approach is applied. In some settings, there is a straightforward implementation of

---

[1] Yalom (1983) indicated that the groups he observed were primarily in training settings in which there were abundant resources for the development of therapeutic programs.

the agenda or focus group models (e.g., Mushet, Whalan, & Power, 1989; Weiner, 1987). In other settings, therapists use an interpersonal approach within the context of a relatively unstructured session much as therapists did prior to 1983 (e.g., Griffen-Shelley & Wendel, 1988; Kahn, Webster, & Storck, 1986). Currently, there is no basis in the outcome literature for endorsing one application of the interpersonal approach over another. For this reason, although we give some special emphasis to the agenda and focus group versions, we also attempt to capture the richness of the interpersonal approach by reflecting the diversity of its applications in the field. The therapist's awareness of the various ways in which the interpersonal approach has been used will empower him or her to adapt any of the versions of this model to the special demands of his or her setting.

## Goals of Treatment

A central goal of the interpersonal model is to foster members' development of effective social behaviors that will enable them to achieve more intimate, gratifying interpersonal relationships. This goal is derived from the Sullivanian position that all psychological problems (no matter how individually centered they may seem) have a social undergirding. For example, although an individual's symptom of depression may seem to reside in the person rather than in his or her relationships, investigation will inevitably reveal interpersonal elements that sustain the symptom. The individual may be depressed because of isolation from others, a perception that others have a negative valuation of him or her, or guilt in relation to negative feelings toward others. Although Sullivan (1953) recognized that certain psychological problems develop within a hereditary matrix, he claimed that even in this instance "life experience may have some influence on the timing of the manifestation of the defect" (p. 314).

To what extent is the modification of maladaptive patterns of social behavior a realistic goal for inpatient groups? In the 1970s, several writers (e.g., Beard & Scott, 1975) explicitly adopted this ambitious goal for their groups. It might be noted, however, that the average duration of hospitalization was longer in the 1970s than it has been in the 1990s. For example, in the Beard and Scott study, group members participated in the group for at least 20 sessions. There continue to exist some clinical contexts in which patients are hospitalized for several months and the group is therefore able to achieve membership stability over time (e.g., see Klein, Hunter, & Brown's, 1986, description of a long-term adolescent inpatient group or Griffen-Shelley & Wender's, 1988, description of a long-term adult group). In these settings, addressing maladaptive patterns of social behavior becomes more feasible. However, in the more typical setting wherein the length of stay is extremely brief, members may not have the opportunity to acquire a new style of relating. In these groups, there are other interpersonally oriented goals that can viably be pursued (Leszcz, 1986a; Yalom, 1983).

For example, one important interpersonal goal is the patient's increased openness to relationships on the unit at large, with a diminution in the negativity and tension attached to such relationships. As has been noted frequently (e.g., Betcher, 1983), many patients exhibit a high level of withdrawal at the time of their hospitalization. Overcoming this isolation is important given that all therapy that a patient receives in the hospital occurs within the framework of a relationship.[2] For example, there is evidence that hospitalized patients see their relationships to other patients on the unit as some of the most helpful experiences during their hospitalizations (Leszcz, Yalom, & Norden, 1985). In an interpersonally oriented group, members have an opportunity to explore their fantasies about catastrophic consequences of relating to others. A group member who assumes that others are secretly laughing at her stammer may discover that although members do notice the stammer, they place little weight on it. She learns that members place much more weight on her forthrightness, a quality that they value highly. This member's greater

---

[2] Recently, there has been recognition that even psychopharmacologic interventions have interpersonal dimensions. See Zaslav and Kalb (1989) for a discussion of the relation between group process in an inpatient psychotherapy group and attitudes and fantasies about medication.

awareness that she has something to offer others is likely to make her more available to others not only in the group but in the unit at large.

The interpersonal model may also accomplish the goal of increasing members' motivation and readiness for outpatient psychotherapy (particularly interpersonally oriented therapy). In fact, the primary goal of Yalom's (1983) agenda and focus group versions is to provide members with a positive experience in therapy so that they will wish to continue treatment after they are discharged. The cultivation of members' preparedness and motivation for outpatient therapy has several dimensions. Within the interpersonal approach, members come to recognize their responsibilities for their difficulties. With this sense of responsibility comes a concomitant hopefulness about the possibility of eradicating problems or at least lessening their severity. The interpersonal approach also heightens members' awareness of the importance of the association between their interpersonal difficulties and their symptoms. Thus, members are led to see the usefulness of carrying on interpersonal exploration in any psychotherapy following discharge. Yalom (1983) emphasized what he called the *problem-spotting function* of the inpatient group (members' delineation of those interpersonal difficulties that can be addressed in a future, more long-term context).

Applications of the interpersonal approach vary in the extent to which they establish insight as a goal. Among those who use an interpersonal approach in an inpatient setting, there seems to be agreement that probing into deeply repressed unconscious contents, even when those contents are relevant to the patient's social dysfunction, is unlikely to be therapeutic (and in the case of low-functioning members may be antitherapeutic). However, applications of the interpersonal approach differ from one another in their estimation of the value of interpreting relatively accessible or preconscious material. Some interpersonally oriented writers (e.g., Kahn et al., 1986) appear to be enthusiastic about the utility of such interpretations. Rosegrant (1988) argued that through these interpretations, the patient is given "an incipient experience of tolerating, and having tolerated by others, parts of themselves which were previously wholly unacceptable" (p. 108).

Another commonly pursued goal in an inpatient therapy group is symptomatic relief. The interpersonal approach is fundamentally incompatible with the direct pursuit of symptom relief as a goal because the former leads the patient to look beyond the symptom to the interpersonal problems precipitating it. On the inpatient unit, many other aspects of treatment such as pharmacotherapy, behavior therapy, and theme-oriented activity therapy are directed toward the treatment of symptoms. The nonsymptomatic focus of the interpersonally oriented group ensures that the contribution of the group will not duplicate those of other modalities (Yalom, 1983).

# Technical Considerations

## The Role of the Leader

The leader of the interpersonally oriented inpatient group necessarily assumes a highly active posture. This posture is required by the here-and-now focus of the group. Group members do not naturally focus on their immediate experience and often avoid it studiously. Instead, they are likely to occupy themselves with other activities such as the discussion of those situational factors that precipitated their hospitalization or the ponderance of abstract issues such as whether people who do not enter treatment are any better adjusted than those who do. A newly formed group in particular requires a certain therapeutic hovering by the therapist to ensure that members accord themselves sufficient opportunity to consider their own transactions. A high level of therapist activity is also required to effect the appropriate balance between affect and cognition, a fundamental technical requirement of the interpersonal approach (Yalom, 1985).

The special features of an inpatient setting demand an even more vigorous intervention style by the therapist than is needed in an outpatient setting. There are a number of respects in which the inpatient therapist must be active (Yalom, 1983). The brevity of members' tenure in the group necessitates that the therapist be active in creating a highly structured session that enables each member to engage in significant interpersonal learning in every session. Members' high level of distress and severity of psycho-pathology require that the therapist provide an abundance of support both to stave off regression and to diminish members' nonproductive anxiety. The interpersonal therapist must be ex-peditious and strongly directive in managing the crises that fre-quently occur in an inpatient group, such as when a member makes a threatening statement to another member.

In addition to maintaining a high level of activity along these lines, the interpersonal therapist must be attentive to other as-pects of his or her leadership style. The therapist must be cog-nizant of his or her own style of relating. The therapist must also pay special heed to the means by which he or she manages conflict in the group.[3] Because these are two areas in which the leadership prescriptions of the interpersonal approach deviates from those of several of the other models described in this text, we give them special consideration.

**Therapist's style of relating.** The therapist of the interper-sonal group must cultivate an interactive style that is strong, authoritative, and yet egalitarian (Yalom, 1983). The authorita-tive aspect is important not only because a highly confident therapist is better able to assuage members' unproductive anxiety but because the therapist's confidence also enhances members' willingness to participate in a process that at the outset of treat-ment may have little credibility as a means of dealing with the difficulties necessitating their hospitalization. The therapist's egalitarianism is important because the interpersonal approach requires that the group members take considerable responsibility for self-disclosing and providing feedback to other group mem-bers. A therapist who is either autocratic or unresponsive fosters infantile behavior on the part of the members who are thereby inspired by the therapist to lie in continual wait for magical

---

[3] The present treatment of leadership does not capture the richness of Ya-lom's (1983) discussion of this topic. Yalom wrote about many features of effective inpatient group leadership that are pertinent to all models of inpatient group. For example, Yalom discussed the importance of the therapist main-taining with vigor and rigor the spatial and temporal boundaries of the group. In this chapter, we have focused on those aspects of leader behavior that are specifically part of the interpersonal model.

provisions. A key means for the therapist to achieve an egalitarian relationship with members is to engage in the activities in which the members are encouraged to engage (Yalom, 1985). For example, just as members are expected to give and receive feedback, so should the therapist contribute observations of members and show a willingness to receive others' comments on his or her own behavior.

Both the need for the therapist to exhibit egalitarianism as well as to model healthy group behaviors requires that the interpersonal therapist take a particular stance toward self-disclosure (Yalom, 1983). Rather than embracing the inscrutability of the Tavistock leader who wishes to fan the flames of leader-centered transference, the inpatient group psychotherapist should engage in "judicious self-disclosure" (Yalom, 1983). Appropriate self-disclosure should have two characteristics. First, it should always be consonant with the goals of the interpersonal group. Second, it should almost always concern the therapist's reaction to some aspect of the group process. An example of judicious self-disclosure is when the therapist acknowledges feeling torn between allowing the group to continue focusing on an obviously distressed but inconsolable member and urging the group to move on to others who may be suffering, albeit less conspicuously so. In this instance, the therapist's acknowledgment of such an internal struggle permits an explicit recognition of all members' needs. Such a recognition reduces both the narcissistic sting and sense of deprivation for a member who is not currently the focus of the group's attention.

In relation to all extant models of group psychotherapy, the interpersonal approach requires a moderate level of leader transparency (Dies, 1977). However, in relation to inpatient models, the desirable level of therapist self-disclosure is somewhat higher than is that of other models. For example, the developmental model (see chapter 6) requires that the therapist maintain a certain separateness so as to be able to interpret more accurately the group process.

**Conflict in the inpatient therapy group.** Anger is an affective state common to inpatient groups. It has many sources. A major source is the hospitalization itself: Members are often angry because of their need for hospitalization and the realities of the hospital situation itself (e.g., loss of privacy, regimentation, exposure to more disturbed patients). Another source of anger is the demand implicitly made on members to share the therapist. The often brief tenure of members in the group and the pressure they feel to change during this tenure also contribute to the intensification of hostile feelings within the group.

In the interpersonally oriented group, members are invited to share openly their reactions to other members. It is natural that along with the positive feelings that members express toward one another, there is an array of negative feelings: irritation, hostility, impatience, exasperation. The interpersonal group therapist is faced with somewhat of a Scylla–Charybdis dilemma in helping the group to respond to the emergence of these feelings. Although it is essential that members learn to communicate their negative feelings effectively, such reactions also have the power to produce further disintegration in the sender and the receiver (and even sideline observers) of such messages.

Interpersonal therapists differ in the ways that they have responded to this challenge. In some interpersonally oriented groups (Beutler et al., 1984), the exploration of members' negative feelings is made the centerpiece of the group. It is possible that consistent focus on negative feelings neutralizes their impact. In other interpersonal group formats, leaders attempt to curtail sharply the expression of negative feelings. For example, Yalom ( 1983) believed that "the inpatient group is not the place for confrontation, criticism, or the expression and examination of anger" (p. 125). Rather, he believed that open, intense, or prolonged manifestation of conflict is destructive to the inpatient group because it feeds members' fearfulness of involvement in the group. He argued that a conflict-ridden, hostile group subverts what for him is the cardinal goal of an inpatient group: to develop members' perception of group as a supportive place in which a high level of comfort with others and understanding is achievable.

Whether the practitioner sees more cost than benefit in the exploration of anger, members' hostility toward one another clearly needs to be modulated. There exists a set of techniques to intervene constructively when conflict arises (Yalom, 1983). For example, the therapist may encourage the angry member to direct his or her hostility toward an abstract issue rather than toward the member associated with the issue. The therapist can offer himself or herself as a target for the anger. The therapist can also encourage a member who gets explosively angry to express hostility when it is in its more nascent form. The common denominator of these and other techniques is that the therapist permits a limited discharge of anger so as to prevent its full flowering (see Yalom, 1983, for other strategies on the management of hostility and conflict in the inpatient group).

Currently, there is no empirical basis for determining what level of conflict can constructively be expressed and explored in an inpatient group, although there is support for the view that a high level of negative expression is undesirable (e.g., Beutler et al., 1984). Most interpersonal group therapists working in an inpatient setting would agree that neither the total squelching nor the full evocation of conflict is desirable. However, apart from these extremes, the therapist has considerable latitude in the degree to which the communication of negative feelings is accorded a place in the group. Until there is more empirical information on this issue, the therapist must titrate negative feelings on the basis of a consideration of the specificities of his or her setting. For example, settings differ from one another in the willingness and ability of staff members (other than the group therapist) to help members cope with their reactions to hostility that had emerged in the session emerging again outside the session.

## Use of the Here-and-Now

Although there are many applications of the interpersonal approach to inpatient group psychotherapy, a sine qua non of all interpersonal applications is the use of the here-and-now as a central focus of the treatment. As we discussed earlier, the focus on the here-and-now is predicated on the position of Sullivan and later Yalom (1985) that most forms of psychopathology have an interpersonal aspect that can be explored within the immediacy of a relationship or, in the case of a group, a set of relationships. A key technical consideration of all interpersonal group therapists is how to use the here-and-now most effectively. From Yalom's (1983, 1985) standpoint, such effective use entails the two-step process that was outlined briefly earlier in this chapter and that we now describe more specifically. The first step, the activation of the here-and-now, involves the delineation to the group of those immediate events that require the group's attention. Although in a mature outpatient group, the group members themselves may perform this task, typically, in an inpatient group, it must be performed by the therapist.

An example of activation of the here-and-now occurred in a session in which a member, Helen, spoke in a very whining tone about her husband's failure to attend to her emotional needs. The therapist observed that while delivering her narrative, Helen did not look at the other members of the group. Note that in sharing this observation, the therapist was activating the here-and-now. The therapist was saying that Helen's *way* of relating her story to the other group members is important. The therapist proceeded to ask the group how it felt about Helen's lack of eye contact. Here, the therapist was keying in on the affective layer of the group, a layer that often emerges vividly during this step. Several group members declined the therapist's invitation by responding intellectually. They said that they inferred that Helen did not want to be interrupted, that she was more invested in simply telling her story than garnering their reactions to it. However, one member, Mary, indicated that she felt vaguely annoyed that Helen was not curious about what she had to say. Other members then followed Mary's lead. One member said she was bored by Helen's monologue. Another said she that felt slightly impatient for Helen to reach her conclusion. Still another said she felt rejected by Helen in response to Helen's evident lack of interest in her opinion. Helen expressed some dismay and shock over both members' perception of her indifference and the feelings in them that these perceptions excited.

Once members had put forth their feelings toward Helen, and Helen her feelings toward them, the group was in a position to be assisted by the therapist in proceeding through the second step, the illumination of the here-and-now. In this case, Helen was encouraged to talk about the expectation that she had about how the group members would receive her disclosures. Helen responded that she had expected exactly what she got: nothing.

The therapist then wondered aloud whether as Helen spoke, members did have thoughts that they might have shared with her but did not. A number of members said that they had many reactions that, in fact, they would have enjoyed sharing with Helen. The therapist then pointed out to Helen that she behaved in accordance with her expectations about the situation rather than with the reality of the situation. That is, because she assumed that others did not care, she actively denied them an opportunity to show their caring for her. The therapist then showed the other group members that, indeed, their behavior was much like Helen's. They assumed that Helen was indifferent to them and thereby denied her the feedback she craved. It can be seen that this second step involves more of a cognitive analysis of what has proceeded in the group. However, so as not to unduly simplify this complex process, it must be recognized that, in both steps, affective and cognitive elements are present. In the present example, Helen's new awareness of members' concern for her prompted her to express feelings of affection for the other members.

In this sequence, the members of the group were given a framework by which their own present affective reactions and those of others could be seen as coherent. Although there was an element of confrontation in the interaction between Helen and other group members, there was also a high degree of support. If the group had merely brainstormed on ways in which Helen could maneuver her husband to be more forthcoming, she would have failed to experience this support so directly. So, too, would she have failed to recognize her responsibility in evoking others' at least seeming disattunement to her. Had the group taken this alternate direction (i.e., a direction toward the there-and-then rather than the here-and-now), the group would have been experienced by members as much less vibrant and compelling. More important, the proceedings would have been perceived as having significance for only those members whose external situations closely paralleled Helen's.

## Content of the Session

For all applications of the interpersonal model to inpatient groups, the content of the session consists of the group's examination of their relationships with one another within and, in some cases, outside the group. In inpatient settings in which relatively unstructured versions of the interpersonal model are used, members bring up material spontaneously. The therapist uses this material to direct members' attention to some immediate aspect of their experience. The therapist guides members in proceeding through the two-stage process just delineated. This format wherein the therapist is primarily reactive to the offerings of members characterizes the entire session. The exception may be some orientation to the group in the beginning of the session, which the therapist may provide or encourage other members to provide, and possibly a go-around in which members introduce themselves to the group.

Alternatively, the therapist can structure a sequence of events within the session. Such structure ensures a focused pursuit of goals in a way that enables them to be fulfilled given the group's limited period in which to work and many members' compromised resources for working (Yalom, 1983). However, the development of such a format requires that the group have a particular composition (i.e., that it be relatively homogeneous in terms of level of functioning).

The notion of creating level groups consisting of members who are relatively homogeneous in terms of level of functioning was formalized by Leopold (1977), although earlier contributors provided some anticipation of this concept. Here, *level of functioning* refers to the patients' behaviors within groups and capacities to use different types of intervention. Although this concept is obviously related to diagnosis and level of adaptation in the extrahospital environment, it is nonetheless different from both of these constructs. Patients are considered to be low functioning when their capacity to relate to others is enhanced by interventions of a primarily supportive, nonexploratory nature (i.e., those designed to effect an immediate lessening in the member's degree of anxiety or other disturbing affects). Patients are viewed as high functioning when they benefit not only from the aforementioned class of interventions but from interventions designed to enhance their awareness of patterns of behavior and the impact of these behaviors on the social environment.

Some treatment settings demand the creation of a group consisting of members who are highly variable from one another in level of functioning. For example, a small psychiatric unit of a general hospital may have too few group members or personnel to justify the organization of groups that are more homogeneous in terms of members' levels of functioning. Yalom (1983) referred to groups of patients at different levels of functioning as "team groups" on the presumption that all members share the same treatment team (although this descriptor may not be accurate in all settings). He argued that the application of an interpersonal approach is inappropriate because the members have diverse interpersonal needs.[4]

A levels approach entails the creation of separate groups and different session formats for high- and low-functioning members. Yalom (1983) proposed the agenda group for high-functioning patients and the focus group for low-functioning patients. Although these models are presented in a highly detailed way, they are not intended as exact blueprints of how other therapists should conduct their groups (Yalom, 1983). Rather, these versions of the interpersonal model provide the therapist with principles and strategies that should be modified on the basis of the particularities of the his or her own setting as well as those of his or her own personality.

## The Interactional Agenda Group

The content of the agenda group is guided by a five-step process. In the first step, orientation and preparation, the therapist provides members with information about the structural features of the group (e.g., length of sessions, frequency of meetings, presence of observers), its purpose, and its mechanics. Group members are informed that the group is designed specifically to assist members in their interpersonal relationships. The therapist also

---

[4] See Yalom (1983) and Vinogradov and Yalom (1989) for suggestions on how such team groups might be conducted. We do not consider them within the present chapter because they require that the therapist deviate significantly from an interpersonal orientation.

explains the notion that by working on their relationships with one another, members can improve their relationships outside of the group. Yalom (1983) saw this orientation as extremely important given the research evidence that patients' knowledge of the goals and working procedures of their groups enhances their performance within the group (Heitler, 1974; Houlihan, 1977).

The second step, the agenda go-around, requires each member to identify some area on which he or she can work during that session. For example, a member might say, "Yesterday, I thought that all of you were secretly laughing at me when I shared my feelings with the group. Today I want to find out if you actually were." Yalom (1983) pointed out that the advantages of the go-around include enabling the therapist to identify the points of greatest tension within the group so that the therapist can recognize problem areas that members can address in concert with one another and support patients in adopting an active participatory stance in the group.

In orchestrating the go-around, the therapist provides members with some instruction on what constitutes an appropriate agenda by allowing the more senior members to formulate their agendas first. Even with such an allowance, it is almost certain that some members will have difficulty formulating their agendas. In such cases, the therapist must help members to isolate problem areas, translate problems into interpersonal terms, and develop problems in such a way that they can be addressed within the here-and-now context of the group.

An example of this agenda-sculpting process is one wherein a group member offers as her agenda, "I'm sick of feeling worthless." The therapist (in some instances assisted by other group members) would engage in a discussion with the member leading to the development of an agenda that is realistic, interpersonal, and here-and-now focused. The member's problem may be rendered less abstract and more interpersonal through the following translation: "I want to place myself more on a par with others." Its contextualization within the group may be, "I want to speak up more today and not always defer to others who are also trying to speak."

cf. Bandler + Grinder,

The formulation of agendas is envisioned to be a step that has immense therapeutic value (Yalom, 1983). Clearly, it accomplishes the problem-spotting function of the group and requires that members take control of their therapy (Leszcz, 1986b). Moreover, to the extent that members can see themselves as having specific interpersonal problems that can be addressed in the group, their motivation to continue group therapy following discharge is enhanced. Finally, members' formulations of agendas is experienced as a success that fosters positive feelings toward the group.

The third step is that of agenda fulfillment. Either group members or the therapist may initiate this process. However, what is important is that the therapist remain alert to the possibility of integrating as many agendas as possible into the field of action. For example, one member may have established as her agenda learning to focus on other members rather than on herself, and another member may have announced his wish to be more open in disclosing to the group his sense of humiliation in relation to his stammering. The therapist might encourage the former to "draw out" the latter. Although most agendas are filled within the session, the therapist may give a member a "homework assignment" to complete on the unit between sessions. For example, if a given number of members wish to practice taking initiative in relationships, the therapist may suggest that the members initiate conversations on the unit with another group member who is striving to overcome his withdrawal.

The fourth step, the wrap-up, consists of a two-part retrospective analysis of the session. In the first part of this step, the group is analyzed by the therapist and any other individuals who have observed the group. The inclusion of observers in an inpatient psychotherapy group is not uncommon. Frequently, students or members of the treatment team request to observe the group for training or treatment coordination purposes. In the literature (e.g., Oldham, 1982), observers are portrayed typically in passive roles with respect to the group process, although they may make active use of the knowledge acquired from witnessing the group elsewhere on the unit. The passivity of the observers often leaves members feeling exploited and fearful about the preservation of their confidentiality (Yalom, 1983). Yalom suggested an active role for the observers so that (a) the aforementioned negative effects of observers can be obviated, (b) the clinical and training functions of having observers can be preserved, and (c) the observers can actively advance the goals of the group. The observers' activity takes the form of sharing their observations about the group with the group members in the initial segment of the wrap-up period. Although the observers strive to be candid, they withhold any perceptions that might be narcissistically damaging or anxiety arousing to the group.

The therapist's role in this discussion is to give consideration to each member's progress in the session as well as to the overall climate of the group. The therapist should emphasize any appraisal of his or her own activity in the group that would help to demystify the therapeutic process and provide a model of openness. If there are co-therapists, their discussion of their relationships also provides members with a demonstration of constructive interpersonal exploration.

In the second part of the wrap-up, group members have an opportunity to bring the meeting to an end. Final events may include a discussion of their reactions to the observers' feedback or the therapist's analysis, the further processing of an unresolved issue from an earlier point in the session, or a focus on those members who have not had an opportunity to speak earlier. Group members are permitted to determine which direction to pursue because such an allowance fosters responsibility taking. At the same time, the therapist must seek opportunities to use this final period to support a self-review process in which members come to recognize more clearly what is effective work in psychotherapy. For example, the therapist may explicitly state that a given session was an especially valuable one because of members' obvious willingness to offer one another honest feedback. (See Yalom, 1983, for a more complete description of this model and a detailed clinical example.)

## The Focus Group

The focus group model was designed for lower functioning group members who are sufficiently organized to sit in a group with others but whose ego functions are too disrupted by their symptoms to permit them to profit from the more demanding agenda group. Although the activities of the focus group are quite different from those of the agenda group, they are nonetheless consistent with the general goals and principles of the interpersonal orientation. The group is directed toward constructively exploring members' interactions in the group so as to foster their willingness to continue with therapy after discharge, their recognition of the helpfulness of talking and concretely identifying problems, and their capacity to engage with others both on the unit and outside the hospital (Yalom, 1983).

The particular activities of the focus group are designed with an awareness of the special limitations of these members. Because many individuals in this group will have exceedingly brief attention spans, activities are pursued for very brief periods of time. Members' capacities for further decompensation necessitate that the exploration of conflictual areas are avoided assiduously. In view of members' vulnerabilities to extraordinarily high levels of anxiety, specific exercises such as muscle relaxation are used to enable members to feel safer and more comfortable. Because members are likely to be threatened specifically by group ambience, the therapist must create ways in which the members can experience success in the group instantly to diminish that threat. That is, the therapist must be attuned to, and poised to emphasize, all positive aspects of members' behavior, including their courage in simply attending the group.

Each session in the focus group is organized into four segments. The first segment, orientation and preparation, is essentially the same in content as that of the agenda group. Information pertaining to the time, place, goals, and methods of the group is shared. Even if there are no new members in a particular session, the therapist must never bypass this step given members' likely high levels of confusion.

The second segment, the warm-up, involves members' engagement in brief exercises that ease them into positive interaction with one another. Examples of such exercises are a ball toss, a go-around in which members describe a positive or negative feeling that they experienced that day, or a go-around in which each member makes observations of another member of the group. It is important that the therapist ascertain the mood of the group in selecting a particular exercise. This emphasis is different from the agenda group in which the therapist has less flexibility in structuring the session.

The third segment consists of a set of structured exercises, each of which lasts from 5 to 15 minutes. Again, the particular exercise chosen (as well as its duration) is determined by the therapist's perception of the special needs and level of task endurance of each group. Yalom (1983) provided examples of various exercises and games in each category. Some exercises have a strong interpersonal focus (e.g., exercises that develop members' capacities for relating to others), whereas others do not (e.g., a didactic discussion about a shared problem). The exercises can be tailored to enable members to process some event on the unit that may have upset them.

The fourth and final segment involves a review of the session. Given the difficulty that these members have in organizing their experience, they are likely to profit from the opportunity to recollect the sequence of events that constituted the session. Following this memorial exercise, the group then conducts an exploration of its reactions to the events of the session, much as is done by the agenda group. Observers are not used because their mere presence may exacerbate members' inevitable difficulties with trust. For a more complete description of this model with clinical examples, see Yalom (1983) and Vinogradov and Yalom (1989).

# Clinical Illustration

The vignette presented in this chapter illustrates an unstructured version of the interpersonal approach. The group was composed of relatively high-functioning members. In this session, the therapist had already oriented the members to the group with the help of the more senior members. Although there were eight members in the group, for ease of exposition, we describe only five members.

## Group Members

Marv, a middle-aged man, had been hospitalized for 3 weeks after his revelation to his outpatient therapist that he had a suicidal plan that the therapist deemed very serious. He had entered the hospital in a mournful mood but in the past week appeared filled with bombast. On the unit, he was consumed with a zeal to help all who encountered him, staff and patients alike, and did so in a way that was so intrusive and condescending that others were avoiding him steadfastly. He had been in the group for four sessions.

Hazel, an elderly group member, was participating in her second group session. In the previous day's session, members commented that although they found her to be very amiable, they noticed that when several members had made some complaints about their life on the unit, Hazel attempted to minimize their concerns. At the end of that session, Hazel congratulated members on having been so perceptive of her during the prior session because her inability to acknowledge to herself or express to others any negative reactions had much to do with her unhappiness in her marriage and her need for hospitalization. With the therapist's help, she formulated a plan that when she experienced even minor dissatisfaction in the group, she would speak up.

Gabe was a young man who had been in the hospital for a week. He was preoccupied by perverse, harm-wishing thoughts toward other people and because of his fearfulness that others might somehow become aware of them, he had progressively isolated himself from his family and friends. Despite an initial refusal to join the group, he became more and more comfortable as he experienced himself being helpful to others. In the previous day's session, he had surprised other members of the group by disclosing about his fears of rejection. He articulated a goal to test in the group the legitimacy of these fears.

Sally, an extremely sociable young woman, revealed in her 2 weeks of being in group an ease in connecting with others. She was a highly liked and admired member of the group, and members frequently commented that she seemed more like a staff member than a patient. Members did not understand why she was in the hospital and assumed it had resulted from a practitioner's misjudgment.

Portia, a woman in her late fifties, had been hospitalized for 4 weeks for symptoms related to bipolar depression. Over the course of her 3-week group participation, she had become considerably less withdrawn.

## The Session

The members proceeded through a brief orientation about the nature and scope of the group.

|        |   |
|--------|---|
| Sally: | What's wrong with you? |
| Marv: | Nothing. |
| Sally: | Well, something's wrong. |
| Marv: | Nothing's wrong. |
| Sally: | You look . . . I don't know . . . miserable today. |
| Marv: | I do? |
| Gabe: | I think you do. |
| Marv: | Well, maybe I'm feeling pretty crummy about what has been going on on the unit. Last night I walked into the TV room and I noticed that one person left, one person started reading a book, like it was real interesting all of a sudden, and the only other person I could talk to said, "Sorry, Marv, I'm watching the show right now." These are all people who seemed glad to talk to me when I first came in the hospital. |
| Therapist: | You said that people are avoiding you on the unit. Perhaps it would be important to see if the same thing is going on in here. |

(In this comment, the therapist is placing Marv's problem within the here-and-now, encouraging him to take responsibility for his behavior, and bolstering him in that effort.)

|        |   |
|--------|---|
| Marv: | Out there it's a jungle . . . in here people seem nicer but there is something that makes me suspicious. Yesterday when I was asking Hazel some questions, Sally said, "Stop badgering her." Now maybe you were kidding, but you used to have lunch with me and you don't anymore. |
| Therapist: | So you're wondering what is going on? |

Marv:   I suppose.

Sally does not respond immediately, but as she sees members staring expectantly at her, she responds in a perfunctory tone.

Sally:   I know you were trying to help and, in fact, I think you were doing a good job.

Gabe:   But you did say "Stop badgering her."

Sally:   Well . . . maybe . . . I just wondered if you weren't coming across a little too strongly. After all, it was Hazel's first session.

Portia:   Yes, I remember you saying that too.

Hazel:   (giggles with embarrassment) Don't worry about me, dear.

Therapist:   It looks like we have a nice opportunity here since Marv wanted to get feedback on whether there was anything he was doing to alienate others in the group. Sally thought maybe Marv had scared you (to Hazel) but we really don't know unless you tell us how you felt toward Marv. And, Hazel, you did say that one of your goals was to be more open with the group members about your feelings, particularly your negative feelings.

(Here, the therapist is attempting to weave the therapeutic needs of group members.)

Hazel:   Well, Marv asked me a lot of questions. I know he was just trying to be helpful . . . and he was . . . he was very helpful.

Gabe:   But, remember that you said last night that you had a headache when you left here.

Portia:   Yes, I remember you saying that too.

Hazel:   (giggles) The session sort of left my head buzzing.

Therapist:   Hazel, Marv is really eager to find out if there is something he did to make you feel that way.

Hazel:   Nothing in particular.

Sally:   Oh come on, Hazel.

Hazel:   Well, like I said . . . all the questions.

Sally:   (asking Hazel) But how did that make you feel? You didn't say how you felt when he did that.

Hazel:     I guess I just felt a bit overwhelmed. I can't say I felt annoyed at Marv. He just was trying to help me.

Therapist: You said you felt overwhelmed by Marv's rapid-fire questioning. What would have been more helpful to you?

(Hazel had identified for Marv a behavior that induced in her a negative reaction. Here, the therapist is encouraging Hazel to identify a positive behavior in which Marv might engage both to assist his interpersonal experimentation within the group and to avoid the pain that might be attached to a more prolonged focus on negative behaviors.)

Hazel:     I really don't know . . . well, I think I would feel more at ease if Marv would let me recover a little bit from one question before he asks me another one. Sometimes I need a time-out.

Marv:      Now why is that the first time that someone around here has said that to me?

Therapist: So let me just check out, Marv, what you think Hazel is asking of you. What change is Hazel asking you to make in how you help her?

(Having Marv paraphrase the feedback both helps Marv to conceptualize it in terms coherent to him and provides him with additional opportunities to correct any misimpressions of what others are attempting to communicate to him.)

Marv:      She says she would feel more comfortable if I would ask her something, let her answer, and maybe move onto someone else for awhile and then maybe get back to her later.

Sally:     (to Hazel) Is that right?

Hazel:     Pretty much. I didn't mean you could ask me only one question. It's just that as soon as I finish answering one, you have another one . . . it's like my husband . . . he always wants more than I can give him.

Therapist: (to Hazel) With Marv you didn't realize that you can let him know when he's asking too much.

|  |  |
|---|---|
| Hazel: | I don't know if he'd accept it like Marv did? |
| Gabe: | You might as well give it a try! |
| Therapist: | (to Marv) So maybe it's not just the number of questions. Sounds like when Hazel gives you an answer to a question, she wants something more from you than another question. |
| Marv: | That's cool. I didn't even realize I was shooting one question after another at her . . . like I'm the prosecuting attorney and I have her on the stand. (with a voice of authority) "Where were you the night he was shot?" |
| Hazel: | That's exactly how I felt: like I was on the stand! |
| Therapist: | Marv, you did something today that I haven't seen you do before. You took the lead in asking for feedback from another member, and then you really listened when it was given to you. I think that Hazel was able to put her finger on something that you can continue to work on even after you leave the hospital: recognizing when your own beliefs about what's best for another person get in the way of being sensitive to what that person actually needs. And Hazel, you, too, took an extraordinary step in clarifying for yourself what you need from Marv. |
| Sally: | Yea, Hazel. Way to go! |
| Therapist: | Another step was that you let Marv know about what you need and don't need from him. |

(This intervention was directed to support members' engagement in risk taking. Within this approach, the therapist necessarily takes a highly active role in establishing the norms of the group and educating patients on what constitutes work in the group.)

|  |  |
|---|---|
| Therapist: | But there were other members who, like Hazel, wanted to work on being more open with the group. I wonder if you have any reactions to what went on between Marv and Hazel. |

(This intervention supports members' ability to learn vicariously.)

|  |  |
|---|---|
| Gabe: | First, I want to say that I really admire what you did, Hazel, because I know how hard it is. |

Therapist:  What makes it so hard?

Gabe:  Okay, well, this is a perfect example of what goes on with me. When Hazel and Marv began to have their exchange, I felt like maybe there would be a big blow-out. And then when they resolved it, peacefullike, I felt sort of . . .

Marv:  (slightly indignantly) You mean you were disappointed?

Gabe:  Not disappointed, no, I would say "let down."

Marv:  Big difference.

Gabe:  Well, whether there's a difference or not, it's still the reaction of a lunatic—a crazy, sick person. Even when I share that with people who have problems too, I know that you're thinking, "They should lock this guy up," but I'm already in here.

Marv:  And that's locked up.

The group laughs.

Sally:  Big deal! (shaking her head)

Gabe:  What do you mean, "big deal"?

Sally:  I mean, really, big deal. Don't you think that there might be other people who felt that way. You're too hard on yourself.

Portia:  I agree—my doctor says everyone has thoughts like that sometimes.

Therapist:  Gabe said he was worried that we would think he was a lunatic, a crazy person. I wonder how members are feeling about Gabe right now?

(Although members have implied acceptance of Gabe, the therapist is working to enable Gabe to obtain more direct feedback about his perception of their view of him.)

Portia:  Are you kidding? I liked you yesterday, and I like you today.

Marv:  Yeah, well, what he said, I like him even better for it.

Other members nod in agreement. Sally laughs.

Hazel:      Something tickling your funnybone, dear?

Sally:      Never mind.

Marv:       Come on, tell us what's so funny?

Sally:      I just had this picture of dainty Hazel in army boots and a bayonet skewering Marv, well, not really Marv . . . more like Marv in the shape of a balloon with all the air rushing out.

Marv:       Thanks a lot, Buddy!

Therapist:  Sally, I wonder how you're feeling right now?

Sally:      I guess when I thought about how he was yesterday with Hazel, I felt slightly annoyed. Just a little.

Marv:       Aw, come on, admit it, you *still* feel that way.

Therapist:  Marv, maybe Sally does feel some irritation toward you, but given that you and Hazel have pretty much worked things out, I wonder if your irritation (speaking to Sally now) doesn't have something to do with me. Yesterday, you said that group was pleasant enough but that you weren't sure it was helping you. I wonder if you don't hold me a little bit responsible.

(Here, the therapist is deflecting Sally's anger from Marv onto herself. If the therapist perceived that Marv were able to tolerate more negative feedback, she might have accorded Sally an opportunity to continue expressing feelings toward Marv. This juncture would be one of considerable variation among interpersonal group therapists in terms of their response to Sally's anger.)

The members are silent for a moment.

Sally:      Maybe I do . . . I don't know . . . I just come here everyday and think, "These people seem so very unhappy and maybe I am too but not as much. "

Therapist:  Perhaps not as obviously?

Sally:      Yes, maybe that's it. Maybe everyone looks sadder because it's harder for me to show it. But because you all look sadder, I feel I have to spend my time in here helping you.

Several members acknowledge that indeed Sally helped them a great deal in previous sessions.

Therapist:   Sally, it sounds like many members in the group are grateful for your many insights and perceptions and, frankly, so am I. But, I wonder, what would it be like for you to be on the receiving end of the help?

Sally:   (with a tone of belligerence and bitterness) This group is just like my family. They want me to be doing for everybody, always. I'm good only so long as I can help.

Marv:   Wait a minute, you don't give us a chance. You come in here and act like everything is fine with you so we figure, "This lady is here for a vacation." Maybe we should have known better, maybe we shouldn't have been fooled. But we know now. You need our help just as much as we need yours.

Several members echo Marv's expression of eagerness to help Sally. (The therapist senses Sally's anxiety that the group's esteem for her will drop if she departs from her helper role.)

Therapist:   How would it feel to members to have Sally be a little less of a helper in here?

Gabe:   I admire you a lot. You're so competent all the time. And if you let us know when you weren't feeling so confident, heck, I wouldn't admire you any less. I'd just feel closer to you.

Marv:   I second the motion!

Therapist:   (noticing the time is up ) We have to end our session now. I think it is worth noticing that a lot of important work was accomplished today. I know that both Hazel and Gabe took some big risks in sharing parts of themselves with the group. Hazel made a real effort to express some of the feelings she has toward others—in this case, Marv—that she usually keeps inside. Gabe shared some of the painful feelings that he has about himself. I think that both of you found out that nobody rejected you for what you offered. Certainly, Marv, what you did in here was great. You asked for feedback, and members responded. I was impressed with how you used members' comments to change yourself in a positive way rather than to get down on yourself. Sally, I think you're aware of the strides you've made today, too. You can see that you don't have to be everybody's helper to have them appreciate you and feel close to you. I'll see all of you later at community meeting.

## Comment on the Session

In the beginning of the session, members appear to be well socialized in the norms of a process-oriented group, as is seen in Marv's amenability to exploring parallels in the group with his problems on the unit. Of course, in many cases, the therapist will be presented with the task of helping a patient like Marv to formulate what he, in the vignette, expressed spontaneously. For example, had Marv merely indicated that he felt "crummy," it would have been encumbent on the therapist to shape this complaint into a concern that could be addressed directly within the group. The therapist might have wondered aloud whether there were something on the unit or in the group that provoked in Marv this unpleasant feeling. Had Marv (or another member) managed to produce an association between a unit or group irritant and his dysphoric feeling, the therapist might then have assisted Marv in drawing parallels between provocations outside and inside the group.

After helping Marv to create a meaningful here-and-now focus, the therapist's next intervention involved providing encouragement to Hazel to give feedback to Marv. This intervention was an effort to weave the therapeutic needs of different members, in this case, Marv and Hazel. The therapist also underlined the value of direct communication among members by implying that only Hazel (not Sally) could accurately report on how Hazel reacted to Marv. When Hazel spoke in general terms about Marv's behavior toward her, the therapist helped her to articulate her perceptions in a more specific way. This greater specificity on Hazel's part was necessary for Marv to acknowledge particular behaviors that he could attempt to modify. Later, the therapist encouraged Hazel to reframe her response to Marv in positive rather than negative terms (a behavior that he could do rather than try not to do). The motive for this intervention was to assist Marv's interpersonal experimentation within the group and to protect him from the pain that might be attached to a more prolonged focus on negatively perceived behaviors.

Once Hazel and Marv had finished their exchange, the therapist reminded other members that some members among them had expressed having a difficulty in communicating openly that was similar to Hazel's. Through this intervention, the therapist facilitated further sharing by members and fostered a process of vicarious learning. Vicarious learning (Yalom, 1985) is a mechanism that maximizes the extent to which members can profit from participation in a group despite the typically short-term nature of that participation in an inpatient setting. If a member does not have an opportunity to address a particular problem within a given session, that member can be helped if he or she can identify with the work of a member who was more active during that session. Although this process often occurs spontaneously, the therapist's invitation to members to identify with one another ensures its occurrence.

The therapist's urging of members to identify with Hazel's reticence led Gabe to respond. After Gabe articulated his fears about his "forbidden" thoughts, members responded supportively but vaguely. The therapist's encouragement of members to be more specific was important given the likelihood that Gabe's high level of anxiety and readiness to self-criticism would lead him to use the vagueness in some fashion to his detriment.

The group moved on to address Sally's concerns. Sally persisted in expressing irritation toward Marv despite his recognition of, and willingness to change, those behaviors that put off some other members. The therapist deflected Sally's annoyance from Marv to herself. This intervention was based on the therapist's perception that because Marv had already tolerated considerable negative feedback from the group, its continuation might have led him to see the group as a wholly aversive situation. Some interpersonal therapists, however, might have allowed Sally to explore further her reactions to Marv. Such a decision might be based on a variety of factors. For example, the therapist might consider Marv's level of fragility, the remaining length of his hospitalization (i.e., number of sessions available to deal with possible fallout from the confrontation), Sally's likely responses to her confrontation (e.g., guilt versus sense of mastery), and the level of group cohesion. In the present example, Sally was able to make good use of the therapist's willingness to be the object of her irritation because she then attempted new behaviors within the group. The therapist sensed Sally's anxiety that the group's esteem for her would drop if she departed from her role as helper. To help Sally determine whether this anxiety had a realistic basis, the therapist provided Sally with an opportunity to obtain feedback on members' reactions to her new role.

At the end of the session, the therapist provided a summary of members' progress in the session. Such a summary serves a number of functions. First, it provides a cognitive framework by which members can organize their perceptions of the group thereby promoting the consolidation of learning. Another function is to help members identify concerns or problem areas that may require further attention on an outpatient basis (Yalom, 1983). Finally, by citing members' progress in addressing these issues during that particular session, the therapist fosters their hopefulness about even more substantially successful work in these areas in the future.

## Status of the Research

This review of the research covers three areas in relation to the interpersonal approach: outcome studies, curative factor studies, and studies relating to specific features of the interpersonal approach, such as the here-and-now focus of the group.

### Outcome Studies

There have been only a smattering of studies that have addressed the comparative efficacy of an interpersonal approach in relation to alternate approaches or no group therapy.[5] Beard and Scott

---

[5] The authors did not base their inclusion of outcome studies on the use of

(1975) randomly assigned chronic patients in a Veterans Administration hospital to either an interpersonally oriented group or a no-group condition. A major focus of the interpersonal groups was to place members' interactions within a communications framework (see Marram, 1973). They found that the subjects who participated in interpersonal group therapy showed greater social competence than did the no-group subjects. More specifically, the interpersonal group members showed greater ability to vary their behaviors in relation to a goal, to understand the complexities of a social system, and to reality test their distorted perceptions.

Beutler et al. (1984) randomly placed subjects of mixed diagnoses into one of three focus group conditions—interpersonal, emotional/expressive, and behavioral—or into a control (no-group) condition. The interpersonal model was distinctive in that it involved the exploration of members' here-and-now experiences with the goal of delineating each member's role within the group. The researchers found that the interpersonal group exhibited the greatest degree of symptomatic change, and this change had sustained itself at a 13-month follow-up. The investigators also found that subjects in the emotional/expressive group, which strongly emphasized the affective rather than cognitive aspects of experience, showed a worsening of symptoms. This finding supports Yalom's (1983) view of the importance of keeping cognitive and affective elements in balance in an inpatient group.[6]

---

the terms *interactional group* or *interpersonal group* alone. The group had to be defined as one in which members learned about themselves through their exploration of their interactions with other members. For example, there were articles in the literature in which the group was labeled *interactional* but in which no emphasis was placed on the exploration of the here-and-now.

[6] In general, the Beutler et al. (1984) study was very well designed. However, certain aspects in the methods lead to some ambiguity in the interpretation of the results. To effect the optimal use of each model, the investigators gave the therapists an opportunity to choose the model that they would use in the study. However, two therapists, both leaders of emotional/expressive groups, received their models through assignment rather than choice. Given the relative inferiority of the emotional/expressive model, questions must be raised if the

Testing a group of somewhat higher functioning members than in the prior two studies, Coché, Cooper, and Petermann (1984) compared problem-solving group therapy with interactional group therapy. Although the groups were drawn from a diagnostically mixed population, the vast majority of subjects had some type of affective disorder diagnosis. The two forms of therapy were equivalent overall. However, problem-solving therapy was more helpful in alleviating subjective distress and the manifestations of thought disorder. As might be expected, interactional therapy was more helpful in improving members' interpersonal adjustment.

All of the aforementioned studies examined interpersonal therapy in a short-term group. Yehoshua, Kellerman, Calev, and Dasberg (1985) had chronic schizophrenic subjects participate in interpersonally oriented inpatient group therapy that spanned a 3-year period (360 sessions). Although they used a quasi-experimental design without a comparison or control group, their results nonetheless suggest variables that might be examined in future studies with greater methodological rigor. All subjects in the study easily met the Research Diagnostic Criteria (Spitzer, Endicott, & Robbins, 1985) for schizophrenia. However, some subjects were so regressed that they were unable to give even the most minimal verbal response in relation to a question; others were much more responsive. Staff who had been on the unit over the 3 years but who had had no direct involvement with the group rated members' change on a number of interpersonally oriented variables such as degree of verbalization and amount

---

poor results were even in part due to some aspect of the therapists' performance, such as subtle manifestations of a lack of conviction about the efficacy of the model. Another problem is that the therapists, primarily interns and residents, were relatively inexperienced. Although the investigators cited this feature as a problem, they also pointed out that in inpatient settings, inexperienced individuals often lead groups. Yet, it is possible that certain models require a higher level of expertise on the part of the therapist. For example, the therapists of the emotional/expressive group were presented with the highly challenging task of encouraging the intensive expression of a wide range of affects in a way that would not promote regression. This may have been a task more appropriate for a more senior therapist.

of interaction with other patients. They found that only those schizophrenics who (a) had some modicum of verbal responsivity (e.g., answered questions) and (b) attended the group with regularity exhibited positive change. This study shows that with some fairly regressed patients, the interpersonal approach is potentially effective.

The preceding very limited group of studies supports the efficacy of the interpersonal approach in the inpatient group in promoting symptomatic change (not generally seen to be a major goal of the interpersonal approach) and interpersonal effectiveness. However, none of these studies considered the question of whether participation in an interpersonally oriented group promotes the development of a positive attitude toward therapy in general and toward group therapy in particular. Certainly, if members made all the positive changes they were observed to make in the aforementioned studies, one would think that they would tend to appreciate the group experience. However, it is conceivable that members might not be entirely cognizant of these positive changes; consequently, it is necessary to obtain a more direct measure of their valuation of the group experience. Because the interpersonal approach (especially the agenda and focus group versions) establishes participation in outcome outpatient therapy as a goal of the treatment, members' attitudes toward group therapy after termination is an important outcome measure.

Leszcz, Yalom, and Norden (1985) attempted to assess members' attitudes toward group therapy by having the members rank order the relative worth of 11 treatment components including an agenda group.[7] They found that group psychotherapy was valued second only to individual psychotherapy sessions. Also, members who characteristically seek out interactions involving a high level of affective exchange (e.g., borderline patients) seemed to value the group more than those who do not

---

[7] The specific procedure the investigators used was to have subjects rank order 10 therapeutic factors by allocating a prescribed number of chips among the factors according to their relative worth. The investigators then conducted discussion with members about the factors.

seek out such interactions. Using the same methodology, Kahn et al. (1986) found that participants in either an awareness group (a group combining interpersonal and insight elements) or a focus group ranked these interventions seventh and fifth, respectively, in relation to 10 other elements of treatment on the unit.

In summary, then, the outcome data that exist are extremely limited. They have rarely involved a comparison of the interpersonal approach with alternate approaches and have never involved a comparison of different versions of the interpersonal model with one another. Moreover, the patient populations and diagnostic groups with which the interpersonal model is most effective have not been determined. The sparse data that do exist suggest that the application of an interpersonal model is associated with positive symptomatic and interpersonal change as well as the cultivation of a positive attitude toward therapy.

## Mechanisms of Change

The greatest concentration of studies on the interpersonal approach has been on the mechanisms of change in group therapy, or therapeutic factors. This classification scheme, which was initially devised by Corsini and Rosenberg (1955) and was later extended by Yalom (1975) and Bloch, Reibstein, Crouch, Holroyd, and Themen (1979), is described in chapter 3 in connection with the educative model. For present purposes, it is sufficient to note that early in the history of the investigation of therapeutic factors, the subject's attesting to the use of a particular factor was seen as adequate proof of its importance in mediating positive change. Currently, there is recognition that the subject's self-report of the value of a factor is a statement of belief rather than fact about its presence and usefulness (Bloch, 1986).

Therapeutic factor research can in one respect address the efficacy of the interpersonal model. One of the goals of this model is to develop members' awareness of the importance of interpersonal exploration. The presumption is that members' recognizing the usefulness of the kinds of therapeutic processes that can be used in an interpersonally oriented group will increase the likelihood of their continuing such an involvement on an outpatient basis. Therapeutic factor research can provide information on whether terminating members see factors that are more interpersonally oriented (e.g., learning from interpersonal actions) as having been more crucial to their progress than those factors that are more individually oriented (e.g., self-understanding).

Table 1 lists five therapeutic factor studies of interpersonally oriented groups. The groups on which these studies were based varied in structure. For example, the groups of Mushet et al. (1989) and Leszcz et al. (1985) used Yalom's (1983) highly structured agenda model in the context of an open-ended group. Brabender, Albrecht, Sillitti, Cooper, and Kramer (1983) studied closed-ended groups with unstructured sessions. Despite this considerable variability, inspection of Table 1 reveals some consistency across the studies. Although there is no therapeutic factor that emerges in the top-five list of each study, the factors of interpersonal learning, vicarious learning, and universality appear with greatest consistency. These factors all pertain to the relationships between or among members. This finding suggests that as a consequence of being in an interpersonally oriented group, members do indeed adopt the perspective that the study of relationships is important. Moreover, it is unlikely that subjects' endorsements of interpersonally oriented factors were due to any mind-sets that they brought to the group experience; investigators have found that in groups conducted according to other theoretical models, other therapeutic factors are subsequently endorsed by members (see Marcowitz & Smith, 1983; Whalan & Mushet, 1986).

Further evidence of the success of the interpersonal approach in preparing members for outpatient therapy is the high degree of overlap found by several investigators between the factors that members endorse as inpatients and the ones that they endorse as outpatients in psychotherapy groups (Kapur, Miller, & Mitchell, 1988; Leszcz et al., 1985; Mushet et al., 1989). Such concordance augers well for patients' ease of transition from one therapeutic setting to the other.

Although existing research suggests that group members tend to be consistent in their endorsements of certain therapeutic factors over others, this accord is never complete. For example, as Leszcz et al. (1985) found, there are certain individuals (partic-

## Table 1

*Five Leading Therapeutic Factors in Interpersonally Oriented Inpatient Groups*

| Measurement Technique | | |
|---|---|---|
| Critical incident[1] | Chip sort[2] | Questionnaire[3] |
| **Brabender et al. (1983)**<br>1. Vicarious learning<br>2. Acceptance<br>3. Learning from interpersonal actions<br>4. Universality<br>5. Hope | **Leszcz, Yalom, & Norden (1985)**<br>1. Interpersonal learning<br>2. Expressing feelings<br>3. Self-understanding<br>4. Vicarious learning<br>5. Responsibility | **Kapur, Miller, & Mitchell (1988)**<br>1. Cohesiveness<br>2. Altruism<br>3. Existential factors<br>4. Universality<br>5. Interpersonal learning |
| **Mushet, Whalan, & Power (1989)**<br>1. Universality<br>2.5 Hope<br>2.5 Vicarious learning<br>4. Acceptance<br>5. Self-understanding | | **Kahn, Webster, & Storck (1986)**<br>1. Universality<br>2. Catharsis<br>3. Altruism<br>4. Hope<br>5. Dynamic insight |

[1] Critical incident technique: Each group member describes the most important or critical event in the session. Their descriptions are then categorized according to a therapeutic classificatory scheme.
[2] Chip sort technique: Members allocate chips to different therapeutic factors on the basis of their importance.
[3] Questionnaire technique: Patients are given the opportunity to rate as more or less helpful the description of different processes within the group.

ularly depressed patients) who, after participating in the agenda group, emphasize the importance of mechanisms of change that are not central to the interpersonal model in general. Flowers (1987) found that those members who did not respond to the modally endorsed curative factors in a short-term group did not derive as much from the group. Future research might be directed toward discovering how these individuals can be identified prior to their assignment to group so that an optimal match can be made between the characteristics and needs of the prospective inpatient group member and the group to which he or she is assigned.

## Specific Features of the Interpersonal Approach

**Leadership style.** The interpersonal approach calls for a highly active, supportive leader who emphasizes esteem-building interventions over more negatively toned confrontative or judgmental interventions. The conclusions of Dies's (1983) review of the research literature on short-term groups strongly supports this leadership posture. He cited a number of studies that show that inactive, withdrawn, or laissez-faire leadership styles (e.g., Cooper, 1977; Lundgren, 1971, 1973) are associated with negative outcomes, as are styles that emphasize negative interventions such as judgmental pronouncements about group members (Flowers, 1978; Flowers & Booraem, 1976; Lieberman, Miles, & Yalom, 1973). Although most of these studies were not performed on inpatient groups, they span such a variety of short-term group situations that the generalizability of their findings to inpatient groups is likely.

Yalom's (1983) position on self-disclosure might be given some consideration in light of the rather ample research literature on this topic. As Dies (1983) pointed out, there are a variety of factors that determine the effect of therapist self-disclosure. One factor is the phase of development of the group. Groups that are relatively mature value a therapist's self-disclosure more than do groups that are newly formed (Dies, 1973; Dies & Cohen, 1976). These findings are important because the inpatient group, particularly one with open membership, is always an immature group because there are always members who are relatively new.

Another factor is the nature of the client population. For example, encounter groups rate leader self-disclosure as more favorable than do members of treatment groups (Dies & Cohen, 1976). The content of the disclosure also appears to be an important factor. Group members see therapist self-disclosure that emphasizes positive or negative feelings in the normal range of experience as more helpful than those reactions that suggest undue professional insecurity or instability on the part of the therapist. Taken together, these findings suggest that although therapist self-disclosure may have some value to group members, the therapist must exercise particular caution in using this type of intervention in view of the typical developmental immaturity of the inpatient group and the relatively high degree of psychopathology of the group members. Although Yalom and others have emphasized the positive effect of therapist self-disclosure in modeling openness, Dies (1977, 1983) pointed out that this positive effect can also be achieved through the therapist's reinforcement of those members who exhibit openness.

**Here-and-now orientation.** Central to all interpersonal models is the focus on the here-and-now. An essential feature of interpersonal groups is members' examination of their interactions with one another. Research cited in chapter 3 on the efficacy of here-and-now statements also has relevance for the interpersonal model. These studies show that here-and-now interpretations are effective when they concern not only the members' behavior in the group but also their present behavior outside the group (Abramowitz & Jackson, 1974; Flowers & Booraem, 1990a, 1990b). Moreover, a theme analysis of the content of inpatient group psychotherapy sessions suggests that members actively question whether they will be able to apply their learning within group to their lives outside the hospital (Silverman & Powers, 1985). All of these results suggest that the interpersonal model is more useful to members when the model supports the establishment of linkages between members' behavior in the group and their behavior on the unit or outside the hospital. The establishment of such linkages has not been an aspect of the methodology of the agenda or focus group models. Such linkages are more likely to emerge from the more free-flowing unstructured versions of the interpersonal model.

In the latter, when a member talks about an external problem, the therapist might gradually develop an awareness of how that problem is relevant to the member's experience within the group. Alternatively, within the unstructured versions, the members themselves may sometimes draw out the implications of their experience in the group to their lives outside the hospital (or on the unit). The research would suggest that the therapist should support members in drawing such connections.

Here-and-now interpretations can be divided into those that entail a delineation of the patient's pattern of behavior versus those that specify the impact of the patient's behavior on others. The former have been found to be made more frequently in psychotherapy groups and are associated with better outcomes (Flowers & Booraem, 1990a). Although the structured and un-structured versions of the interpersonal approach both allow for these types of interpretation, no version has endorsed one type over the other.

Although these results may be seen as mandating that therapists who apply the interpersonal model make an effort to emphasize pattern interpretations over impact interpretations, two points of caution must be raised. First, these results, obtained from the study of outpatient groups, should be replicated with inpatient groups. Second, it would be useful to know why a particular type of intervention is more effective than another. One reason may be that subjects' awareness of their patterns of behavior is a precondition for their use of information about the effect of their behavior on others. Another reason may be that if subjects can clearly see the nature of their behavioral patterns, they may be able to readily and accurately anticipate how others would respond to these patterns. For example, if Alex can see that he constantly interrupts others, it may be obvious to him that this behavior would engender annoyance. Finally, it may be that specification of the impact of an individual's behavior inflicts a narcissistic injury in the individual receiving this information, which heightens defensiveness in relation to the feedback. Knowledge of the reasons why a particular type of intervention is effective makes a difference in planning interventions. For example, if members find the description of the impact of their behavior on others to be upsetting because it is often a negative impact, then the therapist can make an effort to use this intervention only when members are likely to give positive reactions to others' behavior.

Earlier in this chapter, it was noted that the different versions of the interpersonal model vary in the extent to which the analysis of the here-and-now includes the exploration of the motives underlying members' maladaptive social behaviors. Although there has been limited exploration of this issue, the results of one study (Flowers & Booraem, 1990a) suggest that interpretation of motives can actually have a detrimental impact on group members. From their incidental observations of therapy groups, the investigators noted that frequently those interventions involving the discussion of motives were negatively toned. As was indicated in the preceding section, there is considerable literature that suggests that positively toned interventions are more effective than are those that threaten the members' self-esteem.

**The agenda and wrap-up format.** Because most practitioners of inpatient group therapy recognize the need for the inpatient group to be focused and manifestly purposive, therapists of a number of different persuasions (e.g., cognitive–behavioral and behavioral) have incorporated the agenda and wrap-up as important structural elements in the inpatient group. Although these structural elements are particularly crucial to the agenda model that Yalom (1983) recommended for high-functioning inpatients, most studies have examined the effects of structure on the group behaviors of low-functioning inpatients. A number of studies on inpatient samples (e.g., Goldstein, 1971; Gruen, 1977; Jensen & McGrew, 1974) show that particularly with disturbed patients, a high level of structure promotes positive interactions among members. Other studies (e.g., Bednar, Melnick, & Kaul, 1974; Kinder & Kilmann, 1976) suggest that a high level of structure is most appropriate for a group in the earliest phase of development, in which an open-ended inpatient group with rapidly changing membership is likely to reside most of the time.

Given that a high level of structure is an important component of an inpatient model, what conclusions might the research reveal about the efficacy of the particular structure provided by the agenda model? A primary purpose of the agenda go-around and wrap-up procedures is to help members to frame cognitively their affective/interpersonal experience in the sessions. Each member's problem is stated in clear, concrete terms, and later in the session, each member's progress in addressing his or her problem is reviewed. The importance of presenting a strong cognitive framework was demonstrated by Lieberman el al. (1973), who tested subjects in 18 short-term personal growth groups. They found that a sine qua non of positive change was the group's provision of a means for members to label (hence, cognitively organize) their affective experience. Although their population was quite different from an inpatient group, the likelihood is that inpatients are even more dependent on such a framework. Studies have found that inpatient groups emphasizing catharsis or an intense level of affective expression are associated with poorer outcomes than are groups that provide members with some organizing scheme (e.g., Beutler et al., 1984; Pattison, Brissenden, & Wohl, 1967).

Research suggests that the agenda go-around and wrap-up are effective means by which such cognitive structuring may occur. Flowers and Schwartz (1980), working within a behavioral format, found that when subjects indicated on an index card problems that they would like to address in that session, their active participation increased. Leszcz et al. (1985) conducted exit interviews with individuals who had completed an agenda group experience. The interviewees frequently cited the agenda go-around and wrap-up as being especially significant in enabling them to benefit from the group. Specifically, members valued the containment function of agendas: The agendas helped them to restrict their focus in any one session to a single problem. There were, however, some subjects who found the demand to become quickly involved in the group threatening to such an extent that they were driven to terminate their participation in group therapy precipitously.

Yalom (1983) made clear his perception that to be helpful to members, agendas must fulfill three criteria. They must be realistic rather than abstract, here-and-now focused rather than there-and-then focused, and interpersonal rather than intrapersonal. Kivlighan and Jauquet (1990) examined whether variability on these three dimensions was associated with variability in the perceived emotional atmosphere of the group. Participants in personal growth groups were required to develop written agendas for each of 26 sessions. Raters evaluated the degree to which each agenda was realistic, interpersonal, and focused on the here-and-now. The investigators found that what aspects of an agenda are important depend on the developmental status of the group. Early in the group, members' constructions of highly realistic agendas made them feel more engaged by one another and by the group. As the group progressed, the realism factor lost importance. More crucial to members' sense of involvement was the development of agendas that had a here-and-now, interpersonal context. The extent to which Kivlighan and Jauquet's results apply to the inpatient interpersonal group are a matter for future study given that their study investigated nonpatients in a long-term group setting with a stable membership. However, if replicated, their results would suggest that group developmental considerations (e.g., the likelihood that the inpatient group is in the earliest stage of development) bear on which features of an agenda to emphasize.

The limited research that exists suggests that agendas may indeed give members a stronger sense of purpose and a greater capacity to assimilate their group experience. However, additional work needs to be done to determine what characteristics agendas must possess for different types of group composition and for different stages of group development so that their positive effects can be realized and their negative effects can be minimized.

# Critique of the Model

## Strengths

The interpersonal model has much to recommend its use in the inpatient setting. The goal embraced by all versions of the interpersonal approach of enhancing members' interest in pursuing outpatient treatment is an important one. Its importance has been demonstrated by those studies showing that patients who are successful in remaining out of the hospital are those who continue with treatment after discharge (see Yalom, 1983, for a review of this research). This approach shares a strength of the educative model in complementing rather than duplicating other components of the patient's treatment package.

Outcome research has demonstrated that the interpersonal model also lends itself to adaptation to individuals at different levels of functioning (e.g., Beutler et al., 1984). It is flexible in terms of the level of stability of group membership: The interpersonal approach has been applied in groups, the membership of which changes daily and in groups with great longevity.

The unstructured and structured applications of the interpersonal approach each have their own distinctive strengths. The unstructured applications accord the group members the greatest latitude in exhibiting their dysfunctional behaviors within group. In unstructured applications, members have greater opportunity to show rather than report on their difficulties with others. Another strength of the unstructured applications is that they require the members to take a great deal of responsibility. They thereby serve as an antidote to the sense of helplessness that is so often attendant on hospitalization and give members practice in deploying their coping resources—a skill that is essential on discharge.

The two structured versions of the interpersonal model have as a major strength their grounding in the realities of the inpatient situation. These models do not demand that members do more than they can in a relatively brief period of time and in the absence of many of the sources of stability that characterize the typical outpatient group. Another strength is not so much inherent in these models as in the way they have been developed. This strength is the level of specificity with which Yalom (1983) has described the agenda and focus groups. His 1983 text in conjunction with his recently released tapes (Yalom, 1990) serve as a training program for the neophyte group therapist. This contribution is extremely important given that training opportunities are lacking in the settings in which many inpatient therapists work. Yalom's highly detailed presentation not only helps the beginning group psychotherapist but also the researcher interested in comparing Yalom's models with other models. Using both Yalom's text and his recently released tapes

(Yalom, 1990), the researcher can be relatively confident that he or she is implementing the model as Yalom proposed.

Another strength of the structured versions, particularly the agenda version, is that they provide a clear cognitive framework by which members can organize their experience. The importance of this component has been discussed in the previous section. A highly innovative feature of the agenda model is the designation of an explicit role to the observer. Both research (Foster, 1978) and common sense suggests that when observers are required to give something back to the group, their presence is more enriching than when they are in an entirely receptive position.

## Weaknesses

The unstructured and structured approaches each have weaknesses. The unstructured applications lack development both in terms of goals and methods. Most writers who have claimed to be using an interpersonal model simply reference Yalom's 1975 text to provide the reader with more direction concerning how the group was conducted. The discussion of how the interpersonal approach has been applied to take into account the special features of an inpatient setting has been woefully insufficient. The interpersonal approaches that have appeared in the literature have appeared to embrace the Sullivanian goal of the modification of interpersonal behaviors. This goal may be viable in circumstances in which the group is able to achieve some level of cohesiveness through stability in membership and leadership. Such groups do exist in some settings (e.g., Griffen-Shelley & Wendel, 1988). However, the goal of modifying members' maladaptive behaviors in situations in which members are present for only a single session or a few sessions is highly unrealistic.

The major weakness of the agenda and focus group models is the rigidity of structure that they impose on the therapist. Unquestionably, the research literature, some of which was cited earlier, supports the presence of a high level of structure for inpatient groups. However, we question whether the model accords the therapist sufficient latitude in departing from the prescribed structure so as to deliver one of the most important ingredients of effective group therapy: the conveyance of empathy. Yalom (1983) repeatedly emphasized the importance of the therapist's communication of empathy to the group members. However, in Yalom's (1990) videotaped sample session of an agenda group, it appears that the requirement placed on the therapist to assist each member in structuring an agenda interfered with the therapist's establishment of a strong empathic connection with each group member. For example, there were several instances in which members expressed intense feelings of hopelessness and sadness. The therapist, rather than acknowledge these feelings, quickly informed these members that tackling the members' depression was beyond the ken of the group; they were then directed toward developing a more manageable goal. It was hard for us to believe that some members would not experience such an interaction with the therapist as a rejection.

Along similar lines, the process of agenda formation may interfere with providing support. Group members generally are not able to structure their own agendas and require a great deal of input from the therapist so that the agendas are concrete, interpersonal, and here-and-now oriented (Yalom, 1983). Early in the session, a group member might experience failure because his or her ideas for an adequate agenda are met with rejection by the therapist. Admittedly, many patients may not experience this agenda-shaping process as a rejection, particularly when the therapist is able to find and deftly communicate some element of value in whatever effort the member makes in this process. The fact that participants in the agenda group frequently and spontaneously cited the agenda as one of the helpful elements of the treatment would suggest that a sense of rejection may be relatively uncommon (Leszcz et al., 1985). However, some members in the same study reported having left the group early because they found the demand to develop an agenda too intimidating. This finding suggests that the narcissistic tension created by this requirement is worthy of further exploration.

Another limitation is not only a function of the high level of structure of the agenda and focus groups but also of the failure of either systems or developmental thinking to have any significant impact on the interpersonal perspective. In the agenda and focus groups, events in the group are understood concretely rather than symbolically. They are conceptualized on an individual, interpersonal level but never group-as-a-whole level. Although it is claimed that the group can be a context in which to alleviate members' iatrogenic anxiety, no theoretical or practical tools are provided by which to accomplish this objective. Where in the structured format of developing and pursuing agendas is there an opportunity to address these tensions?

Suppose, for example, that in a given session many members had some difficulty with the requirement to create an agenda. Imagine further that the therapist knew that there was some anger on the unit in relation to a staff decision to curtail temporarily the period that patients could remain off the unit. Unless the therapist is able to establish linkages between this group-as-a-whole resistance and the event on the unit, how likely would it be that the therapist could enable the formulation of meaningful agendas? The agenda and focus group models provide no means or direction by which a therapist could conduct such an exploration.

Another weakness of the agenda and focus group models is the complete absence of a developmental focus. Yalom (1983) declared that the life of the group is a single session. This notion is useful when it motivates the therapist to structure the group in such a way that each member benefits from each session. It is not helpful when it discourages the therapist from considering how prior events in the group may be affecting the group in the present. To alter the prior example slightly, consider again the problem of members' difficulty in forming agendas. Perhaps in the prior session, members achieved a significantly higher level of closeness than they had experienced in earlier sessions and were now banding together in an act of shared self-assertion. The therapist cognizant of this connection need not turn the session over to its exploration as would be the case if the developmental model (chapter 6) were applied. However, through a consideration of a shared wish to defy the therapist, the therapist can intervene in a way that does not undermine members' newly formed cohesion. For example, the therapist (recognizing the group's effort to assert itself against authority) may wish to give the group a choice as to how, or even whether, to pursue agendas that day.

One consequence of Yalom's eschewal of group-as-a-whole phenomena is his position on anger. We agree with Yalom that great care must be exercised when the focus is on a particular member's anger toward another member. However, a given member's anger may be a reflection of an affective reaction existing at the level of the group-as-a-whole, and when this reaction is treated as a shared reaction, it can be expressed and explored much more safely. It is our view that Yalom's admonition to therapists to avoid assiduously the eruption of anger in the inpatient group conveys implicitly to members that anger is an unacceptable affect (Hannah, 1984; Kibel, 1984). In fact, members' guilt in relation to the enormity and intensity of their anger is a common intrapsychic contributor to the need for hospitalization.

It may appear that we are advocating that the agenda and focus group models become something other than what they are. This is not the case. Rather, we see the interpersonal approach as having the potential to be integrated with other theoretical motifs. Such an integration will enhance the contribution of that which is particular to the interpersonal approach. Moreover, we recommend that the level of structure for any one session be based not on some preordained and rigidified format but on the therapist's perceptions of the needs of the group in that session.

Another area in which the model might be developed further concerns the nature of the therapist's interventions. Frequently in an inpatient setting, patients have a very difficult time grasping the importance of processing their immediate experience (Froberg & Slife, 1987). The notion of working on personal relationships with people in the group seems to some odd if not outright absurd. For the therapist to give this process more credibility in the eyes of the members, it may be necessary, either in a pre-group orientation or during the group itself, to make comments that establish a link between how a member relates within the group and his or her reported difficulties outside the group (Froberg & Slife, 1987). Research (e.g., Flowers & Booraem, 1990a, 1990b) suggests that members' receptivity to here-and-now comments is enhanced if the comments contain a reference to members' difficulties in relationships outside the group.

A final related area in need of investigation is the transparency of the inpatient group therapist. Yalom (1983) advocated that the therapist, in the interests of authentic respectful treatment of the patient and the modeling of self-disclosure, share with the group some of his or her reactions to the events in the group. In our view, there has been in the literature insufficient recognition of the potential usefulness of this type of intervention. At the same time, we believe that there has been insufficient articulation of the possible dangers of such communication. For example, there is evidence that early in the life of the group, members find those therapist disclosures that reveal the therapist's vulnerability to be unhelpful (Dies, 1973; Dies & Cohen, 1976). Yalom (1983) described a vignette in which a fledgling therapist talks about his insecurity in leading the group. Although the members were reported to respond positively to this revelation, the research suggests that their reactions were not typical.

In our opinion, the most important element missing from Yalom's discussion of self-disclosure is the recognition that self-disclosure, although perhaps eminently justifiable, can arise out of the therapist's countertransference (Rachman, 1990). For example, a neophyte therapist may disclose a sense of insecurity purportedly out of an interest in relating to the members of the group in an authentic way. However, such a communication may be an effort to fend off the attack that the therapist believes his or her self-perceived incompetence invites. In general, little value is assigned to the exploration of the therapist's reactions in terms of their ability either to instigate nontherapeutic behaviors or to serve as cues to the more hidden aspects of group life such as members' barely palpable anger toward the therapist.

# Demands of the Model

## Clinical Mission

In contrast to the educative model, for example, the interpersonal model requires a relatively high level of support from the unit staff. For any particular version of the interpersonal model to be effective, the members of the treatment team must embrace its goals and understand the methods by which it enables their achievement. This support is seen to be essential for several reasons. First, the boundary separating the interpersonal group from the unit is generally a fluid one. Interactions with members and other staff outside the group may be brought within the group and vice versa. To support rather than to undermine such explorations, the staff must see a value to them. Second, the members of the group may be given interpersonal homework assignments that include the staff. Third, in the case of the agenda group, the members of the treatment team may be involved in observing the group; if so, they must have a willingness to assume an active role during the review phase.

## Context of the Group

In the optimal application of this model, the group is embedded in a treatment unit and the therapist is a member of the unit staff. This circumstance provides the therapist with the greatest opportunity to collect information on members' social functioning on the unit that may be relevant to their interpersonal activity within the group. However, this model has been effectively used in other contexts, such as that in which patients have been combined from several units (e.g., Coché et al., 1984).

## Temporal Variables

The interpersonal model places few temporal demands on the setting; some versions have been designed to be applied in a group lasting a single session (Yalom, 1983) and others in groups of members who remain over considerably longer periods of time. For example, Griffen-Shelley and Wendel (1988) described an inpatient interpersonal group in which members remained in the group for 5 to 6 months. The frequency of the meeting is also not a limiting factor. Yalom believed that the group should meet as frequently as possible, preferably daily. However, frequency of meeting should not determine whether the interpersonal model is used. Beutler et al. (1984) reported positive outcomes with an interpersonal group that met only twice weekly.

A temporal factor that is likely to be more constraining is the length of the session, particularly for the structured models. Within the agenda model, the format requires that each member develop an agenda. In an average-sized group (6–10 patients), a session of at least 75–90 minutes is necessary to accommodate this requirement. As Froberg and Slife (1987) noted, some settings are not able to guarantee a session of this length because of scheduling conflicts with other activities. We suggest that one way to alter structured versions of the interpersonal model to make this feature less constraining is to have only a subset of members of the group form agendas.

## Size

Although a more unstructured application of the interpersonal approach would enable the inclusion of a large number of group members, the agenda group is more constrained in size. If the group were to go beyond 10 members, even in a 90-minute session, the therapist may find it impossible to proceed through all the designated stages of the session. On the other hand, Yalom did not see a small group (e.g., one with 3 members) as a contraindication for holding the group. Holding the group whether the group happens to be large or small establishes the dependability of the group.

## Composition

Unstructured applications of the interpersonal approach have been developed for depressed patients (Coché et al., 1984), chronic regressed patients (Beard & Scott, 1975), diagnostically mixed patients (Beutler et al., 1984), and schizophrenics (Kanas, 1991; Yehoshua et al., 1985). Beutler et al. found that the efficacy of an interpersonal approach is not dependent on diagnostic category or degree of psychological disturbance. In general, then, it appears that the unstructured version of the interpersonal approach is somewhat catholic in its ability to accommodate different types of patients. Although some writers have addressed the issue of whether an unstructured interpersonal approach works better with groups that are diagnostically homogeneous or heterogeneous, this issue is in need of empirical study (e.g., Kanas, 1991).

The agenda and focus group versions are more stringent in their composition requirements. Probably the most fundamental requirement is that it be possible to divide patients into groups according to level of functioning. As we pointed out in chapter 2, settings in which there is a relatively small number of patients, such as a 12-bed psychiatric unit of a general hospital, may not have the critical mass at either level of functioning to enable the formation of either an agenda or a focus group. The agenda and focus group versions of the interpersonal model seem to be effective when members have a wide range of diagnoses and symptom patterns. Particularly for the agenda group, diversity in symptomatology might be useful. Slife, Sasscer-Burgos, Froberg, and Ellington (1989) showed that individuals who are depressed show great difficulty in giving and receiving feedback. Other research suggests that individuals with borderline character structure have an affinity for this type of processing (Leszcz et al., 1985). Certainly, the work of a group of vegetatively depressed patients could be potentiated by the presence of patients who have such a processing proclivity. Although this type of variability may be useful for the application of the agenda model, it may not be essential. Weiner (1987) found the agenda group to be highly useful in groups of patients, all of whom shared substance-abuse disorders.

Even more important than diagnostic or symptomatic variability is diversity in the interpersonal styles present in the group. Such diversity facilitates the interlocking of members' stated or unstated agendas that is so vital for efficient work with the inpatient group. In the clinical vignette presented earlier, Marv, who was working on asking questions in a more sensitive way, could be encouraged to interact with Sally, who wanted to be able to be more receptive to others' helping efforts. Most applications of the interpersonal model have been with adult patients, although there have been some attempts to apply the agenda model to adolescent populations (see Barber, 1988). We suspect that an adolescent population in particular would find the agenda model to be very appealing given that the process of peer validation is very much alive with this age group. In a geriatric population, patients with organic brain syndromes may be especially helped by the format of the focus group. The systematic review, held at the end of the session, is specifically designed to reduce confusion. Hence, the interpersonal approach appears to have sufficient flexibility to accommodate all age groups, from adolescence onward.

## Therapist Variables

All versions of the interpersonal model require that the therapist be skilled in helping members to relate to one another. This ability is probably even more important in the unstructured version in which members have greater opportunity to engage in member-to-member interaction. The therapist must also have an ability to help the group focus on and explore the here-and-now. Frequently, therapists fail to recognize what phenomena in the here-and-now are worthy of exploration. For example, Yalom (1983) noted that in visiting inpatient groups, therapists infrequently helped their groups to recognize their responses to having an observer in the group. In addition to the previously stated requirements, focus group leaders need to have an understanding of the psychotic experience.

The interpersonal group can be led either by a co-therapy team or by a single therapist. Co-therapy can be useful in enabling the therapists to perform the many tasks associated with the agenda group. For example, after one therapist helps a member to formulate an agenda, another therapist can integrate that agenda with the agenda of another member. In the focus group model, co-therapy may be helpful in the monitoring of individual members' anxiety levels to ensure that each member experiences the group as supportive rather than threatening or disorganizing.

# Summary

The interpersonal orientation has led to the development of a set of approaches that embraces the Sullivanian position that psychological problems are problems in relationships. To further the well-being of the individual, it is necessary to alter in a positive direction an individual's way of relating to others. In psychotherapy, such alteration can most readily be achieved, so the interpersonal position holds, if the individual works on his or her immediate experiences with others. Yalom (1985), who extended the Sullivanian perspective on psychopathology and its treatment to the psychotherapy group, emphasized the importance of group members' processing their here-and-now experiences with one another in a way that balances cognitive and affective elements. All contemporary applications of the interpersonal orientation to inpatient group have been informed by Yalom's thinking.

Existing versions of the interpersonal model differ from one another in their degree of structure. Prior to the 1980s, those inpatient group psychotherapists who applied the interpersonal orientation to their group work did so in a somewhat loose fashion. Although these practitioners emphasized interpersonal learning within the here-and-now context of the group, they did not use a highly structured session. There is indication from the literature that some practitioners continue to apply the interpersonal orientation in this way.

Yalom (1983) devised two formats for interpersonally oriented groups, each of which is characterized by a high level of structure, particularly in terms of the format of the session. The agenda group for high-functioning inpatients is designed to foster a positive attitude toward therapy, to enable the members to appreciate that talking is beneficial to their well-being, to isolate problems that might be addressed in long-term therapy, and to relieve iatrogenic anxiety. The focus group, designed for low-functioning inpatients, embraces the aforementioned goals but also emphasizes the need to help members socialize in a nonthreatening way and to bolster their orientation to reality.

Although the outcome data on the interpersonal model are rather thin, the empirical support for this approach in an inpatient setting is more substantial than that for many other models described in this text. Strengths of the interpersonal model include the appropriateness of its goals for an inpatient population, its use of those resources that are unique to group, its ability to accommodate extremely brief tenures of members in the group, and its adaptability to a wide range of patients at different levels of functioning.

# References

Abramowitz, S. I., & Jackson, C. (1974). Comparative effectiveness of there-and-then versus here-and-now therapist interpretations in group psychotherapy. *Journal of Counseling Psychology, 21*, 288–293.

Bailine, S. H., Katch, M., & Golden, H. K. (1977). Mini-groups: Maximizing the therapeutic milieu on an acute psychiatric unit. *Hospital and Community Psychiatry, 28*(6), 445–447.

Barber, W. H. (1988). Inpatient adolescent group therapy as a social system. *Group, 12*(4), 233–240.

Beard, M. T., & Scott, P. Y. (1975). The efficacy of group therapy by nurses for hospitalized patients. *Nursing Research, 24*(2), 120–124.

Bednar, R. L., Melnick, J., & Kaul, T. J. (1974). Risk, responsibility, and structure: A conceptual framework for initiating group counseling and psychotherapy. *Journal of Counseling Psychology, 21*, 31–37.

Benne, K. (1964). History of the T-group in the laboratory setting. In L. P. Bradford, J. R. Gibb, & K. D. Benne (Eds.), *T-group therapy and laboratory method: Innovation in re-education* (pp. 80–135). New York: Wiley.

Betcher, R. W. (1983). The treatment of depression in brief inpatient group psychotherapy. *International Journal of Group Psychotherapy, 33*(3), 365–385.

Beutler, L. E., Frank, M., Schieber, S., Calvert, S., & Gaines, J. (1984). Comparative effects of group psychotherapies in a short-term inpatient setting: An experience with deterioration effects. *Psychiatry, 47*, 66–76.

Bloch, S. (1986). Therapeutic factors in group psychotherapy. In A. J. Frances & R. E. Hales (Eds.), *American Psychiatric Association annual review* (Vol. 5, pp. 678–698). Washington, DC: American Psychiatric Association.

Bloch, S., Reibstein, J., Crouch, E., Holroyd, P., & Themen, J. (1979). A method for the study of therapeutic factors in group psychotherapy. *British Journal of Psychiatry, 13*, 257–263.

Brabender, V., Albrecht, E., Sillitti, J., Cooper, J., & Kramer, E. (1983). A study of curative factors in short-term group psychotherapy. *Hospital and Community Psychiatry, 34*, 643–644.

Coché, E., Cooper, J. B., & Petermann, K. J. (1984). Differential outcomes of cognitive and interactional group therapies. *Small Group Behavior, 15*(4), 497–509.

Cooper, C. L. (1977). Adverse and growthful effects of experiential learning groups: The role of the trainer, participant, and group characteristics. *Human Relations, 30*, 1103–1129.

Corsini, R., & Rosenberg, B. (1955). Mechanisms of group psychotherapy. *Journal of Abnormal and Social Psychology, 51*, 406–411.

Dies, R. R. (1973). Group psychotherapy: An evaluation by clients. *Journal of Counseling Psychology, 20*, 344–348.

Dies, R. R. (1977). Group therapist transparency: A critique of theory and research. *International Journal of Group Psychotherapy, 27*, 177–200.

Dies, R. R. (1983). Leadership in short-term groups. In R. R. Dies & K. R. MacKenzie (Eds.), *Advances in group psychotherapy: Integrating research and practice* (Monograph 1, pp. 27–78). New York: International Universities Press.

Dies, R., & Cohen, L. (1976). Content considerations in group therapist self-disclosure. *International Journal of Group Psychotherapy, 26*, 71–88.

Fallon, A. E., & Brabender, V. (1992). *Trends in articles on inpatient group psychotherapy over twenty years*. Manuscript in preparation.

Flowers, J. V. (1978). The effect of therapist support and encounter on the percentage of client–client interactions in group therapy. *Journal of Community Psychology, 6*, 69–73.

Flowers, J. V. (1987). Client outcome as a function of agreement or disagreement with model group perception of curative factors in short-term structured group psychotherapy. *International Journal of Group Psychotherapy, 37*, 113–118.

Flowers, J. V., & Booraem, C. D. (1976). The use of tokens to facilitate outcome and monitor process in group psychotherapy. *International Journal of Group Psychotherapy, 26*, 191–201.

Flowers, J. V., & Booraem, C. D. (1990a). The effects of different types of interpretation on outcome in group psychotherapy. *Group, 14*(2), 81–88.

Flowers, J. V., & Booraem, C. D. (1990b). The frequency and effect of different types of interpretation in psychodynamic and cognitive–behavioral group psychotherapy. *International Journal of Group Psychotherapy, 40*(2), 203–214.

Flowers, J. V., & Schwartz, B. (1980). Behavioral group therapy with clients with heterogeneous problems. In D. Upper & S. M. Ross (Eds.), *Handbook of behavioral group therapy* (pp. 145–170). New York: Plenum Press.

Foster, T. (1978). Inpatient group therapy with observer feedback: A pilot study. *Psychiatric Forum, 7*, 23–27.

Frank, J. D. (1963). Group therapy in the mental hospital. In M. Rosenbaum & M. Berger (Eds.), *Group psychotherapy and group functions* (pp. 453–468). New York: Basic Books.

Froberg, W., & Slife, B. D. (1987). Overcoming obstacles to the implementation of Yalom's model of inpatient group psychotherapy. *International Journal of Group Psychotherapy, 37*(3), 371–388.

Goldstein, J. A. (1971). Investigation of doubling as a technique for involving severely withdrawn patients in group psychotherapy. *Journal of Consulting and Clinical Psychology, 37*, 155–162.

Griffen-Shelley, E., & Wendel, S. (1988). Group psychotherapy with long-term inpatients: Application of a model. *Small Group Behavior, 19*, 379–385.

Gruen, W. (1977). The effects of executive and cognitive control of the therapist on the work climate in group therapy. *International Journal of Group Psychotherapy, 27,* 139–152.

Hannah, S. (1984). The words of the therapist: Errors of commission and omission. *International Journal of Group Psychotherapy, 84*(3), 369–376.

Heitler, J. (1974). Clinical impressions of an experimental attempt to prepare lower-class patients for expressive group psychotherapy. *International Journal of Group Psychotherapy, 29,* 308–322.

Houlihan, J. (1977). Contributions of an intake group to psychiatric inpatient milieu therapy. *International Journal of Group Psychotherapy, 27,* 215–223.

Jensen, J. L., & McGrew, W. L. (1974). Leadership techniques in group therapy with chronic schizophrenic patients. *Nursing Research, 23,* 416–420.

Kahn, E. M. (1986). Discussion: Inpatient group psychotherapy: Which type of group is best? *Group, 10*(1), 27–33.

Kahn, E. M., Webster, P. B., & Storck, M. J. (1986). Curative factors in two types of inpatient psychotherapy groups. *International Journal of Group Psychotherapy, 36*(4), 579–585.

Kanas, N. (1991). Group therapy with schizophrenic patients: A short-term homogeneous approach. *International Journal of Group Psychotherapy, 41*(1), 33–48.

Kapur, R., Miller, K., & Mitchell, G. (1988). Therapeutic factors with in-patient and out-patient psychotherapy groups: Implications for therapeutic techniques. *British Journal of Psychiatry, 152,* 229–233.

Kibel, H. D. (1984). Symposium: Contrasting techniques of short-term inpatient group psychotherapy. *International Journal of Group Psychotherapy, 34*(3), 335–338.

Kinder, B. N., & Kilmann, P. R. (1976). The impact of differential shifts in leader structure on the outcome of internal and external group participants. *Journal of Clinical Psychology, 32,* 857–863.

Kivlighan, D. M., & Jauquet, C. A. (1990). Quality of group member agendas and group session climate. *Small Group Research, 21*(2), 205–219.

Klein, R. H., Hunter, D. E., & Brown, S. (1986). Long-term inpatient group psychotherapy: The ward group. *International Journal of Group Psychotherapy, 36*(3), 361–380.

Leopold, H. S. (1977). Selective group approaches with psychotic patients in hospital settings. *Journal of Psychotherapy, 30,* 95–105.

Leszcz, M. (1986a). Inpatient groups. In A. J. Frances & R. E. Hales (Eds.), *American Psychiatric Association Annual Review* (Vol. 5, pp. 729–743). Washington, DC: American Psychiatric Association.

Leszcz, M. (1986b). Interactional group psychotherapy with nonpsychotic inpatients. *Group, 10*(1), 13–20.

Leszcz, M. (1992). The interpersonal approach to group psychotherapy. *International Journal of Group Psychotherapy, 42*(1), 37–62.

Leszcz, M., Yalom, I. D., & Norden, M. (1985). The value of inpatient group psychotherapy: Patients' perceptions. *International Journal of Group Psychotherapy, 35*(3), 411–433.

Lieberman, M., Miles, M., & Yalom, I. (1973). *Encounter groups: First facts*. New York: Basic Books.

Lundgren, D. C. (1971). Trainer style and patterns of group development. *Journal of Applied Behavioral Science, 7,* 689–709.

Lundgren, D. C. (1973). Attitudinal and behavioral correlates of emergent status in training groups. *Journal of Social Psychology, 90,* 141–153.

Marcowitz, R., & Smith, J. (1983). Patient perceptions of curative factors in short-term group psychotherapy. *International Journal of Group Psychotherapy, 33,* 21–37.

Marram, G. D. (1973). *The group approach in nursing practice*. St. Louis, MO: C. V. Mosby.

Moreno, J. (1934). *Who shall survive? Foundations of sociometry, group psychotherapy, and sociodrama*. Boston: Beacon Press.

Mushet, G. L., Whalan, G. S., & Power, R. (1989). In-patients' views of the helpful aspects of group psychotherapy: Impact of therapeutic style and treatment setting. *British Journal of Medical Psychology, 62,* 135–141.

Oldham, J. M. (1982). The use of silent observers as an adjunct to short-term inpatient group psychotherapy. *International Journal of Group Psychotherapy, 32*(4), 469–478.

Pattison, E. M., Brissenden, A., & Wohl, T. (1967). Assessing specific effects of inpatient group therapy. *International Journal of Group Psychotherapy, 17,* 283–297.

Rachman, A. W. (1990). Judicious self-disclosure in group analysis. *Group, 14*(3), 132–144.

Rosegrant, J. (1988). A dynamic/expressive approach to brief inpatient group psychotherapy. *Group, 12*(2), 103–112.

Silverman, W. H., & Powers, L. (1985). Major themes in brief inpatient group psychotherapy. *Journal of Group Psychotherapy, Psychodrama, and Sociometry, 38,* 115–122.

Slife, B. D., Sasscer-Burgos, J., Froberg, W., & Ellington, S. (1989). Effect of depression on processing interactions in group psychotherapy. *International Journal of Group Psychotherapy, 39*(1), 79–104.

Spitzer, R. L., Endicott, J. E., & Robbins, E. (1985). *Research diagnostic criteria (RDC) for a selected group of functional disorders* (3rd ed.). New York: New York State Psychiatric Institute, Biometrics Research.

Sullivan, H. S. (1940). *Concepts of modern psychiatry*. New York: Norton.

Sullivan, H. S. (1953). *The interpersonal theory of psychiatry*. New York: Norton.

Vinogradov, S., & Yalom, I. D. (1989). *Concise guide to group psychotherapy*. Washington, DC: American Psychiatric Association.

Weiner, H. D. (1987). An innovative short-term group therapy model for in-patient addiction treatment. *Employee Assistance Quarterly, 2*(4), 27–30.

Whalan, G. S., & Mushet, G. L. (1986). Consumers' views of the helpful aspects of an in-patient psychotherapy group: A preliminary communication. *British Journal of Medical Psychology, 59,* 337–339.

Yalom, I. (1975). *The theory and practice of group psychotherapy*. New York: Basic Books.

Yalom, I. (1983). *Inpatient group psychotherapy.* New York: Basic Books.

Yalom, I. (1985). *The theory and practice of group psychotherapy* (3rd ed.) New York: Basic Books. (Original work published 1970)

Yalom, I. (1986). Interpersonal learning. In A. J. Frances & R. E. Hales (Eds.), *American Psychiatric Association annual review* (pp. 699–713). Washington, DC: American Psychiatric Association.

Yalom, I. (1990). *Understanding group psychotherapy: Process and practice* [Film]. Pacific Grove, CA: Brooks/Cole.

Yehoshua, R., Kellerman, P. F., Calev, A., & Dasberg, H. (1985). Group psychotherapy with inpatient chronic schizoprhenics. *Israeli Journal of Psychiatry and Related Sciences, 22*(3), 185–190.

Zaslav, M. R., & Kalb, R. D. (1989). Medicine as metaphor and medium in group psychotherapy with psychiatric patients. *International Journal of Group Psychotherapy, 39*(4), 457–468.

# 5

# The Object Relations/Systems Model

T he object relations/systems model is a psychoanalytic approach to inpatient group psychotherapy that was first proposed in the late 1970s and has been the object of increased
interest over the past decade. This approach differs markedly
from earlier analytic approaches to inpatient group psychotherapy in that the goals are highly specific, the intervention strategy
well defined, and the recommended therapist posture highly active.

A central tenet of the object relations/systems model is that
the tenor of members' interactions with one another on the hospital unit and in the psychotherapy group are reflective of the
organization of their internal lives. According to this model, because a person's intrapsychic organization determines the quality
of his or her relationships, it is this organization that is the target
of change. Unlike the majority of models presented in this text
that aim to modify behavior, especially social behavior, this
model seeks to modify how individuals perceive and experience
themselves and other people.

Group member residency on the psychiatric unit is more crucial to the workings of the object relations/systems model than
it is to those of any of the other models described in this text.
According to this model, the inpatient unit is a complex social
organization with a vast array of features, any of which may
impinge on the treatment taking place within it. Some features
promote the patient's reconstitution, whereas others stimulate

regression and invite the full-blown manifestation of the more toxic aspects of the patient's internal life. Because the inpatient group is a subsystem of the larger system (the unit), it activates the same primitive reactions as are evoked by the unit. However, the group possesses qualities (e.g., its smallness relative to the size of the unit) that enable these reactions to be explored safely and systematically. Such an exploration renders members' reactions comprehensible and manageable. This exploration advances the process of reconstitution, thus lessening members' terror and enhancing their capacity for pleasure and satisfaction in their relationships with others.

In the following section, we offer a brief exposition of the two theoretical frameworks on which the present model is based: object relations theory and general systems theory. Following this discussion, we describe how these theoretical motifs are integrated within the object relations/systems model of inpatient group psychotherapy.

# Theoretical Underpinnings

## Object Relations Theory

Object relations theory has its roots in the work of M. Klein and other writers in the British school of psychoanalysis (e.g., Balint, 1965; Fairbairn, 1952) who sought to replace an instinctual, intrapsychic, and almost monadic perspective with one that was primarily interpersonal. *Object relations* refers to the complex interrelations between the self or images of the self and others or images of others. An "object" can be either a real person or the image of a person. Within this theory, the human ego, that psychological center of organization of the human person responsible for adapting to the environment, is person seeking or object seeking. That is, whereas earlier psychoanalytic theory portrayed human beings as motivated by the urge to satisfy drives, object relations theory sees human beings as motivated by the desire to have relationships (Fairbairn, 1952). As we show, this historical shift from the intrapsychic to the interpersonal (particularly as the interpersonal relates to the intrapsychic) has made psychoanalytic concepts more compatible with those group psychotherapy orientations that emphasize the experiential exploration of relationships and their vicissitudes (Alonso & Rutan, 1984).

Central to object relations theory is the notion that individuals form internal schemata or mental templates of their experiences with others. This process is called *internalization.* These templates shape the individual's future social experiences, determining their quality and tenor. Although changes in an individual's templates can occur throughout life, those social experiences that are most formative of an individual's organizational schemata occur in the first few years of life. For example, if the infant has interactions with his or her mother that are primarily positively toned, then the scheme that the infant constructs from this experience with her will reflect this tone. The infant will then use this scheme to organize new experiences not only with his or her mother but with other people as well. Consequently, new interactions are likely to be experienced as positive.

Object relations theorists have attempted to describe the vicissitudes of the mental life of infants to account for their eventual acquisition of the capacity to have satisfying and stable attachments to others. These accounts of normal intrapsychic development have been found to have great explanatory power in understanding how interpersonal development goes awry in those severely disordered patients typically encountered in the inpatient psychiatric unit. Such object relations theorists as M. Klein (1952), Balint (1965), Winnicott (1955), Fairbairn (1952, 1954), and Kernberg (1976) have provided somewhat different emphases in their developmental accounts of object relations development. Nonetheless, they all stress the importance of the infant's use of the two processes of splitting and projective identification in the organization of experiences with the mother. Although it is beyond the scope of this chapter to offer a comprehensive account of object relations development,[1] what is

---

[1] For a more detailed account of development from an object relations perspective, the reader is urged to read the works of any of the cited object relations

important is that the reader grasp how the infant's use of these processes, particularly splitting, is essential to his or her psychological growth. The understanding of the role of these processes in development is important because it is these very processes that are disrupted in people who require psychiatric hospitalization.

**Normal development.** The earliest representations of experience occur when the infant lacks the capacity to discern where he or she begins and the mother ends. Hence, the initial schemata or representational units are not of a distinct self and a distinct mother but of a self–mother unit. Although the infant cannot distinguish between self and mother until much later, from the very first moments of life, the infant can distinguish what he or she likes or dislikes, what is pleasurable, and what is painful.

The period of normal symbiosis (extending approximately from 1 month to 6 or 8 months of age) is so named because the infant enters this period fusing images of self and mother. It is only on this period's completion that the infant reliably differentiates self from mother. Another important achievement is the infant's gradual construction of associative networks of positive and negative self–mother representations. For example, the infant may associate the mother's gentle touch with her soothing voice and all other pleasure-evoking aspects of her person. The increased ability of the infant to synthesize various images of mother and self creates a potential crisis for the infant. If the infant were to associate positive images of the mother with negative images of her, the infant would be at risk of losing his or

---

theorists such as M. Klein (1952), Kernberg (1976), and Mahler (1968). A secondary source on object relations theory with many practical applications is Cashdan's (1988) *Object Relations Therapy*. A general discussion of object relations theory and group psychotherapy can be found in Ganzarain (1992). The developmental model presented here reflects heavily the work of Otto Kernberg. Although Kernberg's model is less detailed than those of some other object relations theorists such as Mahler, it is particularly useful for understanding individuals with severe psychopathology. Kernberg's theoretical notions reflect his clinical work with borderline and psychotic patients and are particularly relevant because this is precisely the patient population of an inpatient setting.

her sense of a positive tie with the mother. The reason for this risk is that, as indicated, the associative network of positive self–mother representations is very much still under development in this stage. If the infant were to engage in integration of positive and negative images at this time, he or she would experience aggression toward this positive self–mother associative network as an act of destruction. Later on, as this positive associative network acquires more prominence and strength in the infant's intrapsychic life, the infant is able to experience continuity in the existence of this network despite his or her aggression toward it. To protect the positive self–mother images, the infant uses the mechanism of splitting, a defensive operation wherein opposite-valenced representations are actively kept apart.[2] The infant's use of splitting ensures that the good representations will coalesce with one another, the bad representations will coalesce with one another, and never shall the two meet—at least during this developmental period.

The ever-increasing integration of positive self–mother images during the symbiotic period is an achievement of great significance for the developing personality of the infant. This integration of positive self–mother representations is the foundation of the good ego core, which comprises both the individual's emerging positive sense of self as well as his or her ability to adapt to the environment. Kernberg (1976) described this good ego core as "the nucleus of the self system of the ego and the basic organizer of integrative functions of the early ego" (p. 60). As the constellation of positive representations acquires a more focal, central position in the infant's intrapsychic world, the negative representations, through the infant's use of splitting, are expe-

---

[2] *Defenses* are intrapsychic mechanisms operating outside of conscious awareness that assist the individual in mitigating various types of psychological pain and in controlling impulses. *Higher order defenses* are those that enable the individual to express a given impulse in a modulated way. The expression is based on a reasonably accurate view of reality and does not compromise unduly the individual's well-being. An example of a higher order defense is intellectualization. *Lower order defenses* such as splitting, projection, and projective identification often involve a distortion of reality and generally do not serve well the individual's long-term adjustment to the environment.

rienced as more peripheral to the self. The expurgation of negative representations does not mean that the infant fails to experience them but rather that they are less prominent in his or her awareness. When these negative representations are activated or experienced, they frequently possess the quality of being foreign or "out there."

In addition to splitting there is a second class of mechanisms, the projective mechanisms, that enable the infant to give what is unwanted a less central place in his or her experience. They consist of projection and projective identification. Their use during this period is based on both the infant's burgeoning ability to distinguish internal from external, self from other, as well as the imperfection (or the only partial accomplishment) of these discriminations. Although we delineate the differences between projection and projective identification later in this chapter, for the present it is sufficient to note that both of these mechanisms involve the placement of some unwanted aspect of the self on another or, more accurately, upon one's perception of another (Grotstein, 1981). Specifically, the infant is at this stage able to project on the mother his or her own feelings. The infant's projection is reliant on both some pristine sense of the mother being "out there" and also a sense of primal connection with the mother. That is, the infant's perception of being at once one and not-one with the mother makes the mother the object of projection par excellence. This act of projection serves a valuable function for the infant: In seeing the mother (rather than himself or herself) as having these unwanted feelings, the infant spares himself or herself the full force of their burden. The mother serves as a repository or a container for the infant's disturbing feelings until such time as he or she can accept these feelings as his or her own (Bion, 1959).

As indicated, during the symbiotic period, the infant learns not only to distinguish more fully between good and bad representations but also between self and others. However, because of the infant's continued use of splitting during this period, what is perceived is not a whole self or a whole mother but a self and a mother each split into good and bad. Object relations theorists refer to this mode of organizing one's perception of self and others as *part object perception*, which is to be distinguished from *whole object perception*, a later developmental achievement.

Over the period of 6 to 8 months of age, the infant begins to accomplish the integration of the good and bad images of the mother (and others) and the good and bad images of the self. This accomplishment is generally completed sometime between the 18th to the 36th month of age. At this time, the child comes to realize that the image of the loathed mother and the image of the loved mother are images of one, self-same mother. This realization requires the child's abandonment of the idealized (all-good) mother, and with this abandonment comes a sense of responsibility for having brought about her demise. It is this sense of responsibility that gives rise to the feelings of remorse, shame, and guilt (M. Klein, 1952).

The developmental feats of prior stages assist the child in accomplishing the integration of positive and negative images and help the child withstand the temptation to retreat to an earlier, perhaps more comfortable, stage. For example, the child's ballast of integrated good self and mother representations, the foundation of the good ego core, ensure that negatively toned representations will not overwhelm the positive representations. In addition, the child is increasingly able to evoke those positive images of the mother in the absence of her or the stimuli that earlier in life led him or her to develop positive representations. Also, the child's use of projective mechanisms is helpful in attenuating negatively charged elements.

The child's newfound ability to integrate positive and negative aspects of experience of self and others is important because it renders the child's perception of self and others more stable and more realistic given that neither the self nor others are indeed all good or all bad. Through this process, the child also acquires a more robust self-concept. That is, the self is no longer defined narrowly but is perceived to include a range of aspects (Kernberg, 1976).

**The development of psychotic and borderline organizations.** The object relations/systems model allows for a developmental characterization of both borderline personality-disordered[3] and psychotic individuals during their premorbid

---

[3] In this context, *borderline* refers to a level of personality organization de-

states and during regressive episodes. In the premorbid state, individuals with borderline personality disorder have failed to complete the integration stage of object relations development just described. That is, in this state, the individual organized at the borderline level maintains an internal equilibrium and adapts to the environment through the use of splitting. For such an individual, the process of decompensation (i.e., the breakdown of the individual's ability to perform everyday adaptive tasks) is the result of the failure of splitting. With decompensation is an erosion of distinctions between self and others and of separations between benevolently and malevolently toned representations. The associative networks developed over the symbiotic period deteriorate so that the individual's perceptions of self and others become highly fragmented. In contrast to the borderline individual, the psychotic individual in a premorbid state is unable to make the distinctions that the borderline individual can make between self and other, thoughts and their referents, and so on. However, the psychotic individual can make some rudimentary differentiation between positive and negative representations. Through this differentiating and separating process, the psychotic is able to achieve some modicum of inner harmony. For the psychotic patient, as for the borderline patient, regression involves the loss of ability to organize representations according to their affective valence. For both borderline and psychotic patients, the loss of splitting places the individual in great peril in responding to the demands of the environment. As was previously described, the ego's ability to function is based on the coalescence of positive representations and the expurgation of negative representations. It is precisely because the ego has been immobilized that the structure of the hospital becomes essential, performing for the individual the functions that he or she can no longer perform independently.

The terror that an individual experiences on being under siege by his or her own negative representations is something akin to

---

scribed by various analytic writers, particularly Kernberg (1976), rather than the diagnostic category within a symptom-based diagnostic scheme such as the *Diagnostic and Statistical Manual of Mental Disorders* (3rd ed., rev.; American Psychiatric Association, 1987).

what a community would feel on being invaded by a powerful, hostile neighboring community. Certainly, the attacked community would feel pressed to defend itself; the individual under intrapsychic attack does as well. Borderline and psychotic individuals, having by definition lost their more habitual defense of splitting, will use more primitive means to expel threatening elements from the good ego core. For psychotic individuals, hallucinations and delusions represent radical attempts to move what is terrifying on the inside to the outside. For borderline individuals, the perception of others as hostile and bad (projection) and the coercion of others into being so (projective identification) are means of reinstating positive or libidinally laden images of self and objects.[4]

The use of projection and projective identification (concepts that we describe in more detail later) "permits the individual to maintain some degree of internal tranquility, albeit on a regressed level, by means of the unconscious fantasy that noxious images have been deposited into another person or persons" (Kibel, 1990, p. 252). This object relations description of regression has implications for treatment. If regression involves the deterioration of the organizational aspects of the ego, then treatment must be directed toward their reconstitution. However, the particularities of how this goal might be accomplished require knowledge of the inpatient environment itself and of how the environment is likely to interact with the patient's pathology. A framework that can be used to describe the inpatient environment and its relation to the psychotherapy group is general systems theory.

## General Systems Theory

General systems theory is a scientific model that describes the organization, workings, and interrelations of living systems. The roots of general systems theory can be traced as far back as the

---

[4] M. Klein (1952) referred to this experience of the psyche under siege and the primitive defenses used by the individual to lessen the terror attached to this experience as the *paranoid–schizoid position*.

writings of the Greek philosopher Heraclitus in 500 B.C. (Marmor, 1983). However, in the early 1950s, the principles of this model were developed formally in application to biological systems by von Bertalanffy (1950, 1966) and Miller (1978). Subsequently, these principles were extended to psychological systems (e.g., Thomas & Chess, 1980) including organizations (Kernberg, 1975) and psychotherapy groups (H. E. Durkin, 1982; J. Durkin, 1981). The following sections offer a basic exposition of general systems theory, followed by a discussion of its application to the inpatient psychotherapy group.

**Properties of systems.** A *system* is a set of elements and processes that interact with one another in a manner that is both predictable and consistent over time. Of course, what these elements are depends on the nature of the system itself. In the system of a psychotherapy group, an example of an element is a subgroup of the group (Agazarian, 1989). In a large organization, an element may be a department of the organization. A system is capable of growth and self-regulation. Growth in a psychotherapy group may be seen in the development of cohesiveness among members over time. Self-regulation may be seen in the group's ability to modulate the level of tension in the sessions. By providing a holistic rather than reductionistic perspective of causation, general systems theory emphasizes the interdependency among elements of a system: Changes in a given element of a system affect all other elements. For example, if a member of a department leaves, the status of all other members with the department is manifestly or subtly altered. Moreover, systems have emergent properties (Bunge, 1977); the total configuration of events, elements, and processes within the group may produce effects beyond those of any individual event, element, or process or those of their additive contribution. An example of such a group-level phenomenon is the group polarization effect (Moscovici & Zavalloni, 1969), wherein group members' average responses following group discussion tend to be more extreme than the average of members' pre-group responses (although they tend to be in the same direction as pre-group responses).

Any given system exists within a set of other systems, rather than being freestanding. These systems are hierarchically and dynamically related (Kernberg, 1975). The hierarchical aspect of their relation refers to their embeddedness in one another. For example, a person is a living system embedded in another living system, the family. However, that person also comprises various psychological and physiological subsystems. Among the systems within a hierarchy is an *isomorphism*, wherein certain structural elements existing in a system are also found in those systems that are superordinate and subordinate to it. For example, a parental dispute about discipline, with one parent advocating leniency and the other rigid reinforcement of rules, may be re-created within the child who is the object of this conflict. For this child, the expression versus control of impulses is likely to be highly conflictual.

The relations among systems is also dynamic: Just as elements of a system are interrelated with one another, so too are systems within a hierarchy of systems. For example, the closing of state hospital systems affected the nature of psychiatric admissions in general hospitals. However, the extent to which systems can affect one another is determined by the permeability of boundaries of each of the interacting systems. A *boundary* is that which delimits a system, separates it from other systems, and contains the tension within a system (Agazarian, 1989). Some systems have highly permeable boundaries, admitting much energy and information from other systems. Such systems discharge high levels of energy and information to other systems. Other systems have relatively closed boundaries, keeping information and energy within the group.

**The inpatient psychotherapy group.** Over the past 20 years, general systems theory has been applied to long-term outpatient psychotherapy groups (e.g., Agazarian & Peters, 1981; H. E. Durkin, 1972), day-hospital groups (e.g., Greene, Rosenkrantz, & Muth, 1985), and long-term and short-term inpatient groups (e.g., Kibel, 1978, 1981; Rice & Rutan, 1987). General systems theory is particularly appropriate for the inpatient setting because it provides a language to describe the inpatient group and a set of principles to explore the reality that it does not stand alone. Rather, the inpatient psychotherapy group is embedded in a series of hierarchically and dynamically related systems. It typically takes place on a residential unit and may be regarded as a subsystem of the unit. The unit is a system within the larger system of the hospital. Within the suprasystem of the hospital, there are other systems that overlap in membership and function (Levine, 1980). For example, each staff member may be both a member of the treatment team and a member of a discipline-related department such as a department of nursing. There may be other systems within the hospital, such as the business office, that share neither membership nor function with the unit system but affect the unit system nonetheless. The psychotherapy group, although a subsystem of the unit, also comprises various sub-systems. For example, there is the patient subgroup and the therapist subgroup. Each individual member (therapist or patient) can be viewed as a separate system and as a subsystem of the group.

General systems theory contributes to the understanding of the inpatient psychotherapy group the notion that the workings of the group must be viewed within the context of the hierarchy of systems in which the group is embedded. If, for example, at the level of the suprasystem of the hospital, there exists among key administrators or factions of the hospital a conflict concerning philosophy of treatment, then this conflict will appear in some fashion within all systems, subsystems, and their inter-relations.

For example, one hospital that had been long known for its adherence to psychodynamic goals and methods of treatment had been placed under increasing pressure from various ac-crediting groups to provide treatment plans with behavioral objectives. Some administrators felt that this pressure should be addressed simply through the creation and completion of forms that would give the appearance of satisfying the requirements of these external groups. Others felt that some more substantive programming efforts should be made to effect the kinds of symptomatic and behavioral changes in patients that could easily be measured and documented. The latter group was successful in arranging the hiring of a number of behaviorally oriented staff. Some of these new staff were given the responsibility of running psychotherapy groups. Much to their dismay, these group psy-chotherapists found that patients were continually pulled from their groups for individual therapy sessions with their psychiatrists. They also observed that patients within the group expressed an inordinate level of doubtfulness about the value of a behavioral approach. Between sessions, members rarely completed their homework assignments, which were central to the group's effective working. During discharge interviews, many patients continued to express puzzlement about how therapy works and what is truly helpful.

In this example, one can see that the conflict existing between the accrediting groups and the hospital, and within the suprasystem of the hospital, filtered down to all systems and subsystems of the hospital. From a systems perspective, the individual patient's puzzlement concerning or ambivalent reaction to the different approaches to treatment can be understood through recognizing the ambivalence of the institution concerning treatment philosophy. Another way to understand on a broader level the interpersonal processes involved in this example is that the hospital organization reduced the anxiety associated with an external threat by placing it within the organization where it could more effectively be mastered (Hirschhorn, 1988).

Although all hospital systems affect and are affected by all other systems and subsystems, the interrelatedness among systems can most readily be seen in those systems and subsystems that are adjacent to one another. Consequently, although all systems of the hospital (including the suprasystem of the hospital itself) have reverberations within the psychotherapy group, that system to which the psychotherapy group has closest and most obvious ties is the unit on which the group takes place. Throughout this chapter, we outline the important dimensions of the relation between the unit and the group. However, at this point, we discuss several facets of this relation to show the high level of interrelation between the group and the unit and the necessity of viewing the dynamics of the group from the standpoint of its residency on the unit.

One respect in which the group is obviously related to the unit is in terms of composition. Typically, all of the group members are residents of the unit. Frequently (although not invariably), the therapists are members of a treatment team on the unit. The tenor of members' relationships with one another on the unit as well as the issues that emerge in their relationships on the unit cannot help but be carried into the group. For example, on one psychiatric unit, patients were treated by a large group of attending psychiatrists, each of whom spent widely varying amounts of time (from 5 minutes to 1 hour) on individual therapy with their patients. Quite naturally, feelings of envy were rampant on the unit. Within the psychotherapy group, rivalry among members was intense, with much attention given to how many minutes of group time each member received. Frequently, members would devise schemes to ensure fairness in time allotment. Occasionally, members who were enjoying more generous attention from their psychiatrists (and no doubt anxious about being in such a privileged position) would suggest that the group give more prolonged consideration to the concerns of apparently neglected members. Clearly, members' reactions to the evident variability in their relationships to their psychiatrists permeated the group.

Another related aspect of the relation between the group and the unit is the high level of information exchange between the two. Expressed in the language of general systems theory, the boundary between the group and the unit is a highly permeable one, and the flow of information is bidirectional. For example, in one group session, several members managed to convey to the group therapist, a psychiatry resident, the insult inflicted on them by his pattern of leaving the group several times during each session to answer his beeper. They found his behavior to be highly disruptive despite the fact that the co-therapist, a psychology intern, provided some continuity of leadership. The members' reactions to his departures were especially intense because his behavior was emblematic for them of the staff's chaotic and fragmented approach to their treatment on the unit. Indeed, staff members' disorganization in their approach to patients was due to a clash between a biological approach embraced by psychiatry and a psychodynamic–interpersonal approach embraced by the other disciplines represented on the unit. The group therapist was dramatizing this conflict by leaving the group to attend to what he saw as medical emergencies. Yet, when the group confronted him with their extreme displeasure, the resident responded with a high level of openness and agreed to make alternate arrangements for his emergencies. The group's success in addressing this problem was carried onto the unit. Members on the unit (including those not in the group) became more confident that efforts to communicate their confusion and resentment in relation to staff members' behavior would not be met with staff retaliation or indifference.

In this example, the specific interaction between the psychotherapy group and the unit was obviously a favorable one. Within the group, members were able to challenge fears that immobilized them both in the group and on the unit. However, such interactions are not inevitably favorable. Had the resident responded with a high level of defensiveness, a different message would have been taken from the group to the unit. The challenge for the object relations/systems therapist is to use knowledge about the interrelations among the unit, the group, the group's subgroups, and the group members to enable these systems to function synergistically for the furtherance of the members' well-being. The integration of object relations theory and systems theory provides a conceptual framework that facilitates the achievement of such synergy.

## Object Relations and Systems Theory: An Integration

**The inpatient unit.** The reconstitutive aspects of inpatient psychiatric hospitalization are well known (Rice & Rutan, 1987). The hospital unit offers sanctuary from everyday stressors, relief from decision making, and a diminished requirement to attend to the responsibility of everyday life. Those inpatients who are bereft of social supports outside the hospital find such supports in greater abundance in their new setting. The institution of a regime of medication frequently reduces the intensity of symptoms. All these forces are aimed to help patients regain their premorbid level of functioning.

Yet, there exist another set of forces, typically unprescribed, that not only fail to support reconstitution but work to induce an even deeper level of regression (Adler, 1973; Friedman, 1969; Kibel, 1978; R. H. Klein & Kugel, 1981; Rice & Rutan, 1981). As many writers have noted, the structure of the interpersonal situation on the inpatient unit is regression promoting apart from the psychological characteristics or proclivities of the individual patients on the unit. The inpatient unit is generally a large group configuration with rarely fewer but typically more than 50 staff and patients. Turquet (1975), Springmann (1976), and others have documented the regression-promoting effect of the large group. Additionally, the fact that the unit is a setting in which individuals have multiple roles in relation to one another can also promote regression (Ogden, 1981). The nurse who in the group session encourages the expression of disturbing feelings may also be the same person on the unit who imposes sanctions when residents communicate too loudly or vociferously. Inevitably, role multiplicity creates role ambiguity. Patients often experience confusion about what staff roles will emerge when. Staff members also feel uncertain about when a particular role or stance is appropriate. Structural features of the unit such as the large size and the multiplicity and ambiguity of roles all conspire to make staff and patients alike anxious. The high levels of anxiety present on the unit are conducive to the emergence of more primitive modes of psychological functioning than those in which members might engage elsewhere.

The potential for a patient's regression while on a psychiatric unit is further heightened by the particular psychological characteristics of other patients as well as, paradoxically enough, the goal of hospitalization itself, the restoration of the premorbid personality. Individuals enter the hospital because they are unable to handle the tasks of everyday life. Their very natural feelings of ineffectuality lead them to look outside of themselves for nurturance, soothing, and protection. Staff and some other patients offer ready candidates for the fulfillment of such expectations. This expectation is intensified by the fact that it is a shared one among patients. It is also strengthened by the relative isolation of the inpatient unit (Rice & Rutan, 1987) and patients' separation from familiar objects of dependency.

The consequence of the intensity of both patients' dependency wishes and their (and to some extent staff's) expectations that they will be gratified within this setting leads to the development of characteristic types of cultures on the unit. Such cultures that activate primitive modes of psychological functioning were labeled *basic assumption groups* by Bion (1959), who extended M. Klein's (1952) object relations concepts to the group situation. A basic assumption group is a theoretical construct used to describe a type of group in which members behave as if they have accepted a particular unconscious fantasy that is something other than the stated goal. Such groups are to be contrasted with the *work group*, in which the group's actions are in conformity to the explicitly stated goal of the group (in the case of the inpatient community, an example of a work group goal might be members' acceptance of greater responsibility for their difficulties).

One type of culture that commonly develops on an inpatient unit is the *basic assumption dependency group*. In such a group, members act as if they are about to be rescued by an omnipotent leader who will care for all of their needs. Members of the group behave with great passivity, eager to acquiesce to the real or imagined demands of authority figures who are idealized not for what they are presently giving but for the potential of what they might give. Staff (who are as much a part of the culture as patients) often unwittingly participate in this fantasy. One reason that staff are propelled to involve themselves in this fantasy has to do with the structure of the inpatient situation (e.g., the large group size, the multiplicity of the roles). In addition, however, the aforementioned typical separateness of the inpatient unit from the community and in some cases, the rest of the hospital strengthens the pull on staff to become absorbed in whatever unconscious fantasy is ruling the group at the moment (Rice & Rutan, 1981). Staff members' particular proclivities to involve themselves in the basic assumption dependency group are due to the overlap of this fantasy with the realistic task of the staff: to provide nurturance and assistance of various sorts. Given that by design, this is the clinical mission of the staff, it is not difficult for staff members also to embrace the ideal of the perfect caretaker.

Inevitably, staff are unable to fulfill the enormous expectations of the basic assumption dependency group. Soon, both patients and staff (but particularly the former) come to experience intense disappointment in reaction to the continued presence of symptoms and life difficulties. Such disappointment is made more acute by inpatients' typically limited abilities to tolerate frustration and by some of the potentially disturbing events on a unit (e.g., patient elopement, the departure of staff from the unit, and acting-out episodes of other patients). Such events lead patients to question both the availability and competence of the staff in providing for their needs. The shared disappointments of patients and staff promote a culture that resembles Bion's (1959) description of the *basic assumption fight/flight group*.[5] The fight/flight group acts according to the unconscious belief that the group is under siege by an enemy who is threatening the survival of the group. The enemy may be any person or agent who is perceived by the community or a subgroup of the community as an obstacle to the realization of the ideal of perfect caretaking on the unit. The enemy may be a particular staff member who is seen as powerful but cold and depriving or may be a patient whose obstreperousness is viewed as singularly destroying the serenity of the unit. It may be a hospital policy that is seen as excessively handicapping staff in carrying out their nurturing functions. As some of these examples suggest, staff are in no way immune to these collective perceptions. For example, it is not unusual for staff members at a team meeting to speak wistfully about the halcyonic aura of the unit prior to the arrival of some particularly unlikable or difficult patient.

Whereas the dependency group gives rise to passivity as patients wait for expected provisions, the fight/flight group exhibits behaviors that are typical of people confronting an enemy: fighting and fleeing. For example, one inpatient unit showed a mixture of both fighting and fleeing behaviors in a community meeting occurring after an incident in which an adolescent female patient on a mixed-age unit found an instrument with which she cut herself extensively. Whereas some patients sat in the meeting cowering, others decried the staff for their lack of vigilance. Al-

---

[5] We are describing two common cultures that develop on an inpatient unit. This description of group cultures is not intended to be in any way exhaustive nor is the presumption made that any culture is pure (i.e., not containing elements of other cultures). Rather, life on an inpatient unit, particularly a short-term unit, is such that cultures shift rapidly in response to the quickly changing interpersonal scene of the unit, with the dominant culture containing elements of both its predecessor and successor. We are not describing Bion's (1959) basic assumption pairing group, although we do discuss this type of group in the next chapter, which describes the developmental model.

though members of the community were understandably upset by the young patient's successful self-destructiveness, their response was particularly strong because it challenged the assumption of the group in its basic assumption dependency mode.

The fact that cultures on inpatient units at times resemble Bion's (1959) description of the basic assumption groups shows that regression can occur on a group-as-a-whole level, with each member and major subgroup covertly or overtly embracing the group's assumption. Given the permeability of boundaries between the unit and the psychotherapy group, such group-level regressive forces on the unit necessarily infuse the group. Hence, the inpatient group therapist is likely to see the kinds of configurations that are characteristic of the dependency and fight/flight groups. However, regression also occurs on an individual level based on the patient's unique response to the special features of the inpatient setting. As previously discussed, individuals who have undergone the degree of regression that necessitates hospitalization are often unable to use defenses such as splitting, which protects positive self and object images from negative ones. The unhappy coexistence of contradictory perceptions of self and others is sufficiently confusing to the individual that he or she continually seeks ways in the inpatient situation to eliminate the confusion. A primary means of achieving a more consistent and tolerable self-perception is through the use of *projection* and *projective identification*. The understanding of these mechanisms is important so as to grasp not only the meaning of the patient's behavior on the unit but also the value of the object relations/systems group in fostering individual reconstitution. Hence, these concepts are described in some detail.

Both projection and projective identification entail the individual's placement of some intolerable element of intrapsychic experience onto another person. An example of simple projection occurs when Mary, finding her own envy to be unacceptable, projects it onto others and sees individuals around her (or perhaps a particular individual) as being envious of her. Projective identification is a more complicated maneuver in which the individual not only extrudes some loathed part of the self (as Mary did) but also unconsciously acts in a coercive way to elicit an internal (or experiential) and external (or behavioral) response from the recipient of the projection that corresponds to the content of the projection (Goldstein, 1991). It is because of this second step that projective identification can be seen as a mechanism that connects the intrapsychic with the interpersonal (Meissner, 1980; Ogden, 1979).[6] Consider the former example. If Mary is using projective identification in her relationship with Tom to rid herself of her unwanted envy, it is not enough for her to see Tom as envious of her. She must treat him in such a way that he will act and feel envious. When Tom does so, he serves, in Bion's (1962) terminology, as a "container" or receptacle for Mary's envy. The completion of this process of projective identification occurs when the projected content is reinternalized. That is, Mary will proceed to structure her intrapsychic experience of envy using her perception of Tom's experience and expression of envy as a model. If Tom's envy appears relatively unthreatening to himself and others, then Mary's experience of her own envy is neutralized relative to her initial experience of it, that is, prior to her use of projective identification. On the other hand, if Tom responds with excessive hostility, then Mary's reinternalization of the projected content is made even more toxic by virtue of her use of projective identification.

On an inpatient unit, patients' use of projective mechanisms is nearly constant. As discussed earlier, both projection and projective identification require some blurring of boundaries between self and others (Goldstein, 1991), and a weakness in the differentiation between self and other is a critical aspect of the regression that inpatients have undergone prior to hospitalization (Rice & Rutan, 1981). Moreover, inpatients, particularly

---

[6] The distinction made here between projection and projective identification is somewhat controversial. Whereas some theoreticians (Meissner, 1980; Ogden, 1978, 1979) make a strong distinction between these two constructs, others see the distinction as somewhat arbitrary (Grotstein, 1981), arguing that all projections have an interpersonal aspect and that all projective identifications are fundamentally intrapsychic given that the individual does not project into the object but into the image of the object. Although we recognize the irresolution of the issue, we see this distinction as having clinical utility because in some instances patients' interpersonal maneuvering in relation to the projection is much more evident.

those organized at the borderline and psychotic levels, frequently use these mechanisms as means of eradicating both the contradictions in their perceptions and images of self and others and the confusion and anxiety that attend these contradictions. Through projection of that which is seen as negative, the internal is rendered more consistently positive. However, the processes of projection and projective identification occur commonly on an inpatient unit not only because of the facility of the patients to engage in these processes but also because the setting evokes such engagements. The diversity of personalities in the inpatient setting and the presence of conspicuous authority figures often evokes transferential reactions related to early parental figures (Kibel, 1981). Patients attempt to get others to play crucial roles in their internal psychodramas in an effort to produce more favorable outcomes than those outcomes that occurred in the past.

In fact, when inpatients use their interactions with patients and staff on the unit to rid themselves of their own rejected parts, rarely do such attempts bring relief; frequently, they increase anxiety and stimulate further regression. The anxiety in part is inherent in the processes of projection and projective identification. According to Horwitz (1983),

> The subject's projections often lead to persecutory anxieties concerning retaliation by the external object; hence the process may be accompanied by a heightened need to control and dominate the object. A frequent fantasy is that parts of the self are intruding into alien territory and, therefore, run the risk of becoming entrapped, much like a spy dropped behind enemy lines. (p. 263)

When patients attempt to use other patients as repositories for unwanted feelings, impulses, and images, the anxiety that typically accompanies the use of such mechanisms is intensified further because the other patients are unlikely to serve as adequate models of containment. Not only do the other patients lack the ego resources to contain and exhibit the modulated expression of these contents but they too are motivated to rid themselves of the same or similar experiences. Their inevitably extravagant responses to being the recipient of others' projections reinforces others' fears of retaliation, leading the unit to be perceived as more of a war zone than a sanctuary.

Certainly, the staff have greater capacity than patients to tolerate each patient's projections and projective identifications. However, the primitive nature of the material being projected on them and the extreme pressure placed on them to act in accordance with these projections evokes in staff strong countertransference reactions. (In this context, *countertransference* is defined as the therapists' reactions to the patients' transferences). While pursuing the goal of managing the unit, staff rarely have the luxury of adopting the kind of neutral attitude that would enable them to put these reactions to therapeutic use. Staff may be prone to act on their reactions to patients' projections and projective identifications in ways that could bolster patients' fears about the dangers of certain psychic states. For example, when Jean raises the volume of her radio to a level that is intolerable to all so as unconsciously to provoke the on-duty nurse to rage and the nurse responds to her extreme annoyance with excessively harsh limit setting, then Jean's anxiety about the connection between the expression of rage and others' retaliation for such an expression increases. Jean's anxiety then increases her capacity for regression on the unit.

**The psychotherapy group.** The restitutive and regressive forces on the unit are also contained within the psychotherapy group. However, within the psychotherapy group relative to the unit, these forces are more identifiable and as such are more amenable to exploration and alteration (Kibel, 1981). One reason for the greater clarity of these forces in the group is that the group is seen as uniquely providing a net of safety that facilitates the less disguised appearance of regressive reactions. In individual therapy, for instance, the patient is unable to fully express angry feelings toward the therapist because such expressions induce concern over the potential of such feelings to obliterate the therapist. Patients in the midst of their self-perceived helplessness cannot, they believe, afford such an obliteration. In the psychotherapy group, members can express negative feelings toward the therapist and still retain a positive perception of the group (Kibel, 1987a). In addition, the group is conducive to the full-blown manifestation of conflict because the group encourages verbal expression of affect and thereby renders the extent and nature of the affect clearer to all (Kibel, 1987b). Whereas the unit is large and diffuse with many different interactions occurring simultaneously, the inpatient group is small and focused. These latter qualities create an inescapability wherein members are forced to respond to feelings in a more direct fashion. Expressing a similar notion, R. H. Klein and Kugel (1981) commented,

> The harnessing of emotional conflicts and energy can be accomplished with a small-group structure with identifiable boundaries; that factor not only reassures both patients and staff members about their fears of loss of control but also protects the sanctity of other unit boundaries. (p. 322)

Finally, while functioning within the confines of the group, staff are relieved of other burdens and responsibilities, thereby facilitating their assumption of an analytic attitude toward patients' communications and abetting their capacity to serve as healthy containers for members' projections.

Because the psychotherapy group symbolically contains the issues experienced by the unit, it is a place in which important work can be done with effects on all systemic levels including that of the unit. Through the analysis of members' reactions to the regressive-promoting features of the unit in the psychotherapy group, the restitution-fostering features of the unit can be actualized most completely.

## Goals of the Group

The object relations/systems model[7] seeks to promote the necessary intrapsychic change to enable members to return to their

---

[7] The reader may wonder why this model is termed the *object relations/ systems model* rather than simply the *object relations model* given that most contemporary psychodynamic group therapists pay heed to the context in which the group takes place. The term *systems* is critical because it reflects the priority that this model gives to the analysis of group–unit relations over the

premorbid level of functioning. More specifically, this model views the primary impediment to members' reattainment of their former healthier level of functioning to be their inability to use splitting; that is, patients fail to differentiate and segregate good and bad images of both themselves and other people. In the absence of splitting, infusion of the central ego core with aggression occurs. The goal of the object relations/systems model follows quite directly from the statement of the problem. The goal is to neutralize and circumscribe group members' aggression. As the use of splitting is restored and as aggressive images of self and others become less consuming, the individuals' capacities to summon positively toned representations are enhanced. Although there are some object relations theorists (e.g., Rusakoff & Oldham, 1984) who think that some group members may even be able to move beyond splitting to the developmentally more advanced integration of positive and negative images of self and other, most theorists (e.g., Hannah, 1984b; Kibel, 1981) regard this goal as more appropriately pursued by the outpatient therapist.

There are several concrete manifestations of members' greater access to positively toned representations. A first manifestation is that members' experiences of others and members' social behaviors become more benign. In contrast to behavioral models, the alteration of social behaviors is understood within the present model as an effect of intrapsychic change. That is, the social behaviors are not themselves a target of intervention.

A second manifestation of members' successful group participation is that they become more capable of adapting to their environment, of coping with the stressors of everyday life including those on the inpatient unit. During regression, the infiltration of the good ego core by negative images of self and

---

analysis of intragroup dynamics. Moreover, for those trainees interested in learning this model, the systems aspect is actually more crucial than is the object relations component. According to Kibel (personal communication, April 17, 1992), as long as the trainee has an awareness that events on the unit impinge on the group, this model could be applied at some basic level.

other stymies the ego from performing those ego functions (e.g., reality testing, judgment, and the regulation and control of drives, affects, and impulses) that are essential to adaptation (Bellak, Hurvitch, & Gediman, 1973). The return of splitting enables the ego to perform these functions unhampered.

One borderline patient exhibited both of the aforementioned manifestations of intrapsychic change over the course of her group participation. On entering the hospital, she had been so enraged by the frequent nightly bedchecks performed by the nursing staff that she remained awake all night. She would appear on the unit the next morning in a state of fury, ready to hurl castigations at all who approached her, patients and staff alike. Within the psychotherapy group, she was given a forum for her complaints. As she railed against the staff for their intrusiveness and insensitivity, she found that she was joined by other group members who saw the staff's insistence on patients' attendance of community meetings and other activities as further indication of their overbearing stance vis-à-vis the patients on the unit. Although initially this member's dismissal of others on the unit was pervasive, gradually and begrudgingly she differentiated between the staff and the patients, with only the latter being tolerable. Eventually, her irritation was directed only at those staff members who actually performed the checks at night. The lessening of her hostility enabled her to sleep through the night and hence be more prepared for the next day's activities. The outlet for and validation of her anger in the group had enabled her to have more sanguine relationships with both patients and staff and to cope adequately with the stressor of the nightly checks.

A third manifestation of the positive intrapsychic change that occurs with participation in this type of group psychotherapy is the individual's increased willingness to be involved in outpatient group psychotherapy. The restitution of the good ego core (based on positive internalizations) enables the use of those processes such as self-reflection that were casualties of regression. Such a function as self-reflection is critical not only for the patient's participation in exploratory psychotherapy but also for his or her awareness of the value of such an exploration.

## The Change Process

The interventions of the object relations/systems model are targeted toward (a) segregating and reducing the intensity of the members' negative images of self and other and (b) bolstering the good ego core, which is the organized totality of the positive images of self and others. A primary strategy to accomplish the first goal is to help members to establish linkages between present emotional reactions and recent events, particularly events related to the experience of being hospitalized (Kibel, 1978; Rice & Rutan, 1987). What follows is an example in which the therapist provided such a linkage in an inpatient group. An analysis of the hypothesized intrapsychic effects of such an interpretation follows.

Members of a psychotherapy group on an adolescent unit became quite irritated with the therapist for "invading their space" by allegedly asking questions that they deemed to be too personal. The therapist found this to be a curious criticism because he had not within that session asked members any questions, personal or otherwise. He had made some reflective comments but felt that they went little further than what members had actually said directly. However, in thinking about one member's use of the term *invade*, the therapist drew an association between members' irritation and a recent drug screen that had taken place for all adolescents on the unit because of suspicions of the staff. The therapist shared this connection with the members. He also commented that anger in response to a sense of being invaded was quite understandable. After members decried the staff for this action, they proceeded to express fears about being found the culprit whether or not they had ingested illicit drugs during their tenure on the unit. Members who were surprised that others feared being proclaimed guilty despite innocence laughed and developed a fantasy of the patients on the unit taking the same action on the staff.

The therapist's establishment of a linkage between members' experience in the group and precipitating events on the unit had a number of positive effects. It helped members recognize that their emotional reactions were comprehensible rather than mysterious, confusing, and bizarre. Another effect of such an intervention was to validate members' reactions by claiming that their irritation was not an unreasonable reaction to have given the situation at hand. This validation removed other painful affects such as shame and guilt from the anger and thereby diminished the intensity of the latter. Such an intervention altered in a positive way the patients' representational world because it harnessed and somewhat neutralized those aggressive introjects that had invaded the good ego core.

Splitting is effected not only by diminishing the bad but by bolstering the good. Members in the group are given an opportunity to respond to one another in a nurturant fashion. Such displays of caretaking of others are esteem enhancing and strengthen the individual's self-perception of being good. Kibel (1987a) referred to this process as *narcissistic reinforcement*. Even more important, however, is that members' positive self-images are strengthened through their identifications with one another. When a group becomes cohesive through these identifications, the self-images of the members coalesce into a kind of collective group ego (Kibel, 1987a) that is better able than that of any one individual to ward off aggressive introjects. These hostile introjects are also bound by the members' identification of common complaints pertaining to their lives within the group and on the unit. The intermember binding of positive and negative representations enables the group to accomplish externally the splitting that is so crucial for the members' returns to their premorbid states.

# Technical Considerations

## The Role of the Leader

This section discusses three aspects of the leader's role. The first aspect is the set of functions performed by the leader. The second is the therapist's use of countertransference reactions as a basis for interventions. The third is the contribution of the co-therapy relationship to the application of this model.

**The leader's interventions.** The leader operating within the context of the object relations/systems model performs a number of functions: administrative, supportive, and interpretive. In the language of systems theory, the inpatient group psychotherapist has the administrative assignment of managing the boundaries of the group, both external and internal (Rice & Rutan, 1981). With respect to external boundaries, the therapist must operate in such a fashion so as to achieve stability and the optimal level of boundary permeability between the psychotherapy group and the unit. The therapist's maintenance of external boundaries is exemplified in the group's possession of a regular meeting time and place as well as freedom from disruption by other hospital activities (Borriello, 1976; Rice & Rutan, 1981, 1987). Although all models presented in this book attest to the importance of these sources of regularity, the present model provides a unique explanation for their contribution to the effective working of the group. Within the object relations/systems model, the goal of hospitalization—the restoration of splitting—entails patients' reacquisitions of the ability to make differentiations (e.g., between self and other, thoughts and their referents). Predictable boundaries between the psychotherapy group and the unit (or other systems of the hospital) provide an external model of differentiation for members' intrapsychic lives. Lack of such boundary maintenance only furthers the nondifferentiating process of regression (Rice & Rutan, 1981).

For example, two therapists were conducting a psychotherapy group on a psychiatric unit of a general hospital. During the middle of the group, a physician entered the room and announced to one of the therapists that he had to procure from the closet a set of slides for a lecture that he was about to deliver. During his noisy 5-minute search, members appeared uncertain as to whether they should continue to speak. After he left, a heretofore withdrawn psychotic member muttered incomprehensibly about UFO's, and the group responded with an unusual level of interest in this topic. Clearly, the physician's intrusion in the group made more confusing for members distinctions between inside and outside, self and others, fantasy and reality.

As a "boundary manager" (Agazarian, 1989; Kernberg, 1973), the therapist also strives to maintain an optimal level of permeability between the psychotherapy group and the unit. For several reasons, it is important that information flow from the psychotherapy group to the treatment team on the unit. First, the group therapists are in a position to get important information about patients from the standpoints of diagnosis, dynamics, and progress in treatment (Kibel, 1987b). Second, because the psychotherapy group stands in isomorphic relation to the unit on at least some dimensions, communication of knowledge about the psychotherapy group's dynamics can help clarify the dynamics of the unit. Staff are thereby facilitated in working with patients in all aspects of the therapeutic community. Third, the treatment team's reception of helpful information enhances their appreciation of the value of the group and their understanding of its workings. These are ingredients for a pro-group climate, an environment in which the psychotherapy group is protected and supported and in which "group therapy is accepted as part of the fabric of the hospital" (Rice & Rutan, 1981, p. 307). Of course, information must also flow from the unit to the group. For instance, if a group psychotherapist were to lead a group without any knowledge of important recent events on the unit, he or she would be sorely handicapped in the effort to decode the meaning of events in the group.

The therapist must also maintain the internal boundaries of the group. Internal boundaries refer to important sources of regularity within the meetings themselves, such as the membership of the group, its focus, and the rules that members observe during and between sessions. Like the external boundaries, internal boundaries provide members with a sense of safety and a model for internal organization.

In conducting the psychotherapy session, the group leader also makes various types of supportive interventions. Relative to the long-term outpatient therapist, the inpatient group psychotherapist is active in involving the members in the group. To stimulate discussion, the therapist may ask questions, seek clarifications, or even address a unit-related topic. An important supportive activity is to help members bond with one another through a recognition of commonalities in one another's experiences. For example, if a new member expresses anxiety about entering the group, the therapist might remind other members that they had similar feelings several days prior. The therapist thereby facilitates the establishment of a bridge between new and old members. The therapist also offers support by exhibiting and fostering in others a nonjudgmental attitude toward members' contributions (Kibel, 1987b).

The therapist provides not only support but understanding through the use of *clarifying interpretations*.[8] Here, the therapist assists the group in seeing how members' communications in the group are reflective of reactions (often overreactions) to the broader therapeutic milieu. An example of this process was given in the preceding section in which the therapist decoded for members the symbolism in their irritation over his putatively probing questions. In encouraging members to ventilate their anger, the therapist offered himself as an object for this displaced anger. This displacement occurred readily because the therapist was inevitably seen as a representative of the hospital and the treatment team. The therapist was then able to "contain" (Bion, 1962) the aggression for the members. That is, the therapist demonstrated a capacity to tolerate being the target of such feelings. When members use projective identification vis-à-vis the therapist and see that the therapist does not respond with vengeance, they are then able to reinternalize a diluted, less frightening form of anger.

By directing anger toward the therapist, members can test out their concerns about the consequences of being angry and expressing anger in a real context. For example, members may come to see that the manifestation of anger does not necessarily lead to retaliation or abandonment. This process of testing is extremely important because members' concerns about the catastrophic consequences of expressing anger are a major factor in causing their aggressive impulses to be so intolerable. The therapist should take an active role in helping members articulate and test their fears. In some cases, it may be beneficial for the therapist to reassure members that certain negative anticipations

---

[8] Kibel (personal communication, April 17, 1992), although having used the term *clarifying interpretation* in past writings, has indicated that this term may not be entirely apt. More recently, Kibel has leaned toward the use of the term *clarification* or *decoding*. Because this term has achieved some acceptance in the literature, we have chosen to use it.

will not be met. For example, the therapist may make it very clear to members that he or she will not delay their discharge from the hospital simply because they express anger toward him or her.

**The therapeutic use of countertransference.** The object relations/systems model places emphasis on the leader's analysis of his or her own reactions to people and events in the group as a means of understanding the dynamics of the group. The systems aspect of this model enables the therapist's cognizance that as a member of the group, he or she is a subsystem of a subsystem. As such, the therapist's full range of reactions in the group—perceptual, emotional, and cognitive—will be affected by the group's dynamics, which in turn reflect the unit's dynamics. The reflective quality of the therapist's reactions makes them an important source of data for the therapist. However, the therapist is not simply a member of the group. He or she is also a figure of authority who activates members' associations to and memories of early caretakers. Because one function of early caretaking is to contain for the child his or her unwanted parts, the therapist is a prime candidate for projective identification in the group. The group gives to the therapist those feelings, impulses, and other psychological commodities that it cannot yet manage. Although these projective identifications can create intense discomfort in even the most seasoned group therapist, in a sense, they are gifts from the group. They serve as signposts to understanding what it is that group members can least accept within themselves at any one moment within the group session. What is important within this model is a position of therapeutic neutrality, which involves a commitment on the part of the therapist not to act on the uncomfortable reactions that the group can induce but to use them for the purpose of understanding the group further (Hannah, 1984a).

**The co-therapy relationship.** Preferably, an inpatient group is co-led. The presence of two therapists is important both from the standpoint of the therapists and the patients. From the perspective of the therapists, co-leadership is important because each therapist can support the other in tolerating and understanding the primitive projective identifications of which each therapist is likely to be a target (Kibel, 1992). Moreover, co-therapists' comparisons of their differential countertransference reactions can often serve as additional information about the dynamics and defensive posture of the group. For example, Greene, Rosenkrantz, and Muth (1986) argued that wide divergency between co-therapists on their views of patients within the group is often an indicator that the group is using the mechanism of splitting in organizing their group experience. From the view of the patients, co-leadership creates a kind of safety net. A group can acknowledge a perception of certain undesirable qualities in one therapist while it retains a fantasy that the other therapist is perfect. Through this splitting process, the members can hold onto the image of a good therapist.

## Level and Locus of Intervention

The object relations/systems approach requires a certain flexibility on the part of the therapist in two respects. First, the therapist must be flexible in his or her ability to use interventions at individual, interpersonal, and group-as-a-whole levels. Individual interventions have considerable supportive value; that is, they help make members more comfortable in the group. For example, the therapist might pose a question to a reticent group member to diminish that member's sense of isolation. The therapist might help another member recognize a way that she can relate to a theme that the group is exploring so to make the group more cohesive. Interpersonal interventions from the therapist can be used to foster nurturant interactions among members—interactions that are important sources of narcissistic reinforcement. Another function of interpersonal interventions applies only to the treatment of fairly high-functioning members. Through the use of this level of intervention, a process of feedback can be instigated wherein members may be able to see how they contribute to the unhappy outcomes of interactions with others (Kibel, 1981). Kibel emphasized, however, that this process of interpersonal learning is typically most viable in long-term outpatient therapy once splitting has been reinstituted.

Group-as-a-whole interventions, therapist comments directed toward the group as a unit, can be used to "clarify the way in which group behavior is reactive to confluent environmental and transference influences" (Kibel, 1990, p. 252). It is particularly important that interpretations of how the group symbolically reflects reactions to the entire unit be made on a group-as-a-whole level. If such interpretations were made on an individual level, they might be narcissistically injuring to the recipient of the interpretation; that is, they may lower the member's self-esteem and increase his or her sense of vulnerability. Group-as-a-whole interventions, on the other hand, reduce members' levels of defensiveness. When members are able to see that their feelings and reactions in the group are determined by the dynamics of the unit, they are able to recognize that their reactions to present events (although having some realistic basis) are over-reactions.

Second, the locus of intervention is also an important area of therapist flexibility. The therapist must ably move from a focus on events and reactions within the group to those on the unit. This movement is helped by the therapist's consideration of potentially important events on the unit prior to the group psychotherapy session. For example, if a successful suicide occurred on the unit, the therapist might expect that this event would be represented in some manner in the material of the group session.

Within the object relations/systems model, an exclusive and intensive focus on in-the-room transactions would not be desirable because such an in-depth exploration of, for example, the transference patterns would be threatening to members and would induce regression (Kibel, 1987a). Also contraindicated is a historical focus, which can not only raise members' anxiety but also limit their capacity to bond with one another. Members have the unit and the group in common, although their individual histories may be very different. Finally, emphasis on precipitating circumstances of members' hospitalizations ("What brought you into the hospital?") is discouraged because such a discussion entails an emphasis on the members' liabilities in a way that demoralizes them (Kibel, 1984).

## Content of the Session

The object relations/systems approach provides members with the opportunity to bring up material spontaneously within the format of an unstructured session. Early on in the session, the therapist uses a variety of interventions to get members to respond to one another and to establish identifications with one another. For example, if a member remained relatively silent while another member talked about feelings of anger, the therapist might remind that member that the silent member had talked about difficulty with anger in an earlier session.

Throughout the session, the therapist fosters a here-and-now focus by encouraging members to talk about immediate reactions. In this context *immediate* refers to reactions occurring on the unit or in the group. If a member describes a reaction in the there-and-then (i.e., outside the hospital), the therapist might seek a parallel between that reaction and one in the here-and-now: "You say you have been angry at your boss, but as the session ended yesterday, you talked about a similar feeling toward Dr. Suds." Thus, the therapist makes linkages between immediate reactions and events on the unit. Therapists might be facilitated in this process by forming a mental checklist of recent significant events on the unit (Kibel, 1990).

Typically, the reason the group has warded off recognition of its emotional reaction in relation to some event on the unit or some aspect of hospital life is because of a fear that acknowledgment of the connection will bring about some catastrophe. The "working through" of a group-as-a-whole interpretation generally involves some attention to the fears that members have about the awareness of particular feelings and the events that provoked them. Members should be encouraged to test their fearful anticipations of what the consequences of such expressions would be inside or outside of the group. Particularly common are fears of retaliation by the person to whom a certain feeling is expressed.

In summary, the content of the sessions run according to an object relations/systems framework is the expression of immediate affective reactions and the analysis of their precipitants in the group and on the unit. Because this model emphasizes emotional expression and understanding, it involves a balance of cognitive and affective aspects of intrapsychic life. A unique aspect of this model in relation to the other models presented in this text is its facilitation of group members' expressions of their immediate negative feelings, particularly anger. Within a successful session, members are able to say what they thought could not be said.

# Clinical Illustration

The vignette presented in this chapter illustrates the object relations/systems approach in the context of an open-ended group that took place on a unit of a psychiatric hospital. There were seven members in this group, two therapists, and three student observers behind a one-way mirror.

## Group Members

Ruby, a woman in her late twenties, entered the hospital after slashing her wrists. Precipitating this suicide attempt was the discovery that her boyfriend of 3 months was having an affair.

Kathy, a woman in her midtwenties, entered the hospital after having sustained several weeks of vegetative symptoms of depression following the birth of her second child. She had been in the hospital for a week but in the past 2 days had begun to show manic symptoms.

Ralph, a middle-aged, retired Marine entered the hospital after being consumed by the unfounded belief that his military career was being investigated by the FBI. He believed that his neighbors were part of an FBI connection, and his repeated attempts to spy on their spying led to his commitment. He had been treated at a Veterans Administration (VA) hospital, but when staff judged that the setting was exacerbating his fears, he was transferred to a private facility where he claimed to feel safe.

Lizbeth, a young anorextic woman in her late teens, had entered the hospital after her landlord, who lived in her building, noticed that she had not been leaving her apartment. Her summoned relatives learned that she had not eaten in a week. The event appeared to have been precipitated by a grade of B+ in one of her college examinations—a grade that she perceived as unacceptable.

Frank, an extremely obsessive individual, entered the hospital because intensification of sexual preoccupations and his fear that others were aware of them prevented him from going to work.

Serena, a woman in her early thirties, had attempted to kill herself and her baby by falling off a bridge. Both were rescued. She claimed to have heard voices telling her to take this action.

## The Session

This psychotherapy group met daily for 50 minutes. It was led by a psychiatric resident and a psychology intern. Although there were no new members in the group during the reported session, Lizbeth returned to the group after a 3-day stay in a general hospital, where she was tube fed after her weight fell below a certain point. The group began with several members greeting Lizbeth, who said she was glad to be back at this hospital.

> Kathy: So what do you mean it makes this place look like the Garden of Eden?
> Lizbeth: It was just a pit, that's all. It was dirty and disgusting . . . and there was just no reason I had to go there . . . unless, of course, the staff just needed a break from me.
> Kathy: So, how was the food?

The other members laughed. The laughter was at Lizbeth's expense because it was common knowledge on the unit that she had been tube fed at the other hospital.

> Therapist: How did you feel about that question and the group's laughter?

Lizbeth shrugs.

(At this point, the therapist is aware that Lizbeth's departure from and return to the unit was a highly significant event for the group members. The goal of the therapist is to help the group unlock the significance of this event and its effect on the group.)

Ruby:   So, were there any cute doctors there? I heard there were cute doctors at that hospital.

(Lizbeth stands up to leave.)

Lizbeth:   I really don't feel like being here today.

Therapist:   Wait a minute, Lizbeth, maybe there are some things that have been upsetting you and, in fact, may be upsetting other members too. I think it's important for you to stay here so we can explore them.

(The departure of Lizbeth from the group would not only intensify her sense of failure already stimulated by her need for medical hospitalization but would make members more self-critical because they would have proof within the group that their show of aggression has destructive consequences.)

Therapist:   The group has been focusing on Lizbeth's having left the hospital. There's been some joking about it, but perhaps it made people feel jittery.

Ruby:   (sighs with annoyed weariness) Can't you take *anything* at face value?

Ralph:   I'll admit . . . this group is making me feel jittery. I think I felt okay before I came in here today. (then in slightly more authoritative voice) Maybe we were taking a bit too lightly what we should have taken seriously. Young lady, there is *nothing* about what's been happening to you that's funny. We all care about you. I have a daughter your age. In fact, you remind me a little bit of her. How old are you?

Lizbeth:   Nineteen.

Serena:   God bless you.

Ruby:   I didn't mean anything by what I said. I was just trying to get her to see the funny side of it.

Kathy:   Yeah, well, the real reason you mentioned the cute doctors is because you want to get transferred there like Lizbeth did to Scott Hospital since your own dream doctor left for the Bahamas yesterday . . . You've been edgy all morning. I think you miss him.

Ruby:    (petulantly) I'm glad he's gone because he got you-know-who out of my face.

(Here, Kathy and Ruby are referring to an announcement made by Ruby's attending psychiatrist and a nurse on the unit that they would be gone the following week on their honeymoon.)

Frank:    I've been at many psychiatric hospitals, and it's quite common for staff to marry one another. I've heard that 65% of all marriages are forged in the workplace.

Therapist:    Maybe so, but it sounds like this particular marriage may be upsetting to group members.

Ruby:    I don't care who or what he marries . . . and just like I said, I'm glad he got rid of her for me because she was a pain.

Kathy:    Yes she was!

Ruby:    But the one thing I *don't* like is him running off to the Bahamas when I just have one more week to spend in this joint.

Frank:    Be realistic. Would you expect him to make arrangements around your hospitalization.

Ruby:    I didn't say that I expected anything. I don't expect *nothing*!

Therapist:    In the beginning of our session, the group had a very difficult time keying into Lizbeth's feeling of having been abandoned by everyone, but particularly the staff when she was sent to Scott Hospital. It's not a pleasant feeling at all. But I'm sensing that right now there's a shared sense of abandonment here in the group and here on the unit with the departure of two of our staff members.

Ruby:    It's not that easy for me to open up to someone. Last week it took me about four days before I said even one word in here. And then I got to like . . . sort of trust this doctor and he just . . . evaporates! So this morning, I started feeling sad, but then I said to myself, "You're just a hardluck case. You don't have anybody to care about you . . . no family or nothing . . . so you get upset about this doctor like he's family." Like someone on my unit said, "Therapy is like buying a friend."

Frank:    The saying is, "Therapy is the purchase of friend-ship," and it is (a) true and (b) very pathetic.

Lizbeth:    I don't think it's pathetic at all. I think it's very natural to care about your therapist.

Therapist:    Perhaps you know what it's like to miss your therapist.

Lizbeth:    Of course I do . . . that's one reason I was so glad to come back. You know, they had a shrink who was seeing me at Scott, but I didn't say that much to her. I just saved my thoughts . . . made a mental checklist for when I got back.

Ruby:    (looking relieved) That's how I feel! But . . . well, I can't save things up like you could because he's going to be away for 2 weeks. I just have to decide about this new lady, his fill-in, she seems real nice but, I don't know . . .

Kathy:    She's not him, right?

Ruby:    Yeah, and she's young and . . . like maybe she has milk and cookies after our sessions.

Frank:    Yes, she's so obviously green. Did you notice the other day . . .

Ralph:    I would give *anything* to have these sorts of problems. Right now, my home is under surveillance. And I was at the VA trying to get better, but they soon infiltrated that place, which is very easy for them to do because it's a government establishment.

Many of the members of the group have heard this story before and roll their eyes as if to say, "Here we go again."

Frank:    Well, you're here now, so just don't worry about it.

Ralph:    Yeah, I'm here now, but I won't be here for long because wherever I am, they find me. And even as I'm talking now . . . (he turns around and looks at the one-way mirror through which the group is being observed by several students) I bet they're getting information to use against me. So what I'm saying is I don't give a (expletive) about whether Dr. P. goes or stays or what . . . I want these people off my back!

Frank: (with a flippant tone) So your hunch is that the observers are not what or whom they seem to be? Very interesting, indeed!

Kathy: (thinking Frank was taking Ralph's suspicions seriously) Give me a break . . . he's paranoid.

Ruby: Come on . . . how could you think those observers are FBI agents . . . it's crazy!

Ralph: I have enough people after me without this group getting after me.

Kathy: Well, you make people attack you. I used to be like that . . . I'm not that way now. You know, you're so scared of the FBI, but I think you're pretty scary.

Ruby: Yeah, Ralph, I picture you shooting someone someday because you think they're following you but guess what . . . it turns out the person is only walking his dog.

Several members snicker, and Ralph shakes his head.

Therapist: There seems to be some friction right now, but let's go back and understand what happened here. Ruby, what were you feeling as Ralph began speaking a few minutes ago . . . right when you were talking about Dr. P. leaving and the new therapist taking his place?

Ruby: Well . . . I started to feel better, and then he just interrupted me.

Therapist: So perhaps you were feeling a bit annoyed about the interruption?

Ralph: I didn't mean to interrupt you. I shouldn't have done that . . . there's no excuse . . . just a lack of discipline on my part.

Therapist: But maybe the sequence of events was important. Ralph, I notice that Ruby and Frank were talking about how Dr. D. may be different from Dr. P, and they're not happy about it. And then you started worrying aloud about the FBI . . . I know it's on your mind a lot. Perhaps, though, what Ruby and Frank were saying was making you a little uneasy. By the way, wasn't Dr. P. your psychiatrist too?

Ralph: Yes . . . well . . . I think you have to give people more of a chance. This new doctor doesn't need

|  |  |
|---|---|
|  | Ruby's flap. I like her . . . she really listened to me, and she didn't get bored. . . . *I* noticed she's younger, but how would you feel if you were her . . . she's trying her best, and this other guy is put on a pedestal, and everyone is around boo-hooing that he's gone while you're trying to help them. |
| Serena: | I think Ralph is right. |
| Therapist: | So if Dr. D. were a fly on the wall in our session today, how might she feel? What might happen? |
| Frank: | We'd swat her and bring back the other doctor . . . Okay, I'll be serious. My professional opinion is she wouldn't care. Negative feelings towards therapists are commonplace . . . and since these little reactions of ours don't change her paycheck . . . I don't think we should flatter ourselves to think it would bother her even slightly. |
| Lizbeth: | I think she would care . . . especially if she is, as you say (nodding toward Ruby), not all that experienced. |
| Kathy: | Doctors are human. . . . They have feelings. |
| Therapist: | So what if you hurt her feelings . . . what then? |
| Serena: | Well, if she realized that some of her patients don't like her . . . |
| Ruby: | (interrupting) Wait a minute . . . I never said I don't like her . . . I just said she was . . . what did you say Frank . . . green . . . yeah, she's just green. |
| Serena: | (tentatively) Okay . . . but still . . . I still think she could lose confidence. |
| Ruby: | Like what do you mean? |
| Serena: | (somewhat more confidently now) Lose confidence and stop trying. Just like I lost confidence in myself as a mother. |
| Frank: | As long as she doesn't hold up my discharge . . . what is that expression . . . something about fury and a woman scorned? |
| Therapist: | Earlier in our session, some members expressed a disappointment in seeing their therapist go and a resentment at having to adjust to a new therapist. Let's face it: Life for many of you would have been a whole lot easier it your doctor had stayed. But once you find the courage to express these understandable reactions, then you get scared that some- |

thing awful is going to happen, as if you're not entitled to feel the way it is very natural to feel. Reminds me of yesterday when Kathy thought I would be terribly offended because she told me she was put out that I was late.

Kathy:   (smiling) You were cool about it. And I notice that today you got here on time.

Ralph:   We only have a few minutes left and I'm worried about Serena because of what she just said about losing confidence in herself as a mother. I know about everything that was in the paper when you made the headlines. I read the story too. But I saw you on the unit the other night holding her . . . and you looked like a fine mother. Heck, when people are under stress, they can do a lot of things . . . like when I was in Nam . . . I wouldn't even want to tell you some of the things I . . . anyway, you're little girl loves you a lot and *that* should give you confidence.

Other members agreed with Ralph, and the group briefly laughed about the antics of the baby on the unit.

## Comment on the Session

The therapists entered the session recognizing that over the past several days, there had been some major events on the unit that potentially might affect members in the session. The therapists were particularly sensitive to the departure of the two staff members. They were aware that among the staff, feelings of resentment and confusion were prevalent particularly because the departing physician served as a primary supervisor for many of the residents (including one of the therapists).

Early in the session, members showed a lack of empathic attunement to Lizbeth that discouraged her from talking about her feelings of abandonment. They also acted toward her in such a way that made it intolerable for her to remain within the group. The therapists viewed Lizbeth as a container for something painful in the group. That is, through a group projective identification process, Lizbeth was pressured into feeling in an extreme way an affect that other members were seeking to ward off. The therapists proceeded to examine subsequent events in the group to learn more about the meaning for the group members of both her anorexia and her transfer from the unit. Note that before the therapists were able to assist the group in understanding the significance of the transfer, they made some general comments emphasizing that (a) members' behaviors may be linked to possible discomfort over Lizbeth's departure and (b) such discomfort could be understood. Such comments are helpful in establishing a here-and-now focus (through an emphasis on the importance of immediate reactions) and creating a sense of safety in the group (through the conveyance of confidence that these reactions would in time become comprehensible). Although such comments were not and could not have been sufficient to get the group to own the psychological content projected onto Lizbeth, they were successful in helping the group to take a somewhat more nurturant posture toward her, which enabled her to remain in the group.

Later material in the group led the therapists to see that Lizbeth was chosen as a group container for at least two reasons. First, her anorexia, a rather evident manifestation of internalized aggression, symbolized psychological content that members both identified with and feared. For example, Kathy's harsh behavior toward Lizbeth may have been a result of her eagerness to disavow her own self-destructive urges. In view of her postpartum depression, these urges may have been rooted in repressed aggression toward her second child. Serena, given her recent suicide/murder attempt was in a position to identify with Lizbeth's self-directed hostility (H. D. Kibel, personal communication, April 17, 1992). Second, members appeared to draw a connection between Lizbeth's sense of abandonment by the staff who arranged her transfer and their own sense of abandonment in relation to the complex event of the marriage and vacation of two staff members. To a large extent, the group's difficulty in acknowledging the impact of this event mirrored that of the staff. Once there was some group acknowledgment of the importance of Dr. P.'s departure, group members were able to come forth with a diversity of reactions. One especially common theme that was present among inpatients was members' intolerance of their own dependent strivings. It was this intolerance that created the need for a group container in the form of Lizbeth, the member perceived by others as most abandoned and most vulnerable. The group also exhibited intolerance of their sadness through the use of a hypomanic defense wherein they trivialized and sexualized their relationships with Dr. P.

Another element that emerged with particular prominence was members' disappointment with the replacement therapist. The members' specific complaint about this therapist was noteworthy in view of the in-training status of the therapists leading the group. Although it might have been useful for the therapists to have drawn this parallel, any intensive exploration of members' reactions to the therapists' neophyte statuses would have increased the level of tension in the session. In a long-term outpatient situation, the exploration of the parallel could have been very productive. In the inpatient situation, the value of the exploration must be weighed against potential of such an exploration to stimulate regression (Kibel, 1987a).

The group's discussion of their reactions to the replacement therapist was interrupted by Ralph, who essentially offered himself up as a scapegoat and a repository for others' projections. His anxious and paranoid-flavored ruminations appeared to be stimulated by his and others' concerns about the possibility of retaliation by the relevant authority figure. Members' identification with him was evident in both their nonverbal expression of annoyance and in Ruby's statement of having "once" been like him. As Kibel (1978, 1981, 1987a) pointed out, it is important for leaders to help members to articulate the feared consequences of the expression of hostile feelings. These articulations go a long way, he believed, in the "detoxification of negative affects." During this exploration, the therapist had Ruby share with Ralph her reaction to his interruptions. This may have sounded to the reader like a kind of intervention that would be more consistent with an interpersonal approach. Note, however, that, whereas the goal of the interpersonal model is to enable the member to get feedback so as to change his or her social behaviors, the goal of the object relations/systems model is to show the member that there is a coherence in even those interpersonal responses that seem puzzling or irrational.

During members' exploration of their fears of retaliation by the replacement therapist, the group therapist focused on the surfacing of a similar concern in a member's relationship with her, namely Kathy's protestation over the therapist's lateness to the previous session. This reference provided the group with an opportunity to reality test their concerns about staff's likely retaliation. This illustrates how within the object relations/systems model the therapist can fluidly move from the unit to the group and back to the unit using one arena to illuminate the other. In this example, the therapist also used a technical maneuver that Feilbert-Willis, Kibel, and Wikstrom (1986) identified as being helpful in the group treatment of severely disturbed patients. While underscoring members' retaliatory fears, the therapists acknowledged the courage required of group members to talk about negative reactions toward the therapist. Such a coupling of the positive with that which is potentially perceived as negative spares the member from feeling criticized by the therapists' interventions. One manifestation of the usefulness of the therapist's comments was Kathy's willingness to talk about the therapist's prior lateness.

The group ended with Ralph offering comfort to Serena and other members joining in. The group's exploration of their fears of retaliation by an authority figure and the assuaging of these fears freed the group to have benevolent and even playful interactions with one another. Ralph's taking an active role in this effort suggests that at least for the moment, he had reconstituted and was no longer serving as the repository for group members' anxiety over their manifestations of aggression.

## Status of the Research

### The Effectiveness of the Model

Various reviews of the research literature (Greene, 1988; Lettieri-Marks, 1987) have failed to reveal any outcome studies in which an inpatient group run according to the object relations/systems approach is contrasted with either groups run according to alternate models or control groups. Although the research on most of the models reviewed in this book is fairly sparse, it is particularly so for this model, perhaps because the target of change for the model is intrapsychic. Concepts such as the "bolstering of the healthy ego" and "the detoxification of aggression" are not readily translated into operational terms.

Certainly, the nature of the change sought within this model is more difficult to measure than, say, the frequency of a member's compulsive checking rituals during a day. However, such an investigation would be possible through the design of technically and conceptually sophisticated, theory-based research that uses measures not common in group psychotherapy research. For example, Lerner and Lerner (1980) have devised a well-validated Scale of Defense that is based on the analysis of Rorschach responses and reveals the degree to which the subject uses splitting as well as a host of other defenses. However, because this measure requires a pre- and posttest Rorschach, it may not be practical in many settings. Another measure of splitting was developed specifically for group psychotherapy (Greene et al., 1985). This measure reflects the divergence in the member's rating of co-therapists using a semantic differential technique. The greater the disparity in the rating of the therapists, the greater the use of splitting. Preliminary validation data, which show significant correlations between this measure and measures of members' self-representations, appear quite promising (Greene, 1988).[9] Using such a measure, the clinician can determine whether splitting increases as a function of participation in an inpatient group run according to the object relations/systems model.

Another goal of the model is to deintensify members' typically strong transference reactions to people and aspects of life on the unit. Members are helped to see the unit as a less terrifying and

---

[9] Splitting may not manifest itself as a divergence in perception in the two therapists. The advantage of the inpatient setting for the reinstitution of splitting is that there are many types of splits possible (e.g., between the group and the rest of the unit, between the nurses and the physicians). The technique used by these investigators might be further developed to enable other types of splitting to reveal themselves. According to Greene (personal communication, February 1991), such work is underway.

more comfortable place. Scales such as the Ward Atmosphere Scale (Moos, 1974) or the Group Climate Questionnaire (MacKenzie, 1983) should be useful in tapping members' perceptions of the affective climate of the unit as a function of being in a particular type of group.

Finally, the exponents of this model expect that its successful application will render members more willing to enter an outpatient treatment situation, an arena in which more substantial psychological restructuring is possible. Whether this model promotes entry into outpatient group psychotherapy could be determined by a follow-up on members several months after discharge.

## Components of the Model

**Theoretical postulates.** Like any model, the object relations/systems model makes a number of theoretical assumptions that cannot be tested. An example of such an assumption is the notion that psychopathology is rooted in conflict among different parts of the personality (Kibel, 1987a). However, there are other suppositions in this model that are amenable to empirical scrutiny. One major supposition is that the events, issues, and aura of the unit affect the nature of the process of the inpatient psychotherapy group. This assumption has received some support from a series of studies (Astrachan, Harrow, Becker, Schwartz, & Miller, 1967; Astrachan, Harrow, & Flynn, 1968; Becker, Harrow, Astrachan, Detre, & Miller, 1968; Harrow, Astrachan, Becker, Miller, & Schwartz, 1967) that show that "the social system of the ward with its norms, expectations, and values, plays a particularly important role in determining patient behavior in group meetings and has a significant impact on the therapeutic process" (R. H. Klein, 1977, p. 201). A more recent study (Karterud, 1989), which we discuss in greater detail later, found that the group-as-a-whole defenses of the community were perfectly mirrored by the groups within the community. These studies support the notion that the inpatient psychotherapy group is not so much a system in its own right but a subsystem within a system (Kibel, 1981).

**The focus on aggression.** A distinctive feature of the object relations/systems model is the encouragement that members are given to focus on hostile feelings, particularly toward the therapists, staff members, and aspects of the community and hospital life. Although there has been a great deal of theoretical writing about the expression of anger in groups, there have been few good empirical studies.

One question that has been addressed in the inpatient literature is the extent to which anger is a common affect expressed in the inpatient group. This line of investigation is important for the object relations/systems model because this model assumes that the experience of anger is accessible in the inpatient group on a fairly reliable basis. The literature suggests that groups are highly variable on this dimension. In some groups, the expression of anger is fastidiously avoided, and interpretive lines that seek to help the group clarify the source of anger seem to have little success (Richmond & Slagle, 1971). Whether a group is able to show anger may depend on the level of cohesion of the group. Braaten (1990) found that members of highly cohesive groups described important events in the group as those involving positively toned processes, such as self-disclosure and feedback, attraction, and bonding. Low-cohesive groups focused more on negatively toned events and were characterized by avoidance, defensiveness, conflict, and rebellion. Because most inpatient groups are short term and do not have time to develop a high level of cohesion, it is likely that the latter type of events and processes predominate in the sessions. Hence, the object relations/systems model focuses on phenomena that are commonplace in the inpatient group.

Karterud (1989) categorized group sessions held on various units according to Bion's (1959) scheme of basic assumption groups. He found that the group sessions frequently assumed a fight/flight character in which aggression was directed toward the group therapists and the staff at large. This pattern was particularly common on a unit that had many involuntarily committed members. Karterud reported that some (he did not specify what percentage) members clearly showed a greater capacity to use splitting and projective identification as a function of their group participation. Concomitant with the use of these defenses was a greater ability to participate in community life in positive ways. However, in some of these groups, the anger became extremely intense (certainly more intense than what would be recommended by any exponent of the object relations/systems model), and these groups appeared to precipitate self-destructive activity.

In this same study (Karterud, 1989), there were some groups that developed a dependency culture characterized by members' high levels of engagement with and trust in one another. Karterud's observers noted that when the therapists made efforts to help group members approach negative affect, these efforts (like those of the therapists in the Richmond & Stagle, 1971, study) were instantly quashed by the group. The observers also noticed that the unit on which these groups took place emphasized patient and staff engagement in extremely positively toned interactions and discouraged the free-flowing expression of hostility and other negative feelings. One might speculate that something about the structure of the unit itself in combination with the kind of patient admitted to the unit leads to the reinstitution of functional splitting at an early point in the patient's hospitalization. Perhaps within some settings, the other patients, the staff, the psychotherapy group, the unit, and the hospital can quickly become associated with the activation and coalescence of members' positive self- and object representations. In such an environment, questions might be raised as to whether the therapists' concentration on members' hostility would promote regression rather than restitution.

A study by Koch (1983) provided evidence that the processing of hostility within an analytically oriented psychotherapy group leads to positive outcomes in at least in some instances. These investigators taped sessions from a day-hospital psychotherapy group and analyzed the degrees of different types of affects. Koch found that the degrees of expressed hostility and affection were good predictors of successful outcome as measured by increased self-esteem and diminished subjective anxiety.

Two general conclusions may be drawn from the research on aggression. The first is that the focus of the object relations/ systems model is generally an appropriate one, given the abundance of aggression on an inpatient unit. However, there may be some group cultures organized specifically around the inhibition of aggression. How this organization would affect the group therapist's success in helping members explore aggression must be studied further. The second conclusion is that there is some suggestion from the research that the exploration of aggression in a psychotherapy group is associated with positive outcome.

**The diagnostic use of countertransference.** One feature that distinguishes the object relations/systems model from most of the models described in this text is the view that the therapist's own emotional and cognitive reactions to group members' behavior frequently serve as information about important aspects of the group's and individual members' functioning (Hannah, 1984a). There have been many anecdotal examples of therapist's and treatment team's productive examinations of countertransference reactions (e.g., Book, Sadavoy, & Silver, 1978; Brown, 1980), although recently this area has received more systematic empirical study.

Greene et al. (1986) studied whether the degree to which psychotherapy group members used splitting and projective identification in their organizations of perceptions of the co-therapists was mirrored by the levels of disparity in co-therapists' perceptions of the members. Their psychotherapy groups took place in a day-hospital setting and were run according to an object relations/systems model. Splitting was measured using the same method as in the Greene et al. (1985) study. The disparity in the co-therapist's perceptions of members was operationalized by having the therapists rate the level of severity of each member's presenting complaints. The investigators found that when a member saw the therapists in polarized terms (i.e., one bad, one good), the therapists were twice as likely to give widely divergent ratings of the severity level of that member's problems as when the member saw the therapists as being similar.

Although the Greene et al. (1985) study was pilot in nature, it provides some empirical support for the object relations position that the group therapist's reactions (or, in this case, disparity in co-therapists' reactions) can provide important information, such as the extent to which a member or a group relies on a certain type of defense mechanism.

# Critique of the Model

## Strengths

The object relations/systems model of inpatient group psycho-therapy has as a major strength its high level of conceptual development. To a greater extent than most of the models presented in this book, it offers an explicit description of the assumptions about psychopathology on which it is based. It also establishes clear linkages between the kinds of changes that are expected as a function of a member's involvement in group and the processes in the group that produce these changes. Finally, it offers the therapist a highly comprehensive explanation for common sequences of events in the inpatient group.

Related to these strengths is the power of the model to take into account the complex pattern of interrelations between the hospital, the unit, the group, and the individual. This power is important in at least two respects. First, it enables the therapist to bring a vast array of information to bear in understanding events in the group and in formulating interventions. In contrast to most other models, the therapist is never put in a position of having to declare some domain of the member's experience in the group as irrelevant to the group. Second, the integrative nature of the model provides the therapist with a perspective by which to transport information from the group to the therapeutic milieu. For example, developments in the group may clarify dynamics of the unit that may have been confusing to staff. In sharing these clarifications, perhaps at a staff meeting, the group therapist enhances the therapeutic value of life on the unit and thereby helps foster a pro-group climate (Rice & Rutan, 1981), one in which the group is seen as strengthening and complimenting (rather than subverting) other therapeutic efforts (Borriello, 1976).

A key advantage of this model is that it is based on a realistic assessment of the characteristics of the inpatient setting and group. The object relations/systems approach puts to therapeutic use what might be deemed as antitherapeutic in other systems. Although the inpatient therapist is exhorted to keep consistent spatial and temporal boundaries in the group (e.g., Rice & Rutan,

1981), the object relations/systems model makes the inevitable inconsistencies and boundary ruptures a central area of exploration in the treatment. No longer are the intrusions of the unit into the group an obstacle to treatment; they and their analysis *are* the treatment.[10]

The object relations/systems model enjoys an adaptability to a range of clinical circumstances on an inpatient unit. For instance, although tailored most specifically for borderline and schizophrenic patients, the model can be altered to serve the needs of higher functioning patients. The latter are better able than are the more regressed patients to do some limited exploratory work within the group. For example, high-functioning patients can use the group to recognize when certain of their emotional reactions (although rooted in realities of the inpatient environment) are overreactions. They can also appreciate more fully and tolerantly their own contributions to the negative patterns of interaction that develop between themselves and other people (Kibel, 1981). However, as we discuss later, we believe that this aspect of the model could be developed further.

The object relations/systems model is also flexible in that it makes no assumptions about the patient's tenure in the group. Potentially, a member could profit from involvement in even a single session. However, the model is also capable of being used in a long-term inpatient group and can be adapted to more fully use this group's greater potential cohesiveness. For example, members of long-term groups tend to be more tolerant of exploring the significance of "in-the-room" events (Kibel, 1986).

## Weaknesses

Like most of the models presented in this text, the object relations/systems model suffers from a lack of empirical validation

---

[10] This is not to say that object relations therapists oppose the therapists' efforts to create stability within the group. In fact, therapists of this theoretical persuasion are particularly aware of the disruptive effect of boundary violations (Rice & Rutan, 1981). Because constancy in leadership, membership, place, and time all contribute to group cohesion and because a cohesive group is a desirable achievement, such forms of constancy should be cultivated. Nonetheless, what the object relations/systems model has that other models lack is a framework to handle the fractures in constancy.

in terms of both its comparative efficacy and the descriptive power of certain of its central postulates. One tenet that is especially central to this model is the notion that events in the group symbolically mirror the dynamics of the unit. This principle, which is derivative of a general systems perspective, has an uncertain epistemological status. At times, it is treated as axiomatic. Because the inpatient group is a subsystem of the system of the unit, the events of the former must necessarily reflect unit dynamics. At other times, it is treated as an empirical postulate. For example, exponents of this model routinely cite the previously described research of Astrachan and colleagues (e.g., Astrachan, Schwartz, Becker, & Harrow, 1967) showing patterns of similarity between the group and the unit in emotional tenor, characteristic defensive structures, and so on to support its veracity.

We believe that accepting the principle of isomorphism as axiomatically true for inpatient groups and their relation to the unit forces the therapist into a conceptual straightjacket. The therapist is then predisposed to a kind of robotic interpretation of the meaning of events within the group. For example, if two members are in conflict with one another, any therapist operating within an object relations/systems framework will attempt to determine how this conflict may symbolically contain a conflict at the level of the unit, perhaps between subgroups of patients or between patients and staff. The therapist may then use a highly liberal criterion for judging the adequacy of interpretations that link this in-the-room conflict to conflict on the unit and may reject other kinds of interpretations out of hand. Perhaps the conflict between the members relates to the group's phase of development, which, although having ramifications for the group's relation to the unit, is not a direct reflection of unit dynamics (Beeber, 1988). We believe that the optimal use of the object relations/systems model occurs when the therapist regards the principle of isomorphism as a heuristic device rather than as a statement of necessity. Moreover, further development of this model would entail the discovery of what elements are most likely to repeat themselves and when they are likely to do so. Research might pursue hypotheses such as that advanced by Fulop and Schuman (1987) that the greater the tension in a hierarchy of hospital systems, the more likely it is that thematic repetition will occur from one system to another in the hierarchy.

We also believe that this model might profit from further technical development in certain important areas. Exponents of the object relations/systems perspective provide the therapist with little direction on how to select and prepare members for the group experience. Is there some group composition that is more desirable than others? Should members at different levels of functioning be placed in the same or different groups? Is preparation for group important, and is there some format for pre-group training that is especially compatible with the object relations/systems model? These questions have been largely unarticulated in the literature and research.

# Demands of the Model

## Clinical Mission

Although the object relations/systems model is based on modern psychoanalytic thinking, it does not require that the unit at large embrace a psychoanalytic perspective concerning psychopathology and its treatment. Were this the case, the model would be quite limited in its arenas of potential application. Nonetheless, the model does demand that the group take place in a therapeutic community or milieu. As Rice and Rutan (1987) described them, therapeutic milieus and communities, although similar, have some different characteristics and historical origins. A therapeutic milieu is an environment in which staff see life on the unit and all of its aspects as an important therapeutic instrument. It might be distinguished from a unit that embraces a medical model in which only one intervention (e.g., the patient's medication) is seen as useful. A therapeutic community has the features of a therapeutic milieu. Additionally, however, the therapeutic community typically has a community meeting that is attended by all patients and staff and that emphasizes the community wide analysis of all social events, egalitarian relationships among patients and staff, the effort to establish free communications among all levels, and the examination of roles by all members of the community but especially staff (Clark, 1965; Jones, 1952; Karterud, 1988; Main, 1977). Although the notion of the therapeutic community has fallen into some disfavor, therapeutic milieus continue to exist and be nurtured in many settings.

The application of the object relations/systems model is also aided by the staff's endorsement of those therapeutic processes emphasized by the model (Borriello, 1976). The first process is the expression of negative affect. A unit and staff that conspire to assist patients in obtaining control over feelings through the institution of a highly structured regime would see this group as working at cross-purposes with its mission. A second related process is the exploration of members' experiences on the unit, particularly as they relate to members' reactions in the psychotherapy group. Failure to accept the value of such an exploration is likely to stimulate a level of mistrust of the group that can hamper its working. Some staff may regard members' opportunities to ventilate complaints about the unit in the group as the group therapist's readiness to indict the unit and its staff. It is true that any adverse attitudes of other staff on the unit toward the group can serve as grist for the group's mill. However, when these negative attitudes are integral to the philosophy of the unit, staff can operate in a way that may seriously jeopardize the effective working of the group. As Borriello (1976) pointed out, sabotage of the group by the staff can take many forms. Patients may not be referred to the group. Individual sessions may be scheduled during the group sessions. It would seem that such challenges cannot be addressed only within the group; mechanisms must be developed to enable staff to be educated about the nature of the group and to compare with reality their impressions about the group. In circumstances in which such an incompatibility exists between unit philosophy and the assumptions of the model, and an educative effort is not feasible, an alternative model may be more appropriate than the object relations/systems model.

## Context of the Group

The object relations/systems model as it is currently described in the literature assumes that the group has little autonomy from the unit. Any structural factor that increases the group's autonomy requires some adaptation of the model for its optimal application. This model can be applied most easily when the group takes place on the unit. A group that is held off of the unit and that combines members of different units is much more likely to achieve the status of a system rather than a subsystem. It may develop goals, values, and norms that differ from those of other systems in the hospital. Certainly, the dynamics of each residential unit as well as those of the various departments of the hospital affect the group, as does the broader system of the hospital itself. However, these influences are more indirect, interacting, and complicated. Linkages between in-the-group and on-the-unit experiences to which all (or most) members can relate are less readily drawn.

This model is also more readily applied in open-membership than closed-membership groups. Closed-membership groups, too, enable the group to achieve more autonomy from the unit. In closed-membership groups, developmental phenomena emerge with particular clarity. The stage of development in which the group is residing may be as important as are the issues emerging on the unit. However, the introduction of the developmental factor does not preclude the use of an object relations/systems model. In fact, many group psychotherapists who use an object relations/systems framework think in terms of group development (e.g., Rice & Rutan, 1987). The clearer presence of developmental stages simply requires the therapist's recognition of the importance of this factor and readiness to see how members' experiences on the unit determine the way in which a group proceeds through a particular developmental stage.

## Temporal Variables

This model places few if any temporal demands on a patient's participation in the group. It can be adapted to varying lengths of hospitalizations and, at least hypothetically, a member could profit from attendance of even a single session. However, to the extent that a group does possess membership stability, the therapist can be more ambitious in taking an exploratory approach to the transferences within the group.

## Size

This model could be used with a relatively small number of members (e.g., 4 members) or with a much larger group (e.g., 12 members). The fact that the most potent interventions of this model are directed to the group as a whole and deal with a common reality among members enables the group to "reach" members who may not have had an opportunity to speak during the session. However, the effectiveness of the model depends on the therapist's ability to create a sense of safety in the group. If the size of the group makes it appear to members as a forbidding place, then the group is too large. Leszcz (1989), working within an object relations framework, recommended that when the group is composed only of severely character-disordered patients, only 4 to 6 members may be an acceptable size for the group.

## Composition

The object relations/systems model was developed with a particular inpatient population in mind: the population of patients organized at the schizophrenic or borderline levels. Although this model seems to have great usefulness for this population, it is not clear how applicable it may be to individuals who have milder forms of character pathology or who are depressed. If, indeed, these higher functioning members have achieved on a premorbid level some integration of positive and negative self and object images, then is it of any value to them to participate in a group that fosters splitting? Because most inpatients are organized at the borderline level at best, this problem applies to an extremely small percentage of hospitalized patients, among whom, no doubt, are individuals who could have been maintained in outpatient treatment.

There are several contraindications for the placement of a patient in an object relations/systems group (Kibel, 1992). Many of these contraindications are shared by other models. A potential member should be excluded from the group if he or she lacks the cognitive resources to grasp the group's proceedings. For example, some individuals who are experiencing the effects of recent electroshock therapy may be unable to attend fully to the group. Individuals with various organic conditions may also experience the group with more confusion than understanding. The group is also contraindicated for individuals who may undermine the integrity of the group. Individuals who are acutely manic, assaultive, or actively suicidal frequently fall into this category. The acutely suicidal require some comment because there are many patients who need hospitalization precisely because of their acute suicidality on admission. For most suicidal patients, the structure and support of the unit rapidly diminishes the threat of self-destructive activity. It is for that small group of patients with whom staff (and often patients) maintain a heightened state of vigilance for signs of imminent suicidal action that group psychotherapy is contraindicated.

The issue of heterogeneity and homogeneity of membership is not one that has received any significant attention in the inpatient object relations literature. A number of writers (e.g., Borriello, 1976; Leszcz, 1989) argue against the creation of a homogeneous group of severely character-disordered or psychotic members because of the high regressive potential of such groups and the immense demands that such groups place on the therapist to manage powerful countertransference reactions. Although there might be some benefit in the inclusion of higher functioning members, fluctuations in the composition of the inpatient population may not permit the creation of a heterogeneous group along the dimension of ego functioning. However, we believe that the absence of heterogeneity should not preclude the use of the object relations/systems model. In fact, we believe that this model is better suited than most other models presented in this text to deal with the regressive phenomena that emerge in the group.

The object relations/systems approach can be applied with different age groups ranging from children to the elderly. Soo (1985) described an object relations activity therapy approach for children. The children engage in activities of varying levels of structure. Inevitably, the activities stimulate the emergence of conflicts among members that can then be explored therapeutically. Setterberg (1991) specifically addressed the use of an object relations/systems model with inpatient children and adolescents and described how the developmentally expected dependency needs of this population will even intensify the dependent aspect of the unit culture beyond what is seen in an adult population. Setterberg discussed how the psychotherapy group's maintenance of stable boundaries vis-à-vis the unit (thereby differentiating the group from the unit) supports the growth processes of differentiation and the establishment of autonomy in its group members.

## Therapist Variables

**Therapist training.** The full understanding and use of this model require a good grounding in and acceptance of psychoanalytic principles in general and object relations and systems theory in particular. Moreover, the therapist must be capable of discerning the dynamics of the group and be able to work with them in the aforementioned theoretical framework. As such a list of competencies suggests, the object relations/systems model places greater demands on the therapist than do some of the other models described in this book, such as educative and problem-solving models. Yet, this model is not at all unapproachable by the therapist in training (Kibel, 1992). The neophyte practitioner can apply this model by attempting to (a) discern and communicate parallels between the material in the group and the events and issues of the unit and (b) foster an atmosphere of tolerance for the full range of feelings that members are likely to express. Although the therapist may not fully grasp the relation between these intervention strategies and, say, the reinstitution of splitting, he or she may be able to accomplish the goals of the model nonetheless. As indicated earlier, the trainee's mastery of principles of general systems theory is more critical to the application of this model than is a grasp of object relations theory (H. Kibel, personal communication, 1992).

   **Co-therapy.** Although the use of this model does not require the presence of two therapists, such an arrangement is highly desirable. The therapists can assist one another in managing difficult countertransference reactions. Differences in co-therapists' countertransference reactions can provide dynamic information about the group. Finally, the presence of two therapists lessens the strength of members' fears that they will be abandoned if they acknowledge aggression toward the leadership.

# Summary

The object relations/systems model is a framework for conceptualizing and supportively treating members' relational pathologies in the inpatient group to enable them to return to their premorbid level of interpersonal and adaptive functioning. The object relations perspective entails accounting for members' failures to have gratifying relationships with others in and out of the group in terms of the self and object images that mediate these relationships. Within this model, hospitalization is seen as a result of the failure of splitting, which is the defensive ability to separate positive and negative images of self and others. The interpersonal consequence of the loss of splitting is that negative affects and impulses, particularly aggressive ones, pervade interactions. This pervasion is seen vividly on the inpatient unit. The ambiguity and multiplicity of relationships on the unit invite members to act out in a chaotic way their negative transferences.

The systems component of this model enables the recognition that the inpatient psychotherapy group is a subsystem of the system of the unit. As such, it contains the elements of the system as a whole. As in the larger system, the group stimulates members' primitive transference reactions. However, the small-group aspect enables the exploration of members' reactions to the regressive influences of the unit. Such exploration of the here-and-now (with the here-and-now including any experience on the unit) enables the deintensification of members' negative feelings with a concomitant strengthening of positive reactions to others. Members' opportunities to express with impunity their dissatisfaction with the various aspects of the treatment, the staff, and unit life supports their reacquisition of splitting. This internal reorganization permits their conduct of more benign relationships with others and more accepting attitudes toward self.

The object relations/systems model has a number of strengths including (a) the clarity of its theoretical base; (b) its recognition and precise characterization of the ego-functioning deficits of many inpatients, particularly the deficits affecting interpersonal relations; (c) its analysis of how patients' interpersonal pathologies interact with the common features of the inpatient environment; (d) its establishment of realistic goals for short-term treatment; and (e) its provision of a line of intervention that is wholly consistent (at least on a conceptual basis) with these goals. Weaknesses of this model include (a) the lack of outcome studies to support its efficacy, (b) the lack of technical development of certain aspects of inpatient group psychotherapy such as selection and pretraining, and (c) the uncertain usefulness of this model in its present form with higher functioning inpatients.

# References

Adler, G. (1973). Hospital treatment of borderline patients. *American Journal of Psychiatry, 130,* 32–36.

Agazarian, Y. (1989). Group-as-a-whole systems theory and practice. *Group, 13,* 131–154.

Agazarian, Y., & Peters, R. (1981). *The visible and invisible group: Two perspectives on group psychotherapy and group process.* London: Routledge & Kegan Paul.

Alonso, A., & Rutan, J. S. (1984). The impact of object relations theory on psychodynamic group therapy. *American Journal of Psychiatry, 141*(11), 1376–1380.

American Psychiatric Association. (1987). *Diagnostic and statistical manual of mental disorders* (3rd ed., rev.). Washington, DC: Author.

Astrachan, B. M., Harrow, M., Becker, R. E., Schwartz, A. H., & Miller, J. C. (1967). The unled patient group as a therapeutic tool. *International Journal of Group Psychotherapy, 17,* 178–191.

Astrachan, B. M., Harrow, M., & Flynn, H. R. (1968). Influence of a psychiatric setting on behavior in group therapy meetings. *Social Psychiatry, 3*(4), 165–172.

Astrachan, B. M., Schwartz, A. H., Becker, R. E., & Harrow, M. B. (1967). The psychiatrist's effect on the behavior and interaction of therapy groups. *American Journal of Psychiatry, 12,* 1379–1387.

Balint, M. (1965). *Primary love and psychoanalytic technique.* New York: Liveright.

Becker, R. E., Harrow, M., Astrachan, B. M., Detre, T., & Miller, J. C. (1968). Influence of the leader on the activity level of therapy groups. *Social Psychology, 74,* 39–51.

Beeber, A. R. (1988). A systems model of short-term, open-ended group therapy. *Hospital and Community Psychiatry, 39*(5), 537–542.

Bellak, L., Hurvitch, M., & Gediman, H. (1973). *Ego functions in schizophrenia, neurotics, and normals.* New York: Wiley.

Bion, W. R. (1959). *Experiences in groups.* New York: Basic Books.

Bion, W. R. (1962). *Learning from experience.* New York: Basic Books.

Book, H. E., Sadavoy, J., & Silver, D. (1978). Staff countertransference to borderline patients on an inpatient unit. *American Journal of Psychotherapy, 32,* 521–532.

Borriello, J. F. (1976). Group psychotherapy in hospital systems. In I. R. Wolberg & M. L. Aronson (Eds.), *Group therapy* (pp. 99–108). New York: Stratton Intercontinental Medical Books.

Braaten, L. (1990). The different patterns of group climate critical incidents in high and low cohesion sessions of group psychotherapy. *International Journal of Group Psychotherapy, 40*(4), 477–493.

Brown, L. J. (1980). Staff countertransference reactions in the hospital treatment of borderline patients. *Psychiatry, 43,* 333–345.

Bunge, M. (1977). Emergence and the mind. *Neuroscience, 2,* 501–509.

Cashdan, S. (1988). *Object relations therapy: Using the relationship.* New York: Norton.

Clark, D. H. (1965). The therapeutic community—Concept, practice and future. *British Journal of Psychiatry, 111,* 947–954.

Durkin, H. E. (1972). Analytic group therapy and general systems theory. In C. Sager & H. Kaplan (Eds.), *Progress in group and family therapy* (pp. 9–17). New York: Brunner-Mazel.

Durkin, H. E. (1982). Change in group psychotherapy: Therapy and practice. A systems perspective. *International Journal of Group Psychotherapy, 32*(4), 431–439.

Durkin, J. (1981). *Group psychotherapy and general systems theory.* New York: Brunner/Mazel.

Fairbairn, W. (1952). *Psychoanalytic studies of the personality.* London: Tavistock.

Fairbairn, W. (1954). *An object relations theory of personality.* New York: Basic Books.

Feilbert-Willis, R., Kibel, H. D., & Wikstrom, T. (1986). Techniques for handling resistances in group psychotherapy with severely disturbed patients. *Group, 10*(4), 228–238.

Friedman, H. J. (1969). Some problems of inpatient management with borderline patients. *American Journal of Psychiatry, 126,* 299–304.

Fulop, G., & Schuman, E. P. (1987). Process parallels in related groups. *Group, 11*(2), 78–84.

Ganzarain, R. (1992). Introduction to object relations group psychotherapy. *International Journal of Group Psychotherapy, 42*(2), 205–223.

Goldstein, W. N. (1991). Clarification of projective identification. *American Journal of Psychiatry, 148*(2), 153–161.

Greene, L. R. (1988). Implications of object relations theory for research on group psychotherapy of borderline patients. In N. Slavinska-Holy (Ed.), *Borderline and narcissistic patients in therapy* (pp. 499–519). Madison, CT: International Universities Press.

Greene, L. R., Rosenkrantz, J., & Muth, D. (1985). Splitting dynamics, self representations and boundary phenomena in the group psychotherapy of borderline personality disorders. *Psychiatry, 48,* 234–245.

Greene, L. R., Rosenkrantz, J., & Muth, D. (1986). Borderline defenses and countertransference: Research findings and implications. *Psychiatry, 9*(3), 253–264.

Grotstein, J. S. (1981). *Splitting and projective identification.* New York: Jason Aronson.

Hannah, S. (1984a). Countertransference in in-patient group psychotherapy: Implications for technique. *International Journal of Group Psychotherapy, 34*(2), 254–272.

Hannah, S. (1984b). The words of the therapist: Errors of commission and omission. *International Journal of Group Psychotherapy, 34*(3), 369–376.

Harrow, M.E., Astrachan, B. M., Becker, R. E., Miller, J. C., & Schwartz, A. H. (1967). Influence of the psychotherapist on the emotional climate in group therapy. *Human Relations, 20*(4), 9–64.

Hirschhorn, L. (1988). *The workplace within: The psychodynamics of organizational life.* Cambridge, MA: MIT Press.

Horwitz, L. (1983). Projective identification in dyads and groups. *International Journal of Group Psychotherapy, 33*(3), 259–279.

Jones, M. (1952). *Social psychiatry (The therapeutic community).* London: Tavistock.

Karterud, S. (1988). The influence of task definition, leadership and therapeutic style on inpatient group cultures. *International Journal of Therapeutic Communities, 9*(4), 231–247.

Karterud, S. (1989). A comparative study of six different inpatient groups with respect to their basic assumption functioning. *International Journal of Group Psychotherapy, 39*(3), 355–376.

Kernberg, O. F. (1973). Psychoanalytic object-relations theory, group processes and administration. *Annals of Psychoanalysis, 1,* 363–386.

Kernberg, O. (1975). *Borderline conditions and pathological narcissism.* New York: Jason Aronson.

Kernberg, O. (1976). *Object relations theory and clinical psychoanalysis.* New York: Jason Aronson.

Kibel, H. D. (1978). The rationale for the use of group psychotherapy for borderline patients on a short-term unit. *International Journal of Group Psychotherapy, 28*(3), 339–358.

Kibel, H. D. (1981). A conceptual model for short-term inpatient group psychotherapy. *American Journal of Psychiatry, 181*(l), 74–80.

Kibel, H. D. (1984). Symposium: Contrasting techniques of short-term inpatient group psychotherapy: Introduction. *International Journal of Group Psychotherapy, 34*(3), 335–338.

Kibel, H. D. (1986). From acute to long-term inpatient group psychotherapy. *Psychiatric Journal of the University of Ottawa, 11*(2), 58–61.

Kibel, H. D. (1987a). Contributions of the group psychotherapist to education on the psychiatric unit: Teaching through group dynamics. *International Journal of Group Psychotherapy, 37*(1), 3–29.

Kibel, H. D. (1987b). Inpatient group psychotherapy—Where treatment philosophies converge. *Yearbook of Psychoanalysis and Psychotherapy* (Vol. 2, pp. 94–116). New York: Gardner Press.

Kibel, H. (1990). The inpatient psychotherapy group as a testing ground for theory. In B. E. Roth, W. N. Stone, & H. D. Kibel (Eds.), *The difficult patient in group: Group psychotherapy with borderline and narcissistic disorders* (pp. 245–264). Madison, CT: International Universities Press.

Kibel, H. (1992). Inpatient group psychotherapy. In A. Alonso & H. Swiller (Eds.), *Group therapy in clinical practice* (pp. 93–112). Washington, DC: American Psychiatric Press.

Klein, M. (1952). *Contributions to psycho-analysis: 1921-1945.* New York: Anglobooks.

Klein, R. H. (1977). Inpatient group psychotherapy: Practical considerations and special problems. *International Journal of Group Psychotherapy, 27,* 201–214.

Klein, R. H., & Kugel, B. (1981). Inpatient group psychotherapy from a systems perspective: Reflections through a glass darkly. *International Journal of Group Psychotherapy, 31*(3), 311–328.

Koch, H. C. H. (1983). Correlates of changes in personal construing of members of two psychotherapy groups: Changes in affective expression. *British Journal of Medical Psychology, 56,* 323–327.

Lerner, P., & Lerner, H. (1980). Rorschach assessment of primitive defenses in borderline personality structure. In J. Kwawer, H. Lerner, P. Lerner, & A. Sugarman (Eds.), *Borderline phenomena and the Rorschach test* (pp. 257–274). Madison, CT: International Universities Press.

Leszcz, M. (1989). Group psychotherapy of the characterologically difficult patient. *International Journal of Group Psychotherapy, 39*(3), 311–335.

Lettieri-Marks, D. (1987). Research in short-term inpatient group psychotherapy: A critical review. *Archives of Psychiatric Nursing, 1*(6), 407–421.

Levine, H. B. (1980). Milieu biopsy: The place of the therapy group on the inpatient ward. *International Journal of Group Psychotherapy, 30,* 77–93.

MacKenzie, R. (1983). The clinical application of a group climate measure. In R. R. Dies & K. R. MacKenzie (Eds.), *Advances in group psychotherapy: Integrating research and practice* (pp. 159–170). Madison, CT: International Universities Press.

Mahler, M. (1968). *On human symbiosis and the vicissitudes of individuation.* Madison, CT: International Universities Press.

Main, T. (1977). The concept of the therapeutic community: Variation and vicissitudes. *Group Analysis, 10,* 2–12.

Marmor, J. (1983). Systems thinking in psychiatry: Some theoretical and clinical implications. *American Journal of Psychiatry, 140*(7), 833–838.

Meissner, W. W. (1980). A note on projective identification. *Journal of the American Psychoanalytic Association, 28*, 43–68.

Miller, J. G. (1978). *Living systems.* New York: McGraw-Hill.

Moos, R. (1974). *Evaluating treatment environments: A social ecological approach.* New York: Wiley.

Moscovici, S., & Zavalloni, M. (1969). The group as a polarizer of attitudes. *Journal of Personality and Social Psychology, 12*, 125–135.

Ogden, T. (1978). A developmental view of identifications resulting from maternal impingements. *International Journal of Psychoanalytic Psychotherapy, 7*, 486–508.

Ogden, T. (1979). On projective identification. *International Journal of Psychoanalysis, 60*, 357–373.

Ogden, T. (1981). Projective identification in psychiatric hospital treatment. *Bulletin of the Menninger Clinical, 45*(4), 317–333.

Rice, C. A., & Rutan, J. S. (1981). Boundary maintenance in inpatient therapy groups. *International Journal of Group Psychotherapy, 31*(3), 297–309.

Rice, C. A., & Rutan, J. S. (1987). *Inpatient group psychotherapy: A psychodynamic perspective.* New York: Macmillan.

Richmond, A. H., & Slagle, S. (1971). Some notes on the inhibition of aggression in an inpatient psychotherapy group. *International Journal of Group Psychotherapy, 21*, 333–338.

Rusakoff, L. M., & Oldham, J. M. (1984). Group psychotherapy on a short-term treatment unit: An application of object relations theory. *International Journal of Group Psychotherapy, 34*(3), 339–353.

Setterberg, S. R. (1991). Inpatient child and adolescent therapy groups: Boundary maintenance and group function. *Group, 15*(2), 89–94.

Soo, E. S. (1985). Applications of object relations concepts to children's group psychotherapy. *International Journal of Group Psychotherapy, 35*(l), 37–47.

Springmann, R. (1976). Fragmentation as a defense in large groups. *Contemporary Psychoanalysis, 12*, 203–213.

Thomas, A., & Chess, S. (1980). *The dynamics of psychological development.* New York: Brunner/Mazel.

Turquet, P. (1975). Threats to identity in a large group. In L. Kreeger (Ed.), *The large group: Dynamics and therapy* (pp. 87–144). London: Constable.

von Bertalanffy, L. (1950). The theory of open systems in physics and biology. *Science, 3*, 23–29.

von Bertalanffy, L. (1966). General system theory and psychiatry. In S. Arieti (Ed.), *American handbook of psychiatry* (Vol. 3, pp. 705–721). New York: Basic Books.

Winnicott, D. W. (1955). The depressive position in normal emotional development. *British Journal of Medical Psychology, 28*, 29–100.

# 6

# The Developmental Model

The developmental model is a psychodynamic approach that is based on the view that psychotherapy groups proceed through stages of growth. Each stage is characterized by a conflict or a set of conflicts that the group must resolve before proceeding to the next stage. These conflicts emerge commonly in the course of human relationships and frequently pose obstacles to members' enjoyment of stable and satisfying relationships in their lives outside the hospital. Because the conflicts that the group addresses reside not exclusively within any individual but within the group itself, all members participate (albeit to varying degrees) in their resolution. The supportive atmosphere of the group enables the group to discover collective resolutions that are generally more favorable than are those that members have achieved in their lives outside the group. These resolutions enhance members' capacities to have more positively toned relationships with others. Moreover, insofar as the resolutions require greater acceptance of some previously rejected part of the self, members' work in the group leads to more positively toned experiences of the self.

## Theoretical Underpinnings

Psychodynamic theory and general systems theory provide the conceptual underpinnings for the developmental model of group psychotherapy. In this chapter, we describe the contribution of each of these frameworks. Because the developmental model shares some theoretical roots with the object relations/systems model, this chapter revisits some of the concepts discussed in the object relations/systems chapter. We thus assume that the reader has some familiarity with these concepts from reading chapter 5.

## The Contribution of Psychodynamic Theory

Psychodynamic theory is inherently a theory of development. Its application to the group setting enables an understanding of what intrapsychic processes are stimulated by the psychotherapy group and what particular themes members address as the group moves from stage to stage. The first psychodynamic account of group development was that of Freud, who saw group development as recapitulating individual development. In *Group Psychology and the Analysis of the Ego*, Freud (1921/1955) described the process of group development as one wherein members form bonds with one another (and thereby become a group) through their common libidinal attachment to the leader, who is perceived as a parental figure. His emphasis on the importance of members' relationships with authority has been incorporated into later models of group development, as has his delineation of the important role of identification both in members' relationships with the leader and with one another.

Bion (1959) extended the observations of Freud by applying the object relational framework of M. Klein (1946). Whereas Freud thought that group psychology could be based on the psychology of the individual, Bion argued that there are processes that transcend the psychology of the individual and are unique to the life of the group. Like Freud, Bion sought to find the essential features that define a group and how members come to form relationships with one another. He argued that the driving force behind members' willingness to maintain a group and relate to the leader and one another is different on a covert level from what it may appear to be on an overt level.

On an overt level, members come together because they have some job to perform and because their activities are motivated by consistency with the demands of this job. For example, members of a psychotherapy group may see themselves as coming together to solve problems. They engage in the discussion of problems because this activity conforms to the explicit goal of the group. In fact, Bion (1959) thought that at times, a group's behavior can be motivated by the stated mission of the group. He referred to a group whose behavior was consistent with its explicit goal as a work group. However, he thought that this state is rare in group life. What makes the work group difficult to achieve is members' perceptions of the similarity between their relationship to the group and the infant–mother relationship. That is, the image of the group as a whole seems to members like a maternal agent and is therefore evocative of members' most infantile anxieties, needs, and fantasies. On a covert level, members bond with one another out of an expectation that by so doing, their need states will be gratified. When a group's activity is primarily motivated by an identifiable need state, then a basic assumption culture is present.

Bion (1959) delineated three basic assumption cultures: dependency, fight/flight, and pairing. A dependent basic assumption culture is one wherein members' behaviors are motivated by the wish to be cared for by an all-powerful parental figure.[1] In the fight/flight basic assumption culture, members act on the unconscious wish to find a leader who will direct them into either fight or flight when the group is threatened. The pairing basic assumption culture is motivated by members' beliefs that their interactions (typically sexual) will produce a messianic figure. For all of these basic assumption cultures, the cognitive processes that members use are akin to Freud's description of primary process, which is characterized by a failure to distinguish between self and other, to observe the laws of logic, and to appreciate the realities of space and time. The work group, on the other hand, uses secondary process, which involves members' deployment of more mature forms of mentation. Bion's concept of basic assumption group cultures ultimately became incorporated into most (if not all) subsequent developmental models.

---

[1] The dependency and fight/flight basic assumption groups are described in greater detail in chapter 5.

Bion's (1959) extension of the Kleinian concept of projective identification to the group situation also has had an impact on developmental models. The concept takes as its point of departure the mother–infant relationship wherein the infant, to maintain a sense of well-being, projects onto the mother his or her unmanageable or disturbing experiences. The mother contains these experiences until such time as the infant can safely re-own them. Bion saw the group as a maternal environment that serves as a container for members' disavowed elements (e.g., affects, impulses). The group (or some part of the group) is perceived by members as connected to, but vaguely separate from, the individual members. Their sense of the group as being somewhat "out there" enables the group to function as a repository for disorganizing elements. The group contains these elements until members can sufficiently tolerate them as parts of themselves. The notion of the group as having a nurturant ambience with resources for containing different types of psychological elements has figured prominently in subsequent theories of group development.

Other observers have noted that the basic assumption themes emerge not randomly but in a predictable order that is consistent with the emergence of themes in individual development. Bennis and Shepard (1956) postulated the existence of developmental phases in the life of the group. They outlined two broad sequential phases: the dependency–power and interdependent personal orientations. The first phase, the dependency–power orientation, incorporates Bion's (1959) dependency and fight/flight basic assumption groups as distinct subphases. Both of these subphases involve members' efforts to address problems with authorities. Members can progress to the next phase only after they have achieved some resolution of the problems of this phase. In the second phase, the interdependent personal orientation, members focus on conflicts that arise in their relationships with one another. Bennis and Shepard (1956) incorporated Bion's pairing culture into this phase. Their concept of subgrouping is also akin to Bion's notion of containment (the process of developing a container) in that it describes how members can project onto a subgroup of members their own rejected impulses and affects.

However, although subsequent developmental writers have seen value in the earlier analytic formulations of group life, they have also seen an important limitation that is epitomized by Bion's (1959) work. Although others (e.g., Ashbach & Schermer, 1987; MacKenzie & Livesley, 1984) recognized that Bion identified certain important phenomena that are unique to group life, they argued that the kind of conceptual scheme he proposed has as its starting point the individual rather than the group itself. For example, MacKenzie and Livesley (1984) wrote,

> Bion fails to conceptualize the group as a social system developing a unique organizational structure. His point of view is derived from the application of a theory of individual psychology to a group setting. His view of the individual/group boundary is from the side of the individual. (p. 284)

A comprehensive model of group dynamics and development requires the use of the group itself as a primary frame of reference. Within such a framework, the group is regarded as a complex organizational system that has properties that are beyond those of the individual but that affect the individual. It is only through a thorough understanding of these properties that the resources of the group can be used fully to further the well-being of the individual group members. Recent models of group development (e.g., Agazarian & Peters, 1981; Ashbach & Schermer, 1987; Beeber, 1988; MacKenzie & Livesley, 1983) build on the work of Freud, Bion, Bennis and Shepard, and others by integrating their analytic notions with the theoretical framework of general systems theory, which advocates the exploration of the group as a social system.

## The Contribution of General Systems Theory

General systems theory (von Bertalanffy, 1950) provides a conceptual vehicle for understanding the complex interrelations among the group, its various subgroups, and the individuals within a subgroup. Use of this conceptual framework expands the psychotherapist's range of resources in effecting individual change. Thus, a systems perspective fosters an awareness that interventions directed at the subgroup and group can change the individual. Because the terms *group* and *subgroup* are critical to this discussion, we will briefly defined them. A group is a social system that is defined by its boundary with respect to the environment external to it. According to Ashbach and Schermer (1987),

> a group is defined by a singular boundary around it which delineates inclusion and exclusion of members and separates it from the extra-group environment. Such a boundary surrounds an unformed aggregate of persons until connections are made among those who are within it. These connections form a matrix through which further differentiation takes place. (p. 116)

The differentiation to which Ashbach and Schermer (1987) referred occurs not only between the group and the environment outside the group but also within the group. Differentiation within the group results in the emergence of subsystems of the group called *subgroups*. A subgroup forms when a perceived boundary is formed between a subset of group members and the rest of the group. Subgroups can occur when members perceive a distinction based on any conceivable variable: age, race, cultural background, or, as is often the case in a psychotherapy group, position on some interpersonal issue. Von Bertalanffy (1950) noted that over time, living systems become more complex. The differentiation of the group into subgroups is one aspect of this complexity. The other aspect, integration, is discussed subsequently.

In view of the apparent physical and psychological boundaries that exist between group members, individual members can accurately be regarded as subsystems of the group. However, because subgrouping occurs as such a natural part of group life, the individual will also generally be a subsystem of some subgroup. The image of a series of progressively smaller concentric circles, from the group to the subgroup to the individual, captures part of the interrelations among these entities.

Another feature of any accurate depiction of these relations is that the boundary separating each entity (or, in this case, circle) from another is not continuous (or closed) but is broken (or open). The open-boundary representation reveals an important phenomenon concerning the relations among these entities: There is a flow of information from one unit to another. Although it would be possible for a system to be completely bounded, such systems are rarely seen in nature (Rice & Rutan, 1987). Permeable boundaries between related systems (or groups and their subgroups) are much more common. That is, there is an ingress and egress of information from one system (or subsystem) to another.

Considering two aspects of system/subsystem relations helps the practitioner recognize how the individual can be treated through interventions directed at the subgroup and group levels. The first aspect to consider is the isomorphy in organizational attributes between systems that exist within the same hierarchy of systems. As discussed in chapter 5, *isomorphy* refers to the repetition of structural features of systems within a given hierarchy. The principle of isomorphy would lead one to expect that dynamics that are present at the group (or macro) level are likely to exist at individual or subgroup levels and vice versa. The second aspect is that as a subsystem of these larger units, the individual group member necessarily has boundaries that are permeable in both directions. For example, if a heightened level of anxiety characterizes the unit on which a group takes place and the group shares a permeable boundary with the unit, then anxiety is likely to infuse the group, its subgroups, and individuals within the subgroups. If some change is made at any one of these levels, reverberation at the other levels occurs. Hence, if anxiety is quelled on the unit, the unit's newfound tranquility is also likely to enter the group and all of its subsystems. Likewise, within the group itself, as the therapist intervenes to help the group move toward a more effective level of organization, the individual whose boundaries are permeable in relation to the other members of the group and the group-as-a-whole is also so led (Durkin, 1982).

A general systems approach is necessarily a developmental approach given that an intrinsic property of any living system is that it is capable of growth and development (von Bertalanffy, 1950, 1968). There are two processes by which growth occurs:

differentiation and integration. *Differentiation*, which has been described previously in terms of the formation of subgroups, refers to the process whereby single units divide into multiple units. *Integration* is the process of synthesis whereby the parts of the whole connect with one another to maintain the integrity of the system.[2] It is within the context of the cycle of differentiation and integration in the evolution of a living system that the concept of *stage* or *phase* is useful to describe the maturation process. From a systems perspective, a stage is a period in which a group is reorganized through the occurrence of differentiation and integration. A group is reorganized when its structure has been altered.

The structural alteration that occurs with development (i.e., as the group proceeds from stage to stage) is by definition a boundary alteration. The process of differentiation entails the creation of new internal boundaries. In contrast, the process of integration is one wherein the flow of information from one subgroup to another increases to such an extent that the boundaries between subgroups dissolve. Once one subgrouping structure becomes obsolete, the group becomes ripe for the emergence of a new form of differentiation. Although the internal boundary configuration of the group changes as the group proceeds from stage to stage, the external boundary structure changes over the course of a stage. When the group is in a highly polarized condition, as occurs when subgroups crystallize, members perceive themselves as primarily affiliated with their subgroup and as having little in common with the members of the group at large. At such times, the boundary between the group and the extragroup environment tends to be weak. This phenomenon is seen, for example, when one subgroup of members is dissatisfied with the group and complains to staff on the unit about the group. As the group proceeds to integrate its differences, members perceive themselves to be more clearly part of the group itself rather than citizens of one of its subdivisions. Members' sense of solidarity

---

[2] Integration does not occur inevitably: The dividing systems may split off and become autonomous systems. Even so, integration of differences between reasonably autonomous systems is likely to occur.

with one another frequently leads to diminished permeability of the external boundary relative to its status prior to the group's integration of subgroup differences. That is, members have a renewed and strengthened sense of we-ness.

In addition to boundaries, there are other structural features of the group social system that may also change from stage to stage, namely goals, roles, norms, and level of cohesion. The goals of the group are a particularly important structural feature. Across all stages, the primary goal for the group is to survive, grow as a system, and master the environment (Agazarian, 1989, 1992). However, within each stage, this primary goal can only be achieved through members' differentiation and integration in relation to the specific conflicts of that stage, whether it be one relating to trust, authority, intimacy, or so on. Because the goal of each stage is to resolve the conflictual differences of that stage and because the conflicts vary, the goals change from stage to stage. The roles that members perform are those behaviors that are required by the system for it to fulfill its goals. The constancy of some goals (e.g, the survival of the system) over the life of the group requires that roles are actively present at all times. However, the presence of some variation in goals from stage to stage is accompanied by variation in the role structure. For example, within a given stage, the system may require the resources of members who can express defiance toward the leader. At another stage, the system may demand the contributions of members who can express tender sentiments toward other members. Group norms refer to implicit rules concerning what patterns of behavior are acceptable or unacceptable. Norms are related to goals in that, as a system matures, the norms become increasingly appropriate to the goal of the group (Agazarian & Peters, 1981). For example, early in the life of a group, members may avoid exploring their difficulties in any serious way despite the fact that this is the expressed purpose of the group. As the group matures, avoidant behavior become less and less acceptable to members and, hence, less common in the group.

A final important structural feature is cohesiveness, which is the degree of connection between subsystems of a system; it is "the degree of magnetism a group has for its members" (Agazarian & Peters, 1981, p. 113). Cohesiveness varies within and between stages. Generally, the cohesiveness of a group tends to reach a nadir early in a stage prior to the differentiation of the group into subgroups. As the group proceeds through the processes of differentiation and integration, cohesion increases. There is also variation from stage to stage. As the group successfully resolves each set of conflicts, enabling them to progress to the next stage, members' senses of attachment to the group as a whole increase. However, at all times in the life of the group, there must be some modicum of cohesiveness to sustain the group through the various developmental challenges that it will encounter.

In summary, then, as a group moves from one stage to another, it undergoes changes in its structural features, particularly its internal and external boundaries. Within each stage, the group is confronted with some common tension or pressure in relation to which members take different positions. Members identify with other members whose positions are similar to their own. As these identifications coalesce, subgroups emerge. To preserve its own existence, the group then proceeds to integrate the differences among the subgroups (Agazarian, 1989). Groups vary from one another on the depth of the integration and the extent to which each individual member participates in this activity. However, for the group to progress to the next developmental stage, the integration must be adequate to dismantle the subgrouping structure of the present stage. Members must come to experience themselves not primarily as members of a subgroup but rather as members of one unified group (Beck, 1974).

## Application of Developmental Concepts to the Inpatient Setting

Developmental concepts have particular applicability to the inpatient psychotherapy group. As a population, individuals requiring psychiatric hospitalization exhibit interpersonal difficulties resulting from their failure to have resolved satisfactorily the earliest conflicts of individual development. Because group development to a large extent recapitulates individual development (Agazarian & Peters, 1981; Saravay, 1978; Schutz, 1958), the early conflicts in individual development are mirrored in the early conflicts arising in the group. Because the inpatient group enjoys membership stability for only the briefest time, it is inevitably these earliest stages in which the inpatient group predominantly resides. As such, the inpatient group provides members with the opportunity to address the conflicts that are most pressing and problematic.

For example, in the first stage, members are occupied with the conflict related to the challenge of trusting others. In this stage, members with prominent paranoid symptoms have the opportunity to circumscribe their use of the projective defenses (i.e., projection and projective identification), thereby expanding their potential for positive relations with others. In the second stage, members work toward the resolution of conflictual stances toward authority. As discussed in the previous chapter, many borderline patients require hospitalization because of the breakdown in the defense mechanism of splitting (Kernberg, 1975; Kibel, 1981). Their failure to differentiate positive and negative self and object representations leads to the perception of others, particularly authority figures, in extremely malevolent terms. The second stage provides members with the opportunity to express and explore their negative feelings toward one another and to an even greater extent toward the therapist. Members' recognizing and accepting their previously "dangerous" feelings fosters their reacquisition of splitting. Hence, proponents of this model regard developmental stages as an area of great potential for the therapist. These stages entail activating those longstanding conflicts that pose a threat to inpatients' interpersonal adjustments and, hence, to their survival in the community.

We describe four stages of group development in the following section. The reader might notice that the number of stages is fewer than that typically described for outpatient groups. For example, Beck (1974) outlined nine stages for a long-term outpatient group. The likely reason for the tendency of writers on inpatient groups (e.g., Beeber, 1988; Brabender, 1988; Rice & Rutan, 1987) to specify fewer stages is that development takes considerable time. Outpatient groups, which generally have greater membership constancy, arrive at developmental stages rarely reached by the inpatient group.[3]

---

[3] The relation between the duration of the group and the number of stages

As in all developmental models, inpatient or outpatient, the stages described do not occur inexorably. Whether a group progresses, regresses, or remains locked within a given stage depends on a variety of factors (Hill & Gruner, 1973). Such factors include, but are not limited to, the characteristics of the membership, the events within the group, and the consistency and permeability of the boundary between the group and the broader environment. Stated simply, inpatient groups have more regressive potential than do outpatient groups. In the inpatient setting, the multiplicity of roles between staff and members, the constant change in membership, and the inevitability of violations of the external boundary of the psychotherapy group (e.g., a group session is canceled for the sake of some "more important" activity) can all hinder the psychotherapy group from making consistent progress through the stages. The therapist who uses a developmental model in the inpatient setting must expect the phenomenon of rapid recycling through the stages. In fact, it may be of some benefit to members to be exposed to this recycling because the conflicts of each stage are never fully and optimally resolved by group members (Bion, 1959; Schutz, 1958). Returning to earlier stages enables members to approach prior conflicts more constructively and thus solidify earlier gains. However, insofar as it is beneficial to members to address a range of interpersonal issues, the group therapist should do what he or she can to foster the kind of group stability that promotes the group's development (Beeber, 1988).

To some extent, the application of the developmental model results in many of the same interventions that a psychodynamically oriented therapist who is not attuned to developmental phenomena would make (MacKenzie, Livesley, Coleman, Harper, & Park, 1986). However, because the developmental model provides the therapist with a framework for anticipating what themes are likely to emerge next in the group, it enables the

---

that a group can complete is not entirely understood. Tuckman (1965) pointed out that in some instances, it is possible for a group to truncate its involvement with each stage and thereby rapidly proceed through what he would consider a full developmental cycle of four stages.

therapist to respond with greater alacrity. This consideration is important given the short-term nature of inpatient group therapy. More rapid detection of group themes and conflicts enables more active intervention on the part of the therapist. The developmental perspective also has the potential to broaden the group psychotherapist's information base in the formulation of interventions. Because boundary structures, goals, roles, and norms vary from stage to stage, the therapist can use any of these structural features to infer the key dynamics of the group at any point in its life. The use of the vast fund of data required by a developmental perspective enhances the therapist's ability to develop an accurate understanding of events in the group.

## Goals of the Model

The general goal of any group developmental model is to help each member more adequately resolve the conflict of each developmental stage than he or she has in the past. Developmental models generally accept the phenomenon of recycling described by Erikson (1950), wherein individuals revisit again and again old conflicts, resolving them more satisfactorily each time. Certainly, the inpatient in a short-term group cannot make the same kind of resolution as can an outpatient who, in a long-term group, has the luxury of exploring these conflicts in depth. The inpatient on entrance into the hospital has resolved many basic intrapsychic and interpersonal conflicts in a manner that has led to the total submergence of one pole of the conflict either through denial, projection, massive repression, or some other primitive defense. Their progress in the group involves making peace with the warded-off side of the conflict, thereby enhancing their awareness of reality and their potential for adapting to the environment. Whereas the goal for outpatients in a long-term group might be a full integration of both sides of a conflict, the goal for inpatients would be their greater acceptance of the existence of dichotomies with their personalities.

Within a developmental model, the therapist helps members gain greater acceptance of all aspects of the self by assisting the group as a whole to work toward accepting differences within the group. Within each stage, the group is presented with a specific set of differences. The goal of each stage is for the group to recognize and accept the presence of a particular type of polarity or conflict. The stage-specific goals are summarized in Table 1.

**Stage 1.** The therapeutic goal of Stage 1 is for members to resolve in a more satisfactory way than they have done in the past the conflict between involvement with others and isolation. Frequently, in the initial sessions of a time-limited group, members will appear eager to get to know one another and to work together. Very typically, members will exchange stories about what brought them to the hospital. Although the initial circumstances and symptoms described will be highly varied, members will gradually move toward articulating a very limited set of themes. Members become struck with how much they have in common (Rice & Rutan, 1987). The particular commonality identified will depend on the group itself. For example, members may excitedly identify a shared difficulty in enduring the pain of a recent loss, or members may ascertain that what binds them together is their boredom with their marital relationships. This search for commonalities reveals a longing on the part of members to bond with one another and to be relieved of the painful perception of themselves as being alone with their difficulties.

Typically, on a more covert level, there are many manifestations of negative feelings about the prospect of involvement with others. For example, despite its vigor, Stage 1 discussion rarely involves members' exchanges of immediate reactions to one another. Furthermore, members often exhibit insensitivity to the genuine emotional reactions of other members. If a member introduces a painful topic, other members may treat it perfunctorily and quickly move on to something more cheerful. Among the many flight behaviors exhibited by members in Stage 1 is a high level of moralizing, intellectualizing, "yes-butting," and advice giving (Agazarian & Peters, 1981; Clapham & Sclare, 1958; Wender, 1946). One feature that all of these behaviors share is that, on the surface, they create the illusion that members are highly involved with one another. However, all of these behaviors close rather than open the boundaries to communication among members (Agazarian, 1992). If any of these devices were to lay bare members' negativity toward involvement, then paradoxically

**Table 1**

*The Goals and Intervention Strategies of the Four Developmental Stages*

| Stage | Goal | Intervention strategy |
| --- | --- | --- |
| 1 | Resolution of conflict between involvement and isolation | a. Support development of healthy norms<br>b. Foster subgroup development in relation to attitude toward involvement in group |
| 2 | Resolution of conflict between fear and hostility toward authority figures and other group members | a. Interpret derivatives of feelings toward therapist<br>b. Explore fantasies of consequences of expressing anger toward therapist<br>c. Emphasize group-as-a-whole and subgroup-level interpretations |
| 3 | Resolution of conflict between overpersonal and counterpersonal orientations | a. Emphasize interpersonal interventions<br>b. Support constructive feedback process<br>c. Identify fears in relation to establishment of intimacy |
| 4 | Resolution of conflict between idealizing and devaluing of group experience | a. Interpret loss-related derivatives<br>b. Interpret subgroup level defensive reactions to loss<br>c. Help members articulate perceptions of progress in the group |

such exposure would force members into a discussion of this fact and into a more genuine level of relating with one another. Hence, members' best defense against involvement is to create the pretense of involvement.

Each inpatient group will show some individuality in the means that it uses at once to hide and to express the wish to avoid interaction. For example, a group may persist in the engaging in the behavior of leaving the door to the group room open, which leaves the group vulnerable to intrusions from the outside. Another group may take flight in the rhetoric of Alcoholics Anonymous. Still another group may focus unduly on the difficulties of a particular member, often one who appears especially helpless. A particularly common strategy that inpatient groups use in conjunction with some of the aforementioned tactics is the development of an inactive subgroup that is distinguished by its silence and its apparent unresponsivity to the events in the group. The member or members who constitute this subgroup refrain from speaking up spontaneously. Occasionally, they are called on solicitously by other members and are asked to account for their silence. Indeed, when they report that they are simply too frightened to speak or regard themselves as having nothing in common with other members, other members respond to them in a way that makes them even more reticent. For example, if members of this inactive subgroup talk about being afraid, other members may then trivialize their concerns or contrast their fears with other members' avowed total confidence in communicating openly. The inactive subgroup serves as a container for members' fears and reservations about involvement in the group. Through the creation of such a container, the group can act as if negative attitudes toward the group exist only within the subgroup; in fact, they exist within the group as a whole.

The many diverse behaviors of Stage 1 suggest that there is conflict between two forces: the wish to engage and the wish to remain apart. MacKenzie and Livesley (1983) described the surfacing of this tension in these very terms:

> The characterological dimension that is particularly important during this stage falls along the lines of sociable/with-

> drawn and trust/distrust. The basic issue for members is
> whether they can accept themselves as interacting social
> beings. (p. 105)

As we discuss, each element in the conflict is multidetermined.

Many factors lead group members to wish to engage with one another. A factor operative in all human bonding is the natural inclination that human beings have to enter into relationships with others (Scheidlinger, 1964; Yalom, 1985). Group participation is also seen by members as a means of satisfying their dependency needs. The members of an inpatient group regard their group participation as an involvement that conforms to the wishes of the staff. They imagine that through this act of conformity, they will be the object of staff's approval, nurturance, and curative powers. Another engagement-fostering factor is members' needs to render whole and consistent their self-perceptions, which have been fractured as a consequence of the process of regression (Kibel, 1978, 1981). Members interact with other members to obtain information that enables them to clarify their own confusing self-perceptions. Finally, as members begin to participate in the group, they quickly learn that many of their difficulties are shared by other members. Particularly when members have a sense of shame attached to these difficulties, they experience a high level of relief, which fosters further engagement. Yalom (1985) labeled this factor, which he saw as therapeutic in its own right, *universality.*

There are also many factors that lead members to wish to maintain their separateness from one another. This wish is derivative of the urge that all human beings share to be autonomous and individuated. As members experience their yearnings to connect and even fuse with one another, such wishes stimulate "anxiety over total loss of the self and, thus, lead to compensatory needs for distance, autonomy, and independence" (Greene, 1983, pp. 4–5). It also has its roots in members' more concrete fears of the consequences of involving themselves with one another. Although members see their acts of involvement as conforming to authority's demands, they also fear that such involvement will limit their capacity to receive on an individual, personal level what authority figures can provide. Moreover, involvement with one another requires that members take responsibility for their own and one another's progress. If they were to assume such responsibility, members' actions would be at odds with their belief that help can come only from authority figures. Hence, members' strong dependency wishes conflict with their desires to enter into relationships with one another. They see the formation of relationships with one another as jeopardizing the possibility of having their dependency needs gratified within the group. Members also recoil from commitment to the group because the poor boundary differentiations of many of the members who enter inpatient groups give rise to the fear that they may catch one another's symptoms. Members also fear being rejected by other members of the group. They dread the anticipated feelings of shame and guilt that they imagine will follow their exposing certain loathed parts of the self.

In many inpatient groups, members' desires to connect are more conspicuous than are their wishes to remain separate and individual. However, there are some inpatient populations such as narcotic addicts (Osberg & Berliner, 1956) and "institutionalized delinquents" (Shellow, Ward, & Rubenfeld, 1958) that show blatant hostility and negativism on entrance into a group. Their reactions have led to the postulation of a pre-Stage 1 in some populations, particularly antisocial ones, in which members need to be "won over" before they are willing to engage with one another (Tuckman, 1965). We see such a postulation as unnecessary because all groups demonstrate an admixture of the two opposite-poled wishes. In populations whose members have experienced chronic and severe frustration of dependency needs, the expectation that compliance brings fulfillment is not a strong one and, consequently, must be cultivated within the group itself. We address variations in therapist interventions for these different groups in the technique section.

Regardless of which wish is more conspicuously present, the goal for the therapist is to help members effect a reconciliation between the opposing forces of connection and separateness. Certainly, for the group to continue, the wish to connect must prevail over the wish to remain separate. The primary means by which this goal can be achieved is through the clear expression of both poles of the conflict and the identification by all members with each of the poles. In other words, members are likely to make a full commitment to working with one another through the acknowledgment of not only positive but also negative feelings toward group involvement. The importance of group-as-a-whole recognition of members' positive feelings toward involvement is perhaps obvious: The articulation of these feelings enhances members' hopefulness and motivation to work within the group. Less obvious may be the usefulness of members' expressions of negative feelings about the group. It is important for members to recognize that negativity toward involvement exists as a force within each member and within the group as a whole: As long as a subgroup contains a significant affect, impulse, or fantasy for the group, the group cannot become cohesive. Moreover, the group's failure to take seriously members' fears about the group hinders the application of group-level reality-testing activities in response to these fears. Hence, what members consciously disavow or trivialize, they are doomed unconsciously to accept.

In Stage 1, when members see that they can express the unspeakable truth of fearing the group, with impunity, their trust of the other members and of the group as an entity is enhanced. This trust is exhibited by greater openness not only within the group but elsewhere in the hospital as well. Hence, like both the object relations/systems model and the interpersonal model, the developmental model predicts that successful engagement with the group will enhance members' involvement in all aspects of hospital life. As indicated earlier, successfully completing Stage 1 is particularly important for those group members who either chronically or through regression use paranoid defenses. Although Stage 1 completion does not lead these patients to abandon the use of projective defenses, they do begin to contemplate the possibility that other oases of safety do exist.

**Stage 2.** The goal of Stage 2 is to help members develop greater tolerances of their feelings of anger and envy toward one another and the leader through awareness of the ubiquity of these feelings in the group and through actively testing the anticipated consequences of expressing such feelings. This greater tolerance makes less necessary their use of projection and projective identification in ways that lead to further deterioration of their relationships with others.

The special challenges of this stage have their roots in Stage 1. Although members find relief in their identification with one another during Stage 1, they do not perceive such identifications as leading to the furtherance of their well-being in any substantive way. In Stage 1, members are united in the undeclared expectation that if any real help is to be obtained, it will come from the therapist. As Agazarian and Peters (1981) wrote in describing the dependent stance of the fledgling group, "The basic assumption . . . is [that] the benevolent leader will somehow rescue the group and each and every one of its members" (p. 133). In Stage 1, much of the group's vibrance is borne out of the expectancy that the ministrations of the therapist will soon be forthcoming; during this stage, the therapist is an idealized figure who is seen as capable of effecting not only the cessation of psychological pain but also the satisfaction of infantile longings for nurturance.

As many have noted, the group moves from a focus on issues related to engagement and trust to a focus on negative feelings toward both the authority figures in the group and one another (Beeber, 1988; Powdermaker & Frank, 1948; Rice & Rutan, 1987; Shellow et al., 1958; Tuckman, 1965). The group's transition to Stage 2 occurs as members experience nascent concerns about what the group and the leader are not providing. Entrance into Stage 2 is signaled by members' disguised expressions of resentment toward the therapist. Often, these expressions take the form of dissatisfaction with authority figures outside the group (e.g., the hospital, bosses, parents). As dissatisfaction builds, members usually become bolder in their expressions of feelings toward the therapists by focusing on authority figures within the hospital such as attending psychiatrists or the head nurse of a unit. Members also express their dissatisfaction by violating the external boundary of the group through lateness or absence. During this time, members put greater effort into encouraging the therapist to expand his or her range of provisions to the group (Kaplan & Roman, 1963). For example, members may ask the therapist technical questions about the side effects of certain drugs. The members' success in getting the therapist to provide what the other members cannot renews members' hopefulness that the therapist will exhibit magical powers on their behalf. It also gives members a temporary and illusory sense of control over the therapist's actions.

In Stage 2, the group gradually differentiates into characteristic subgroups. Typically, a counterdependent subgroup (Bennis & Shepard, 1956) develops that rejects the leadership of the group as well as the group's norms. This subgroup often takes the position that the group does not need the therapist. This message may be conveyed by members' blatant disregard of the therapist's comments or, as K. Dies (1991) described for adolescent groups, by behavior that members expect will win the therapist's disapproval (e.g., putting their feet up on the furniture, chewing gum noisily). It may also be shown by verbalized criticism of the therapists or by members' attempts to create an alternative structure to that presently existing within the group. For instance, someone may propose a round-robin format for a group that had been to that point an open forum. The emotional tone of the communications of members in this subgroup is generally antagonistic.

Another common subgroup is distinguished by its compliant stance toward the leader. This dependent subgroup (Bennis & Shepard, 1956) attempts to execute what they believe to be the wishes of the leaders. This subgroup responds to the expression of any negative feelings toward the staff either with disapproving silence, commendations of the staff, or explanations for staff members' seemingly objectionable behaviors. Such a vigorous response to angry expressions is necessitated by members' convictions, usually unconscious, that other members' hostile manifestations will lead to retaliation by authority. For example, the leaders of the group may withhold help or expose members' weaknesses to the other group members.

Although these two subgroups are invariably present in Stage 2, there are also other types of subgroups that commonly develop; the membership of these subgroups may overlap with that of the aforementioned subgroups. For example, very often, the group subdivides into the "haves" and the "have nots." One group may complain that a particularly monopolistic member is "getting all the attention." Another group may identify those members who have sufficiently severe problems to warrant the group's attention and others who appear to be able to manage on their own. Still another group may classify the members into who has and has not been helped by hospitalization.

The various subgroups of Stage 2 represent the group's different strategies for dealing with hostility toward and disappointment in the therapist as well as feelings of envy and competition toward one another. Each subgroup embraces a particular defensive strategy that masks an array of negative feelings and thereby allows members to preserve their ties with the idealized therapist. For example, the dependent subgroup attempts to manage negative feelings through unquestioning compliance and rationalization. At the same time, they can act out competitive impulses toward other members by striving for perfection as group members and thereby vanquishing (at least in their imagination) their peers in the eyes of the therapist. The therapist's goal during this stage is to diminish the strength of each subgroup's intolerance of negatively perceived affects (e.g., anger and envy) by fostering the recognition that their negative feelings are shared. Through this recognition, members experience increasing freedom in expressing their negative feelings directly. Such freedom eventually leads members to a group-as-a-whole confrontation with the leader. This confrontation signals a shift from a competitive to a cooperative mode of relating. With the group-as-a-whole acknowledgment of the therapist's imperfections and limitations as well as the anger and disappointment that such frailties have stimulated, members no longer see themselves as needing to wait for the therapist's divine ministrations. The abandonment of the view of the idealized therapist permits a more realistic appraisal of the many resources that members have to help one another. In a sense, then, in Stage 2, the members supplant the figure of the therapist with the image of the group.

Progress in Stage 2 is particularly important for borderline inpatients in particular because during regression, they are overwhelmed with aggressively toned impulses and feelings (Kibel, 1981). Through the establishment of a target for these feelings and through the validation of these feelings by members' awareness that they are shared by other members, the intensity of members' aggression is diminished. Such an attenuation permits the emergence of more positively toned and harmonious interactions with others. Group members also profit from the therapist's maintenance of a consistent posture in the face of their testing of limits (K. Dies, 1991). The therapist's consistency reinforces the internal boundaries of the group and thereby lessens members' fearfulness of the dangers of being with others.

**Stage 3.** During this stage, members experience working cooperatively as a group (Beeber, 1988; Grotjahn, 1950; Mann & Semrad, 1948; Powdermaker & Frank, 1948; Rice & Rutan, 1987; Thorpe & Smith, 1953). According to Rice and Rutan (1987), the members have "moved beyond a stage of simply sharing their experiences, or criticizing the group, to attempting to understand their experiences together" (p. 59). In this stage, the goal for members is to have experiences of accepting and being accepted by other members as individuals. As we discuss later, the main vehicle for the accomplishment of this goal is the process of feedback.

As the group enters Stage 3, the emotional climate of the group is extremely positive. It is frequently characterized by joyfulness, playfulness, and tranquility. At no time in the prior life of the group are members more open to communication with one another. After having been under the yoke of the preoccupation with the leader in the last two stages, members are now able to discover other group members in a genuine way and to attend to the specificities of one another's interpersonal styles. That is, the members learn that other members of the group have distinctive manners of relating and that these manners differentially affect each member of the group (Beeber, 1988; Brabender, 1985; Livesley & MacKenzie, 1983).

The sunny atmosphere of Stage 3 leads members to be struck by one another's positive qualities. Members may notice that one member is able to articulate others' feelings well, that another member is skilled at breaking tension, and that still another member effectively confronts members whose behaviors divert the group from its work. The therapist may notice that much of the positive feedback that members offer one another is superficial and even inaccurate. Members convey positive feedback not so much to give useful information but to build an illusion that the group is a sanctuary where members will find unconditional acceptance. As this illusion comes to be challenged, a subgroup of members, representing an overpersonal orientation (Bennis & Shepard, 1956), will band together to protect it.

Rarely does the group's exclusive focus on one another's positive qualities last: The group gradually recognizes one another's more negatively perceived features. Bennis and Shepard (1956) and Agazarian and Peters (1981) hypothesized that the greater closeness among members in early Stage 3 stimulates anxiety that connection or intimacy with others will involve loss of the self. Typically, a subgroup of members representing a counterpersonal stance (Bennis & Shepard, 1956) will use the group's newfound ability to recognize differences defensively (Agazarian & Peters, 1981; Beeber, 1988; Burnand, 1990). They will engage in behaviors that are at odds with the group norms as a means of establishing distance between themselves as individuals and other members (Beeber, 1988). Although some members may retreat from the intimacy of the group through silence or manifestations of boredom, others may do so by offering other members negative feedback.

As in the case of positive feedback, the specific content of the negative feedback is of limited therapeutic value because it is based on a superficial level of observation. That is, members share little more about one another than first impressions. In this regard, the inpatient group is different from the outpatient long-term group wherein the particular content of the feedback is highly important in effecting change. However, when the therapist shapes the feedback so that it is operational (i.e., highly concrete) and reasonably unchallenging to the self-esteem of its recipient (much along the lines advocated by Yalom, 1983, in the interactional agenda version of the interpersonal model described in chapter 4), the negative feedback is of potential benefit to members. The careful molding of negative feedback by the therapist allows the overpersonal subgroup to recognize that the identification of differences does not require the traumatic dissolution of self-esteem. In fact, such members have an opportunity to see that negative feedback can be esteem bolstering. It enables the recipients to substitute globally condemnatory thoughts such as "Others find me totally worthless and contemptible" with more specific and hence less disturbing thoughts such as "Others find it difficult to take an interest in what I am saying when I speak at length and show no interest in others." Hence, in defining what parts of themselves others find objectionable, these parts are delimited and a healthy process of splitting furthered.

The counterpersonal subgroup also profits from the opportunity to offer negative feedback. Other members' tolerances of their communications helps the counterpersonal members feel that their self-protective efforts will be accepted in the group. Their experience of connection without engulfment challenges the necessity of the strong defensive barriers that they have erected between themselves and others. This experience paves the way for their engagement in nonthreatening, more libidinally toned exchanges with other members of the group. Moreover, when the deliverers of negative feedback see that the expression of their contained aggression leaves the recipient intact, the interaction reduces the individual's sense of his or her destructive capability and the concomitant guilt and anxiety.

Hence, for both the overpersonal and counterpersonal subgroups, successful Stage 3 participation increases members' openness to a greater range of communications and affective experiences in relationships. Through their Stage 3 work, members' capacities to achieve intimacy in relationships deepens.[4]

**Stage 4.** Stage 4 does not occur as a natural developmental outgrowth of Stage 3. In a closed-ended group, it occurs in re-

---

[4] The reader may notice that *feedback* is regarded in a very different way in this model than it is in the long-term outpatient interpersonally oriented group. In the latter, the content is crucial in helping members to correct distorted perceptions of self and others. In the inpatient group, members use feedback to address problems in the acceptance of positive and negative affects in peer relationships. Sometimes, however, a particular piece of feedback serves an additional function. The first author had an opportunity to treat members in a short-term inpatient group and to continue to treat them in a long-term outpatient group. Occasionally, members would use an observation from the inpatient group as a kind of transitional object (Winnicott, 1965). That is, the piece of feedback that members would mention frequently (almost like a mantra) would serve as a device to cull up their image and positive feelings about the inpatient group.

action to the impending conclusion of the group. In an open-ended group, Stage 4 is precipitated by the departure of one or more members who have become well-established in the group.[5] Indeed, members' exploration of Stage 3 issues ends without their full resolution. Members of inpatient groups are unable to accomplish the task of integrating positive and negative views of self and others that can (and should) be pursued on an outpatient basis. Behaviorally, Stage 4 is marked by a reduction in the frequency and intensity of group interactions. Members become more focused on symptoms and are less inclined to engage in here-and-now exploration. Gradually, loss-related themes emerge in the group's discussion, but rarely at this time do group members directly examine the loss of the group itself. Instead, members talk about extragroup losses such as the death of significant figures in their lives, the loss of youth, or the loss of a job. As the date of termination approaches, members increasingly focus on losses related to the experience of hospitalization itself such as the departure of a friend or a favorite staff member from the unit or their own discharge from the hospital. As the sadness in relation to these losses becomes more fully palpable, an especially sensitive member or the therapist will raise the possibility that the group's sadness is also linked to the loss of the group.

The introduction of the notion that the loss of the group constitutes a significant event challenges members (a) to explore their range of emotional reactions in relation to this loss and (b) to assess the group's usefulness in furthering members' well-being and preparing them for discharge. However, never do groups perform these tasks willingly. Quickly, subgroups emerge that perform some aspect of the task of dealing with loss while ignoring other aspects. Two subgroups are especially prominent during this stage. One subgroup disavows the importance of the group experience and the intensity of members' emotional reactions toward one another. The particular form of dismissal of the group varies from member to member of this subgroup. For

---

[5] Beeber (1988) observed that in an open-ended group, the departure of one or two members did not necessarily influence group development.

example, one member may articulate the sentiment, "This has been very nice but how important could an experience be that lasts only two weeks?" Another member may use devaluation by invidious comparison: "I don't mind so much that the group is ending because my individual therapist is back from vacation."

The other major subgroup idealizes the group experience. During the last stage, members tend to compare the group experience with other life experiences (MacKenzie & Livesley, 1983). For this subgroup, such comparisons commonly lead to a deprecation of other groups and people outside of the present group. Comments such as "No one has ever accepted me the way this group has" or "People in here are just more sensitive than people on the outside" are common.

Each subgroup's response is a way of denying the reality of the loss of the group and the feelings (fear, sadness, anger, guilt, etc.) associated with this reality. The idealizing subgroup acts on a common unconscious fantasy that if the group is not criticized, it will not be destroyed. Such members deny their negative feelings toward others as means of holding onto valued relationships. Frequently, those members who idealize the group during this last stage of group development are individuals who are unable to grieve significant losses in their lives. They maintain an active relationship with their idealized image of the lost object. In contrast, those members who devalue the group spare themselves the experience of loss through their obliteration of the memory of the good group (e.g., "What did not happen cannot be missed"). At the same time, they do not incorporate what was positive about the group experience. Again, there are other subgroups that may develop. For example, some members may have a very intellectualized reaction to the loss; other members may become very absorbed with postdischarge plans as if the group has ended already. For all subgroups and for the group as a whole, the acknowledgment of both positive and negative feelings toward the group experience is important. For the devaluing subgroup, the capacity to identify certain positive aspects of the group enables them to reestablish the boundary between the "good" and the "bad." It provides them with practice in reevoking splitting in the face of loss. For the idealizing subgroup, the ability to articulate the negative component of their emotional experiences in group leads to further fortification of their positive image of the group and themselves. That is, the threat of the aggressive images of the group are neutralized through their overt expression in the group.

Although the effort to help members acknowledge negative and positive reactions to the group and its loss may appear to be aimed at the goal of fostering integration of positive and negative self-images and object images, such a goal is generally regarded as too ambitious for most inpatients (e.g., Kibel, 1981). However, the ability to integrate good and bad self-images and object images exists on a continuum. Some group members will have a greater capacity to engage in integration than will others. The members who can use the inpatient group to move toward integration of representations are those who in their outpatient lives have already made some progress toward this goal. However, for the vast majority of inpatients, a more realistic goal of this stage is the reinforcement of the process of splitting, which is also served by helping members express with impunity positive and negative feelings toward the group.

## The Change Process

Within this model, each stage presents the group with a fundamental conflict pertaining to human relationships. These conflicts are ones that emerge inside and outside of the group for all people. Inevitably, members will hold different positions in relation to these conflicts. These differences will lead to the formation of subgroups wherein members who take the same position on an issue ally with one another.

The group's differentiation into subgroups creates tension within the group. Each subgroup finds another subgroup expressing with disturbing vividness its own most unacceptable psychological contents (i.e., forbidden thoughts, impulses, feelings, fantasies). At each stage, members are faced with the option of responding to this tension by dissolving completely into different subgroups or by integrating the differences among them and thereby remaining a group. Members are compelled to maintain the group by their attachment to one another and by the sense of loss that would attend the group's dissolution. Members

are led toward dissolution by their anxieties over the consequences of recognizing within themselves the psychological contents expressed by the other subgroups. Within a long-term outpatient group, there are certain natural forces that operate to
lessen members' anxiety about identifying with one another;[6] in
the inpatient group, the group's movement toward integration
rather than fragmentation depends more crucially on the activities of the therapist. It is essential that the therapist help members articulate their fears of particular impulses and feelings and
engage in active testing of their fearful anticipations. However,
even without such therapist interventions, members of each
subgroup are ever-watchful of the consequences that members
of other subgroups face in expressing what they perceive to be
the forbidden. As they see that such members are able to do so
with relative impunity, members' tolerances for their own
warded-off experiences increase.

Because the individual member is a subsystem of both his or
her subgroup and the group as a whole, as the subgroups move
toward the acceptance of previously renounced psychological
experiences, so does the individual. The consequence of this
movement for the individual is a lessening of the use of the
primitive defenses of projection and projective identification to
ward off unacceptable affects and impulses. As a healthy form
of splitting supplants the more primitive projective defenses, the
individual's acceptance of both self and others increases.

# Technical Considerations

## The Role of the Leader

In long-term outpatient groups, the therapist who applies a developmental model can respond in a relatively nondirective fash-

---

[6] For example, in writing about a training group, Bennis and Shepard (1956)
discussed the important role of the "independent person" or individual un-
conflicted in the area in which the group was working in moving from one
stage to another. In the inpatient group, one cannot count on the presence of
such individuals among the group members. The therapist must perform the
functions served by these independent individuals as described by Bennis and
Shepard.

ion and can allow certain processes inherent to group life to move the group forward from one stage to the next. In the short-term inpatient group, the therapist must be much more active in assisting the group to resolve the developmental conflicts of each stage and ensuring that all members of the group participate in this resolution. Although there are some intervention strategies that are specific to each developmental stage, there are others that are useful in all stages. The latter consist of (a) the regulation of the external and internal boundaries of the group, (b) the creation of an emotional climate of acceptance and openness through the therapist's demonstration of tolerance for and empathy with members' feelings, and (c) the facilitation of the processes of differentiation and integration of subgroups. We describe each type of intervention in turn.

The developmentally oriented inpatient group therapist must pay constant attention to the external and internal boundaries of the group to ensure their stability. Although a stable external boundary is important for most of the models described in this text, its absence in this model may more sharply limit the model's viability. For the developmental model to be applied, the group must possess sufficient autonomy to be a bona fide group (i.e., a system that has the capacity to develop its own structural properties that may be distinct from those of the system in which the group is embedded). The group's emergence as a distinct system requires that the therapist safeguard the time, meeting place, and frequency of group meetings. According to Beeber (1988), "useful techniques for highlighting the group's boundary are closing the door on time, leaving empty chairs for absent members (patients assigned to the group, but too disturbed to attend), and enlisting group members' support in encouraging latecomers to be on time" (p. 583). The predictability of changes in membership also contributes to the delineation of the group's external boundary. In most short-term settings, the pressure to place incoming patients in a group immediately makes closed-ended groups unfeasible. However, the external group boundary is made more salient if there is an order to members' introductions to and departures from the group (e.g., new members begin the group on Monday). Finally, the external boundary of the group is also fortified through the existence of a supportive position of the broader system vis-à-vis the group (Rice & Rutan, 1981). The best assurance against violations of the group boundary by the broader system is the system's understanding and endorsement of the goals, framework, and methods of the group (Borriello, 1976).

Maintenance of the group's internal boundaries is also important because stable internal boundaries support the group's growth. The boundary between acceptable and unacceptable group behaviors must be drawn clearly by the therapist. The therapist must outlaw those behaviors that would undermine members' sense of safety. Whereas in a mature long-term outpatient group, it may be appropriate for the group to interpret the rules, in the inpatient group it is essential for the therapist to assume this responsibility so as to ensure members' comfort. The internal boundaries of the group should also be fortified through members' clear awareness of the group's mission. During the orientation, the therapist should outline what the group is and is not designed to accomplish.

Second, the therapist must promote the development of an atmosphere wherein members feel that their communications are accepted. In each stage, members are called on to express affects that are unacceptable to themselves and that they expect to be unacceptable to others. The therapist should respond to such communications with supreme equanimity, understanding, and compassion because the self-disclosing individual, particularly in the initial two stages of development, will be exquisitely attuned to how the therapist is receiving his or her disclosures. In fact, many of members' fears about the possible negative consequences of certain types of expression will pertain specifically to how the therapist is likely to react (e.g., will the therapist get angry and reduce the patient's privileges on the unit?). In addition, other members are likely to take the therapist's lead in formulating their own responses to those self-disclosures that seem especially foreign and frightening. Probably the most important requirement for the therapist's achievement of consistent empathy is the mastery of his or her countertransference. It is generally the therapist's effort to ward off unpleasant identification with members' conscious or unconscious feelings or impulses that prevents him or her from maintaining a strong empathic tie with members' experiences (Hannah, 1984). The therapist must accept that unpleasant countertransference reactions are common fare. Part of therapist training within this model involves learning how to approach such reactions with an exploratory rather than a defensive stance (Brabender, 1987).

Third, the therapist must nurture the processes of the differentiation of members' positions on the central issue of each stage and the integration of these positions. The therapist can catalyze the process of differentiation—or, as Agazarian (1992) referred to it, *functional subgrouping*—by helping each group member ally with one or more other group members. For example, the therapist might say, "Sheryl, you've been talking today about being peeved with me because I was called out of group for an emergency. It reminds me of how you, Anna, commented on my appearing preoccupied yesterday. It seems that some members wonder if the group has my full attention." The intervention not only links the reactions of different members but also helps the subgroup articulate its position. Such an articulation is necessary if ultimately members outside the subgroup are able to identify with it in some respect.

Once subgroups have differentiated themselves from one another, the group can either move toward greater fragmentation (ultimately leading to the physical or psychological disbanding of the group) or reconcile their different positions in some higher order configuration. The latter resolution will lead to an even greater sense of closeness among members than at any prior point in the life of the group. To help members engage in integration rather than fragmentation, the leader must take an actively interpretive role by assisting the group to recognize the fears that prevent the group as a whole from explicitly identifying with the psychological content being expressed by a given subgroup. Also, the therapist might use techniques that make members' acknowledgment of a particular element less threatening. For example, if a group is exhibiting difficulty expressing anger, the therapist might use the subjunctive form, saying, "Suppose you did feel angry toward me. How would you expect me to react?" (Brabender, 1985; Yalom, 1983). In other words, the therapist must skillfully titrate the distance between members and their own experiences so that experience becomes more tolerable rather than more threatening.

## Assessment and Preparation

In chapter 4, the concept of the levels group was introduced. In the levels group, individuals are placed in a group on the basis of their receptivity to different types of intervention (Leopold, 1977; Yalom, 1983). In Yalom's (1983) scheme, potential group members are viewed as low functioning if their ability to relate to others is enhanced primarily by nonexploratory or supportive interventions. Although higher functioning patients benefit from supportive interventions, they also are able to benefit from interventions that raise their awareness of how their interpersonal styles affect others. The developmental model is optimal for use with the higher functioning inpatient. The good candidate for this group is a patient who profits from greater awareness of the effects of his or her social behaviors as well as from insight into how social behaviors are linked to warded-off (but relatively accessible) fantasies, feelings, and impulses.

Exclusionary criteria for the developmental model include the presence of cognitive disorganization due to any number of factors including acute psychosis, central nervous dysfunction, or the effects of recent electroshock therapy. Extreme agitation or threatening behavior toward others should also preclude the patient's placement in a group of this type.

The recommended mechanism for selecting group members is the screening interview, which enables the therapist to determine the suitability of each patient for group and provides potential members with basic information about the group. Preferably, the interview is conducted in a small group in which 4 to 5 members are interviewed simultaneously. The small group format has the obvious advantage of efficiency over individual interviews because the therapist does not have to repeat the presentation of the group for each prospective member. This time-saving feature enables the therapist to give a more elaborated presentation of the group than would typically be possible in a series of individual interviews. Another advantage of the small group interview is that it is possible to obtain a sample of a patient's group behavior, which may be relevant to the decision of whether the patient is appropriate for the group.

The interview is divided into three parts. In the first part, the therapist gives a didactic exposition of the group and clearly delineates the goals and methods of the group. Members should also be told which potential goals will not be pursued in the group (e.g., symptom relief, solutions to practical problems). In the second part, the therapist provides information about logistical and structural features of the group such as time, place, and rules. Patients are given an opportunity to have answered any questions about the group. In the third part, the therapist individually interviews each patient in the presence of others about the circumstances that precipitated hospitalization, any prior group psychotherapy experiences, and the attitudes formed toward group psychotherapy from these experiences. Often, the patients' accounts of the reasons for their hospitalizations provide some indication of their capacities to engage in self-exploration. Patients who focus on their symptomatology and adamantly reject the notion that difficulties in relationships might be related either to their symptoms would probably fare better in another type of group. Often, other patients will respond spontaneously to the patient who is being interviewed. These responses are almost always supportive and should not be discouraged because they serve to enhance all participants' motivations to enter the group.

## Locus and Level of Intervention

Whereas some models presented in this text have a constant locus of intervention (e.g., exclusively within the here-and-now) or a single level of intervention (exclusively individual, dyadic, or group-as-a-whole centered), the locus and level of intervention of this model are highly variable. Both locus and level depend on the group's stage of development. In the following section, we discuss the types of interventions that are appropriate for each stage.

**Stage 1.** One of the most important goals for the therapist during Stage 1 is the establishment of healthy group norms. Norms are those explicit or implicit rules that guide members' behaviors. There are three norms that are particularly important to establish during Stage 1: (a) the group's focus on immediate experience (i.e., their present reactions to one another, the therapist, and events in the group), (b) the expression of feelings and impulses in words rather than actions, and (c) the group's maintenance of consistent internal and external boundaries. Although we discussed the importance of stable boundaries, we make several comments about the first two norms.

Helping the group focus on its own immediate experience constitutes a considerable part of therapist activity during Stage 1 because generally groups will discuss concerns ostensibly lying outside the group. For example, in the earliest sessions, members will focus on the circumstances that precipitated their hospitalizations. The group therapist strives to gradually shift the group's focus from outside to inside the group by using a combination of individual, interpersonal, and group-level interventions. For example, the therapist might ask a member what he or she experienced while another member was poignantly describing her experiences prior to hospitalization, direct a member to comment on an especially nurturant interaction between two members, or make group-level comments about the caring that members are showing one another. Movement toward an immediate focus is likely to stimulate considerable anxiety. To keep members' anxiety within tolerable limits, the therapist must encourage esteem-enhancing communications among members.

The therapist encourages the expression of affects and impulses by assisting members who are exhibiting some feeling states nonverbally to label their experiences. For example, rather than allow a member to sob for a protracted period in the session, the therapist should quickly assist him or her in describing exactly what this uncomfortable experience is like and what event in the group precipitated it. Such comments should be followed by an exploration of how the group-as-a-whole participates in the feeling or impulse that has now been expressed verbally so as not to allow an individually centered comment to diminish cohesiveness.

In Stage 1, the therapist must also help the group achieve cohesiveness because cohesiveness enables members to accept previously disavowed parts of the self. That is, as members come to value the group-as-a-whole and the other members of the group and come to recognize that others share the feelings and impulses that they reject, they are better able to accept these previously unacceptable contents. It is also through cohesiveness that members are able to retain a perception of themselves and the group as being acceptable in the face of their attack on authority in Stage 2. The cornerstone of cohesiveness is the process of identification or the recognition of some shared elements of experience. The gradual building up of identifications from the individual level to the subgroup level to the group-as-a-whole level transforms a collection of individuals into a bona fide group.

In the earliest moments of a group's life, members identify with one another on individual bases. In early Stage 1, a diversity of issues and concerns are presented and most members show an ease in finding one or more other members with whose experiences they can identify. Invariably, there will be members who fail to identify with other members of the group. The therapist must help these individuals to identify with at least one other group member. In fact, when members do not achieve at least one identification, they are highly vulnerable to premature terminations (Dugo & Beck, 1984). If the majority of members in a group show greater interest in isolation than in involvement, the therapist must avoid the kind of deductive group-as-a-whole approach described by Ezriel (1973) wherein a group-as-a-whole concern is identified followed by an exploration of how each individual member relates to this concern (e.g., the previous example of the therapist leaving for an emergency). Despite the value of group-as-a-whole comments in promoting cohesiveness in many groups, this type of intervention intensifies such members' fears that involvement will lead to the dissolution of the boundaries between themselves and others. With groups composed of members who show a high level of fearfulness about group involvement, the therapist should rely more heavily on the inductive group-as-a-whole approach suggested by Horwitz (1977). Using this approach, the therapist responds to individual concerns and slowly (but inexorably) moves toward identification of the group-level issue. For example, the therapist might help a single member identify a feeling, help another member associate to it, and ultimately help all members see that the feeling is a force within the group at large.

In addition to helping each individual become involved in the group, the therapist supports the crystallization of the engaged and the nonengaged subgroups of Stage 1. Although one of these subgroups will develop more conspicuously than the other, the therapist must place his or her investment in helping the less conspicuous, complementary subgroup develop. In the most typical inpatient group, it is the engaged subgroup that achieves prominence in Stage 1. The therapist's effort, then, must be to get the subgroup expressing the opposite wish to achieve its own cohesiveness. This can be done by showing members how different manifestations (e.g., getting lost on the way to group, not speaking in the group, a member's commenting that he or she is completely different from all other group members) may reflect a common underlying disposition of not wanting to be involved with other group members.

The group's differentiation into these positions creates a tension within the group for reconciliation. The tension derives from members' tacit recognition that the differentiation threatens the integrity of the group. Inpatient groups are highly variable in the extent to which they are able to effect an integration of these positions without the intervention of the therapist. Generally, the more polarized the subgroups, the more reliant they are on the therapist's conflict-resolving interventions. Moreover, the less skilled that individuals in the engaged subgroup are at expressing affect and showing empathy with others' experiences, the more the therapist needs to assist them in identifying with the positions of others that are ostensibly different from their own. Flexibility is essential in responding to each group's unique resources for conflict resolution.

One type of intervention that is very helpful in moving the group toward an awareness of the conflict between engagement and nonengagement is the pairing of group-as-a-whole and individual interpretations (Brabender, 1985). Such a pairing involves identifying a common underlying motive and the individual positions that members hold in relation to this motive.

An example of the combined interpretation would be the following:

> There was a part of each group member that felt like running out of the room. Yet, each of you covered up your fear of being in the group in a different way. Mary's way was to philosophize about the meaning of life; Margaret's way was to giggle when anything serious was said in the group; Harold's way was to declare the group as "boring." Perhaps you are using these means to hide from yourselves and one another the very understandable fear of being involved with one another.

This type of intervention serves many purposes. It presents as legitimate members' desires for separateness and recognizes members' individualities (i.e., each member has an individual defense), thereby lessening their fears of fusion. At the same time, it brings members together and fosters cohesiveness through the articulation of commonalities.

**Stage 2.** In Stage 2, the therapist helps the group move toward a collective expression of dissatisfaction with the therapist through a combination of interpersonal and group-as-a-whole interventions. Early in Stage 2, some members will be more undisguised in their expressions of dissatisfaction than will other group members. For example, whereas one member may openly criticize the therapist for not providing sufficient direction, another may express discontent by looking at the clock frequently. The therapist supports these members in coalescing as a subgroup by pointing out that all of these behaviors are variations on a single theme.

The therapist must also actively support the coalescence of the subgroup that contains fear in relation to the expression of aggression. Depending on the diagnostic composition of the group, this subgroup may be less conspicuous and may require more of the therapist's nurturance than may the overtly angry group. Failure of the former subgroup to cohere adequately may lead individual members to feel trepidation over the risk of becoming the target of the aggression of the more overtly hostile subgroup. One challenge that the therapist faces is the tendency of the fearful group to act out their affect through an array of overly compliant behaviors that have won the acceptance of past authority figures.

Another major activity of the therapist in Stage 2 is undermining the occurrence of scapegoating. Although scapegoating can occur in any stage, its potential in Stage 2 is particularly great (Dugo & Beck, 1984), and the consequences for the scapegoated individual as well as for the group are more damaging. Many members find their own hostile feelings to be repugnant and dangerous; as a consequence, they use one another's expressions of anger as opportunities to project their own hostile feelings onto this individual (Scheidlinger, 1982). Such a figure becomes a scapegoat when members perceive this person as uniquely expressing hostility and then reject the person for so doing. Members may develop the fantasy that the group would be a perfect place if this angry member were not present. If the scapegoating is fully consummated by the scapegoat being expunged from the group, then members will feel intensified guilt rather than relief. The scapegoat will have received confirmation of his or her perhaps most dreaded fear in relation to the consequences of experiencing and expressing hostility: Hostility leads to loss and rejection.

To obviate the unfolding of this dynamic, the therapist must help members recognize that individual expressions of hostility as well as fears of hostility are reflective of forces present within the group-as-a-whole. The therapist can avert scapegoating in a number of ways, only a few of which we cite. First, the therapist can exhibit an accepting attitude toward members who are expressing hostility, verbally or nonverbally. Second, the therapist can restate members' complaints in the most general terms possible to facilitate other members identifying with the complaint. For example, if a member complains about the group therapist's failure to give him or her a diagnosis, the therapist might comment, "I bet there are others who feel that the staff, including perhaps, the staff in this room, have information they are withholding from you." Generally, some other members will be able to relate to this general formulation of dissatisfaction. A third method is to establish as "grist for the mill" not a given member's hostility but other members' difficulties in relating to this hostility. Framing the problem in this fashion sets the stage for analyzing members' fears in relation to the expression of hostility.

In addition to managing scapegoating in Stage 2, the leader is challenged by the group's efforts to get him or her to be more forthcoming. As discussed in the goals section, in this stage, members will pose technical questions to the therapist (e.g., "Does Halcion make people jittery?") or make unmasked bids for the therapist to provide advice to concrete problems (e.g., "Do you think I should leave my husband?"). Within this model, the therapist offers support and understanding but never specific directives. In Stage 2, direct answers to members' questions have a number of negative consequences. They interfere with members' burgeoning expressions of hostility toward the therapist (in fact, frequently the therapist's "answers" are motivated, usually unconsciously, by the wish to avert such an expression). They also weaken the internal boundaries of the group by clouding the purpose of the group. That is, in this model, members are in the group to learn to deal with the emotions that emerge in interpersonal relationships, not to get answers to problems. Finally, answers undermine members' senses of their own coping resources by removing from them the responsibility to solve their own problems.

Once clear subgroups have formed in Stage 2, the therapist's task is one of supporting the group in integrating both sides of the conflict between fear and hostility. One of the greatest contributions that the therapist can make to this integration is the demonstration of an even-handed attitude of acceptance of both of the dominant subgroups. However, once the subgroups have consolidated, the therapist should foster cross-subgroup identifications. For example, the therapist might select a member in the fearful subgroup who expressed a more moderate position than did others in that subgroup and encourage this member's empathic grasp of the expressions of some members of the hostile subgroup. Finally, the therapist might urge each subgroup to articulate its fantasies of the consequences that the other subgroup is likely to face for the position that it espouses in the group. For example, the subgroup that adopts the counterdependent position will often anticipate that members of the dependent subgroup will become like helpless infants. Once these fantasies surface, they are available for comparison with reality.

**Stage 3.** In Stage 3, members have the opportunity to experience many of the psychotherapeutic processes that are characteristic of an outpatient group. In this stage, the group faces issues that pertain to the establishment of intimacy in the group, with some members expressing a yearning to develop close emotional ties (overpersonal subgroup) and other members trying to ward off that effort (counterpersonal subgroup). In helping members differentiate into subgroups, the therapist should work primarily at the interpersonal rather than at individual or group-as-a-whole levels given that in this stage, members are keenly interested in their relationships with specific other members. It is because of this interest that members for the first time in the life of the group have the opportunity to partake of the process of giving and receiving feedback.

Early in Stage 3, the overpersonal subgroup coalesces easily with little or no therapist intervention. The members of this subgroup spontaneously offer others positive feedback that results in large part from the sanguine feeling that follows the resolution of Stage 2 authority issues. The egosyntonic nature of the feedback can be used by the therapist to teach members to offer comments that refer to member behavior (rather than traits or abstract qualities) and to acknowledge their own reactions to other members' behaviors (thereby reducing the judgmental aspect of the feedback). For example, if a member says, "I like Alice—she's such a kind person," the therapist might encourage not only that member but others to specify what behaviors of Alice's seem kind and what feelings these behaviors evoke in other group members. When members' enchantment with one another fades and when members become more sensitive to one another's negative qualities, these skills will enable them to deliver a full range of observations, positive and negative, in a constructive manner. Yalom (1983, 1985) provided additional suggestions for the therapist's support of a healthy feedback process. Some of these suggestions are cited in chapter 4 on the interpersonal model.

As the group continues, those members who feel anxiety in relation to the group's expression of loving, tender feelings toward one another become more active. They attempt to curtail the intimacy that the group has achieved by using negative feedback defensively. That is, negative comments about others are used not to convey useful information to other members but to subvert the group's sense of closeness. The therapist's response to this development is crucial to the group's progress. On the one hand, the therapist must discourage any communication that would be narcissistically wounding to other members. On the other hand, the therapist must support the emergence of this side of the conflict so that the group as a whole can better address it.

There are several means by which the therapist can negotiate this therapeutic dilemma. One is to hold members to the guidelines for delivering feedback that are established early in Stage 3 (e.g., the feedback must refer to specific behaviors rather than to qualities of the person). Another means is to solicit actively the feedback of other members to convey the notion that there are a diversity of views on each member. Still another means is to encourage members to give feedback primarily to those who are in their subgroup. The counterpersonal members often find relief not only in the dispensation of negative feedback but also in the reception of it. In either case, they feel protected against the libidinal feelings that are stirred up early in this stage. As in the earlier stages, the therapist might assist each subgroup in recognizing the fears attached to identification with the other subgroup's position. Finally, the therapist might work to assist members in each subgroup in discriminating differences in their positions (Agazarian, 1992). For example, some group members who earlier were content to exchange positive feedback with one another will find the contributions of the more counterpersonal subgroup members to be intriguing. These members may recognize the potential utility of negative as well as positive comments. Their views of what types of information are helpful in the group might be differentiated from those of other members in their subgroup who insist that only narcissistically bolstering comments are helpful. This differentiation of positions within a subgroup and the support of cross-subgroup identifications paves the way for the integration of the differences among the subgroups. However, given the typical membership instability in the inpatient group, rarely does the group complete the integrative task of Stage 3.[7]

**Stage 4.** In Stage 4, the therapist pursues the goal of helping members accept a diverse set of affects that are related to the loss of the group by working on a primarily group-as-a-whole level. The imminent ending of the group leads to the rapid emergence of subgroups. The therapist's activity must be directed toward supporting the crystallization of the subgroups by aiding members who have similar positions in relation to the event of loss identify with one another. Each subgroup is organized to defend against some affect and fantasies in relation to loss, typically the affects and fantasies associated with the perception of the group as either beneficial or inadequate, perhaps even damaging. As mentioned in the Goals section, the imminent loss of the group stimulates a variety of fantasies (e.g., the belief that if they acknowledge sadness in relation to the ending of the group, they will have caused its ending). Members can be encouraged to articulate these beliefs and, to whatever extent possible, test them out in the group. For example, if the members express a belief that their lavish praise of the group will lead to its indefinite continuation, the therapist can assure the group that the group will end at the prescribed time regardless of their sentiments toward it.

In the final stage, the therapist should nurture members' positive dispositions toward continuing treatment on an outpatient

---

[7] In a long-term outpatient group, the issues that emerge in this stage provide the therapist with opportunities to work on a more interpretive level with members to promote the integration of positive and negative self and object images. As discussed earlier, such a goal is inappropriate for inpatients because most group members have regressed to a position at which the defense of splitting is no longer functioning. Consequently, each developmental stage must be used to bolster splitting, thereby creating a foundation for the outpatient therapist to do more interpretation and integrative work. What the inpatient group therapist can feasibly do is interpret the motives that are attached to the rejection of particular psychological contents. What the outpatient group therapist can do beyond this level of interpretation is explore the motives attached to the maintenance of splitting (e.g., avoidance of abandonment anxiety) and the fears associated with the integration of self and object images of different valences.

basis. Members' appraisals of both the group and their progress should be supplemented by feedback from other group members. When a member hears other group members describe the strides that he or she has made, it reinforces that member's perception that therapy is a valuable tool in enhancing one's well-being. Such reinforcement is particularly potent when members use this newfound ability (from Stage 3) to formulate feedback in operational or concrete terms.

## Content of the Session

The developmental model involves the conduct of an unstructured session in which members are encouraged to express spontaneously their thoughts and feelings. The content of what members express is associated with the developmental stage in which the group is residing. The group moves from an exploration of commonalities and issues related to trust (Stage 1), to a focus on authority issues (Stage 2), to an examination of peer relationships (Stage 3), to an analysis of loss-related issues (Stage 4).

The content of a session using the developmental model shares with the unstructured version of the interpersonal model a focus on members' immediate reactions within the group session. However, relative to the interpersonal model, the developmental model places greater emphasis on the feelings and impulses that members are attempting to ward off through the formation of subgroups and the use of other group-level defenses. Relative to the developmental model, the interpersonal model focuses more intensively on the study of the social consequences of behavior (i.e., whether particular behaviors lead to more positively toned or negatively toned relationships). Except for in Stage 3, behaviors are of interest in the developmental model only in their capacity to reveal feelings, fantasies, and impulses.

In comparison with the object relations/systems model, the developmental model places less emphasis on establishing linkages between events in the group and issues on the unit. However, the developmental model by no means precludes the analysis of group–unit relationships. Whereas the object relations/ systems model treats members' reactions to the group as symbolic expressions of their responses to events on the unit, the developmental model treats members' discussion of events on the unit as symbolic expressions of their reactions to the group. Relative to the object relations/systems model, the developmental model places more emphasis on internal boundary analysis through its focus on subgroups. In attending to group–unit relations, the object relations/systems model focuses more intensively on the group's external boundary. Finally, the developmental model involves a more continuous and intensive focus on how the group's history affects current interactions within the group. Although the object relations/systems model does not preclude interventions that focus on the group's history, its emphasis on group–unit relations would make such historical comments less common.

# Clinical Illustration

This clinical illustration of the developmental model is drawn from a closed-ended, eight-session group in a private psychiatric hospital. The group was in its third session. Each session lasted 90 minutes. All group members had been referred to the group by their attending psychiatrists. They had all proceeded through a screening interview. The group members came from four different residential units.

## Group Members

Vance, a lawyer in his late thirties, entered the hospital following a severe depression that appeared to be precipitated by having been "busted" for selling cocaine and subsequently being disbarred. This highly intelligent young man was prone to mood swings. Although staff complained of his demanding behavior on the unit, in his first two group sessions, he was exceedingly deferential. He frequently indicated that he found merit in the leaders' comments, particularly those of the senior leader.

Millie, a woman in her midforties, indicated during the screening interview that she was attempting to "get over" the ending of her marriage 4 years prior. Over the past 4 years, she had made a number of suicide attempts. The most recent one was apparently associated with her former husband's announcement of his upcoming wedding. As in the case of her earlier hospitalizations, Millie assumed an extremely buoyant mood on being hospitalized. During the first two sessions, she frequently asserted her prior connection with the senior therapist while reserving the terms *honey* and *dear* for the therapist in training.

Herman, a man in his early sixties, was forced into early retirement by his brother-in-law, who engineered a buy-out of their co-owned furniture business. Herman was brought to the hospital by his daughter, who found him to be exhibiting the same irritability and cognitive disorganization that preceded a full-blown manic episode 5 years ago. During the first two sessions, he tended to ramble about his difficulties and showed little attunement to others' contributions.

Ron, a man in his early thirties, lived with his parents and was unable to work because of chronic and frequent epileptic seizures, which were only partially regulated by antiseizure medication. His social adjustment was marginal. Although he had a few friendships with other men, he lacked the social skills to initiate a relationship with a woman, although he was highly desirous of such a relationship. He came to the hospital because his parents observed that he had been forgetting to take his medication, was sleeping excessively, and was neglecting his physical appearance. There was no clear precipitant to his decline, although his parents noted that Ron had increasingly articulated despair about ever being able to achieve an intimate relationship. He was on the same unit as Millie and had been taken "under her wing." In the prior sessions, Ron had exhibited little discomfort on the frequent occasions when she had spoken for him.

Barbara, a woman in her midthirties, entered the hospital because of the mixed symptoms of depression and anxiety associated with a recent mastectomy. Despite having been given a "clean bill of health," Barbara was constantly tearful and everwatchful of new signs of illness. Her depression and somatic ruminations interfered with her return to work. During the first two sessions, she was highly active and skillful in articulating her own feelings and those of the other members.

Kate, a woman in her midfifties, had been a nun since her early adulthood and had worked as a head nurse in a Catholic hospital. In her work as a nurse, she had been exhibiting excessive suspiciousness of her subordinates and accusing them of stealing drugs and making denigrating comments about her to the patients. Her symptoms appeared to be temporally linked to the recent death of her mother. During the first two sessions, she had been somewhat withdrawn. However, she had had several positive interactions with Barbara, to whom she was obviously drawn. She eagerly assured Barbara of her high prospects for good health.

Jenny, a young woman in her early twenties, was adolescent in both appearance and manner. She ran away from home when she was 14 and since then had lived independently of her parents. She had been hospitalized repeatedly and was chronically suicidal. She was reasonably active during the first two sessions and frequently disarmed the other members by her willingness to comment on the group's process.

## The Session

The session begins with only six of the seven members and two therapists present.

> Therapist: I didn't receive a message from Herman.
> Millie: He's probably trying to sell someone a couch. He'll be here. (she notices that Ron seated next to her is continuing to solve a crossword puzzle) You can stop now.
> Vance: (sighs loudly and puts his leg on the arm of his chair speaks in a weary tone) Don't expect anything from me today . . . Bad night!
> Millie: (sarcastically) Don't worry . . . we never expect anything from you. (She then laughs at her own joke.)
> Jenny: (addresses Vance sympathetically) I heard you arguing with that nurse. She's a bitch!
> Vance: (shakes his head with disgust and then begins haltingly) I was . . . going to leave this morning. My doctor . . . he came . . . persuaded me to stay. But

|        | I don't know. I might not stay . . . I might stay. I don't know. |
|--------|------------------------------------------------------------------|
| Millie: | (solicitously) What happened, babe? I saw you at dinner last night. You went back for seconds of turkey and stuffing. I saw you do it. You looked fine then. So what happened, hon? Tell Mama Millie! |
| Vance: | (winces and says bitingly) Just what I need . . . another mother. (Millie giggles) Anyway . . . last night after dinner . . . after my second helping, I go back to my room and I'm not sitting there two minutes and in comes Mr. Undergraduate Psychology Major, B.S., Extraordinaire and he's going to counsel me on my problems. "How are you feeling today, Vance? Are you still feeling depressed, Vance? Do you still feel like you need some crack, Vance?" Now let me take a little poll. Who here is paying $650 a day to have a psych tech advise you on the fine points of life and love? |

There is a brief discussion wherein members express confusion and disagreement over what the per diem charge is. Vance does not participate.

| Vance: | Okay, so that was just the first thing. Then, I bring in this little TV . . . you know, the mini-portable type and Sergeant Head Nurse, otherwise known as Your Royal Highness of Kookland, says, "I am very sorry but those are not allowed here . . . if you wish to view a show . . ."—can you believe that, she said, *view a show?*—"you must join the others in the community room. Now I don't know how to put this delicately . . . I don't want to offend anyone . . . but some of these people are just not my cup of tea. |
|--------|--------------------------------------------------------------------------------------|
| Jenny: | Talk to me after group. I know this place. I know how to get around in it. (Barbara and Kate exchange glances.) |
| Vance: | And then . . . when I go to use the phone, I'm told, "fifteen minute limit" . . . now you're not going to tell me that everyone who gets on that phone stays on for only 15 minutes. I think these nurses have something against me . . . maybe because I'm a |

professional . . . I don't know . . . but I was thinking about these things all night. I couldn't sleep so I got up early and packed my bags.

Kate: (responds with a cautious tone, apparently attempting to be diplomatic) You know, Vance . . . I've worked in a hospital for over 30 years. I can't help but to see it from the side of the administration. If you don't have rules, you have chaos. The rules may not always meet everyone's individual needs but they do bring order and safety.

Vance: (with a dismissing tone) Yeah, well I think they have special rules for me.

Barbara: I'm not on your unit, Vance, so I can't comment on how things are there, but I do want to react to something else you said. The psych techs on my unit are among the most helpful, sensitive people I've met here. I don't think it matters what degree a person has. The first night I got here, I was so upset. My psychiatrist left and the aide sat and held my hand all evening. I'll never forget that.

Millie: (nodding her head as Barbara speaks, quickly and ebulliently responds) Yeah, there are some really nice people here. But I have a wonderful relationship with my doctor and that's what's important to me. He's the one who holds my hand when I feel like jumping off a bridge. When I have trouble with the nurses on my unit . . . some of them are a little, um, uptight about certain things, he comes to my defense immediately. Like the time they wouldn't let me keep my cat on the unit and he told them it was okay . . .

Kate: (interrupts with incredulous and slightly disapproving tone) A cat on the unit? From a hygiene perspective . . .

Millie: (shrugs) Well, I couldn't find any place for her to stay, and I wouldn't put her in a kennel. It was just for one night anyway. (After Millie delivers her comment, members ask her to identify her doctor and she does so. She proceeds to give several other instances of her psychiatrist's special treatment of her.)

| | |
|---|---|
| Ron: | (shifts in his seat and says in a monotone voice) I have the same doctor. (There is a brief silence in the group.) |
| Jenny: | (looking increasingly disturbed as Millie was speaking) My doctor spends 5 minutes with me . . . if I'm lucky. |
| Ron: | (nodding) Sometimes 5 minutes would be a lot. |
| Millie: | (proudly) I've just never had that problem . . . I've never had a session that lasts less than 45 minutes. |

Several members, Ron, Jenny, and Herman begin to speak at once.

| | |
|---|---|
| Herman: | (prevailing over the other voices speaks with a tone of annoyance) Is there any way to change psychiatrists? |
| Therapist: | It looks to me that a number of members are quite understandably hurt and angry and frustrated. It is quite painful to discover that other group members are receiving more time, attention, and special favors from the staff . . . |
| Barbara: | (speaking before the therapist can complete her thought) Well, I use to get frustrated because my doctor would come in and he would be so rushed and so obviously in a hurry to get to the next person that I would forget what I wanted to tell him. (Members nod) But then, I figured that if I make a checklist, I wouldn't forget. So that's what I've been doing and it has really worked out. |
| Kate: | That's a great idea. I'll try that tomorrow. |
| Herman: | (furrowing his brow) This whole place . . . I mean, she says she gets 45 minutes. I get 2 minutes. He (pointing to Ron) has the same doctor and he gets 5 minutes? So where's the fairness in that? I'm disgusted with this whole place . . . just like Vance is. |
| Therapist: | And maybe the group is part of that disgust. After all, in the two sessions we've had so far, certainly some members have gotten more of the group's attention than others. |
| Millie: | This is my favorite group. |
| Herman: | Well, if you ask me it hasn't exactly been earthshattering. |

Barbara:   (puzzled and hurt) What do you mean? I thought you got a lot off your chest yesterday. We tried to help you. Were we just wasting our time?

Herman:   I'm worried that I may be wasting my time . . . I still have a brother-in-law who took my business away. I'm still depressed. In fact, I think talking about it in here made me even more depressed. (turning to the therapist) What am I supposed to do? (gestures vaguely to the other group members) I mean, you're nice people but how are you supposed to know what I should do?

Millie:   I told you yesterday, just forget about the company. Start a new life for yourself. Anyway, what do you expect the therapist to do about your predicament?

Vance:   Well, obviously, she can't do anything about it, but she can say something about it . . . what is she being paid for anyway?

Therapist:   Vance, you sound annoyed and so did Herman a moment ago. And I think there are others in the group who are feeling the same way, too.

Jenny:   (turning away from the therapist, speaking to Herman) You're not going to get answers in here. I've been in group before and it's always the same way. Face reality. Everything you do here is on your own.

Vance:   Well, if we have to do everything on our own, why did we bother coming here anyway?

Jenny:   Ask them!

Vance:   I will . . . Okay, what are we doing here waiting for you to give us answers when you're not going to give us an answer?

Barbara:   (nervously interceding) Well, no one can really give you answers. They can listen . . . they can guide you a bit perhaps. And the therapists have been doing that.

Millie:   That's right . . . these therapists have gone to school and are highly trained. My doctor says that he has a lot of respect for them.

Vance:   (with a derisive tone) Yeah, but if I just needed someone to listen to me, I could talk to your cat, Millie.

Several group members snicker.

Kate:    I have a suggestion. What if we work on each person's problem for 5 minutes. We'll tell the group a
problem and then the group can develop a plan for
that person. The therapist can then let us know if
it is a good one.

A long pause occurs. One member looks at the clock.

Therapist:    Throughout this session, I've been hearing a lot of
frustration and exasperation with first the unit and
then with the therapists. Right now it seems you're
angry with us for a number of things but especially
for not giving you clear and specific solutions to
your problems, solutions which you feel you very
much need. You feel that we have something that
you need and we're keeping it from you. Naturally,
that's infuriating. At the same time, I'm sensing that
it has been a bit frightening, maybe to some members more than others, to let us know that you feel
anger toward us.

Kate:    (with a matter-of-fact tone) It's not our position to
tell you what to do.

Therapist:    (addressing the entire group) But what if you did?

Ron:    (tentatively) You might get disgusted and leave . . .
like this therapist I had last year. He gave me assignments to do between sessions. But they seemed
dumb to me so I didn't do them and it was like,
"Who are you to challenge my authority? I am the
doctor and you are the patient." So you know what
he did? He transferred me to someone else. And
that's not the first time I've been transferred.

Jenny:    That stinks . . . although I'm not surprised!

For the next few minutes, members exchange stories about therapists abandoning patients including some pertaining to the staff
of their units.

Therapist:    So perhaps one concern that Ron may have and
perhaps others have is that if the group challenges
us by either criticizing the group or doing things in

|  | here the way you want them done, that we'll abandon ship. |
| Barbara: | Ron, I just don't think that's true. I mean, I don't understand why that therapist did what he did but I don't think that will happen here. |
| Co-therapist: | Barbara, maybe you have a different picture of how I might react if you or another member express your feelings and opinions about the group. |
| Barbara: | Well if I did think you were not being as helpful as you might . . . I . . . I . . . wouldn't really say anything! |
| Therapist: | Because if you did say something, I would . . . ? |
| Barbara: | You're so calm in here all the time and I think that probably you wouldn't do anything but act very pleasant. But I'd still . . . I don't know . . . feel foolish. |
| Therapist: | Perhaps you think we would see you as being foolish. |
| Kate: | That's the worst thing . . . having people see you as a fool. Before I came in here I thought everyone was seeing me as a fool. |
| Barbara: | And now? |
| Kate: | I'm not sure of anything anymore . . . I never thought I would say something like that but it's true. |
| Vance: | You know, Sister, that's not the . . . |
| Kate: | I asked you to call me Kate . . . |
| Vance: | Whatever . . . that's not the worst thing . . . not to me . . . hey, you know these staff members are talking about us when we walk out the door. I take it for granted. Like what happened to me last night. First thing this morning, my doctor was in my room saying, "Now, I hear there were a few problems last night?" So she, I mean the head nurse, must have written me up. She must have. |
| Co-therapist: | And we might do that too? |
| Millie: | Not you, Honey! |
| Vance: | Well, I know you do that because my doctor already mentioned to me something that you wrote. |
| Therapist: | Yes, we do write progress notes every day, but it sounds as though you're worried that we might use them as weapons to retaliate against you if you upset us. That's a pretty frightening thought. Naturally |

|  |  |
|---|---|
|  | it's going to want to make you be very careful with us. Perhaps others feel that way also. |
| Ron: | I do. (He laughs nervously.) |
| Barbara: | (turns to the therapist) Why don't you tell us that you won't laugh at us and maybe we'll feel better. |
| Therapist: | I could do that, but I'm not sure that just saying it, you would believe me. I think that as the group goes on, if you see any evidence of me laughing at you, even in a subtle way, you should let me know. I, in turn, will let you know if I am laughing at you. |
| Jenny: | I don't know what all the fuss is about. I say, so what if you laugh at us? So what if you tell my doctor? What is he going to do about it anyway? I can sign myself out whenever I want to. |
| Vance: | (laughs) You know, you're right. I mean, this morning, he seemed more worried that I would leave than anything else. |
| Jenny: | They need us more than we need them. In fact, I think about that movie *One Flew Over the Cuckoo's Nest* and how they all got on that bus and had a great time and no one felt depressed or sick anymore. |
| Millie: | (with exuberance) That's who we need in here, McMurphy. (then, turning toward the therapist) Sorry, you'll have to be Nurse Ratchet. (The entire group giggles.) |
| Vance: | Not ratchet, Ratched! |
| Jenny: | How about wretched? (Kate laughs—Jenny looks at her with astonishment and then with pleasure.) |
| Ron: | Yeah, that movie was great. I saw it nine times. |

Other members talk about the movie in positive terms and briefly pursued the fantasy of where they would go if they had access to a group bus. The group members now appear more relaxed and engaged. There is some discussion of the upcoming weekend and some leisure activities scheduled in the hospital. The session is coming to a close.

|  |  |
|---|---|
| Therapist: | Earlier in the session, you had the courage to talk about your dissatisfaction with the group. Some talked about the lack of answers, others talked |

about the inadequate order or structure. But, in a way, I think you felt you had to walk on eggshells in sharing with us these complaints because of a fear that we might respond to them by using our authority against you . . . leaving you, laughing at you, reporting you.

Vance:  All of the above.

Therapist:  Perhaps these fears were so strong because of some of the feelings you explored in yesterday's session . . . that being hospitalized makes you feel helpless . . . like you need to lean on others. Yet, toward the end of this session, I have been hearing something a little different. Some awareness has been developing in here that maybe you can help yourselves more than you thought but also maybe you can help one another in powerful ways. And when you think of it in that way, perhaps letting us know what is on your mind and what you don't like isn't such risky business after all. See you tomorrow.

## Comment on the Session

Early in the session, there were some behavioral manifestations of the group's move to Stage 2: one member's lateness (Herman), another member's expression of fatigue (Vance), another member's absorption with his crossword puzzle (Ron). Vance's complaints about the unit were also a derivative or displaced expression of his concerns about the group: concerns about control, the competence of the authority figures, the impact of the pathology of other members. Certainly, the therapists might have moved more quickly to explore parallels in the group with his outside experience. However, there were two benefits to be had from allowing other members' to react to his complaints and to formulate complaints of their own. The first benefit was that it enabled members to approach authority issues with less anxiety than if they, in early Stage 2, had focused on their relationships with authority directly. As members expressed their dissatisfaction, they had an opportunity to witness the therapist's reactions to determine whether the therapist would accept or disapprove of their negative feelings toward authority. Members experience the disclosure of negative feelings toward the therapist as less risky if they observe the therapists' acceptance of their displaced expressions of negative feeling toward the therapist.

The second benefit of allowing the group to elaborate on the derivations of their concerns about the therapists is that it enables the group-as-a-whole conflict to emerge with greater clarity. In this example, what seemed most evocative for members was their sense of deprivation by caretakers as well as their perception that others were getting more from caretakers. Such clarity assists the therapists in formulating interventions that will have significance for many group members.

In this particular session, subgroups emerged very quickly as members talked about their frustrations with their lives on the unit. Several members (Vance, Herman, and Jenny) were united by their counterdependent posture, revealed in their mistrust of authority and their relative ease in expressing negative feelings toward authority. This subgroup's activity stimulated the emergence of another subgroup (Millie, Barbara, and Kate), which performed the function of opposing and thereby holding in check the former subgroup's expressions of hostility. Herman's rather global expression of dissatisfaction with the hospital provided the therapist with an opportunity to move the group to an exploration of authority themes within the group. The therapist endeavored to help members express angry feelings more directly within the immediate context of the group. Once the major subgroups crystallized, the therapist consistently interpreted members' reactions to staff on the unit as derivative of their responses to the therapist. This strategy represents a departure from the object relations/systems approach in which the therapist might be just as likely to encourage members' elaborations of their reactions to staff outside the group. Within the present model, a major aspect of the therapist's facilitation of members' direct expressions of negative feelings toward the therapist was her encouraging members to identify fears associated with the expression of hostility.

As is often the case in this group, the identification of the fears led to some effort to test their reality basis in the experience of the group. The therapist attempted to provide support to this process by encouraging members to notice and comment on her reactions to their communications. Regardless of how much effort a group puts into the reality-testing process, the mere identification of the fears associated with certain types of communications leads to their abatement. Concomitant with the lessening of fear is the greater acceptance of hitherto-rejected affects, impulses, and fantasies. Such psychological contents no longer need to be rejected because they are no longer perceived as dangerous. One manifestation of members' increased tolerances of their own psychological experiences is the weakening of the subgrouping structure and the growth of cohesiveness in the group as a whole. In this example, members' participation in the bus fantasy, which expressed a successful repudiation of authority's wishes, illustrated this process of group unification.

# Status of the Research

## Effectiveness of the Model

To date, there are no well-designed studies that address the effectiveness of the developmental model in inpatient settings. Like the object relations/systems model, the present model poses a challenge to the outcome researcher in that the expected change is intrapsychic and hence less easily measured than are changes in other domains (e.g., behavioral, interpersonal, physiological). Given that the model is designed to help members experience greater tolerances of themselves and more benign perceptions of others, it is necessary to have measures that can both reflect these aspects of personality and be applied in a group setting. Some methodologies have been developed to reflect these kinds of changes. For example, Greene (1990) discussed the success of studying the group setting using the semantic differential methodology, wherein the individual describes the self and others on various 7-point bipolar adjective-rating scales (e.g., good–bad, valuable–worthless).

There is some suggestion from the literature that groups that exhibit development (i.e., show a progression beyond Stage 1) are associated with better outcomes than are those that do not. MacKenzie, Dies, Coché, Rutan, and Stone (1987) divided training groups of group psychotherapists into those who were successful in facilitating development and those who were not. They found that the groups of the successful psychotherapists were more likely to show changes over the course of the group that were consistent with developmental predictions than were the other groups, which appeared static in members' manners of relating to one another. If these results generalized to the short-term inpatient group, they would support the importance of the therapist's effort to catalyze the group's development according to this model.

## Components of the Model

**Theoretical assumptions.** The developmental model makes the assumption that developmental stages exist and can unfold within the typically brief period in which inpatient psychotherapy groups take place. In fact, there does exist some empirical support for the existence of developmental stages in short-term groups.

An early empirical investigation of group development focused on four "self-analytic" groups that met in the context of a college course on interpersonal relationships (Mann, 1967). The investigators had observers rate a group using a complex categorical scheme that reflected various dimensions of the leader–member relationship. For example, observers rated the extent to which members resisted, identified with, and accepted the leaders. The data were consistent with the postulation of six phases of group development. During each stage, a distinctive pattern of leader–member behaviors was observed, with characteristic subgrouping in each phase. Although we refer the reader to Mann for a more thorough exposition of the results, in brief these findings support the common view in the literature that as group development proceeds, members become less intensely focused on the leader and more concerned with member–member relationships. One finding, however, that may have particular implications for the inpatient group is that the members in Mann's study never fully resolved their feelings toward authority. Although reactions to the leader became less focal, conflictual elements still remained. If, indeed, college students continue to worry about their relationships with authority, one would expect inpatients, who typically have high levels of dependency, to do the same. Although Mann's study suggests that the notion of a shift from a leader-centered to a member-centered group accurately describes how groups operate, he found that the stages did not exist in mutual exclusion of one another.

Another relevant set of studies was conducted by Beck and her colleagues on leadership patterns across developmental stages (Beck, 1981; Beck, Eng, & Brusa, 1989; Beck & Peters, 1981). Beck tested hypotheses derived from her nine-stage model of group development concerning the relation between the number of sessions that the group meets and the type of contributions made by members who are highly active during a particular stage. Beck's findings thus far are consistent with general group developmental theory and her specific four-leader typology.[8] Her results across a number of studies show that over the life of the group, the pattern of leadership changes in predictable ways.

MacKenzie (1983) also investigated the existence of developmental stages by examining the vicissitudes of the group emotional climate using the Group Climate Questionnaire–Short Form (GCQ-S). The GCQ-S is a 12-item questionnaire that reflects three dimensions of group life: level of engagement (or sense of involvement with one another), conflict, and avoidance. On the basis of group developmental theory, MacKenzie and Livesley (1983) made predictions about a group's fluctuation on these dimensions over time. For example, in early group sessions, engagement was expected to build quickly as members came to identify with one another's experiences. During this period, conflict was expected to stay at a very low level because members are motivated to deny differences. In later sessions, conflict was expected to increase as members faced their differences with one

---

[8] A detailed exposition of Beck's model is beyond the scope of the present chapter. In brief, Beck believed that every group requires a four-leader structure. Each of the four leaders performs functions that are essential to its progress. These leaders are "the members who tend to explicate and develop the group-level issues of that phase" (Beck, Eng, & Brusa, 1989, p. 157). Whether a given leader is active at any time depends on the group-level issues that the group is addressing or is about to address.

another and with the leader. At the same time, members were predicted to show less engagement and less willingness to take responsibility for the work of the group (i.e., a high level of avoidance). Still later, as the group members resolve conflicts related to authority, one would expect their degree of conflict and avoidance to diminish and their level of engagement to increase. MacKenzie (1983) obtained completed GCQ-S forms for 35 sessions from 75 members placed in 12 therapy groups. He found that across groups, the aforementioned predictions were upheld.

MacKenzie's (1983) pattern of results was replicated by Brabender (1990), who administered the GCQ-S to seven closed-ended inpatient psychotherapy groups. However, Brabender found that groups that started out very high in engagement relative to other groups in her sample did not go on in immediately subsequent sessions to become more fully engaged. Rather, they showed a diminution in engagement and an early surfacing of conflicts. However, by the end of the eight-session life of the group, groups highest in engagement in the initial sessions remained so. She also observed that groups that were relatively high in engagement often had a subgroup of members who very actively socialized with one another on one of the units. This observation highlights the fact that members' relationships on the unit affect the developmental life of the inpatient group even when the group is composed of members from different units.

Another study supporting the existence of developmental stages in inpatient groups was done using an adolescent sample followed for a 7-month period (Bernfeld, Clark, & Parker, 1984). The investigators distinguished between task roles, which help a group accomplish its task; group roles, which help a group maintain itself as an entity; and individual roles, which refer to individuals' idiosyncratic behaviors that do not help the group in any respect. On the basis of Dimock's (1971) group developmental theory, they predicted that early in group development, task roles would be high and individual roles would gradually increase as individuals gained comfort and established themselves within the group. As the group proceeds further, group roles would increase in frequency as members come to value the group and work to ensure its existence. The investigators obtained results consistent with their predictions.

In addition, the investigators rated the appropriateness of the members' behaviors in the group over time (Bernfeld et al., 1984). They found that of the 11 members who remained in the group for fewer than 15 sessions, approximately 50% improved. Of the 11 members who remained for 15 or more sessions (to a maximum of 40), 73% improved. Because the investigators did not include a control group, these results cannot uniquely be ascribed to specific effects of group psychotherapy as opposed to the general effects of hospitalization. However, they do suggest that there may be some critical period of tenure in the group that is necessary before positive effects can be realized from the model. This period may exceed the length of many patients' hospitalizations.

Although the majority of extant studies are consistent with the notion that developmental stages exist, there are a few studies that provide disconfirming evidence. For example, Reed (1986) made predictions about inpatients' observations of their groups on the basis of Brabender's (1985) theory of inpatient group development and R. Dies's (1983) model of leadership dimensions. R. Dies distinguished between the technical aspects of leadership, which consist of structuring activities and providing cognitive input, and the personal aspects of leadership, which relate to providing emotional support through the Rogerian qualities of empathy, genuineness, and warmth. In considering the technical and personal dimensions, Reed predicted that in the earliest stages when the therapist provides considerable structure, technical interventions are of greater importance than are personal interventions. Later in the group, personal interventions (e.g., individual feedback) are more valued by the group members because they entail a recognition of the member's individuality.

Reed (1986) classified groups as being in particular stages of development of the basis of members' GCQ-S, which members completed after every session. She measured perceptions of the leadership using the Leadership Profile, a 14-item questionnaire about the leaders' behaviors and members' wishes for changes in the leaders' behavior (R. Dies, 1983). Reed tested 10 inpatient groups over eight sessions and failed to find systematic variation in the members' perceptions of leadership behavior across developmental stages. Instead, she found that the members perceived the leaders to score high on the technical and personal dimensions throughout the four stages.[9]

Kanas, Stewart, Deri, Ketter, and Haney (1989) also questioned the existence of developmental stages in the short-term setting in their study that measured group climate using the GCQ-S in 12-session psychotherapy groups with outpatient schizophrenics. Kanas et al.'s study is relevant to the present discussion because the groups were short term and had a level of severity of disturbance comparable to that of inpatients. According to these researchers, the groups did not show a sequence of stages. Over the 12 sessions, members' engagement with one another increased, whereas conflict and avoidance of responsibility decreased. Hence, the groups did not show the increase in conflict that signals entrance into Stage 2. Although Kanas et al. interpreted their results as showing a lack of group development, an alternate hypothesis can be raised. Schizophrenic subjects are more likely than are other patient populations to exhibit difficulty with trust and, hence, would need to spend a greater number of sessions addressing Stage 1 issues (K. R. MacKenzie, personal communication, February 1989). Their increasing engagement and diminishing conflict and avoidance scores were consistent with the explanation that the group was slowly progressing through Stage 1.

**Other components.** The empirical support for certain elements of the developmental model has been described in earlier chapters on models that share these elements. One element, the emphasis on the exploration of members' here-and-now experiences, was discussed in conjunction with the interpersonal model in chapter 4. Although the research generally supports the efficacy of a here-and-now approach, several studies suggest

---

[9] This study does show that group members require an intervention style that is highly affective and cognitive throughout the life of the short-term group. The importance of the strong presence of these factors in all of the stages may preclude their variation from stage to stage.

that here-and-now explorations are especially effective if the member's present way of dealing with others in the group is linked to his or her behavior outside the group (Abramowitz & Jackson, 1974; Flowers & Booraem, 1990a, 1990b). Within the present model, members' discussion of material outside the group is often seen as a symbolic expression of concerns about the group and is interpreted as such. However, the establishment of specific linkages between in-the-room and out-of-the-room behavior is not a tactic of this model. Whether such linkages would enhance the effectiveness of this model or merely overwhelm inpatients who may be struggling to organize one sphere of experience can be determined only by further research.

The developmental model requires that in Stage 2, the therapist facilitate members in expressing and understanding their anger in relation to the therapist or group leader. As we discussed in chapter 5 in regard to the object relations/systems model, there is evidence that processing anger is associated with enhanced self-esteem and diminished anxiety (Koch, 1983).

Finally, the developmental model places particular emphasis on the fostering of cohesiveness. Within each stage, the therapist assists members in identifying with one another once they have differentiated themselves into subgroups on group-level issues. Moreover, the developmental model contains a number of technical means by which to enhance cohesiveness such as the use of group-as-a-whole interpretations. There is considerable research literature (e.g, Braaten, 1989; Lieberman, Yalom, & Miles, 1973; Yalom, Houts, Zimerberg, & Rand, 1967) suggesting that highly cohesive groups produce better outcomes than do low-cohesive groups on a wide range of outcome measures including interpersonal efficacy and symptom reduction.

## Generalizability of the Model

Often, developmental models are described in relation to closed-ended groups, which by definition enjoy membership constancy. Schopler and Galinsky (1990) attempted to determine whether the movement of a group past Stage 1 occurs in open-ended groups. This issue is particularly relevant to inpatient groups because most are open ended. The investigators identified 11 formative tasks, the completion of which would be necessary for the group to move past the initial stage of development. An example of such a formative task is, "Group purpose and/or goals are clear to most members." The leaders of 116 open-ended groups, both inpatient and outpatient, rated the extent to which their groups completed each of the tasks. The researchers found that half of the groups made substantial progress toward completing their formative tasks, leading them to conclude that these groups had achieved considerable development. Moreover, the groups' degrees of progress were inversely related to membership change: The greater the change, the less the progress.

McLees, Margo, Waterman, and Beeber (1992) used the GCQ-S over a 12-week period to assess the reactions of inpatients to weekly community meetings. Over the course of a week, the membership of the community would change considerably given that admissions ranged from 4 to 12 per week and discharges ranged from 2 to 14 per week. These investigators found a progression from Sessions 5 through 9 that approximated a "normal sequence of group development" (p. 26). Sessions 5 and 6 were characterized by high scores on the engagement dimension and low scores on the conflict and avoidance dimensions. In Session 7, engagement declined and conflict and avoidance increased. Sessions 8 and 9 showed an increase in engagement with diminished avoidance. The conflict dimension remained stable. Although the group investigated was a large community meeting rather than a small psychotherapy group, these findings are important because they suggest that a group with rapidly changing membership can nonetheless undergo development.

Stockton, Rohde, and Haughey (1992) used the GCQ-S to investigate the reactions of outpatients to different degrees of structure in a group. Patients were randomly assigned either to a highly structured group in which members performed exercises in the beginning of the session designed to "facilitate involvement, greater emotional expressivity and interaction with others" (p. 165) or to a no-exercise control group. For both groups, the investigators obtained a pattern of GCQ-S scores that supported the developmental stages postulated by MacKenzie and Livesley (1983). However, the subjects in the experimental groups exhibited patterns that suggested less recycling back through earlier developmental stages relative to those of the control group. Their findings are important because they suggest that structure within the session is not incompatible with, and may even facilitate, group development. However, it would be important for this study to be replicated with an inpatient group.

# Critique of the Model

## Strengths

A main strength of the developmental model is its use of natural forces within the group to foster the psychological growth of its members. The kinds of conflicts that are described in this chapter emerge in groups of every possible format including structured groups (Runkel, Lawrence, Oldfield, Rider, & Clark, 1971; Stockton et al., 1992). Usually, their activation leads to resistance to whatever task is required by the model. For example, in a cognitive–behavioral model, members sometimes fail to do homework assignments or do them minimally as a means of expressing negative feelings toward authority. Within nonanalytic models, there are seldom means for addressing the basis of this resistance.

From a technical standpoint, the present model is also reasonably well developed. There is a clear format for pretraining and orientation of members. For each stage, there are specific guidelines for intervention. However, the model also affords the therapist considerable flexibility in working at different levels of intervention (i.e., individual, interpersonal, and group-as-a-whole levels). The model provides the therapist with specific intervention strategies to deal with the phenomenon of scapegoating, an ever-present danger in inpatient groups given inpatients' common reliance on the projective defenses.

The model entails the group therapist's attendance to many different aspects of group life: norms, goals, boundary structures, and so on. The multidimensionality of perspective demanded by this model provides the therapist with a number of converging operations by which to test the accuracy of interpretations.

Finally, this model provides excellent preparation for members' entrance into dynamically oriented outpatient group therapy. Relative to most outpatient groups, the inpatient group therapist applying this model is more active and pursues a more restricted set of goals. However, both inpatient and outpatient dynamically oriented groups (a) emphasize an exploratory or insight-oriented process involving cognitive and affective elements and (b) require considerable responsibility taking on the part of group members. Hence, the patient is unlikely to experience a major paradigm clash that may hinder the important transition from inpatient to outpatient therapy.

## Weaknesses

The major weakness of the developmental model is that frequently a setting's inability to satisfy the many demands of this model may preclude its use. We elaborate on the demands of the model in the following section. However, some of the more critical demands are the presence of reasonably high-functioning members who are able to use an exploratory process effectively, some stability in membership at least across several sessions, the opportunity to prepare patients for group, and the presence of therapists who have a knowledge of theory and technique within the psychodynamic and systems frameworks.

This model is also limited in that it makes minimal use of the therapeutic milieu. On the one hand, it requires a strongly pro-group climate to nurture the stability of the group. On the other hand, it demands that the group be treated as a somewhat separate entity from whatever system in which it is embedded. To the extent that the boundaries between the group and the milieu are highly permeable, what occurs within the group may be more critically dependent on the forces at play in the broader system (e.g., the unit) than on those residing exclusively within the group itself.

Like any model that relies on conceptualizations at the group-as-a-whole and subgroup levels, this model faces the danger of losing sight of the individual group member. The progression of the group does not necessarily mirror the progression of the individual. This model places a special demand on the therapist to monitor constantly whether each individual's personal boundary is permeable to the input of other members. This monitoring process is made difficult by the fact that the goals of this model are less operational than are those of other models such as the social skills training version of the behavioral model.

The model also suffers from the lack of any outcome data to demonstrate its efficacy in inpatient groups. Although there is considerable support for the existence of developmental stages in short-term groups, the support for development in inpatient groups, even in those with constancy of membership, is limited.

# Demands of the Model

## Clinical Mission

The developmental model requires a clinical context that is strongly supportive of its goals and methods. Support from the context is essential in two ways. First, the group's growth is dependent on the existence of a clear and stable boundary between the group and its context. Boundary instability leads to constant regression and limits the array of developmental issues that the group can address. Yet, the maintenance of a consistent external boundary requires a collaborative effort by both those outside and within the group. For example, the attending psychiatrist who considers the termination date of a time-limited group in planning a patient's discharge helps maintain the boundary between the group and its context. The staff who refrain from using the washer and dryer that happen to be located in the group room during the period the group is meeting also assist in boundary maintenance.

The second way in which staff members support the effective application of the developmental model is through their tolerance of the members' changing emotional reactions in relation to the group. Application of this model leads members to a heightened awareness of the affects and impulses stimulated by the group process. Consequently, members are likely to express their reactions, inside and outside the group, in a more intense way than they would with other models, particularly the cognitively structuring models such as the cognitive–behavioral and problem-solving models. For example, at one point in the group's life, members inevitably complain on the unit about the inadequacy of the group or its leaders. Staff are in a better position to respond sensitively to members' criticisms, frustration, and anger if they recognize that the reactions are a natural part of a developmental process. In a unit or institution that is philosophically aligned with the position that an individual's emotional life should be subdued, staff are not likely to greet this model with acceptance.

## Context of the Group

This model differs from most of the models described in this book in that it is most effectively applied when the group takes place off the unit and is composed of members of different units. These features promote the group as an emergent system in its own right rather than simply a subsystem of the unit. However, some inpatient group therapists have reported the viability of using a developmental model with groups that do take place on a unit with group members who are drawn exclusively from the unit (Beeber, 1988; Rice & Rutan, 1987).

## Temporal Variables

The application of the developmental model is facilitated by the use of a closed-ended format (Kaplan & Roman, 1963) because such a format ensures constancy of membership, a feature strongly conducive to group cohesiveness (Brabender, 1988). Moreover, members are given a common set of stimuli to which they can respond, which encourages the developmental stages to emerge with greater clarity (Kaplan & Roman, 1963; MacKenzie, 1990). For example, in Stage 1, all members are faced with the task of getting to know one another. Even if they have a familiarity with other members from situations outside of the group, they still must come to know one another as members of this particular group. However, even though the closed-ended structure facilitates group development, research cited in this chapter suggests that group development can exist in an open-ended group. Hence, this feature does not preclude the use of the developmental model.

Group meetings should be held as frequently as possible, preferably daily. Sessions should occur at least three times a week because fewer sessions seriously disrupt the continuity of the group. The therapist who makes an interpretation on Friday about the group's reaction to events in Tuesday's session is likely to find that in the busy hiatus, the group has forgotten the contents of Tuesday's session. If the group is open ended, it is important that there be consistency of membership at least across several sessions. For both open-ended and closed-ended groups, the greater the number of sessions in which the membership is stable, the further the group can progress (Schopler & Galinsky, 1990) and the more likely members are to realize benefits from group participation (Bernfeld et al., 1984).

## Size

The optimal size of the group is 6 to 10 members. This model is difficult to apply with fewer than 6 members because the model relies on the formation of subgroups, each with several members. If a single member is singularly left to represent a position in a conflict (a common occurrence in the extremely small group), then this member is highly vulnerable to being ostracized by the group. If many more than 10 members are included in the group, it becomes an inordinately burdensome task for the therapist to track each member and to ensure, especially in Stage 1 when it is critical, that each member has successfully bonded with at least one other member.

## Composition

The successful application of the developmental model requires the selection of members who are able to use constructively the exploration of interpersonal and intrapsychic experience. Such members are to be distinguished from those patients who can tolerate only supportive techniques. Although low-functioning borderline and schizophrenic patients are often found in the latter group, there are some individuals in these diagnostic categories who can make good use of this type of group. This model group is not suited for individuals who are actively psychotic, violent, or vulnerable to a moderate to severe level of confusion as a consequence of drugs, electroshock therapy, or central nervous system damage.

Heterogeneity of symptomatology is preferable to homogeneity within this model. Group members being too alike in terms of symptoms or presenting problems can lead to the quick development of a pseudo-cohesiveness that interferes with the emergence of subgroups in Stage 1. When subgroups fail to crystallize, the group is hindered in exploring members' reservations about group participation and in establishing a more genuine sense of cohesiveness that is the product of such an exploration. MacKenzie et al. (1986) described the use of a short-term developmental model with an outpatient group of bulimic patients. The investigators reported that the members quickly formed a sense of connection in relation to their eating symptoms but resisted other forms of identification. The investigators indicated that after 7–10 months of treatment, the group showed significant improvement on various symptom measures. Such a finding suggests that homogeneity of symptoms does not preclude use of a developmental approach. On the other hand, Opalic (1990) reported that group developmental stages in a group of hospitalized psychotics were barely discernible. Hence, the viability of a developmental approach for a diagnostically homogeneous group may depend on the level of functioning of the members.

The developmental model has most commonly been applied with a mixed-gender group. Brabender's (1992) observations of the differing behaviors of men and women in a short-term inpatient group suggests that each gender brings a distinctive set of resources to the group. For example, whereas women contribute their skills in helping members connect, men offer greater comfort in acknowledging negatively toned affects. Because subgroups frequently form along gender lines (e.g., the engagement subgroup of Stage 1 often comprises mainly women), the presence of both men and women catalyzes the process of differentiation. However, there is some evidence, such as the previously cited study by MacKenzie et al. (1986), that same-gender groups can also show development. Hence, the use of this model is not precluded in a same-gender group.

The model is most suitable for members who agree (however reluctantly) to be in the group. No particular age demands are made by this model. A developmental framework with inpatients has been used with adults (Brabender, 1985) and adolescents (Bernfeld et al., 1984; Ghuman & Sarles, 1988; Powles, 1959). We are unaware of any report of use of this model with a geriatric population.

Two final considerations concerning membership pertain to the overall composition of the group. Preferably, there should not be included in the group any individual who is a clear outlier on some dimension (e.g., age, gender, race) that is likely to be conspicuous to the group members unless the individual in question shows a particular ease in bonding with others. An individual who is deviant along some conspicuous dimension is in a prime position to be scapegoated by other members. An additional consideration is the balancing of the group along interpersonal lines. Because the developmental model requires that members articulate different positions in relation to a set of conflicts and because there are characteristic interpersonal styles associated with these positions, it is ideal to have a diversity of interpersonal styles present in the group. Different interpersonal styles bring different resources to the group for purposes of conflict resolution (Whitaker & Lieberman, 1964). For example, if all members of the group are inclined toward a passive–dependent style, there will be little challenging of authority in Stage 2 and the group will become fixated within this stage.

## Therapist Variables

This model is most successfully applied by therapists who accept fundamental psychodynamic principles and who have training in group dynamics, psychodynamic theory (particularly object relations theory), and systems theory. Hence, among the models we have presented in this text, the developmental model is one of the most demanding in terms of the therapist's training and experience.

With respect to the structure of the group leadership, although the presence of a co-therapy team is not essential, it is highly recommended because frequently when one therapist is the target of a projection, it is often more effective if the other therapist takes an active role in facilitating members in exploring this issue. Another advantage of co-therapy is that it is extremely useful as a means of enabling each therapist to have the necessary emotional support to tolerate the stage-specific array of intense affects and impulses that are likely to emerge in such a group (Brabender, 1987). Co-therapy also provides each therapist with a means to obtain feedback on the reliability of their perceptions of the group. Moreover, when therapists differ in their perceptions about the group, the discrepancy itself has diagnostic value. For example, Greene, Rosenkrantz, and Muth (1986) demonstrated that when members of a group use the defense mechanism of splitting, therapists are likely to form widely different impressions of the group. In relation to other models, it is essential that there be stability of leadership. A high level of leadership flux will, like high membership turnover, create considerable potential for fixations and regressions.

## Summary

The developmental model of inpatient group psychotherapy is a psychodynamically based model that supports members' here-and-now explorations of a series of conflicts that are activated through their interactions over time. Although the conflicts are expressed at the level of the group, they also have resonance at the interpersonal and intrapsychic levels. This model proposes the existence of four stages of development. Each stage is organized in relation to some major issue toward which members take different positions. The elaboration of differences among members leads to the crystallization of subgroups. It is through members' increasing tolerances for and identifications with the positions of the different subgroups that the goals of the model are realized. These goals are (a) increased self-esteem based on a greater acceptance of diverse parts of the self and (b) a more positive view of others as well as a stronger anticipation of satisfaction from relationships with others.

This model is more suited to the treatment of high-functioning inpatients than are many of the models described in this text. It is especially useful in a treatment setting in which members of different units are combined for group therapy. The model demands a setting in which there is considerable support for the creation of a group with membership stability.

Currently, there exist data to support the central concept of the model, the existence of developmental stages in the short-term group. However, the model still awaits an empirical test of the utility of a development perspective.

# References

Abramowitz, S. I., & Jackson, C. (1974). Comparative effectiveness of there-and-then versus here-and-now therapist interpretations in group psychotherapy. *Journal of Counseling Psychology, 21,* 188–293.

Agazarian, Y. (1989). Group-as-a-whole systems theory and practice. *Group, 13,* 131–154.

Agazarian, Y. (1992). Contemporary theories of group psychotherapy: A systems approach to the group-as-a-whole. *International Journal of Group Psychotherapy, 42,* 177–203.

Agazarian, Y., & Peters, R. (1981). *The visible and invisible group: Two perspectives on group psychotherapy and group process.* London: Routledge & Kegan Paul.

Ashbach, C., & Schermer, V. L. (1987). *Object relations and the self, and the group: A conceptual paradigm.* London: Routledge & Kegan Paul.

Beck, A. (1974). Phases in the development of structure in therapy and encounter groups. In D. Wexler & L. N. Rice (Eds.), *Innovations in client-centered therapy* (pp. 421–463). New York: Wiley.

Beck, A. (1981). The study of group phase development and emergent leadership. *Group, 5*(4), 48–54.

Beck, A., Eng, A. M., & Brusa, J. A. (1989). The evolution of leadership during group development. *Group, 13,* 155–172.

Beck, A., & Peters, L. N. (1981). The research evidence for distributed leadership in therapy groups. *International Journal of Group Psychotherapy, 31*(1), 43–71.

Beeber, A. (1988). A systems model of short-term, open-ended group therapy. *Hospital and Community Psychiatry, 39*(5), 537–542.

Bennis, W. G., & Shepard, H. A. (1956). A theory of group development. *Human Relations, 9,* 415–438.

Bernfeld, G., Clark, L., & Parker, G. (1984). The process of adolescent group psychotherapy. *International Journal of Group Psychotherapy, 34*(1), 111–126.

Bion, W. (1959). *Experiences in groups.* New York: Basic Books.

Borriello, J. F. (1976). Group psychotherapy in hospital systems. In L. R. Wolberg & M. L. Aronson (Eds.), *Group therapy* (pp. 99–108). New York: Stratton.

Braaten, L. J. (1989). Predicting positive goal attainment and symptom reduction from early climate dimensions. *International Journal of Group Psychotherapy, 39*(3), 377–387.

Brabender, V. (1985). Time-limited inpatient group therapy: A developmental model. *International Journal of Group Psychotherapy, 35,* 373–390.

Brabender, V. (1987). Vicissitudes of countertransference in inpatient group psychotherapy. *International Journal of Group Psychotherapy, 37*(4), 549–567.

Brabender, V. (1988). A closed model of short-term inpatient group psychotherapy. *Hospital and Community Psychiatry, 39*(5), 542–545.

Brabender, V. (1990). Short-term group psychotherapy. In R. MacKenzie (Chair), *Therapeutic strategies in brief group therapy.* Symposium conducted at the meeting of the American Group Psychotherapy Association, Boston, MA.

Brabender, V. (1992). The psychological growth of women in a short-term inpatient group. *Group, 16*(3), 131–145.

Burnand, G. (1990). Group development phases as working through six fundamental human problems. *Small Group Research, 21*(2), 255–273.

Clapham, H. I., & Sclare, A. B. (1958). Group psychotherapy with asthmatic patients. *International Journal of Group Psychotherapy, 8,* 44–54.

Dies, K. (1991). A model for adolescent group psychotherapy. *Journal of Child and Adolescent Group Therapy, 1*(1), 59–70.

Dies, R. (1983). Clinical implications of research on leadership in short-term group psychotherapy. In R. R. Dies & K. R. MacKenzie (Eds.), *Advances in group psychotherapy: Integrating research and practice* (pp. 1–26). Madison, CT: International Universities Press.

Dimock, H. G. (1971). *Leadership and group development: Part 2. How to observe your group.* Montreal, Quebec, Canada: Concordia University.

Dugo, J. M., & Beck, A. P. (1984). A therapist's guide to issues of intimacy and hostility viewed as group-level phenomena. *International Journal of Group Psychotherapy, 34*(1), 25–45.

Durkin, H. (1982). Change in group psychotherapy: Theory and practice: A systems perspective. *International Journal of Group Psychotherapy, 32*(4), 431–439.

Erikson, E. H. (1950). *Childhood and society.* New York: Norton.

Ezriel, H. (1973). Psychoanalytic group therapy. In L. R. Wolberg & E. K. Schwartz (Eds.), *Group therapy: 1973, An overview.* (pp. 183–210). New York: Intercontinental Medical Book Corp.

Flowers, J. V., & Booraem, C. D. (1990a). The effects of different types of interpretation on outcome in group psychotherapy. *Group, 14*(2), 81–88.

Flowers, J. V., & Booraem, C. D. (1990b). The frequency and effect of different types of interpretation in psychodynamic and cognitive–behavioral group psychotherapy. *International Journal of Group Psychotherapy, 40*(2), 203–214.

Freud, S. (1955). Group psychology and the analysis of the ego. In J. Strachey (Ed. and Trans), *The standard edition of the complete psychological works of Sigmund Freud* (Vol. 18, pp. 67–143). London: Hogarth Press. (Original work published 1921)

Ghuman, H. S., & Sarles, R. M. (1988). Three group psychotherapy settings with long-term adolescent inpatients: Advantages and disadvantages. *Psychiatric Hospital, 19*(4), 161–164.

Greene, L. (1983). On fusion and individuation processes in small groups. *International Journal of Group Psychotherapy, 33*(1), 3–19.

Greene, L. (1990). Relationships among semantic differential change measures of splitting, self-fragmentation, and object relations in borderline psychopathology. *British Journal of Medical Psychology, 63*, 21–32.

Greene, L., Rosenkrantz, J., & Muth, D. (1986). Borderline defenses and countertransference: Research findings and implications. *Psychiatry, 9*(3), 253–264.

Grotjahn, M. (1950). The process of maturation in group psychotherapy and in the group therapist. *Psychiatry, 13*, 63–67.

Hannah, S. (1984). Countertransference in in-patient group psychotherapy: Implications for technique. *International Journal of Group Psychotherapy, 34*(2), 257–272.

Hill, W. F., & Gruner, L. A. (1973). A study of development in open and closed groups. *Small Group Behavior, 4*, 355–381.

Horwitz, L. (1977). A group-centered approach to group psychotherapy. *International Journal of Group Psychotherapy, 27*(4), 423–439.

Kanas, N., Stewart, P., Deri, J., Ketter, T., & Haney, K. (1989). Group process in short-term outpatient therapy groups for schizophrenics. *Group, 13*(2), 67–73.

Kaplan, S. P., & Roman, M. (1963). Phases of development in an adult therapy group. *International Journal of Group Psychotherapy, 13*, 10–26.

Kernberg, O. (1975). *Borderline conditions and pathological narcissism.* New York: Jason Aronson.

Kibel, H. (1978). The rationale for the use of group psychotherapy for borderline patients on a short-term unit. *International Journal of Group Psychotherapy, 29*, 339–358.

Kibel, H. D. (1981). A conceptual model for short-term inpatient group psychotherapy. *American Journal of Psychiatry, 181*(1), 74–80.

Klein, M. (1946). Notes on some schizoid mechanisms. *International Journal of Psychoanalysis, 27*, 99–110.

Koch, H. C. (1983). Correlates of change in personal construing of members of two psychotherapy groups: Changes in affective expression. *British Journal of Medical Psychology, 56*, 323–327.

Leopold, H. S. (1977). Selective group approaches with psychotic patients in hospital settings. *American Journal of Psychotherapy, 30*, 95–105.

Lieberman, M. A., Yalom, I., & Miles, M. (1973) *Encounter groups: First facts.* New York: Basic Books.

Livesley, W. J., & MacKenzie, K. R. (1983). Social roles in therapy groups. In R. R. Dies & K. R. MacKenzie (Eds.), *Advances in group psychotherapy: Integrating research and practice* (pp. 117–135). Madison, CT: International Universities Press.

MacKenzie, K. R. (1983). The clinical application of the group climate measure. In R. R. Dies & K. R. MacKenzie (Eds.), *Advances in group psychotherapy: Integrating research and practice* (pp. 159–170). Madison, CT: International Universities Press.

MacKenzie, K. R. (1990). *Time-limited group psychotherapy.* Washington, DC: American Psychiatric Association.

MacKenzie, K. R., Dies, R. R., Coché, E., Rutan, J. S., & Stone, W. N. (1987). An analysis of AGPA Institute groups. *International Journal of Group Psychotherapy, 37*(1), 55–74.

MacKenzie, K. R., & Livesley, W. J. (1983). A developmental model for brief group therapy. In R. R. Dies & K. R. MacKenzie (Eds.), *Advances in group psychotherapy: Integrating theory and research* (pp. 101–135). Madison, CT: International Universities Press.

MacKenzie, K. R., & Livesley, W. J. (1984). Developmental stages: An integrating theory of group psychotherapy. *Canadian Journal of Psychiatry, 29,* 247–251.

MacKenzie, K. R., Livesley, W. J., Coleman, M., Harper, H., & Park, J. (1986). Short-term therapy for bulimia nervosa. *Psychiatric Annals, 16*(12), 699–708.

Mann, J. (1967). *Interpersonal styles and group development.* New York: Wiley.

Mann, J., & Semrad, E. V. (1948). The use of group therapy in psychoses. *Journal of Social Casework, 29,* 176–181.

McLees, E., Margo, G., Waterman, S., & Beeber, A. (1992). Group climate and group development in a community meeting on a short-term inpatient psychiatric unit. *Group, 16*(1), 18–30.

Opalic, P. (1990). Group processes in short-term group therapy of psychotics. *Small Group Research, 21*(2), 168–189.

Osberg, J. W., & Berliner, A. K. (1956). The developmental stages in group psychotherapy with hospitalized narcotic addicts. *International Journal of Group Psychotherapy, 6,* 436–447.

Powdermaker, F., & Frank, J. D. (1948). Group psychotherapy with neurotics. *American Journal of Psychiatry, 105,* 449–455.

Powles, W. E. (1959). Psychosexual maturity in a therapy group of disturbed adolescents. *International Journal of Group Psychotherapy, 9,* 429–441.

Reed, K. (1986). *Members' perception of therapists' behavior in short-term psychotherapy groups.* Ann Arbor, MI: Dissertation Information Services.

Rice, C., & Rutan, S. (1981). Boundary maintenance in inpatient therapy groups. *International Journal of Group Psychotherapy, 31*(3), 297–309.

Rice, C., & Rutan, S. (1987). *Inpatient group psychotherapy.* New York: MacMillan.

Runkel, P. J., Lawrence, M., Oldfield, S. Rider, M., & Clark, C. (1971). Stages of group development: An empirical test of Tuckman's hypothesis. *Journal of Applied Behavioral Science, 7*(2), 180–193.

Saravay, S. M. (1978). A psychoanalytic theory of group development. *International Journal of Group Psychotherapy, 28*, 481–507.

Scheidlinger, S. (1964). Identification, the sense of belonging and of identity in small groups. *International Journal of Group Psychotherapy, 14*, 291–306.

Scheidlinger, S. (1982). On scapegoating in group psychotherapy. *International Journal of Group Psychotherapy, 32*, 131–143.

Schopler, J. H., & Galinsky, M. J. (1990). Can open-ended groups move beyond beginnings? *Small Group Research, 21*, 435–449.

Schutz, W. C. (1958). *FIRO: A three-dimensional theory of interpersonal behavior.* New York: Holt, Rinehart & Winston.

Shellow, R. S., Ward, J. L., & Rubenfeld, S. (1958). Group therapy and the institutionalized delinquent. *International Journal of Group Psychotherapy, 8*, 265–275.

Stockton, R., Rohde, R. I., & Haughey, J. (1992). The effects of structured group exercises on cohesion, engagement, avoidance, and conflict. *Small Group Research, 23*(2), 155–168.

Thorpe, J. J., & Smith, B. (1953). Phases in group development in treatment of drug addicts. *International Journal of Group Psychotherapy, 3*, 66–78.

Tuckman, B. W. (1965). Developmental sequence in small groups. *Psychological Bulletin, 63*, 384–399.

von Bertalanffy, L. (1950). The theory of open systems in physics and biology. *Science, 3*, 23–29.

von Bertalanffy, L. (1968). *General systems theory.* New York: Brazillier.

Wender, L. (1946). The dynamics of group psychotherapy and its application. *Journal of Nervous and Mental Disease, 84*, 54–60.

Whitaker, D. R., & Lieberman, M.A. (1964). *Psychotherapy through the group process.* New York: Atherton Press.

Winnicott, D. W. (1965). *The maturational processes and the facilitating environment: Studies in the theory of emotional development.* Madison, CT: International Universities Press.

Yalom, I. (1983). *Inpatient group psychotherapy.* New York: Basic Books.

Yalom, I. (1985). *The theory and practice of group psychotherapy.* New York: Basic Books.

Yalom, I., Houts, P. S., Zimerberg, S. M., & Rand, K. H. (1967). Predictions of improvement in group therapy. *Archives of General Psychiatry, 17*, 159–168.

Chapter

# 7

# The Cognitive–Behavioral Model

There are many models or systems of psychotherapy that take into account an individual's cognitions. These include several of the psychoanalytic schools of thought such as the Sullivanian, Adlerian, Horneyan, and Freudian schools (Freeman, 1987). Of course, cognitions have a prominent place in the cognitive and cognitive–behavioral models such as Ellis's (1962) rational–emotive therapy, Lazarus's (1981) multimodel therapy, Beck's (1967/1972, 1976) cognitive therapy, and Meichenbaum's (1977) cognitive–behavior modification. Even those models that seek primarily to modify behavior accept that cognitive symbolic processes are often necessary mediators of behavior (Bandura, 1969; Mahoney & Kazdin, 1979) and that the effectiveness of behavior modification can be enhanced by considering cognitive factors (see Schwartz, 1982). Thus, although cognitions are now included in most therapeutic systems, the position accorded them varies substantially (Perris, 1988a). In this chapter, we review the cognitive and cognitive–behavioral models, both of which belong to a class of models in which the cognitions are a central focus for change.

Cognitive–behavioral psychotherapy is a comprehensive and empirically based theory and therapy of psychopathology, the philosophical origins of which can be traced to the ancient Roman Epictetus, who emphasized the subjective side of reality and the value of introspection (Perris, 1988a). Modern cognitive–behavioral psychotherapy is historically grounded in two dif-

ferent theoretical schools—the behavioral and the psychoanalytic. Some propose that cognitive therapy grew out of the behavior modification model, with the work of Bandura (1969,
1977a, 1977b) being an important milestone. Cognitive–behavioral therapists have adopted from the behavioral school the
scientific method (i.e., clearly defined goals, emphasis on empirical outcome, low to moderate levels of inference from the
behavior), a focus on behavioral change, and a variety of behavioral techniques and strategies such as graded task assignments, scheduled behavior rehearsal, and role playing (Beck &
Weishaar, 1989; Freeman, 1987).

The psychoanalytic foundations and contributions are equally
unequivocal. Within psychoanalysis, the trend toward increased
emphasis on the role of cognition culminated in the foundation
of the cognitive–volitional school (Arieti, 1974) and the approach
of cognitive psychoanalysis (Beiber, 1980; Erdelyi, 1985). However, both Arieti and Beiber maintained their basic psychoanalytic approaches and continued to focus on unconscious processes. The inception of cognitive psychotherapy as a separate
school of thought coincided with Beck and Ellis (traditionally
trained psychoanalysts) departing from the domain of psychoanalysis and developing a new therapy system in the early 1960s
(Perris, 1988a). From the psychoanalytic schools of thought, cognitive psychotherapy has embraced the importance of understanding the individual's characteristic (subjective) perceptions
of himself or herself and the world; the concomitant internal
dialogue and process (often outside of awareness) that can influence one's perception of past, current, and future situations;
and the importance of insight (i.e., bringing automatic thoughts
into awareness).

The influences of two very different traditions (psychoanalysis
and behaviorism) have resulted in a number of different variations and combinations of cognitive and cognitive–behavior therapy models. The term *cognitive–behavioral therapy* could include
Beck's cognitive therapy (Beck, 1967/1972, 1976; Beck, Rush,
Shaw, & Emery, 1979), Ellis's rational–emotive therapy (Ellis,
1962), Goldfried's systematic rational restructuring (Goldfried,
DeCanteceo, & Weinberg, 1974), Meichenbaum's self-instructional training (Meichenbaum, 1977) and stress inoculation train-

ing (Meichenbaum, 1975), Maultsby's rational behavior therapy (Maultsby, 1975), Lazarus's multimodal therapy (Lazarus, 1981), cognitive appraisal therapy (Wessler & Hankin, 1988), interpersonal problem-solving therapy (Spivack, Platt, & Shure, 1976), Rehm's self-control therapy (Rehm, 1977), structural cognitive therapy (Liotti, 1987), covert conditioning (Mahoney & Arnoff, 1978), personal science (Mahoney, 1977), or Bandura's more cognitively mediated view of social learning (Bandura, 1977a, 1977b). The assumption that all of these therapies have the same theoretical underpinnings and treatment methods is naively misguided (Kiesler, 1966). There have been a number of attempts to systematize and characterize the essential features of this model (Kendall & Bemis, 1983). For clarity, we use Hollon and Beck's (1986) definition of cognitive and cognitive–behavioral therapies, hereafter referred to as the *cognitive–behavioral therapies*. According to this definition, these therapies include "those approaches that attempt to modify existing or anticipate disorders by virtue of altering cognitions or cognitive processes" (Hollon & Beck, 1986, p. 443) This definition excludes approaches that rely predominantly on techniques that are considered more behavioral in focus (e.g., systematic desensitization). It also does not involve techniques that clearly involve a cognitive process (e.g., imagery) but that do not have as the intended goal-changing cognitions per se (Hollon & Beck, 1986). In this chapter, we consider only those therapies that have as an explicit goal targeting and changing the "cognitive processes."[1]

One of the most familiar and well-researched forms of cognitive–behavioral therapy is that using an individual format with outpatient depressed individuals (Beck, 1967/1972; Dobson,

---

[1] Our definition is more circumscribed than that of Kendall and Bemis (1983), who included all those approaches that share the goal of correcting a maladaptive relationship between events and cognitions on the basis of the premise that "disturbance in mediational processes give rise to maladaptive emotional states and behavior patterns" (p. 52). We have opted not to use this definition because to add the additional types of groups suggested by this more inclusive definition to this chapter would obscure, rather then illuminate, the distinctions we make with regard to the cognitive–behavioral, problem-solving, and behavioral (social skills) models.

1989; Haaga & Davison, 1989). The use of a group format and the utility of cognitive therapy with a wider range of psychiatric problems (Freeman, Simon, Beutler, & Arkowitz, 1989), particularly the more severe disorders typically found in an inpatient setting, is relatively new (Bowers, 1989; Glantz, 1987, 1989; Greenwood, 1987; Grossman & Freet, 1987; Schrodt & Wright, 1987; Scott, Williams, & Beck, 1989; Wright & Schrodt, 1989; Wright, Beck, These, & Ludgate, in press).

The procedure and process of cognitive–behavioral group therapy vary depending on which model out of the diverse set available the therapist follows; the models differ on the goals, responsibilities and styles of the leader, assessment and patient categorization, content and focus of the session, and the importance of the therapeutic alliance. The models each can be broadly categorized into one of three classes of group approaches: a structured psychoeducational approach, a problem-solving approach, or an experiential–affective approach (Wessler & Hankin-Wessler, 1989). The psychoeducational group is a highly structured, time-limited approach in which the primary objective is imparting information and emphasizing self-help techniques, with the task of applying them left to the individual. By design, little or no attention is paid to the particular concerns of the individual. Although this can be an efficient way of teaching a large, highly motivated group, it cannot be used exclusively with moderately or severely disturbed individuals without the support of other therapeutic techniques (Wessler & Hankin-Wessler, 1989). (See Sank & Shaffer, 1984, for more specific information on how to conduct such groups.) Problem-solving groups too have educational aspects; however, their main objective is working on the individual's practical and psychological problems. We discuss this type of group in more detail in the next chapter. The experiential–affective group relies on both direct teaching and more indirect methods (e.g., guided imagery, exercises, role playing). Its goal is to help patients identify and understand the connections between cognitive appraisals and resulting emotions and to promote changes in behavior, affects, and personality. It is this latter class of models that is the focus of this chapter. The distinction between these classes of groups is, of course, an artificial one; various combinations of the techniques that each class offers can be flexibly combined depending on member characteristics and type of inpatient setting in which the therapist practices (Wessler & Hankin-Wessler, 1989).

## Theoretical Underpinnings

Central to the cognitive–behavioral model of therapy is the premise that there is an interaction among the manners in which individuals conceptualize and construe themselves, their worlds, and their futures. The focus is primarily on cognitions and the correction of faulty cognitions. As Ellis (1959) explained, "We feel that certain things are good or bad because we believe or think that they are" (p. 57). However, the popular misconception that this model avoids or dismisses emotions and behavior is untrue. In fact, Beck's (1967/1972) model was designed to treat an "emotional" problem, namely depression. Although the emphasis is on how cognition influences emotion and behavior rather than on the inverse (Beck et al., 1979; Ellis, 1962), reciprocal connections are also acknowledged in a cognition–emotion–motivation–behavior loop (Beck, 1991).

People are likened to social psychologist Kelly's (1955) image of a "personal scientist," constantly ferreting out relevant information from the environment, using it to create and modify theories about himself or herself and the environment, and behaving and feeling in a manner consistent with those theories. Psychopathology involves the development probably during infancy or childhood of incorrect, unrealistic, or distorted theories (called *dysfunctional schemas*); these are often activated by the impact of particular external events that then distort newly acquired information and further distort the individual's self-perception and view of the world. A basic tenet of the theory is that individuals search for truth and strive for logical consistency. When individuals recognize that there are inconsistencies between their views of themselves and contrary evidence, they evaluate the evidence and often change their self-perceptions. Changes in behavior and emotions result from such efforts to resolve inconsistencies and inaccuracies (Arkowitz & Hannah, 1989). *cf. dissonance theory*

Although there have been a number of different theoretical contributions to the cognitive–behavioral theory of emotion (e.g., Ellis, 1962), Beck and his followers have provided the most extensive description and investigation of its application to inpatient group therapy (Freeman & Greenwood, 1987; Freeman et al., 1989; Haaga & Davison, 1989; Hollon & Beck, 1986). Our theoretical discussion therefore concentrates on the work of and the terms used by Beck and his colleagues.

The model proposes that an individual's perceptions or cognitions (usually negative) about himself or herself, the world, and the future (together referred to as the *cognitive triad*) are the result of cognitive distortions (i.e., thoughts, images of loss, negative interpretations of ambiguous events). These distortions arise when a stressor (either internal or external) activates or energizes an underlying cognitive structure or schema (i.e., an attitude or assumption, which can be an irrational or rational belief). These schemas become the substrate from which the cognitive distortions emerge. Central to the understanding of the formation and maintenance of psychological disorders are the three related concepts of the cognitive triad, cognitive distortions, and cognitive schemas (Beck et al., 1979).[2]

## Core Concepts

**Cognitive triad.** The cognitive triad refers to the negative or distorted views that individuals may have about (a) themselves (e.g., "I'm a loser"), (b) the world (e.g., "Life's unfair"), and (c) the future (e.g., "It's hopeless"). This concept was initially developed to account for the idiosyncratic verbalizations of depressed patients (Beck, 1991).

The severity of the level of distortion and the extent to which the distortion is negative may vary for each element of the triad. The therapist can develop a refined conceptualization of the pa-

---

[2] For a more in-depth understanding of the theoretical underpinnings, the reader is referred to Ellis (1992), Beck (1991), Beck and Emery (1977, 1985), Freeman (1990), and Beck et al. (1979).

tient's problem by assessing the degree to which each of the three factors makes a contribution to the patient's cognitions.

**Cognitive distortions.** Because most environmental events have some ambiguity, people often have latitude in the meaning and value that they attribute to the events; thus, all people have a capacity to distort reality in significant ways. These distortions are the result of underlying schemas or belief systems. The ability to assess and monitor the veracity of the distortion becomes important. When a belief is held in spite of disconfirming evidence or when there is an inflexible application of a belief, the belief becomes dysfunctional (Ellis, 1962; Freeman, 1987).

In the context of cognitive–behavioral theory, cognitive distortions are the dysfunctional thoughts and images generated by an event that activates a certain schema (Freeman, 1990). Thoughts or cognitions can be conscious or nonconscious. Nonconscious cognitions, or automatic thoughts, are ones that are outside one's awareness and are often not verbalized; however, the psychoanalytic notion of the unconscious is not applicable here (i.e., no emphasis is placed on hidden motives or "ego-protecting" mechanisms). Some examples of cognitive distortions are catastrophizing and overgeneralization (see Appendix A for a more inclusive list).

**Schemas.** Schemas are underlying assumptions and irrational beliefs that serve as the source of cognitive distortions. Because schemas are theoretical constructs, they must be deduced from automatic thoughts made conscious by exploration and from the observation of behavior. Schemas are highly inferential and because their articulation and elaboration vary depending on the patient's presentation and the therapist's skill and inclination. For example, a therapist may view an individual with an addiction to drugs as having a set of assumptions that form the following schema: "I am a romantic, intellectual individual who is sensitive and cognizant of the injustices and contradictions of the cruel world and cannot bear the harsh realities without a drug to deaden the pain" (Moorey, 1989). Another therapist may say that the schema is more likely to be the following: "Drugs feel good, and therefore taking drugs is OK" (A. Freeman, personal communication, March 3, 1992).

A schema can start with an innate predisposition and begin to influence cognitions and behavior from the earliest moments of life (Ellis, 1992). For example, a depressed mood may be the result of an inability to reach perfect standards that were originally endorsed by a mother who was disappointed in herself for her lack of personal accomplishments. Assumptions continue to evolve and be modified throughout life; new assumptions can develop later in life in response to emotionally important events even without childhood antecedents (Perris, 1988a). These beliefs and values are the accumulation of the individual's social, familial, school, work, and religious learning and experience.

The totality of schemas that an individual possesses becomes how that individual defines himself or herself. Schemas can act individually or in combination with each other. For example, two contradictory schemas can coexist because one can be dormant while the other governs day-to-day behavior. Moreover, silent schemas may be activated only in certain situations by a specific external event (Freeman, 1987). This notion of dormancy does not invoke the Freudian concept of unconscious, nor does cognitive–behavioral therapy subscribe to the psychoanalytic concept of "phase-specific" fixation/regression (Perris, 1988a). The impact of a schema on an individual's thoughts, perceptions, emotions, and behavior depends on (a) how central to the individual's sense of self the schema is; (b) how important the individual perceives the schema to be for personal safety or well-being; (c) how actively the individual disputes or struggles with the schema when it is activated; (d) how young was the individual when the schema was internalized; (e) the relative importance and meaning of the individuals from whom the schema was acquired; and (f) how strongly the schema has been reinforced (Freeman, 1990).

As a schema develops, environmental information and experience are incorporated only to the extent that the individual can assimilate it into his or her own subjective experiences. Schemas thus become self-selective because individuals may ignore data that they are not able to render consistent with the schema. The greater the number of dysfunctional schemas a person has, the wider the range of situations that will activate one of them and thus the more vulnerable the individual will be to becoming disturbed. Once activated, schemas can produce biases in memory for past events, in perception of current ambiguous situations, and in anticipation of future events.

Perceptions, thoughts, images, beliefs, and other cognitive phenomena are considered important in the origin and maintenance of psychiatric disorders and in particular types of depression (Freeman, 1990). The cognitive–behavioral model suggests that beliefs and schemas may render a person more vulnerable to a psychiatric disorder when faced with a stressor; the combination of a dysfunctional belief and a stressor may lead a chain of cognitive events to occur with increased frequency and intensity, which may help precipitate a symptomatic episode. For example, individuals who are overinvested in maintaining warm, interpersonal relationships to satisfy intimacy needs may be more vulnerable to stressors such as interpersonal losses than may individuals who are high in autonomy and have more investment in the acquisition of personal power (Beck, 1991).

There is considerable controversy over whether cognitive distortions and underlying schemas actually cause any psychiatric disorders or whether they are secondary to other causal agents. Regardless of the primary or secondary role of cognitions in causing symptoms, cognitive theory still has much to offer in the treatment of psychopathology. By whatever means psychiatric symptoms arise, negative thoughts, images, and interpretations do have subsequent effects on mood and behavior. Thus, even in cases in which such cognitive phenomena are secondary symptoms of some biological psychiatric disorder, they can still play a role in maintaining disturbing emotions and behaviors (Williams & Moorey, 1989). For example, biologically based disorders such as psychosis and attention deficit disorder in adolescents can be exacerbated, attenuated, or maintained by cognitions. Even though reality testing and rational thinking are particularly difficult for schizophrenics, many cognitive–behavioral therapists would take the position that a patient may have developed cognitive distortions or dysfunctional self-instructions that allowed him or her to exaggerate his or her difficulties so as to avoid performing unpleasant tasks (Grossman & Freet, 1987).

## Goals of Treatment

Cognitive–behavioral therapy is a coping model as opposed to a mastery model of psychotherapy (Freeman, 1987). The goal of the therapy is not to "cure" but to help the patient become more functional in the world and experience greater control and self-efficacy by developing better coping strategies to manage life's everyday problems. Initially, patients learn the strength and the impact that their dysfunctional thoughts have on their lives. Therapists then help patients to test the veracity or adaptiveness of their thinking and behavior and to build more effective techniques for responding both intrapersonally and interpersonally (Freeman, 1990).[3] Later, more long-term goals include helping patients learn that their cognitive distortions are manifestations of their underlying schemas and that more long-lasting change will be the result of therapeutic work on the schemas.

Many of the cognitive–behavioral therapy models have a significant educative function. (The degree of emphasis depends on the model.) Underlying this function is the assumption that incorrect decisions concerning and inferences about reality are a source of psychopathology (e.g., depression results when one mistakenly sees a situation as hopeless). The correction of misconceptions is accomplished as a result of grasping new or corrective information. The approach in which the therapist's task is to help patients identify their irrational beliefs and to replace them with more rational ones is called the *rationalistic approach* (Mahoney & Gabriel, 1987). In contrast, the *constructivistic approach* involves members' creation rather than reconstruction of reality. The therapist helps each individual develop less prob-

---

[3] Versions of the cognitive–behavioral model vary in the breadth of change sought. At the most specific level, variants such as self-instructional training and stress inoculation offer particular techniques and have well-articulated steps with the goal of acquiring specific behaviors. More broadly, variants such as Beck's cognitive therapy attempt to transform more dysfunctional cognitions and problematic schemas into more functional beliefs and schemas. The variant that is most encompassing in it goals, rational–emotive therapy, seeks to present and modify a philosophy of life for patients to use on their own long after therapy has formally ended.

lematic and more useful cognitions about the self, the world, and the future. Whereas in the rationalistic approach, the concern is with the accuracy of one's depiction of reality, in the constructivist approach, it is the utility of one's portrayal of reality (Wessler & Hankin-Wessler, 1989). Whether the therapist attempts to depict reality more accurately or to reconstruct reality, most agree that the introduction of new information alone often has little effect in changing the individual's behavior or cognitions. This is because the organization of new information may be altered to fit preexisting schemas rather than new knowledge, evidence, or logic changing the cognition or schema. Hence, as illustrated in the methodological section, additional techniques (i.e., cognitive and behavioral strategies) are necessary to make cognitions and schemas more functional and accurate.

## Target for Change and Process of Change

Cognitive–behavioral therapies view factors within the individual rather than the individual's transactions with the environment as important causal agents. In cognitive–behavioral therapy, the manifest cognitive distortions are the "thematic directional signs that point to the underlying cognitive schema" (Freeman, 1990, p. 66). Cognitive–behavioral therapies view these inner dispositions as targets for assessment and change (Arkowitz & Hannah, 1989). The cognitive distortions (and underlying assumptions or schemas) are the causal mediators that are associated with different psychiatric symptoms. The automatic thoughts and schemas that underlie the problem need to be evaluated and modified because they are assumed to precipitate or at least maintain the symptoms.

**Cognitions.** At least two types of cognitive difficulties have been differentiated as targets for change (Kendall & Braswell, 1985): (a) distortions that are based on an existing but dysfunctional belief system and (b) deficits that result because the individual lacks appropriate mediating cognitions. In the case of the former, change occurs as a result of revising the current belief system. There are at least three ways of accomplishing this: disconfirmation (presenting the patient with logic or evidence that contradicts current beliefs), reconceptualization (providing the patient with another construction to account for existing observations or experiences), and insight (helping the patient understand and recognize the method or process followed to arrive at a belief; Hollon & Beck, 1986). It has been suggested that those cognitive–behavioral models that emphasize processes such as empirical disconfirmation, alternative conceptualizations, and process insight (e.g., rational–emotive therapy, Beck's cognitive therapy) are most effective in changing an individual's beliefs and behaviors when there are evident distortions in the current belief system such as depression (Hollon & Beck, 1986).

In the case of cognitive deficits (e.g., impulsive children), wherein the goal is to create or strengthen appropriate cognitive mediators when none currently exist, repetition-based approaches may be more effective. Approaches entailing the modifications of statements about the self such as self-instructional training and stress-inoculation training rely heavily on repetition and place less emphasis on influencing the validity of an individual's belief system. Repetition is thought to increase the likelihood that the individual will think a certain thought in a given situation (Hollon & Beck, 1986).

Although it is clear that individuals' cognitions are a result of their past experiences, the focus of cognitive–behavioral therapy is on what maintains or reinforces dysfunctional behavior (Freeman, 1987). Cognitive–behavioral therapies place little emphasis on insight or understanding the symbolic or historical meaning of one's maladaptive behavior. Past occurrences and early childhood events are not considered "causes" of an individual's difficulties; rather, these difficulties are caused by the individual's evaluation of prior experience and the centrality of that evaluation (underlying schemas; Ellis, 1962; Garfield, 1989). There has been some recognition that certain abused or personality-disordered individuals may have longstanding, recalcitrant maladaptive beliefs and hence require a limited degree of historical reconstruction, but this is more likely to be done on an outpatient basis (Freeman, Schordt, Gilson, & Ludgate, in press).

Schemas are generally strongly and habitually held ideas that have typically endured for long periods. These schemas require a number of powerful cognitive, emotive, and behavioral techniques to change them, and techniques addressing a single domain—whether cognition, affect, or behavior—are of limited utility (Ellis, 1990; Freeman, 1990). Changing schemas may require the individual to view them from as many different perspectives as possible; a purely cognitive strategy would leave affect, motivation, and behavior untouched. Of course, except for long-term treatment, only limited exploration of schemas is possible in an inpatient setting.

**Cognition and behavior.** According to cognitive–behavioral theorists, the modification of cognitions can occur in several ways. It can occur through the verbal analysis of experience wherein patients are directed to report their automatic thoughts with a focus on what they say to themselves rather than to others (Beck, 1991). Rational–emotive therapists often use group exercises involving imagery or guided fantasy to invite the manifestations of "nonconscious algorithms" (Ellis, 1992). In both procedures, automatic thoughts are brought into the patient's awareness and focus. This bringing into awareness may be similar to what Freud described as making conscious the preconscious material. However, unlike a psychoanalytic therapist, the cognitive–behavioral therapist does not attempt to uncover and deal with material that is defended against.

Modification of cognitions can also occur with the use of behavioral techniques or experiments designed to allow the patient to have new experiences.[4] Various cognitive–behavioral approaches differ in the manner in which and degree to which they incorporate behavioral procedures; that is, some combine cog-

---

[4] Even though both cognitive–behavioral and behavioral therapists may use behavioral interventions, the target for and mechanism of change differs. For example, both behavioral and cognitive–behavioral therapists might choose the lack of social skills of the schizophrenic as their target symptoms. Behavioral therapists would develop therapeutic strategies to help patients learn and modify behaviors (see chapter 9 for further discussion of this). Improvement of social skills for cognitive therapy is done in the context of attempting to correct the dysfunctional cognitions underlying these deficits. A role play, for example, in behavioral therapy is used to acquire and practice certain skills in a particular situation. The same role play in cognitive–behavioral therapy is used primarily to elicit the patient's distorted thoughts and concomitant feelings, with the goal of bringing them into the patient's conscious awareness rather than changing behavior itself (Perris, 1988a).

nitive and behavioral components in an additive or sequential fashion, whereas others integrate these components with one another. Rational–emotive therapy and systematic restructuring combine a cognitive approach with behavioral interventions. The behavioral interventions, usually in the form of homework, serve as practice or behavioral rehearsal inside and outside of therapy to strengthen the newly learned material. In contrast, other approaches integrate behavioral work with cognitive work by use of empirical hypothesis testing (e.g., Beck's cognitive therapy). The behavioral homework is an attempt to gather additional information concerning the validity of a particular belief.

Compared with the object relations/systems and developmental models, cognitive–behavioral therapy places little emphasis on affective arousal as crucial to the change process. However, some cognitive–behavioral therapists have emphasized the role of emotion in cognitive and behavior change (Greenberg & Safran, 1987). Beck and Weishaar (1989) postulated that the presence of affect arousal renders cognitions more accessible and therefore testable, thus enabling more lasting therapeutic change.

## Cognitive–Behavioral Therapy in a Group Setting

The focus of the cognitive–behavioral group session is primarily the individual rather than group dynamics or relationships that develop among members of the group or with the therapist (Wessler & Hankin-Wessler, 1989). Despite the individual focus, the group is not regarded as inferior to an individual format (Brown & Lewinsohn, 1984; Covi, Roth, Pattison, & Lipman, 1988; McKain, 1984; Sank & Shaffer, 1984). Cognitive–behavioral models are seen as suited to the group format for two reasons: (a) A number of patients can be taught efficiently by a single therapist, and (b) a group format allows patients to teach, supervise, and practice the model with others and thereby master it better themselves. For example, when Hollon and Shaw (1979) presented cognitive theory during their first session, they used examples furnished by group members.

The small group is often more effective than is individual therapy in helping people tackle and minimize their dysfunctional attitudes and behaviors (Ellis, 1990). Group therapy, even more than individual therapy, provides the forum for both members and the therapist to obtain information about a patient's beliefs and social behaviors by observing his or her interactions and by making comments about the beliefs and behaviors (Wessler & Hankin-Wessler, 1989). The group can provide a supportive setting in which individuals can have corrective emotional experiences by being able to observe their own behaviors and receive feedback about them from both members and the therapist:

> A group provides a unique pool of experience that can prove to be very influential, a safe, shallow pool where, under the caring vigilance of experienced supporters, a person may learn to swim and develop style before plunging into the deep end of the real world. (Wessler & Hankin-Wessler, 1989, p. 573)

Members can then plan and practice novel responses both within and outside of the group. This risk taking and behavioral rehearsal, although possible in a dyadic situation, often is enhanced in a group format (McKain, 1984). Not only is the group a safer place in which to institute new responses, but it is also likely to have a heightened generalization effect compared with that of a dyadic relationship (Covi et al., 1988).

## Technical Considerations

Cognitive–behavioral group therapy is an active, directive, collaborative therapy that is an amalgam of the dynamic therapies and the behavioral and social learning therapies (Freeman, 1990). It is a here-and-now therapy that maintains an individualized focus on the contents of patients' problems. Although it is not disputed that individuals' cognitions are results of their past experiences, the focus of cognitive–behavioral therapy is on "what is" and what maintains or reinforces dysfunctional thoughts and behaviors (Freeman, 1987). The here-and-now orientation is created by the use of tasks (both within and outside of the session) designed specifically to create the everyday conditions wherein more information can be gathered to reality test attitudes, thoughts, and images (Williams & Moorey, 1989).

## Types of Models

The cognitive–behavioral therapy models have well-delineated and well-articulated treatment procedures and manuals for each of the treatment components (Barlow & Craske, 1991; Beck & Emery, 1977, 1985; Beck et al., 1979; Covi et al., 1988; Ellis, 1962; Glantz, 1987; Heimberg, in press; Kendall & Braswell, 1985; Linehan, 1987a, 1987b; Meichenbaum, 1977; Perris, 1988b). The various approaches are diverse with regard to the model of change adopted.

What follows is a brief description of each of the major models of cognitive–behavioral therapy. It is apparent that different cognitive approaches have been developed for different forms of psychopathology. The inpatient group therapist who uses this type of model can plan to incorporate elements or processes from the various approaches depending on the diagnostic composition of his or her group.

*Rational–emotive therapy* (Ellis, 1962, 1985; Ellis & Grieger, 1985) is both a cognitive theory of disorders and a set of procedures designed to alter a person's philosophy of life and reconstruct his or her personality. This total alteration is more encompassing than are the other cognitive–behavioral approaches (Hollon & Beck, 1986). The procedures mainly involve direct instruction, verbally forceful persuasion, and logical disputation (Zimmer & Pepyne, 1971). Patients are taught to recognize their own irrational beliefs and to dispute them. The therapist models rational thinking and provides feedback to the patient. Homework and behavioral assignments are used as practice rather than as a means of producing change. There is little emphasis on empirical testing because the theory posits that the major life questions that patients face are rarely amenable to empirical inquiry (Hollon & Beck, 1986). This therapy has been used with such diverse populations as sociopaths, schizophrenics, and substance abusers (Ellis, McInerney, DiGuiseppe, & Yeager, 1988; Garfield, 1989).

*Systematic rational restructuring* was initially conceptualized as an attempt to operationalize rational–emotive therapy (Goldfried et al., 1974). There are four structured components to this procedure: presentation of the rationale of treatment, an overview of basic (irrational) assumptions thought to underlie all symptoms and subjective distress, an analysis of specific instances of the patient's difficulties in rational–emotive terms in an effort to determine which irrational assumptions are operating, and teaching patients to modify their internal self-statements. As with rational–emotive therapy, logic, reason, and persuasion are the primary processes used to effect change. Although it offers promise for inpatient treatment, it has primarily been used in treating social and test anxiety (Goldfried, Linehan, & Smith, 1978; Goldfried, Padawer, & Robins, 1984; Wise & Haynes, 1983).

*Cognitive therapy* (Beck, 1976; Beck et al., 1979), like rational–emotive therapy and systematic rational restructuring, endorses a cognitive rationale and makes use of persuasion and logic. However, it differs from both rational–emotive therapy and systematic rational restructuring in that it uses empirical hypothesis testing as a way of changing existing beliefs. Old beliefs are challenged and new beliefs are proposed by having patients do prospective empirical testing of the validity of their beliefs through behavioral assignments and homework. Alternative conceptualizations often are developed prior to prospective hypothesis testing. There is also a focus on various systematic distortions in information processing; the content is differentiated from the way in which distortions are processed. Although this type of therapy has been traditionally associated with the treatment of depression, its scope has been widened to include personality disorders, schizophrenia, and substance-abuse disorders.

*Self-instructional training* combines graduated practice with aspects of rational–emotive theory (Meichenbaum, 1977). Central to change is the repetition in which a sequence of overt verbalizations are transformed by the patient into covert self-verbalizations or thoughts. The procedure includes the therapist modeling the task by verbalizing the steps involved, the patient executing the task while the therapist articulates the steps, the patient performing the task while inaudibly moving his or her lips, and the patient completing the task while thinking the task through to himself or herself (Meichenbaum & Goodman, 1971). The repetition may facilitate the development of a mediating cognition. Similar to rational–emotive therapy, this therapy deals with distorted or irrational existing beliefs by relying largely on persuasion. Self-instructional training has been used most extensively with schizophrenics and impulsive, nonself–controlled children (see Hollon & Beck, 1986, for a review).

*Stress-inoculation training* combines a skills-training acquisition phase with subsequent practice (Meichenbaum, 1975). The procedure involves the following three main steps: educating the patient about the nature of stressful or fearful reactions and presenting a cognitive rationale for treatment; having the patient acquire and rehearse coping statements and behavioral self-control skills, such as progressive relaxation, that the patient can use when confronted by stress; and having the patient test and practice these skills in actual or stress-provoking role-play situations. The first two steps involve some combination of cognitive restructuring based on reason, persuasion, and the development of cognitive mediation or cognitive replacement based on repetition (Hollon & Beck, 1986). This approach has been used with elderly depressed patients in the consolidation phase of a more encompassing group treatment (Glantz, 1989).

## The Role of the Leader

The role and procedures that a therapist uses vary in relation to the cognitive–behavioral model chosen and the nature of the therapist–patient–group interaction. There are obvious procedural differences in the relative emphasis placed on the didactic presentation of material, problem-solving methods, degree of encouragement of strong affect, insights, fantasy material, and level of activity. For example, rational–emotive group therapists are much more likely to use group exercises that involve guided imagery than are the cognitive therapists who follow Beck's model. In addition, there are differences in the therapist's focus on content and the therapist's level of transparency. Nevertheless, some general statements can be made about the role of the therapist in this group of models. Comparatively, the cognitive–behavioral group therapist takes a verbally active approach (Garfield, 1989). This level of intervention may be even greater with certain patient populations such as chronic schizophrenics (Greenwood, 1987), the elderly (Glantz, 1989; Yost, Beutler, Corbishley, & Allender, 1986), and adolescents (Schrodt & Wright, 1987). Therapists are active in teaching the theoretical model, proposing methods of coping, and teaching strategies for testing hypotheses and solutions. The therapist also orchestrates each session to ensure that new members do not dominate, that no one becomes disruptive, and that antitherapeutic statements and actions by members are not permitted to affect other group members in a detrimental way (Wessler & Hankin-Wessler, 1989). The therapist also actively monitors the intensity of the emotional expression and the level of distress. For example, members often endorse and escalate each other's gloomy perceptions. Rather than allow members themselves to gradually establish realistic perceptions, the therapist is active in Socratically guiding patients to consider a more adaptive viewpoint (Covi et al., 1988). This active role is evident in every session unless the therapist elects to be silent or to function as a coach. If the group cannot adequately maintain its focus on the task, the therapist intervenes rather than allow members to struggle.

However, the group leader is not merely a facilitator for the creation of conditions for positive exploration. Rather, he or she is highly directive in structuring the sessions, both in form and content. Specifically, the leader (a) teaches a model for understanding dysfunction, (b) proposes hypotheses and strategies for testing the veracity of members' newly discovered ways of viewing their "symptoms," (c) directs feedback, and (d) proposes homework (Freeman, 1987; Wessler & Hankin-Wessler, 1989).

An assured and authoritative style of relating is essential for many of the cognitive–behavioral therapy group approaches (Garfield, 1989). For some groups of patients, such as those with borderline personality disorders, the therapist must present himself or herself as indestructible (Swenson, 1989). Ellis is reported to be even verbally forceful in presenting a direct, concerted, sustained attack on patient irrationality (Becker & Rosenfeld, 1976). Others, however, suggest an interactively warm but more formal environment (Glantz, 1989). Almost all cognitive–behavioral therapies advocate an active restructuring of rather than a restatement of feelings or cognitions (Freeman, 1987).

Some of the cognitive–behavioral approaches encourage monitoring of relevant aspects of the patient–therapist relationship and attending to the dynamics and process of the group despite the model's focus on individual change; at the very least, group dynamics are important insofar as they affect the individual's thinking, feelings, and actions (Covi et al., 1988). Group norms, communication patterns, and emerging leadership roles can be used to enhance the therapeutic process or can encourage continued maladaptive thinking, feelings, and actions (Wessler & Hankin-Wessler, 1989). For example, if group members do not confront each other or if they begin to concentrate on only practical and not psychological and cognitive aspects of a problem, the group leader must recognize and actively comment on such a process and then propose an alternative (Ellis, 1992).

## The Role of the Patient–Therapist Relationship

Although the importance of a satisfactory patient–therapist relationship to the progression of therapy is recognized by most theoretical orientations presented in this book, the specific quality of the therapeutic alliance required and the role that is attributed to it in the change process vary across theoretical models as well as within the versions of cognitive–behavioral therapy groups.

The founders of the cognitive–behavioral models did not focus on the therapeutic alliance; the perception by the patient of the therapist as a warm and genuine person who exhibits unconditional positive regard was not considered a prerequisite for success with at least some patients (Ellis, 1959; Greenwood, 1987). However, most theorists now acknowledge the significance of a therapeutic alliance (Ellis, 1985; Freeman et al., in press; Garfield, 1989; Greenwood, 1987; Wessler & Hankin-Wessler, 1989; Westen, 1991). Rapport, empathy, genuine human caring, warmth, and active listening have been specified as being essential to the maintenance of a therapeutic alliance and successful treatment (Freeman, 1990). Rational–emotive therapy differentiates *acceptance* from *warmth* or *approval* and encourages the former. Warmth is given with extreme caution so that patients do not think that they are "good people" simply because the therapist approves of them (Ellis, 1980).

One striking difference between cognitive–behavioral models and the object relations/systems and developmental models is in what has been termed *therapeutic* or *technical neutrality*. In technical neutrality, the therapist encourages neither a more positive, gratifying relationship nor a negative, frustrating relationship. Therapists do not "contaminate" the therapeutic interaction with their own advice, praise, or scolding (Swenson, 1989). Technical neutrality is quintessentially analytic. In contrast, some of the cognitive–behavioral therapy techniques (e.g., validation, coaching, cheerleading) not only have the effect of creating a positive therapeutic climate but also can improve the patient's self-esteem (Swenson, 1989). Rather than setting the stage for an exploration of the patient's internal world, as the developmental model might encourage, the cognitive–behavioral therapist guides the patient to explore dysfunctional or deficit cognitions to learn more functional cognitions and behaviors. From the cognitive–behavioral perspective, technical neutrality would present an additional invalidating experience. Consonant with this lack of technical neutrality, cognitive–behavioral models do not object to therapists' personal disclosures. The use of therapist self-disclosure, particularly when the therapist reveals the similarity of his or her problems to the patient's (e.g., communicating with others, feeling put down, loneliness), is considered an appropriate intervention that can reduce a patient's denial and improve his or her self-esteem (Greenwood, 1987).

A positive therapeutic alliance can enhance therapeutic effectiveness (Wessler & Hankin-Wessler, 1989).[5] The patient's specific reactions to the therapist are used in the context of examining

---

[5] The therapeutic alliance is considered important because the therapist–patient interaction, as well as therapist characteristics that may appear "irrelevant" to the patient's beliefs, may influence the patient's acceptance of alternative ways of thinking. That is, patients may accept a therapist's comment and change their opinions because they admire or respect the therapist rather than because of evidence presented (Wessler & Hankin-Wessler, 1989).

distorted assumptions by having the patient look at the cognitions that are generating the response or behavior (Freeman, 1987). Similarly, the obstacle of noncompliance or resistance to treatment, which impedes collaboration, can be viewed as the result of irrational beliefs, which the therapist can then actively confront and dispute (Ellis, 1985).

## The Use of Co-Therapists

A co-therapy team is strongly advised, particularly for groups with more than six members (Glantz, 1987; Hollon & Evans, 1983). The high level of therapist activity in the group session and the multiple tasks of the therapist are eased by a dyadic therapeutic team that can share the burden. In addition, some of the behavioral techniques such as modeling and role playing work best with the presence of at least two therapists. A division of therapeutic attention and labor helps therapists attend to and then challenge distortions of the participant whose problem is being discussed while also monitoring other group members (Greenwood, 1987). There are many ways to divide the labor depending on the relative strengths of each of the therapists. This model especially is accommodating to a training facility wherein a trainee may be paired with a senior therapist. The specificity of the role assignment enables the therapists to work together more easily. Covi et al. (1988) recommend that one member of the team assume the position of the primary therapist ∧ who begins and ends the session, initiates and directs the discussion of various agenda items, and summarizes the work of the session. The co-therapist reviews and organizes the homework while the primary therapist asks members to describe their agendas (Hollon & Evans, 1983). The co-therapist also monitors the group process and tracks the primary therapist's interactions and manner with the group (Covi et al., 1988). Despite the division of labor, the therapists should have a collaborative posture toward the group and equivalent access to each member of the group and the group as a whole.

## The Role of Technique

The cognitive–behavioral model presents an overall framework or strategy, not just a series or group of techniques. The followers of Ellis and Beck, in particular, rely heavily on the inductive method and a Socratic style of questioning to facilitate change by helping members develop greater awarenesses of their distorted thinking and perceptions. The variety of behavioral and cognitive techniques used are important devices for effecting cognitive change. Therapist and patient collaborate to design specific, structured learning experiences to teach patients to bring into awareness conscious and nonconscious algorithms; monitor dysfunctional thoughts; recognize the link between thoughts, mood, and behavior; scrutinize the data supporting inaccurate or irrational assumptions; and substitute more accurate or realistic interpretations of their experiences. Behavioral techniques or assignments (e.g., role playing) primarily are used to elucidate the patient's thoughts and to provide novel experiences; that is, the emphasis is on discovering and changing cognitions, rather than changing the behavior (Arkowtiz & Hannah, 1989).

## Member Selection and Group Composition

Cognitive–behavioral groups work best with 4 to 12 members depending on the composition and availability of patients (Hollon & Evans, 1983). Sessions should range from 1 to 2 hours each depending on the attention span of the members and the group size. The greater the number of members, the longer the time period required to adequately attend to each member's agenda. The model is most effective when group attendance is voluntary. However, sanctions for nonattendance or privileges for attendance have not hindered its utility (Greenwood, 1987; Grossman & Freet, 1987).

There are reports of successful treatment with cognitive–behavioral therapy for many diagnostic categories such as severe depression (Blackburn, 1989; Miller, Norman, & Keitner, 1989), general anxiety (Freeman & Simon, 1989), panic disorders (Barlow & Craske, 1991; Greenberg, 1989), phobias (Heimberg, 1990; Hope, Herbert, & Bellack, 1991), eating disorders (Channon & Wardle, 1989; Garner & Bemis, 1982), obsessional disorders (Salkovskis, 1989), alcohol dependency (Ellis et al., 1988; Glanz, 1987; Sanchez-Craig, Annis, Bronet, & MacDonald, 1984), drug addiction (Ellis et al., 1988; Moorey, 1989), impulsive disorders

(Meichenbaum & Asarnow, 1979), borderline personality and other personality disorders (Beck, Freeman, & Associates, 1990; Freeman, 1988; Freeman & Leaff, 1989; Freeman, Pretzer, Fleming, & Simon, 1990; Linehan, 1987a, 1987b), and acute and chronic schizophrenia (Greenwood, 1987; Perris, 1988a). Unfortunately, most of this research reports on use of this therapy with outpatients in an individual format. Moreover, group research that does exist reports on groups with diagnostically homogeneous compositions (e.g. Glantz, 1987; Greenwood, 1987; Heimberg, 1990; Linehan, 1987a, 1987b; Meichenbaum, 1977). On the one hand, frequently the structure of an inpatient setting necessitates the creation of a diagnostically heterogenous group. On the other hand, the focus on the individual and the extent to which the treatment can be tailored to the specific dysfunction in a group setting attenuate the central relevance of diagnostic composition more so than in approaches that emphasize group-level interventions. There are a few reports of diagnostically mixed groups (Coleman & Gantman, 1991; Freeman, 1987; Freeman et al., in press). These groups have taken advantage of a heterogenous composition in that such a composition more closely approximates real life and allows for a greater variety of perspectives.

With respect to age, there have been reports of the successful use of cognitive–behavioral group therapy with adolescents, adults, and geriatric patients (Blackburn, 1989; Bowers, 1989; Covi, Roth, & Lipman, 1982; Glantz, 1989; Grossman & Freet, 1987; Rush & Watkins, 1981; Steuer & Hammen, 1983; Yost et al., 1986).

In principle, an inpatient can benefit from cognitive–behavioral group therapy if his or her difficulties can be conceptualized in terms of irrational, unrealistic, or dysfunctional thoughts and beliefs. The inpatients who are most likely to profit from this intervention are those who are motivated to change (e.g., work hard in sessions and complete homework assignments); accept and understand the general cognitive–behavior model; seem able to use the theory to reconceptualize their problems; can use the reconceptualizations to change their dysfunctional thoughts; and are able and willing to complete tasks that require role playing and guided exercises in self-monitoring (Bowers, 1989; Glanz, 1987).

In the past, patients with extensive delusional systems, who are disruptive because of active psychosis, who do not think that they are psychiatrically impaired, who attribute their illnesses to physical causes, who are unable to establish a rapport with the therapist, or who are unable to collaborate are considered not suitable for this type of group (Wessler & Hankin-Wessler, 1989). In addition, patients whose interpersonal styles are verbally disruptive (e.g., overly verbose, hostile, demanding of attention; Heimberg, in press) or whose cognitive deficits are significant (e.g., Alzheimer's disease, mental retardation, learning disabilities) have also traditionally been thought to be poor candidates for cognitive–behavioral group therapy.

However, more recently, a number of cognitive–behavioral group therapy researchers have instituted some modifications in techniques that have permitted a wider range of patients to benefit from this form of therapy. For example, Williams and Moorey (1989) reported the successful use of cognitive–behavioral group therapy with brain-damaged individuals if the procedures were simplified in such a way as to be comprehensible to these patients. They suggested that there is a greater need to rely on behavioral methods during the treatment than perhaps one would for other groups and that most of the cognitive work needs to be done during the session. The greater the severity of the cognitive deficit, the greater the ratio of behavioral to cognitive interventions needed (Williams & Moorey, 1989). Similarly, Greenwood (1987) reported the successful use of cognitive–behavioral group therapy with chronic hospitalized young adult schizophrenics, a group that is often seen as unable to establish a rapport with the therapist or collaborate in a problem-solving approach. There are also some reports of success with patients who attribute their illnesses primarily to physical difficulties (Coleman & Gantman, 1991).

## Assessment

Assessment and preparation prior to the member's first group meeting are essential to the success of this model. Formal diagnosis is less important than is the evaluation of the member's ability to understand the cognitive–behavioral model and make use of feedback from the therapist and other members and his or her motivation to participate in homework assignments. Thus, information from other staff may not be adequate to assess the member's potential for functioning in the group. The main aims of this assessment are to evaluate whether the patient is capable of using cognitive–behavioral concepts to describe problems so that the therapist can arrive at a cognitive conceptualization of the case. If the patient is to join an ongoing group, assessment and preparation need to be done prior to the patient's first meeting. If a new group is forming, the assessment and preparation can be rendered more efficiently in the group rather than in an individual format. Cognitive–behavioral therapists favor the use of questionnaires in their initial and ongoing assessments to supplement the interview. The assessment begins with an exploration of each patient's presenting problems; formalized assessments such as the Beck Depression Inventory (BDI; Beck, 1978), the Beck Anxiety Inventory (BAI; Beck, Epstein, Brown & Steer, 1988), and the Hopelessness Scale (Beck, Weissman, Lester, & Trexler, 1974) evaluate target symptoms. The Dysfunctional Attitude Scale (Oliver & Baumgart, 1985; Weissman, 1979) and the Automatic Thoughts Questionnaire (Hollon & Kendall, 1980) assess the patients' main cognitions, appraisals, and irrational and unrealistic beliefs. The Life History Questionnaire (Lazarus, 1981) collects background information (e.g., developmental, social, family history).

In preparing the patient for the group, the need for specificity of target symptoms and goal setting cannot be overemphasized. Their delineation should be concertized collaboratively with the patient in the form of developing a detailed prioritized problem list.[6] With short-term hospital stays, it is usually possible to work on only a few specific problems. The first problem that a patient

---

[6] Some advocate that the problem list and the problem to be worked on in group should be negotiated in an individual session to personalize intervention targets and to prevent members from being influenced by other members' choices of problems (Covi et al., 1988). Others feel that this a luxury that a successful inpatient model cannot afford and may not require (Coleman & Gantman, 1991).

should usually focus on is one that can be resolved within the hospital stay and that plays a central role in patients' symptoms.

For example, a 40-year-old man who has a 10-year history of alcohol abuse was hospitalized after a suicide gesture. In interviewing the patient for group, the therapist found four possible areas for intervention: the drinking behavior itself; the concurrent depression (low mood, helplessness), although the direction of causation between the depression and drinking was unclear; the reliance on the use of alcohol as a primary coping mechanism; and the social environment (his wife) that permitted and even may have supported his drinking (Glantz, 1987). Depending on the patient's length of stay, the patient's depression and the concomitant automatic dysfunctional thoughts that contribute to the depression or his reliance on alcohol as a primary coping mechanism to solve problems may be targeted as goals. This patient perceived his drinking as a means to "resolve" or "dissolve" dissatisfaction at work (lack of promotions, inability to assert himself) and conflicts with his wife. The alcohol also served to reduce his anxiety and anger by terminating fantasies and facilitating the forgetting of or distortion of a memory of past events (his drinking began 10 years ago after an affair). The therapist hypothesized that the maladaptive conceptualizations (both cognitive content and processes) had a central role in the etiology, maintenance, and exacerbation of the alcohol abuse. Both the maladaptive conceptualizations surrounding the development and maintenance of the alcoholism and depression were thus the primary targets of the cognitive–behavioral psychotherapy.

Further exploration with this patient revealed that his maladaptive processing included drawing arbitrary inferences, creating selective distortions, and making gross overgeneralizations; his thinking was either global, abstract, and undifferentiated or highly narrow, concretized, and specific depending on the circumstance (Glantz, 1987). His self-evaluations were based on a single criterion (his affair 10 years ago), demonstrating a narrow focus of attention on a single aspect of the situation. He believed that alcohol was the only alternative to bad feelings and difficult problems. For this patient, the focus in the preparation and initial phases of therapy were then his cognitive distortions in a specific area (e.g., his home life, wife, or job). As part of his assessment, he may complete the BDI, the BAI, the Hopelessness Scale, and perhaps the Automatic Thoughts Questionnaire. He may then repeat all or some of these at regular intervals. He may also be given *Coping With Substance Abuse* (Beck & Emery, 1977) or *Coping With Depression* (Beck & Greenberg, 1974) to read as part of the initial preparation.

The initial goals for this patient in the inpatient group, similar to those of other patients, were to introduce the following premises: (a) the way an individual thinks strongly affects the way he feels and behaves and therefore his ability to cope with and enjoy life, (b) there are alternative ways to view life that can lead to more desirable feelings and behaviors, (c) and by changing thinking, one can control feelings and behaviors (Glantz, 1987). The content chosen for therapy discussions should focus on one of a member's specific interpersonal problems, with the overall goal being to help the member identify his or her particular maladaptive conceptualization processes. The next step is to help the member understand the negative consequence of these maladaptive conceptualizations and to recognize alternatives and the concomitant improvement that will result from this reconceptualization. The goal then becomes helping the member develop more functional alternative coping and self-regulatory skills. Additionally, patients are supported in replacing maladaptive conceptualizations and behavioral symptom patterns with more functional behaviors and thoughts rather than being encouraged to simply stop drinking (Glantz, 1987). This general intervention strategy applies to all patients with alcohol problems. However, the specific goals and techniques used for each individual are based on a patient's particular dysfunctional thinking, coping strategies, personality, symptoms, social resources, and drinking history. The primary goal is to teach generalized coping and reconceptualizing skills that extend beyond what is discussed in the group.

## Preparation

The goal of preparation is to facilitate the patient's entry into group. If a new group is being formed, cognitive–behavioral theory can be taught at the initial session. However, in the inpatient setting, typically the patient joins an ongoing group and must therefore be given an education regarding the principles of cognitive–behavioral therapy prior to beginning group. The content emphasis of the preparation needs to be adapted to the particular patient population and the resources that such a population brings to treatment. For example, with young disturbed chronic inpatients, the willingness to participate cannot be assured. The cognitive change desired during this initial phase would be from rejection (e.g., "I don't want to be here") to acceptance (e.g., "This group is OK. I can talk here"; Greenwood, 1987). However, for some depressed inpatients, this issue may not be relevant and the initial focus may be on definitions and examples of automatic thoughts and schemas and the relation between thoughts and feelings (see Beck et al., 1979, for examples of how to present this material). This introduction provides a common language and conceptual framework for group members. An essential part of the model is to conceptualize the relation of the members' target symptoms to their dysfunctional or irrational thought patterns. Once the member can identify the dysfunctional thought pattern, he or she is asked to develop an awareness of the frequency of this maladaptive thinking. To assist with this process, members can be given a relevant reading (see Appendix B, Bibliotherapy) and perhaps an activity schedule such as that included in *Mastery and Pleasure* (Blackburn, 1989) to rate their own activities. The more completely the cognitive–behavioral conceptual framework is understood at a practical level, the more able the patient will be to make use of the group experience.

It is important to assess and review patients' expectations, particularly those related to concerns such as discomfort in groups, judgments about others' reactions to their problems, or fear of talking or getting help in the group. Although other models concentrate on exploring expectations, the emphasis in this model is on the cognitive distortions or irrationality of the cognitions that would preclude the patient's successful group participation. One thing that the therapist can do to instill hope in the patient concerning group experience is to talk about treatment efficacy studies (Covi et al., 1988). Patients are also familiarized with the format of the session and the importance of the homework requirement (Coleman & Gantman, 1991).

## The Structured Agenda Format

Groups can be closed-ended or open-ended. In a close-ended group, both the course of therapy and each therapy session is structured. In an open-ended or ongoing group, it is possible to structure only the format of each session. Rather than permitting members' interactions or topics to emerge as the group progresses (as in the interactional version of the interpersonal model or the object relations/system model), sessions are structured through the use of a consistent format. Part of the rationale for this is that many patients become hospitalized because they are unable to structure their thinking or their overall life experiences, particularly during stressful times (Freeman, 1990).

The session usually begins with the members' completion of structured assessments that evaluate their current status. As these forms are reviewed by one of the therapists for significant changes in clinical status, the other therapist may establish an agenda by soliciting members' thoughts about the previous session and inviting members to review their activities since the previous session, to report on the success of the homework assignments, and to state briefly personal items on which they wish to work in this session. Each of these segments can be divided into separate go-arounds or combined into one go-around. Agenda setting usually takes 5–15 minutes. Because members frequently have unresolved business from previous sessions, a review of unfinished agenda items from previous sessions is included in the session structure; until these cognitions and associated feelings are examined, a member may get little out of the session (Covi et al., 1988). The therapists then attempt to highlight common experiences, illuminate complicated or difficult-to-grasp principles, or illustrate a topic that will be discussed that session (Covi et al., 1988).

Most of the group session is devoted to discussing personal agenda items through the patient–therapist interchange.[7] Al-

---

[7] While one member of the group is actively working on his or her personal

though the agenda is set, it can be modified. If the group or a member digresses, the therapist can ask whether the member (or the group) wishes to continue with this digression or return to the previously set agenda (Freeman, 1987). An effort is made to cover all agenda items; a disproportionate amount of time spent with one or more members can be compensated for at subsequent sessions (Covi et al., 1988). The body of the session depends somewhat on group composition, the nature of the problems, how much each member has accomplished in previous sessions, and whether the group is closed-ended or open-ended. The therapist can take one of two strategies. He or she can attempt to work a little with each member or concentrate in depth on a few members in a single session, recognizing that those members not receiving the group's attention will have their opportunities in the next session (Coleman & Gantman, 1991). Part of the group time may be spent introducing a new technique or concept (Covi et al., 1988). The particular cognitive–behavioral strategies introduced and used by the therapist will depend on the type and severity of the members' problems, their knowledge and understanding of their problems in cognitive–behavioral terms, the number of sessions that the group has existed or that an individual member has attended and the additional number he or she is expected to attend, and the therapist's preferences. The final few minutes of the session can be used as a wrap-up to evaluate the session, assign homework for the next session, get feedback from the members about the session, and have members summarize what they have learned during the session. The structured format permits patients to anticipate the group session and allows for a more gradual conclusion of the session than "We have to stop here" (Freeman, 1987).

---

agenda, some therapists prefer to have other members involved initially by "active listening" (trying to understand the general therapeutic principles used by the therapist and applying them to their own similar problems). At the end of the patient–therapist interchange, other members of the group can comment on what they discovered and offer feedback (Covi et al., 1988). Other therapists request that members "jump in" whenever they feel that they can contribute (Coleman & Gantman, 1991).

## Homework

A fundamental tenet of the cognitive–behavioral model is that much of the therapeutic change takes place outside of the group therapy session (Covi et al., 1988). Individualized self-help exercises (i.e., homework) facilitate this process. Homework extends the therapy session and can reinforce newly learned skills. It is believed that the members who diligently complete self-help tasks make progress and are able to meet their stated therapy goals more quickly (Freeman, 1990).

In addition, the completion of written homework for each session makes the process of group therapy available to many members who may be otherwise too uncontrolled and unskilled to participate actively in the group. For example, Grossman and Freet (1987) required adolescents to complete written homework as a prerequisite for attending group. The adolescents could get help on their homework from the hospital staff and teachers. Having written homework assignments completed ahead of time so that they were available to read during the session made social interaction possible for adolescents who were too reticent, psychotic, or socially inept to make spontaneous valuable contributions. Structured homework made group sessions more productive, improved adolescents' relationships with staff, and increased their self-esteem.

The therapist must take care that an assignment can be completed given a member's behavioral repertoire and level of functioning. The creation of the particular self-help exercise should be a collaborative effort between the member, the therapist, and the group; it should be relevant to the material discussed in the session (Covi et al., 1988). To increase compliance with assignment completion, other hospital staff should be aware generally of homework requirements and, when possible, should be informed of the specific assignments. Patients might also be assisted either by the group or other staff members in scheduling time to complete their assignment during a day that may be full of other hospital activities. The assignment of homework is not always feasible. Certain groups, such as the elderly, do not readily do therapy work between sessions (Glantz, 1989).

## The Course of Therapy and Content of the Session

Cognitive–behavioral group therapy is problem oriented rather than process oriented. That is, there is little pressure placed on the member to understand the interactions between himself or herself and the therapist or other group members. Cohesion, a cornerstone of change for many of the models (e.g., the educative model, the interactional agenda version of the interpersonal model, and the object relations/systems model), is facilitated or discouraged depending on the goals for the individual group members. The cognitive–behavioral variants do not usually focus on phenomena such as dominance, group-as-a-whole dynamics, and affectivity that are prominent in other models (e.g., those just mentioned) unless they illustrate an individual's distortions or highlight the relevance of cognitive principles (Hollon & Evans, 1983).

**Cognitive and behavioral strategies.** As shown in Appendixes B and C, cognitive–behavioral therapy has a plethora of cognitive strategies and many behavioral techniques available as part of its repertoire.

The techniques can be divided roughly into cognitive and behavioral techniques, although there is some blurring of the boundaries between the two.

Although the format for inpatient therapy does not vary from outpatient therapy, the type of techniques used depends on the group members' assets, skills, severities and types of symptomatologies, and treatment goals (Bowers, 1989). Suppose, for example, that the therapist wishes to demonstrate to a group of young chronic schizophrenics the centrality of cognitions in determining one's reactions to an event. The therapist may use the strategy of performing skits that model an emotional episode wherein the activating event and emotional components are clearly labeled. The task of the group members would be to generate self-statements that would have led to the emotional sequence (Greenwood, 1987). Alternatively, the therapist may lead moderately depressed patients through a guided fantasy in which they are asked to imagine squeezing toothpaste all over a friend's bathroom. Each member then shares his or her emotional experience of the exercise. From such exercises, members learn that they have particular cognitions that accompany their emotional experiences.

Most types of cognitive–behavioral therapy entail a characteristic plan of progression. In closed-ended groups, initial sessions are more generally behavioral in orientation, whereas later sessions involve more explicit cognitive techniques. For example, with adolescents in a state hospital, Grossman and Freet (1987) found that group sessions required specific and structured behavioral guidelines, which were referred to as *group therapy rules* and *constructive behavior tools*. The tools and rules became the foundation for teaching rudimentary social skills and provided guidelines for evaluating larger segments of behavior. After gaining behavioral control, the adolescents were encouraged to explore feelings and learn self-observational skills (Grossman & Freet, 1987). In contrast, a group primarily composed of depressed adults might begin with exercises to improve self-observation.

In general, the particular behavioral techniques used change across sessions in a closed-ended group. Initially, specific behavioral tasks are assigned to increase activity, to improve self-observational skills, and to teach members that there is a connection between thoughts and resulting feelings. To accomplish these tasks, such techniques as activity scheduling, self-monitoring of mood events, mastery and pleasure ratings, graded or partial task assignment are used. As the sessions progress and the goals shift to focusing on discovery, evaluating, and empirically testing various automatic thoughts and underlying assumptions, the particular behavioral techniques used change (e.g., shame-attacking exercises, role playing). Similarly, initial cognitive strategies (e.g., reattribution, advantages–disadvantages, alternative techniques, labeling distortions, identifying idiosyncratic meaning) are generally aimed at identifying specific automatic thoughts and gradually increasing attention toward discovering and changing underlying belief systems (e.g., through guided fantasy, as–if technique, downward-arrow technique; Hollon & Shaw, 1979). This latter cognitive shift seldom occurs during a short-term hospital stay. Patients are often discharged from the hospital having learned to recognize and correct specific faulty cognitions but not to change the underlying beliefs or assumptions.

In an open-ended group, this cognitive and behavioral progression occurs at an individual level only. In the beginning or when the patient has more severe symptomatology, a relatively greater proportion of behavioral techniques are used. As therapy progresses, more cognitive techniques are used. Within each of the cognitive and behavioral components, therapy proceeds from the relatively more simple to the more complex. As therapy progresses, behavioral tasks proceed from graded or partial task assignments to whole task assignments. Similarly, cognitive strategies shift from processing current cognitive events or distortions (thoughts, images, particular interpretations) to accessing (if possible) nonconscious beliefs and schemas (Williams & Moorey, 1989). Similarly, there may be a higher number of patient–therapist interactions during the earlier part of the treatment than in the later phases when individual consolidation and self-initiative should be taking place (Covi et al., 1988).

**The course of therapy.** There are several manuals that detail the sequence and time frame of the sessions in closed-ended outpatient or day-hospital groups (Covi et al., 1982, 1988; Glantz, 1989; Moorey, 1989). In short-term inpatient settings, a closed-ended group with a specific time frame is less feasible. However, the phases are still somewhat applicable, and the progression can be followed at an individual level. The first phase of therapy is characterized by the process of understanding the basic tenets of cognitive–behavioral theory and therapy and learning to think in cognitive and behavioral terms (Covi et al., 1982). The therapist facilitates members' understanding by illustrating the theory with examples from their experiences and by introducing techniques aimed at identifying distorted and irrational thoughts and modifying dysfunctional behavior (Covi et al., 1982). Members learn the relation between their target symptoms or problems and their dysfunctional thoughts. They are then trained to identify and test the accuracy of their cognitions and to dispute problematic cognitions through the use of structured exercises (Heimberg, 1990). With short-term inpatient stays, this may be all that can be accomplished in the three to six sessions available.

During the next phase of group treatment, members use their newly acquired background of cognitive therapy to develop an understanding of their particular symptoms. This involves identifying the particular negative cognitions that accompany the symptoms, formulating the type of cognitive distortion they represent, and discovering the underlying assumptions that are at the core of such dysfunctional thinking (Covi et al., 1982). Therapy then proceeds on two levels: Techniques are taught and applied to the entire group (e.g., all members can be trained to identify, recall, and initiate mastery/pleasure activities), and treatment is individualized by matching techniques with personal goals (Covi et al., 1988).

For example, Grossman and Freet (1987) presented how cognitive–behavioral techniques can be adopted to the special needs of different diagnostic groups of inpatients. They taught all adolescents in their group to differentiate among their thoughts, feelings, and actions and to then label their internal experiences and check feedback from other group members for accuracy so as to discover the systematic ways they distort what they hear. All group members were taught this skill even though the pace of learning for each member varied; members differed in the emphasis they required. Adolescents whose major problems were due to hyperactivity seemed to backslide easily even after they understood the whole process; practice at identifying and checking the accuracy of their thoughts was imperative for their success. With adolescents of below-average intelligence, the learning was slow; these members had to be helped to put their feelings into words and taught to use some alternative sentences that were chunked into very small steps and then repeatedly practiced. However, once they understood their distortion processes, they were able to retain this understanding. For psychotic adolescents, learning new sentences was only part of the task. They also had to learn to identify the exaggerations and the advantages gained by their distortions; because they had not learned basic coping skills, they had to be taught more effective ways to achieve their goals. Adolescents with personality disorders had distorted responses that were more consciously aimed at achieving some short-term objective than were those the other adolescents. The task with these adolescents was to point out the exaggerations implicit in their distortions and to discuss with them the consequences of their behavior. Sentences that had enough emotional impact to be remembered were used to make the adolescents aware of how they gave themselves excuses to act out so that they would immediately get what they wanted but would destroy their long-term relationships with important people. Long-run consequences of their behavior were thus emphasized (Grossman & Freet, 1987).

The last phase of the group treatment is consolidation and working on issues of termination. The cognitive–behavioral model is mindful of relapse prevention as an essential part of *Marlatt* the therapy. Preparation for termination begins in the first session. Members learn a model and a series of techniques that they can use during stressful times. They are encouraged to understand the need for monitoring their moods and are taught how to be watchful of indications of need for further cognitive therapy. Depending on the length of time in group, at least 1 or 2 sessions need to be devoted to an exploration of significant termination issues. Members are encouraged to express and discuss their concerns about leaving the hospital and the group. The cognitive–behavioral model is applied to termination issues in that the accuracy of members' posttreatment predictions (e.g., they will experience future symptomatology, they are not yet well) needs to be questioned. As part of this, a member's progress with respect to target symptoms is reviewed. Members identify procedures that were helpful in attenuating symptoms. They are also encouraged to design and implement their own self-help cognitive therapy programs for residual symptoms and possibly continue therapy after hospitalization so as to maximize the likelihood that therapeutic gains will be maintained (Covi et al., 1988).

In an open-ended diagnostically heterogenous group, pacing is one of the most arduous tasks that the therapist faces. Experience and supervision are irreplaceable aids in this area. Somehow, the healthier members' needs must be accommodated at the same time as those who are new or more severely disturbed are allowed to learn the basics. Members' disparities can be somewhat attenuated if at each session basic principles are reviewed, the majority of the session is pitched to the "average patient," and remedial or advanced work is done between sessions (Freeman et al., in press).

## An Alternative Form: Rotating Theme Group

Freeman (1987; Freeman et al., in press) developed a theme-focused cognitive–behavioral group approach for use in inpatient settings. The model was developed to alleviate some problems inherent in inpatient groups: the variety of diagnostic and educational backgrounds, the variation in individual articulateness, different levels of comfort with social interaction and speaking in a group format, and the disruption that occurs in the group when members frequently come and go without notice. Although homogeneity of age, severity of symptoms, and diagnosis is preferred, it is not essential to the utility of this approach. Its structured nature allows for patients with cognitive confusion to participate. Each group session is self-contained, with closure at the end of each session; sessions are not cumulative. The approach has maximum flexibility in its structure so that the group is designed first by estimating the average number of sessions attended by members (e.g., if the average length of stay is 16 days and it is possible to have three sessions per week, the number of sessions in the cycle will be about seven). Staff members then generate a list of topics for the group to discuss totaling no more than the computed number of sessions. Members' input about topics can be sought after the initial series of group meetings. The group is run in continuing cycles (e.g., seven sessions per cycle). Some examples of topics include the stigma of being in a hospital, impulse or anger control, family problems, and relationships and friendships (see Freeman, 1987, for other examples).

The topic for each session is posted on the unit prior to the meeting. Each group member prepares in advance by writing two of his or her own problems related to the topic of the day and brings the list to the group meeting. In the group, one member functions as a secretary, writing on the blackboard the problems that are read by each member at the beginning of the session. The therapist combines issues that overlap to establish a group agenda. Each problem is then discussed. Written notes can be brought to the session, especially for those less comfortable with talking in a group. Aside from the selection of a specific topic, the group is conducted using the principles and techniques previously described in this chapter (see Freeman, 1987, and Freeman et al., in press, for a detailed exposition of this model).

Another variation of the rotating theme group is the *programmed group*, which is similar to a closed-ended structured educational group in that it is designed to teach specific information about cognitive therapy but unlike the closed-ended group allows members to enter at any point. Freeman et al. (in press) provided a sample schedule for such a program. The skill in designing one of these programs is to present topics that do not require preexisting knowledge. This type of program is the most efficient way of providing basic information about cognitive–behavioral therapy but restricts significantly the interactions among group members and the therapists.

## Clinical Illustration

This was an open-ended group in an acute care psychiatric facility. To enter the group, the patient and treating psychiatrist must have made a six-session commitment (the equivalent of 2 weeks at three sessions per week). New group members were added only at the beginning of the week. Sessions were 90 minutes long.

Each member was interviewed prior to beginning group (in a group format if there was more than one patient joining); patients were given information about the group, taught cognitive–behavioral theory, and were required to make a commitment to attend and do homework. The therapist made a tentative case conceptualization in cognitive–behavioral terms. If additional time was available, the patient and the therapist formulated specific problems to work on in group. If time was not available, this was the work of the first session. Often, the patient was given reading such as *Coping With Depression* (Beck & Greenberg, 1974) or *Coping With Substance Abuse* (Beck & Emery, 1977).

## Group Members

Al, a 45-year-old man, was a manager for a construction company. He had a 25-year history of alcohol abuse but had stopped drinking 6 months prior to his hospitalization. He had been experiencing increasing anxiety since he had stopped drinking, feeling overwhelmed at work and yelling at his children and wife. He was hospitalized after he had gotten into a physical fight with one of his subordinates, had gone on a drinking binge, and then had made a suicide gesture because he felt hopeless about his ability to keep from drinking. The therapist assessed he that had inadequate skills to cope with the difficulties of daily life in addition to exhibiting some distorted cognitions (e.g., all-or-nothing thinking). This was his second group session. This member is included to show how drug and alcohol problems may be tackled within a cognitive–behavioral framework.

Sally was a 60-year-old widow who had been in long-term treatment for anxiety and depression. She complained that she was lonely and that her siblings and children did not visit her. A number of antidepressants had been unsuccessful in ameliorating her chronic dysphoria (she regularly called her psychiatrist and had numerous physical complaints). Her hospitalization was the result of her relatives' frequent calls to the psychiatrist complaining about her worsening condition. This was her second group session. This member illustrates how one can work with a patient who has little acceptance of her difficulties (e.g., Coleman & Gantman, 1991).

Patricia was a 39-year-old mother of 8-month-old twin boys. Before her pregnancy, she had been a very successful engineer in a consulting firm and had received many awards for her designs. Despite only having a BA, she had been the youngest member of the large prestigious firm to be made a senior consultant—managing her own team of engineers. She had recently returned to her job full time. She had been hospitalized after an overdose of psychotropic medication that had been given to her by her general practitioner (she had complained of weight loss, insomnia, and loss of concentration on her job). This suicide attempt resulted in a comatose state of almost 1 week. She had no other psychiatric history or experience with therapy. This was her second session. This member is included to show how the cognitive–behavioral model can be used with a depressed patient.

Sutton was a 25-year-old single man from a wealthy family. He had been hospitalized for a suicide gesture after being accused by his girlfriend's father of stealing some of her jewelry. After graduating with average grades from a prestigious university, he could not hold a steady job. He had been staying in bed, with no energy, and getting into disagreements with his mother and the various household helpers. He had had numerous short-lived friendships. In the hospital, his depression quickly dissipated. Group treatment for him focused on building more socially responsible behaviors. No effort was made to restructure his underlying schema of "I will get what I want." Rather, the goal was to modify it to "I will get what I want over the long haul." This modification enabled the therapist to continually point out that his "winning" in the short run damaged his long-term goals and relationships. This was his eighth group session. This member illustrates the technique used in working with personality-disordered patients.

Phoebe was a 45-year-old single, attractive, bright, soft-spoken woman who was recently promoted in her job as an executive secretary to the president of a company. She had been experiencing increasing anxiety at work since her promotion and had become more socially isolated outside of work. A week ago, she had stopped going to work. One of her co-workers visited her at home and found her in a confused and somewhat paranoid state, having taken too much over-the-counter sleeping medication. On inquiry, the therapist discovered that the anxiety related to having to frequently entertain clients when the president was tied up by showing them the city in the company limousine. The patient and therapist agreed to work on her social anxiety and the dysfunctional thoughts that maintained this dysfunctional and avoidant behavior. This was her fifth session. This patient is included to illustrate the use of cognitive–behavioral techniques developed by Heimberg (1990) for treating social phobia.

## The Session

This was the second session of the week. Members had completed the BDI and BAI when they arrived. The therapist reintroduced himself and the co-therapist, and members repeated their names while the co-therapist collected and reviewed the questionnaires.

> Therapist: This is a cognitive–behavioral therapy group. Last time we learned through the toothpaste exercise that there is a connection between what a person thinks and feels. When you get upset, it is often related to what you are thinking. If you think differently, you will often feel better and be able to do things differently. From the behavioral perspective, the idea is to solve things and do things differently a little at a time. It is a bit structured; we have an agenda (co-therapist writes this on the blackboard). Our agenda is to check with everyone and find out what has been happening since last we met. You might make a brief comment about how your homework went. Then after touching base with everyone, we'll go over homework in more detail, and continue working on our goals by developing specific strategies to help you think, feel, and behave differently. Does anyone have any questions about what I said right now or thoughts or questions from yesterday? (Therapist structures the session format.)
>
> Sally: I have a question about something I noticed in our last meeting. It sounds like this is more between doctor and patient than other therapies that I've had.

(Patient articulates one of the differences between this group and the psychodynamic group that she had been involved with in her last hospitalization.)

> Therapist: You mean the therapist is more active here? In other types of groups, the therapist may be more quiet and group members are free to talk about whatever

seems important at the time. Yes, that's perceptive. Here it's more structured. We have a certain format. (silence) Now I made it so structured that no one wants to say anything. (giggles from the group members) Let's go around and find out how everyone is doing and how the homework went. It's important for us to find for each of you a manageable chunk of your goal that you can accomplish today. Please feel free to give feedback when other people present what they are working on. After all, we have so much collective wisdom here. Let's start with Patricia. Did you do your homework?

Patricia: (Homework was to pick two times when she felt upset and write what the automatic thoughts were. She was to complete a form that she had been given the previous group meeting requiring the specification of the situation, her feelings, and her automatic thoughts.) Yes, it went OK. I feel fine.

Therapist: Good. How about you Sally?

Sally: Oh no, I forgot. What was I supposed to do? I left it in the locker. I've been having a bad day. I was just so upset after talking to my doctor.

Therapist: Did you write it down?

Sally: Well, I guess. Some of it. I started to anyway. I have such a bad memory. I just can't seem to remember anything anymore.

Therapist: I'm glad that you wrote it down (reinforces the importance of written homework).

Co-therapist: (takes a piece of paper from a nearby pile) Here is some paper. Today you can write your assignment down so that you do not forget. Homework is important because it's like continuing the therapy after you leave. We know from research that the more a person is participating in the therapy process, the sooner that they can achieve their goals.

(Co-therapist uses this as an opportunity to reinforce the essential aspect of homework, reinforcing Sally for her attempts without exposing her.)

Therapist: Al, how about you?

|           |                                                                                                                                                                                                                                                                             |
| --------- | --------------------------------------------------------------------------------------------------------------------------------------------------------------------------------------------------------------------------------------------------------------------------- |
| Al:        | I'm jangled. I'm constantly being bombarded with these events, thoughts. I wrote it down as part of my homework.                                                                                                                                                            |
| Therapist: | Great. I'm glad you wrote them down so we can review them. We'll talk about your jangledness when we go over your homework in detail. Sutton?                                                                                                                                |
| Sutton:    | You know what concerns me? Does anyone here feel those symptoms that they came in with now? I don't feel them anymore. I was not sleeping. I couldn't concentrate or work. I was depressed. I couldn't eat. But I don't feel any of them now.                                |
| Al:        | I see it this way. Ever see sad kids in Disney World? It ain't the real world.                                                                                                                                                                                              |
| Sally:     | It's not usual to be away from your problems the way that you are here. There's no pressure here.                                                                                                                                                                           |
| Therapist: | I'll fix that. You're all saying that the pressure is off. Maybe that will allow you a moment to take a breath to figure things out. Perhaps it is a sign that we're not working hard enough.                                                                                |
| Sutton:    | I'm wondering whether I should even be here, in the hospital. It's really boring.                                                                                                                                                                                           |
| Therapist: | Well that's certainly something we need to address. In fact wasn't that your assignment? To talk to each of your parents, a staff nurse, and one other staff member and write down what areas they felt you needed to work on.                                               |
| Sutton:    | Well sorta. I didn't write it down.                                                                                                                                                                                                                                         |
| Therapist: | Today, we were going to evaluate your hypothesis that you don't need to be here. I wonder what you must have said to yourself that let you off the hook for your homework? Maybe you can think about that while we check in with some other people. Phoebe?                    |
| Phoebe:    | I'm feeling pretty good. I picked a person to talk to. The conversation went OK.                                                                                                                                                                                            |
| Therapist: | Terrific! Tell us about it.                                                                                                                                                                                                                                                 |
| Phoebe:    | Well, I thought about who would be the most difficult person for me to talk to. It was this woman on the unit, Joan. I wasn't even sure why she was here since she never appeared to have any problems. When she was sitting in the day room, I just started talking to her. I was amazed that she was |

|  | willing to talk. It turns out she has a lot of problems with her family. Her kids are so demanding, and her husband is too busy for her. I always wanted to have a family, but her life doesn't seem so great. |
|---|---|
| Therapist: | So you made your assignment even more difficult and succeeded. You also learned that everyone has problems even if it doesn't seem so at first. Why don't we start with you then. We'll role play a situation with Phoebe. Your boss has just called from his car phone and says, "Phoebe, a client is coming into the office this afternoon from Paris. I'm stuck in a traffic jam in London on the way to the airport. I'm going to miss my flight and the next one is 6 hours away. Can you take him about the town?" Would he say something like that? |
| Phoebe: | And he'd say, "I knew I could count on you. Don't know what I'd do without you." |
| Therapist: | What are your automatic thoughts? |
| Phoebe: | I'd think, "Oh my God, now what?" |
| Co-therapist: | (writing on the board) You're thinking, "I won't know what to do." |
| Phoebe: | He'll be bored by what I come up with. It'll be a strange situation. |
| Therapist: | Define *strange* (attempts to get the Phoebe to articulate her meaning in behavioral terms). |
| Phoebe: | Tense, awkward. |
| Therapist: | How do you know it will be tense or awkward (goes for further behavioral specification)? |
| Phoebe: | The conversation won't flow, I'll jump from one thing to the next. |
| Co-therapist: | Anything else? (Phoebe shakes her head no.) Anything else in terms of your speech? |
| Phoebe: | I'll be so self-conscious. He'll see I'm uncomfortable . . . like I'll talk in a monotone and talk too softly. The more uncomfortable I'll be, the longer the pauses will be. |
| Therapist: | What if all those things are true? So what if he does notice? You could have symptoms and he may notice. Now what would be the worst if he notices? |
| Phoebe: | I will start to feel worse about myself. It will bother me. |
| Therapist: | It would probably bother you a lot. It may bother most people, but it sounds like it would bother you |

|  |  |
|---|---|
| | a lot more. It could bother different people for different reasons. For what reasons would it bother you? |
| Phoebe: | It would reinforce the fact that I'm a loser socially. |
| Therapist: | Having symptoms that other people would notice would show that you are a social loser. Socially incompetent? (Phoebe nods.) What kind of cognitive distortion is going on? Can anyone help Phoebe out? (Here, therapist uses the technique of labeling as a way to identify the distortion.) Sutton? |
| Sutton: | It's an inference that is arbitrary. Who says nervousness means being a social loser? |
| Al: | All-or-nothing thinking, you're either skilled or socially inept. |
| Patricia: | A social loser is an extreme overgeneralization. |
| Therapist: | Yes, you may have done something socially awkward. I know I have. But to say you're socially incompetent? You are overgeneralizing to make that one awkward moment an expectation about all events in the present and future. |
| Phoebe: | I guess there is a "should" in there, that I expect myself to have total control over the conversation and always have it proceed smoothly. |
| Therapist: | That's a remarkable automatic thought (laughter). Let's get some rational responses. |
| Phoebe: | I don't know. I'm trying to think if there have ever been times when I've not had symptoms and it's been OK. With the clients. I can't think of any. Maybe I've had similar circumstances and there have been times that I've had to take out clients and not had symptoms that it has been OK. |
| Therapist: | Perhaps if you keep in mind that you don't always get symptoms, but it is likely that you also might have symptoms. So what if you've had symptoms? |
| Phoebe: | Well once I get symptoms, they just feed on themselves and I get off on the wrong track. It's like taking the wrong exit and you just keep making additional mistakes that get you more lost. There's a threshold that I cross and its hard to get back once I have crossed it. |
| Therapist: | What happens if you cross the threshold? |
| Phoebe: | I withdraw. |

Therapist: Which means what? (The therapist tries to get patient to behaviorally define her use of terms.)

Phoebe: I pull back.

Therapist: You are quiet and you pull back? (The therapist attempts to further behaviorally describe "pull back." Phoebe nods.) If someone withdraws, they are quiet, are they socially inept?

Patricia: I feel that if I am quiet that other people will know that there is nothing there.

Therapist: So you, Patricia, can relate to this also. But what I am asking is if you have symptoms, is that socially inept? Do symptoms equal social ineptness? (Acknowledges the similarity between Patricia's and Phoebe's feelings but avoids having the group reinforce each other's gloomy perceptions.)

Sally: If someone is withdrawn, society labels them as socially inept.

Therapist: If you are at a party and someone was quiet, they could be socially inept, but what else could they be? What other reasons might they be quiet? (Again avoids reinforcing these self-perceptions as truth by suggesting an alternative interpretation of the data.)

Patricia: They just don't have anything to contribute to that particular conversation.

Co-therapist: (writes on board) Does (blank) have to equal (blank)? Fill in the blanks.

Phoebe: Does being quiet and reserved mean ineptness? No.

Therapist: Say it the way you might think it.

Phoebe: Being quiet, not talking, doesn't necessarily equal being socially inept.

Therapist: Let's set up a role play. Your boss calls you from his car phone and tells you, (therapist hesitates) . . . help me with the details, Phoebe.

Phoebe: He says that he's not going to be able to get back and would I take Mr. Smith, who is a very important client, so I already feel additional pressure, to dinner and he would like a guided tour around the town and he'll call me on the limo phone when he is ready to meet him.

Therapist: So what is your goal?

Phoebe: To entertain him.

Therapist: Can you objectify entertain? (Phoebe shrugs.) Anybody?

Al:   To tell him first what happened and what the game plan is. Pick two things to talk about and make suggestions about what you could do between now and then.

Therapist:   Your thoughts are good, but let's be even more specific. How about suggesting two places to go. (Phoebe nods.) Other ideas?

Al:   Pick two topics of conversation.

Therapist:   Good. OK Phoebe? (Phoebe nods.) What is your baseline level of anxiety (referring to a 1–100 scale measuring subjective anxiety, 0 being no anxiety at all and 100 being "can't stand it") and what is your rational response?

Phoebe:   My anxiety level is 40. My rational response is "Being quiet doesn't mean being a social loser or incompetent."

The co-therapist plays the part of the client, and Phoebe plays herself. Periodically, the therapist interjects to ask for Phoebe to say aloud her rational response and to give a numerical value to her anxiety level. Then the role play continues. After approximately 5 minutes of the role play, the therapist asks Phoebe one more time to say the rational response to herself and make one final measurement of her anxiety. The role play serves three purposes. (First, it tests the hypothesis that Phoebe is inept at managing her boss's clients by allowing other members to give feedback about whether she is presenting herself as socially inept. It is the first step in correcting cognitive distortions. Second, it provides a new mediating self-statement that Phoebe can add to her repertoire of responses to manage stressful situations. Third, it gives Phoebe practice in responding in a relatively safe environment.)

Therapist:   How do you think it went?

Phoebe:   I think it went OK, but I talk too much.

Therapist:   Sounds like you're damned if you do and damned if you don't. First you berate yourself for not talking enough, and then when you talk you berate yourself for talking.

Phoebe:   Well anyway, I think that this was easier than I suspect it would be really talking to a client. I may not have much in common with the client and it wouldn't be as easy talking to a client as talking to the co-therapist.

Therapist: Did the co-therapist make it easy for Phoebe?

Patricia: No, she was hard on her, maybe harder than someone actually would be.

Al: Heck no, she made her carry the conversation a lot.

Therapist: Did you meet your goals, two topics of conversation and two places to go?

Phoebe: Yes. I suggested two topics of conversation and two places to go.

Therapist: You suggested more than two things. How do the others think that Phoebe did?

Sally: At the beginning she looked uneasy. But as time went on, she looked better and better.

Therapist: Does uneasy mean "socially incompetent?" (Sally says no.) Do you think that most people would be uncomfortable in that situation? (silence) It would make me uncomfortable (group laughs). There are plenty of reasons for the discomfort. What could you take from this?

Phoebe: It seems like my fortune-telling abilities need some fine tuning. I guess that I don't have to take all the burden of responsibility.

Therapist: Good. I agree. Shall we continue around in order? (to Al) We didn't have much chance to work with you last time. You told us last time that you drank your whole life and that you had stopped drinking 6 months ago and that work was overwhelming.

Al: Yeah. I don't know who I am anymore.

Therapist: What's it feel like being abstinent?

Al: I used to just drink and let life go by. I didn't know what it was like to not drink. I guess these problems used to be around, but I didn't know about them. I was too drunk all the time. Without the booze, I feel lost. Don't know how to do anything.

Therapist: Let me say that from a psychologist's point of view that you were using alcohol to self-medicate so you wouldn't see and feel the difficult issues of life.

Al: Sounds good.

Therapist: So now he's a baby. (Group members giggle.) Al has a million upsets each day because he doesn't

have booze. (to Al) All those things that you
shielded yourself from, you're going to have to
problem solve in new ways besides drinking the
booze. For homework, you were going to write
down two events, and we were going to scrutinize
them in our cognitive–behavioral therapy way.

Co-therapist goes to board and draws four columns labeled situation, feelings, automatic thoughts, and rational responses and
enters members' responses in the appropriate columns.

| | |
|---|---|
| Therapist: | Say you have an argument with a nurse, you may get sad or nervous. (Co-therapist enters the incident under situation. Enters nervous and sad under feelings.) Then you evaluate whether it's accurate. That is, whether the situation needs fixing or your thoughts need fixing. Now Al, what was your example from your homework? |
| Al: | A nurse was late with the medication. I was supposed to go to the program for recovering alcoholics. I was getting nervous. I was also supposed to be at psychological testing at the same time, and shoot, they don't know where I'm supposed to be. |
| Therapist: | So we have the upset with the nurse for not knowing where to send you (entered under situation). How were you were feeling? |
| Al: | Sad, nervous. |
| Therapist: | Automatic thoughts are brief, fleeting thoughts of which you may be barely aware. |
| Al: | I thought, I gotta be somewhere for two activities at the same time. |
| Therapist: | Anything else? |
| Al: | I started saying the Serenity Prayer. |
| Therapist: | OK. You made a rational response to this situation. Or another way to look at it is to say that you developed a behavioral strategy to manage the situation. The behavioral strategy was saying the Serenity Prayer. The automatic thought is one step earlier. Do you remember, however fleeting, what the thought might have been? |
| Al: | I can't control this situation. How can I be at two places at the same time? |

Sutton:  What would happen if you weren't able to?

Al:  I don't know. I feel like maybe I could get into trouble.

Therapist:  You have to stay in the hospital one more day (Face indicates joking manner. The therapist feels free to joke to highlight the distorted aspects of the patient's thinking.) Al says, "I gotta be in two places at once. I can't control it." He thought he could get into trouble. (to Al) Evaluate whether the thought is a faulty one. Sometimes just putting out the thought—recognizing and labeling it—is helpful. Let's develop a treatment plan for Al. Let's say that without booze you're a worrier. You have to learn how to handle a lot of these situations without worrying. Does that seem like a reasonable and realistic plan to you?

Al:  Sounds good to me.

Therapist:  First you frame the situation. Label your feelings. Then focus on that automatic thought that you may never have concentrated on before. Then evaluate whether that thought is a reasonable or an accurate one. You are on your way to understanding how to use cognitive–behavioral therapy (silence). Let's go on to your other homework situation.

Al:  The situation was that we went to the AA meeting last night. When we got back to the unit, the doors to enter the unit were locked. I felt anxious. I thought I'm going to have to go through all this garbage to get in. I'll draw attention to myself. They'll ask me a lot of questions.

Therapist:  This is a good one. What's the issue around being the center of attention?

Al:  I don't like being the center of attention. I don't know why. They'll ask me a lot of questions. Everyone will be wondering about me. I won't be able to explain myself. I don't like to draw attention to myself.

Therapist:  What would happen if you did? What's wrong with a lot of questions?

Al:  I just wouldn't like to do it. It's like I couldn't explain myself. Like they would think, what was I doing? Fooling around?

Therapist:   You mean you'd feel guilty. Al is afraid he will be accused of something. Al predicts trouble for himself. How did you get back in?

Al:   Well that's the crazy thing. I was with another guy. He had the right idea. I wish that I could have reacted like he did. He was mad. He said, "Why the heck did they lock the doors? They know we went to a meeting." He just rang the door bell, which was right there, and they let us in and they didn't even ask any questions.

Co-therapist:   Your tests indicated, yesterday and today, that you get anxious about a lot of things and that you are anxious much of the time.

Therapist:   Now that you've stopped drinking, you're raw in the world. You're anxious, and you don't know how to manage it. What rational response can he say to himself?

Sally:   Well, you can ask what is the worst that could happen.

Al:   Well, I know. I could kick myself for getting so bent out of shape.

Therapist:   It's a good thought, but it doesn't work for Al. He just feels worse. Could you stand being anxious for 3 to 6 months and not give yourself such a tough time?

Al:   Well, I have to.

Therapist:   If you are able to put up with being anxious for a few months, as you get more experience in the world without drinking, that anxious feeling will lessen to some degree. It's going to be many months of work, and you're going to have to do it yourself. Some people don't want to work on it, but with a lot of effort and cognitive–behavioral therapy, it will get better. So your rational response would be to say, "Let me step back and see if I can handle this. I don't need booze to handle this" (writes on board). You anticipate many bad things happening. You're like a weather man predicting rain 95% of the time. Remind yourself of your ability to predict.

Al:   Not great.

Therapist:   You are working very hard. Continue to collect examples and automatic thoughts for next time (assigns homework). Let's talk to Sally. Yesterday, she told us that she has no problems that we could help with (Sally giggles). (to Sally) You're depressed. You see yourself as being in the hospital so your doctor can regulate your medication. You think that you have pain from the medication. Your doctor thinks you have something else.

Sally:    Well, she knows I have pain, but she says it's not due to the medication. But every time I take my medication, I get sick, physically sick. I have a lot of pain. She wanted me to come into the hospital, but I felt that we could have done this on an outpatient basis.

Therapist:    Then you wouldn't have met us.

Sally:    Yes, well. She says that I am psychosomatic. I don't see it that way. I think that my case is much more complicated than she says. But she intimidates me. I think we should be partners. She should take me seriously and think that these symptoms are real or at least evaluate them.

Patricia:    It scares me because she is my doctor also. How long have you been seeing her? Did you trust her in the past?

Sally:    I've seen her for years, off and on. I trusted her. Maybe you won't have the same problem with her. (They appear to wander. The therapist returns them to the agenda.)

Therapist:    Let's talk about your homework that you forgot. You felt your psychiatrist doesn't listen to you. That makes you feel frustrated. Your automatic thought was that you felt helpless and that she didn't respect you. Last time, other members helped to evaluate that response. Is it a reasonable response to feel frustrated if you feel that you have not been listened to? (Sutton and Al nod yes.) So then we were going to have you check out the accuracy of your perception that your psychiatrist wouldn't listen to you. So the group suggested seeing if she would talk with you about your symptoms, and you agreed that it was a reasonable test of whether she listens. Part of your homework was to see if your psychiatrist would talk with you about your symptoms.

Sally: Well, that's why I'm so upset and forgot my homework, because of my meeting with my psychiatrist. I can't be right with her. She thinks she's the doctor—she knows best and she doesn't listen. (laughing) I'm laughing because she says that I don't listen to her. I wrote her this letter, which she told me to bring here and share with the group. It says that I think that we should be partners. I know my body better than she does. I know when things are real, and she should listen and take what I say seriously. I think that sounds reasonable.

Therapist: Does it to you?

Al: Naah. The doctor is always right.

Sally: She says that I don't admit to my problem. She says that I'm angry. I don't feel angry. I'm willing to work on it, but how can I work on something I don't feel?

Therapist: (breaks in to stay on track) Part of your homework was to test whether she would listen to you. She listened to you by reading the letter. You may not like her opinion, but your idea of collaboration was that she was to listen to you, which she did by allowing you to present your case through the letter. You feel that your symptoms are real side effects, and it sounds like she thinks that they are due to your depression. (Having a specific criterion for evaluating whether someone is listening helps eliminate the "yes–but" response from the patient.)

Al: Isn't it a matter of perspective? My wife is a pharmacist, and if I get a drug from a doc I just take it. I say the doctor is an authority—she went to medical school, and she should know. My wife says, "What are you crazy? Taking a drug without knowing anything about it?"

Therapist: (to Al) So you would take the drug, and if you had these pains, you would say to yourself that you were not going to worry about it. The drug is supposed to work and these pains must be something else or you would just ignore them. (Al nods.)

Sally: I told her that I had pains in my body, but she said these pains are not the usual side effects for medicines I am taking.

Therapist:  So she listened to your complaint and told you that these pains you have aren't side effects. You checked out what the usual side effects are?

(The cognitive distortion in question, "My psychiatrist doesn't listen to me" has been disproved through this empirical demonstration. The patient then attempts to go on to another complaint about her doctor, which implicitly takes a yes–but form. Some therapists may attempt to handle this new complaint in the same manner as the previous one. Sally, however, had a two-part assignment. This deliberate shift, although appearing to focus away from the patient's complaint about her psychiatrist, actually removes the therapist from the yes–but struggle that is beginning to emerge in the interaction with this patient. The question about the side effects begins the transition into the second part of Sally's assignment, which was to write down the circumstances surrounding the pains. That is, when Sally developed these pains, she was to write down the situation around the development and termination of these symptoms and what she was thinking and feeling.)

Sally:      Well yes, she told me.
Therapist:  Which symptoms did you write down that make you sick?
Sally:      Well, I feel sick in my stomach, and I have lots of pain here in my shoulder, and my neck hurts, and I sometimes have tingling in my feet, and I feel like sometimes that there is this tight collar around my neck and . . .
Therapist:  These were all from yesterday, and you wrote them down? (Sally shakes her head no.) Which ones were from yesterday? (Therapist attempts to narrow the field of discussion and keep it specific.)
Sally:      Throat burning, weakness in the legs, but the symptoms seemed to have lessened. I know these are side effects.
Therapist:  Which ones?
Sally:      I had them before, the weakness in the legs.
Therapist:  What was the feeling like?

Sally:        I don't know if I can describe it. It's like a drawing feeling, the energy just drawing away.

Therapist:    What do you mean by a "drawing feeling"? (Again, the therapist tries to get the patient to be as behaviorally specific as possible and focus on the specific qualities of the feeling rather than on the pervasive feeling of not being listened to.)

Sally:        I don't know, like a draining feeling.

Therapist:    (co-therapist writing on the chalkboard in the appropriate columns situation, feelings, and thoughts) So what did you do? (The therapist also could have addressed what else was going on at that moment.)

Sally:        I just tried to ignore it.

Therapist:    Good. What were you doing at that moment?

Sally:        Well, I was listening to the radio, and then I decided to take a nap and went to bed.

Therapist:    Good. So you had these symptoms, and you had the automatic thought of not worrying. Your rational response was to ignore it and to think that it would go away. This went better than I thought. (to the group) Her bodily symptoms are diminishing, and the ones that she still has she copes with by ignoring them. We asked her to talk with her psychiatrist. Sally wrote her a letter and was able to get her psychiatrist to listen to her. If this continues, we need to revise your goals. Let's move on to Patricia. Do you have your homework?

Patricia:     Yes. I wanted to ask you a question. Do I have a goal? We were talking about goals last time and today.

Therapist:    Good point. The goal for Al is to be able to cope with worrying. The goal for Sally is to learn how to evaluate whether her symptoms are side effects or a manifestation of her anxiety and depression. Her other goal is to learn to communicate better with her psychiatrist. The goal for Phoebe is to tolerate her symptoms of anxiety when she is in her work situation. For you, Patricia, yesterday we were talking about your perfectionism and doing two things at once. What would you say your goals are? (This summary is a useful way to keep a simple focus.)

Patricia:   Maybe the inadequacies I feel and realizing they are normal?

Therapist:   Is the inadequacy you feel the result of your pessimism or that you really are inadequate? In other words, you feel you haven't done a good job with any task. But an outsider would say that the job is fine, or would they agree that you haven't done a good job? We have to figure out whether your thoughts are erroneous. Or if they are accurate, then we need to problem solve so that you feel more adequate. We'll have to gather more data and look at situations to see whether you are inadequate or are not. Let's look at your first situation and set of feelings.

Patricia:   I feel down and depressed. I can't be what I am supposed to be.

Therapist:   What do you mean more specifically?

Patricia:   I am not a good mother. Jason and Jacob seem totally dependent on me. I can't do anything right. I can't seem to do everything that I used to do. If I had been a better mother, then they would have developed a little more independence. I haven't done a good job.

Therapist:   (co-therapist writes on the board) So you're automatic thought is "My little boys are dependent upon me." What it the feeling?

Patricia:   I feel anxious, scared, and overwhelmed. I thought everything would be instinctive.

Therapist:   Are you an instinctive person?

Patricia:   I guess not.

Therapist:   You strike me as being a thinking person. You think things through. You plan carefully. Would you say that's true?

Patricia:   Well, yes. I thought I should be a loving mother.

Therapist:   Did you think that you were not?

Patricia:   I guess I was at first, but not now.

Therapist:   You thought you were supposed to be loving all the time? (Patricia nods.) You're supposed to be loving all the time and if you are not, you're terrible? (Patricia nods.) You are a terrible person for not being a loving mother 100% of the time?

Sally:    You're trying to be a supermom. Trying to be perfect. If you're not perfect, you are horrible. No room to be human.

Al:    You're feeling guilty. You're like me, if it rains I feel guilty and worry even though I know it's not my fault really. You got it in your head that you're supposed to be super all the time. Well, that just ain't possible. My kid is now 18. When he was young, he was a royal pain. I remember when he was 5 on a Saturday watching these boring cartoons. I would rather have been doing something else. If you think that you're not supposed to be bored some of the time, well, it is boring. You gotta admit it.

Therapist:    Maybe you're a perfectionist. You want to do it 100% of the time. Be a loving mother, plan the perfect consultations for your firm.

Patricia:    I have a problem with doing two things at once. If I'm not with my sons, I can't concentrate on what I'm doing. I feel like I should be with them. I feel like they need me even if they are doing OK without me. When I'm in the office, I feel like I should be home.

Sally:    You're very hard on yourself.

Therapist:    You have trouble dividing your time, doing two things 100% of the time perfectly. (Patricia nods.) What was the second situation?

Patricia:    Working.

Therapist:    What you told us yesterday was that you are an engineer in a consulting firm. You have just been promoted to be the senior consultant for one of the consulting teams, even though you only have a BA in engineering and everyone else has a master's. What is your feeling about your work situation?

Patricia:    Anxiety.

Therapist:    What was the automatic thought?

Patricia:    I can't do it. I'm not smart enough to do this anymore.

Therapist:    Anymore?

Patricia:    That's it. Can I bring up something stupid? The major problem with me is that I can't do it.

Therapist:    You said, "I can't do it." What can't you do?

Patricia:    Before I had children, I could spend any amount of time to get the job done.

Therapist:   You mean without the babies, you could take nights, weekends, vacations to get the job completed.

Patricia:   Well, I did take vacations.

Therapist:   The way you got ahead was to work extra, no matter what it took. Now when you went back to work were you depressed? (Patricia says yes.) So you were already handicapped. Do you know what I am talking about? Part of the depressive symptoms are that you don't feel motivated, you can't concentrate. (Therapist educates.) What part of the job was overwhelming?

Patricia:   I wrote the final report with the findings and recommendations. I told my boss that I wasn't sure that I could do it. She thought I could. She thought I was already doing it.

Sally:   Were you already doing it?

Patricia:   I guess I was, but I had my boss who was checking it and who I could go to when I didn't know, but I was really helping her do it. She was the one in charge.

Al:   Well, before you were the helper to the person. Now you are the one who is supposed to write the report. Who is your helper?

Patricia:   Our company is trying to cut back. We lose people who leave for better jobs.

Therapist:   You've done these write-ups before, but it has taken you awhile. Can it still take you awhile? Is that OK with you?

Patricia:   No, it's not OK with me. It can't take longer. I have babies to get home to. Maybe I'm not being honest. I don't want the responsibility that I used to have anymore.

Therapist:   Sounds OK to me. Does that sound OK to you? (Patricia nods.) Does it sound reasonable for a woman who just had twins to not want the responsibility at work that she had before? What stopped you from talking to your boss?

Patricia:   Well, I feel my boss pulling on me. She is about 60, and she said she really had to go to bat for me to become a partner and that the others had not liked the idea about me being out so long on a pregnancy leave, but she told them that I was a very hard worker and that I would more than pull my share in the company. She said she's doing everything she can to keep me in the top position that I'm in, and then I'm going to tell her I don't want to work like I used to. You know, I don't know if she even cares about me.

Therapist: You don't know if she cares? Is that true? Or is that a dysfunctional thought. Dysfunctional thoughts are ones that are negative and inaccurate.

Patricia: I'm afraid she will be disappointed in me.

Therapist: You don't like to disappoint people or maybe you don't like them to get angry? (Patricia nods.) You'd be like Sally, who can't talk to her psychiatrist. You wouldn't be able to talk to the psychiatrist either.

Patricia: No, I wouldn't. That's why I was asking about her experience with her doctor.

Therapist: I'd like you to write rational responses to automatic thoughts and collect more data.

Patricia: You mean you'd like me to call my boss.

Therapist: Well, you can think about doing it, but for next time, for each of the two situations you presented today, the one about feeling inadequate at work and feeling inadequate as a mother. I want you to list a rational response to them. Then collect two more situations. Was that helpful? (Patricia nods.) Are you saying that so you won't disappoint me? (Patricia laughs and says no.) Let's move on to Sutton. Sutton, you told us that you weren't sure you should stay. What originally brought you into the hospital?

Sutton: Well, I was depressed and my parents wanted me to come in because they feel that I have problems. But I don't feel bad now. I'm not experiencing any depression.

Therapist: What problems did they feel that you have?

Sutton: Well, I can't stand working with my father, and my parents just don't know why since it would be easy street they say.

Therapist: You told me it bugs you even to have to go to the office. I also remember you told us the first day that your girlfriend left you and that it had to do with your "borrowing" her jewelry and not letting her know.

Sutton:     Well yeah. I don't need her now. I guess I'm just tired of trying to work on my problems. Last night some nurse bitched at me because I was late getting back from my pass. I was having a good time with a girl I met on the unit. I really didn't see the reason to get back so soon. The nurse said that I missed the evening group. So what. I just didn't feel like going to hear people belly-ache about their problems.

Therapist:  This is a pattern for you. You were having a good time. You said to yourself "Who needs to work on problems?" You go for the short-run goodies and ignore the long-term consequences. Go for the fun and ignore the long-term damage that it might cause to you, your parents, your reputation in the community, with the ex-girlfriend. What thoughts are in your mind that give you an excuse to grab it all now, whatever you feel like taking, and let the future be damned? (Emotional and direct confrontation may be necessary for individuals whose distortions allow them the excuse to consciously manipulate their situation for immediate gratification at the expense of long-term growth.)

Sutton:     Yeah. It's hard for me to keep in focus the long-term downside of what I do.

Therapist:  I think that you tell yourself something distorted about the situation that then gives you an excuse to immediately get what you want, but you don't keep in mind that there is long-term damage. Take the situation of wanting to leave the hospital. What are you telling yourself that gives you an excuse to leave?

(Here, the therapist is using a variation of self-instructional training in which there is an attempt to get the patient to articulate the self-instructions that allow him or her to engage in self-destructive behavior.)

Sutton:     I guess that I don't have any problems.
Therapist:  Do you?

Sutton: Sometimes I see that I do—I don't have much motivation to work. I don't know why I even took the jewelry. I can't wear it (group laughs). My dad could buy the jewelry store that she got it from. I guess I also have some trouble getting along.

Therapist: So when you think about it, you know you have problems. Maybe you're telling yourself that everyone seems to be exaggerating how bad the situation is for you.

Sutton: (smiles) You got it, sir. I say, I could change if I wanted. What's the harm in taking what I want?

Therapist: Now, let's look at the long-term damage.

Sutton: I'm not really sure there is any. I just gotta smooth things over with my girlfriend. I just gotta tell myself not to do things like take the jewelry.

Therapist: Now this is where it is really important that you check out the consequences of your actions with others because you don't see it the same way as others, but you have to exist in their world, so you better check it out. Do it right now with the group.

Sutton: OK group, help me out.

Patricia: Well, if you leave the hospital now, your girlfriend might see that you just are trying to get out of stealing and so may press charges.

Al: Your parents are paying for this parade. They may get fed up since you don't seem to be making an effort.

Sally: Your reputation in the community, as the doctor said—if you ever want to get another job. Your friends will be influenced.

Therapist: Good. We're just about out of time, Sutton, I'd like you to make a list of the long-term consequences of leaving the hospital and a list of what you need to work on. Maybe we'll do a little empirical testing next time. We will look at those statements that you tell yourself that give you the excuse to get what you want at the expense of damaging your longer term relationships or your own growth and test their validity. Everyone know what they will be doing for homework?

Sally: What do I have to do for tomorrow?

Therapist: I want you to again record any instances when you get these pains. I want you to use the chart that the

co-therapist has given you to indicate the surrounding circumstances—what you were thinking, how
you were feeling. Really concentrate on those automatic thoughts. Next time we will try to focus
more on your automatic thoughts also. You're going
to do it? (to Sally and Sutton—they nod) How did
it go today?

Al:     Feels like a real good AA meeting, the same kind
of good feeling.

## Comment on the Session

The example presented is lengthier than what we provided for
other models for two reasons. First, although a few practitioners
(e.g., Coleman & Gantman, 1991; Freeman, 1990; Freeman et
al., 1992) have written and presented methods for applying the
cognitive–behavioral model to a heterogenous inpatient population, clinical illustrations are not available in the literature. This
is in part because cognitive–behavioral groups first developed
in an outpatient setting in which inclusion in a specific population (e.g., patients with depression or panic disorder) or problem with a single theme (e.g., weight loss, anger) were the criteria
for member selection. This composition criteria may have occurred because there is a high degree of specificity in the techniques used according to the disorder or problem being addressed. It is only recently that cognitive techniques have been
applied to an inpatient group setting wherein members often
have different problems and diagnoses.

Second, because this model has many techniques available
and because specific interventions are often used with particular
disorders, an effort was made to endow the clinical example with
a diversity of patients to illustrate how interventions vary on the
basis of the special problems of each member. For example,
Heimberg's (1990, in press) treatment of social phobia was illustrated in the work with Phoebe. Sally was an example of the
very difficult somaticizing patient and how Coleman and Gantman (1991) might have successfully managed this patient in a
diagnostically mixed group. Sutton was used to illustrate the very
recent contributions to the literature on the ways in which both
adolescents with sociopathic tendencies and adults with signif-

icant personality pathologies can function within the cognitive–behavioral group (Freeman & Leaff, 1989; Grossman & Freet, 1987). Al represents a method of conceptualizing and working with the alcoholic within this model (Glantz, 1987). Finally, Patricia illustrates how a bright, seriously depressed, and passive individual begins to tackle some of her dysfunctional cognitive distortions.

## Status of the Research

The efficacy of the cognitive–behavioral therapies in treating a wide range of psychiatric disorders in an outpatient setting has been established (for reviews, see Dobson, 1989; Haaga & Davison, 1989; Hollon & Beck, 1986; Lyons & Woods, 1991). A significant number of outpatient studies have suggested that a group format is effective with a homogeneous patient population for patients with depression, eating disorders, addictions, and phobias. To the extent that the therapy in a group remains individualized with a content focus, the results are relevant and provide information about the kind of patients that might potentially benefit from cognitive–behavioral group in an inpatient setting.[8]

---

[8] For depression, there is overwhelming evidence that cognitive–behavioral group therapy is better than no therapy at all (Blackburn, 1988; Hollon & Beck, 1986). In studies that compared cognitive–behavioral group therapy with other treatments for depression, cognitive–behavioral group therapy was either superior to or equivalent to psychodynamic therapy (Covi & Lipman, 1987; Jarvik, Mintz, Steuer, & Gerner, 1982; Steuer et al., 1984) and to behavioral therapy (Shaw, 1977).

For social phobia, cognitive–behavioral group therapy was shown to be to be more effective than no treatment (Heimberg, 1990; Heimberg, Becker, Goldfinger, & Vermilyea, 1985; Turner, 1987), equivalent to or more effective than systematic desensitization (Emmelkamp, Brilman, Kuiper, & Mersch, 1985; Malkiewich & Merluzzi, 1980), and more effective than discussion/support (educational) group therapy (Heimberg et al., 1990). It is not likely, however, that a patient would be hospitalized solely for social phobia. The efficacy of group therapy is considerably diminished with a social phobic who also displays a personality disorder, a combination more likely to precipitate hospitalization (Turner, 1987). The treatment of agoraphobia in a group format using

## Inpatient Outcome Studies

Despite the numerous clinical reports of its utility with a group format, there is a paucity of studies on short-term, open-ended inpatient groups with severely disturbed patients. We are aware of only one inpatient cognitive–behavioral group therapy out-

---

cognitive–behavioral interventions has also been disappointing. Cognitive interventions alone (relabeling, discussing irrational beliefs, and self-instructional training) were less effective than was a purely behavioral approach (in vivo exposure), and the combination of cognitive and behavioral techniques together was not superior to behavioral therapy alone (Emmelkamp & Mersch, 1982; Emmelkamp et al., 1985; Emmelkamp, Mersch, Vissia, & Van Der Helm, 1985). It is possible that behavioral assignments are themselves a potent way of changing the dysfunctional cognitions in these patients (Beck, 1991; Williams & Moorey, 1989).

The cognitive–behavioral group therapy outcome studies evaluating treatment of addictions (drug and alcohol) have yielded mixed results. Some studies suggest that cognitive–behavioral group therapy is at least as effective as are psychodynamic or interactional treatments (Kadden, Cooney, Getter, & Litt, 1989; Oei & Jackson, 1982; Sanchez-Craig, 1980), whereas other studies have reported that cognitive–behavioral treatment is not superior to no treatment in prevention of relapse (Chaney, O'Leary, & Marlatt, 1978).

For outpatient groups of patients with eating disorders, a cognitive–behavioral model has been shown to be more effective than no treatment (Gray & Hoage, 1990; Dedman, Numa, & Wakeling, 1988; Luka, Agras, & Schneider, 1986; Schneider & Agras, 1985) and at least as effective as medication (Kirkley, Schneider, Agras, & Bachman, 1985) or nondirective supportive group therapy (Gordon & Ahmed, 1988). About two thirds of the patients who received cognitive–behavioral group therapy continued to do well 2 to 5 years after treatment (Mitchell et al., 1989). See Cox and Merkel (1989) for a review of this literature.

The influence of population heterogeneity on the efficacy of treatment is unknown. Only one study has demonstrated that a diagnostically mixed group (anxiety and depression) can be an effective treatment (Lipsky, Kassinove, & Miller, 1980).

With respect to age, the majority of the studies have used adults under 65 year of age. However, cognitive–behavioral group therapy has been shown to be effective with children, adolescents (Thorpe, Amatu, Blakely, & Burns, 1976), and geriatric patients (Beutler et al., 1982; Jarvik et al., 1982; Keller, Croake, & Brooking, 1975; Steuer et al., 1984).

In terms of intellect, whereas higher education remains a positive predictor of treatment response to cognitive–behavioral therapy (Blackburn, 1988), some come study. In this study, hospitalized adolescent males were presented with an 8-week (12-session) group training course using cognitive–behavioral techniques (e.g., live modeling, behavioral rehearsal, practice, role playing, negative and positive symbolic modeling) with the goal of decreasing anger and aggressive behavior (Feindler, Ecton, Kingsley, & Dubey, 1986). Adolescents received training in relaxation, self-instruction, use of coping statements, use of assertive social interactions, the evaluation of one's own behavior, the self-monitoring of anger and conflict experiences, and problem solving. Compared with subjects in a waiting-list control group and in another control group composed of other ward adolescents, the adolescents receiving the active cognitive–behavioral group treatment exhibited increased self-control (rated by staff), increased appropriate verbalizations, decreased hostile verbalizations during conflict situations (using role play), and increased reflective responding on a cognitive task and received fewer fines and restrictions on the unit. A second study with moderately to severely depressed geriatric patients (aged 66–72) from a nursing home compared patients attending a cognitive–behavioral therapy or a music therapy group or receiving standard care (control group; Zerhusen, Boyle, & Wilson, 1991). Groups were held twice weekly for 10 weeks. At the end of treatment, patients from the cognitive–behavioral therapy group were significantly less depressed on an inventory than were patients in either the music group or the control group.

In light of the limited empirical evidence of the effectiveness of the group cognitive–behavioral therapy, it is helpful in gleaning some knowledge about its efficacy to briefly review the research on the application of the model with an inpatient population using an individual format. DeJong and his colleagues (DeJong, Henrich, & Ferstal, 1981; DeJong, Treiber, & Henrich, 1986) compared cognitive–behavioral therapy (cognitive restructuring with social skills training) to cognitive therapy with no behavioral interventions and to a waiting-list control condition. After 5–6 weeks of treatment, both patient conditions receiving

---

evidence suggests that average intelligence is not required for a successful outcome (Benson, Johnson, & Miranti, 1986; Lipsky et al., 1980).

therapy did better than did waiting-list patients on self-report and observer-rated measures of depression. Patients from the cognitive–behavioral group reported that they were less depressed than did those from the cognitive therapy group. In a third study, depressed inpatients received standard care (pharmacotherapy, clinical management, and milieu therapy) or standard care and cognitive–behavioral therapy (Miller et al., 1989). Significantly more patients in the cognitive–behavioral therapy group than in the standard care group had an amelioration of symptoms. Treatment continued for 4 months after discharge. At a 1-year follow-up, if patients received the additional cognitive–behavioral treatment, they remained improved. Similarly, Bowers (1989) administered nortriptyline alone or in combination with either cognitive therapy or relaxation therapy to a group of 30 depressed inpatients. All three groups improved. However, those receiving cognitive therapy and relaxation therapy both reported less depression and less depressive thought content than did those receiving only medication. Observers also reported that patients receiving cognitive–behavioral therapy appeared less depressed than did those receiving medication alone or in combination with relaxation training. The efficacy of cognitive–behavioral therapy in an inpatient setting is supported further by the systematic observation of improvement in refractory depression either with cognitive–behavioral therapy alone or in combination with medication (Bowers, 1989; Miller, Bishop, Norman, & Keitner, 1985).

It has been speculated that the presence of vegetative symptoms makes the application of cognitive–behavioral therapy more difficult. Several studies suggest that despite the presence of an endogenous depression, cognitive–behavioral therapy has been effective (Blackburn, Bishop, Glen, Whalley, & Christie, 1981; Beck, Hollon, Young, Bedrosian, & Budenz, 1985; Kovacs, Rush, Beck, & Hollon, 1981). Some have even questioned whether the addition of antidepressant medication improves the response to cognitive–behavioral therapy (Covi, Lipman, Derogotis, Smith, & Pattison, 1974; Simons, Lustman, Wetzel, & Murphy, 1985; see Blackburn, 1988, and Hollon & Beck, 1986, for reviews of the literature).

Self-instructional training (SIT) has also been studied with an inpatient schizophrenic population (Meichenbaum, 1977; Meichenbaum & Cameron, 1973). Schizophrenic patients were taught to attend to the facial and behavioral cues of others to help them monitor their own psychotic thinking and behavior. SIT helped schizophrenics improve appropriate attention to the task by preventing internally distracting stimuli from interfering with their performance on specified tasks. However, attempts to replicate these findings using a larger sample were unsuccessful (Margolis & Shemberg, 1976).

## Components and Parameters of the Treatment

**Changing cognitions.** The premise of cognitive–behavioral therapy is that symptoms lessen as dysfunctional cognitions are retrieved in the presence of affect, evaluated through empirical testing and logic, and changed with the help of behavioral enactment (Arkowitz & Hannah, 1989). There is indeed evidence that cognitive–behavioral methods are effective in ameliorating symptoms (Blackburn, 1988; Haaga & Davison, 1989; Hollon & Beck, 1986). Cognitive–behavioral therapy is purported to work directly to change cognitions and schemas; through its modification of the cognitive mediating system, it is believed to have a prophylactic effect on relapse of symptoms. Several researchers have achieved promising results concerning the efficacy of cognitive–behavioral therapy in preventing relapse (Blackburn, Eunson, & Bishop, 1987; Hollon & Najavits, 1988; Simons, Murphy, Levine, & Wetzel, 1986). Despite its prophylactic effect on relapse, there is no evidence that the presence or development of certain cognitions significantly contributes to the development of symptoms; cognitive measures (e.g., locus of control, expectancy of positive and negative outcomes, inventory of irrational beliefs, and perception of control) do not predict onset of symptoms (Lewinsohn, Steinmetz, Larsen, & Franklin, 1981). Rather, some cognitions precede or change concomitantly with the attenuation of symptoms (Hope et al., 1991; Reda, Carpiniello, Secchiaroli, & Blanco, 1985; Rush, Weissenburger, & Eaves, 1986; Simons, Garfield, & Murphy, 1984). There is also evidence (Simons et al., 1986) that people who have similar behavioral and emotional responses to active treatment have different probabilities of relapse depending on the extent of their dysfunctional attitudes at treatment termination (Williams & Moorey, 1989). Thus, although dysfunctional cognitions do not seem to predict who will develop symptoms, they do seem to be related to recovery and vulnerability to relapse. Although the efficacy of cognitive-behavioral group therapy could be demonstrated by showing a significant reduction in dysfunctional cognitions by the end of treatment, there would be no evidence that cognitive change was specific to the cognitive interventions.

**Number of sessions required.** Research studies with depressed outpatients using an individual format have unequivocally demonstrated that there is a significant decrease of symptoms after 12 to 20 sessions (Blackburn et al., 1981; Murphy, Simons, Watzel, & Lustman, 1984; Rush, Beck, Kovacs, & Hollon, 1977). However, with trends toward decreasing lengths of stay, an important consideration for instituting this model is whether there is any evidence that it can be effective if only a few sessions are possible. Some empirical reports have suggested that four to six sessions may be helpful if the goals are limited. Cognitive-behavioral methods in a group format have been successful in four sessions (Carson 1986; Deardorff & Funabiki, 1985; Keller et al., 1975), five sessions (Malkiewich & Merluzzi, 1980), six sessions (15 hr; Emmelkamp et al., 1985), and eight sessions (17 hr; Shaw, 1977). However, these studies used healthier study populations (e.g., anxiety and mild depression in otherwise functioning individuals), none of which included patients with severe or chronic symptoms.

**Homework.** A unique feature of the cognitive-behavioral model is its prescription of homework. No empirical studies have addressed the utility of this aspect. However, to the extent that homework increases the patient's involvement in treatment, it may be important given that there is a positive relation between measures of patient involvement and outcome (Gomes-Schwartz, 1978; O'Malley, Suh, & Strupp, 1983). A specific type of homework that is unique to the cognitive-behavioral model is the use of bibliotherapy. Although there are no studies that tested the utility of bibliotherapy within the context of an inpatient group, the effectiveness of bibliotherapy alone was tested in a community mental health center waiting-list situation (Kassinove, Miller, & Kalin, 1980). Neurotic patients during 8 weeks of waiting for a therapy assignment received either no contact or 16 sessions of coming to the mental health center to read (bibliotherapy) or listen (audiotherapy) to materials that described the philosophy of rational–emotive therapy. Bibliotherapy and audiotherapy treatments were superior to no treatment in decreasing irrational thinking. However, only patients receiving bibliotherapy reported less anxiety and neuroticism than did those receiving no treatment.

# Critique of the Model

## Strengths

The cognitive–behavioral therapy models are an extremely well-developed set of models. The goals of treatment are clear—to discover the dysfunctional or irrational cognitions that contribute to or cause the specified symptoms and to master a set of techniques that allows the individual to cope better with those symptoms and the problems of everyday life. Compared with most other models, there is an abundance of treatment manuals available. These manuals clearly delineate a set of techniques. Many of them spell out in detail the format and goals of each session. There are many articles that label and describe in observable and measurable terms the implementation of a wide range of techniques and their variants. (Appendixes B and C describe only a partial list of the techniques available.) Even if a clinician chooses not to use the models in their entirety, mastery of these techniques can augment the clinician's clinical armamentarium. There are clear methods of assessment that can aid in the determination of discharge. When co-therapy is indicated, the co-therapy roles are well delineated and differentiated. Although therapist training is advised for the implementation of these models, trainees do not need tremendous psychological sophistication. Research has indicated that a wide variety of students (e.g., nursing and mental health students) can be taught to deliver this type of treatment effectively in a group format (Chaisson, Beutler, Yost, & Allender, 1984). Objective measures of therapists' attitudes and competency (e.g., therapy preference scale, cognitive therapy scale) have been developed for this model (Shaw & Wilson-Smith, 1988).

Versatility in treating a wide range of human problems is one of the major strengths of this group of models. The myriad techniques give tremendous flexibility to the therapist's repertoire and style. Like behavior therapy, cognitive–behavioral therapy has the potential to effectively treat specific problems (e.g., social phobia, depression). To a lesser extent, cognitive–behavioral therapy also has the potential to promote self-exploration and to develop self-awareness, a goal that it shares with psychodynamic and humanistic approaches.

The many versions of the cognitive–behavioral model are an empirically based set of approaches; their design has been influenced and supported by much of the research in social and developmental psychology (Hollon & Garber, 1988). There is some support for the efficacy of cognitive–behavioral therapies as treatment for certain disorders particularly using an individual format. However, it is distinctive in that it is the only model that when compared with pharmacotherapy in clinical trials is equally effective in reducing depressive symptoms.

These models have the potential to serve a wide age range of patients. Techniques for treatment of children, adolescents, adults, and the elderly have been established. There is also clear delineation of the variations in implementation of the techniques that need to take place in response to differences in developmental issues.

The cognitive–behavioral theory of emotion, symptoms, and psychopathology has much face validity for both patients and staff. It is understandable and believable to the psychologically unsophisticated patient, and it does not require the patient to have access to his or her unconscious or to have an understanding of beliefs outside of his or her awareness as do other models. For patients, cooperation is clearly and concretely spelled out in terms of the requirements for homework, participation, and attendance. The present problem-oriented focus of cognitive–behavioral therapy reassures patients that their problems are being directly addressed. Patients readily experience themselves as actively involved from the start of treatment. Stylistically, inpatients appreciate and often request the active, reassuring, and encouraging stance of the cognitive–behavior therapist. The therapy allows the problems to be broken down into manageable steps. It facilitates the achievement of tangible results and provides the experience of success early in the course of therapy. It is an especially good set of models for those patients who like to feel that they are doing something for themselves.

## Weaknesses

Descriptions of cognitive–behavioral group therapies have included both closed-ended and open-ended groups. The open-ended groups require some stability of membership—at least a three- to five-session commitment (often more for patients with psychotic disorders) and low turnover. Without some membership stability, the gains for individual members are limited. Most of the shorter term groups described in the literature were closed-ended (for exceptions, see Coleman & Gantman, 1991; Freeman, 1987). In addition, the implementation of cognitive–behavioral group therapies as currently reported in the literature requires a time frame that most inpatient facilities cannot accommodate. Hence, these models as presently designed may have limited utility in most inpatient settings. However, many inpatient cognitive–behavioral group practitioners disagree with this and report their impressions that it is clinically useful even if only a few sessions can be attended (K. Barber, personal communication, May 28, 1992).

There are myriad studies using group format with volunteers, college students, and to a lesser extent outpatient depressives. Despite how well researched this model is for outpatient depressives and other nonclinical populations, it is striking how few of the empirical trials have actually used a population with the severity and chronicity typical of most hospitalized psychiatric patients. There is very little evidence that cognitive–behavioral techniques in a group setting are effective with low-functioning patients. The one empirical study with inpatients in a group had a specific problem focus (Feindler et al., 1986). Even if empirical trials with outpatient and volunteers are included, there are few studies that have compared a cognitive–behavioral group with a group using an alternative model (medication compared with cognitive–behavioral therapy is an exception). In the instances in which the cognitive–behavioral group is more effective than are its alternatives, the conditions studied did not resemble most of the inpatient population in terms of characteristics, group composition, and time frame available in an inpatient setting.

The cognitive–behavioral approaches are most easily instituted with patients who desire change. Like the other verbal psychotherapies, treatment is hindered by conditions under which patients do not actively collaborate (e.g., antisocial personality, psychosis, somatization) or demand too much individual attention. The models work best with the educated, intelligent, and articulate patient (Garfield, 1989). Although there are clinical reports of its applicability to patients with limited intellectual endowment in an individual format, there is limited empirical evidence of its efficacy in a group setting with such patients and no evidence that cognitive–behavioral therapy would work in the diagnostically mixed short-term group.

Unlike other models of therapy that require mastery of an entire new lexicon or an understanding of unfamiliar theoretical constructs, a good many of the technique articles and treatment manuals are comprehensible to a high school graduate. The techniques have been operationalized so that the procedure can be reliably repeated. However, in our opinion, the concepts and procedures appear deceptively simple. Despite the detailed and well-articulated description of the model in terms of goals, assessments, formats, and techniques, there are few guidelines on when and under what circumstances to use a particular technique. Although the majority of the sessions are spent working on the "problem," there is limited information on how this process should proceed.

Because the focus is the individual and not the group, few writings address those aspects of treatment that are specific to a group setting (e.g., patients' interactions with and reactions to each other). This lack of articulation is in part because the model does not emphasize what is specific and unique to a group format (e.g., patients' mutual support of, advice to, collaboration with, and reactions to other members). Thus, unless the cognitive–behavioral group therapist has other additional training, the group tends to have little patient-to-patient interaction and the therapist fails to make therapeutic use of the group setting.

Cognitive–behavioral writings do not address or acknowledge the impact that the larger hospital system or unit (both staff and patients) can have on the efficacy of the group; there is no inclusion of the importance of the milieu. That is, the cognitive–behavioral model assumes that the group can function relatively independently of the rest of the hospital treatment. However, if a patient is given more than one orientation, he or she may become totally disoriented. This is more likely in a teaching hospital wherein treatment is administered by multidisciplinary teams among which widely different orientations may exist. There may be no one to aid the patient in integrating the various orientations. Although it is certainly possible to integrate pharmacotherapy with cognitive–behavioral therapy, the integration needs to be endorsed by the staff psychiatrist prescribing the medications. The cognitive–behavioral therapy model works best if the rest of the treatment team has a similar orientation. At the very least, the model requires a supportive environment to be effective and preferably an explicit, articulated interface with the rest of the treatment. Additional staff training programs and staff discussions may be required to change deleterious effects that a lack of support may have on the efficacy of cognitive–behavioral therapy and to increase acceptance of the model as a place within the treatment setting (Schrodt & Wright, 1987).

The cognitive–behavioral approaches assume that the correction of dysfunctional or irrational cognitions is the key to symptom amelioration or change. Although the success of the cognitive–behavioral methods in attenuating symptoms is known, the mechanisms of action are not. There is no evidence that these approaches to a group work differently than do other alternative interventions. It may be that cognitive–behavioral therapy operationalizes the essential elements of therapy to a somewhat greater extent than do other therapies and is more explicit about them (Arkowitz & Hannah, 1989). The absence of empirical evidence of specificity of effect for the cognitive–behavioral approaches supports and encourages future research to explore explicit comparisons with other psychosocial alternatives (e.g., dynamic or humanistic interventions).

Although the model clearly articulates the role of the therapist and the co-therapy team, with few exceptions (e.g., Ellis, 1992;

Freeman et al., 1992) it does not acknowledge or provide adequate guidance for how to manage patients' reactions to the leader or the therapist's reactions to the patients. As an exception, Ellis (1992) viewed patients' reactions to the leader or other group members as samples of the distorted cognitions (e.g., overgeneralizations) that can be addressed. With regard to countertransference, Freeman advised the therapist to use the same techniques as the patient to explore and cope with what is evoked by the group experience (Freeman et al., 1992). In some circumstances, Ellis (1992) may even confront the patient (e.g., "I try not to hate you, but I really do dislike some of your behavior, and I hope for my sake, the group's sake, and especially your own sake, that you change it"; p. 68). Relative to other models, however, the treatment of these concepts is not as thoroughgoing. This model would profit from a more complete articulation of the manner in which these reactions could be used in furthering the work of the group.

The cognitive–behavioral group therapist approaches members with encouragement, collaboration, and active "cheerleading." This style encourages the suppression of certain types of affect such as hostility. However, this suppression may hinder the analysis of these affects in relation to their controlling cognitions. When affects such as hostility emerge outside the group, the member may be less skilled in using cognitive–behavioral techniques to modify them relative to those affective states (e.g., depression) that have been explored in group.

# Demands of the Model

## Clinical Mission of the Hospital

The utility of the cognitive–behavioral therapy model is somewhat limited by the clinical mission of the hospital. It is not highly compatible with a setting that completely endorses the biological etiology of all symptoms given that the cognitive–behavioral therapy model requires that patients view dysfunctional or irrational cognitions as important causes in the etiology and maintenance of their symptoms. The success of this model requires, at the very least, a supportive environment and preferably an explicit collaborative interface with the rest of the treatment. That is, without a supportive milieu, its efficacy is compromised. The development of a supportive milieu may require additional staff training, supervision, and discussions to increase the acceptance of the model within the treatment setting (Schrodt & Wright, 1987). The model is best suited for a setting in which the group therapy is just one component within the framework of an entire cognitive–behavioral program.

## Context of the Group

The cognitive–behavioral model functions autonomously from unit activities and thus it does not require group members to live on the same unit. It does not presuppose that the therapist know the unit atmosphere or what happens on the unit because in general unit events are not part of the content of the session. This independence from the unit more readily permits the group therapist to be an outside consultant than would be possible with other more unit-based models (e.g., the object relations/systems model). It still remains valuable for the therapist to be in liaison with unit staff to inform them about the current efforts and problems being discussed in group and get feedback from them about patients' behaviors. Knowledge of group goals and aims will also enable staff to more readily encourage patients to complete homework or to actually aid them carrying out the assignments (savvy staff may know to help patients without the group therapist's specific instructions). Conversely, it is not necessary that the patient's goals in group exactly parallel those of the rest of his or her treatment.

## Temporal Variables

As mentioned, perhaps the factor that is most likely to limit the use of this model is its required time frame. Although there are no formal treatment trials that have evaluated the minimum time required to achieve benefit in an inpatient group using this model, some outpatient studies suggest that it takes between 12 and 20 sessions before significant symptom attenuation can be derived. The applicability of these studies is limited, however, because they used the cognitive–behavioral model as the only intervention (this is usually not the case in an inpatient setting wherein group is just one of the many avenues of intervention pursued). Clearly, this is not a model that can be used in a single session. The amount of group time required by this model depends on the patient composition, whether other concurrent treatments use the cognitive–behavioral model, the number of group members, the stability of the group, whether assessment has been accomplished prior to beginning group, and how extensive the preparation is. Little or no benefit can be gained from less than three or four sessions (1 week). The completion of an assessment and then preparation for group are strongly advised, although it is possible to minimize preparation prior to beginning a closed-ended group. Similarly, membership stability is important. It is accomplished more readily if the group is closed-ended. If, however, the group is open-ended, turnover cannot occur at every session unless the leader structures into the session an introduction of new members and teaches the relevant techniques and theory.

## Size

Group size constraints are between 4 and 12 members. The greater the turnover, the more difficult it is to accommodate the upper range of members because time is not available to adequately work on all the problems and handle the initial sessions for new members who may require much teaching. Group size is also constrained by the availability of a co-therapist. A single therapist cannot manage more than six patients.

## Composition

Cognitive–behavioral therapy has been used most frequently with higher functioning patients (e.g., those with depression without psychotic features), with only very few examples of its success with lower functioning or psychotic patients. Greenwood's (1987) work with young chronic schizophrenics and Meichenbaum's (1977) work with schizophrenics are exceptions. The former, although using a model similar to Beck's (1976), requires some modification, whereas the latter is a specific self-instructional training. Recently, patients with borderline personality disorder have also been successfully treated in a year-long group

(Linehan, 1987b). Although most examples of cognitive–behavioral groups in the literature have been homogeneous, it is not clear the extent to which this bias reflects a demand of the model. The model seems best suited for homogeneous groups given that the focus of the teaching may be vastly different depending on members' intelligence, levels of ego strength, and presenting symptoms. What seems most difficult from the therapist's point of view would be a mixed– ego strength, mixed-diagnostic group. The model does not require that members be psychological sophisticated. It mostly requires time to prepare and teach theory and application. There is little research to support that one sex does better than the other in this type of therapy. Only patients who voluntarily agree to attend group are suitable for this type of group, although it does not hinder the therapy to have privileges extended or revoked for attendance. With some modification, this model can be suited to a wide age range (from adolescents to elderly patients).

## Therapist Variables

The use of a co-therapist is highly recommended. The role of the therapist is articulated more than in most models so that it is possible to have different co-therapists if the therapist remains the same (as in the case of co-therapists who are nurses on rotating shifts).

The successful use of the cognitive–behavioral model requires that both patients and staff understand principles of cognitive therapy. This means that staff must be trained in cognitive therapy techniques (which may require the hospital to provide formal training and supervision). Data from a National Institute of Mental Health collaborative study by Shaw and Wilson-Smith (1988) suggest that this model requires therapists to see patients in therapy for 13 to 18 months (72–100 hours) and have 34 to 54 hours of supervision to learn this model. It has been shown, however, that individuals with less than advanced degrees (e.g., nurse trainees and other mental health students) can be successfully trained and can then effectively implement cognitive–behavioral therapy. Competency of the therapist and members' improvement is significantly correlated, which suggests that therapists' competency is an important variable in successful cognitive–behavioral therapy (Chaisson et al., 1984).

## Summary

The cognitive–behavioral model of inpatient group therapy is a recent addition to the models of inpatient psychotherapy. The therapy is aimed at enabling the patient to cope better with his or her symptoms and problems in life. The target of change is the individual's dysfunctional cognitions and behaviors. The focus of the group is on the individual patient. The therapist uses a wide variety of cognitive and behavioral strategies to aid each member in identifying dysfunctional cognitions, testing their accuracy, and practicing new ways of thinking and acting that will enable him or her function better.

Different versions of the models are well documented and well articulated in procedures manuals. There is voluminous literature of empirical support for the efficacy of the cognitive–behavioral model with various diagnostic populations, although there is little knowledge about its effectiveness in an inpatient setting with groups composed of members with mixed diagnoses or of patients of the severity and chronicity typical of psychiatrically hospitalized patients. The most severe constraint on the use of this model in an inpatient setting is time. The approach requires assessment and preparation prior to beginning group. Clinicians report that some stability of membership and more than a few number of sessions are required for members to benefit from the group experience; however, future research is needed to confirm these clinical observations. If these demands of the model can be fulfilled, this model is likely to show much promise in terms of its contribution to the care of hospitalized psychiatric patients.

## References

Arieti, S. (1974). The cognitive–volitional school. In S. Arieti (Ed.), *American handbook of psychiatry* (2nd ed., Vol. 1, pp. 877–903). New York: Basic Books.

Arkowitz, H., & Hannah, M. T. (1989). Cognitive, behavioral, and psycho-dynamic therapies: Converging or diverging pathways to change? In A. Freeman, K. Simon, L. Beutler, & H. Arkowitz (Eds.), *Comprehensive hand-book of cognitive therapies* (pp. 143–167). New York: Plenum Press.

Bandura, A. (1969). *Principles of behavioral modification.* New York: Holt, Rinehart & Winston.

Bandura, A. (1977a). Self-effacy: Toward a unifying theory of behavioral change. *Psychological Review, 84,* 191–215.

Bandura, A. (1977b). *Social learning theory.* Englewood Cliffs, NJ: Prentice-Hall.

Barlow, D. H., & Craske, M. G. (1991). *Mastery of your anxiety and panic.* Albany, NY: Graywind.

Beck, A. T. (1972). *Depression: Causes and treatment.* Philadelphia: University of Pennsylvania Press. (Original work published 1967)

Beck, A. T. (1976). *Cognitive theory and the emotional disorders.* Madison, CT: International Universities Press.

Beck, A. T. (1978). *Depression inventory.* Philadelphia: Center for Cognitive Therapy.

Beck, A. T. (1991). Cognitive therapy: A 30-year retrospective. *American Psychologist, 46*(4), 368–375.

Beck, A. T., & Emery, G. (1977). *Cognitive therapy of substance abuse.* Philadelphia: Center for Cognitive Therapy.

Beck, A. T., & Emery, G. (1985). *Anxiety disorders and phobia: A cognitive perspective.* New York: Basic Books.

Beck, A. T., Epstein N., Brown, G., & Steer, R. A. (1988). An inventory for measuring clinical anxiety: Psychometric properties. *Journal of Consulting and Clinical Psychology, 56,* 893–897.

Beck, A. T., Freeman, A., & Associates. (1990). *Cognitive therapy of personality disorders.* New York: Guilford Press.

Beck, A. T., & Greenberg, R. L. (1974). *Coping with depression.* New York: Institute for Rational Living.

Beck, A. T., Hollon, S. D., Young, J. E., Bedrosian, R. C., & Budenz, D. (1985). Treatment of depression with cognitive therapy and amitriptyline. *Archives of General Psychiatry, 42,* 142–148.

Beck, A. T., Rush, A. J., Shaw, B. F., & Emery, G. (1979). *Cognitive therapy of depression.* New York: Guilford Press.

Beck, A. T., & Weishaar, M. (1989). Cognitive therapy. In A. Freeman, K. M. Simon, L. E. Beutler, & H. Arkowitz (Eds.), *Comprehensive handbook of cognitive therapy* (pp. 21–36). New York: Plenum Press.

Beck, A. T., Weissman, A., Lester, D., & Trexler, L. (1974). The measurement of pessimism: The Hopelessness Scale. *Journal of Consulting and Clinical Psychology, 42,* 861–865.

Becker, I. M., & Rosenfeld, J. G. (1976). Rational–emotive therapy: A study of initial therapy sessions of Albert Ellis. *Journal of Clinical Psychology, 32,* 872–876.

Beiber, I. (1980). *Cognitive psychoanalysis.* New York: Jason Aronson.

Benson, B. A., Johnson, M., & Miranti, S. V. (1986). Effects of anger management training with mentally retarded adults in group therapy. *Journal of Consulting and Clinical Psychology, 54*(5), 728–729.

Beutler, L., Scogin, F., Kirkish, P., Schretlen D., Corbishley, A., Hamblin, D., Meredith K., Potter, R., Bamford, C., & Levenson, A. (1987). Group cognitive therapy and alprazolam in the treatment of depression in older adults. *Journal of Consulting and Clinical Psychology, 55*, 550–556.

Blackburn, I. M. (1988). An appraisal of comparative trials of cognitive therapy for depression. In C. Perris, I. M. Blackburn, & H. Perris (Eds.), *Cognitive psychotherapy: Theory, and practice* (pp. 160–178). New York: Springer-Verlag.

Blackburn, I. M. (1989). Severely depressed in-patients. In J. Scott, J. M. G. Williams, & A. T. Beck (Eds.), *Cognitive therapy in clinical practice* (pp. 1–24). New York: Routledge.

Blackburn, I. M., Bishop, S., Glen, A. I. M., Whalley, L. J., & Christie, J. E. (1981). The efficacy of cognitive therapy in depression: A treatment trial using cognitive therapy and pharmacotherapy, each alone and in combination. *British Journal of Psychiatry, 139*, 181–189.

Blackburn, I. M., Eunson, K. M., & Bishop, S. (1987). A two-year naturalistic follow-up of depressed patients treated with cognitive therapy, pharmacotherapy, and a combination of both. *Journal of Affective Disorders, 10*, 67–75.

Bowers, W. A. (1989). Cognitive therapy with inpatients. In A. Freeman, K. Simon, L. Beutler, & H. Arkowitz (Eds.), *Comprehensive handbook of cognitive therapy* (pp. 583–596). New York: Plenum Press.

Brown, R. A., & Lewinsohn, P. M. (1984). A psychoeducational approach to the treatment of depression: Comparison of group, individual, and minimal contact procedures. *Journal of Consulting and Clinical Psychology, 52*, 774–783.

Burns, D. (1980). *Feeling good.* New York: William Morrow.

Carson, T. P. (1986). Assessment of depression. In A. R. Ciminero, K. S. Calhoun, & H. E. Adams (Eds.), *Handbook of behavioral assessment* (2nd ed., pp. 404–445). New York: Wiley.

Chaisson, G., Beutler, L., Yost, E., & Allender, J. (1984). Treating the depressed elderly. *Journal of Psychosocial Nursing, 22*, 25–30.

Chaney, E. F., O'Leary, M. R., & Marlatt, G. A. (1978). Skill training with alcoholics. *Journal of Consulting and Clinical Psychology, 46*, 1092–104.

Channon, S., & Wardle, J. (1989). Eating disorders. In J. Scott, J. M. G. Williams, & A. T. Beck (Eds.), *Cognitive therapy in clinical practice* (pp. 127–156). New York: Routledge.

Coleman, R., & Gantman, C. (1991, February). *Inpatient cognitive–behavioral groups.* Paper presentation at the meeting of the American Group Psychotherapy Association, San Antonio, TX.

Covi, L., & Lipman, R. S. (1987). Cognitive–behavioral group psychotherapy combined with imipramine in major depression. *Psychopharmacology Bulletin, 23*(1), 173–176.

Covi, L., Lipman, R. S., Derogotis, L. R., Smith, J. E., & Pattison, J. H. (1974). Drugs and group psychotherapy in neurotic depression. *American Journal of Psychiatry, 131,* 191–198.

Covi, L., Roth, D., & Lipman, R. S. (1982). Cognitive group psychotherapy of depression: The closed-ended group. *American Journal of Psychotherapy, 36*(4), 459–469.

Covi, L., Roth, D. M., Pattison, J. H., & Lipman, R. S. (1988). Group cognitive–behavioral therapy of depression: Two parallel treatment manuals for a controlled study. In C. Perris, I. M. Blackburn, & H. Perris (Eds.), *Cognitive psychotherapy: Theory and practice* (pp. 198–222). New York: Springer-Verlag.

Cox, G. L., & Merkel, W. T. (1989). A qualitative review of psychosocial treatments for bulimia. *Journal of Nervous and Mental Disease, 177*(2), 77–84.

Davis, M., Eshelman, E. R., & McKay, M. (1988). *The relaxation and stress reduction workbook* (3rd ed.). Oakland, CA: New Harbinger.

Deardorff, W. W., & Funabiki, D. (1985). A diagnostic caution in screening for depressed college students. *Cognitive Therapy and Research, 9,* 277–284.

Dedman, P. A., Numa, S. F., & Wakeling, A. (1988). A cognitive behavioural group approach for the treatment of bulimia nervosa: A preliminary study. *Journal of Psychosomatic Research, 32*(3), 285–290.

DeJong, R., Henrich, G., & Ferstal, R. (1981). A behavioral treatment programme for neurotic depression. *Behaviour Analysis and Modification, 4,* 275–287.

DeJong, R., Treiber, R., & Henrich, G. (1986). Effectiveness of two psychological treatments for inpatients with severe and chronic depressions. *Cognitive Therapy and Research, 10*(6), 645–663.

Dobson, K. S. (1989). A meta-analysis of the efficacy of cognitive therapy for depression. *Journal of Consulting and Clinical Psychology, 57*(3), 414–419.

Ellis, A. (1959). Rationalism and its therapeutic applications. In J. Barron (Ed.), *Annals of psychotherapy monograph* (No. 2, pp. 55–62). New York: American Academy of Psychotherapists.

Ellis, A. (1962). *Reason and emotion in psychotherapy.* Secaucus, NJ: Lyle Stuart and Citadel Press.

Ellis, A. (1977a). Discomfort anxiety: A new cognitive–behavioral construct. In A. Ellis & R. Grieger (Eds.), *Handbook of rational-emotive therapy* (Vol. 2, pp. 105–120). New York: Springer.

Ellis, A. (1977b). Rational emotive therapy and cognitive behavior therapy: Similarities and differences. In A. Ellis & R. Grieger (Eds.), *Handbook of rational-emotive therapy* (Vol. 2, pp. 31–45). New York: Springer.

Ellis, A. (1980). Rational–emotive therapy and cognitive–behavior therapy: Similarities and differences. *Cognitive Therapy and Research, 4,* 325–340.

Ellis, A. (1985). *Overcoming resistance: Rational-emotive therapy with difficult clients.* New York: Springer.

Ellis, A. (1988). *How to stubbornly refuse to make yourself miserable about anything—Yes anything.* New York: Carol.

Ellis, A. (1990). Rational–emotive therapy. In I. L. Kutash & A. Wolf (Eds.), *The group psychotherapist's handbook* (pp. 289–315). New York: Columbia University Press.

Ellis, A. (1992). Group rational–emotive and cognitive–behavioral therapy. *International Journal of Group Psychotherapy, 42*(1), 63–79.

Ellis, A., & Becker, I. (1982). *Guide to personal happiness*. North Hollywood, CA: Wilshire.

Ellis, A., & Grieger, R. M. (1977). *Handbook of rational–emotive therapy* (Vol. 2). New York: Springer.

Ellis, A., McInerney, J. F., DiGuiseppe, R., & Yeager, R. J. (1988). *Rational–emotive therapy with alcoholics and substance abusers*. New York: Pergamon Press.

Emery, G. (1984). *On your own life: How the new cognitive therapy can make you feel wonderful*. New York: NAL/Dutton.

Emmelkamp, P. M. G., Brilman, H., Kuiper, H., & Mersch, P. (1985). The treatment of agoraphobia: A comparison of self-instructional training, rational–emotive therapy, and exposure in vivo. *Behavior Modification, 10,* 37–53.

Emmelkamp, P. M. G., & Mersch, P. P. (1982). Cognition and exposure in vivo in the treatment of agoraphobia: Short-term and delayed effects. *Cognitive Research Therapy, 6,* 77–90.

Emmelkamp, P. M. G., Mersch, P. P., Vissia, E., & Van Der Helm, M. (1985). Social phobia: A comparative evaluation of cognitive and behavioral interactions. *Behavioral Research Therapy, 23*(3), 365–369.

Erdelyi, M. (1985). *Psychoanalysis: Freud's cognitive psychology*. San Francisco: Freeman.

Feindler, E. L., Ecton, R. B., Kingsley, D., & Dubey, D. R. (1986). Group anger control training for institutionalized psychiatric male adolescents. *Behavior Therapy, 17,* 109–123.

Freeman, A. (1987). Cognitive therapy: An overview. In A. Freeman & V. Greenwood (Eds.), *Cognitive therapy: Applications in psychiatric and medical settings* (pp. 19–35). New York: Human Sciences Press.

Freeman, A. (1988). Cognitive therapy of personality disorders: General treatment considerations. In C. Perris, I. M. Blackburn, & H. Perris (Eds.), *Cognitive psychotherapy* (pp. 223–254). New York: Springer-Verlag.

Freeman, A. (1990). Cognitive therapy. In A. Bellack & M. Hersen (Eds.), *Handbook of comparative treatments for adult disorders* (pp. 64–87). New York: Wiley.

Freeman, A., & Greenwood, V. (1987). *Cognitive therapy: Applications in psychiatric and medical settings*. New York: Human Sciences Press.

Freeman, A., & Leaff, R. C. (1989). Cognitive therapy applied to personality disorder. In A. Freeman, K. M. Simon, L. E. Beutler, & H. Arkowitz (Eds.), *Comprehensive handbook of cognitive therapy* (pp. 403–434). New York: Plenum Press.

Freeman, A., Pretzer, J., Fleming, B., & Simon, K. M. (1990). *Clinical applications of cognitive therapy.* New York: Plenum Press.

Freeman, A., Schrodt, G. R., Gilson, M., & Ludgate, J. (in press). Cognitive group therapy with inpatients. In J. Wright, A. Beck, M. These, & J. Ludgate (Eds.), *Cognitive therapy with inpatient populations.* New York: Guilford Press.

Freeman, A., & Simon, K. M. (1989). Cognitive therapy of anxiety. In A. Freeman, K. M. Simon, L. E. Beutler, & H. Arkowitz (Eds.), *Comprehensive handbook of cognitive therapy* (pp. 347–366). New York: Plenum Press.

Freeman, A., Simon, K. M., Beutler, L. E., & Arkowitz, H. (1989). *Comprehensive handbook of cognitive therapy.* New York: Plenum Press.

Gambrill, E. (1985). Bibliotherapy. In A. S. Bellack & M. Hersen (Eds.), *Dictionary of behavior therapy techniques* (pp. 48–51). New York: Pergamon Press.

Garfield, S. L. (1989). The client–therapist relationship in rational–emotive therapy. In M. E. Bernard & R. DiGiuseppe (Eds.), *Inside rational–emotive therapy* (pp. 113–125). San Diego, CA: Academic Press.

Garner, D. M., & Bemis, K. M. (1982). A cognitive–behavioral approach to anorexia nervosa. *Cognitive Therapy and Research, 6,* 123–150.

Glantz, M. (1987). Day hospital treatment of alcoholics. In A. Freeman & V. Greenwood (Eds.), *Cognitive therapy: Applications in psychiatric and medical settings* (pp. 51–68). New York: Human Sciences Press.

Glantz, M. (1989). Cognitive therapy with the elderly. In A. Freeman, K. Simon, L. Beutler, & H. Arkowitz (Eds.), *Comprehensive handbook of cognitive therapy* (pp. 467–489). New York: Plenum Press.

Goldfried, M. R., DeCanteceo, T., & Weinberg, L. (1974). Systematic rational restructuring as a self-control technique. *Behavior Therapy, 5,* 247–254.

Goldfried, M. R., Linehan, M. M., & Smith, J. L. (1978). Reduction of test anxiety through cognitive restructuring. *Journal of Consulting and Clinical Psychology, 46,* 32–39.

Goldfried, M. R., Padawer, W., & Robins, C. (1984). Social anxiety and the semantic structure of heterosexual interactions. *Journal of Abnormal Psychology, 27,* 86–97.

Gomes-Schwartz, B. (1978). Effective ingredients in psychotherapy: Predictions of outcome from process variables. *Journal of Consulting and Clinical Psychology, 46,* 1023–1035.

Gordon, P. K., & Ahmed, W. (1988). A comparison of two group therapies for bulimia. *British Review of Bulimia and Anorexia Nervosa, 3*(1), 17–31.

Gray, J. J., & Hoage, C. M. (1990). Bulimia nervosa: Group behavioral therapy with exposure plus response prevention. *Psychological Reports, 66,* 667–674.

Greenberg, R. L. (1989). Panic disorder and agoraphobia. In J. Scott, J. M. G. Williams, & A. T. Beck (Eds.), *Cognitive therapy in clinical practice* (pp. 25–49). New York: Routledge.

Greenberg, R. L., & Safran, J. D. (1987). *Emotion in psychotherapy: Affect, cognition, and the process of change.* New York: Guilford Press.

Greenwood, V. B. (1987). Cognitive therapy with the young adult chronic patient. In A. Freeman & V. Greenwood (Eds.), *Cognitive therapy: Applications in psychiatric and medical settings* (pp. 103–116). New York: Human Sciences Press.

Grossman, R., & Freet, B. (1987). Cognitive approach to group with hospitalized adolescents. In A. Freedman & V. Greenwood (Eds.), *Cognitive therapy: Applications in psychiatric and medical settings* (pp. 132–151). New York: Human Sciences Press.

Haaga, D. A. F., & Davison, G. C. (1989). Outcome studies of rational–emotive therapy. In M. E. Bernard & R. DiGuiseppe (Eds.), *Inside rational–emotive therapy* (pp. 155–198). San Diego, CA: Academic Press.

Heimberg, R. G. (1990). Cognitive behavior therapy. In A. Bellack & M. Hersen (Eds.), *Handbook of comparative treatments* (pp. 203–218). New York: Wiley.

Heimberg, R. (in press). *Treatment of social fears and phobias*. New York: Guilford Press.

Heimberg, R. G., Becker, R., Goldfinger, K., & Vermilyea, J. A. (1985). Treatment of social phobia by exposure, cognitive restructuring and homework assignments. *Journal of Nervous and Mental Disease, 173,* 236–245.

Heimberg, R. G., Dodge, C., Hope, D., Kennedy, C., Zollo, L., & Becker, R. (1990). Cognitive–behavioral group treatment for social phobia: Comparison with a credible placebo control. *Cognitive Therapy and Research, 14,* 1–23.

Hollon, S., & Beck, A. T. (1986). Cognitive and cognitive–behavioral therapies. In S. L. Garfield & A. E. Bergin (Eds.), *Handbook of psychotherapy and behavior change* (pp. 443–482). New York: Wiley.

Hollon, S. D., & Evans, M. D. (1983). Cognitive therapy for depression in a group format. In A. Freeman (Ed.), *Cognitive therapy with couples and groups* (pp. 11–42). New York: Plenum Press.

Hollon, S., & Garber, J. (1988). Cognitive therapy. In L. Abramson (Ed.), *Social cognition and clinical psychology* (pp. 204–253). New York: Guilford Press.

Hollon, S., & Kendall, P. (1980). Cognitive self-statements in depression: Development of an automatic thoughts questionnaire. *Cognitive Therapy and Research, 4*(4), 383–395.

Hollon, S., & Najavits, L. (1988). Review of empirical studies of cognitive therapy. In A. J. Frances & R. E. Hales (Eds.), *American Psychiatric Press review of psychiatry* (Vol. 7, pp. 643–666). Washington, DC: American Psychiatric Press.

Hollon, S. D., & Shaw, B. F. (1979). Group cognitive therapy for depressed patients. In A. T. Beck, A. J. Rush, B. F. Shaw, & G. Emery (Eds.), *Cognitive therapy of depression* (pp. 328–353). New York: Guilford Press.

Hope, D. A., Herbert, J. A., & Bellack, A. S. (1991, November). *Social phobia subtype, avoidant personality disorder and psychotherapy outcome.* Poster presented at the meeting of the Association for the Advancement of Behavior Therapy, New York.

Jarvik, L., Mintz, J., Steuer, J., & Gerner, R. (1982). Treating geriatric depression: A 26 week interim analysis. *Journal of the American Geriatric Society, 30,* 713–717.

Kadden, R. M., Cooney, N. L., Getter, H. G., & Litt, M. D. (1989). Matching alcoholics to coping skills or interactional therapies: Posttreatment results. *Journal of Consulting and Clinical Psychology, 57*(6), 698–704.

Kassinove, H., Miller, N., & Kalin, M. (1980). Effects of pretreatment with rational–emotive bibliotherapy and rational–emotive audiotherapy on clients waiting at community health centers. *Psychological Reports, 46,* 851–857.

Keller, J. F., Croake, J. W., & Brooking, J. Y. (1975). Effects of a program in rational thinking on anxieties in older persons. *Journal of Counseling Psychology, 22,* 54–57.

Kelly, G. A. (1955). *The psychology of personal constructs.* New York: Norton.

Kendall, P. C., & Bemis, K. M. (1983). Thought and action in psychotherapy: The cognitive–behavioral approaches. In M. Hersen, A. Kazdin, & A. Bellack (Eds.), *The clinical psychology handbook* (pp. 565–592). New York: Pergamon Press.

Kendall, P. C., & Braswell, L. (1985). Cognitive–behavioral self-control therapy for children: A components analysis. *Journal of Consulting and Clinical Psychology, 50,* 672–689.

Kiesler, D. J. (1966). Some myths of psychotherapy research and the search for a paradigm. In A. P. Goldstein & N. Stein (Eds.), *Prescriptive psychotherapies* (pp. 102–126). New York: Plenum Press.

Kirkley, B. G., Schneider, J. A., Agras, W. S., & Bachman, J. A. (1985). Comparison of two group treatments for bulimia. *Journal of Consulting and Clinical Psychology, 53*(1), 43–48.

Kovacs, M., Rush, A. J., Beck, A. T., & Hollon, S. D. (1981). Depressed outpatients treated with cognitive therapy and pharmacotherapy: A one-year follow-up. *Archives of General Psychiatry, 38,* 33–39.

Lazarus, A. A. (1981). *The practice of multimodal therapy.* New York: McGraw-Hill.

Lewinsohn, P. M., Steinmetz, J. L., Larsen, D. W., & Franklin, J. (1981). Depression-related cognitions: Antecedent or consequence? *Journal of Abnormal Psychology, 90,* 213–219.

Linehan, M. M. (1987a). Dialectical behavioral therapy: A cognitive–behavioral approach to parasuicide. *Journal of Personality Disorders, 1*(4), 328–333.

Linehan, M. M. (1987b). Dialectical behavior therapy for borderline personality disorders. *Bulletin of the Menninger Clinic, 5*(3), 261–276.

Liotti, G. (1987). Structural cognitive therapy. In W. Dryden & W. L. Golden (Eds.), *Cognitive–behavioral approaches to psychotherapy.* New York: Hemisphere.

Lipsky, M. J., Kassinove, H., & Miller, N. J. (1980). Effects of rational–emotive therapy, rational role reversal, and rational–emotive imagery on the emotional adjustment of community mental health center patients. *Journal of Consulting and Clinical Psychology, 48,* 366–374.

Luka, L. P., Agras, W. S., & Schneider, J. A. (1986). Thirty month follow-up of cognitive–behavioural group therapy for bulimia. *British Journal of Psychiatry, 148,* 614–615.

Lyons, L. C., & Woods, P. J. (1991). The efficacy of rational–emotive therapy: A quantitative review of the outcome research. *Clinical Psychology Review, 11,* 357–369.

Mahoney, M. J. (1977). Personal science: A cognitive learning therapy. In A. Ellis & R. Grieger (Eds.), *Handbook of rational psychotherapy.* New York: Springer.

Mahoney, M. J., & Arnoff, D. B. (1978). Cognitive and self-control therapies. In S. L. Garfield & A. E. Bergin (Eds.), *Handbook of psychotherapy and behavioral change: An empirical analysis* (2nd ed., pp. 689–722). New York: Wiley.

Mahoney, M. J., & Gabriel, T. J. (1987). Psychotherapy and the cognitive sciences: An evolving alliance. *Journal of Cognitive Psychotherapy, 1*(1), 39–57.

Mahoney, M. J., & Kazdin, A. E. (1979). Cognitive behavior modification: Misconceptions and premature evaluation. *Psychological Bulletin, 86,* 1044–1049.

Malkiewich, L. E., & Merluzzi, T. V. (1980). Rational restructuring versus desensitization with clients of diverse conceptual levels: A test of a client–treatment matching model. *Journal of Counseling Psychology, 27,* 453–461.

Margolis, R. B., & Shemberg, K. M. (1976). Cognitive self-instruction in process and reactive schizophrenics: A failure to replicate. *Behavior Therapy, 7,* 668–671.

Maultsby, M. C., Jr. (1975). *Help yourself to happiness.* New York: Institute for Rational-Emotive Therapy.

McKain, T. L. (1984). Coping skills training and cognitive–behavioral therapy. In L. I. Sank & C. S. Shaffer (Eds.), *A therapist's manual for cognitive behavior therapy in groups* (pp. 9–24). New York: Plenum Press.

Meichenbaum, D. (1975). A self-instructional approach to stress management: A proposal for stress inoculation training. In I. Sarason & C. D. Spielberger (Eds.), *Stress and anxiety* (pp. 337–360). New York: Plenum Press.

Meichenbaum, D. (1977). *Cognitive–behavior modifications: An integrated approach.* New York: Plenum Press.

Meichenbaum, D., & Asarnow, J. (1979). Cognitive–behavior modification and metacognition development: Implications for the classroom. In P. C. Kendall & S. D. Hollon (Eds.), *Cognitive–behavioral interventions: Theory, research and procedures* (pp. 11–36). San Diego, CA: Academic Press.

Meichenbaum, D., & Cameron, R. (1973). Training schizophrenics to talk to themselves: A means of developing attentional controls. *Behavior Therapy, 4,* 515–534.

Meichenbaum, D., & Goodman, J. (1971). Training impulsive children to talk to themselves: A means of developing self-control. *Journal of Abnormal Psychology, 77,* 115–126.

Miller, I. W., Bishop, S. B., Norman, W. H., & Keinter, G. I. (1985). Cognitive/behavioural therapy and pharmacotherapy with chronic, drug-refractory depressed inpatients: A note of optimism. *Behavioral Psychotherapy, 13,* 320–327.

Miller, I. W., Norman, W. H., & Keitner, G. I. (1989). Cognitive–behavioral treatment of depressed inpatients: Six- and twelve-month follow-up. *American Journal of Psychiatry, 146,* 1274–1279.

Mitchell, J. E., Pyle, R., Hatsukami, D. K., Goff, G., Glotter, D., & Harper, J. (1988). A 2–5 year follow-up of patients treated for bulimia. *International Journal of Eating Disorders, 8*(2), 157–165.

Moorey, S. (1989). Drug abusers. In J. Scott, J. M. G. Williams, & A. T. Beck (Eds.), *Cognitive therapy in clinical practice* (pp. 157–182). New York: Routledge.

Murphy, G. E., Simons, A. D., Wetzel, R. D., & Lustman, P. J. (1984). Cognitive therapy and pharmacotherapy, singly and together, in the treatment of depression. *Archives of General Psychiatry, 41,* 33–41.

Oei, T. P. S., & Jackson, P. R. (1982). Social skills and cognitive behavioral approaches to the treatment of problem drinking. *Journal of Consulting and Clinical Psychology, 51,* 390–395.

Oliver, J., & Baumgart, E. P. (1985). The Dysfunctional Attitude Scale: Psychometric properties and relation to depression in an unselected adult population. *Cognitive Therapy and Research, 9,* 161–167.

O'Malley, S. S., Suh, C. S., & Strupp, H. H. (1983). The Vanderbilt Psychotherapy Process Scale: A report on the scale development and a process-outcome study. *Journal of Consulting and Clinical Psychology, 52,* 581–586.

Perris, C. (1988a). The foundations of cognitive psychotherapy and its standing in relation to other psychotherapies. In C. Perris, I. M. Blackburn, H. Perris (Eds.), *Cognitive psychotherapy* (pp. 1–42). New York: Springer-Verlag.

Perris, C. (1988b). Intensive cognitive–behavioural psychotherapy with patients suffering from schizophrenic psychotic or post psychotic syndrome: Theoretical and practical aspects. In C. Perris, I. M. Blackburn, & H. Perris (Eds.), *Cognitive psychotherapy* (pp. 324–375). New York: Springer-Verlag.

Reda, M. A., Carpiniello, B., Secchiaroli, L., & Blanco, S. (1985). Thinking, depression, and antidepressants: Modified and unmodified depressive beliefs during treatment and amitriptyline. *Cognitive Therapy and Research, 9*(2), 135–143.

Rehm, L. P. (1977). A self control model of depression. *Behavior Therapy, 8,* 787–804.

Rush, A. J., Beck, A. T., Kovacs, M., & Hollon, S. D. (1977). Comparative efficacy of cognitive therapy and pharmacotherapy in the treatment of depressed outpatients. *Cognitive Therapy and Research, 1,* 17–38.

Rush, J., & Watkins, J. T. (1981). Cognitive therapy with psychologically naive depressed outpatients. In G. Emery, S. Hollon, & R. C. Bedrosian (Eds.), *New directions in cognitive therapy: A casebook* (pp. 5–28). New York: Guilford Press.

Rush, J. A., Weissenburger, J., & Eaves, G. (1986). Do thinking patterns predict depressive symptoms? *Cognitive Therapy and Research, 10*(2), 225–236.

Salkovskis, P. M. (1989). Obsessions and compulsions. In J. Scott, J. Mark, G. Williams, & A. T. Beck (Eds.), *Cognitive therapy in clinical practice* (pp. 50–77). New York: Routledge.

Sanchez-Craig, M. (1980). Random assignment to abstinence or controlled drinking in a cognitive–behavioral program: Short term effects on drinking behaviour. *Addictive Behaviours, 5,* 35–39.

Sanchez-Craig, M., Annis, H., Bronet, A. R., & MacDonald, K. R. (1984). Random assignment to abstinence and controlled drinking: Evaluation of a cognitive–behavioral program for problem drinkers. *Journal of Consulting and Clinical Psychology, 52,* 390–403.

Sank, L. I., & Shaffer, C. S. (1984). *A therapist's manual for cognitive behavior therapy in groups.* New York: Plenum Press.

Schneider, J. A., & Agras, W. S. (1985). A cognitive behavioural group treatment of bulimia. *British Journal of Psychiatry, 146,* 66–69.

Schrodt, G. R., & Wright, J. (1987). Inpatient treatment of adolescents. In A. Freeman & V. Greenwood (Eds.), *Cognitive therapy: Applications in psychiatric and medical settings* (pp. 69–82). New York: Human Sciences Press.

Schwartz, R. M. (1982). Cognitive–behavior modification: A conceptual review. *Clinical Psychology Review, 2,* 267–283.

Scott, J., Williams, J. M. C., & Beck, A. T. (1989). *Cognitive therapy in clinical practice.* New York: Routledge & Kegan Paul.

Shaw, B. F. (1977). Comparison of cognitive therapy and behavior therapy in the treatment of depression. *Journal of Consulting and Clinical Psychology,* 45(4), 543–551.

Shaw, B. F., & Wilson-Smith, D. (1988). Training therapists in cognitive–behavioral therapy. In C. Perris, I. M. Blackburn, & H. Perris (Eds.), *Cognitive psychotherapy: Theory and practice* (pp. 140–159). New York: Springer-Verlag.

Simons, A. D, Garfield, S. L., & Murphy, G. E. (1984). The process of change in cognitive therapy and pharmacotherapy for depression. *Archives of General Psychiatry, 41,* 45–51.

Simons, A. D., Lustman, P. J., Wetzel, R. D., & Murphy, G. E. (1985). Predicting response to cognitive therapy of depression: The role of learned resourcefulness. *Cognitive Therapy and Research, 9,* 79–89.

Simons, A. D., Murphy, G. E., Levine, J. E., & Wetzel, R. D. (1986). Cognitive therapy and pharmacotherapy for depression. *Archives of General Psychiatry, 43,* 43–48.

Spivack, G., Platt, J. J., & Shure, M. B. (1976). *The problem-solving approach to adjustment.* San Francisco: Jossey-Bass.

Steuer, J. L., & Hammen, C. L. (1983). Cognitive–behavioral group therapy for the depressed elderly: Issues and adaptations. *Cognitive Therapy and Research,* 7(4), 285–296.

Steuer, J. L., Mintz, J., Hammen, C. L., Hill, M. A., Jarvik, L. F., McCarley, T., Motoike, P., & Rosen, R. (1984). Cognitive–behavioral and psychodynamic group psychotherapy in treatment of geriatric depression. *Journal of Clinical and Consulting Psychiatry, 52,* 180–189.

Swenson, C. (1989). Kernberg and Linehan: Two approaches to the borderline patient. *Journal of Personality Disorders,* 3(1), 26–35.

Thorpe, G. L., Amatu, H. I., Blakely, R. S., & Burns, L. E. (1976). Contributions of overt instructional rehearsal and "specific insight" to the effectiveness of self-instructional training: A preliminary study. *Behavior Therapy, 7,* 504–511.

Turner, R. M. (1987). The effects of personality disorder diagnosis on the outcome of social anxiety symptom reduction. *Journal of Personality Disorders, 1*(2), 136–143.

Weissman, A. (1979). The Dysfunctional Attitude Scale: A validation study (Doctoral dissertation, University of Pennsylvania, 1979). *Dissertation Abstracts International, 40,* 1389–1390b.

Wessler, R. L., & Hankin, S. (1988). Rational–emotive therapy and related cognitively oriented psychotherapies. In S. Long (Ed.), *Six group therapies* (pp. 159–216). New York: Plenum Press.

Wessler, R. L., & Hankin-Wessler, S. (1989). Cognitive group therapy. In A. Freeman, K. Simon, L. Beutler, & H. Arkowitz (Eds.), *Comprehensive handbook of cognitive therapy* (pp. 559–582). New York: Plenum Press.

Westen, D. (1991). Social cognition and object relations. *Psychological Bulletin, 109*(3), 429–455.

Williams, J. M. G., & Moorey, S. (1989). The wider application of cognitive therapy: The end of the beginning. In J. Scott, J. M. G. Williams, & A. T. Beck (Eds.), *Cognitive therapy in clinical practice: An illustrative casebook* (pp. 227–250). New York: Routledge.

Wise, E. H., & Haynes, S. N. (1983). Cognitive treatment of test anxiety: Rational restructuring versus attentional training. *Cognitive Therapy and Research, 7,* 69–77.

Wolpe, J. (1973). *The practice of behavior therapy* (2nd ed.). New York: Pergamon Press.

Wright, J., Beck, A, These, M., & Ludgate, J. (in press). *Cognitive therapy with inpatient populations.* New York: Guilford Press.

Wright, J. H., & Schrodt, G. R. (1989). Combined cognitive therapy and pharmacotherapy. In A. Freeman, K. Simon, L. Beutler, & H. Arkowitz (Eds.), *Comprehensive handbook of cognitive therapy* (pp. 267–282). New York: Plenum Press.

Yost, E. B., Beutler, L. E., Corbishley, M. A., & Allender, J. R. (1986). *Group cognitive therapy: A treatment approach for depressed older adults.* New York: Pergamon Press.

Zerhusen, J., Boyle, K., & Wilson, W. (1991). Out of the darkness: Group cognitive therapy for depressed elderly. *Journal of Psychosocial Nursing, 29*(9), 16–21.

Zimmer, J. M., & Pepyne, E. W. (1971). A descriptive and comparative study of dimensions of counselor response. *Journal of Counseling Psychology, 18,* 441–447.

# Appendix A
## Examples of Cognitive Distortions

1. Evaluating oneself or situation in all-or-nothing (extreme) thinking.
2. Catastrophizing—overestimating difficulty to disastrous proportions.
3. Overgeneralization from a single negative event to many negative events.
4. Developing conclusions based on a few pieces of information that validate ideas while ignoring all of the other available information.
5. Discounting the positive.
6. Concluding an arbitrary, negative inference that is not justified by the presented evidence or that is in direct contradiction to the facts. Two types of arbitrary inference are mind reading (others should be able to read one's mind or know what one is thinking without confirming it) and negative prediction (predicting negative events without appropriate documentation).
7. Magnification of imperfections or minimization of good points.
8. Taking one's immediate emotional responses as evidence for the way things really are (e.g., "I feel overwhelmed. Therefore, I won't be able to complete the task").
9. Absolutist, unconditional, rigid "should/must/ought" statements, which have the effect of producing guilt.
10. In an extremely overgeneralized way, labeling a situation or oneself with inaccurate and negatively and emotionally loaded words (e.g., "I'm just a lousy person").
11. Taking events that have nothing to do with oneself and making them personally meaningful (e.g., "This always happens to me whenever I want something and I'm rushed").
12. Underestimating or overestimating the extent to which one has control of self, others, or the world.
13. Belief in "heaven's reward" (i.e., "If I do everything right, I will be rewarded later").
14. Externalization of one's self-worth.
15. Belief that worrying will prevent bad events from happening or that it will make them go away.

411

16. Belief that life is fair.

(From Beck, Rush, Shaw, & Emery (1979); Ellis, 1990; Freeman, 1987, 1990.)

# Appendix B
# Examples of Behavioral Techniques

The goal in using behavior techniques is threefold: (a) to change behavior through the introduction and practice of a broad range of behavioral techniques (Beck & Weishaar, 1989; Beck et al., 1979), (b) to use the behavioral techniques as short-term interventions with the goal of long-term cognitive change, (c) to collect data and then empirically test the veracity the underlying assumptions and beliefs. (Followers of rational–emotive therapy do not use empirical testing because they tend to believe that irrationality is ultimately not testable.)

**Activity scheduling.** This technique assesses the patient's current use of time. It can be used in the preparatory phase of group as an assignment to get the patient accustomed to the idea of doing homework. It can also be used prospectively to plan more productive use of time later in the course of therapy (Freeman, 1987).

**Mastery and pleasure ratings.** The patient can begin to examine his or her mastery (the sense of accomplishment in doing the activities) and pleasure (how much he or she enjoys the activities) by means of the activity schedule. These ratings are made using a 5- or 10-point scale and can be used to plan more mastery and pleasure activities as well. This schedule provides data with which to identify cognitive distortions by exploring the discrepancies between what was actually accomplished and the feeling of mastery and whether the reasons for this difference are realistic or distorted (Beck et al., 1979).

**Behavioral rehearsal.** This technique allows the patient to practice interactions with other group members. The therapist and group can coach and model new behaviors. Both group members and therapist can give feedback on the patient's performance (see chapter 9).

**Externalization of voices.** This technique has the therapist role play the patient's dysfunctional voice and then an adaptive response. Patient and therapist role play together so that the therapist can, in a stepwise manner, become an increasingly more dysfunctional voice of the patient and the patient through successive approximation can get practice in adaptively responding.

**Bibliotherapy.** For some patients, reading can aid in the induction phase to educate the patient about principles of cognitive–behavioral therapy. Books such as *Feeling Good* (Burns, 1980), *Cognitive Therapy and the Emotional Disorders* (Beck, 1976), *Coping With Depression* (Beck & Greenberg, 1974), *Coping With Substance Abuse* (Beck & Emery, 1977), *Own Your Own Life* (Emery, 1984), *Guide to Personal Happiness* (Ellis & Becker, 1982), and *How to Stubbornly Refuse to Make Yourself Miserable About Anything—Yes Anything* (Ellis, 1988). Bibliotherapy is only a small part of the therapy unless the group is mostly an educational one. The reading material chosen should be carefully selected with the characteristics and limitations of the patient population in mind (Gambrill, 1985).

**Graded task assignments.** The therapist assigns tasks in a stepwise fashion from simpler to more complex. Each assignment is accompanied by an exploration of the patient's doubts and encouragement of realistic evaluation of his or her accomplishment (Freeman, 1987).

**In vivo work.** This technique consists of having the patient practice his or her newly learned skills outside the group setting. It is used often with agoraphobia, social phobia, or social difficulties. It also can be used within the session to simulate real-life circumstances (e.g., having the patient hyperventilate to learn that many symptoms he or she has are the result of the hyperventilation; Williams & Moorey, 1989).

**Progressive relaxation.** The use of progressive relaxation, focused breathing, and meditation help anxious patients begin to gain a sense of control over their anxiety. *The Relation and Stress Reduction Workbook* (Davis, Eshelman, & McKay, 1988) is an excellent resource for both patients and therapists.

**Shame-attacking exercises.** This technique consists of having patients test their distorted beliefs in regard to how others view them by performing shameful or foolish activities. The goal is for the patient to realize that others tend not to scrutinize and evaluate his or her behavior with the same critical eye that he or she does (Ellis, 1985).

# Appendix C
# Cognitive Strategies

**Rational coping statements.** These statements are also referred to as *constructive adaptive self-statements.* Patients are taught to use self-statements or instructions (first verbally out loud and then silently) to help them through a stressful situation. These statements should be meaningful to the patient and ideally should be chosen by them. This technique can be the entire therapy, or it can be used in combination with other techniques (Meichenbaum, 1977).

**Cognitive distraction.** This technique enables the individual to temporarily stop ruminating by having him or her focus on complex counting, addition, or substraction. Engaging in mental imagery, physical activity, or humor are also used as distractions that provide temporary relief and allow patients to detach from their anxiety and establish control over their thoughts (Freeman, 1990). Ellis (1980) cautioned that cognitive distraction should always be used as an adjunct to other methods given that patients may not want to continue to work on their problems if this alleviates the majority of their distress.

**Thought stopping.** This technique teaches patients to stop dysfunctional thoughts at their inception rather than letting them accrue. Patients are usually taught to use a sensory cue (e.g., visualizing a stop sign, hearing the therapist's voice) as a way to stop the thoughts (Wolpe, 1973).

**Semantic analysis.** This technique challenges patients who overgeneralize and misuse language (Ellis, 1990).

**Guided imagery or guided fantasy.** This technique is specifically designed to raise certain issues such as anxiety, guilt, shame, and joy. It raises affect and clarifies cognitions and can demonstrate the interrelations among cognition, affect, and behavior. Initially, the technique is used to illustrate the relation between cognitions and resulting emotions. Later, in the therapy process, during guided group fantasy, each member works separately on his or her own problem area and then participates in a group discussion. Group members who had similar emotional experiences find that they had similar cognitions, whereas others are surprised that they responded in unpredictable ways (Wessler & Hankin-Wessler, 1989).

**The discomfort anxiety concept.** A technique used especially by rational–emotive therapists to dispute the irrational belief that one should not experience discomfort or unease. For some patients, this is manifested in their low frustration tolerance of their symptoms (e.g., depression and anxiety) and a desire for immediate relief. Rational–emotive therapists philosophically endorse long-term rather than short-term hedonism. Patients are encouraged to remain in an uncomfortable situation for discrete periods of time to encourage the development of frustration tolerance (Ellis, 1977a, 1977b, 1990). Discomfort anxiety can take an interpersonal form as well manifesting itself as a manipulation to obtain immediate gratification. Grossman and Freet (1987) attempted to help adolescents deal with this by listing as one of the goals "Building up your emotional bank accounts [with people]." The goal was to have enough in one's "emotional bank accounts" to get what one wants from them "off the interest." When adolescents manifested discomfort anxiety and manipulated the situation, therapists asked, "What must you have been thinking to allow yourself to get away with that?"

**Active disputing.** This popular technique of rational–emotive therapy involves vigorous disputing or debating by challenging, questioning, and expressing skepticism of the patient's irrational and absolutist thinking and then teaching the patient how to do his or her own disputing. This technique is less applicable for mentally retarded and severely psychotic individuals (Ellis, 1980). Freeman (1990) advocated using this technique only when the issue of suicide is prominent because this technique has the potential to lead to a power struggle with the patient and because patients with chronic symptoms are often reluctant to give up a problem that will leave them with no way to cope.

**Idiosyncratic meaning.** This technique involves the clarification of terms and statements to ensure that the group, the patient, and the therapist have the same understanding (Freeman, 1987). By doing this, the therapist models the importance of "active listening" and provides a method for questioning and confirming assumptions.

**Questioning the evidence.** This technique teaches patients to question the "data" that they are using to continue a belief or strengthen an idea. It is a less confrontational technique than is active disputing (Freeman et al., 1992).

**Reattribution.** This technique is used when patients inaccurately attribute negative events to all of a personal deficiency (e.g., "It's all my fault that my son did not get into Harvard"). The therapist guides the patient to recognize all responsible individuals (Freeman, 1987).

**Examining alternatives.** This technique helps patients learn to solve problems by use of additional options. Other group members' participation can be particularly helpful in this regard (see chapter 8).

**De-catastrophizing** (also called the *what-if technique*). This helps patients recognize that they are overestimating the catastrophic nature of a situation. The therapist asks the patient questions like, "What if it did occur?" and " What is the worst that would happen?" (Freeman, 1987). Imagined events or interactions that might happen often illustrate the dysfunctional thinking that distorts patients' perceptions.

**The "as-if" attitude.** This technique can be used when the patient appears to be following some nonconscious belief or holding a particular cognition that is irrational or dysfunctional. The therapist states that the patient is acting "as if" he or she holds a belief and then presents evidence to support the "as-if" statement. Other group members can add further support for the therapists' interpretation and offer speculations about each other's nonconscious cognitions (Wessler & Hankin-Wessler, 1989).

**Advantages and disadvantages** (also called *referenting*). Patients list the pros and cons of a belief or behavior to help gain a balanced perspective. This is often effective with adolescents (Schrodt & Wright, 1987).

**Reframing.** This technique helps patients reframe a negative experience. Patients learn to see the positive side of unfortunate events. For example, losing one's job may be seen as an opportunity for growth (Ellis, 1990).

**Labeling of distortions.** Identifying and labeling cognitions aids in monitoring dysfunctional thinking. Often, patients are given a list and description of types of distortions that can be referred to during the session (Heimberg, 1990).

**Downward arrow.** In this guided association approach, patients articulate their thoughts and fears of the significance of events so they can understand the underlying assumptions. The technique follows each patient's statement with questions like "Then what?" or "What would happen then if that were true?" (Freeman, 1987).

**Replacement imagery.** This technique helps patients develop more effective positive imagery and dreams to replace the ones that generate anxiety or depression (Freeman, 1987).

**Cognitive rehearsal.** Patients imagine each step in a sequence to an event or task as a way to rehearse cognitively before a task is behaviorally performed (Freeman, 1987).

**Direct questioning.** This technique can be used when a patient does not acknowledge a feeling that is apparent from his or her demeanor. The patient is asked what just went through his or her mind (Williams & Moorey, 1989).

# 8

# The Problem-Solving Model

T he capacity to resolve the plethora of situational problems
that abound in every individual's life is related closely to
effective daily functioning. Generally, everyday problems can be
classified into one of two categories. Problems can be of an impersonal nature (e.g., anagrams, mathematical problems); in this
case, the subject of study usually does not contain an affective
component, and problems can usually be solved by intellectual
assessment and resolution. Alternatively, problems can be of an
interpersonal or personal nature; the subject contains more affective components, and the dilemma often involves the self and
others (e.g., getting married, changing jobs). The assessment,
potential consequences, and solution often involve an appreciation of mutuality that includes understanding and empathy
with the other's perspective and comprehension of and skill in
interpersonal exchange. Skills in solving both kinds of problems
are essential to one's ability to manage one's life; yet, the processes in resolving each kind appear to be quite different (Meichenbaum & Goodman, 1971; Spivack, Platt, & Shure, 1976).
The relation between problem-solving capabilities and psychopathology appears to hold only for interpersonal problem solving
and not for impersonal problem solving (Gotlieb & Asarnow,
1979). Therefore, the focus of the model presented in the chapter
is primarily interpersonal problem solving because psychiatric
patients—whether they are children, adolescents, or adults—have
been shown to have deficits in interpersonal problem-solving

abilities when compared with their normal cohorts. Almost all the models of group psychotherapy presented in this book can be seen as attempting to aid patients in resolving interpersonal problems in some manner, albeit sometimes indirectly. Models range in their efforts to do this from attempting to expose, redefine, or resolve the unconscious conflicts surrounding a problem to improving the basic social skills of interpersonal exchange that may make interpersonal problem solving difficult. Interpersonal problem solving is also a major feature of all the cognitive and cognitive–behavioral therapies (E. Coché, 1987;[1] Mahoney & Arnkoff, 1978). The problem-solving model presented in this chapter focuses on teaching effective, rational problem-solving steps in a direct, straightforward manner. This approach emphasizes the significance of cognitive processes that mediate the individual's ability to perceive, appreciate, and think through the alternatives and consequences of an interpersonal problem before taking action as a way to improve psychological functioning.

# Theoretical Underpinnings

## The Relation of Problem-Solving Capabilities to Psychiatric Illness

Through the ages, philosophers and students of human behavior have noted that the ability to solve problems is closely and perhaps directly related to human adjustment. As early as the fifth century B.C., Socrates observed that competent people are those who manage their daily circumstances, "possess a judgment which is accurate in meeting occasions as they arise, and rarely miss the expedient course of action" (Socrates quoted in D'Zurilla & Goldfried, 1971). The study of problem solving has a long and respected history in the psychology literature (Davis, 1966; Duncan, 1959; Heppner, 1978; Simon & Newell, 1971). Socrates's

---

[1] We regret the untimely death of Dr. Erich Coché, who was a colleague to both of us during our tenures at Friends Hospital, Philadelphia, PA.

viewpoint has also been expressed in the contemporary world; Jahoda (1953, 1958) offered as one criterion for "positive" mental health the capacity to solve problems in real-life situations. Certainly, ability to think rationally and flexibly is an important part of psychological health (Hartmann, 1939, 1964; Kubie, 1954). An individual's incapacity to resolve certain problematic situations has been viewed as abnormal behavior; an inability to solve problems has further undesirable effects such as the development of anxiety, depression, and additional problems, as well as the promotion of the belief that future problems cannot be resolved (D'Zurilla & Goldfried, 1971; Goldfried & Davison, 1976).

The seminal research of Spivack (1984) and his colleagues supports the link between interpersonal problem-solving abilities and emotional health.[2] Some of the skills required to negotiate interpersonal exchanges and to solve problems that arise from them are acquired at least by 4 years of age (Shure & Spivack, 1982; Shure, Spivack, & Jaeger, 1971). The development of each of these skills has been articulated elsewhere in considerable detail (Spivack et al., 1976). The capacity to solve problems is a socially required and adaptive cognitive/interpersonal ability that makes possible successful functioning throughout the life span; it is important for children (Shure & Spivack, 1972; Spivack et al., 1976), adolescents (Platt, Spivack, Altman, Altman, & Peizer, 1974; Spivack & Levine, 1963), and adults (Platt, Scura, & Hannon, 1973; Platt & Spivack, 1972a; Platt, Siegel, & Spivack, 1975). For all of these age groups, there exists a functional relation between psychopathology and certain aspects of

---

[2] Additional evidence such as the positive relation of interpersonal problem solving to the number of close friendships and degree of family support available (Hansen, St. Lawrence, & Christoff, 1985) buttress the link between interpersonal problem-solving ability and emotional health, although certainly other explanations of these findings can be advanced. It should be noted that psychiatric patients have poorer social networks and fewer intimate relationships than do individuals who have never been hospitalized. Interpersonal problem solving appears to be positively correlated with social competence (Platt & Spivack, 1972b). Social skill competence, a related area, is positively correlated with intrapsychic foundations (Bellack, Morrison, Mueser, Wade, Sayers, 1990; Mueser, Bellack, Morrison, & Wixted, 1990).

problem solving; this has been demonstrated by the differences in problem-solving competence between groups that differ in their levels of demonstrated emotional adjustment (e.g., impulsive adolescents in residential treatment versus normal high school students, adult psychiatric patients versus healthy adults). That is, for example, when emotionally maladjusted children[3] or adolescents[4] are compared with their healthy counterparts, the emotionally disturbed groups display deficiencies in their abilities to overcome particular problematic aspects that block the successful achievement of a personal goal. Although the relation between successful problem solving and capacity for interpersonal exchange seems to be obvious, the association between problem-solving ability and psychopathology is not; the latter association attempts to account for something that has a social and affective component (symptoms of psychopathology) by cognitive process.

Empirical work with adult psychiatric populations suggests that these patients are deficient in addressing and solving problems of daily life (Platt & Spivack, 1972a, 1972b, 1974). Adult

---

[3] Shure and Spivack (1972) found that regardless of social class and intellectual functioning, 10–12-year-old children in schools for the emotionally disturbed generated fewer alternatives to problem situations and their expressed solutions were more impulsive and required physical aggression compared with normal children. Socially maladjusted boys (aggressive or isolated) generated fewer alternative solutions than did popular boys, although there were no differences in their abilities to evaluate presented solutions (Richard & Dodge, 1982).

[4] Adolescents with problems of impulse control and acting out had inadequate and inflexible problem-solving skills when compared with normal adolescents (Levenson & Neuringer, 1971; Spivack & Levine, 1963). In particular, poorly adjusted children in this age group seemed less capable of conceptualizing different alternative solutions, exhibited less proclivity to evaluate the negative and positive aspects of the actions before decision making, and were less able to generate spontaneously the possible sequelae of a hypothetical transgression or positive action (Spivack & Levine, 1963). Although adolescents with psychiatric difficulties seemed to be equally capable of problem recognition and causal and consequential thinking, they were deficient in generating alternatives, evaluating options, and role taking (Platt et al., 1974). These differences in problem solving were not the result of intellectual or social class differences.

psychiatric patients produced significantly fewer alternative solutions to problems and elaborated less on the alternatives than did the hospital employee controls (Platt & Spivack, 1972a). The patients also produced proportionately fewer relevant responses in contrast to the controls. Studies on specific psychiatric disorders are consistent with studies on general psychiatric inpatients: Heroin addicts provided fewer solutions to problematic situations than did nonaddicted controls (Platt et al., 1973); depressed individuals also showed deficits in their abilities to generate multiple alternatives and to make effective decisions concerning real interpersonal problems (Nezu, 1986).

Thus, these studies demonstrate that differences in problem-solving abilities are discernable among groups that differ grossly in their levels of adjustment. There is also evidence that differences in problem-solving abilities are discernable among individuals within a homogeneous group who differ only in their degrees of social competence (Platt & Spivack, 1972a, 1972b). For example, reformatory inmates who were identified by their peers and institutional officials as being misfits and as having disciplinary problems were found to be more deficient in problem-solving skills than were other inmates (Higgins & Thies, 1982). For a psychiatric population, patients' abilities to address themselves to problem situations and to generate alternative solutions (and provide more relevant ones) were positively associated with their attainments of higher levels of social competence prior to the onset of their illnesses (Platt & Spivack, 1972b).

With a heterogeneous psychiatric population, there is a relation between severity of psychopathology (or level of social maladjustment) and problem-solving capability. Particularly for men, the more severe their psychopathology, the more deficient their problem-solving skills (Gilbride & Hebert, 1980; Platt & Siegel, 1976).[5] Compared with other psychiatric inpatients, suicidal children, adolescents, and adults have even greater deficiencies in problem-solving skills; specifically, they have proclivities to solve problems actively and spontaneously and are

---

[5] The relation of problem-solving skills to severity of psychopathology for women has been less well supported by research (Platt & Siegel, 1976).

deficient in their efficiencies of responding, their flexibilities of shifting response sets, and the quality of their cognitive problem-solving skills (Cohen-Sandler, 1982; Levenson & Neuringer, 1971; Linehan & Wagner, 1990). When faced with interpersonal problems, suicidal individuals are rigid in their conceptualizations of the problems, generate only a limited number of viable alternative solutions, and narrowly and impulsively focus on the goals rather than evaluate ways to achieve them (Cohen-Sandler, 1982; Levenson & Neuringer, 1971).

Although substantial empirical research supports the thesis that interpersonal problem solving plays an important role in healthy functioning (and that good problem-solving skills are positively correlated with emotional well-being), no causal effect has been established. That is, the fact that there is an association between good problem-solving skills and mental health does not mean that the former causes the latter. At the very least, one conclusion that can be drawn from these studies is that individuals with psychiatric disorders are ineffective at interpersonal problem solving. A stronger conclusion might be that ineffective problem solving decreases human social and personal functioning and may exacerbate existing psychiatric disorders. The most controversial conclusion, with the least empirical support, is that ineffectual coping with problematic circumstances has personal and social consequences that often result in emotional or behavioral disorders that require psychiatric treatment (Goldfried & Davidson, 1976).

Thus, the capacity to think about interpersonal exchange may make a significant contribution to an individual's actual psychological and social adjustment (Platt & Spivack, 1975; Spivack, 1984). The nexus of the problem-solving model is that such thinking can be altered by direct intervention (Platt & Spivack, 1975); parallel to this supposition is the view that altering this thinking leads to change in problem-solving capabilities. This assumption was tested in a study that evaluated the efficacy of the problem-solving model's training procedures (Nezu, 1980). The results indicated that formal and extensive training specifically in problem formulation improved people's abilities to subsequently generate effective alternative solutions to real-life problems. Formal instruction in the production of alternative solutions also enhanced individuals' abilities to generate effective solutions (Nezu, 1986). Finally, direct training in the decision-making process also improved individuals' capacities to make better decisions (Nezu, 1980). One can conclude from these studies that a person's general interpersonal effectiveness (whatever his or her psychiatric status) may be facilitated by specific and formal training in skills that allow him or her to solve everyday problems.

Together, the aforementioned lines of research compellingly establish the relevance of problem-solving training to the treatment of psychiatric disorders. The relation of such training to treating psychiatric disorders is based specifically on the following assumptions: (a) Individuals with psychiatric disorders have deficiencies in problem-solving skills (and, more specifically, the presenting complaint results from the patient's inability to cope with the problem); (b) the capability to think about problem solving may contribute to a person's actual adjustment; and (c) training in this skill can specifically and directly enhance a person's ability to solve current and future problems, improve daily functioning, increase self-esteem, and ameliorate some psychiatric symptomatology (Goldfried & Davison, 1976; Platt & Spivack, 1975; Spivack, 1984).

## The Locus of Deficient Problem-Solving Skills in the Psychiatric Population

The design of an adequate problem-solving training program requires some attention to the specific nature of the deficiencies. Psychiatric patients do not differ from healthy individuals on all the skills required for adequate problem solving. For example, on tasks measuring problem recognition and causal thinking, adolescent psychiatric patients did not differ significantly from their healthy counterparts (Platt et al., 1974).

The major differences between psychiatric patients and their emotionally healthy counterparts seem to be primarily in the areas of generation, evaluation, and implementation of possible solutions. In the area of generation, there are substantial qualitative and quantitative differences. When compared with healthy individuals, psychiatric patients exhibited deficiencies in their abilities to generate spontaneously possible solutions to personal and interpersonal problems (Nezu, 1986; Platt et al., 1973; Platt & Spivack, 1972a, 1972b; Richard & Dodge, 1982; Shure & Spivack, 1972). In addition, healthy individuals produced a greater proportion of effective solutions to the total number of solutions than did the psychiatric patients (Platt & Spivack, 1972a).[6]

In addition to a relative deficiency in generating solutions, psychiatric patients differ from healthy individuals qualitatively in the content of their responses to common problematic situations (Platt & Spivack, 1974). Healthy individuals were more likely to include the element of introspection in the decision-making process before resolving the problem with an action. In contrast, psychiatric patients tended to give more responses that reflected taking immediate, impulsive, concrete, and physically aggressive action (Platt & Spivack, 1974; Shure & Spivack, 1972). The latter were less likely to weigh the pros and cons of possible solutions before taking action and were less likely to spontaneously generate consequences of hypothetical transgressions or good deeds (Spivack & Levine, 1963).

With respect to evaluation, the differences were more complicated. When psychiatric patients were presented with an array of possible solutions to various interpersonal problems, they were as able to place these solutions in a hierarchy of effectiveness as were healthy individuals (Platt et al., 1975; Richard & Dodge, 1982).[7] However, the psychiatric patients were not able to generate alternative consequences of a given act or solution (e.g., "If I express my displeasure to her about her behavior, she might see how serious I am or she might not listen to me because I made her feel bad or she might refuse to be my friend"). This

---

[6] For both healthy and psychiatrically impaired individuals, the ability to generate responses was related to the effectiveness of the solution; those subjects who were more likely to give a lower number of responses gave many more ineffective responses than did those who gave a larger number of responses (Platt & Spivack, 1972a).

[7] Adolescent psychiatric patients may be the exception in that there is evidence that they do have more difficulty evaluating the effectiveness of alternative solutions than their healthy counterparts (Platt et al., 1974).

type of consequential thinking is a significant component of social adjustment from a very early age (Shure & Spivack, 1982) and differentiates impulsive from nonimpulsive children (Spivack & Shure, 1974).

The subsequent process of implementation consists of articulating the sequence of the means of solving a problem. This involves recognizing obstacles and appreciating that goal achievement may take time. It becomes significant in social adjustment sometime during grade school and remains important for adequate social adjustment throughout the life span (Shure & Spivack, 1972). In several studies, psychiatric patients were not able to create and elaborate to the same extent this sequence and rationale as were their healthy counterparts (Gotlieb & Asarnow, 1979; Platt et al., 1975; Shure & Spivack, 1982). That is, psychiatric patients were not as skilled in recognizing the multiple tiny steps that are required to carry out a solution to a problem.

These deficiencies in both adolescents and adults cannot be accounted for by lack of general intelligence (Siegel, Platt, & Peizer, 1976) or originality of thinking (Gotlieb & Asarnow, 1979) and are independent of social background or social class (Platt & Spivack, 1974). Regardless of level of education, social background, or sophistication, healthy individuals from widely differing cultural backgrounds agree on what constitutes a hierarchy of effective and socially appropriate ways of solving problems (Platt & Spivack, 1974; Siegel, Platt, & Spivack, 1974).

The findings of these studies clearly suggest that successful therapeutic intervention with psychiatric patients must focus on the development and practice of problem-solving skills related to the generation (both amount and kind) of potential solutions (Platt & Spivack, 1975).

## Mechanisms of Change

The major contributors to this model's development view problem-solving training as affecting social adjustment. However, they have disparate views on what they consider to be the crucially operative mechanisms. Some view interpersonal problem solving as fundamentally involving social judgments and cognitive processes (social cognition) and thus view problem-solving training as cognitive or cognitive–behavioral therapy (Wessler & Hankin-Wessler, 1989). Other contributors view problem-solving training to be within the purview of a psychodynamic framework and believe the critical mechanism of change to be in the regulation of self-esteem (E. Coché, 1987; Platt & Spivack, 1975; Spivack et al., 1976). That is, problem-solving training works by making people more interpersonally effective. The individual is likely to have more success and less failure in the interpersonal realm. This greater effectiveness is likely to enhance self-esteem. An adequate level of self-esteem in turn immunizes an individual from the development or exacerbation of symptoms. This process is outlined in Figure 1.

Others view problem-solving training as primarily a behavioral process (overt or covert) in that although the development of the skills is important, there is a significant emphasis on solving problems through the behavioral implementation of a decision; thus, they view problem-solving training as a method of behavioral intervention for target problems (D'Zurilla & Gold-

**Figure 1**

*The Problem-Solving Conceptualization of Psychopathology and its Treatment*

| Problem | Treatment |
| --- | --- |
| Poor problem-solving skills | Improvement in problem-solving skills |
| ↓ | ↓ |
| Adaptive failures | Greater success in adaptive situations outside hospital |
| ↓ | ↓ |
| Low self-esteem | Higher self-esteem |
| ↓ | ↓ |
| High vulnerability to symptoms (Other factors may predispose a person to symptoms) | Diminished long-term vulnerability to symptoms |

fried, 1971; Goldfried & Davison, 1976). The theory that a particular therapist embraces to some extent determines the way in which the model is implemented. We discuss these differences in emphasis and procedure in the technical section.

## Goals of Treatment

Problem-solving training can be conceptualized as helping the individual develop a "learning set" that increases the probability that he or she will cope more effectively with a wide range of situations (Goldfried & Davison, 1976). The primary goal in the training is to have patients acquire a specific method of problem solving so as to improve their abilities to resolve problems, specifically, to learn to formulate problems, generate solutions, and identify the most effective alternatives. Problem-solving training increases the availability of a variety of potentially effective alternative solutions to problems and improves the patient's likelihood of selecting the most effective response from among these alternatives (D'Zurilla & Goldfried, 1971). Thus, the goal of training is not to provide specific solutions to specific situations but instead to teach a general coping skill so that patients are in a better position to manage more effectively a wide variety of social circumstances (Kanfer & Busemeyer, 1982).[8] Thus, neither immediate symptom reduction nor symptom alleviation during hospitalization is a major goal of this model. However, there is an expectation that the acquisition of problem-solving skills will enrich the range of coping responses available to the individual

---

[8] Kanfer and Busemeyer (1982) proposed a broader view of problem solving and decision making than what is used currently. In addition to encouraging the change of specific behaviors, the approach emphasizes attention to the responses and environmental variables that may influence the maintenance of the newly acquired responses and thus may help protect this new behavior from factors that could precipitate a relapse. The patient is aided in examining his or her current circumstances and behaviors by comparing them with a desired criterion and initiating self-correcting responses to attenuate any difference between present and desired states. This view of problem solving highlights and incorporates self-regulation or self-management processes into the therapy.

and will lead to fewer failures in adaption to problematic situations. Although sometimes no appropriate solution or course of action is immediately apparent, the extent to which a person expects to be able to manage his or her difficulties increases the likelihood that he or she will be successful eventually in obtaining an acceptable resolution. Increased confidence in problem-solving ability has been associated with improved problem-solving and decision-making skills (Kanfer & Busemeyer, 1982). On a more long-term basis, a decreased perceived vulnerability to failure renders individuals more resistant to the acquisition or exacerbation of symptoms.

**Rationale for use of the group setting.** Even though the focus in this training is on the individual rather than either the group or the developing relationships among group members, the goal of this technique in the group setting is to provide a supportive ambience that allows members to observe and comment on social interactions within the group (Wessler & Hankin-Wessler, 1989). Thus, the group setting provides an opportunity for group members to observe first-hand the interactions that particular members report to be problematic.

## Problem-Solving Steps

The problem-solving steps in the training have been described by D'Zurilla and Goldfried (1971); Goldfried and Davison (1976); Spivack et al. (1976); and E. Coché (1987). There is general concurrence among these authors on the steps that should be taught. These problem-solving steps are not intended as a model of human problem solving. That is, in specifying the problem-solving stages, there is no implication that these are the processes that individuals spontaneously use. In real life, an individual may move from one stage to another and back again. With more complex problems, one may also work simultaneously on several subproblems, each at a different stage of development (Kanfer & Busemeyer, 1982). Therefore, the sequential approach as presented in the ensuing discussion must be viewed not as a description of how individuals without deficits solve problems in real life but rather as a heuristic and efficacious way for organizing therapeutic procedures (Goldfried & Davison, 1976).[9]

## Technical Considerations

### Group Composition and Patient Selection

Problem-solving groups function most successfully when they consist of 4–12 voluntarily attending participants. Patients with a wide variety of psychiatric disorders have been found to benefit from the training, including patients with depression (Nezu, 1986), schizophrenia (Bedell & Michael, 1985), borderline personality disorder (Linehan & Wagner, 1990), antisocial tendencies (E. Coché & Douglass, 1977; Kazdin, Esveldt-Dawson, French, & Unis, 1987), and alcohol and drug abuse (Glantz, 1987). Patients recovering from acute psychotic episodes, as well as chronic schizophrenics, also appear to profit from participation in this type of group (Waldeck, Emerson, & Edelstein, 1979). Both homogenous as well as heterogeneous diagnostic groups benefit from this model.

The single most important variable on which to match patients is level of cognitive development. The model functions less effectively when members are at radically different levels of cognitive functioning (e.g., J. Coché & Coché, 1986). For this reason,

---

[9] Kanfer and Busemeyer (1982) noted that the model for problem-solving training presented here is static as opposed to dynamic. A static model conceptualizes the individual as confronted with a set of unchanging goals and alternative solutions. The individual chooses an alternative and carries it out, and that particular problem is terminated. Examples are committing suicide, having a baby, making a career choice, or having an abortion. In each of these examples, because the opportunity to modify or correct one's course of action is limited, there is little generalized learning from solving the specific problem. In contrast, in the dynamic problem-solving model, the individual objectives may change over time. In addition, the individual may find it necessary to search for new solutions in response to feedback received as a goal is approached and environmental vicissitudes that change the probability of particular consequences occurring. For example, the goal of developing a new relationship is one that may continuously be improved on.

most groups are designed to be homogenous with respect to age. Children, adolescents, adults, and geriatric patients have been able to improve their problem-solving skills with this training (Hussian, 1987; Spivack et al., 1976).

Although not imperative, mixed-gender groups are more desirable than are same-gender groups given that interpersonal problems often involve both sexes and each sex characteristically offers a different perspective. Similarly, diagnostically heterogeneous groups are preferable to homogenous groups because the former brings a greater array of interpersonal resources to bear on the group's work (G. Spivack, personal communication, January 23, 1992). Diagnostically heterogeneous groups also generate a wider variety of problems for members to attempt to solve. This variability both gives members more practice in applying the problem-solving steps and cultivates their awareness that what is important are the skills they develop, not the specific solutions that they acquire.

Although some patients benefit more from this model than do others (E. Coché, Cooper, & Petermann, 1984; E. Coché & Flick, 1975), the exclusion criteria are minimal. The inclusion requirements are (a) a reasonable degree of intellectual capability and verbal facility, although efficacy has been demonstrated with mentally retarded adults (Benson, Johnson, & Miranti, 1986); minimal short- and long-term memory; (b) an ability to effect some change on the environment; (c) and the ability to inhibit immediate responding (E. Coché, 1987; Hussian, 1987). Patients with serious memory disturbances (e.g., those receiving electroconvulsive treatment [ECT] or with serious brain pathology) are excluded (E. Coché, 1987). The moderate degree of memory loss that is commonly found in geriatric psychiatric inpatients does not preclude effective training as long as modifications are made (E. Coché, 1987; Hussian, 1987). For example, although the use of a large visible blackboard may be somewhat disruptive with younger age groups, it is essential for geriatric groups to aid members' compromised memories. Patients whose disruptive or otherwise antisocial behaviors undermine the group's progress are also excluded (e.g., some antisocial personality disorders and manic patients).

## Time Frame

For mixed-gender, mixed-diagnostic acute care populations with no preset content, E. Coché (1987) recommended an eight-session closed-ended group over a 2-week period. A shorter series of sessions for such patients was been found to be less effective, and patients who participated in less than seven sessions did not derive the desired benefits from the training (see E. Coché, 1987). If the content of the sessions (i.e., the problems) is pre-specified, a shorter series of five sessions has been shown to be efficacious (Edelstein, Couture, Cray, Dickens, & Lusebrink, 1980; Hussian & Lawrence, 1981). The length of the session usually varies from 60 to 90 minutes but can be as long as 3 hours (e.g., Linehan & Wagner, 1990) depending on the composition of the group and members' abilities to focus on the material (E. Coché, 1987; J. Coché & Coché, 1986; Wessler & Hankin-Wessler, 1989).

## Preparation

A 30- to 60-minute individual screening interview with the leader is advocated (J. Coché & Coché, 1986). The screening interview functions as a role induction in which prospective group members are taught appropriate member behaviors to enhance their ability to derive benefit from the group. The specifics of the room, the meeting time, and an attendance contract are given. Resistance to being a member of a group is explored (J. Coché & Coché, 1986). Although a private screening session may be most ideal, we think that group preparation prior to beginning the group is not absolutely necessary and could occur as part of the first scheduled group meeting if the group is closed ended. This modification can be made because the principal foundations (theoretical and technical) of the model do not violate patients' general expectations of what a group is supposed to be.

## The Role of The Leader

The goal of this model is to teach a problem-solving method so that members can evaluate a problem, consider the alternatives, make a decision, implement it, and then verify its effectiveness. The therapist's central function is to provide and maintain the structure and boundaries of the group. This is accomplished by teaching and navigating the group through the necessary steps of the problem-solving model and by periodically reminding the group members of their goal to learn how to solve problems (E. Coché, 1987). To pursue the task of guiding members through the problem-solving procedure, the therapist educates members about each of the basic steps of the problem-solving model and stresses the importance of methodically, tenaciously, and consistently following the procedure without deviation. The therapist can impart the basic tenets of the approach by lecturing, modeling, providing direct feedback on members' behaviors in group, acting as a coach, developing homework assignments, and creating new experiences for groups members directly by role playing and indirectly by providing a good group experience (Wessler & Hankin-Wessler, 1989). The therapist takes an active role in each session, whether lecturing, coaching, or remaining silent. If the group does not follow the prescribed order of steps or does not adequately complete a task, the therapist intervenes. This requirement at times creates a demand on the leader to interrupt an ongoing process to prevent the group from skipping a step while not discouraging members' participation.

Generally, a moderate level of directiveness is appropriate for the leader of this type of group. What the leaders should avoid are either extreme on the continuum of directiveness, although their styles will invariably lean to one side or the other. In particular, the leader should avoid insisting on brief, precise verbalizations in which less time is spent on each step and a considerable number of problems are dealt with in each session. With this extremely task-oriented focus, important curative elements of group technique (e.g., cohesiveness) may receive inadequate attention. In addition, some creative solutions are likely to arise only if the atmosphere is relaxed (E. Coché, 1987). The other undesirable extreme is that wherein the leader allows the group to talk as long as it wishes on any particular problem, permitting tangents and digressions. Although the atmosphere that this style creates builds cohesiveness, creates a pleasant experience, and may provide other individual therapeutic benefits, it misses the point of problem-solving training and may even bore some members. Regardless of the therapist's degree of directiveness, he or she must intervene at all times in a manner to enhance rather than undermine the self-esteem of group members (E. Coché, personal communication, September 20, 1980).

An essential component of navigating members through the procedure is the clinical acumen to refocus or rephrase problems in a manner so that they have the potential to be resolved. Frequently, members present a vague problem that must be made more specific and concrete to be workable. For example, in working with borderline patients, Linehan reframed suicidal and other dysfunctional behaviors as part of the members' learned problem-solving repertoire used to manage or ameliorate psychic distress (Linehan & Wagner, 1990). Occasionally, a member will present a problem that is the result of psychotic thinking. The leader's clinical skill is needed to aid the member in reframing the problem in such a way that it becomes a worthwhile problem on which to work (e.g., a paranoid thought that people are talking about a patient can be refocused as a self-esteem problem or a perceptual difference problem). It is rare that a member's verbalizations cannot be reformed to form a significant problem (E. Coché, 1987).

In addition to reframing members' problems, the therapist must organize and prioritize them in a way that is manageable for the group. There is variation in the method of establishing priorities. For example, if a member drops out, the leader can choose to disregard this event and continue, treat the event as a group problem and allow the group to work on it, or speak with the individual member. (We discuss the establishment of content priority in greater detail in the following section.) The therapist must also decide in what way a problem (the level or aspect) is to be addressed. For example, when a member requests help with a problem but then rejects all possible solutions given, this individual can be viewed as having a specific deficiency in problem-solving ability, namely a tendency to reject solutions before thoroughly examining their potential usefulness. If this member can own and recognize this "yes–but" tendency as a problem, it can be worked on in the group as well. One general approach to such a member is to request that the member withhold all criticism during the solution-generating step. If criticism occurs in the evaluating step, the therapist can invite other group members to comment on their success with a particular solution or advise members that any one solution may not work equally well for all (E. Coché, 1987).

The second task of the therapist is the management of the group process. Some therapists who use this model feel that successful group therapy requires attention to the dynamics of the therapy group (E. Coché, 1987; Wessler & Hankin-Wessler, 1989). Similar to the cognitive–behavioral models, problem-solving training views the individual as the focus of change; however, group dynamics (norms, boundaries, cohesiveness, patterns of communication, and emerging leadership roles) are important because they can enhance or detract from members learning to solve problems and translate newly developed skills into appropriate action. For example, the practice of giving here-and-now group problems preference over problems dealing with issues outside the group effectively covers most problems that arise within the group. The therapist encourages the group to "own" a given problem and to work toward its resolution by generating and then evaluating alternative solutions. In this process, the group becomes less dependent on the group therapist—a tack that may arouse anxiety. The anxiety is diminished by the therapist's conveyance and nurturance of an attitude that difficulties can be mastered when approached with the right frame of reference and with the sense of accomplishment that this technique engenders. In addition, members who "own" and resolve their own intragroup problems are more likely to tackle their own intrapersonal problems successfully.

The therapist is also responsible for regulating the emotionally expressive interactions among members (Wessler & Hankin-Wessler, 1989). Even though problem-solving groups are primarily task oriented, emotional reactions are not uncommon during the course of therapy. It is also important that the therapist titrate the level of emotional expressivity and not permit antitherapeutic statements and actions by group members to influence other members in a detrimental way. Management of each session also requires that the therapist ensure that no one or two members dominate or disrupt the session. When such circumstances arise (e.g., when a member deals with social anxiety by incessant talking), the therapist has a number of alternatives. One is to consider it a group problem and let the group address it. This may be effective as long as the group is not too intimidated by the monopolizer and if the monopolizer is willing to listen to the group's comments without becoming too defensive or sulky. However, it is necessary to intervene if there is an attack on the member. A second method is to intervene outside the session by discussing the problem individually with the monopolizer; this intervention can reduce the frequency of the behavior without causing additional anxiety. A third strategy involves the therapist placing himself or herself strategically next to the monopolizer and explaining that whenever the member talks too much, the therapist will motion with his or her arm as a sign that it is time to slow down. Whatever strategy is used, it is important to articulate and to highlight the positive aspects of the high verbal activity level (i.e., that the member is also displaying an interest in the group, often manifesting a good deal of concern for other members by trying to help them, but is working too hard in the group). Finally, as a last resort, it may be necessary to discharge this member from the group (E. Coché, 1987).

The leader may also find it necessary to periodically remind members of their goal to learn how to solve problems. For example, sometimes members present problems in an effort to induce the group leader to take some kind of action, usually to repair something in their environment, rather than work toward a solution themselves. Usually, members wish immediate action but desire to retain a passive role in the process. The therapist must stress that the goal of the group is to teach members how to solve problems themselves rather than have others solve problems for them (Kanfer & Busemeyer, 1982). In the therapeutic process, it is necessary for the therapist to help the member "own" the problem. In most cases, the problem can be redefined so that the member can accept and then work on the problem.

Leaders can either work alone or in co-therapy teams. The basic procedural structure of problem-solving training is relatively easily learned for the neophyte group therapist. A college graduate or graduate student can often function successfully as the co-therapist with a more experienced therapist (E. Coché,

1987). The more structured and preset the agenda and content, the less experience is required. Additional reading of the psychoanalytic and cognitive–behavioral literature and experience with a more seasoned therapist is useful.

## Content of the Session

**Problems to be addressed.** The main focus of the content in this model is the exploration of each member's presented practical or psychological problem. Problem-solving groups resemble multiple individual therapies in that at any one time a single individual is the focus and receives attention from the group leader (and from other group members) for his or her particular problem. Group members participate in helping each other apply the model. They vicariously learn about their own problems by observing other members' attempts to apply the model with their problems (Wessler & Hankin-Wessler, 1989).

There is considerable variation among problem-solving groups in the degree and type of structure used in the sessions to organize the exploration of members' problems. Problem-solving training groups can be designed to have a preset structure and topic modules (Bedell & Michael, 1985; Edelstein et al., 1980; Hussian & Lawrence, 1981; Shure & Spivack, 1978). The particular topic presented is preselected with a knowledge of the problem areas typical for that patient population; the problem is hypothetical but nonetheless germane to members' issues. For example, chronic institutionalized psychiatric patients may participate in a 5-week problem-solving program that discusses problem areas such as banking, budgeting, medication, health, telephone usage, meal planning, transportation, and community resources (Edelstein et al., 1980). Geriatric patients in a nursing home may have problem scenarios that include such topics as "dealing with combative residents, loss of freedom or flexibility, infrequent or disruptive visits by family members, getting attention of the staff for medical or other concerns, fear of being institutionalized for the remainder of their lives, ability of their spouse to function alone, and negative staff attitudes " (Hussian, 1987, p. 206).

Problem-solving training can also be designed to focus on a specific type of problem such as suicidal behavior (Linehan & Wagner, 1990), relationship issues (Pollack, 1992), or loss (Corder, Whiteside, Koehne, & Hortman, 1981) rather than on hypothetical situations. Here, the members bring in their own problems that are variations of these themes. For others (e.g., E. Coché, 1987), it is only the format of each session that is fixed in advance, with the content varying depending on the concerns and problems presented by the members. Although the topics and problems that members present are considered, grouped, and addressed, E. Coché (1987) advocated giving preference to in-house problems over external or noninstitutional problems, the rationale being that greater saliency provides more immediate positive reinforcement. For example, problems with staff members and doctors (e.g., an inability to express certain thoughts and dissatisfactions to one's doctor) should take priority over an inability to express ones' thoughts and dissatisfactions to one's boss. Hussian (1987), on the other hand, stressed the exploration of extrainstitutional problems to help members generalize from the therapy setting to real-life events.

The manner in which the therapist establishes particular problems to explore is a crucial decision. Members have a natural interest in specific solutions, particularly if those problems pertain to their reasons for hospitalization. By focusing on particular problems, the therapist may give the content of the problems and solutions greater salience, thereby distracting members from the all-important task of acquiring the principles of problem solving.

**Therapeutic aids.** The atmosphere of the group can range from a traditional group format with chairs in a circle to an instructional format with a black board, notebooks, self-monitoring cards, and a table in the center. Because there is a significant number of steps and didactic information that group members must absorb, several techniques have been developed to facilitate members in this task. E. Coché (1987) recommended the use of a wall poster display of the problem-solving steps to help members both remember the procedure and ascertain whether the group is skipping any of the steps. Table 1 shows an adaptation of a poster that E. Coché (1987) used with a group

**Table 1**

*Steps in Problem Solving*

1. Bring up the problem
2. Clarify the problem; gather information
3. Generate solutions
   *** No criticism ***
4. Evaluate the solutions
   Advantages/disadvantages
   Long term/short term
   You/others
5. Select the solution(s)
6. Generate methods of implementation
7. Practice
8. Verify the solution; tell the group

Adapted from E. Coché (1987) in Kavoussi, Fallon, & Coccaro (1992).

of personality-disordered patients (Kavoussi, Fallon, & Coccaro, 1992). This technique is especially valuable with patient populations who have difficulties with cognitive organization and memory (E. Coché, 1987).

The therapist keeps a log, either on lined paper or a blackboard, to record all problems and solutions. The log is another technique to aid the members' memories; it can be viewed by any of the group members and is the property of the group. A problem is entered into the log after the group has gained clarity on the problem. All solutions and who has suggested them are recorded, even if ideas are only a variation of a prior solution. A copy of the log can then be given to the member on whose problem the group is working.

Members can individually choose to audiotape the didactic portions of the session and those parts of the session that address their problem. (Care must be taken to record only those portions that are applicable to the particular member so that confidentiality is not breached.) The tapes can be reviewed several times between sessions and are helpful in increasing members' retention about what has been said during the session (Wessler & Hankin-Wessler, 1989).

**Orientation.** The group begins with a basic orientation each time membership changes. This step includes a rationale for the kind of treatment provided by the group and information on how the group proceeds. The extensiveness of the orientation depends on whether pre-group preparation has occurred, the general proclivities of the therapist, and the constraints of the setting. The orientation can include an in-depth introduction to all of the central concepts and principles of problem-solving therapy. For example, in addition to a basic outline of the procedure, the therapist may develop the notion of the importance of being assertive and exerting control over events in one's life. The therapists might also talk about the importance of identifying problems when they occur and about how deficient problem-solving skills are an interpersonal handicap that may lead to depression, withdrawal, and learned helplessness (Goldfried & Davison, 1976; Hussian & Lawrence, 1981). However, if the exigencies of the clinical setting preclude the use of a large portion of the group's session for orientation, a much simpler statement may suffice. For example, the therapist might simply explain that deficient problem-solving skills are an interpersonal handicap, that people get frustrated when they are unable to solve impersonal as well as interpersonal problems, and that the purpose of the group is to help members become experienced in interpersonal problem solving (E. Coché, 1987; J. Coché & Coché, 1986). Once members begin to practice the problem-solving strategy and are successful in coping effectively with actual problem situations, these expectations should be strengthened. Most of the presentation of the rationale, expectations, and relation of problem-solving training to interpersonal difficulties and psychopathology should occur early in the life of the group. The importance of recognizing problem situations when they occur and resisting the tendency to react automatically without thoroughly considering issues should also be stressed at the beginning, as well as throughout the group as necessary for the particular patient population (Goldfried & Davison, 1976).

The following description is a step-by-step outline of the general problem-solving procedure. The steps include (a) preliminary description of the problem, (b) clarification of the problem, (c) generation of alternatives, (d) evaluation of the alternatives, (e) role playing, (f) implementation of the decision, and (g) verification of the correctness of the decision and concomitant correction of actions. Each step is repeated each time a new problem is presented. The emphasis and time spent on each step may vary for different patient populations. For instance, geriatric patients may require more prompting, more concrete examples, and more emphasis on the noncritical generation of alternative solutions than may younger patients (Hussian, 1987). Impulsive adolescents may require a longer period to anticipate long-term negative consequences. The number of problems that the leader anticipates discussing each session will also influence the extent to which each step is emphasized.

If the problems are preset, the steps are taught and the problem is presented. If, however, the content of the session is determined by the members' particular problems, an introduction is needed to encourage members to begin identifying problematic situations from their experiences—past, present, and expected future. Identification of problems that cause distress is often difficult for some members, particularly those with borderline psychopathology who are prone to experiencing generalized distress. To assist patients in identifying specific problem areas, the therapist might give a lecture on the signal value of distress (i.e., that disturbing emotions, whatever their nature, often signal a problem that requires the person's attention; Linehan, 1987a, 1987b). Members can be instructed to observe their own behaviors between sessions and to keep a daily record of problematic situations that produce emotional reactions. The emotional reaction can be a signal for the patient to look for the events (cognitive and external) that may precipitate these feelings (D'Zurilla & Goldfried, 1971). However, such didactic input may be unnecessary when the group contains some verbal, insightful, reality-oriented members who can serve as models for the less verbal, more disorganized members (E. Coché, 1987).

## Problem-Solving Steps

**Presenting a problem.**[10] If the problems have been set prior to the session, then the leader reads the problem situation and addresses the problem either to the group at large or to one particular member who can then ask others for help (Edelstein et al., 1980; Hussian, 1987; Hussian & Lawrence, 1981). The advantage of using a hypothetical problem that is based on problems generated by patients in similar situations or for a particular target problem such as upcoming relocation or new medication is that it eases the acceptance of having problems, prevents a single member from dominating the group proceedings, and allows the group to work on common problem areas sooner than they might using problems spontaneously offered by the members.

If each member is invited to generate his or her own problem, the leader requests volunteers to present a problem, either personal or practical, internal or external. Often, the first few sessions are concerned with problems pertaining to life on the unit and conflicts with aides, doctors, or other patients (E. Coché, 1987). Examples of such complaints are "The T.V. blasts with stupid soaps on my unit, what can be done about it?", "My roommate leaves her dirty clothes on the floor, what should I do?", "I'm bothered by the nurse checking up on me at night when I sleep, can you do anything?" As the group progresses, members are more likely to take responsibility for such problems and confront more threatening material. Occasionally, a member starts with a very personal problem such as "I feel so rejected, my husband doesn't want to have sex with me very much anymore, what should I do?" This high level of openness can either aid the group to continue at that level or make members un-

---

[10] Kanfer and Busemeyer (1982) suggested that before problem definition occurs, the detection of a problem is an essential step. This involves the individual pinpointing a specific set of problematic responses or events as well as learning to read warning signals by social comparison or self-standard. The model presented here does not include this step and to some extent assumes that an individual is capable of detecting his or her own problems.

comfortable and cause them to avoid further discussion of personal issues.

Although the group therapist does not directly ask any particular member to present a problem or provide a solution, other group members sometimes apply pressure to have a silent member present a problem. If the group becomes encumbered by a group dynamic that keeps it from working profitably (such as a monopolizing member or excessive silence), the leader introduces the interfering dynamic as a problem topic (E. Coché, 1987).

Another variation in problem presentation is to combine the aforementioned approaches. The therapist begins with structured hypothetical presentations and progresses through semistructured topics to member-generated problems (Bedell & Michael, 1985; Edelstein et al., 1980).

**Problem clarification and information gathering.** When members present their problems, they are often unable to do so in a clear, concise manner. This is often the most challenging step of the treatment because what the problem is may not at all be what the member deems it to be. Members must be encouraged to restate the problem so that they provide the kind of information that is likely to maximize the outcome in the subsequent step (D'Zurilla & Goldfried, 1971). This problem refinement is accomplished by getting members to define all relevant aspects of the situation. The manner in which this is accomplished and the particular thrust of the focus on content (and level of inquiry) depends on the theoretical inclination of the therapist and the capacities of the members. With respect to the former, problem clarification can proceed as a psychodynamic inquiry, primarily exploring feelings, thoughts, and conflicts that make the situation problematic (G. Spivack, personal communication, July, 27, 1992). Alternatively, the inquiry can proceed at a more behavioral level. The therapist can encourage the member to define the problem in operational terms (concrete and measurable) by specifying the major issues concerning who, what, where, and when in brief and objective terms (Bedell & Michael, 1985). For either type of inquiry, it is important to identify the member's primary goals and the barriers that make the situation problematic and prevent the acquisition of the goal

(D'Zurilla & Goldfried, 1971). Both external situational events and internal events (thoughts, feelings) are important for a thorough description of the problem (Goldfried & Davison, 1976). If the group member is unclear in the initial presentation of his or her problem, the other group members are encouraged to ask specific questions to eliminate the confusion. Reinforcement of the importance of gathering additional information is essential because information seeking is a basic skill in problem solving: It further clarifies members' understanding of the situation, it teaches them to resist impulsively providing obviously inappropriate suggestions, and it conveys to each member that everyone may see the situation differently (G. Spivack, personal communication, January 23, 1992). This step can involve as much exploration as members' resources will allow; that is, the therapist can adjust the problem formulation to the members' psychological sophistication. For example, an adolescent may say, "I get in trouble in school because I am constantly joking around in class and when I'm not doing that, I'm yawning." A reasonably psychologically sophisticated individual may tolerate coming to the awareness that the problem lies not so much in the clowning around but in anxiety about academic performance. For another youth, it may be necessary to stay on the level of the manifest problem.

The tendency of members to attempt to tell their "life stories" during this step often poses a problem for the leader. A lengthy soliloquy often represents the member's misunderstanding of the model and a resistance to a technique that is not designed to focus on past experiences and free associations (E. Coché, 1987). If the verbalizations produced by the member are not necessary to generate adequate solutions, then it is important not to dwell on the step any longer. The therapist can intervene by either asking the presenting member if the information is relevant to solving the problem, encouraging the group to proceed to the next step, or querying the group as a whole as to whether the information is sufficient to solve the problem (E. Coché, 1987).

Some problem-solving training programs encourage a detailed understanding of the events precipitating the problem behavior. For example, Linehan (1987a, 1987b; Linehan & Wagner, 1990) had members identify events and variables that precipitated maladaptive behaviors (e.g., suicide attempts) and then conducted a thorough behavioral analysis of the chain of events that surrounded the reciprocal interaction between the environment and the member's emotional and behavioral responses. This variation in procedure is usually not practical if the inpatient setting is short term in nature.

**Generating solutions.** After the problem has been presented and clarified, the therapist facilitates the generation of solutions. This step is at the core of problem-solving group training given that inpatients are particularly deficient in their abilities to search for alternative solutions to a problem. During this step, the major task is to generate a range of possible solutions among which some may be effective (Goldfried & Davison, 1976). Imagination and creativity are paramount in this process. This step originated from Osborn's (1963) method of *brainstorming*, a procedure designed to facilitate idea finding in group sessions: Criticism is disallowed, and free wheeling, quantity production, and creative combinations are welcomed (D'Zurilla & Goldfried, 1971). There is empirical support for the efficacy of these brainstorming procedures; they are more likely to generate effective responses than is requesting that individuals produce only high-quality responses (D'Zurilla & Goldfried, 1971).

Members of the group generate as many possible solutions as they can without making any judgments regarding risk, possibility of success, practical aspects, or systemwide ramifications (Hussian, 1987). When beginning this step with each new presented problem, the brainstorming method is explained, with particular emphasis on postponing all criticism until the group has moved to the next step (E. Coché, 1987). The leader must repeatedly and in different ways emphasize that all solutions are appreciated. For instance, the leader may use the verbal reinforcement, "This is great—we've come up with 11 different solutions." Wall posters that say, "The More the Merrier" and "No Criticism" are helpful in reinforcing the notion that at this step, quantity is paramount and criticism is not helpful (J. Coché & Coché, 1986). As solutions are presented, the leader records in the log all solutions and the contributing members' names. The written log serves to reinforce that each solution is appreciated and important (E. Coché, 1987). The log also serves as a reference for the group to consult at any time to review solutions already suggested and to help the members to explore other possible alternatives.

E. Coché (1987) suggested that the therapist refrain from making suggestions so that the group does not develop a dependency on the therapist, which could seriously handicap members' abilities to develop problem-solving skills. The therapist actively aids members to see potential solutions in their utterings; in another theoretical framework, this may be referred to as a *reframing process*. All solutions are welcome, whether they are bizarre, psychotic, humorous, completely impractical, or potentially damaging. The therapist need not fear the inclusion of damaging or criminal solutions because data on individuals with sociopathic tendencies suggest that these tendencies decrease after problem-solving training (E. Coché & Douglass, 1977). Occasionally, the therapist may need to review the problem to keep the solutions relevant to the specific problem presented and to maintain clarity of discussion. Sometimes, it may be necessary to return to the previous step to obtain more information to develop a particular solution.

The solutions must be specific so that their quality can eventually be evaluated (Goldfried & Davison, 1976). To achieve specificity, the group first must sometimes generate as many general alternatives or strategies as possible before moving to the decision-making or evaluation step. The group may then need to return to the solution-generation step to produce more specific alternatives. The group may also need to return to the solution-generating step to develop possible tactics for carrying out the particular chosen solution (Goldfried & Davison, 1976).[11] That is, after a solution is selected, there are often a number of options for implementing it. Some authors advocate a two-part process for this step: After a solution is agreed on, the group

---

[11] In the generation of solutions, strategies or general courses of action are differentiated from tactics or the specific ways in which these solutions might be implemented. Whereas in selecting the best strategy, the emphasis is on resolving the major issues, in selecting tactics, the focus is on implementing the strategy. Strategies involve what to do, whereas tactics involve deciding how to do it (Goldfried & Davison, 1976).

returns to generating alternatives or ideas of implementation (Edelstein et al., 1980; Goldfried & Davison, 1976; Hussian, 1987). Others feel that tactics or ideas of implementation should then be raised as a new (or subsequent) problem of the group. This latter strategy has the beneficial effect of teaching members that all problems cannot be resolved by going through the procedure once but that some require two or more rounds (E. Coché, 1987).

**Evaluation and decision making.** Once the generation of all solutions has been exhausted, the leader makes a very clear transition to the next phase by announcing that it is time to examine the ideas and determine which ones are feasible. The leader then reads the problem and solutions from the log. The group members are asked to give opinions on which solution they think is most likely to be successful. If no one volunteers to begin, the therapist can call on the member who presented the problem to give the first opinion. Therapists who use this model usually have their own favorite methods of giving the discussion a focus, attempting to determine the utility of a decision in light of the values of the individual who presented the problem, and preventing that member from getting into a "yes–but" interchange. E. Coché (1987; J. Coché & Coché, 1986) focused on the "weighing" of solutions (i.e., which ideas are most likely to be successful and what will be the cost if one solution is chosen rather than another). Cost can be defined in terms of money, hard work, pain, hurt feelings, disturbed relationships, loss of prestige, and other similar concepts. The weighing of solutions is an important skill that implies that most solutions are not without a price; concomitantly, the lesson aids members to avoid a flat rejection of others' solutions. Weighing is an extremely useful step for adolescents with sociopathic or impulsive tendencies because it enables them to learn that immediate solutions to problems often require some significant long-term cost (e.g., stealing gets you what you want, but you might end up in jail; J. Coché & Coché, 1986).

Different therapists use different means to help members compare the weight of different solutions. For example, Hussian (1987; Hussian & Lawrence, 1981) developed a scale ($-2$ to $+2$) that group members use to rate the dimensions of personal benefits, benefits for others, short-term advantages and disadvantages, and long-term positive and negative consequences. The four sets of scores that accompany each presented solution are tallied, and the most viable solutions are chosen. Whether one elects to use a numerical approach, the utility of a decision should be assessed keeping in mind the individual's particular values, the values of significant others who often label and influence what is effective in a particular environment, and the various expected consequences and their estimated likelihoods of occurrence (D'Zurilla & Goldfried, 1971). Sometimes during this phase a new alternative emerges. The suggestion is acknowledged, is entered into the log, and its feasibility is discussed in a manner similar to that of the other solutions.

One problem that may arise during this period is when a member is too interested in foisting his or her favorite solution onto the group. It may be necessary for the leader to carefully remind that individual that not all solutions work for all people. The therapist too must guard against his or her own eagerness that the member who presented the problem come up with the right solution. For instance, a member may decide that the best solution to dealing with feelings toward a disliked staff member is to avoid the staff member. Certainly, it would be appropriate for the therapist to question this member about the consequences of this line of action. However, care must be taken not to discourage the group from finding creative solutions to this or another problem. After sufficient discussion of the consequences of the various alternatives, the member selects a solution that is likely to most effectively resolve the major issues while maximizing other positive consequences (Goldfried & Davison, 1976). The group then discusses specific implementation of the chosen solution. As indicated previously, if there are a number of options for implementation, then either implementation itself can be raised as another problem for the group to address (i.e., Coché's method) or the group can return to the solution-generating step to produce ideas for implementation. Tactics are generated and weighted in the same manner as are the solutions.

**Role playing.** Cognitive and behavioral rehearsal (also called *role playing*) can give members the psychological preparation that they need to withstand challenges and obstacles that they are likely to encounter outside of the group setting (Wessler & Han-kin-Wessler, 1989). This step is optional, although with geriatric patients (Hussian, 1987) and more severely disturbed patients (Douglas & Mueser, 1990) it is usually necessary. The leader typically decides whether the presented problem and perhaps one or more of the proposed solutions lends itself to role playing in the group. Although there may be resistance to role playing when it is first introduced, members' willingness to participate can be increased by an explanation of the advantages of partic-ipation and by a willingness of the leader to participate as well (E. Coché, 1987). Usually, the presenting member takes his or her own role and enacts the chosen solution. This experience allows the member to practice a behavior never used before and gives him or her a feeling of mastery before the real-life situation occurs. Sometimes, the presenting member plays the role of the opponent with whom an issue is to be addressed. This exercise gives the member the other individual's perspective and can provide ideas for additional strategies in dealing with such peo-ple (E. Coché, 1987). If the leader takes the member's role, he or she can model particular behaviors that the member may adopt.

**Verification and reporting back to the group.** After the mem-ber accepts and decides to act on a solution, he or she is invited, but not required, to report back to the group in subsequent ses-sions on its effectiveness.[12] This procedure encourages members to observe the consequences of their actions and to match out-comes against their expected predictions. It also highlights the real-life quality of the work done in the group sessions. In ad-dition, it rewards other members for producing solutions and stimulates them to produce more (E. Coché, 1987). Sometimes

---

[12] Verification includes the execution of the decision and evaluation of its efficacy. In the model presented in this chapter, evaluation of the success or failure of the solution chosen occurs only after the solution has been tried (E. Coché, 1987; D'Zurilla & Goldfried, 1971). Kanfer and Busemeyer (1982) sug-gested that verification should be an ongoing evaluation of feedback to monitor which components in the sequence are effective and which require change. The dynamic problem-solving model allows for continuous adjustments in strategies and tactics (Kanfer & Busemeyer, 1982).

a participant will report that a chosen solution was not successful. This information can be accepted by the group as a challenge to generate a new problem, and the steps begin anew.

# Clinical Illustration

## Group Members

This is the fourth of eight sessions in a closed-ended, diagnostically heterogenous group in an acute care psychiatric hospital.

Mary, a homemaker, was admitted to the hospital because she was unable to take care of her four children (all under 10 years) or manage her household. Her oldest son's teacher first noticed that the child was increasingly disheveled and frequently appeared at school without a packed lunch. On inquiry, she ascertained that his mother remained in bed all day and minimally performed parenting functions. Her husband, a traveling salesman, denied noticing any deterioration and did not want his wife hospitalized. When she was admitted to the hospital, she had an elaborate plan of suicide that also involved killing all her children. The unit staff suspected that she had an underlying psychosis. Since her admittance, she had said little to anyone.

Aura was admitted to the hospital 1 week ago. Recently, she and her husband had moved to a larger house that required her an additional commute over a river to get to work. She had become intensely phobic, fearing that the bridge would collapse. The enormity of her fear prevented her from commuting to her job. In previous group sessions, she had focused on her anger at her husband for wanting to move.

Larry, a man in his midthirties, was admitted to the hospital after he had been unable to continue his job as a middle manager in a large office because of severe migraine headaches that were unresponsive to medication. He exhibited insomnia, pacing, and a preoccupation with events at work. He was very irritable with his wife and three children. His wife insisted that he go into the hospital. He had been helpful in past sessions to other members but had not introduced any of his own problems.

Jerry, an attractive man in his late thirties, was a somewhat successful local television producer. He stated that he had been looking for a permanent relationship. Having dated many women, he initially was enthralled with all of them. However, within 1 year, he became disenchanted and terminated the relationship with each of them. His hospitalization was precipitated by two events: the cancellation by the networks of one of his shows that had received much critical acclaim but could not maintain adequate ratings and the recent breakup of a relationship by a woman whom he had dated for a few months. She had left him for another man who appeared to be a faster "rising star." He became very depressed, hopeless, and suicidal. He felt helpless, was unable to get out of bed, had insomnia and weight loss, and had become preoccupied with finding ways to get even with the man whom he believed took this woman away from him. It seems that his self-esteem and narcissism had been badly bruised by this rejection. In past group sessions, he had been very interactive, presenting a problem at each session involving either how to get over this woman, his annoyance with the hospital staff for not allowing him to conduct his business affairs, and his inability to eat the "lousy" hospital food.

Martha, a woman in her fifties, had been married for 15 years to a man 20 years her senior. In the past 3 years, her husband had developed Alzheimer's disease, was now bedridden, and was unable to recognize her. She had single-handedly managed his care. Although her husband had siblings in the area, they had not offered to help and she had not been able to ask them to do so. Recently, she developed murderous fantasies that scared her, and she voluntarily admitted herself to the hospital. In previous group sessions, she had presented the problem of how to ask for help and had begun to make efforts to contact some of her husband's siblings.

Mark, a 28-year-old schizophrenic, had had multiple psychotic breaks. He lived with his mother and was admitted to the hospital after thinking that his mother was poisoning his food. This recent break seemed to be precipitated by his joining a softball league and being unable to attend games because his mother became "ill." Most of his breaks seemed to have been precipitated by his efforts to develop some independent interests. In a previous group session, he had presented the problem of being unable to have the courage to ask a woman on a date and then have sex with her. At the end of the discussion, it became clear that he was able to ask women on dates but that he was unable to find a way of telling his mother not to interfere, a problem that he agreed to tackle in a later group session.

Karen, a woman in her early thirties, was admitted to the hospital after an acute psychotic break. She lived alone and worked in a typing pool for a large law firm. She had recently gone to see the movie *Jaws* and had become preoccupied with the fear that her bosses at work were plotting to throw her to the sharks. This had begun after one of the lawyers had reprimanded her for some typing errors in an important brief and a little later she overheard him quipping to a colleague that they were going to throw one of their competitors to the sharks. On the unit, she began having the same fear about some of the nurses and had to be heavily medicated and physically restrained after verbally and physically trying to protect herself from the staff. In previous sessions, she had been almost silent, except for an occasional question.

## The Session

Therapist:  Who would like to start?

Martha:  I just wanted to let the group know that I called Jane, my husband's sister, last night and told her I was in the hospital. She gave me her usual, "Oh, you poor thing, if only I had known," but didn't offer anything else. I told her that when I got out of the hospital, I wasn't certain that I could care for my husband all by myself. She said that maybe she could relieve me sometime. But I felt like she was putting me off. The previous me would have just said, "Oh thanks" and waited forever for an offer that never materialized. But the new me said, "When could you do that?" She actually gave me a time, and I said that I would plan an afternoon to go food shopping and get my hair done.

Therapist:  (clapped) I am happy to hear that. It sounded like you had been clear, straightforward, and insistent without being pushy.

The group clapped also, and several members verbally congratulated Martha.

Jerry: At the sound of clapping and praise, I yearn to get back to my job.

Karen: I didn't think that there were any sharks in here, just a peacock.

There is some snickering in the group, with members uncertain whether Karen was psychotic or joking.

Larry: (stuttering) My doctor says I have to start talking in here or things won't change. I have been here 10 days, and when I think about going back to work, I still get a terrible headache. I don't feel so hopeless anymore. I can sleep at night, thanks to the medication. I should go home. My wife is alone with the kids and is starting to get angry with me. But, when I think of dealing with my boss, I get tense and a headache. I feel I won't be able to change the situation. He's always on my case.

Jerry: I empathize with your circumstances. I grind my teeth; my orthodontist said I should wear a night guard. Of course, I work under incredible pressure, not just the usual office work (glancing at Aura and Larry).

Therapist: Jerry, since you feel that you have a similar problem, it will be important for you to listen closely to this discussion . . .

(The therapist makes the decision to discourage Jerry from presenting his problem given that in previous groups he had presented several problems and decides not to tackle the issues of his monopolization at this point.)

Jerry: Well, my circumstances are considerably worse . . .

Therapist: (holds up her hand to indicate she is not finished) Right now we are helping Larry with his problem. One advantage of our group format here is that sometimes people's problems are similar enough so that after a discussion about some problems, another member can often solve a problem on his own, without bringing it up. However, if after we have finished with Larry and you feel that your problem is different from his and you were not able to arrive at your own solution from this discussion, then of course you are free to bring it up for a problem for the group to discuss. OK. Let's take the directive of Larry's psychiatrist and get to work on Larry's problem. Larry, perhaps you could clarify for the group exactly what you see the problem to be. (The therapist attempts to get Larry to further define and specify the problem.)

Larry: My boss has a temper. Sometimes it's undeserved.

Jerry: (interjects) Believe me, it's always undeserved.

Mary: (interrupts) My husband used to have a temper, and I used to get frightened. Is that how you feel?

Larry attempts to speak but is overpowered by Aura.

Aura: So you feel overwhelmed? My boss makes me feel that way sometimes, and I feel so worthless.

Therapist: Each of you is trying to aid Larry in formulating his problem as he struggles to figure out what he feels and then struggles to say it. Perhaps that is part of his problem. It would be important for us to let Larry struggle with exactly what it is that he is feeling so that we can be most helpful. Larry, what is it that you feel?

(The group has the basic idea of further defining the problem, but their attempts to help Larry are personalized and they collude with Larry's passive style. The therapist eludes to the parallel between his difficulties in his presentation to the group and his difficulties with his boss.)

Larry: Both of those things, overwhelmed and inadequate.

Therapist: So let's hear how you would describe your problem to the group. (The therapist asks Larry to formulate the problem.)

Larry:      My boss yells at me. When he does, I feel over-
            whelmed and inadequate. Sometimes it is over
            things that are not really my fault. I'm at a loss as
            to how to respond. I get tense and speechless and
            start to stutter like I'm doing now. Then I leave and
            get these bad headaches. I'd like to know how to
            handle my boss's anger.

Therapist:  (writes in the log) Now this is a workable problem.
            So Larry presents the problem that his boss gets
            angry at him for things that are undeserved and he
            does not know what to do or how to respond.

Jerry:      Just engage in what I call the "Three Stooges num-
            ber" (gives imitation and accompanying sounds and
            everyone laughs).

Therapist:  That's one solution. Before we look at the solutions,
            is there any other information that we need to know
            to answer this problem?

(The therapist treats Jerry's interruption as a serious contribution,
even though Jerry is probably not serious and the solution is a
socially undesirable one. In taking Jerry's suggestion as serious,
the therapist can use this opportunity to reinforce the importance
of following the prescribed order of steps. She then asks the
group to further clarify the problem.)

Martha:     Does your boss do it in front of your co-workers?
            (Larry nods yes.)

Aura:       How often does he yell at you?

Larry:      It's hard to say. He goes through these moods.
            Maybe once a week.

Therapist:  Do you see this as important to evaluating what
            needs to be done? (She attempts to keep the group
            focused on only essential information.)

Aura:       Ah, maybe. I guess that I was thinking that if it
            were frequently, then the guy is probably a jerk and
            you could report it to his boss, but if it is less fre-
            quently, then maybe you have to adjust to it.

Mark:       Does he yell at everyone that way?

Larry:      Yeah, they just don't seem as bothered by it.

Therapist:  Do we have sufficient information to resolve the
            problem? (silence) Let us now focus on the different

alternatives. Does anyone have any thoughts? (There is a definite transition from one step to the next.)

The leader records each solution in the log and says aloud the name of the person and his or her contribution.

Aura:    Tell him you have a headache.

Mark:    Just listen, maybe use ear plugs or something and try not to get upset. Like just try not to take it in.

Mary:    Listen and take notes. Then when he is done tell yourself how wrong he is on each point.

Martha:    Take notes, then figure out, as Mary says, each point of the argument and then make an appointment with him and tell him, even if you have to write it all out and read it to him.

Jerry:    Sir, Mr. Bogus Boss, I just wanted to tell you . . . (caricature the reading of such a statement to the boss).

Therapist:    I guess what you're implying, Jerry, is that you think that maybe Larry should learn his lines so to speak.

Jerry:    Au contraire, Madame, I was just joking. What I really think is that he could tell him in a clever way where he could stuff it. You shouldn't take that garbage. You know, one time my boss did that to me and . . .

Therapist:    Jerry, by giving your experience with it, you are in a way evaluating the effectiveness of it. It's important to save your evaluation of the alternatives until a little later, in the next step. (The leader remains focused on the task and this particular step, reminding Jerry that personal experiences help with evaluation but that this step does not permit even implied criticism.)

Mark:    If it's his fault, he should just say he's sorry. It's your right.

Karen:    I don't think he should do anything, it's too dangerous. You can't tell when people are going to get something to go after you. I didn't even do anything and I'm being sought after by the sharks. The boss might threaten him.

| | |
|---|---|
| Martha: | Just listen to what he had to say. At a later time, when he seems like he is in a better mood, tell him that you don't like being treated that way and you are not going to tolerate it anymore. |
| Jerry: | Tell him you have a friend who could get some real-type sharks after him, ha, ha! (The group giggles.) Seriously, imply without being openly admitting—after all you don't want to be dishonest—that a member of your family has controlling stock in the company or in a company that your employer deals with. |
| Mark: | Just quit your job. Maybe your wife can go out to work. (Despite how impractical, humorous, and incredible the idea is, there is no comment on its non-viability in this step.) |
| Jerry: | Seriously, gang. Why don't you give him a gift of my tapes? |
| Therapist: | Well, we have come up with a number of methods. Great. Can anybody add or combine any of the alternatives? (Creative combinations are actively encouraged.) |
| Mary: | Maybe you could quit this job, but not until you have found another job. |
| Martha: | Listen to him, later tell him that you don't like it, and that if he does not change you will leave. But it's important to have another possibility lined up before you say that. (silence) |
| Therapist: | Terrific. It's time for us to move onto the next step of evaluating all of these alternatives. We have lots of alternatives to consider. (The therapist provides reinforcement for the quantity of alternatives, a clear transition to the next step, and clear instructions on how to evaluate the alternatives. In this illustration, the evaluation of alternatives is done in the more informal manner of Coché.) |
| Therapist: | It's important for us to look at these alternatives in terms of their advantages, both short and long term, and the cost. |
| Larry: | I think that it might be best for me to keep quiet. I mean, I would rather not. I mean, the other alternatives sound good for someone else, but I know myself. I just don't think that I will be able to stand up to him at the time or even later. |

Martha:     But that's what you've been doing, and look where
            you ended up. And you still have headaches.

Larry:      So maybe there is no alternative but just to endure.

Aura:       Then you'll have more symptoms, but if you feel
            that way, you could take sleeping pills or even take
            tranquilizers or ask for a medication you could take
            on the job.

Therapist:  Perhaps this is another alternative that we had not
            mentioned in the previous step. One could take ad-
            ditional medication (writes in the log) in order not
            to feel overwhelmed. What are the costs and ben-
            efits of that?

Mark:       I wouldn't take any more pills than I had to—with
            all the problems with medication being poisoned,
            like Tylenol.

Therapist:  So you run the risk of getting bad side effects. Any
            other side effects?

Mark:       Yeah, and other types of side effects too, like being
            tired. The point of a tranquilizer is to tranquilize.
            You can't have one that just makes you less anxious
            and doesn't mellow everything else out.

Aura:       And you're not really doing it on your own. Sup-
            pose you forgot your medication one day or ran out
            and you wouldn't want others to know that you
            had to take pills in order to deal with that bully.

Mary:       You could get hooked, too, like there is a girl on
            the unit who is hooked on Xanax and it is really
            hard to stop. Her doctor wanted her to come into
            the hospital to get off of it.

Larry:      Yeah, I guess I don't want to take pills.

Jerry:      Tranquilizers are for the weak, and they make you
            weaker. In my celebrated (ha ha!) opinion, you
            should extricate these emotions from your being. In
            the language of the hoi polloi, get it all out. I know
            I should tell people a thing or two also. Tell him
            what's on your mind!

Therapist:  What are the advantages and disadvantages of this
            strategy?

Mark:       You could get put in jail, or fired.

Jerry:      Not if you do it in the politically correct way. You
            could make it more subtle so that only he would
            know (with some anger in his voice). Listen, I've

|  |  |
|---|---|
|  | done it before. There's not a thing that he could do if you do it right. |
| Mark: | He's still your boss, he could fire you. |
| Jerry: | Well, how about being sarcastic or humiliating him in a more subtle way. Or a joke at his expense. |
| Therapist: | Karen, you were saying earlier that you thought it was too dangerous because of retaliation in subtle ways. (Karen nods affirmatively.) |
| Aura: | But, like maybe you wouldn't get a promotion and no one would tell you that was the reason. |
| Larry: | Yeah, I'm definitely not the type to be able to do that either with brawn or brains. I'm not quick enough and I can't even defend myself. It's not realistic for me to think that I could actually go on the offensive. |
| Therapist: | What are you thinking now about the alternatives? |
| Larry: | Well, I'm not going to just take it, but I'm not going to attack back. I don't want to take medication, so I guess that leaves me with some form of listening to it and later saying something. My wife can't work; we have small children. I guess I could also consider another job, too. There are lots of openings in the computer field. Maybe it would be easier for me to consider saying something to him, if I knew that I had another job possibility. As long as I don't burn my bridges. |
| Therapist: | So Larry is thinking of a two-pronged approach, one of checking out his options in the job arena and secondly saying something to the boss. It looks like we have generated two new tasks for you—looking for a new job and figuring out what to say to your boss. |
| Larry: | I don't think that I'll have trouble with how to find another position. I'm not sure that I really want to leave, but I guess it is a good idea to look. The other problem. I don't know what to say to my boss or how to say it. |
| Therapist: | Let's do a role play. We'll see if that helps. |
| Larry: | Maybe (with some hesitation). |
| Therapist: | Perhaps I will play you—you can be my coach. Who wants to play the boss? |

(With a commitment from Larry as to his selection, the leader moves to the next step. Not every situation needs to be role played, but in this instance, it is necessary to help Larry overcome a rather passive style.)

|     |     |
|-----|-----|
| Martha: | Jerry, it's the perfect part for you (laughs). |
| Jerry: | What do you mean by that? |
| Martha: | You're an actor of sorts, or at least know the mind of an actor. You'd be able to really play it. |
| Jerry: | Well, I thought you'd never ask. Let me talk to my agent about a contract (laughs, then seriously). It's about time that someone recognized my talents. |
| Therapist: | Give us a specific incident to work from: what, when, how, and over what issue. |

(A situation is role played for the next 6 minutes. After the leader is coached by Larry and goes through the role play, Larry and the leader switch places and Larry plays himself, with the leader coaching when necessary. Jerry plays the part of the boss with great gusto.)

|     |     |
|-----|-----|
| Therapist: | Well that was terrific! Do you think that you have some idea of what you are going to do? |
| Larry: | (nods) I think so. I didn't mean to take up so much time. |
| Martha: | We're all in the same boat—you helped us. Besides, I learned something from the suggestions you got. |
| Therapist: | So you got some ideas even though it isn't your specific problem. You were able to make the appropriate modifications in your head. The other important aspect to remember is that learning how to solve a problem is more important than remembering exactly what the specific solutions are. The steps are more important than the specific solution. Once you know the steps, you can always find the solution that is uniquely good for you. Does anyone else have a problem they would iike to discuss? |
| Mary: | I do. I would like to get the group to help me with getting my husband to spend more time with me. My husband and I have been married 10 years. We |

have four children. My oldest, Timmy, is 10. My youngest child is now 9 months old. During the past 6 months, my husband has had to work late in the evening every night until around 10:00; when he gets home, he is too tired and goes right to bed. When we first got married it wasn't like this. He was so attentive . . .

Therapist: You want your husband to spend more time with you. Why would you like more time? (The therapist attempts to focus a problem that is not yet well defined.)

Mary: Why? (startled). I would like a little conversation. I haven't spoken to a grown-up all day. He has to continue to work. We need the money with this last child. I have the kids all day. By 6 p.m., I'm beat. I want to hand them off to someone. The house is a wreck. I can't get any cleaning done. When I finally get the kids in bed, I am exhausted. I should then try to clean up and get some time to myself, but I just find that I want a drink. I have been increasingly lonely, afraid, and low in the evenings after our children are in bed. My husband and I used to watch T.V. together or just talk. I try to watch T.V. by myself or read, but I can't concentrate. And i would really rather be with someone else. There aren't many people on the street so I can't even go out in the evenings and visit on the block. I'm also worried that someone will know I'm all alone and will try to break in. I don't like being alone every night. I can't manage the kids by myself. I can't go out because the kids are there. I can't even use the bathroom . . .

Therapist: OK. What prevents him from getting home earlier?

(It is the therapist's judgment that Mary has inundated the group with much unfocused information and that the problem could more expediently be pursued if she becomes active in attempting to clarify the problem rather than expecting the group to do this. Another therapist who judges that the group can benefit from the struggle to clarify Mary's problem may not intervene as quickly.)

Mary: Since the birth of the last child, we've been finan-
cially strapped, and so he has to work. He is just
too tired when he comes home. I can't really expect
him to be much of a conversationalist. Actually, he
has never had the gift of gab.

Therapist: So it is not realistic to expect that your husband will
come home earlier and provide you the kind of support and conversation that you would like.

Mary: But I am still lonely.

Therapist: So your problem is, how can you get your needs
for adult companionship met under your current
circumstances?

Mary: Yes, that's it!

Therapist: Is there other information we need? Anyone in the
group?

Larry: Do you have friends and relatives around?

Mary: Not many friends who don't have commitments
themselves, but I do have one sister who I sometimes speak with on the phone. My mother-in-law
lives in the area.

Aura: Can you get babysitting help?

Mary: Well . . . money is really tight, so I can't pay for one
very much of the time.

Larry: How would your husband feel about your working
to make some of the money?

Mary: I don't think that he would care as long as the children were well taken care of. (silence)

Therapist: Any more questions? (silence) Well, if there are no
more questions, let's move on to generating some
ideas and solutions (records each solution and its
contributor).

Martha: She could get a job one night a week, where there
are other people, that way she could kill two birds
with one stone: be with people and make some
money also.

Aura: She could ask her mother-in-law to sit with the kids
for one night while she either works or goes to the
movies or out with a friend.

Mark: She could swap babysitting services with a friend
so that they could each go out one night a week.

Jerry: She could have a Tupperware party after the kids
go to bed and invite other people. Ha ha! Those

|  |  |
|---|---|
|  | tupperware ladies would love you. Hey, maybe Mary Kay makeup—then eventually you could drive around in one of those pink Mercedes. |
| Aura: | She could adopt grandparents and then invite them over every other week or so. |
| Jerry: | No way could I stay at home at night with the kids and be so isolated. I gotta hand it to you Mary, it's not for me. Every time I meet a woman and she starts talking about how much she wants kids, that's the beginning of the end. |
| Therapist: | I'm not sure what solution you are suggesting. |
| Jerry: | (throws his hands up) Sorry . . . just making a comment. It's too late for her now. |
| Therapist: | Your statement sounded like an evaluation. That is best saved for the next step. |
| Jerry: | I have a very serious suggestion. Why don't you rent a movie so you wouldn't be so bored with T.V. all the time. There are award-winning videotapes of my Emmy-worthy shows. What do you think of that? |

(The therapist writes this solution down also and does not evaluate it. Jerry appears somewhat crestfallen that no one responds to his suggestion. The therapist, noticing this, attempts an intervention to soften the narcissistic blow without deviating from the steps.)

|  |  |
|---|---|
| Therapist: | That's a creative solution, one that not everyone would think of, Jerry. We're not quite ready to evaluate the suggestions. Any other solutions? |
| Mark: | She could put a lock on the door so no one could get in. |
| Therapist: | Any other solutions? (silence) OK. Let's move on to the next phase. Mary, do any of these look like possibilities for you? |
| Mary: | Well, all of them seem pretty good. I wonder if I could get a job for one night a week. I guess if my mother-in-law could babysit, then I wouldn't have to worry too much how much money I would make. I mean, I would like to make some, but anything would probably be a help and if I made enough, |

maybe my husband could work a little less, or I could spend a little more. I think that I'll talk with my husband when he comes to visit me on the weekend and see what he thinks. Also, maybe I'll call my sister and ask her to come over instead of just talking on the phone.

Therapist: Are there any disadvantages to each of these possible solutions? (silence) Mary? (She shakes head no.) Do you think it will help with your loneliness? (She nods her head yes.) Anyone else see any problem with what Mary has put together? (silence) Let us know how you do. It is likely that there are other aspects that may need to be looked at when you talk it over with the various people involved (implies that a new problem may develop out of talking it over with her spouse and that this is to be expected). It looks like we have time for one more problem today. (Jerry is sighing heavily and noticeably sulking. Some of the group members glance at him.)

Martha: (looks at Jerry, but says tentatively) Karen has not really talked at all this week, and it's the end of the week. She has not had a chance at all to present a problem.

Jerry: (gets up) I don't know if I can stay. My secretary should be calling soon.

Martha: Jerry, the group is almost over. Can't that wait? Why would you leave so close to the end of group? You know the rules. Are you upset with us?

Jerry: Not really. I forgot that my secretary was supposed to call, and since they won't let me have a private line installed in my room, I have no choice but to ask her to call at the times when no one else is on the unit.

Therapist: You seemed to become upset after you offered your tapes as a solution and no one said anything.

Jerry: I don't care if you people are not sophisticated enough to recognize the value in those tapes. *The New York Times* said my shows were creative and . . .

Mary: I liked your suggestion—really I did. You do have good ideas. I didn't mean to cause . . .

Larry:    Oh, is this my fault? I will give the tapes as a present to my boss, if you think that would do it.

Karen:    You can have the floor, really you can. I can wait until Monday.

Jerry:    Don't patronize me (somewhat angrily). I'm above all of this and you. More people would recognize my name on the street than all of your names put together. Too late for you people.

Several members had stunned expressions on their faces. There was silence. Jerry moves toward the door.

Therapist:    Let's wait a minute. This is an important group problem and a very important problem of PR (public relations) for you, Jerry. If you leave Jerry, we really won't be able to work on it. We would appreciate your help. (Jerry sits down, but looks distrustful of the therapist.)

Jerry:    How is this a PR problem? I thought this was confidential.

Therapist:    Oh, it definitely is. Jerry you have a PR problem in that you made this very creative and interesting suggestion, which you felt that people should have recognized for its value (Jerry nods). I think you wanted the people here to recognize you. No doubt about it . . . You certainly have talents that should be recognized. But what about the way that you went about it, getting people to recognize you? Well look at everyone: Instead of getting them to recognize what you contributed and be able to appreciate you for it, you have stunned them. You have pushed them away by telling them they don't count. If you had a product to sell, you'd hardly sell anything if you told people that their opinion about the product didn't count. You have an advertising problem so to speak. You see what I mean?

Jerry:    Well, they certainly don't appreciate me and my talents, that's for sure!

Martha:    Weren't you telling us that your girlfriends don't appreciate you? And that the television station didn't appreciate all that you gave to them?

Jerry:   They certainly don't appreciate me.

Mark:   Does the king appreciate the queen?

Martha:   Well isn't this the same thing as what we're talking about in group?

Therapist:   Martha is saying she sees the same thing happening in group as with your girlfriends and work. You feel the group does not appreciate you. You have talents. You feel that people don't recognize or appreciate them. Your problem is how to get people to recognize and appreciate you. Are you willing to work on that? Your girlfriends point out that you wish to be appreciated but do not reciprocate that appreciation in that they say you don't listen to them. Follow me so far? (Jerry nods.) Martha and Mark are saying they see the same thing happening in group. You feel you make special contributions and the group does not appreciate them or the contribution. Perhaps we should work on this. What do you think, group?

Karen:   It's fine with me.

Therapist:   So Jerry, maybe you could rephrase the problem in your own words.

Jerry:   Like you said, it's a PR problem. So what do I do wrong?

Martha:   Well, I wonder whether Jerry is really interested in anyone. Like, do you really care about these girlfriends?

Jerry:   Of course I do!

Therapist:   We have two problems here. How to show people, us, your girlfriends that you are listening, that you are considering what we say. The other problem is the PR problem, how to get people to recognize what you are giving them and to get them to acknowledge your talents.

Jerry:   I really shouldn't have to figure out how to get people to notice; they should just do it on their own.

Mark:   Matel advertises Barbie doll.

Therapist:   Yes, as Mark suggests, even good products need to be advertised.

Jerry:   OK. I guess that's the problem I want to work on. How to get people to notice an already good product.

| | |
|---|---|
| Therapist: | Should we use a specific example, like how could you get people in this group to acknowledge your contributions? (Jerry nods.) Let's consider some alternatives. |
| Karen: | I think it's important that you consider what each person says instead of just what you're trying to promote. Like when you offered the tape to Larry. Larry was try to tell his boss off, and you were suggesting that he give your tapes to him for Christmas. Now if he liked the guy, that's one thing, but he didn't. Like you should have suggested that he give them to his wife, not some guy he hates. |
| Martha: | I think that it is important that you say why your tapes were relevant. I mean, maybe they were, but we didn't see why. Like, for example, you know Aura likes comedy and one of them was a comedy. See, like you really thought about someone's interests in particular. |
| Aura: | Maybe you should say more flattering things to people about them and keep it focused on them. You're very sharp, and I am sure that you could think of things to say to each one of us that would make us feel that you had considered us. |
| Martha: | I guess I feel a little afraid of you, Jerry, like you might get angry at me, and you're so quick that I'm afraid that you would make fun of me. |
| Jerry: | I'm only kidding around, it's just my nature. |
| Martha: | You know you could just try saying, "I feel like you guys don't appreciate me." I know I would respond to that. I know I could say a lot of good things about you because you can be a nice guy. |
| Jerry: | Geez, I don't know if I like this, maybe I should leave. |
| Therapist: | Well, that's one solution. We need to consider all others before you act on it, so just sit down until we get to the discussion of the alternatives. |
| Mary: | Maybe we could help him figure out why he does that and then he wouldn't do it any more. Maybe when we feel that he isn't paying attention, we could tell him that we need him to pay attention. |
| Karen: | Maybe we could reserve a certain amount of time for him, since he is pretty special. |

Therapist: I think we have a number of possible solutions to Jerry's problem of feeling unacknowledged by the group members. Jerry, what looks good to you?

Jerry: Well, I guess I would like to just be frank. But it's not really practical in the business world or with these women. What kind of guy will they think I am. They'll think I'm a wimp telling them that I feel like they don't appreciate me. And sometimes I have too much to do to think of other people. Here it's different. You people have so many problems you can't really hurt me.

Martha: Then maybe you're with the wrong women.

Therapist: We are just about out of time for today. I know we are at the evaluation stage with Jerry's issue, but it will have to be saved. Jerry, maybe you can think about these different solutions this weekend, and on Monday, you can tell us what looks good to you. Also on Monday, we want to get to Karen. OK? Maybe some of you will have things to report then.

## Comment on the Session

Problem-solving training can be used to deal with problems arising outside and inside the group. Most problems that members introduce will be ones originating on the unit or outside of the hospital. In this illustration, the problems that Larry and Mary introduced dealt with issues that brought them into the hospital. In the case of Jerry, his behavior in the group reflected a similar problem that he experienced in his personal life. That is, the group became a social microcosm of his experience with the world. When this happens, the problem can be addressed by focusing on the behavior as it is manifested in the group (e.g., Jerry's wish for attention and approval from other group members and his resulting sulking when appreciation was not forthcoming in the form that he felt that he deserved). Alternatively, the problem could have been addressed in the same way that Larry's and Mary's problems were addressed (i.e., Jerry's desire for approval from his girlfriends and his disappointment in their lack of appreciation of him). Although not presented in this vignette, a group-as-a-whole problem can also be successfully addressed in a problem-solving group. For example, in one group of inpatients, two of the members formed a subgroup that was flirtatious in nature, eating together, spending free time together, and speaking only to each other in group. Other members of the group felt left out and envious. The problem was addressed when several members expressed their anger toward the subgroup for their lack of interest in other members' problems.

## Status of the Research

There is much evidence to support the problem-solving model as effective in the inpatient group setting. The model presupposes that, compared with nonclinical populations, psychiatric populations are deficient in particular problem-solving abilities. Problem-solving training has been shown to improve problem-solving abilities and often ameliorate symptomatology as well. There is also evidence that other diagnostic groups not previously tested in a group setting can benefit from problem-solving group training. In this section we discuss the efficacy of problem-solving training with various clinical populations and review its effective implementation in the inpatient setting.

### Inpatient Group Outcome Studies

The problem-solving model has considerably more empirical support for success in the inpatient setting than do most other models presented in this text. In a series of empirical studies, E. Coché and his colleagues evaluated the efficacy of group problem-solving training with a mixed-gender, mixed-diagnostic population in an acute care inpatient facility. Closed-ended groups were conducted for eight sessions (60–90 minutes each). In the first study, patients received either the problem-solving training or participated in a play reading group (reading and discussing comedies; E. Coché & Flick, 1975). These groups, along with a sample of patients receiving standard hospital care, were compared on paper-and-pencil problem-solving measures (Platt & Spivack, 1975) before and after group treatment. Results indicated that although hospitalization alone improved patients' problem-solving abilities as measured by improved capacity to generate relevant means (the sequence of steps to achieve an endpoint) and a reduction in generating irrelevant means, participation in problem-solving groups additionally enhanced their abilities to produce an even greater number of alternative solutions. In fact, more disturbed patients made greater gains than did less disturbed ones. Hospital stays for patients in both the play reading groups and the problem-solving groups were significantly shorter than were those of patients not receiving either of the group treatments.

In the second study, E. Coché and Douglass (1977) extended the first study to involve additional outcome measures beyond the assessment of problem-solving skills. The study included the same experimental groups (play reading, problem-solving training, and no group treatment). Whereas both of the active treatments were helpful in reducing depression and general psychopathology (e.g., psychotic thinking), the problem-solving training group was more successful than were the other two conditions in improving patients' impulse controls. Perhaps the most notable aspect of the problem-solving training was the improvement in patients' self-esteem and subjective feelings of competence; patients were less critical of themselves, less worried and frightened, and less dependent on other people and felt better able to handle the exigencies of everyday living than were either patients in the play reading group or the no-treatment group. There was also some evidence that those who participated in the problem-solving group were more interested in and able to form and maintain interpersonal relationships.

In the third study, problem-solving training was compared with interpersonal psychoanalytic group therapy similar to the unstructured version of the interpersonal model presented in chapter 4 (E. Coché et al., 1984). Although neither of these approaches appeared clearly superior, women seemed to gain more from the interpersonal approach and men more from the problem-solving training. The authors interpreted these results to mean that men are more comfortable with a problem-oriented, rational approach, whereas women prefer an interpersonal approach that encourages the expression of feelings and provides the opportunity for closeness with others.

Problem-solving training in an inpatient psychiatric setting also has been compared with social interaction groups in which interpersonal skills are taught with the goal of creating behavioral change (Cohen, 1982). Both problem-solving training and social interaction training were superior to the placebo control treatments (reading plays or no group treatment). Overall, problem-solving training was more effective than were all the other treatments in improving psychological health. However, when analyzed by diagnostic category, schizophrenics showed significantly greater gains with social interaction training, whereas depressed patients made greater progress with problem-solving training.

The superiority of group problem-solving training to other interventions in an acute care inpatient setting is not without exception. D. E. Jones (1981) compared a six-session problem-solving training program (similar to the Coché program) to a attention-placebo group (group recreational activities) and to control (no-treatment) group. The study failed to confirm that the problem-solving group was more effective than were the two other groups in reducing the number of problems patients perceived in daily living or in increasing their displays of more adaptive social behaviors (as measured by a checklist) on the inpatient unit. However, the problem-solving training group scored higher on paper-and-pencil cognitive problem-solving skills (e.g., increased relevant means, decreased irrelevant means) than did the other groups. Two factors could account for the lack of unequivocally positive results: It may be that fewer than eight sessions are not adequate to effect behavioral change in this population (E. Coché, 1987) or that an outcome measure of changed behavior is not sensitive enough to capture the improvement in problem-solving ability.

These studies together suggest that group problem-solving training is superior to no treatment in improving problem-solving abilities and ameliorating symptomatology. The training provides more therapeutic benefit than merely positive nonspecific effects of a group setting (e.g., play reading groups). There is limited evidence that certain diagnostic groups of patients seem to profit from problem-solving training more than do others (e.g., depressed patients do better than schizophrenics, and men do better than women).

**Schizophrenics.** Although there is evidence for the effectiveness of this model for those with acute schizophrenic episodes (E. Coché & Douglass, 1977; E. Coché & Flick, 1975), its efficacy with chronic schizophrenics has been more difficult to demonstrate. The original design of problem-solving training by Siegel and Spivack (1976) suggests that chronic schizophrenics have significant problem-solving deficits and can improve their problem-solving skills with individual training. When chronic schizophrenic patients were compared with control patients after both were taught a considerably expanded version of problem-solving training, the former improved their abilities to generate alternatives to a greater degree than did the latter (Siegel & Spivack, 1976). These findings contrast with those of McLatchie (1982), who compared group problem-solving training with relaxation training in a population of chronic schizophrenics in a long-term facility; the investigator found no significant differences in improvement between the groups on measures of psychotic symptomatology or paper-and-pencil measures of problem-solving ability. Although it is also possible that the small number of patients who participated obscured the small improvement that may have occurred, the author attributed the lack of positive results to staff apathy and impoverished resources. There is some support for the author's interpretation given that in a similar setting, a like number of patients were shown to benefit from problem-solving training even though the staff were untrained (Edelstein et al., 1980). However, caution must be exercised in drawing conclusions from this study because it did not contain an adequate control group.

Increasing the length of training may be necessary for effective treatment of a chronic population; chronic psychiatric patients may need additional training or structure that is not required for psychiatrically healthier patients. In support of this notion, Pierce (1980) compared group problem-solving training (11 sessions, 80 minutes each) with a control group in a day-hospital psychiatric population and found that problem-solving training significantly increased patients' abilities to generate relevant means but not alternative solutions. In a study with chronic day-hospital psychiatric patients, problem solving-training was taught (twice a week for 15 sessions) by requiring patients to master each step completely before tackling the next (e.g., problem definition, generation of alternatives) instead of having them complete all the steps with a single problem (Hansen et al., 1985). Each step included instruction, rationale, modeling, behavioral rehearsal, feedback, and verbal reinforcement.

This method effectively improved problem-solving abilities for these patients on trained situations and did generalize to novel situations. Improvement was largely maintained at 1- and 4-month follow-ups, although there was decreased retention of individual component steps. Although no separate control group was used, careful measures were taken before, throughout, and after the study.

**Substance-abuse patients.** Although none of the studies just reviewed included substance-abuse patients, there is evidence that patients with drug and alcohol problems are deficient in problem-solving skills compared with normal individuals (Platt & Spivack, 1975) and that the latter can significantly benefit from problem-solving training when placed in a homogeneous group. Male alcoholics participated in either a problem-solving group, a discussion group, or a standard hospital treatment control group in two separate studies (Chaney, O'Leary, & Marlatt, 1978; S. L. Jones, Kanfer, & Lanyon, 1982). Groups met twice weekly for six 90-minute sessions. In both studies, the problem-solving group showed improved performance at the end of treatment. This improvement was further confirmed at a 1-year follow-up, at which time the problem-solving group showed decreased duration and severity of relapse episodes. The results of the studies differed in their findings about the discussion group. In the Jones et al. study, there was no difference between the problem-solving group and the discussion group at posttreatment or at 1-year follow-up. In the Chaney et al. study, the problem-solving group was superior at posttreatment and at 1-year follow-up. These authors suggested that one difference between the studies was the level of patient functioning. The Jones et al. study had higher functioning (e.g., higher socioeconomic class and more likely to be married) subjects than did the Chaney et al. study. It may be that lower functioning alcoholics require more specific and concrete training than do higher functioning alcoholics.

In another study, male alcoholics were assigned to either a standard treatment or a standard treatment plus a 10-session, 4-week problem-solving training group (Intagliata, 1978). At discharge, patients participating in the group treatment had made significantly greater improvement on paper-and-pencil measures of problem-solving thinking than had the control group patients and were significantly more likely to anticipate, plan for, and cope with postdischarge problems and maintain these skills at 1-month follow-up. This improvement was not due to improved verbal proficiency. Similarly, Platt et al. (1973) reported on the use of a problem-solving skills training program with incarcerated heroin addicts. Although subjects were not randomly assigned to group treatments, there was a significant relation between completing a problem-solving skills training program and successful parole performance.

## Other Relevant Outcome Studies

**Geriatric patients.** Many of the outcome studies have included a wide age range of adult patients (up to 70 years of age; Coché et al., 1984; E. Coché & Douglas, 1977; Coché & Flick, 1975; Cohen, 1982; Intagliata, 1978). Although geriatric patients were not excluded, a separate analysis was not performed probably because the number of geriatric patients in each study was too small. Toseland and Rose (1978) used subjects 55 years and older from a nursing home to compare a role-playing (interpersonal skills training) group with a problem-solving group and a social work group. They found that the role-playing and problem-solving groups showed significant gains compared with the social work group. These findings are consistent with those of another study that found that subjects 60 years and older who participated in an individual format of problem-solving training for at least 1 week exhibited reduced depression and improved problem-solving ability compared with subjects who participated in behavioral reinforcement schedule and waiting-list control groups (Hussian & Lawrence, 1981).

**Children.** Much of the original work on problem-solving training was designed to teach primary grade-school children a problem-solving style that could help them cope more successfully with their day-to-day problems (Spivack & Shure, 1974). Children who received the training were able to generate more solutions to problems. They had superior anticipatory and consequential thought and used less aggressive solutions to problems. They also exhibited more concern for the feelings of other children, more initiative in the classroom, and increased abilities to complete activities and overcome problems without adult assistance than did those children who had not received the training. The former were also better liked by their peers. Similarly, when antisocial inpatient children were given problem-solving training, relationship therapy, or treatment contact for 20 sessions, problem-solving training led to a decrease in externalizing and aggressive behavior at home and school immediately after discharge and 1 year later in comparison with the other treatment conditions (Kazdin et al., 1987). Although Sessions 12 and 20 in the training programs had individual formats, there is much support from other studies for the use of problem-solving training with children in a group setting.

Emotionally disturbed preadolescent boys in a residential treatment facility were given in a group setting either problem-solving training, interpersonal skill training, the combination of these two, or discussion only (Small & Schinke, 1983). Results indicated that boys in the combined problem-solving and interpersonal skill training conditions had better conceptual abilities and social behavior than did boys in the problem-solving training or discussion-only conditions. Similar positive results were obtained when children receiving 12 sessions (6 weeks) of problem-solving training or another social–cognitive training approach (social perspective taking) were compared with those receiving a behavioral contingency approach without cognitive training in children (Urbain, 1980). Results indicated that all three approaches led to increases in performance on the social–cognitive measures (problem solving and perspective taking) but not on teacher ratings of socially impulsive behavior.

Variations of the original problem-solving method have been successfully used. The use of videotapes with concurrent group discussions (twice weekly for 5 weeks) in teaching problem-solving skills to emotionally disturbed boys (ages 7–15 years) led to improvement in emotional control, impulsivity, and overall personality problems and to greater self-initiated learning compared with a control group (Elias, 1983). Following a 23-week program with 45 scripted social problem-solving lessons, a group of latency-age children (average age 10 years) of low socioeconomic backgrounds with histories of behavioral disorders were able to generate a significantly greater number of alternative solutions than were similar children who did not receive the training (Natov, 1981). The children with training also demonstrated a significant improvement in classroom learning compared with the control group. Their ability to articulate the steps required to achieve a stated goal, however, did not improve.

**Adolescents.** The benefits of either direct didactic problem-solving training, a role-playing approach (videotaped role playing with corrective feedback), a combined didactic problem-solving and videotaped corrective feedback approach, or the making of a documentary film (attention-control group) for seven sessions (10.5 hours) were evaluated with a group of male adolescent offenders (Chudy, 1981). Results revealed that all three training groups were equally effective in improving the adolescent offenders' interpersonal problem-solving skills and decreasing their use of aggressive solutions. Follow-up indicated that training groups had a 10% recidivism rate compared with a 33% rate for the attention-control group.

Overall, data concerning the efficacy of problem-solving training are fairly positive. In most instances, problem-solving training with emotionally maladjusted children and adolescents improves their problem-solving abilities more than does no treatment at all. When compared with other forms of therapy such as social skills therapy or a combination of different therapies, problem-solving training is as or more effective. There are many variations in the training such as the use of videotapes, didactic teaching, and prepared scripts, all of which have been shown to have utility.

**Mentally retarded patients.** Because problem-solving training involves considerable cognitive processing, one reasonable question might be the extent to which an individual with less-than-average intelligence could benefit from this type of treatment. Although there have been no studies examining this treatment with the psychiatrically impaired cognitively compromised adult, there have been three studies with mentally retarded adults attending vocational training programs.

In the first study, subjects received either no treatment or 14 1-hour sessions over 7 weeks of problem-solving training (Ostby, 1982). (Subjects were shown a videotape that emphasized conceptualizing the problem, identifying relevant social cues, generating solutions, selecting positive responses, and then having members role play the implementation of the solutions chosen by the group.) Subjects who received the training demonstrated improved problem-solving ability compared with controls for some measures.

In the second study, mildly and moderately retarded young adults were randomly assigned to one of three treatment groups or a control group based on a pretest assessment (Castles, 1982). The three treatment groups, which included a social skills group, a problem-solving group, and a group combining social skills training and problem-solving training, each received 15 1-hour training sessions. Results were equivocal in that mildly retarded subjects showed some improvement regardless of whether they received training. For the moderately retarded adults, all types of training significantly improved their abilities to generate a variety of solutions. However, although all subjects improved their effectiveness in the training situations, none were more successful in new situations. Those subjects receiving the problem-solving training component were rated more positively by leaders in personal and social responsibility.

In the third study, attempts to reduce aggressive responses were studied by comparing the effects of a relaxation group, a self-instruction group (members practiced repeating coping statements aloud and silently and were taught to discriminate trouble statements from coping statements), a problem-solving group, and a combined anger management group (combining other treatments; Benson et al., 1986). Dependent measures included self-report, supervisor ratings, and role playing. All three groups decreased in aggressive responses over time, with no significant differences between groups.

Thus, for mentally retarded adults who function within a vocational training setting, problem-solving training may aid in improving social functioning, but it is not clear that such training is more effective than are other types of training or even the nonspecific effects of attention to the problem.

## Using an Individual Format With Special Populations

Although outcome studies with inpatient groups are limited to those discussed earlier, there is considerable additional evidence for the efficacy of the problem-solving training using an individual format. The fact that problem-solving training is individually focused even within a group setting allows the reasonable extrapolation from studies using an individual format to its possible utility with patients in a group setting. In addition, problem-solving training with other characteristic populations suggests the potential utility of the therapy with a wide range of patients and therapeutic settings. With these assumptions, we discuss the treatment of specialized populations. Suicidal patients are discussed because they remain a crucial group that requires hospitalization and needs to be managed inside the hospital.

**Suicidal adults.** Patients who have attempted suicide or have suicidal ideation also have been found to have defective problem-solving skills (Schotte & Clum, 1982) or a certain trait of inflexibility in their thinking associated with difficulty in generating solutions to problems (Patsiokas & Clum, 1985). Problem-solving training would seem to be especially important for this population. When compared with supportive therapy with a small number of suicidal patients, problem-solving therapy was more effective than was supportive therapy in reducing depression and in improving interpersonal problem solving (Lerner, 1989). At a 3-month follow-up, differences continued to exist in symptomatology (depression, loneliness, and hopelessness) but not in problem-solving ability.

Patsiokas and Clum (1985) randomly assigned 15 hospitalized suicide attempters to treatment consisting of either Beck's cognitive–behavioral restructuring or problem-solving training or to a nondirective (reflection) control group; treatment consisted of 10 1-hour individual sessions over a 3-week period. Results in-

dicated that although there were no differences in suicidal ideation, suicidal intention, or impersonal problem solving among
the three groups at the end of treatment, subjects in the problem-
solving training exhibited better interpersonal problem-solving
abilities and less hopelessness than did either the cognitive restructuring or nondirective control group.

Thus, preliminary work in an individual format with hospitalized suicidal patients suggests that problem-solving training
improves interpersonal problem-solving abilities and reduces
symptoms of depression more than does supportive therapy and
perhaps general cognitive–behavioral therapy. Linehan (1987a)
provided some additional evidence that problem-solving training
is effectively applicable in a group format within an outpatient
setting with suicidal patients. Future research will be needed to
confirm the efficacy of problem-solving training with suicidal
patients in an inpatient group setting.

**Suicidal children.** Twenty suicidal and nonsuicidal psychiatrically hospitalized children (8–13 years) were each given seven
individual 45-minute training sessions of problem-solving training (Cohen-Sandler, 1982). Nonsuicidal psychiatrically hospitalized children without training were used as a control group.
The training was effective in improving means–ends thinking of
suicidal children; generation of alternatives for both interpersonal and impersonal problems was enhanced for suicidal and
nonsuicidal children. Those suicidal children who prior to treatment were significantly more deficient in generating alternative
solutions to interpersonal problems than were nonsuicidal children dramatically improved with training (Cohen-Sandler,
1982).

In summary, problem-solving training has a more substantial
base of empirical support for its efficacy within an acute care
setting than do most models. Moreover, the benefits accrued from
training have been shown to be maintained for at least some
follow-up period. In instances in which the treatment has not
been effective, it is unclear whether a specific modification in the
procedure, such as an increased number of training sessions or
more emphasis on the role-playing aspect, would have aided its
efficacy. This project remains for future research.

# Critique of the Model

## Strengths

The problem-solving model is an extremely well-articulated model. There are several available manuals and procedural articles for the interested clinician (E. Coché, 1987; Goldfried & Davison, 1976; Platt & Spivack, 1975; Rosenblum, 1983; Siegel & Spivack, 1976; Tannenbaum, 1991). These specify in detail each of the steps involved in the acquisition of problem-solving skills, a step-by-step therapeutic procedure for acquiring them (often including the specific scenarios), and the tasks and techniques required of the leader. This level of specificity and detail is unmatched by any of the other models presented in this book and allows the already skilled therapist to replicate the problem-solving training approach without previous supervision in the techniques.

This model has a tremendous range of applicability to many different patient populations. As we have discussed, there is a wide age range (from children to geriatric patients) for which this training is potentially applicable and useful. The modification of techniques required for the transition of use from one group to another is well articulated in the manuals available. This approach also has been applied successfully to populations that are often considered difficult to treat, such as chronic schizophrenics (Edelstein et al., 1980; Siegel & Spivack, 1976), patients with impulsivity disorders (Elias, 1983), patients with suicidal ideation (Lerner, 1989; Patsiokas & Clum, 1985), drug and alcohol addicts (Glantz, 1987; Intagliata, 1978), the mentally retarded (Ostby, 1983), and juvenile delinquents (Chudy, 1982).

In addition, empirical measurement of problem-solving skills (e.g., means–end measures) has been established (Platt & Spivack, 1975; Spivack, Shure, & Platt, 1985). The reliability and validity issues have at least been considered and addressed such that a handy paper-and-pencil measurement of the skill can be applied before and after treatment to a clinical population with some confidence that it is an accurate and valid measure of improvement (Gilbride & Hebert, 1980; Platt & Siegel, 1976; Platt & Spivack, 1975; Spivack, 1984; Spivack et al., 1985). In the previous section, we presented much empirical evidence for the model's efficacy in an inpatient group setting for both acute and long-term care, including its superiority over no treatment and it equivalency or superiority over other types of groups (e.g., social skills, supportive, nonstructured) for improving problem-solving skills. There is even some evidence for its specific superiority for certain populations (e.g., depressives and men) over other forms of treatment.

Relative to the other models presented in this book, this model has considerable flexibility in terms of leadership. Leaders can function alone or in co-therapy pairs. Compared with other models, this model permits the use of relatively untrained personnel who may have limited theoretical knowledge about psychopathology or group dynamics. Classroom teachers (Natov, 1981) and nonpsychology personnel (Rosenblum, 1983) have successfully used this model. College graduates or graduate students can function as co-therapists. There has even been an attempt to use patient "graduates" as therapists (E. Coché, 1987, see demands section for further discussion of this point). The basic procedure of problem-solving therapy is relatively easily learned and gives neophyte therapists a structure to follow and impose on their groups.

Another advantage of problem-solving training is that the focus of the content can vary depending on the needs of the patient population. The training can be a generalized one wherein content is not predetermined. Alternatively, the model may be used with other populations in which a dramatic shift in environment or role status is involved, such as psychiatric patients being discharged, paroled prisoners, and former drug addicts (Goldfried & Davison, 1976).

This training can be used in conjunction with other types of hospital treatments. For example, it can be used either as a prelude or prerequisite to participating in another more traditional inpatient group or concomitantly with another model of group therapy that may or may not have overlapping membership and meet at a different time during the day. Because it can also be used in combination with other techniques, it provides additional clinical armamentarium for therapists to aid patients (e.g., Benson et al., 1986; Glantz, 1987; Mahoney & Arnkoff, 1978; Pekala,

Siegel, & Farrar, 1985). As an example of the latter case, Pekala et al. (1985) combined the problem-solving approach with a somewhat less structured approach of the interpersonal model. The model had as its goal a more generalized accomplishment than simply improving problem-solving skills; in addition to teaching a methodology that further develops problem-solving skills and improving patients' abilities to deal with interpersonal interactions, it helped them to realize how they may have been contributing to their problems (insight), to recognize the universality of some of their difficulties, and to enhance ego functioning with current problems. When problem-solving training is combined with other techniques, a number of outcome studies have suggested an increase in effectiveness (Kanfer & Busemeyer, 1982; Spivack et al., 1976; Urbain & Kendall, 1980).

Finally, this model provides an excellent first group experience. Problem-solving groups can be an enjoyable experience provided that the leader is creative and engaging (J. Cooper, personal communication, November 22, 1991). The procedure has much face validity. Because the need for problem-solving skills and patients' deficits can be easily demonstrated, patients can usually be convinced that the group is worthwhile. Members get a tremendous amount of satisfaction from being presented with a task that they can actually accomplish; they feel better just by virtue of the fact that they have successfully completed a task within the session. The training does not require that members learn or accept a complicated theoretical framework. E. Coché (1987) believed that there was some indication that problem-solving training prepares members to join a less structured, more interpersonal- or intrapsychically oriented inpatient or outpatient group: A highly structured experience allows learning and adaptation to group setting and processes without being too anxiety arousing (E. Coché & Flick, 1975).

## Weaknesses

The most notable weakness of this model is that the number of sessions and the stability of group membership required to complete effective training constrain the model's applicability. Within an acute care setting, clinical reports and empirical evidence support a time frame of no less than six sessions (E. Coché, 1987). Given that the average length of hospitalization is 2 weeks, this is certainly a challenge. The time required for the model's effectiveness to be realized is probably increased with a more chronic population; however, these latter patients often reside in long-term settings. Most clinical and empirical reports support the use of a closed-ended group for good reason. In groups wherein the content is dependent on what problems members choose to present, stability of membership is needed to free the group from addressing every member's concern. A closed-ended group allows for the possibility that a problem tabled one day can be scrutinized the next day. Even when the content is preordained, it takes more than a few sessions to understand and incorporate the problem-solving steps into members' everyday response repertoires to problems.

A second weakness involves a lack of clarity of the nature of the relation between problem-solving abilities and psychopathology or symptoms. It is assumed that part of mental health is the successful ability to resolve problems or difficulties in daily living and that the link between problem-solving abilities may be through self-esteem; that is, when self-esteem is low, people are vulnerable to symptoms, and when one can solve problems, self-esteem improves (G. Spivack, personal communication, January 23, 1992). However, improvement in problem-solving abilities could also merely make day-to-day functioning easier and thus allow less energy to be consumed by daily interpersonal exchange and more efforts to be placed on managing symptoms. Thus, a reduction in symptomatology may come with but not be directly due to problem-solving training.

A third weakness involves the kind of exploration that is done with members' problems. Although some, such as Spivack, emphasized an approach that may allow for considerable uncovering of problems, others appear to be willing to accept members' problems as the members describe them (e.g., Bedell & Michael, 1985; D'Zurilla & Goldfried, 1971). This difference can be illustrated in the following example: A depressed woman may describe her problem as an inability to say no so that she allows her resources to be depleted by her family (i.e., "I give and give and get nothing back"). However, in reality, she may also be an

extremely depriving and rejecting person. Spivack and colleagues may be more interested in her conflict between wanting
to rebuild her own resources and her guilt over depriving her
children of the resources that they are requesting, whereas a
therapist with a more behavioral orientation may concentrate on
strategies for saying no. Although the content may be different
for each approach, both would agree that learning the process
of problem solving is more important than is the specific content;
thus, it is less important that the content be accurate. However,
if members chronically misidentify their problems and are allowed to accept their problems and their formulations at face
value, then their abilities to use their newly learned problem-
solving skills are compromised. For all variants of this model,
further elaboration of the methodology of an effective problem-
clarification step within the short-term frame of the inpatient
setting would enormously improve the applicability. Even the
means–ends test, a method of assessing problem-solving skills,
is more biased toward evaluation of the enumeration and sequence of the means to get from the beginning to the end and
is less focused on problem clarification.

For some patient populations (e.g., borderline patients and
some depressed patients), the problem-solving model may ignore and suppress angry thoughts and aggressive behaviors and
may foster a defensive primitive idealization (particularly when
the therapy is approached from a more behavioral orientation)
because the priority is not the recognition of and effort to understand the patient's aggressive intentions but rather to encourage an analysis of the problem in concrete and measurable
terms. Thus, it may be impossible for these patients to learn to
accept and manage what for them may be a central problem—
the containment of their aggressive impulses (Swenson, 1989).

A fourth weakness of this model relates to the insufficient
attention that the role of the unit or hospital milieu is given. G.
Spivack (personal communication, January 23, 1992) suggested
that the milieu is indeed important and offers the "parent–child
dialogue" paradigm (Shure & Spivack, 1978, 1982) as an important way by which staff can encourage, consolidate, and reinforce the learning of the problem-solving process that occurs in
the group. This process involves helping the patient think

through and appreciate other views of a problem; in this process, there is a shift away from the immediate and concrete problem to a process and interactional way of thinking (both staff's and patients' perceptions change). This, of course, requires that staff members themselves not be unduly invested in the search for specific patient problems. Even better, staff should be trained in "dialoging" (Shure & Spivack, 1978, 1982). Although this idea is very interesting, the mechanics associated with the training and implementation of dialoging on the unit remain to be further delineated in the literature.

The final weakness of this model involves the transfer of learning to the members' lives. The goal of this model, an ambitious one, is to aid the patient in developing a way of processing an interpersonal problem. Although it is clear that members can acquire this skill while in the hospital, there is a lack of evidence that specifically shows the generalization of this skill to real-life settings. Generalization is more important in this model than it is in the object relations/systems model or the interactional agenda version of the interpersonal model. In the latter two, the goal is to alter an aspect of the member's functioning while in the hospital, whereas the problem-solving model has as its goal the alteration in the member's way of processing interpersonal problems. The institution of dialoging on the unit suggested would help strengthen the process learned in group with an experience that is closer to real life, thus increasing the likelihood of generalization.

# Demands of the Model

## Clinical Mission

This model is grounded in the belief that psychiatric populations are deficient in problem-solving abilities. The use of this model is compatible with the mission of any setting that permits this skill to be taught and practiced. This model can coexist with almost any theoretical orientation. Its value may be most salient in a setting that endorses the interpersonal or biopsychosocial view of psychopathology; here, there is likely to be a natural acceptance of the notion that problem-solving deficits can lead to a reoccurrence of symptoms. The hospital staff and administration do not need to actively embrace this model, although its efficacy is likely to be enhanced in a setting wherein members are encouraged to complete homework or review material or suggestions made by the group. It can co-exist with a strictly biological model of etiology of psychopathology in that problem-solving deficits do not need to be viewed as an essential ingredient in the etiology of or recovery from symptoms; rather, the training could be viewed as an additional life enhancer (e.g., with an attitude such as "antidepressants will eliminate your symptoms of depression, but life would be easier if you had better problem-solving skills"). The problem-solving approach may not be very highly regarded in a setting that holds a very strong psychoanalytic orientation; although inpatient psychoanalytic practitioners no longer search for the genetic causes of symptoms, they may regard this model as a band-aid approach. In its more behavioral form, its presence as part of the treatment may encourage the squashing of affect expression and may destroy the nurturing of a deeper and more complex understanding of one's difficulties given that most patients prefer the easier, quicker solution. Furthermore, it may render intensive exploration in outpatient psychotherapy difficult in that it may prematurely seal over areas of conflict.

## Context of the Group

Groups using this approach can coexist with any number of other activities and therapies. The versatility in the range of human problems that can be explored in the group is one of the strengths of this model. The group can focus on problems that members introduce, or it can focus on a particular problem such as discharge planning. Such a group is not constrained by where the patients reside, whether on the same or different units. Examples of each occur in the literature. Although material from the unit can be brought to the group for exploration and discussion, the approach does not necessarily use the context of the unit as a source for material. The group can take place any time of the

day and before or after physical activities or individual psychotherapy.

## Temporal Variables

Stability of membership and the length of time required to complete the training are the factors that most limit the applicability
of this model. As mentioned, research and clinical reports suggest that for a group in which the content is not prespecified, a
minimum of six sessions is required and eight sessions is recommended. When the content is limited to a specific topic or
the group works on hypothetical (but usually relevant) problems,
the number of sessions may be reduced. However, without allowing members to apply the model directly to their particular
problems, members' success in generalizing their learning to
their own lives may be limited. Although closed-ended groups
are not required, some stability of membership is highly recommended to obviate the necessity of a review of the problem-
solving method in every session that someone new attends. Such
a review of the process in its abstract form may not benefit and
may even be tedious to those members who have already attended several sessions. Practically speaking, this may mean that
a new group can only begin every 2 weeks (if held three or four
times each week). At the very minimum, it requires that entrance
to the group occur only once every 7 days. If the recommended
length and stability requirements are observed, a single unit in
a general hospital most likely would not be able to support such
a group given that a sufficient number of members must be
available to begin and end the group at the same time. Thus, its
utility may be largely limited to larger psychiatric facilities.

## Size

Clinical reports suggest that groups should have no fewer than
3 members and no more than 12 (E. Coché, 1987; Pekala et al.,
1985). Most of the research that reports on groups in acute care
setting have used groups with between 4 and 10 members (E.
Coché et al., 1984; E. Coché & Douglass, 1977; E. Coché & Flick,
1975; D. E. Jones, 1981). Studies with chronic psychiatric patients

tend to have groups with fewer members, often around 5 members. (Edelstein et al., 1980; McLatchie, 1982). In their study, E. Coché and Flick (1975) noted that patients were more active and gained more from the experience when they were placed in the smaller groups than when they were placed in the larger groups.

With some populations such as delinquent boys and children with histories of behavioral disorders, a classroom or large group format has been successful (Elias, 1983; Natov, 1981; Spivack et al., 1976; Tannenbaum, 1991), although in both cases, these children were not being treated psychiatrically.

## Composition

This model offers tremendous latitude in terms of appropriate group composition. The approach can be used with all age groups—children (over 5 years old), adolescents, adults (18–70 years old), and geriatric patients. With the exception of the combination of both young and older adults, it is recommended that groups be composed of a single-age category because the problem-solving training in part is dependent on cognitive processing abilities. Moreover, the training for children who have a limited ability to think abstractly is different from that for adults who under normal circumstances are capable of abstract thinking. Similarly, mentally retarded individuals can benefit from this training but should be placed in a group separate from those of average intelligence given that the procedure does require some modification. One group that has been systematically excluded from this model has been those individuals with severe memory impairment or other more severe organic brain impairments. Similarly, those receiving ECT also have been excluded. It is the clinical impression of those clinicians who have used the model that ECT patients would not benefit from the training, although no separate study with these individuals has confirmed this (E. Coché, 1987).

Both sexes have been shown to benefit from problem-solving groups; however, research discussed in the prior sections suggests that men may be better able to use and more comfortable with the training (as opposed to a more interpersonal model) than may women (E. Coché et al., 1984).

Diagnostically, there is a tremendous range of patients who have been shown to benefit from problem-solving training: depressives, schizophrenics, those with impulsive disorders, suicidal patients, alcoholics, drug addicts, and even those with sociopathic tendencies. Within an acute care setting, patient groups can be diagnostically homogeneous or heterogeneous. If individuals with different diagnoses have difficulties at different stages of problem solving, as is suggested by Marx, Williams, and Claridge (1992), there may be some advantage to treating individuals in diagnostically homogeneous groups. Such an arrangement would help the therapist to hone in on that stage of processing in which a particular diagnostic group is most deficient. Effective groups have been conducted with mixed-gender, mixed-diagnostic composition and mixed-adult age ranges. There is some evidence to suggest that patients may benefit from groups that are homogeneous with respect to chronicity and how longstanding and unremitting their symptoms are, although this is seldom an issue because facilities are often segregated along these lines (e.g., acute, chronic, and intermediate care). In addition, some research that we have discussed suggests that depressed patients may respond better to this model than to a social skills model, whereas chronic schizophrenics may respond better to a social skills model (Cohen, 1982).

## Therapist Variables

Leaders can work alone or in co-therapy pairs. The most ideal therapist is someone who has group dynamics training along with some background in cognitive–behavioral therapy. However, compared with other models, this model permits the use of relatively untrained personnel who may have limited theoretical knowledge about psychopathology or group dynamics. Young college graduates, graduate students, untrained social workers, or psychiatric aides can be used as co-therapists; they can learn the model usually by reading literature in cognitive–behavior modification and working as co-leaders in a group with an experienced leader (E. Coché, 1987). When the structure of the training is a classroom format, teachers (Natov, 1981) and nonpsychology personnel (Rosenblum, 1983) have been used.

In fact, E. Coché (1987) reported an unpublished study conducted by Zelazowski (1976) in which the researcher taught the problem-solving training procedure to a number of patients who then, under his supervision, conducted problem-solving training groups for other patients. This arrangement was only partially successful: The patient–therapist did well as long as events proceeded smoothly. However, when resistance among members arose that required attention to group dynamics, attendance dropped and members complained. The researcher–supervisor had to intervene and provide support and counseling to the patient–therapist. The researcher concluded that therapeutic skills were needed to help the groups out of crisis; attention to group dynamics was invaluable.

# Summary

The problem-solving model is a method of enhancing members' adjustments through increasing abilities to address interpersonal problems. The group of techniques developed are based on the assumptions that (a) psychiatric patients are deficient in problem-solving skills, (b) this deficiency in part is responsible for their psychiatric symptomatologies, and (c) problem-solving training will improve their abilities to function effectively in everyday life, increase self-esteem, and potentially attenuate their psychiatric symptoms. Leaders actively impart a specific set of steps and techniques for members to learn and practice in the group setting. Members are given a general orientation and then are taught specific steps to follow after which they immediately begin to apply the techniques to either hypothetical problems or ones from their own lives. The steps include presenting and clarifying the problem, generating alternatives, evaluating the alternatives, role playing, and reporting back to the group at a later time their successes or failures with the particular solutions.

Of all the models presented in this book, the problem-solving model is one of the most well founded in terms of empirical research. There is strong evidence that psychiatric patients are deficient in problem-solving skills. Moreover, there seems to be some relation between the severity of the psychopathology and deficiencies in interpersonal social skills and problem solving. There is also considerable evidence that a wide range of ages and diagnostic categories can benefit from this training. In addition, with some modifications, the model can benefit patients from a wide range of levels of intellectual functioning.

The model can be used in a variety of settings and is minimally constrained by the clinical mission and theoretical orientation of the setting. Compared with other models in this book, much less training of the therapist is required, and the therapist is only minimally required to have a working knowledge of the cognitive–behavioral theoretical framework. Although a working knowledge of group dynamics would be helpful, much could be done in this model without it. The most limiting requirement of this model is the time that is necessary to have members learn and practice the problem-solving technique. This may limit the settings in which this model can be usefully applied. Overall, the model works best if the groups are closed-ended and last for at least six to eight sessions. Perhaps one of the most remarkable aspects of this model is that given its robust empirical base, it has received so little attention in the general group psychotherapy literature.

# References

Bedell, J. R., & Michael, D. D. (1988). Teaching problem-solving skills to chronic psychiatric patients. In D. Upper & S. M. Ross (Eds.), *Handbook of behavioral group therapy* (pp. 83–118). New York: Plenum Press.

Bellack, A. S., Morrison, R. L., Mueser, K. T., Wade, J. H., & Sayers, S. L. (1990). Role play for assessing the social competence of psychiatric patients. *Journal of Consulting and Clinical Psychology, 2*(3), 248–255.

Benson, B. A., Johnson, M., & Miranti, S. V. (1986). Effects of anger management training with mentally retarded adults in group therapy. *Journal of Consulting and Clinical Psychology, 54*(5), 728–729.

Castles, E. E. (1982). Training in social skills and interpersonal problem-solving skills for mildly and moderately mentally retarded adults. *Dissertation Abstracts International, 3*(9), 3023-B.

Chaney, E. F., O'Leary, M. R., & Marlatt, C. A. (1978). Skill training with alcoholics. *Journal of Consulting and Clinical Psychology, 46*(5), 1092–1104.

Chudy, J. F. (1981). The effectiveness of integrated vs. independent training in interpersonal problem-solving and role-taking with juvenile delinquents. *Dissertation Abstracts International, 42*(8), 3411-B.

Coché, E. (1987). Problem-solving training: A cognitive group therapy modality. In A. Freeman & V. Greenwood (Eds.), *Cognitive therapy: Applications in psychiatric and medical settings* (pp. 83–102). New York: Human Sciences Press.

Coché, E., Cooper, J. B., & Petermann, K. J. (1984). Differential outcomes of cognitive and interactional group therapies. *Small Group Behavior, 15,* 497–509.

Coché, E., & Douglass, A. A. (1977). Therapeutic effects of problem-solving and play reading groups. *Journal of Clinical Psychology, 33,* 820–827.

Coché, E., & Flick, A. (1975). Problem solving training group for hospitalized psychiatric patients. *Journal of Psychology, 91,* 19–29.

Coché, J., & Coché, E. (1986). Group psychotherapy: The severely disturbed patient in hospital. *Carrier Foundation Letter, 113,* 1–6.

Cohen, S. R. (1982). A comparison of the effects of interpersonal problem solving training groups and social interaction training groups on hospitalized psychiatric patients. *Dissertation Abstracts International, 42*(7), 2981-B.

Cohen-Sandler, R. (1982). Interpersonal problem-solving skills of suicidal and nonsuicidal children: Assessment and treatment. *Dissertation Abstracts International, 43*(2) 519-B.

Corder, B. F., Whiteside, R., Koehne, P., & Hortman, R. (1981). Structured techniques for handling loss and addition of members in adolescent psychotherapy groups. *Journal of Early Adolescence, 1*(4), 413–421.

Davis, G. A. (1966). Current status of research and theory in human problem solving. *Psychological Bulletin, 66*(1), 36–54.

Douglas, M. S., & Mueser, K. T. (1990). Teaching conflict resolution to the chronically mentally ill. *Behavior Modification, 4*(4), 519–547.

Duncan, C. P. (1959). Recent research on human problem solving. *Psychological Bulletin, 56*(6), 397–429.

D'Zurilla, T. J., & Goldfried, M. R. (1971). Problem solving and behavior modification. *Journal of Abnormal Psychology, 78*(1), 107–126.

Edelstein, B. A., Couture, E., Cray, M., Dickens, P., & Lusebrink, N. (1980). Group training of problem solving with psychiatric patients. In D. Upper & S. M. Ross (Eds.), *Behavioral group therapy: An annual review* (pp. 85–102). Champaign, IL: Research Press.

Elias, M. J. (1983). Improving coping skills of emotionally disturbed boys through television-based social problem solving. *American Journal of Orthopsychiatry, 53*(1), 61–72.

Gilbride, T. V., & Hebert, J. (1980). Pathological characteristics of good and poor interpersonal problem-solvers among psychiatric outpatients. *Journal of Clinical Psychology, 36,* 121–127.

Glantz, M. (1987). Day hospital treatment of alcoholics. In A. Freeman & V. Greenwood (Eds.), *Cognitive therapy: Applications in psychiatric and medical settings* (pp. 51–68). New York: Human Sciences Press.

Goldfried, M. R., & Davison, G. (1976). *Clinical behavior therapy*. New York: Holt, Rinehart & Winston.

Gotlieb, I. H., & Asarnow, R. F. (1979). Interpersonal and impersonal problem-solving skills in mildly and clinically depressed university students. *Journal of Consulting and Clinical Psychology, 41*(1), 86–95.

Hansen, D. J., St. Lawrence, J. S., & Christoff, K. A. (1985). Effects of interpersonal problem-solving training with chronic aftercare patients on problem-solving component skills and effectiveness of solutions. *Journal of Consulting and Clinical Psychology, 53*(2), 167–174.

Hartmann, H. (1939). Psychoanalysis and the concept of health. *International Journal of Psychoanalysis, 20*, 308–321.

Hartmann, H. (1964). *Essays on ego psychology*. Madison, CT: International Universities Press.

Heppner, P. P. (1978). A review of the problem-solving literature and its relationship to the counseling process. *Journal of Counseling Psychology, 25*, 366–375.

Higgins, J. P., & Thies, A. P. (1982). Social effectiveness and problem solving thinking of reformatory inmates. *Journal of Offender Counseling, Services and Rehabilitation, 5*(3/4), 93–98.

Hussian, R. A. (1987). Problem-solving training and institutionalized elderly patients. In A. Freeman & V. Greenwood (Eds.), *Cognitive therapy: Applications in psychiatric and medical settings* (pp. 199–212). New York: Human Sciences Press.

Hussian, R. A., & Lawrence, P. S. (1981). Social reinforcement and problem solving training in the treatment of depressed institutionalized elderly patients. *Cognitive Therapy and Research, 5*, 57–69.

Intagliata, J. C. (1978). Increasing the interpersonal problem-solving skills of an alcoholic population. *Journal of Consulting and Clinical Psychology, 46*(3), 489–498.

Jahoda, M. (1953). The meaning of psychological health. *Social Casework, 34*, 349–354.

Jahoda, M. (1958). *Current concepts of positive mental health*. New York: Basic Books.

Jones, D. E. (1981). Interpersonal cognitive problem-solving training—A skills approach with hospitalized psychiatric patients. *Dissertation Abstract International, 42*(5), 2060.

Jones, S. L., Kanfer, R., & Lanyon, R. I. (1982). Skill training with alcoholics: A clinical extension. *Addictive Behaviors, 7*(3), 285–290.

Kanfer, F. H., & Busemeyer, J. R. (1982). The use of problem solving and decision making in behavior therapy. *Clinical Psychology Review, 2*, 239–266.

Kavoussi, R. J., Fallon, A. E., & Coccaro, E. F. (1992). *Impulsive aggression in personality disorders*. Unpublished manuscript, Medical College of Pennsylvania, Philadelphia.

Kazdin, A. E., Esveldt-Dawson, K., French, N. H., & Unis, A. S. (1987). Problem-solving skills training and relationship therapy in the treatment of antisocial child behavior. *Journal of Consulting and Clinical Psychology*, *55*(1), 76–85.

Kubie, L. S. (1954). The fundamental nature of the distinction between normality and neurosis. *Psychoanalysis Quarterly*, *23*, 167–204.

Lerner, M. S. (1989). Treatment of suicide ideators: A problem-solving approach. *Dissertation Abstracts International*, *51*, 435.

Levenson, M., & Neuringer, C. (1971). Problem-solving behavior in suicidal adolescents. *Journal of Consulting and Clinical Psychology*, *37*, 433–436.

Linehan, M. (1987a). Dialectical behavior therapy for borderline personality disorder: Theory and method. *Bulletin of the Menninger Clinic*, *51*, 261–276.

Linehan, M. (1987b). Dialectical behavioral therapy: A cognitive behavioral approach to parasuicide. *Journal of Personality Disorders*, *1*, 328–333.

Linehan, M., & Wagner, A. (1990). Dialectical behavior therapy: A feminist–behavioral treatment of borderline personality disorder. *Behavior Therapist*, 9–14.

Mahoney, M. J., & Arnkoff, D. B. (1978). Cognitive and self-control therapies. In S. L. Garfield & A. E. Bergin (Eds.), *Handbook of psychotherapy and behavior change: An empirical analysis* (pp. 689–722). New York: Wiley.

Marx, E. M., Williams, J. M., & Claridge, G. C. (1992). Depression and problem solving. *Journal of Abnormal Psychology*, *101*(1), 78–86.

McLatchie, L. R. (1982). Interpersonal problem-solving group therapy: An evaluation of a potential method of social skills training for the chronic psychiatric patient. *Dissertation Abstracts International*, *42*(7), 2995-B.

Meichenbaum, D., & Goodman, J. (1971). Training impulsive children to talk to themselves: A means of developing self-control. *Journal of Abnormal Psychology*, *77*, 115–126.

Mueser, K. T., Bellack, A. S., Morrison, R. L., & Wixted, J. T. (1990). Social competence in schizophrenia: Premorbid adjustment, social skill, and domains of functioning. *Journal of Psychiatric Research*, *24*(1), 51–63.

Natov, I. (1981). An intervention to facilitate interpersonal cognitive problem-solving skills and behavioral adjustment among emotionally handicapped children. *Dissertation Abstracts International*, *41*(12), 5034.

Nezu, A. (1980). Component analyses of three stages of the social problem solving training model. *Dissertation Abstracts International*, *40*(11) 929-B.

Nezu, A.M. (1986). Efficacy of a social problem-solving therapy approach for unipolar depression. *Journal of Consulting and Clinical Psychology*, *54*(2), 196–202.

Osborn, A. F. (1963). *Applied imagination: Principles and procedures of creative problem-solving* (3rd ed.). New York: Scribner's.

Ostby, S. S. (1982). Social problem-solving training with mildly and moderately retarded individuals. *Dissertation Abstracts International*, *43*(7), 2320-B.

Patsiokas, A. T., & Clum, G. A. (1985). Effects of psychotherapeutic strategies in the treatment of suicide attempters. *Psychotherapy*, *22*(2), 281–290.

Pekala, R. J., Siegel, J. M., & Farrar, D. M. (1985). The problem-solving support group: Structured group therapy with psychiatric inpatients. *International Journal of Group Psychotherapy*, *35*(3), 391–409.

Pierce, C. V. M. (1980). Interpersonal problem-solving training for psychiatric patients. *Dissertation Abstracts International, 41*(10), 4339-A.

Platt, J. J., Scura, W. C., & Hannon, J. R. (1973). Problem-solving thinking of youthful incarcerated heroin addicts. *Journal of Community Psychology, 1*(3), 278–281.

Platt, J. J., & Siegel, J. M. (1976). MMPI characteristics of good and poor social problem-solvers among psychiatric patients. *Journal of Psychology, 94,* 245–251.

Platt, J. J., Siegel, J. M., & Spivack, G. (1975). Do psychiatric patients and normals see the same solutions as effective in solving interpersonal problems. *Journal of Consulting and Clinical Psychology, 43*(2), 279.

Platt, J. J., & Spivack, G. (1972a). Problem-solving thinking of psychiatric patients. *Journal of Consulting and Clinical Psychology, 39*(1), 148–151.

Platt, J. J., & Spivack, G. (1972b). Social competence and effective problem-solving thinking in psychiatric patients. *Journal of Clinical Psychology, 28*(1), 3–5.

Platt, J. J., & Spivack, G. (1974). Means of solving real-life problems: 1. Psychiatric patients vs. controls and cross-cultural comparisons of normal females. *Journal of Community Psychology, 2*(1), 45–48.

Platt, J. J., & Spivack, G. (1975). *Means–ends problem-solving procedure (MEPS): A measure of interpersonal cognitive problem-solving skill.* Philadelphia: Department of Mental Health Science, Hahneman Medical College & Hospital.

Platt, J. J., Spivack, G., Altman, N., Altman, D., & Peizer, S. B. (1974). Adolescent problem-solving thinking. *Journal of Consulting and Clinical Psychology, 42*(6), 787–793.

Pollack, L. E. (1991). Problem-solving group therapy: Two inpatient models based on level of functioning. *Issues in Mental Health Nursing, 12,* 65–80.

Richard, B. A., & Dodge, K. A. (1982). Social maladjustment and problem solving in school-aged children. *Journal of Consulting and Clinical Psychology, 50*(2), 226–233.

Rosenblum, B. E. (1983). ROSEBUD: An interpersonal problem solving enhancement program for kindergartners. A primary prevention mental health program. *Dissertation Abstracts International, 23*(8), 2565A.

Schotte, D., & Clum, G.A. (1982). Suicide ideation in a college population: A test of a model. *Journal of Consulting and Clinical Psychology, 50*(5), 690–696.

Shure, M. B., & Spivack, G. (1972). Means-ends thinking, adjustment, and social class among elementary-school-aged children. *Journal of Consulting and Clinical Psychology, 38*(3), 348–353.

Shure, M. B., & Spivack, G. (1978). Dialogues for parent–child problems. In M. B. Shure & G. Spivack (Eds.), *Problem-solving in childrearing* (pp. 131–158). San Francisco: Jossey-Bass.

Shure, M. B., & Spivack, G. (1982). Interpersonal problem-solving in young children: A cognitive approach to prevention. *American Journal of Community Psychology, 10*(3), 341–356.

Shure, M. B., Spivack, G., & Jaeger, M. (1971). Problem-solving, thinking and adjustment among disadvantaged preschool children. *Child Development, 42,* 1791–1803.

Siegel, J. M., Platt, J. J., & Peizer, S. B. (1976). Emotional and social real-life problem-solving thinking in adolescent and adult psychiatric patients. *Journal of Clinical Psychology, 32,* 230–232.

Siegel, J. M., Platt, J. J., & Spivack, G. (1974). Means of solving real-life problems: 2. Do professionals and laymen see the same solutions as effective in solving problems? *Journal of Community Psychology, 2,* 49–50.

Siegel, J. M., & Spivack, G. (1976). Problem-solving therapy: The description of a new program for chronic psychiatric patients. *Psychotherapy: Theory, Research and Practice, 13*(4), 368–373.

Simon, H. A., & Newell, A. (1971). Human problem solving: The state of the theory in 1970. *American Psychologist, 26,* 145–159.

Small, R. W., & Schinke, S. P. (1983). Teaching competence in residential group care: Cognitive problem solving and interpersonal skills training with emotionally disturbed preadolescents. *Journal of Social Service Research, 7*(1), 1–16.

Spivack, G. (1984). *Interpersonal cognitive problem-solving, mental health and prevention: An annotated bibliography.* Unpublished manuscript.

Spivack, G., & Levine, M. (1963). *Self-regulation in acting-out and normal adolescents* (Report No. M-4531). Washington, DC: National Institutes of Health.

Spivack, G., Platt, J. J., & Shure, M. B. (1976). *The problem-solving approach to adjustment.* San Francisco: Jossey-Bass.

Spivack, G., & Shure, M. B. (1974). *Social adjustment of young children.* San Francisco: Jossey-Bass.

Spivack, G., Shure, M. B., Platt, J. J. (1985). *Means–ends problem solving (MEPS): Stimuli and scoring procedures supplement.* Philadelphia: Department of Mental Health Sciences, Hahneman Medical College.

Swenson, C. (1989). Kernberg and Linehan: Two approaches to the borderline patient. *Journal of Personality Disorders, 3*(1), 26–35.

Tannenbaum, M. (1991). *Social–cognitive therapy for children.* Unpublished doctoral dissertation, Institute for Graduate Clinical Psychology of Widener University, Chester, PA.

Toseland, R., & Rose, S. D. (1978). A social skills training program for older adults: Evaluation of three group approaches. *Social Work Research Abstracts,* pp. 873–874.

Urbain, E. S. (1980). Interpersonal problem-solving training and social perspective-taking training with impulsive children via modeling, role-play and self-instruction. *Dissertation Abstracts International, 40*(11), 5424-B.

Urbain, E. S., & Kendall, P. C. (1980). Review of social–cognitive problem-solving interventions with children. *Psychological Bulletin, 88*(1), 109–143.

Waldeck, J. P., Emerson, S., & Edelstein, B. (1979). COPE: A systematic approach to moving chronic patients into the community. *Hospital and Community Psychiatry, 30,* 551–554.

Wessler, R., & Hankin-Wessler, S. (1989). Cognitive group therapy. In A. Freeman, K. Simon, L. Beutler, & H. Arkowitz (Eds.), *Comprehensive handbook
of cognitive therapy*. New York: Plenum Press.

Zelazowski, R. R. (1976). *Hospitalized psychiatric patients as co-leaders of problem-solving training groups: A pilot study*. Unpublished master's thesis, West
Chester State College, West Chester, PA.

# 9

# The Behavioral Model: Social Skills Training

**B**ehavioral therapy is an approach that has evolved considerably over its history. Since its development, there have been many factions based on philosophical, theoretical, and technical differences. Use of the group format by behavioral therapists led to further splinterings, resulting in the generation of many variations in the technical application of the model. This diversity has left the behavioral therapies struggling to find identity and to articulate characteristic features that are common to their many variations. Nonetheless, the behavioral group model, more than any of the other models in this book, offers a preponderance of techniques that aim to change a particular set of behaviors. This model, in all its myriad forms, is unique in its emphatic commitment to empirical methodology as the crucible for acceptable treatment.[1] In this chapter, we highlight a partic-

---

[1] There is considerable controversy over whether the dimension of scientific rigor and the empirical methodology distinguish the behavioral model from other models. These are, however, distinctions that also apply to the cognitive–behavioral model (Ledwidge, 1979; Mahoney & Kazdin, 1979). For many (e.g., Mahoney & Kazdin, 1979) there may not be a difference between the two models in this respect. However, for our purposes, the distinction between the cognitive–behavioral model and the behavioral model is a difference in theory and location of emphasis concerning the target of change. For the former, emphasis is on cognitions, whereas for the latter, emphasis is on behaviors.

ular version of the behavioral model, social skills training, which is applicable to a wide range of inpatients but particularly those who have more severe and chronic psychopathology.

# Theoretical Underpinnings

## The Relation of Behaviorism to Learning Theory and Behavioral Therapy

**Levels of analysis.** The relation of behaviorism to behavioral therapy is often a confused one. *Behaviorism, learning theory* (or the *laws of learning*), and *behavior therapy* are not synonymous terms; rather, they represent three separate levels of analysis. Behaviorism is most generally a philosophy of science that carries with it a philosophy of the mind, specific assumptions about human nature, and a set of values and goals concerning the pursuit and evaluation of scientific activity, including "objectivity" and "empiricism" (Zuriff, 1985). Learning theory, the second level of analysis, uses philosophical assumptions about human nature to develop laws or theories of how organisms learn, modify, and extinguish behavior. Classical conditioning and operant conditioning are examples of theories that attempt to explain and predict observable phenomenon. These theoretical systems influence how therapists perceive and respond to clinical phenomenon. Behavioral therapy, the third level of analysis, is associated with a methodology and set of techniques that are aimed at changing certain behaviors in identifiable and predictable ways. It is likely that a symptom will be treated differently depending on one's theoretical framework. For example, in a case of an individual with a snake phobia, a behavioral therapist might use systematic desensitization, whereas a psychoanalyst might use free association and interpretation to at least attenuate

---

With target of change being the critical factor, many of cognitive or cognitive–behavioral therapists have been less interested in empirical validation (e.g., Ellis, 1990; Wessler & Hankin-Wessler, 1989).

the fear of snakes.[2] In summary, behavioral therapists' clinical practice is informed by their theoretical proclivities. Their conceptual leanings are, in turn, determined by the philosophical lens by which they view the essence of human behavior. Although this notion applies to all of the therapy models that we discuss in this book, it is particularly central in the behavioral model given that a number of the seminal works in behavioral therapy have developed out of disparate philosophical notions of behaviorism.

**Types of behaviorism.** Behaviorism, which originally began as a movement in opposition to introspection, was defined by Watson (1924) as muscle movements and glandular secretions. Mental events or private events such as thoughts or feelings were not the purview of psychology because there could be no public agreement as to their occurrence (Watson, 1920). The implication of this definition for theory and clinical practice was that constructs such as thoughts or feelings were not considered scientifically legitimate and thus not clinically relevant. This philosophy became known as *metaphysical behaviorism* and is reflected in the early writings of Wolpe (1958) and his use of desensitization in a group setting and in the current practice of social skills training, in which the emphasis is on observable behaviors. Skinner (1938, 1974) also rejected the idea that cognitions and emotions were necessary to the prediction and control of behavior; however, his reasoning was based on the notion that those contingencies that give rise to feelings or cognitions are isomorphic to those that produce the concomitant overt behav-

---

[2] Conversely, therapists of different philosophical and theoretical orientations can use the same techniques, recouching them in conceptual language that is consistent with the therapist's theoretical orientation and philosophical bent. For example, a behavioral therapist and a cognitive–behavioral therapist both may use a behavioral technique of requesting that a depressed individual who complains that he or she never "does anything" complete a time log of his or her activities. The behavioral therapist is interested in its completion to gather baseline data for the eventual purpose of changing or increasing the level of activity or the pattern of the way that the individual spends his or her time; the cognitive–behavioral therapist might be looking for a distortion in the individual's perception of his or her time commitments and the way that he or she actually spends his or her time.

ior, rather than Watson's (1920) criteria of public agreement. Thus, for Skinner, the focus in theory and clinical practice was on observable behaviors rather than on an individual's emotions or cognitions. Skinner's philosophy, known as *radical behaviorism*, also deviated from the metaphysical philosophy in that behavior was seen as an interaction between the organism and its environment. Thus, the unit of analysis in the behavioral theories included both an organism's behavior and its context. In contemporary radical behaviorism, context continues to assume a central focus. Unlike Skinner's radical behaviorism, some contemporary radical behaviorists, known as *contextual behaviorists*, see cognitions as having a legitimate status in determining behavior (Hayes, 1987; Hayes & Hayes, 1992). They argue that the cognitive/social history of an individual influences overt behavior in a manner that cannot be predicted simply by knowing the history of reinforcement with the stimulus event (e.g., a man's response to a woman may be influenced not only by his direct experiences with previous women but also by what verbal rules that he has learned in the social context without direct experience). Thus, metaphysical, radical, and contextual behaviorists agree on the acceptable method of study (the empirical method) but vary on the particular unit of study (e.g., public vs. private behavior, overt mechanistic units of behavior vs. behavior and its context, observable behavior vs. cognition or verbalization).

Perhaps more well known than his notion of metaphysical behaviorism is a method that Watson (1924) developed for studying behavior, which has come to be known as *methodological behaviorism*. Methodological behaviorism, which has profoundly influenced the field of psychology throughout this century, has become for the majority of behaviorists the sine qua non of behavioral therapy. Methodological behaviorism claims that science can study only public (observable) events; there is a distinction between (a) thoughts, feelings, and other private events that are not observable and (b) other public events (e.g., overt behavior) that are observable. Hence, this position originally excluded mental events from scientific scrutiny and thus from clinical practice. However, over time, contemporary methodological behaviorists have attempted to deal with cognition and emotion by conceding that the scientifically analyzable world must be used to make inferences about what is scientifically unanalyzable; although thoughts cannot be seen directly, their influence on other types of human behavior can be seen and measured. For example, measuring "cognitive" parameters enhance the predictive validity and therapeutic power of techniques conceptualized previously as purely "behavioral" techniques. Similarly, cognitive mastery of a task or role improves the efficacy of behavioral rehearsal and modeling techniques (Mahoney & Kazdin, 1979). Although they may not necessarily label themselves methodological behaviorists, most group behavioral therapists, including those practicing in inpatient settings, are influenced by this philosophical tradition. Although therapists may vary on the particular behavior or behavioral unit that they believe worthy of study and intervention (e.g., overt behavior, behavior and its context, verbalization and its context), they all agree on the acceptable method of study, namely, the empirical method. In summary, based on philosophical assumptions, theories of how behavior is acquired, modified, and extinguished are put forth and validated or disconfirmed by way of empirical method. Belief in a particular theory of psychopathology and theory of change lends itself to the development of techniques to develop modify or attenuate the identified behaviors. The theory, methodology, and set of techniques constitute the essence that defines each particular behavioral therapy approach.

## Definition of Behavioral Therapy

Although there have been sporadic reports throughout the century of the application of behavioral principles to effect behavioral change, its systematic application did not occur until the 1950s (Masters, Burish, Hollon, & Rimm, 1987). It is not surprising given the diverse philosophies of behaviorism that when the term *behavior therapy* is used, it has a variety of meanings. According to one account (Franks & Barbrack, 1983), the term *behavior therapy* was first used by Lindsley, Skinner, and Solomon (1953) to describe treatment with hospitalized psychotic patients; it referred to the application of Skinnerian operant conditioning to patients' socially dysfunctional behaviors. Although Skinner and his colleagues appear to have been the first to introduce the systematic use of behavioral therapy, Eysenck (1959) and Lazarus (1958) each independently and in a broader context also coined the term *behavior therapy*. Eysenck, using the term as a new therapy for psychological disorders, broadened it to include both operant and classical conditioning principles. Lazarus introduced the term *behavior therapy* with an even broader meaning; it referred to the addition of an objectively validating methodology in a context of more traditional psychotherapy procedures (Franks & Barbrack, 1983). Unlike Eysenck and Skinner, who used the principles of learning theory in a therapeutic context, Lazarus espoused a wide variety of clinical techniques without regard to their theoretical origins. His single requirement was that techniques had to have data supporting their effectiveness and that empirical methods had to be used to monitor therapeutic efficacy. Thus, from its inception as a treatment, there were several variations of behavioral therapy; the term *behavior therapy* could refer to such diverse approaches as operant conditioning (Lindsley et al., 1953), token economy therapy (Allyon & Azrin, 1968), systematic desensitization (Wolpe, 1958), contingency management training (Rimm & Masters, 1979), self-control training, social skills training (L'Abate & Milan, 1985), multimodal therapy (Lazarus, 1976), and social learning (Bandura, 1977a).

With such independent lines of development using the same term and a diversity of thought about what behavioral therapy is, the term defies a single encompassing definition or characteristic (Emmelkamp, 1986; Wixted, Bellack, & Hersen, 1990). The lack of a single defining characteristic for the field has been likened to Wittgenstein's problem of family resemblance (Zuriff, 1985); just as no single feature is common to all family members nor does one common feature differentiate family members from other groups. So, too, with behavioral therapy, there is no single feature that all behavioral therapies have in common, and no single criterion differentiates them from other models. Yet, the set of overlapping features and historical associations that the behavioral models share do constitute the essence of the family resemblance. Most definitions fall into two groups—doctrinal, in which behavioral therapy is linked directly to theories or laws of learning, and epistemological, in which behavior therapy is defined in terms of methods of studying clinical phenomena. The former is a more limiting definition, whereas the latter may be an overinclusive one that encompasses any aspect of the vast mental health field that is data based (Franks & Barbrack, 1983).

## Common Features of Behavioral Approaches

Despite the diversity within the conceptual field, contemporary behavioral therapy can nonetheless be described as an approach that is based on a broad set of theoretical and methodological assumptions and principles rather than either a unitary theoretical framework or a compilation of techniques; it is a therapy in which theory and practice are complementary and scientific rigor and clinical acumen are interwoven (Franks & Barbrack, 1983). The central features common to most types of behavioral therapy include an emphasis on (a) an empirical orientation, (b) a behavioral focus, (c) an action orientation, (d) environmental factors, (e) an ahistorical focus, and (f) an ideographic approach (Wixted et al., 1990). We discuss each of these features in the sections that follow.

**Empirical orientation.** The nexus of all behavioral approaches is an empirical orientation. This orientation entails the application of findings and principles derived from experimental and social psychological research to the design of the treatment. There is a reliance on basic research in psychology as a source of hypotheses about the efficacy of various techniques. The criterion for acceptability of a particular intervention or technique for use in the therapeutic setting is that it has been found to be effective on the basis of empirical validation rather than on the basis of clinical intuition or general impression. In the broadest context, the behavioral therapist has no a priori commitment to any particular therapeutic intervention or theoretical orientation; the only restriction is to an empirically validated method.

Behavioral therapy involves the systematic application of experimentally confirmed techniques within a setting that uses an empirical framework. Such an approach encourages the generation of hypotheses related to the nature of the problem behavior, the use of techniques most suitable to ameliorate the problem behavior, and the collection of data relevant to evaluation of the utility of these interventions for treating the patient's identified problems (Hollander & Kazaoka, 1988). To some extent, all psychotherapy models adopt a set of hypotheses regarding a theory of the nature of abnormal behavior, the role of the therapist, and the specific techniques that will be effective in ameliorating the behavior. However, it is the use of these hypotheses in an experimental paradigm that distinguishes the behavioral model from other models presented in this book. Target populations and problems are clearly delineated and operationally defined. Interventions are concretized and systematically applied and thus can be reproduced (Flowers, 1979). The evaluation of the efficacy of the intervention is specified in objective and measurable terms, with an emphasis on overt change as the main criterion (although some mediational variables such as attributions are considered acceptable). In summary, the essence of the behavioral approach is accountability, openness to alternatives, and an insistence on the existence of data rather than just theory or subjective experience to qualify a technique for inclusion in a treatment program (Franks & Barbrack, 1983).[3]

**Focus on behavior.** Related to the model's empirical foundation and consistent with the philosophy of behaviorism is the focus on behavior or symptoms as opposed to underlying causes. To some extent, all psychotherapy models assume that human response (including behavior, cognition, and affect) can be changed through a process of unlearning or relearning. The par-

---

[3] Although behavioral therapists are guided by generally accepted principles of measurability and an acceptance of data rather than dogma, it is not true that behavioral therapy consistently rests on theory derived from experimental psychology and that the practice of behavioral therapy is invariably empirically based. Some procedures have used the case study technique, whereas others have been subject to even less scientific scrutiny. (For a more extended discussion of these matters, see Mahoney & Kazdin, 1979; Franks & Barbrack, 1983.) In addition, even the behavioral therapy procedures (e.g., aversion therapy, systematic desensitization) originally thought to be based exclusively on the operant and classical learning paradigms involve additional (e.g., cognitive) processes and require the use of nonbehavioral concepts to explain therapeutic effects (Emmelkamp, 1986).

ticular form that this learning process takes depends on the type of therapy model endorsed. It is a commonly held belief that behavioral therapists use only learning theory that contains a concomitant empirical methodology as a conceptual basis for intervention and change (Flowers, 1979). Although this view is not incorrect, there are other theoretical frameworks that affect contemporary behavioral applications (Hollander & Kazaoka, 1988).

At one time, therapists thought that the learning processes that are used to explain the development and continuation of desirable and functional behavior were the same ones that could sufficiently and parsimoniously explain behaviors labeled as "abnormal"; that is, most manifestations of maladaptive behavior were viewed as either the failure of the individual to learn adaptive coping skills or the sometimes accidental acquisition of unacceptable and often self-defeating behaviors (Hollander & Kazaoka, 1988). However, within the past 10 years, most behavioral therapists have come to accept biological contributions to abnormal behavior. How the symptoms are acquired is less relevant because the empirical method cannot easily be applied to a retrospective analysis, and even knowing the cause of maladaptive behaviors does not necessarily lead to effective treatment. Emphasis is on present symptoms rather than distal causes, and there is no assumption that symptoms necessarily reflect underlying psychopathology as is the case in the psychoanalytic tradition. Regardless of how the maladaptive or problem behavior is acquired, it is its present manifestation that is the focus of assessment and intervention; whatever the "cause," behavioral interventions can aid individuals in learning to adapt more effectively.

Maladaptive or problem behaviors can be categorized as (a) behavioral excesses, (b) behavioral deficits, or (c) behavior under inappropriate stimulus control (Hollander & Kazaoka, 1988). Behavioral excesses are those behaviors that in isolation are not unacceptable but become so when an individual uses them to an excessive degree. These are the behaviors that can interrupt the routine of the individual (as in the case of an individual who checks his or her stove so often that he or she is not able to leave the house) and often are threatening or discomforting to others (as in the case of an individual who frequently exhibits aggressive behavior). Behavioral deficits are behaviors that an individual appears unable to perform when appropriate, such as a lack of assertiveness. Behaviors that are problematic because they are under inappropriate stimulus control are not considered abnormal in isolation. They are maladaptive when the circumstances or contingencies under which they occur are undesirable or dangerous. For instance, a person's attempt to acquire emotional support is not abnormal, but when the individual seeking these provisions engages in a series of one-night stands with acquaintances met in bars, the behavior becomes dangerous.

The particular behaviors on which the behavioral approach focuses are ones that can be articulated in the language of empirical psychology and are capable of being altered in measurable ways (Hollander & Kazaoka, 1988). What is considered the appropriate unit of behavior depends somewhat on the clinician's philosophy and theoretical orientation. For example, with social phobia, a therapist using operant conditioning may focus on the behavior at the manifest level, emphasizing the reinforcement of successive approximations of gregariousness. In contrast, a therapist using systematic desensitization might conceptualize a social phobia as a problem concerning underlying anxiety and attempt to ameliorate this internal state (Masters et al., 1987). Similarly, there is considerable controversy over the emphasis that should be placed on making changes in cognitions and affects and to what extent cognitions in particular can be considered measurable behaviors (see the earlier discussion on types of behaviorism). Although most therapists accept that changes occur in the cognitive and affective domains, therapists differ in their relative emphases on, and timing in dealing with, these domains as they relate to behavior and are targeted for intervention. Many therapists believe that it is technically easier and more efficacious to alter behavior, with resultant modifications occurring in cognitions and affects, than it is to change cognitions and affects, with resultant alterations in behavior (Hollander & Kazaoka, 1988). For example, with a patient who is frequently too passive and self-deprecating, a cognitive–behavioral therapist following the teachings of Ellis (e.g., Ellis & Grieger, 1977) may try to persuade that patient to think differently to eliminate the inappropriate behavior. In contrast, a behavioral therapist may attempt to use a social skills approach to teach the patient how to improve his or her social behavior with the expectation that new ways of thinking will emerge from the patient's more effective social interactions.

Whether the commitment is to the measurement of overt behavior only or can include private events, behavioral therapy places great emphasis on an objective (rather than subjective), quantitative behavioral assessment; this enables the therapist to establish a baseline against which to judge the impact of the treatment. A systematic behavioral assessment that emphasizes a focus on antecedents, behaviors, and consequences is also seen as exposing the environmental factors that may be influencing or controlling the identified behavior. When maladaptive behaviors and their antecedents and consequences have been identified, clearly defined and specific treatment goals can be set. When possible, these are mutually agreed to by both therapist and patient. The treatment then flows naturally from the assessment and goal setting.

**Action orientation.** Behavioral treatments are usually designed to aid patients in performing a task rather than discussing the task (i.e., doing rather than talking). Behaviorists believe that behavioral change occurs by actively practicing new targeted behaviors or by being exposed to critical cues rather than by just developing an understanding or insight. Behavioral change is accomplished by rehearsing appropriate behaviors in the session and then supplementing this with in vivo practice (i.e., homework). Although social learning and self-efficacy theories suggest that cognition is important, most behavioral therapies do not place a central focus on cognition and affect.

**Environmental factors: Antecedents and consequences.** The behavioral approach emphasizes the study of the environmental factors and the behavior–environment interaction, which are seen as playing an essential function in shaping and maintaining behavior. A systematic assessment of the behavior in its context is then made to assess whether a behavior is adaptive. This process involves a study of the interactions among antecedents, behaviors, and consequences (Hollander & Kazaoka, 1988). The antecedents determine under what circumstances certain identified responses occur. Antecedent variables of problem behaviors are identified by systematic and careful scrutiny of the factors that exist each time the problem behaviors occur. The evaluation of consequences is also important in clinical assessment because the consequences strengthen, weaken, or maintain previously acquired behaviors.

Human behavior, however, is not just a direct result of consequences; rather, people have the ability to think and process information about external and internal experiences, including the capacity to reflect on and make judgments about the potential benefits and costs of engaging in certain behaviors in future situations. This capability enables individuals to weigh the short-term loss or gain against long-term positive or aversive consequences and defer the immediate rewards if the behavior will produce long-term aversive consequences. Also, when evaluating externally rewarding consequences, individuals recognize and take into account the effect that these behaviors have on their own self-evaluations (Bandura, 1969). Thus, individuals act on their situations to make changes that suit them rather than simply reacting to their environment. Individuals have the capacity to inform themselves, to symbolically enact what they learn from others' experiences, to reinforce themselves for their achievements, and to strive for mastery or competence (Hollander & Kazaoka, 1988). The "self-controlling" behaviors and self-evaluated monitoring of the behavior–environment interaction (Bandura, 1974, 1977a, 1977b, 1978; Bandura, Adams, Hardy, & Howells, 1980) allow some degree of freedom to transcend environmental controls (e.g., the influence of antecedents and consequences).

Linked to the behaviorist emphasis on the impact of the environment is a rejection of classical trait theory, the position that individuals have a predisposition to act similarly in a wide range of circumstances. Behavioral therapists do acknowledge a certain degree of cross-situation and longitudinal stability in behavior, which for them equals "personality." The consistency of behavior across situations and through time, then, is not the result of an assembly of traits or of underlying dynamics but is viewed as the sum total of specific learning histories. Abnormal behavior is usually considered a relatively stable pattern of learned maladaptive interpersonal behaviors. Behavioral therapists differ in the extent to which they believe that a person's behavior is dictated or can be predicted by a situation. This is reflected by variations in different therapists' emphases on situation factors versus acknowledging the importance of an individual's reciprocal interactions with his or her internal environment (e.g., previous history, cognitions, physiological proclivities) and the external situation. In general, behavioral therapists think that the degree of behavioral consistency is not nearly as stable as psychodynamic theories suggest and that stability is a description, not a cause of behavior.

**Ahistorical focus.** There is a focus on the individual's current functioning. Behavioral interventions address contemporary factors rather than historical ones. It is assumed that the critical factors involved in producing dysfunctional behaviors are not necessarily the same factors responsible for maintaining the behavior. For example, a child with autism may be taught to speak using operant methods (cf. Lovaas, 1987; Lovaas, Berberich, Perloff, & Schaeffer, 1991), but behavioral therapists would not claim that autism is caused by operant factors. This ahistorical focus and the belief that an individual's problems are subject to the same processes that influence normal behavior help attenuate the potential for problems to be viewed as manifestations of intrapsychic disease.

**An ideographic approach.** Traditionally, the emphasis in this model is on the prominent features of each individual case rather than on nosological labels. This individually centered approach applies to both assessment and treatment. The rationale for this ideographic approach is that overly general categories can obscure significant differences among individuals. From the perspective of assessment, behavioral therapists are more concerned with how an individual acts or behaves in a situation than with, for example, whether he or she has a diagnosis of bipolar disorder. Such labels are often of little value in correcting or remediating specific skill deficiencies. A diagnosis does not answer questions such as what behaviors are present, when, and where they are enacted. For instance, if an individual is described diagnostically as being depressed, one does not know if that means that the individual is socially isolated, does not make eye contact, does not groom, or does not go out in public or is irritable and angry, suicidal, or hopeless about the future and feels worthless about himself or herself. Thus, by using behavioral observations and criteria rather than broad nosological categories and inferences about a patient's symptoms, skill deficits can more directly be considered and assessed, and training can proceed more directly from the assessment.

From a treatment standpoint, the multitude of behavioral techniques and combinations thereof liberate the therapist from using an "all purpose, single method" therapy with every problem or type of patient (Bandura, 1969, p. 89). For example, whereas with a chronic hospitalized schizophrenic the therapist may set up a token economy to increase the patient's social contact on the unit, a less regressed schizophrenic may receive social skills training to foster more appropriate social interaction. Some enthusiastic proponents of the behavioral model assert that it is one of the most flexible and individualized forms of treatment (Hollander & Kazaoka, 1988). Recently, however, with the advent of descriptive, atheoretical, and measurable diagnostic categories (e.g., the *Diagnostic and Statistical Manual of Mental Disorders*, 3rd ed., rev.; American Psychiatric Association, 1987) and the development of well-specified treatment manuals, there is a growing interest in nomothetic treatment prescription to supplement the individualized approach.

## Behavioral Therapy in a Group Setting

The extent to which behavioral therapists focus on the unique properties of the group varies considerably from a lack of interest in these properties at one end of the continuum to a significant effort to mobilize them at the other. Those practitioners with the least interest in group factors can apply the same behavioral principles and technical interventions used in an individual format to the group context. Lazarus (1961), one of the earliest to apply behavioral principles to a group format, reflected this individual-therapy-in-a-group approach using systematic desensitization with a group of phobic individuals. The trend of applying behavioral interventions to groups of individuals can be seen in the extension of behavioral techniques such as assertion training or social skill training in inpatient groups (e.g., Field & Test, 1975; Magaro & West, 1983). This application often is motivated by the pragmatic effort to conserve resources (economic or personnel). These groups often do not use "group process" or patient–patient interactions to promote change, are generally more didactic, have a structured format, and have patients with homogeneous target problems and similar treatment goals.[4] Goals for these kinds of groups often center on issues of self-management and basic training (e.g., daily-living skills groups; Wallace, Boone, Foy, & Donahoe, 1985). There has been an expansion of procedures developed for the individual setting that can summarily be applied to the group context with little change in the basic technique required. Many have assumed that the behavioral group is essentially multiple individual therapy (i.e., a setting for application of individualized techniques) rather than a vehicle for promoting behavior modification (Shaffer & Galinski, 1989).

Those practitioners showing a keen interest in group factors view the group format as offering a unique structure and context that allows for the modification of behaviors that might not otherwise occur or at the very least would be difficult to change in an individual therapy context. Associated with this perspective is the importance of the "group setting" (i.e., group structure and group process) as a means for change (e.g., Rose, 1989). At the same time, this view pays homage to the essence of behavioral methodology. In this approach, group process is empirically defined as the changes over time in observable and measurable elements of the environment (including interaction of members with each other) that affect members' behaviors; it is assumed that these elements can be systematically structured to achieve

---

[4] Although the social skills group generally falls at this end of the continuum, some practitioners acknowledge the importance of particular group processes. For example, Liberman, DeRisi, and Mueser (1989) acknowledged the importance that cohesion has in enhancing symptom relief. They recognized the role that seasoned members play in providing credibility and expectations and enhancing motivation for new members. These researchers also valued the increased opportunity for observational learning.

modification in the individual group member's behaviors (Hollander & Kazaoka, 1988; Rose, 1989).[5]

## Learning Mechanisms and Group Psychotherapy

Because there is little agreement on a single conceptual framework for understanding and implementing the behavioral group approach, clinicians have applied, part-and-parcel, a variety of theoretical systems to understand the central aspects of behavioral group therapy; they have approached it mainly from an empirical and applied perspective (Hollander & Kazaoka, 1988). In this regard, behavioral group therapists view the treatment as a therapy implemented in or by a group that makes use of principles of learning as the core of its intervention strategies (Cohn & Mayerson, 1985). The operant conditioning approach is one of most well-known and straightforward methods for changing behavior. It is based on the notion that the frequency or intensity of a response will increase if it is followed by a reinforcing event and will decrease if is followed by no reinforcement or by punishment (Wixted et al., 1990). Desirable behaviors in the session can be reinforced by praise from the therapist or other members.

The classical conditioning approach is a more useful intervention when attempting to change maladaptive emotional reactions such as fear or anger. This method is based on the theoretical assumption that a negative emotional response is

---

[5] Liberman (1970) was one of the first to attempt to modify the group dynamics; by a series of selective prompts and reinforcements, he shaped and facilitated verbal behavior of individual members reflecting cohesiveness (e.g., statements of interest, concern, affection, and assistance). It is interesting that patients in this experimental group manifested earlier symptomatic improvement than did those in the comparison group, suggesting that improvement in a group attribute (e.g., cohesiveness) attenuates symptomatology without directly addressing it. Since then, a few others have made notable contributions to the study of group process (e.g., Upper & Ross, 1979) by exploring the role of cohesiveness and attraction (Falloon, 1981), studying the effect of patients' increased capacities to be empathic and remain in the here-and-now (Fromme & Smallwood, 1983), and attempting to understand the impact of types of therapist interventions on the group (Flowers & Booraem, 1990).

acquired when an originally neutral stimulus becomes associated with an unpleasant experience. Thus, when that originally neutral object is presented, it elicits the emotional response as if the original unpleasant experience were going to take place. Systematic desensitization is a technique that uses this notion of classical conditioning in its treatment of fear or anxiety. Wolpe (1958), in his theory of reciprocal inhibition, put forth the idea that if the feared stimulus (e.g., crowds of people) is paired either in vivo or in imagery with the opposite of fear, relaxation, the strength of the original conditioning process will gradually lessen and the emotional response will become extinguished (Wixted et al., 1990).

## Mechanisms of Change

Behavioral group therapists range in their views of the mechanisms responsible for change depending on whether they emphasize the nonmediational and mechanistic basis of behavior and change (e.g., Watson, Skinner) or believe in higher order constructs such as expectancies, cognitions, and symbolic processes (e.g., Bandura's social learning theory). In either case, the primary causal factors are the individual's transactions with the environment, rather than dispositions within individuals (Arkowitz & Hannah, 1989). Behavioral group therapists emphasize environmental determinants of behavior and their interactions with the individual's behavior. They predicate their interventions on the basis of the postulates of traditional learning theory and social learning theory. Learning theory posits that behavior is acquired or modified by information learned either from stimuli–stimuli associations (i.e., classical conditioning) or from the development of associations between stimuli–response connections and particular outcomes (i.e., operant conditioning). Social learning theory additionally suggests that learning may occur indirectly through vicarious or observational experiences as well as through direct behavioral experiences and that individual behavior (and change) is a result of ongoing reciprocal interactions between the environment and the individual's behavioral and cognitive processes (Bandura, 1977a, 1977b, 1978). This "reciprocal determinism"—the notion that individuals act on their en-

vironment, which in turn influences the individual in an interactive loop (Bandura, 1977a, 1977b, 1978)—crucially affects the
interventions of the behavioral group therapist. Learning and
change occur when new behaviors are acquired or when existing
responses are modified (Arkowitz & Hannah, 1989). The change
process is enhanced by the patient's engagement in a self-observation process (by way of self-monitoring). The importance
of the group context is that members provide one another with
both examples of new appropriate behaviors (vicarious learning)
and valued feedback and reinforcements.

Although many behavioral group therapists believe that cognitive change is important in therapeutic change, most view cognitive techniques alone (e.g., providing contradictory information) as less efficacious in facilitating change. Furthermore,
cognition is considered to be either isomorphic to behavioral
change (Skinner, 1974) or simply one part of the behavior–cognition–environment loop in which none of these components is
primary (Arkowitz & Hannah, 1989). In contrast to the cognitive–behavioral model, wherein cognitions are "causes" in
change, social learning theory posits that cognitions are mediators of change (Schwartz, 1982). Thus, behavioral group therapists are likely to endorse interventions that are performance
based rather than cognitively oriented.

Similarly, in behavioral therapy, affective arousal is viewed as
a phenomenon to be changed rather than a mediator of behavioral change as it is in the more psychoanalytically based models
(Arkowitz & Hannah, 1989). In fact, a basic assumption of the
behavioral models is that the subjective experience of an emotion
follows the acquisition of a targeted behavioral manifestation of
the emotion (Liberman et al., 1989). Although some feel that
change in behavior must be accompanied by affective arousal
(e.g., Arkowitz & Hannah, 1989), most proponents of the behavioral model believe that teaching the demonstrable and measurable behaviors of affective expression is a more efficient
means of making an emotional change than is focusing on internal feeling states (Liberman et al., 1989). In fact, there is evidence that the behavioral manifestations of one's ability to manage interpersonal exchange (i.e., one's social skills) is highly
correlated with aspects of intrapsychic functioning such as mo-

tivation, curiosity, and sense of humor (Bellack, Morrison, Wixted, & Mueser, 1990; Mueser, Bellack, Morrison, & Wixted, 1990). Thus, the emphasis remains in providing the patient with new behavioral experiences to modify behavior. Phenomenological changes (e.g., changes in self-esteem, sense of well-being) are assumed to follow changes in overt behavior inside and outside of the group.

## Goals of Treatment

Behavioral group therapy is most noted for the treatment of problems that involve troubled interactions with others. However, proponents of this model believe that most target symptoms amenable to individual behavioral therapy are equally suitable for treatment in the group setting (Hollander & Kazaoka, 1988). In fact, the group environment may be more desirable because even problems that apparently have little to do with social interaction (e.g., snake phobia) often have a social aspect to their maintenance that is likely to remain unnoticed or unaddressed in an individual therapeutic setting.

A central feature of this model is the major emphasis it places on the articulation of observable and measurable goals as conceptualized and agreed on by the patient and therapist (Hollander & Kazaoka, 1988). The goals are individual in nature in that they involve the acquisition or modification of a person's target behaviors. These identified behaviors can be of an individual nature as in the case of a foot fetish, panic attack, or suicidal behavior. Alternatively, identified goals can be interactional as in the case of an individual who is socially avoidant or is inappropriately aggressive. Thus, the target behaviors occur primarily in the context of others. The objective is to change the target behaviors outside the session where they naturally occur.

When the focus is on these individual goals, change is possible whether other members are present or not; the group simply provides the context for change. Although goals are most often individualized, the group setting permits and augments individual behavioral change in ways that are not possible in individual therapy. In addition to the potential for direct learning and experience, the group environment provides the possibility of vi-carious learning with the variety of social stimuli and behavioral repertoires available from other group members (Hollander & Kazaoka, 1988). The group facilitates progress toward individual goals by providing enhanced reinforcement options. Because the group setting is also somewhat sheltered, members can practice newly acquired or modified behaviors spontaneously in a na-turalistic setting without the negative consequences of failure and with continued feedback from members and the therapist; the high level of therapist control over the group process ensures that members respond to one another in approving rather than rejecting ways.

When the targeted behavior is more social or interactional in nature, the group setting has a number of advantages. The format allows the assessment of members' behaviors by "sampling" and monitoring behaviors inside group, which is not as possible in an individual context. That is, problem behaviors are enacted in the group setting so that the therapist and members have first-hand experience of observing the problem behaviors. As with the treatment of individual goals, the group provides abundant opportunities for members to learn and practice new target social behaviors in a safe environment in which they can obtain feed-back and reinforcement from the therapist and other members. The therapist's control over the therapeutic environment allows for members to try new behaviors or modify existing old ones in a setting in which the penalty for mistakes or misjudgments is attenuated. In addition, the presence of multiple individuals makes possible the learning of more flexible response patterns that enable patients to cope better with people in their environ-ment because each group member offers an idiosyncratic style of response as do people outside the group with whom patients will need to interact (Hollander & Kazaoka, 1988; Liberman et al., 1989).

To make best use of the group milieu, the therapist establishes goals that optimize appropriate participation of group members. Group process objectives such as cohesiveness or cooperation are established to aid individual group members in pursuing their goals rather than as ends in themselves; that is, although they are necessary for individual goal attainment, process objectives are not of primary importance (Sundel & Sundel, 1985).

## Technical Considerations

A survey of the burgeoning literature on groups that use behavioral methods reveals that the field defies an easy and parsimonious technical classification system for the varieties of groups. Several attempts have been made, each with a different emphasis. Groups have been differentiated by the number of behavioral techniques they use (single versus multiple) and the degree of homogeneity of target symptoms that members share (Flowers & Schwartz, 1985); the extent to which the behavioral techniques are integrated into the "group process" (Flowers, 1979); and the nature of goal pursued (individual versus interactional; Hollander & Kazaoka, 1988).

There is, however, considerable overlap in these classifications. In focusing on the applicability of this model to the inpatient setting, there are three particular types of groups that we believe deserve highlighting. The first type is groups in which the primary techniques for symptom amelioration are based on an operant or classical conditioning paradigm. The goal is to provide for the individual patient a skill or set of skills that enhances his or her ability to gain control over an identified troublesome behavior. Examples of this type of group are Ferguson's (1976) group for patients with eating disorders and Lazarus's (1961) group for patients with phobias. Ferguson focused on operant principles, attempting to modify behavior through an emphasis on the antecedent and consequent events that may control the presence of target symptoms. Lazarus used classical conditioning principles to reduce fears by teaching patients to systematically desensitize themselves. Each of these groups was homogeneous with respect to target symptoms. The group paradigm varied depending on the particular target goal. Because many inpatient settings do not allow for groups to be so narrowly circumscribed, we refer the reader to other texts for further discussion of these groups.

The second kind of group is one in which there is a great deal of technical eclecticism (Flowers & Schwartz, 1985; Gallagher, 1981; Lazarus, 1976; Rose, 1989). Unlike the first paradigm described, this kind of group involves no step-by-step program that is specified in advance; rather, it is based on methodological behaviorism as a philosophy and may include techniques such as Gestalt awareness exercises and even transference analysis (Hollander & Kazaoka, 1988). Groups can be homogeneous or heterogenous with respect to patient symptoms. What distinguishes this type of group from the other models presented in this book is its attempt to clearly delineate each individual's target problem in measurable and observable terms and to assess it formally before, during, and at the termination of the therapy group (i.e., to track it throughout the lifetime of the group). This approach seems to us to be most suitable for an outpatient setting given that some of the techniques used are more appropriate for healthier patients and require a cohesive group (see Rose, 1977, for the exception). It is for these reasons that we have chosen not to discuss this type of group in detail and invite the reader to seek further reading (Flowers, 1979; Rose, 1989).

The third type of group is the social skills training group. This type of group involves augmenting or modifying the behavioral repertoire (mostly in the domain of interpersonal exchange but also in the realm of practical life skills such as money management).

Because of space limitations, it is not possible in this section to review the technical considerations of each type of group. We have therefore chosen to concentrate in detail in the technical section and clinical illustration on the social skills training group, which we feel complements the other models presented in this book in expanding the therapeutic repertoire of the inpatient group therapist and has enormous potential and flexibility. Moreover, the social skills training model is highly accessible to the practitioner in terms of the skills required for successful application.

Social skills can be defined as those behaviors involved in the interpersonal exchange that enable an individual to fulfill social emotional needs and to achieve independent living in the community (Liberman, Mueser, & Wallace, 1986). There are many excellent skills training programs delineated in detail in various manuals. They have often been referred to as various programs: interpersonal skills training (Goldstein, Sprafkin, & Gershaw, 1976), personal effectiveness training (Liberman et al., 1986), social skills training (Liberman et al., 1989), assertion training (Lange & Jakubowski, 1976), heterosocial skills training (Curran, Wallander, & Farrell, 1985), life skills training (Gazda & Brooks, 1985), response acquisition training (McFall & Twentyman, 1973), replication therapy (Kanfer & Phillips, 1970), communications training, and training in activities of daily living (Baker, Brightman, Heifetz, & Murphy, 1978).[6]

## Selection and Composition

There are no contraindications for specific diagnostic groups. The social skills model has been used with patients with depression (Becker, Heimberg, & Bellack, 1987), acute psychiatric states (Christoff & Kelly, 1985; Monti & Kolko, 1985), posttraumatic stress disorder (Foy, Resnick, Carroll, & Osato, 1990), alcoholism, chronic schizophrenia and chronic psychosis (Benton & Schroeder, 1990; Gordon & Gordon, 1985; Wallace et al., 1985), problems of aggression and anger (Milan & Kolko, 1985), and eating disorders (Chiodo, 1990; Pillay & Crisp, 1981). It has been used with inpatients of all ages—children (Bornstein, Bellack, & Hersen, 1980; Ladd & Asher, 1985; Matson et al., 1980), adolescents (Kolko, Dorsett, & Milan, 1981), adults (Wallace et al., 1985), and elderly patients (Breckenridge, Thompson, Breckenridge, & Gallagher, 1985; Gambrill, 1985; Patterson, Eberly, Harrell, & Penner, 1983). One class of patients who may not be appropriate for this form of treatment are those with attentional difficulties such as those with serious short-term memory limitations, attention deficits, or high levels of agitation (Liberman et al., 1989).

---

[6] There is also a comprehensive skills training program (Austin, Liberman, King, & DeRisi, 1976; Spiegler & Agigian, 1977) that has been applied to more chronic populations and attempts to rehabilitate these patients educationally, behaviorally, and socially. This group uses a "school" model wherein patients attend classes.

When there is uncertainty about the appropriateness of a patient for group, the rule of thumb is to "experiment" by exposing the identified patient to social skills training.

Liberman et al. (1989) suggested that patients have the following capacities: (a) to be oriented, (b) to be able to use and understand simple sentences, (c) to be able to follow three-step instructions and be able to attend to another individual for 3–5 minutes without interrupting, and (d) to express a desire to improve expression of personal feelings. For some populations, such as chronically hospitalized patients, these requirements are too stringent and would preclude them. Wallace et al.'s (1985) guidelines provide more flexibility to include chronic patients. Wallace et al. required that patients not be "acutely ill" and that they have no obvious evidence of organic brain syndrome. However, social skills training can be successfully adapted to the treatment of psychiatric patients with mental retardation (Andrasik & Matson, 1985).

Patients are sometimes clustered into groups in which they have common goals such as improving conversational skills or developing recreational activities. There is an assumption that there is some homogeneity in terms of skill deficits. However, members do not need to be of the same level of functioning. For example, Wallace et al. (1985) required that group members have deficits in at least two areas of community living skills. Most social skills training is conducted with groups ranging in size from 4 to 8 members, although groups have been conducted with as many as 15 members (Liberman et al., 1989). However, very impaired patients require a higher staff to patient ratio (e.g., 1 therapist to 2 patients; Wallace et al., 1985).

## Group Parameters

Group sessions can be conducted for 30–90 minutes each and as infrequently as once a week or as frequently as seven times a week depending on the available time constraints. The shorter the length of the sessions, the more frequent the group should meet (Goldstein et al., 1976). Patients with chronic psychiatric illnesses (e.g., chronic schizophrenia, severe personality disorders) often require more intensive skills training because of the extent of their social and cognitive impairment. Sessions spaced too far apart allow for considerable forgetting. Closer spacing allows for more rapid acquisition and generalization of the skill and increases the durability of the skill (Liberman et al., 1989).

Groups can be open-ended (Douglas & Mueser, 1990; Liberman et al., 1989) or closed-ended (Goldstein et al., 1976; Monti & Kolko, 1985; Sundel & Sundel, 1985) depending on the circumstances of the setting. Groups can teach a series of specific skills such as that of Goldstein et al. (1976), who identified 37 specific skills to be taught and mastered in a closed-ended group, or groups can teach a circumscribed set of skills if the group is limited to a short-term hospital setting (e.g., Douglas & Mueser, 1990, focused on negotiation, compromise, and expression of negative feelings). Alternatively, the selection of specific skills can be tailored to each individual (Liberman et al., 1989).

## The Role of the Leader

Although it is possible to conduct the sessions with a single therapist, a co-therapy team is usually preferred, particularly when the number of patients is at the upper limit of the recommended range. When the recommended co-therapy team is used, at least one of the therapists should be an experienced leader in the social skills model. The second leader can be a co-therapist who is less experienced in the model but has some basic knowledge of clinical psychology and therapy. Co-therapy is preferred because it enables therapists to share the planning and distribution of the many duties required for the implementation of a very active set of techniques. It also enables them to conduct a more objective postmortem analysis of the sessions. The model provides a structure for two individuals with differing views and styles to work together (Flowers, 1979; Hollander & Kazaoka, 1988). An opposite-sex co-therapy team is preferred (Monti & Kolko, 1985). Usually the roles are clearly parceled, although the way in which they are delineated varies depending on the preferences of the therapists. One possible delineation is that one therapist be actively involved with presenting the content of the day's lesson while the other attends to the group dynamics, manages the process, and serves as a role-play partner, with a periodic switching of roles (Monti & Kolko, 1985; Sundel & Sundel, 1985). The co-therapist can also keep records, operate recording equipment, and write homework assignments (Hollander & Kazaoka, 1988; Liberman et al., 1989).

A therapeutic relationship that includes cooperation and collaboration is a necessary prerequisite for the behavioral model. However, the importance of the therapeutic relationship in the change process within the behavioral framework is varied. Some believe that relationship factors do not significantly affect the outcome of behavioral techniques (Arkowitz & Hannah, 1989). Others point to greater efficacy when therapy is implemented by a warm therapist than when it is conducted by an impersonal and unconcerned therapist (Morris & Suckerman, 1974).

Compared with other models, the social skills model places less emphasis on the value of the therapeutic relationship in the change process. Unlike in the more psychoanalytic-based models, the therapeutic relationship is not viewed as a major source or a main vehicle of therapeutic change. Rather, the therapeutic relationship serves to facilitate behavioral change; as a credible and authoritative source of information and education, the therapist is able to motivate members and provide a comfortable environment in which skills can be learned. In this vein, resistance and noncompliance are seen as synonymous and as something to be overcome to carry out the teaching of the behavioral techniques (Arkowitz & Hannah, 1989).

Therapists are most successful when they are expressive, active, lively, and even charismatic participants in the group. An enthusiastic therapist is particularly important for more chronic patients who lack spontaneity and affect. Liberman et al. (1989) likened the therapist to a theater director or an athletic coach. Specifically, therapists are encouraged to gesture broadly and speak with greater volume than usual, even if it seems overdone. In fact, Liberman et al. (1989) suggested that the therapist (or co-therapist if he or she is directing the action) remain standing throughout most of the session, moving freely about the room, unless otherwise required by the practice situation. The ambience should be somewhere "between an elementary school classroom and a revival meeting" (Liberman et al., 1989, p. 75), with plenty of good humor and positive reinforcement, including cheering and applause. Sessions should never be boring; a "boring" session is likely to be the result of too much talking and not enough action. The therapist deemphasizes "whys" and speculation on motives and emphasizes action and behavior. The group therapist closely monitors the group events. For example, during a role play, the therapist moves about the room to observe and direct the member and terminates the role play when (a) it is successfully completed, (b) the main theme gets lost in a myriad of details and irrelevancies, (c) there is too much material presented in a single role play so that the member is overwhelmed with too much information, or (d) the member begins to flounder for other reasons. This type of intervention is particularly important because members' practicing of ineffective responses may make later change even more difficult. Unlike other models in which the first step is the recapitulation of the identified problem within the session, social skills trainers feel that this practice may further ingrain ineffective behaviors.

The therapist makes emphatic efforts to provide a highly reinforcing and comfortable environment for members to learn new behaviors by having an upbeat attitude and providing an abundance of positive reinforcement. Inappropriate social behavior by the members is ignored if possible. For example, if a group member makes a critical comment to another group member, the therapist may ignore the remark and redirect the group's attention. Members are not confronted with their deficits. Rather, the therapist solicits, acknowledges, and socially reinforces constructive or adaptive behaviors by group members. There is little attempt to maintain therapeutic neutrality. In fact, Liberman et al. (1989) suggested that to improve the therapeutic alliance, particularly for lower functioning patients, therapists might provide snacks, use tokens and other rewards, let sessions go longer than the specified time, pat members on the back if it seems comfortable for the therapist and the member, and verbally acknowledge and even send cards on members' important days such as birthdays and anniversaries. With this more disabled group of patients, the therapist is more interested in establishing a comfortable and highly reinforcing environment so that the aversiveness of the training can be minimized; it is more important to reinforce members' earnest interests and efforts than their social skills, especially early in the training (Wallace et al., 1985).

In social skills training, the therapist's task is to teach members the social skills required to effectively communicate their needs and feelings to others in a socially acceptable and productive way. To accomplish this objective, the therapist might provide incentives for members to learn new behaviors, help members change environmental factors that maintain the behaviors, train or educate members in specific social skills, or teach members behavioral techniques that they can use themselves. Specifically, the therapist's role includes (a) assessing the member's strengths and weaknesses in specific skills; (b) developing with members specific short-term (and if applicable long-term) goals for the setting, then identifying and linking the target behaviors that require change to the desired goals; (c) chunking the identified target behaviors into concrete, measurable, and manageable units; (d) promoting positive expectations; (e) being a good role model who illustrates formally and informally appropriate behavior; (f) structuring role-play situations (e.g., building the specific scenes, assigning roles, engaging members in behavioral rehearsal); (g) articulating verbal and if possible visual instructions and prompts for attaining the target behaviors, reviewing the behaviors, and prompting and cuing the patients as often as necessary until they have successfully accomplished the behaviors; (h) encouraging a highly reinforcing setting by providing and soliciting from other group members concrete positive feedback for verbal and nonverbal behaviors and suggesting constructive alternatives for improving; (i) encouraging members to observe and evaluate their own performances and effectiveness in achieving the specified goals; (j) ignoring and cutting off inappropriate or interfering behavior; (k) assigning homework for between the therapy sessions that is functionally related to target behavior and has a good chance for success; (l) rewarding members for their efforts and successive approximations of the behavior; and (m) instilling the notion that practice for members is essential to incorporate the target behaviors into their behavioral repertoires (Liberman et al., 1989).

## Use of Audiovisual Aids

A blackboard or newsprint pad is important for identifying and tracking members' improvement in target behaviors. Wall posters of the day's lessons (steps of the skill), the overall format of the training, or paralinguistic behaviors to be evaluated provide important and useful reminders and allow for visual as well as auditory learning. Videotape can be used as a source of feedback, but with higher functioning patients, it should not be used as a main source because the giving of feedback serves a function for both the giver and receiver (Liberman et al., 1989). With a more chronic population, videotape feedback can serve a valuable function. Although members have more difficulty initially providing each other with feedback, with some prompting and multiple reviewing of the tape, members can often can provide suggestions for improvement (Wallace et al., 1985).

Additional aids during the training itself can be used, ranging from electronic devices to hand signals. Hand signals developed by Liberman et al. (1989) are useful for learning how to say something and add to the general level of activity while allowing the focus to continue to be on the role play rather than on the feedback. Homework assignments are written on 3 X 5 inch cards as a reminder to members.

## Assessment of Social Skills Deficits and Choice of Goals

Similar to an outpatient group, assessment in an inpatient setting occurs most often prior to group entry but always before training; it continues throughout the life of the group. The emphasis on continual assessment distinguishes this model from most models featured in this text. Unlike with the outpatient group, inpatient assessment is much more abbreviated because of the time frame and patient level of functioning. (For in-depth assessments, see Lazarus, 1976, and Flowers & Schwartz, 1985.)

As previously defined, social skills are those interpersonal behaviors that enable an individual to fulfill social–emotional needs and to achieve independent living in the community (Liberman et al., 1986). There are two types of social skills: instrumental skills and affiliative skills. Instrumental skills are work- and service-related social interchange skills that are needed to survive in the community. These are the skills that help an individual achieve independence and material goods such as money, a residence, a job, and goods and services. For example, members can focus on preparing for job interviews or better managing their own medication. Mastering salesperson–customer, doctor–patient, boss–worker relationships constitute further instrumental goals. Affiliative skills are those social–emotional skills that are used to form and maintain friendships and family relationships. These enable a person to enjoy intimacy, receive emotional support, display interpersonal warmth, and engage in reciprocal behaviors with those who are close. Giving and accepting criticism and expressing clearly positive and negative feelings are examples of affiliative skills. The primary goal in training of either type of skill is to improve the member's social competence, which is an important predictor in the course of psychiatric illness (see chapter 8 for a review of the relation of social competence to psychiatric illness). Each skill can be broken down for assessment and training purposes into three components: (a) receiving skills, also known as *social perception* (i.e., the capability to attend to and accurately perceive relevant social cues such as facial expression), which are not usually public behaviors; (b) processing skills (also referred to as *problem-solving skills*), which include the ability to evaluate the information received, identify long- and short-term goals, and plan a behavioral response that anticipates possible consequences; and (c) sending skills, which include the verbal, nonverbal, and paralinguistic behaviors displayed in the social interaction. Psychiatric inpatients can have deficits in one or all three areas.

Deficits can occur in one or more of the following components of a social skill: expressive features including speech content, paralinguistic elements (voice volume, pace, pitch, and tone), nonverbal behavior (interpersonal distance, hand gestures, body shifts and other kinesics, eye contact, and facial expression), and response timing; receptive features including attention, decoding, and knowledge of contextual factors and cultural values; certain life skills including assertiveness, heterosocial skills, and job interview skills; personal goals and values; and affects including anxiety, depression, and anger (Beidel, Bellack, Turner, Hersen, & Luber, 1981).

The focus among the many problem behaviors that a patient presents during the assessment must be sharply delimited. Flowers and Schwartz (1985) referred to this as "narrowing." Sending skills are usually taught before receiving and processing skills if deficits are present in all three domains (Douglas & Mueser, 1990). The more impaired the patient, the more likely he or she will require instruction in paralinguistic and verbal behavioral skills before being taught social perception and problem solving.

There are so many problems for which social skills training can be helpful that no list can be inclusive. Some examples of chronic problems are poor eye contact (infrequent, insufficient, or lengthy duration), little spontaneous speech, low voice volume, interrupting people, inappropriate sexual advances, inappropriately touching others, lengthy talk of delusions, incessant chatter, frequent complaining or unreasonable demands, and begging and badgering. All of these and any other displays of behaviors that are either self-defeating or unacceptable to most adults are suitable to work on.

In choosing the particular goals to work on, the therapist should consider a variety of criteria (Liberman et al., 1989). These goals should be specific, attainable (the first goal should be able to be obtained with ease to ensure continued interest), positive, and constructive (the addition or modification of current behavior rather than a removal of it, such as the acquisition of types of sentences that enable an individual to start a conversation rather than eliminating a psychotic patient's inappropriate laughter). The goals should center on high-frequency, functional behaviors that are likely to occur in the patient's everyday life, such as the ability to express positive feelings toward a spouse rather than toward the therapist. They should be consistent with the patient's cultural and familial values and responsibilities (e.g., teaching dating skills are appropriate only if it is with an age group and a culture that endorses dating). Finally, the goals should be ones that patients can choose and delineate with the help of the therapist to the extent that they are able.

Choosing which skills to teach may not always be so straightforward. Many programs teach a specific set of skills that staff believe are relevant to patients' deficits; however, the patients may not perceive these deficits to be relevant to their current needs. For example, teaching social skills to elderly patients has been a particular problem. An overall review of the studies done with geriatric patients in social skills training indicates that many interventions are flawed in ignoring patients' social and personal goals (Gambrill, 1985). One study cited by Gambrill (1985) found that elderly patients in their study were not concerned about skills like complimenting or requesting information but were very concerned about how to terminate a conversation with a talkative friend and telling a close friend that something is bothering them (Gambrill & Barth, 1982). Unlike other models presented in this book, in which goals can center around events or interactions that occur in the group, the behavioral model has as its primary focus and indicator of success members' functioning outside the group and hospital setting.

Within this model, training begins with a target area in which a successful outcome can readily be effected because a positive outcome is likely to increase the member's willingness to undertake more difficult relationships and situations. For members who experience intrusive, persistent, and chronic symptoms (e.g., severe depression, hallucinations), goals for the addition or modification of target behaviors are developed that have the potential to displace symptoms. The changes targeted can be activities in which members do not currently engage but did before becoming ill. Target behaviors also replace specific dysfunctional behaviors, such as helping a member develop listening skills to shift his or her focus from auditory hallucinations.

There are a number of available techniques for evaluating social skills. Questionnaires and interviews are the easiest but are the least reflective of actual deficits. There are structured assessments available for the group therapist to use to evaluate social behaviors such as the Response, Antecedents, Consequences, and Strength assessment, which can use response rates or duration data (Sundel & Sundel, 1985), the Rathus Assertiveness Schedule (Rathus, 1972), the Skills Inventory (Goldstein et al., 1976), the Semistructured Screening Form (Wallace et al., 1985), the Behavioral Checklist of Social and Independent Living Skills for more chronic patients (Wallace et al., 1985), and the Wolpe-Lazarus Assertiveness Schedule—Revised (Becker et al., 1987; Hersen et al., 1979). Self-report measures require an accurate observer and thus are most suitable for use with the higher functioning patient. Even when a paper-and-pencil assessment is used, further information is gathered by an interview focused on the specific deficient social transactions. Information elicited would include what kinds of difficulties occur, in what kinds of situations, how often, and with whom. The therapist obtains a detailed description of how difficulties arise and what each party did and said and whether the goals for the encounter were accomplished (Liberman et al., 1989).

Often, inpatients are not capable of this level of awareness. Fortunately, this step can be abbreviated or eliminated in favor of more direct observational assessment. One such method of observational assessment, referred to as the *naturalistic test*, is an in vivo evaluation of the social behavior with others. For example, a patient may be asked to make a request of a staff member, and the staff member may be instructed to make the situation mildly stressful by presenting the patient with some obstacles.

An alternative to the naturalistic test is the role-play assessment, in which the patient (either in the group or in an individual session) is presented with a simulated interpersonal situation and asked to respond to it. The Behavioral Assertiveness Test—Revised is a formalized assessment used to assess conversational skills by evaluating positive and negative assertions using a series of role-play scenes (Beidel et al., 1981). Becker et al. (1987) developed a standard 12-scene role-play assessment for use with depressed patients. The scenes are divided into scenes requiring positive or negative assertions, a more or less familiar interaction partner, and male versus females partners.

The disadvantage of the role-play assessment is that because it is more remote from real life, it produces less anxiety than would the real situation. The particular role-play assessment is dependent on the nature of the inpatient setting and the patient's level of functioning, such as whether an individual is hospitalized for a suicide attempt in a short-term facility after being demoted in a job or whether the individual has spent 5 years in a state hospital. For the former, a role-play may be developed around making inquiries into the reasons for demotion. For the latter, a role play may be developed for being annoyed by another patient who is playing the radio too loudly. Social skills evaluation should be macroscopic enough to indicate whether the behavior occurred and whether it was appropriate but microscopic enough to indicate paralinguistic assessment (e.g., eye contact, body posture, distance and physical contact, facial expressions, and voice inflection) and verbal assessment (e.g., latency of response, appropriateness of language, ability to perceive accurately the other person, evidence of appropriate problem solving, and amount of speech and content of response; Liberman et al., 1989). These assessments can then be used for comparison in a later session. In a large hospital, they can be valuable in assigning patients to groups with individuals having similar deficits. Role-play tests and naturalistic tests require more time and effort but more closely approximate the real-life situation than do interviews. Assessments can also be made by examining the tangible products of social life (e.g., a grocery store receipt indicates that an individual is able to manage a grocery shopping task). Nurses or reliable relatives can also be enlisted to assess the patient in vivo and report to the group therapist. This is perhaps the most cumbersome method of assessment but yields the most accurate information.

In some chronic care facilities, there are patients for whom much more basic social skills training is required. It may be necessary to involve them in a more basic group such as one that might practice appropriate eye contact, approaching an individual, where to stand, and knowing how to begin, maintain, and end a conversation. Although it is possible to combine patients lacking these skills with higher functioning patients in a group, it is best if they are treated in a separate, slightly smaller group such as the one described by Wallace et al. (1985) or given discrete trials (Massel, Corrigan, Liberman, & Milan, 1991).

After therapists have assessed the patient's skills, patients themselves must be helped to identify goals that they agree require attention. This appraisal can be done either informally or formally with an instrument such as the Striving Scale (Wallace et al., 1985). This scale requires patients to anchor the scale with descriptions of their imagined best and worst life and place themselves using a 10-point scale on the scale currently, 5 years ago, and 5 years in the future.

## Preparation

Although the evidence to support the efficacy of group preparation is equivocal (Cohn & Mayerson, 1985), preparation for the group experience is likely to result in more effective and efficient learning. Preparation should communicate a rationale for group treatment; provide instruction on appropriate patient behaviors (e.g., homework, giving constructive feedback, sharing personal information, behaving rather than talking, and the importance of observing and imitating others); and help the patient develop positive expectations about the effect that the group experience will have on his or her behavior by, for example, citing positive research findings (Cohn & Mayerson, 1985; Sundel & Sundel, 1985).

Supplemental handouts describing various aspects of the group are often distributed to new patients. This is particularly important for more chronic patients because they are less likely to retain information presented in the preparation session than are healthier patients. Liberman et al. (1989) offered a sample preparatory handout for a high-functioning inpatient population. Beidel et al. (1981) distributed a more extensive manual to all incoming members that included each of the skills to be taught and the steps to perform the skills, as well as a sample homework sheet.

If the therapist thinks that the patient may have some difficulty in attending the session, a contract can be written to include the requirements for the patient (i.e., attendance) and the rights and privileges that may be gained by fulfilling these requirements (e.g., being able to watch a favorite TV program or coupons to use at the canteen for snacks). If it appears that the patient might be resistant to participating in the sessions, it is important for the therapist to address this prior to group: this can be done by articulating and labeling the patient's concerns, giving positive reinforcement for what the patient is able to do (e.g., attend the preparatory session, indicate a wish to get help), or predicting that the individual may experience reluctance to participate (Liberman et al., 1989). The patient also can be allowed not to actively participate in the role plays for the first one or two sessions, with gradually increasing participation by having them give feedback to others, then gradually working them into others' role-play scenes, initially in nonspeaking parts and then in speaking parts.

## Training

Assessment continues throughout the training process. Groups are often thematically organized to teach certain skills such as conversational skills, expressing positive and negative emotions, self-care and skills for community living such as money management, job interviewing skills, dating and friendship skills, anger management, stress management, medication management, and symptom self-management. Once the goals are chosen and the role-play assessment is completed, the essential features of the training are behavioral rehearsal, modeling, constructive feedback from the therapist and fellow group members, self-evaluation, and repeated practice (in the session and through homework).

## Format of the Session

The format varies somewhat depending on whether the group has an open-ended membership and on whether a specific skill is being taught in a series. It also depends on the level of skill deficit. The following is a general summary of the steps; the order, however, may vary depending on group parameters and therapist preferences.

**Introductions.** In an open-ended group, sessions begin with an introduction of new members. A brief description of the goals and methods (both procedure and content) of the group is presented. When possible, this information should be communicated to the new members by the seasoned members of the group. At a minimum, this should include the importance of practice and rehearsal of verbal and nonverbal behaviors, both in the session and for homework. It can also include the importance of developing alternatives to coping and of expressing feelings and thoughts to others in an appropriate fashion. As with all steps, any contributions made by members should be amply rewarded with verbal praise. The therapist fills in any required information not mentioned by members. Members' participation in the orientation increases their sense of responsibility for the group as well as creates for the new members realistic but positive expectations of what the group can do. In an ongoing group, in which most members return, the next step is to check homework assignments and formulate goals. If the group is a series of discrete modules designed to teach specific new skills every few sessions, then this next step is skipped and the new skills are introduced (see the following section).

**Checking homework assignments and formulating session goals.** Checking homework assignments and formulating goals can be done as two separate steps, or these activities can be handled together in one go-around. If the homework report is a separate step, groups with more chronic patients should role play their assignments rather than just have members report about them because such members are often not accurate observers of their own performance. Specific details are requested (e.g., if a member says that an "assignment got all messed up," the therapist needs to find out in what way, at what point, and what else was going on). The success or failure of the homework assignment will influence the goals and situations chosen to address at that particular session. For example, suppose a member was given the assignment of inviting another patient to take a walk. If that member reported that he or she was able to approach and greet the chosen patient but not suggest that they take a walk together, that specific scene might be role played in the session. Members are praised for completing homework regardless of the outcome. At the discretion of the therapist, sometimes members who fail to complete their homework may be asked to perform the assignment in the session. Some therapists have advocated that feedback and an additional role play be done with each member before continuing on to the next person

(K. T. Mueser, personal communication, July 21, 1992). Multiple role plays are particularly important for more chronic individuals.

**Teaching a new skill.** If the group is an ongoing one and no new skills are being taught, the next two steps (teaching a skill and the "dry run") may be skipped. The particular skill taught and the level at which it is presented depends on the level of functioning of the group members. For example, a group of chronic schizophrenics at a state hospital may need to learn how to begin a conversation by first working on eye contact, interpersonal distance, or the different types of greetings. A group of higher functioning depressives may be helped by focusing on generating a variety of topics with which to begin conversations. When teaching a new skill, the therapist presents a brief rationale. This is often in conjunction with some discussion initiated by the therapist. For example, when expressing negative feelings is taught, the therapist first has members identify different negative emotions and then solicits members' speculations about difficulties connected with not being able to express these feelings in an acceptable manner (Douglas & Mueser, 1990). A second example concerns teaching appropriate assertiveness behavior. Members first learn the difference between assertion and aggression and between nonassertion and politeness. They then learn about one's own rights and the rights of others (Lange & Jakubowski, 1976).

After the rationale is presented, clear, concrete, and brief instructions are presented for performing the response; each step of the skill is presented and discussed. When sending skills are taught, specific verbal and nonverbal behaviors can be taught (e.g., when you begin a conversation, make eye contact, stand at an appropriate distance, and give a greeting). When receiving skills are taught, questions that get the individual to think about what the other is thinking and feeling are important (e.g., "Exactly what did George say?", "What do you think George was thinking when he asked you to make up your mind?", "What was he feeling?"). Receiving skills can also involve teaching the "dynamics" of social behavior (Becker et al., 1987); if this is the skill being taught, the initial focus is on learning to detect "floor shifts" (i.e., signals that a person is about to end a message) and topic changes (shifting from one topic to another). Processing skills include having the patient state short- and long-term goals, generate possible alternative strategies, and predict long- and short-term consequences of each of the strategies (e.g., "In the short run, what did you want to accomplish?", "If you gave your boss a piece of your mind, what do you think would happen immediately?", "How do you think that would affect your over-all relationship?", "Are there other alternatives?", "Which ones would help you reach your goal?", "What was your long-term goal?"). However, instructions alone are not sufficient (Jaffe & Carlson, 1976). The skill needs to be modeled by the therapist or by another who is competent in the skill.

There are programs and manuals that identify specific skills to be taught in a group setting. A few examples are the independent living skills program (Wallace et. al., 1985), the structured learning program (Goldstein, Gershaw, & Sprafkin, 1985; Goldstein et al., 1976), the conversational skills program (Monti & Kolko, 1985), attention focusing (Liberman, Massel, Mosk, & Wong, 1985), and social skills for schizophrenics (Beidel et al., 1981) and for depressives (Becker, 1990; Becker et al., 1987). For any of the programs, when new skills are being taught, the therapist must have some criteria for their successful acquisition. For example, Wallace et al. (1985) moved on to the next module when all members had successfully performed all of the behaviors identified in the role play on two successive trials. Beidel et al. (1981) made the criterion that of three flawless performances.

**Behavioral rehearsal.** In this step, also called the *dry run*, each member role plays, receives feedback, attempts the role play again, and receives more feedback. If a new skill is being taught, the therapist aids each member in setting up the role-play scene involving the particular targeted goal. If the group has completed homework and goal formulation only through a verbal mode and no new skill is being taught, this step is next. If two role plays with feedback are done in the initial go-around, then this step and the next (*constructive feedback*) may be skipped. To the extent that members are able, they should participate in delineating and designing the role-play scene. The therapist should begin with the most seasoned and enthusiastic members of the group. Role-play time varies but should not be longer than 5 minutes for higher functioning patients and not longer than 2 minutes for chronically ill patients (K. T. Mueser, personal communication, July 21, 1992). The guidelines for this role play are similar to the ones for role play in the assessment phase. It is even more important in this phase that efforts be made to have group members who resemble the individual with whom the patient has difficulty be active in the role play. As many props as necessary are important to make the scenario realistic. In some settings, the first rehearsal is done with minimal coaching, particularly when no role-play assessment has been conducted; this enables the therapist to assess the member's skill level (Liberman et al., 1989). The dry run can also be used as an initial assessment tool for those groups in which rapid turnover exists. Before beginning the role play, it is important to solicit members' awareness of both the short- and long-term goals and the effects of the situation rehearsed. For example, if a member wants to learn to ask a boss for time off from work, care must be taken to encourage the development and maintenance of a collaborative, trusting working relationship (the long-term goal). The therapist and the members collaborate in giving stage directions and cues to the actors. During the initial rehearsal, the therapist must be acutely aware of both the verbal, nonverbal, and paralinguistic elements of the members' behaviors. The therapist stops the action when enough information is gleaned from the role play to provide useful feedback. Scenes that are rehearsed should contain the basic principles of learning: positive reinforcement of specific behaviors, believable models to demonstrate effective behaviors, small incremental goals to shape effective behavior, and selective inattention for inappropriate behaviors in an effort to extinguish them.

A series of situations should be developed, each slightly more difficult for the member to handle than the previous one. It is important that the member first experience some initial success so that he or she is encouraged to continue working on the response. The therapist must elicit the who, what, when, where, how, and how often of the scene in attempting to select a recent situation or one that is likely to occur in the near future (Flowers & Schwartz, 1985). The emphasis is on expediency—role play the scene, finish, comment on it, and do it again: "Specifics, action, and repetition are the soul of learning" (Liberman et al., 1989, p. 61). The objective is to get the member to provide enough specific information and behaviors to make the role play real but not to get bogged down with irrelevant or redundant details. The more that behavioral rehearsal is similar to real life, the more likely it will be to generalize to the real world. For example, if a member has trouble with his 60-year-old mother, a surrogate in the role play that resembles his mother (e.g., is older, is dominating) is helpful. Surrogates can volunteer, but it is likely to be less anxiety provoking and faster if the therapist makes the choice. When a specific other person is not the target of the behavior and time is available, the role play can be replayed a number of different times with different actors; by having the member react to different kinds of people, an interpersonal flexibility is fostered and a broader behavioral repertoire is possible.

Occasionally, members refuse to participate in a role play. When this happens, it may be best not to confront the member but allow him or her not to role play and set the expectation that he or she will engage in it in the future.

**Constructive feedback.** The therapist uses every available opportunity to provide realistic praise to the member. Positive feedback is also encouraged from other members. If members have more serious deficits in social skills, it may be necessary for the therapist to request feedback about specific things (e.g., rather than "What was positive about the way he handled that situation?" the request may need to be more focused: "How has his voice tone improved from last time?").

If the member's sending skills have improved to an appropriate level, the therapist then helps him or her evaluate the accuracy of his or her perceptions (receiving skills). In the clinical illustration that follows, note how the therapist periodically checks on the members' receiving and processing skills throughout the session. In the absence of major perceptual distortions, the therapist proceeds to problem-solving techniques for generation and evaluation of the options and strategies for achieving the best option (Liberman et al., 1989). With higher functioning patients, the therapist might then invite the member to comment on how another member's response or action might be more effective; constructive comments that members make are acknowledged. Criticisms are reformulated in a constructive manner. With more severely disturbed patients, feedback from other members is usually coached by the therapist in terms of making a "good" performance better. Feedback encourages the members to be active parts of the group even when they are not directly involved in the action. The number of comments that a member can successfully incorporate is related to his or her level of functioning. More chronically impaired patients can only incorporate one or two suggestions. If the member receives more comments than he or she is likely to be able to assimilate, the leader directs the member as to the particular ones to which to attend. Off-topic statements, noncooperative statements, and hostile or negative statements are handled by ignoring them when possible.

**Modeling.** After the member has been exposed verbally to the suggestions and corrections, he or she is ready to see a model that incorporates the comments. Modeling is particularly essential for improving the performance of schizophrenics but may be unnecessary for nonpsychotic patients (Eisler, Blanchard, Fitts, & Williams, 1978). The model can be live (involving therapists or other members), or it can be videotaped (e.g., Wallace et al., 1985). The more disabled the patient, the more likely it is that the co-therapist will find it necessary to model. If patients are higher functioning, it is important to choose a person to model who is actually capable of effectively peforming the skill, preferably someone who has some similarity to the member and his or her manner of responding. The member who is learning the behavior is coached on what to focus attention before the model begins. The therapist requests lower functioning patients to repeat back what they are to observe. The therapist not performing in the role play can provide commentary on the different aspects of the behavior being performed. After modeling has been completed, the therapist requests the member to articulate what she or he saw; this better ensures that the member has understood and observed the demonstrated behaviors. If the member being simulated is likely to be unpredictable or more difficult, the modeling step can be repeated with a target person who is instructed to provide greater resistance to the model.

One advantage of a videotaped demonstration is that it can be stopped at various points along the way and then replayed in its entirety. For the individual with more severe social deficits, a tape can be periodically stopped to allow assessment of whether he or she has comprehended the information being presented. Some examples of questions that the therapist may ask in this situation are "Who was in the scene?", "What was his goal when he started talking?", "How was his voice tone, posture?", "Do you think that he asked the question about salary in an appropriate manner?" When the member responds incorrectly, the tape is replayed until he or she can correctly identify the information being taught (Wallace et al., 1985).

**Behavioral rehearsal with coaching.** The patient then practices the same scene again to determine if he or she has acquired the skill. This is an extremely important step. In fact, there is evidence that improvement in social skills is more closely linked to the number of role plays in which a member participates than the number of sessions that a member attends (Douglas & Mueser, 1990). Details and props make the role play more realistic and foster generalization to real life. If the member has very impaired social skills, it may be important for the leader to play the surrogate in the role play and for the member's attention to be focused on only one aspect of the skill. It is better to minimize the requirements than to expect patients to assimilate several suggestions. Higher functioning patients are likely to improve on several aspects even if their attention is directed to only one aspect at a time. If the member does not improve sufficiently, more active coaching with hand signals may be necessary; this involves positive "on-line" feedback during the role play from the therapist (e.g., "Good eye contact", "Just the right distance"). After the therapist has terminated the role play, specific positive feedback is again solicited from other group members (always including the target member) and the member performing the behavior (e.g., "What were you able to do this time that enabled you to accomplish your goal?"). The self-evaluation is an important step mainly in programs that treat depressed or higher functioning patients (e.g., Becker et al., 1987), whereas it is used much less frequently with more severely impaired patients (e.g., Douglas & Mueser, 1990). Self-evaluation involves having the individual describe himself or herself as competent, with the belief that feelings of effectiveness will follow.

Techniques have been developed to help the therapist to respond to the special problems that may arise at this stage. When some individuals in the group seem to acquire a particular skill quicker than others, the formation of informal subgroups may be necessary, with one group concentrating on acquiring the minimum acceptable response while the other group concentrates on scene variation, uncooperative others, or other exceptions (Beidel et al., 1981). If the member is reluctant to engage in the rehearsal step, the therapist can "double" for the member. The member can then repeat exactly what the therapist has said. The therapist can also play the part of the member and have the member make comments or elaborations on the behavior of the therapist. This latter technique encourages patient involvement and allows vicarious learning to occur without overwhelming anxiety. Before beginning the role play with more chronic patients, it is important to have members clarify roles, goals, what is to happen, and what they are watching. For example, questions from the therapist like "What is your role, Arthur, in this scene?", "What is my role?", and "What are you going to be doing in the scene?" ensure that members understand the task. If skills are being taught in a closed-ended group in which members need to complete training of one skill before beginning another, it may be necessary to supplement the group sessions with individual ones when a single individual appears not to be able to master skills that the others have (Beidel et al., 1981).[7]

---

[7] A relatively new procedure has been developed for use with very chronic psychiatric patients, referred to as the *attention-focusing procedure* (Massel, Corrigan, Liberman, & Milan, 1991; Wong & Woosley, 1989). This consists of repeated practicing until the skill is successfully achieved, three levels of prompts if responses are incorrect ("You can make a positive statement to Marion", "One positive statement you can make is, I like your red hat"), and the consistent use of verbal reinforcement as well as primary reinforcers (e.g., soda and food). Thus, there are a greater number of prompts, reinforcement, and modeling and a smaller number of repeated discrete trials. This procedure is a staff-intensive one given that each patient is paired with both a leader and a surrogate.

**Assignment of homework.** Assignments in the real world help increase the possibility of transfer of learning and overcome the problem of generalization (i.e., performing the behavior in a protected environment in which only positive feedback and constructive comments are permitted is considerably different from real life). Falloon and colleagues have shown that completing daily social homework assignments improves outcome (Falloon, 1981; Falloon, Lindley, McDonald, & Marks, 1977). For assignments to have the best chance of success, it is important for the co-therapist to complete an assignment card for each member that gives clear, simple, detailed instructions. The card is given to the member, who carries it about as a reminder to complete the task before the next group convenes.

Assignments are gradually adjusted to increasing levels of difficulty as the member develops skills and confidence. They should directly follow from the training. For example, if the member has practiced making a request of another patient such as turning down his or her radio, the homework assignment should focus on making the same or similar request of someone else on the unit. To increase the likelihood of success of homework, the specific assignment should be one in which some proficiency has been achieved in the session and that includes guidelines about where, when, and with whom to try the new skill (Becker et al., 1987). About 60–90% of the assignments should be completed successfully (Liberman et al., 1989). Once the assignment has been designed, the member is encouraged to consider whether the assignment is relevant and realistic and should be given the option to turn it down for another one or defer it until more practice occurs. The member is encouraged to think about the potential obstacles to its completion; this process increases the likelihood of success. However, the member should also be prepared for the possibility of failure. In more chronic patients, it becomes critical to involve nursing staff in the selection, monitoring, and carrying out of assignments given that chronic patients often are more damaged by failure and are less likely to carry out an assignment if not encouraged by staff. It is not necessary to provide different assignments each time because repeated assignments can increase the member's sense of effectiveness. With a very chronic population, it has been suggested that twice-daily homework assignments, with intermittent staff prompts, increases the acquisition and generalization of the social skill (Wong et al., in press).

**The next member.** This first member has now completed what he or she might do on this day. The initial rehearsal step is begun with a new patient and proceeds in the manner previously described. It is best if all members have the opportunity to engage in two to four role-play experiences during every group (K. T. Mueser, personal communication, July 21, 1992).

**Evaluation and generalization.** Success is based primarily on specified, measurable, and objective criterion (e.g., being able to complete the role play with all of the behaviors performed appropriately). Success can also be measured by self-evaluation forms, although these are less desirable given that members are often unable to make accurate judgments about their performance. Monitoring of progress can be accomplished by self-report (e.g., Social Skills Distress Scale or a diary), observation by others (family or nursing staff), and permanent products (e.g., pay stub to indicate success at negotiating a job interview). Self-monitoring can help a member be more aware of his or her new skills.

Behavioral therapists have become increasingly concerned about the generalizability of learned skills to real life (Koegel & Rincover, 1977). Social skills training attempts to incorporate those techniques that enhance the transfer of learning. Overlearning by repeated practice aids in this transfer. Transfer is least likely to occur when a second skill is begun before a first is mastered (Goldstein et al., 1976). Goldstein et al. (1985) emphasized the importance of transfer of skills from the learning setting to real life by making the role playing representative and realistic of the problem by using physical props and co-actors similar to the figures of interpersonal strife that the member would encounter in real life and by having members do homework (in vivo practice). In addition, multiple exemplars and trainers are provided by rotating leaders and having the member repeat the role-play scene with multiple actors and then multiple scenes (Goldstein et al., 1985). Monti and Kolko (1985) used adjunct role players to promote transfer of learning; other individuals (preferably therapists in training) attended after the third session for the purpose of providing new and different people with whom members can practice. Reinforcement and prompting the newly learned skills in the natural environment (e.g., with nursing staff, relatives of patients) optimally aid in the generalization of these skills to the member's daily life. Decreasing of training structure, supervision, and reinforcement when the skill is acquired and encouraging the member to use self-reinforcement also aid in helping the member generalize the new skills to real life (Liberman et al., 1989). Goldstein et al. (1985) reported that with these techniques, skill transfer occurred in approximately 50% of their structured learning therapy.[8]

# Clinical Illustration

## Group Members

Tony was a 45-year-old chronic schizophrenic who had been hospitalized a dozen times since he was 22 years old. When he was not hospitalized, he lived in a rooming house, leaving his room only once every 2 weeks to grocery shop; he bought cans of food with his caseworker, which he kept on the radiator and ate without heating. When the caseworker was on vacation for 3 weeks, he did not go out. He also went monthly to the local community mental health center to get medication. He never attended the day program and appeared almost mute. He had no family in the area and rarely spoke with anyone, inside or outside the hospital.

The long-term task was to increase the quantity and quality of Tony's social interactions. To do this, Tony's overall social skills needed improvement. When Tony first entered the hospital, he began with one of the group therapists an intensive individual social skills program to improve the basic building blocks of

---

[8] Interestingly, group therapists are encouraged, like their patients, to evaluate their competence in teaching social skills. Liberman et al. (1989) provided a formal assessment technique for such an evaluation. Therapists are encouraged to evaluate skills that they perform, to identify those that need practice, and to reward themselves as they improve.

social skills (similar to the treatment in Liberman et al., 1984; Liberman et al., 1985); it was felt that a group would be too overwhelming and that he would not be responsive to traditional social skills training. In the first 9 months of the program, he learned how to approach people and make a greeting and make basic requests for assistance. Three months ago, he joined the group. For the first month, he continued his individual training and was gradually integrated into the group, first by watching, then by providing feedback to other members, then by participating as a confederate in other members' role plays, and finally by rehearsing the behaviors himself in a role play in the group. Quite by accident, the group leaders discovered that he had an interest in Parchesi, a game that patients often played on the unit. Tony agreed that he would like to be able to play the game with others. Tony worked in the group on learning how to initiate conversation by greeting and then on learning how to make a positive request to others. With his homework assignments, it was first necessary to have staff prompt him on the unit to make a greeting; later he seemed to be able to make the greeting without a prompt.

WillieMae was 56-year-old woman with a 30-year history of hearing voices. She had had a longstanding delusion that a homing radio had been implanted in her head. This began after she had received a course of electroconvulsive shock therapy 25 years ago. She frequently mumbled and laughed to herself in a way that made others avoid her, particularly people in her boarding house. Her community caseworker felt that one of the reasons for her frequent hospitalizations was that she would experience some difficulty, would gradually deteriorate, and would be unable to use the supports that were already in existence for her (i.e., the caseworker and her outpatient psychiatrist). She then would become more psychotic and act more inappropriately. It would then be several months before she could return to the community. She refused to go to a day program.

In assessing her social skills, WillieMae had good eye contact and a nice smile, was able to appropriately respond to others' greetings in passing but rarely made spontaneous remarks and did not appear to initiate any conversations on the unit. Reports of unit and boarding house behavior indicated that occasionally when she did not get what she desired, such as watching a particular TV show, she became loud and angry, cursing and threatening others. On further assessment, it seemed that although she was able to start an appropriate response to others' questions and requests, she would then have bursts of laughter and begin to refer to some aspect of her delusions. The therapists concluded that in response to her several areas of deficiency in social skills, goals that could be addressed included improving her ability to initiate conversation and to answer questions and respond to others without wandering off into delusional material. Another was to decrease her inappropriate laughter by ignoring it and replacing it with an alternative skill that was incompatible with it, namely, active listening (e.g., "uh-huh" and restatement of what others said). WillieMae had been working in the group for about 4 weeks and had been able to learn to initiate conversations and had developed a small but appropriate repertoire of things about which she could converse. She learned how to call her caseworker and talk to her about feeling poorly. What was apparent in all her interactions was that although her skills had improved remarkably, she had not yet learned how to listen to what others said. The therapists judged that it was now time to work on her listening skills by teaching her active listening.

Gina was a 32-year-old woman who had been making deep cuts in her arms and legs since age 12. She also experienced transient psychotic episodes. The staff suspected that she may have multiple personalities, although she did not appear to refer to the different aspects of her presentations by different names and each "personality" did not seem quite discrete enough to warrant a multiple personality disorder diagnosis. She had been transferred from an acute care facility because of her continued risk of suicide, lack of appropriate placement and lack of consistently adequate reality testing. She had been in and out of hospitals since she began cutting herself and had been in the hospital this time for approximately 2 weeks. Her interpersonal style vacillated between whiny behavior and irritability, with verbally and physically aggressive assaultive behavior. Sometimes she sobbed hysterically in public. When she was angry she would often impulsively cut herself or throw things at people and threaten them. She intimidated others because of her unpredictability and often made them fear for their physical safety.

In assessment of her interpersonal skills, the group therapists felt that she had two short-term goals on which she could work. The first was to be able to be appropriately assertive, that is, to stand up for her personal rights and to express her positive and negative feelings to others; specifically, she would work on developing the ability to make positive and negative assertions. The second goal concerned her frequent perception that others were transgressing against her as a result of her misperceptions of what they were saying or their intentions. The second goal was thus for her to learn skills that would enable her to perceive others more accurately. She initially was somewhat resistant to attending the group. However, she wished to get a job and reside in her own place when she left the hospital. Although she was able to obtain jobs, she always lost them within a short period of time, usually because of an altercation with a co-worker or boss. Even though she was unable to acknowledge that these disputes were the result of her doing, she agreed that she would work on improving her skills of tolerating others' faults so that she could retain a job. At the time this group took place, she had only been in the hospital 2 weeks and was still working on the first goal. She had acquired the skill of saying no and had been working on expressing complaints in her homework assignment.

John, a new group member, was a tall, borderline mentally retarded, chronic schizophrenic man who lived in a group home. When left alone, he would follow grade-school girls and try to touch and caress them in the same way he would with his stuffed animals. If the girls became frightened and would try to run away, he would pursue them without regard to their requests to stay away, most likely attempting to fulfill his own dependency needs. Although he was relatively harmless, he was admitted to the hospital because the community became frightened of his actions and organized petitions for his commitment.

The assessment of John's social skills indicated that he was not afraid of others but needed to further develop a repertoire of appropriate behaviors and to perceive more accurately others' levels of comfort with his behavior. The treatment goals in group for him were (a) to learn to appropriately approach and greet individuals, (b) to learn when to begin and end a conversation, (c) to learn to make verbal requests when appropriate, (d) to listen to others' responses, and (e) to respond appropriately to others' wishes.

## The Session

This group took place in a state hospital setting. The group met daily on the unit for 35–40 minutes. (When members have less severe symptoms, the meeting may be longer—up to 90 minutes.) As each member developed goals and specific skills to be worked on, a poster was used to identify the steps of the skill. Another poster that contained the nonverbal and paralinguistic skills was a permanent wall fixture.[9]

> Therapist:   Since we have a new member, let's start by in-
>              troducing him.

Members introduce themselves and indicate how long they have been in group.

> Therapist:   Let's begin with talking about the goals of the
>              social skills group. (silence) WillieMae, what can
>              you tell John about our group?

(In a higher functioning group, the group would begin by discussing the goals, rules, and operating procedures of the group. A seasoned member may be able to speak about the purpose of the social skills group. When there is no member who is able to do this, it becomes the therapist's responsibility.)

> WillieMae:   (laughs) I did my homework (holding out an as-
>              signment card, which had her assignment on it.
>              She laughs again loudly).

---

[9] The paralinguistic and nonverbal skills poster lists the following: eye contact, body posture, distance and physical contact, gestures, facial expressions, voice volume, voice inflection, and latency of speaking.

| | |
|---|---|
| Therapist: | Good, WillieMae, and we will get to that in a moment. But you told John about an important part of our group. We leave with a homework assignment every day. We have an assigned job that we do before the next time we meet. The more you can practice with other people, the better you will become at the skill and it will be easier too. First, we try out new skills in here. We get some help from the other group members, then we do homework. When you practice out there its more like real life. |
| WillieMae: | Safe (laughs). |
| Therapist: | Yes WillieMae, good thought. It is safer here. What else can we tell John about the way our group works? (silence) |
| Gina: | Geez Louise (with exasperation). Why don't you just tell him. It's such a waste of time to have these people try to struggle through this. It will take the whole group time. And if that's all we're going to do, I'm out of here. It's just too boring. |
| Therapist: | It sounds like you are excited to get started, Gina. Before we do that, we should tell John that what you just illustrated by your request is exactly the kind of thing that we are working on in here. You have been working on making requests of people in a way that they can hear you and respond to you. And that one was a pretty good request. Maybe the group can look at that a little later when we role play with you. But first we need to explain to John what you did that was so good and how that relates to the type of thing we do here. Maybe you can explain to him what you were able to do so much better than when you started. |
| Gina: | Well, I get emotional real easy. When I get mad, I used to let people have it. So I've been working on how to get what I want, you know, make requests so people won't get bent out of shape or uptight. So I guess you're here so that you can work on something that will make it easier for you to get along with other people. (WillieMae laughs in the background.) |

Therapist:  Yes, good Gina, good explanation. Tony, do you have anything you want to add, like what you've been working on?

Tony:  I want to play Parchesi.

Therapist:  Yes, very good Tony. Tony has been learning how to introduce himself to others and to be able to make requests of people. What in particular have you been practicing?

Tony:  Looking at people right and saying the right words.

Therapist:  Right! We try to improve the way we talk to people, both what we say and how we say it (points to poster of paralinguistic skills on the wall). Tony is working very hard to make good eye contact. Did you notice that he looked up while he was speaking? Very good. We work on our facial expressions, and where we should stand (looks at John), and the quality of our voice (looks at Gina). We learn to say what we think and feel, we learn to make requests rather than hoping someone will know what it is that we want. And we also learn (looking at Gina, then WillieMae, and then John) how to better hear what others say to us, because often we don't hear it quite right. (WillieMae starts laughing.) One of the things we do in here is role play. Who can tell John what a role play is? Tony?

Tony:  Pretend.

Therapist:  That's right, Tony. A role play is a pretend interaction. It gives us a chance to practice what we've learned and for others to help by giving us feedback and suggestions about the way that we came across to them.

(This introduction is rather long compared with that of many of the other models. The introduction serves several purposes: It continues both to teach methods of social skills training to old members and to aid in the development of group norms. The members are asked to contribute to the introductions as much as possible. With each contribution comes positive reinforcement from the leader. This process is designed to increase members' abilities to communicate by modeling the giving of positive re-inforcement, which members need to learn to give to themselves and others. It also gives new members positive and realistic expectations of what they can expect from their participation in this group in terms of both personal goals and the basic structure of the group—behavioral rehearsal [role playing], constructive feedback, and homework.)

| | |
|---|---|
| Therapist: | Terrific introduction. Let's go on to each of your homework assignments and see how they went. Let's begin with you, WillieMae, since you told John how important homework is. You have been working very hard, learning how to let others know what you are thinking and feeling and what it is you want from them. (Therapist reads assignment from index card that WillieMae has given him.) Your homework assignment was to call your caseworker to see if she would take you to the public assistance office so you could get your housing situation straightened out. I see that the psych. day aid signed the card that you completed this. Maybe you can show us how it went. |
| WillieMae: | (laughs) Yes (laughs). Yeah and she knew already what I was going to say. Dr. Smith must have wired her (laughs, referring to her belief of the implanted radio tracker in her head). |
| Therapist: | That is great that you were able to carry out the assignment (ignoring the opportunity to get into delusional material and finding something in the performance to reward). Here is a phone you can use in showing us. Were you standing or sitting? |
| WillieMae: | Standing up (laughs). |
| Therapist: | Good. We'll put the phone here. Did the aide say anything? (WillieMae shakes her head yes.) How about if Dr. X (the co-therapist) plays the aid, and you show us where and how he was standing. (WillieMae does and starts laughing.) Now was anyone else in line to use the phone? (nods) Did they say anything to you? |
| WillieMae: | No. He was listening. Dr. Smith couldn't hear with the phone interfering with the transmitter . . . |

Therapist:  (interrupts) OK Tony, how about if you stand in line behind WillieMae and not say anything. Your caseworker is Ms. Yarrow. Gina, how about if you be Ms. Yarrow and go over here with the other phone line. ( WillieMae starts laughing.) Now what did Ms. Yarrow say exactly?

(A great deal of effort is spent to make the role play as realistic as possible to foster generalization. The effort to involve as many people as possible in the role play serves to make it real and to keep the members active in the session, even when they are not themselves working on their skill.)

WillieMae:  I did talk to my doctor about it, and then I knew that Dr. Smith told her to say that.
Gina:  (exasperated) Dr. Smith left years ago. Why do you keep focusing on him? He's not even here.
Therapist:  Well Gina, that's an interesting question, but right now let us focus just on exactly what was said. (Moves away from whys and speculation in favor of observing the behavior.) WillieMae, did Ms. Yarrow say anything else? (WillieMae shrugs.) OK Gina, maybe when we get to that part you can say whatever you think that Ms. Yarrow may have said under the circumstances. Whenever you're ready, WillieMae (she starts to laugh and continues for about 20 seconds). OK WillieMae, what was your goal in this assignment, what are you going to try and do?

(In another model, there may be a focus on WillieMae's discomfort with the role-play situation in an effort to reduce her laughter. This model deemphasizes this feeling state and attempts to refocus her on the task. At the same time, this check provides the therapist with information about whether she understands the activity.)

WillieMae:  Well, it's to talk to Ms. Yarrow to see if she can take me out of the hospital to take care of my housing problem ( laughs).

Therapist:   Yes, very good. Start whenever you are ready.

WillieMae:   Ms. Yarrow, this is WillieMae. I want to go out on a pass cause I got a letter in the mail (laughs). They're gonna take my apartment away.

Gina:   WillieMae, I was thinking about you. Well, I need to see the letter. I could take you, but did you speak to your doctor about getting a pass?

WillieMae:   (laughs) So you know. I will lose my apartment. Does he want me to lose my apartment? (laughs)

Gina:   (looks uncertain, co-therapist whispers what Gina can say) No WillieMae, no one wants you to lose your apartment, but I can't take you out until your doctor gives you permission. Why don't you call me back after you speak with your doctor, or would you like me to call him?

Therapist:   OK, why don't we stop right there. WillieMae, is that what Ms. Yarrow said? (WillieMae nods.) What was very good about WillieMae's performance, Gina?

Gina:   Well, her voice was loud and clear and she had a good start, I mean she said who she was.

Therapist:   Good, Gina. What else do you think she did well, Tony? Did she state the purpose of the call? (Tony nods.) Yes, she did. Thank you, Tony. What would have made what she did even better?

Gina:   I think Ms. Yarrow didn't know that WillieMae already spoke with her doctor. She could have said that she did.

Therapist:   What would that have done?

Gina:   Maybe WillieMae thought that Ms. Yarrow already knew something and was against her, but I think she was just making sure that WillieMae had permission.

Therapist:   Do you see what Gina means, WillieMae? (She nods.) Maybe we can work on adding that piece of information to help you clarify what Ms. Yarrow knew and didn't know. The role play was a good one. We'll see if we can make it even better. (WillieMae starts laughing.) WillieMae, how would you let Ms. Yarrow know that you had spoken with your doctor? What would you say?

WillieMae:   I would say, "Ms. Yarrow, I already asked my doctor."

Therapist: Good, that is a clear way to say it. Let's try it again in a role play. (WillieMae rehearses again with the same actors. This time she makes the above statement but adds at the end that she thinks Ms. Yarrow is in collusion with Dr. Smith.) OK, let's stop right there. Tony, was she able to clarify that she had already spoken with her doctor? (Tony nods.) Yes she did. You did that well, WillieMae. After we finish the homework assignments, we will come back to this with you and see if we can help you to be able to really listen to what Ms. Yarrow has to say. OK good. Gina, how about you next, what was your assignment?

Gina: I was supposed to tell the evening shift nurse that I didn't like the TV shows that were on in the community room, and I did it, but she just asked me why I didn't like them when all the other patients did. I felt like telling her where to get off, but I didn't. I just said I didn't like them. Then she told me to bring it up at community meeting, and that really p.o.'s me. She just didn't want to deal with it, that (expletive)!

Therapist: OK good. You did the assignment, but it sounds like you feel dissatisfied because you didn't get exactly what you wanted. Is that true?

Gina: Of course it's true. What do you think?

Therapist: Let's role play the situation and see how you were able to do it. Tony, WillieMae, and John, I'd like you to sit around the TV watching a show. Gina, what show were they watching?

Gina: I don't know. Archie Bunker. I just can't stand that nurse's voice . . .

Therapist: OK. Dr. X, you be Georgia, the evening nurse. Now Gina, where was Georgia standing, and did you go up to her? (Gina nods.) OK, take it away.

Gina: Georgia, hi, ah, can I talk to you a minute? I don't like Archie Bunker on the TV. Do you think we could watch something else once in a while?

Co-therapist: Gina, you don't like Archie Bunker? Why not? Other patients seem to like it.

Gina: I just don't like it (her voice somewhat irritated). The problem is that I like something different than these guys. I want to watch *Quantum Leap*. Do you think we could do what I want once in a while? (said with increasing irritation) So what's your response? I'm not asking for a trip to Disney World. You owe me an explanation (demanding).

Co-therapist: Perhaps you could bring this up at the next community meeting, because you know that TV is on a first-come-first-serve basis.

Gina: Yeah, that's about how it happened, that woman is a first-class jerk, and I'm only using nice language because you're here (pointing to the new member).

Therapist: OK, Gina. Thanks for being so honest with us and being respectful of the new member. Tony, what did you like about Gina's role play? (pointing to the paralinguistic poster and the expressing a complaint poster).[10]

Tony: She went up to the nurse. She looked at the nurse and said hello and asked if she could speak with her. She used the right kind of voice. She didn't get too mad like sometimes she does. She wasn't afraid of her.

Therapist: Wow, Tony, you really have been paying attention to the training. That is very helpful feedback. WillieMae, did Gina state her complaint?

WillieMae: Yes (laughs). She's not afraid of anyone (laughs).

Therapist: Gina, did you suggest a solution?

Gina: Yes, but she didn't take it.

Therapist: That's true, but you did your job. You stated the problem, you stated how it made you feel, you felt it was unfair, and you stated a solution.

Gina: Yeah, but so what! Big deal! I didn't get what I wanted.

---

[10] The expressing complaints poster lists the following:
1. Think what the problem is and how to solve it.
2. Explain what the problem is to the other person.
3. Suggest a solution or how to solve the problem.
4. Show you understand the other person's feelings by repeating back.
5. Say "thank you" when the person gives a response.

| Co-therapist: | Oh Gina, the nurse listened to you, she suggested that you bring your request to the community meeting, as a more general issue. |
| Therapist: | You are a harsh critic of yourself. What do you think you did well? |
| Gina: | Well, I guess that I did stand up to her (looking sheepish). I looked at her. I did state (looking at the negative assertions poster) my feelings, I said my position. I suggested a compromise. I guess I didn't say that I understood her feelings. |
| Therapist: | Yes, that's very accurate. What could you have said that showed you understood her feelings? |
| Gina: | That she's just too lazy. |
| Therapist: | How might you state that in more positive terms? |
| Gina: | How can you state that in positive terms? She just doesn't like me, and she's lazy. |
| Therapist: | Well, a sugar-coated pill is a lot easier to swallow than a bitter one. Right? |
| Gina: | So you're suggesting that if I suck up to her, she'll do what I want? |
| Therapist: | Well, what are your short-term goals in this situation? |
| Gina: | I want her to hear me and change the channel. |
| Therapist: | I'm saying there is a much greater chance to get what you want if you present it in a way that is easy for others to hear. Well, is there any possible other reason why she might not have agreed to change the channel immediately? For instance, how would you have felt if you were watching your show and she changed it? |
| Gina: | I guess she was thinking of the other people watching the show. |
| Therapist: | So what might you have said? |
| Gina: | I could have said, "I know you're taking what others want into account, but take what I want into account also." |
| Therapist: | Yes, you could say that you know that she is just trying to be considerate of everyone. OK, let's role play again with the same roles. |

Gina and co-therapist role play. This time Gina adds the statement of the nurse's feeling at the end. There is still an irritation in her voice.

Therapist:   OK WillieMae, did Gina let the nurse know that she understood where she was coming from? (WillieMae nods.) Later in the session, we will come back to this and work on a few more ways that you might express your understanding of others. Let's go on. Tony, how did you do with your homework? You were going to start a conversation with someone. (Tony nods.) Terrific Tony. Where was it?

Tony:   In the dining room.

Therapist:   I'd like to see how it went in a role play. Who were you with and exactly where in the dining room was it?

Tony:   Waiting in line for dinner. Said hello to Marvin and asked him what was he going to eat.

Therapist:   What did he say?

Tony:   Meatloaf.

Gina:   (with disgust) Meatloaf is the only choice. (WillieMae starts laughing.)

Therapist:   (ignoring Gina's comment) Good. Let us try it out. WillieMae, will you be Marvin? (She nods.) Good. John, I'd like you to take a place behind Marvin. Do you remember who that was, Tony? (Tony shakes his head no.)

WillieMae:   John.

Therapist:   Well that works out great. John, stand a distance from Tony, not too close. This is a good distance. (Here, the therapist is attempting to begin to involve John before he starts his own role play and to begin to alert him behaviorally to issues of interpersonal distance, a problem of his.) Whenever you're ready, Tony.

Tony:   (in a mechanical voice with some eye contact) Hello Marvin.

WillieMae:   (laughs) Yeah, hi. (laughs)

Tony:   What are you going to have for dinner?

WillieMae:   Meatloaf.

John:   I want meatloaf too.

Therapist:   OK, let's cut the action right there. That's great, Tony. John, very good for your first role play.

|   | What did Tony do well, WillieMae (points to the starting a conversation poster [11])? |
|---|---|
| WillieMae: | He talked to me, and he stood right in front of me (laughs). |
| Therapist: | Thanks, WillieMae. He did give a greeting. Then he even asked a follow-up question. That's beyond what he had to do! What did you feel that you did well, Tony? |
| Tony: | Don't know. |
| Therapist: | (points to the steps of the skill on the poster) Well, think about what you have been able to do since you started. |
| Tony: | I came to the group. I said all the words. I said even more. |
| Therapist: | Yes, you recognized that you were able to greet. Now what would have made it even better? |
| Gina: | He could have asked what else John was going to have for dinner. |
| Therapist: | Yes. Tony, what else would you like to say? |
| Tony: | I could ask what else Marvin was going to have for dinner. How about dessert? |
| Therapist: | Yes, good. Let's try it again. (Tony completes the role play with the same individuals. He is able to ask the additional question.) |

The homework and goal-setting go-around is completed. Clinicians recommend at least two role plays for each homework assignment. The therapist now facilitates transition into the next phase of behavioral rehearsal for members who are continuing to improve their performance on the same skill. If a new skill or a variant of an old skill is being introduced, it is first modeled by the therapist or co-therapist for all members, even the skilled

---

[11] The starting a conversation (with a friend or acquaintance) poster lists the following:
1. Make a greeting.
2. Determine the type of greeting.
   a. Passing greeting
   b. Interactive greeting
3. Ask a general question—small talk.

ones. Modeling is done at other times during the session, particularly when members have great difficulty acquiring aspects of the skill unless they see an example of it. Frequent modeling is particularly important for members with significant social deficiencies. In some instances, members can also be the actors in modeling skills on which they have previously worked and mastered or at which they are already proficient. One advantage of an open-ended group is that there is a greater likelihood that at least one of the members will have previously mastered a skill being taught so that the role play will enable him or her to review as well as provide a good model for the member learning the skill.

| | |
|---|---|
| Therapist: | Good work. We've completed the homework. Everyone completed their homework. This group deserves a round of applause. (Both therapists applaud.) Each of you should applaud for the rest of you (all clap). How about if we continue to work with Tony? Maybe we can begin by having Gina model the incident (waiting in line for dinner) with Dr. X. (They do a 1-minute role play.) WillieMae, what did you notice about the way that Gina did it? |
| WillieMae: | Good. She was good (laughs). |
| Therapist: | You're right, WillieMae, Gina was quite good. Gina, you've been practicing! WillieMae, what was good about the way she said it (pointing to the paralinguistic skills poster)? (WillieMae continues to laugh.) |
| Co-therapist: | I noticed that Gina looked at me while she was talking. I felt like she was really talking to me and was genuinely interested. She came right up to me without hesitation. I felt like she was interested in what I was going to eat. Tony, what did you notice about what she said? |
| Tony: | She said a lot of things. |
| Therapist: | What in particular did she say? |
| Tony: | First, she asked about the food, and then she asked where Dr. X was going to sit. Then, she told what she was going to have. |

Therapist: OK. Let's switch roles. Tony, who would you like to start a conversation with?

Tony: Marvin.

Therapist: OK. Dr. X, would you be Marvin? (Sets up the role play with WillieMae being part of the food line and Gina playing the part of the cafeteria waitress handing out food.) Take it away, Tony. (They role play for 1 minute.) Let's stop right here and talk about what Tony did particularly well in this role play.

WillieMae: He remembered to say everything (laughs), and he even asked him what he was going to drink.

Therapist: Yes, Tony, not only did you ask all the questions we talked about asking, but you also asked an additional question. Very good. Now this time to make it even better, look at Dr. X a little more when he talks to you. (They role play again, and Tony makes better eye contact, saying the same lines as last time.) Very good. Let's stop here. How did Tony do this time? Did he look at Dr. X more when Dr. X talked? (Gina nods.) Did he look at Dr. X when he was talking to Dr. X, John? (John nods.) Yes, thanks John for giving the feedback. Did he remember all the different lines that he used last time, WillieMae? (WillieMae nods and laughs.) Thanks, WillieMae. Tony, how do you think you did? (He shrugs, but he has a smile on his face. Therapist and co-therapist applaud.) Yes, Tony, you are getting better every day. Let's give him a hand (whole group claps). For homework, Tony, how about if you try the same thing that you tried last night with a different person in another place in the cafeteria. (Tony nods.) Can you see any possible problems with that?

Tony: What if I am the last one in line and no one is left to sit with?

Therapist: Good point. I'm glad you're thinking ahead, anticipating possible problems. The cafeteria is one good place to start a conversation. How about if you don't have a chance? What's another place you could choose?

Tony: My room with my roommates.

Therapist: Good. How about another place? If that one doesn't work? (Tony doesn't answer and shrugs.) WillieMae? Where's another place he can start a conversation?

WillieMae: The day room.

Therapist: Thanks WillieMae. Is that a place you could try it if the dinner line and your room turn out not to be possible? (Tony nods.) Let's try it one more time using the day room. Now Tony, what are you going to say to someone in the day room?

Tony: I'll ask'em what they ate for dinner.

Therapist: Good, you could ask them what they ate for the last meal and how they liked it. Shall we try this? (Therapist sets up the role play. Tony is able to perform the new scene with as good a skill as he did in the last one.) Good, very good. Tony was able to do that as well as the one in the cafeteria line.

Gina: Yeah, Tony, you're getting better. (with a slight mock in her voice) Shall we give the man a round of applause, Doc?

Therapist: Thanks Gina. I think you're right. Tony is making real progress. (Dr. X fills out the 3 × 5 inch assignment card and hands it to Tony.) OK, let's go to Gina. Gina, we were going to help you with the evening nurse. You are working on expressing complaints (points to appropriate poster and lists what Gina did last time in the role play). You approached the nurse, you looked at her, you stated your feelings in an appropriate way, and you stated your position. You also suggested a compromise, and now we are going to help you to tell her that you understand her position. We'll have Dr. X play your part and Gina, you play the night nurse. (They role play a 2-minute scene.) OK, what did you notice about the way that Dr. X approached and spoke with the nurse, WillieMae?

WillieMae: He's so nice in the way that he said it.

Therapist: Thanks WillieMae. When he stated his position, he did not get upset or irritated or emotional at all. He spoke very calmly and was not sarcastic.

Gina, what did you notice about what Dr. X said in stating Doreen's (night nurse) position?

Gina: Dr. X said he could understand that others were watching the show and that she probably thought that everyone was happy, (becomes sarcastic) because after all she always wants to make her patients happy. Then he said that he preferred *Quantum Leap* and asked if there was a way that everyone could be happy.

Therapist: Is what Dr. X said something that you might be able to say? Do you want to change or add anything? (Gina nodded, but does not add more.) Did you notice that Dr. X asked how it could be changed rather than just stating that he wanted it changed?

Gina: Yeah. I see it.

WillieMae: Thank you (laughs).

Therapist: Good observation, WillieMae, he said thank you. OK, let's try it with Gina being herself and Dr. X being Doreen, the night nurse. (They role play for 2 minutes, with Gina able to repeat the suggestions of Dr. X.) Good. Let's stop. WillieMae, did Gina successfully follow each of the steps— did Gina look at the nurse? (WillieMae nods.) Did she say her feelings? (nods again) Did she say what she wanted? (nods) Did she say what she thought the nurse's feelings or opinion might be? (nods) Yes, she was thorough with that! Did she say thank you when the nurse said to bring it up at community meeting? (nods) Yes, she was able to do all the steps in a way that was acceptable. Good. Gina, how do you feel it went?

Gina: No big deal. I guess I did OK.

Therapist: Now tonight is the community meeting. You will need to present your complaint again. Gina, let's role play the community meeting so that you can have one practice before the real thing. Dr. X, you can be the doctor who runs the community meeting. Gina, you play your part. John, WillieMae, and Tony, let's all be part of this role play. (Role play is 2 minutes long, with Gina presenting essentially the same information and steps as

| | |
|---|---|
| | above. This ends with a positive review of her performance and applause from the group.) Your homework is to present your complaint to the community meeting. Now, even if you present your position well, that doesn't necessarily ensure that you will get what you want. Right? |
| Gina: | Yeah, I guess so. |
| Therapist: | We'll be waiting to hear how it went. WillieMae, let's go on to you. (WillieMae starts laughing.) Remember, WillieMae was talking to Ms. Yarrow on the phone and was making a request to be taken on a pass to check on her housing situation. She was able to call Ms. Yarrow, which is great, and she made her request, but she got the impression that Ms. Yarrow was preventing her from going out because Dr. Smith had gotten to her first. However, she did not take the extra step of discovering for certain if her assumption or belief was correct. This skill, which is a new skill for you WillieMae, is called active listening. The first step in active listening is to clarify what you think someone else has said by repeating it back to them and asking them if that is what they meant. So Dr. X will now demonstrate this skill for you in a role play. (The co-therapist repeats the homework scene the way that WillieMae had described it, but this time the co-therapist repeats WillieMae's fear and then asks the clarifying question.) WillieMae, what did you notice about the way that Dr. X asked about Ms. Yarrow's intentions? (WillieMae starts laughing.) |
| Gina: | Geez, can't you put a lid on it? |
| Therapist: | (ignoring Gina's comment) WillieMae, did you notice that Dr. X first stated your concern, that Ms. Yarrow had been in contact with Dr. Smith? Then Dr. X asked if that were true. (WillieMae nods.) So what did Dr. X say to Ms. Yarrow? |
| WillieMae: | To say I think you are in contact with Dr. Smith and then . . . (starts laughing. Dr. X leans over and whispers to WillieMae the clarification question) and say "Is that true?" |
| Therapist: | Yes, good. First you repeat what you think is true and then you ask if that is true. OK, WillieMae, |

|             |                                                                                                                                                                                                                                                                |
| ----------- | ---------------------------------------------------------------------------------------------------------------------------------------------------------------------------------------------------------------------------------------------------------------- |
|             | are you ready to try a role play now? (WillieMae laughs.) Dr. X, you be Ms. Yarrow, and WillieMae here is the phone. Whenever you're ready to try.                                                                                                                 |
| WillieMae:  | Hello, is this Ms. Yarrow? This is WillieMae. I need to go on a pass to check on my housing situation. I got a letter. Can you take me?                                                                                                                          |
| Co-therapist: | Well, yes. Have you spoken with your doctor?                                                                                                                                                                                                                  |
| WillieMae:  | (laughs) Did Dr. T radio you?                                                                                                                                                                                                                                   |
| Co-therapist: | No, no one contacted me by radio. I did not speak with your doctor. I'm not sure that I understand what you mean.                                                                                                                                             |
| WillieMae:  | Did you say that you spoke with my doctor and he does not want to let me go? (Therapist gestures approval for this comment.)                                                                                                                                     |
| Co-therapist: | No. Let me clarify what I meant. I just wanted to make sure that you had received permission from your doctor to go on the pass.                                                                                                                              |
| WillieMae:  | (laughs) Oh yeah. He said yes.                                                                                                                                                                                                                                  |
| Co-therapist: | Good then, I will pick you up tomorrow morning to go. (WillieMae continues to laugh.)                                                                                                                                                                           |

Therapist whispers to WillieMae to clarify what she heard Ms. Yarrow say.

|             |                                                                                                                                                                                                                                                                |
| ----------- | ---------------------------------------------------------------------------------------------------------------------------------------------------------------------------------------------------------------------------------------------------------------- |
| WillieMae:  | Did you say that you will pick me up?                                                                                                                                                                                                                           |
| Co-therapist: | Yes, I will pick you up tomorrow at 9.                                                                                                                                                                                                                        |
| WillieMae:  | 9.                                                                                                                                                                                                                                                              |
| Therapist:  | Good. OK, what was good about how WillieMae handled herself? (Points to paralinguistic poster and active listening skills poster.[12] Asks specific members for their feedback on WillieMae's eye contact and points out the contents of her speech.) How do you think you did WillieMae? |

[12] The active listening skills poster lists the following:
1. Look at the person.
2. Show interest in the other's statement.
   a. Smile
   b. Nod
   c. Say "yes" or "uh-huh."
3. Repeat what you heard to make sure you understand.

| | |
|---|---|
| WillieMae: | Fine. I said everything. |
| Therapist: | Are you meeting Ms. Yarrow in the morning or evening? |
| WillieMae: | At 9 (shrugs). |
| Therapist: | Let's try it again. This time find out whether it is 9 a.m. or p.m. (Role played again. This time WillieMae is able to clarify the meaning and time of the rendezvous. The group applauds WillieMae's successful role play. Her homework assignment is to call Ms. Yarrow again to arrange the pass.) OK. Now we are up to you, John. Good to have you. What do you think about this group? |
| John: | Fine. |
| Therapist: | John said he wants to learn how to make friends. The first step in making friends is to be able to start up a conversation. In order to have a conversation, you first have to figure out when is a good time to start a conversation with someone, and before you can do that, you have to know when you greet someone whether they want to have a conversation with you. So let's start with greetings (puts up poster of greetings[13]). Let's try the greetings (pointing to the steps). This will be a good review for the rest of you. Step Number 1, look at the person. Step Number 2, say a greeting. John, what greeting can you give? (John gestures a wave.) Good. What can you say, John? |
| John: | Hi. |
| Therapist: | Good John. Tony, what else could John say? |
| Tony: | Hello, how are you? |
| Therapist: | Good. |
| Gina: | You can also wave if you are far away. |
| Therapist: | Thanks Gina. Those are good ways to greet a person. So let's try that. (Therapist models initiating a conversation with co-therapist in a role |

---

[13] The making a greeting poster lists the following:
1. Choose the right place and time.
2. Approach the person.
3. Look at the person.
4. Greet the person—"Hello," "Hi."

play.) OK, now why don't you try this, John, with Dr. X. (This is role played.) That was very good for your first time. How did he do?

Tony: He looked at Dr. X. and he smiled. (Therapist signals approval with a "thumbs up" sign.)

Gina: You sure do have a nice smile honey!

Therapist: Yes Gina, you noticed that John has an exceptionally warm smile (points to the paralinguistic skills poster). How was his distance from Dr X? (Gina nods.) How about his voice, WillieMae? (WillieMae laughs and says good.) Yes, he did really good (claps and the rest of the group follows). Now, sometimes after you say hello to someone, you continue the conversation, and sometimes people are in a hurry or just don't feel like talking. Let's practice a greeting when you can't stay to talk. Let's do a role play with Dr. X playing the part of John, and Tony could you be the other person who wants to have the conversation? (Dr. X and Tony role play a passing greeting.) Good, let's stop. Now John, how could you tell that Dr. X wanted to just say "hello" and not continue a conversation? (John shrugs.) What did he do with his eyes after he said "hello"?

John: His face looked down.

Therapist: Yes, he looked down and his eyes looked away from Tony's face. Good John. Tony, what did you notice?

Tony: He didn't talk anymore and kept walking.

Therapist: Very good, so if someone does not have time to talk, they may tell you, "Hi, but I don't have time to talk," they may look down, or just continue walking after they said "hello." John, how about if you practice a greeting without continuing the conversation, and Gina you be the other person. (They role play.) Good. What did you like about what John did?

WillieMae: He smiled "hello."

Therapist: Good, WillieMae. He smiled and had a nice greeting and he didn't talk anymore. Try it again, John. This time it will be even better if you continue to walk after you've made the greeting. (Gina and

|  |  |
|---|---|
|  | John role play again.) Good. WillieMae, what was good about the way John greeted but moved on? |
| WillieMae: | He smiled "hello," but walked past and his eyes did . . . (laughs). |
| Therapist: | Excellent, WillieMae. He said hello, nothing more, he looked away, and he walked past. Gina, what do you think? Could he have made it any better? |
| Gina: | Well, if he didn't hesitate, I thought maybe he wanted to talk to me, because he stopped for a moment. |
| Therapist: | Gina, can you show us the difference with Dr. X? (Gina role plays with Dr. X, the first time hesitating and the second without hesitation. When they are performing, the therapist called John's attention to the hesitation and then the movement without the hesitation.) John, try it again this time with Tony. (Both role play.) Now, how did John do? (Therapist nods positively. WillieMae starts laughing and clapping at the same time.) Good. I agree with you, WillieMae. Let's give John a hand. (Everyone claps.) So John has a great smile, he had a nice strong greeting and then looked away, stopped talking and continued walking past Tony (pointing to each of the steps on the poster of greetings). Very good. For your homework, I would like you to say hello and greet someone without continuing the conversation. Do you think you can do that? (He nods.) Now what are you going to do for your assignment? |
| John: | I am going to say hi and nothing else. |
| Therapist: | Yes. That's right. Who could you do it with? (John shrugs.) Dr. X, do you think you could practice with John? (Dr. X agrees as he writes the assignment on the card. The assignment is a repeat of the day's work to help consolidate progress.) Well, it looks like we are about out of time. Everyone have his or her homework? (goes around to each patient reiterating each individual's homework) Any questions? Good job today. You all worked very hard. See you tomorrow. |

## Comment on the Session

After the introduction of the new member, the checking of homework occurs. In this example, checking homework is combined with two behavioral rehearsals and setting of the day's tasks and goals. In higher functioning groups, this initial checking of homework may be merely a verbal check. However, because these patients may be less capable of articulating what happened and better able to show the therapist and group members, a role play was used instead. The second role play permits additional corrective feedback to be given immediately to the patient along with the opportunity for immediate behavioral improvement.

It is important to note the central role that the unit staff play in the success of this group. Staff perform three functions. First, they assist in the execution of the homework. Specifically, they encourage members to do their homework and "sign off" on the homework assignment cards (e.g., WillieMae). They may even prompt the actual use of a newly acquired skill in vivo (i.e., on the ward). They participate in role plays as part of the homework assignments for members when they are beginning their training or when their skills are not sufficient to allow them to successfully complete their assignments with other patients. John is an example of this use of the staff in implementing the model. Generally, the more severe the social skill deficits and chronic the patient population, the more active a role the staff must have in bolstering the importance of the group, in reinforcing group attendance, and in participating in the homework practice (K. T. Mueser, personal communication, August 15, 1992).

A second function is the creation of additional opportunities for members to practice their skills in vivo. This function is crucial because practice increases the likelihood of skill acquisition. Third, unit staff are usually the ones who control privileges and token incentives, which can motivate members to practice and use their newly developing and acquired skills. Of course, to fulfill this function, staff must have a knowledge of skills training and specifically targeted social skills because some of the skills, such as assertiveness, are not generally reinforced in inpatient settings.

In this group, each member had his or her own distinct set of goals and tasks on which to work. This is in part to provide an illustration for the reader of how to work with different types of patient problems using different strategies. Another possibility with this population is to teach a standard set of skills, aiding each person in the level at which he or she has difficulty. For example, all of the members of this group could benefit from training in a core set of social skills including social perception. For WillieMae, this may take the form of learning to listen to what others say by way of repeating what has been said and later by increasing her active listening skills (e.g., nodding and verbally acknowledging that she heard the person in an attempt to lessen the laughing). For John, this may take the form of learning when people wish to socially engage with him and when they do not. For Tony, improving his memory of what others say may be the first step in helping him develop a greater repertoire of socially acceptable conversation. For Gina, her accurate perception of what has transpired may be an important step in decreasing her emotional lability; that is, decreasing her misperception of interactions as transgressions against her may modulate her angry outbursts.

## Status of the Research

Before discussing the research that supports the efficacy of group social skills training in an inpatient setting, a few words are needed about the lack of general agreement as to the definition of social skills. *Social skills* has been defined in many different ways. Definitions vary as to whether social skills refers to a more general or molar notion of social competence or to more specific skills or abilities. Recent evidence has even suggested that competence in social skills (as manifested by role playing) is related to "intrapsychic foundations" (ego functioning) even when premorbid functioning is accounted for (Bellack et al., 1990; Mueser, Bellack et al., 1990). There is also disagreement as to whether it can include an individual's internal states such as feelings, attitudes, and perceptions of the interpersonal situation or whether it should refer only to observed behavior such as eye contact, content of speech, body posture, and so on (Donahoe & Driesenga, 1988; Halford & Hayes, 1991).

Similarly, there is variation concerning what the goal of the training should be. That is, should the goal be to reduce relapse rate by changing the vulnerability of the individual by reducing his or her perceived stress or improving his or her ability to manage stressors? Or should the primary goal be to improve the quality of the patient's life by increasing his or her ability to handle personal affairs and enjoy the rewards of social relationships (Donahoe & Driesenga, 1988)? If the former goal is paramount, then outcome measures should focus on relapse rates. If the latter is important, then it is sufficient to show that the skills are acquired, maintained, and can be appropriately used in the natural environment so that an individual can function.[14]

Thus, the actual skills that researchers and therapists have taught in group studies have varied considerably (see Appendix A). The majority of the skills taught are believed to be significant for conversational or assertion competence. Some of the skills that patients have been taught include "eye contact, speech initiation, duration, fluency and volume; affect, smiling, and other facial mannerisms; latency, frequency, and duration of responding; giving praise, appreciation, and other verbal reinforcement; and gestures" (Donahoe & Driesenga, 1988, p. 148). Few attempted to train individuals to withhold a response (e.g., in-

---

[14] Before social skills training can be shown to be a useful psychiatric treatment, the positive relation between social adjustment and social skills deficiencies must be demonstrated. Indeed, it has been shown that psychiatric patients do have social skills deficits and that these deficits occur even in the absence of positive symptoms such as hallucinations and negative symptoms such as lack of affect or motivation (Bellack, Morrison, & Mueser, 1989; Bellack et al., 1990). In addition, it has been found that premorbid social competence is correlated with treatment outcome. The literature supporting this claim is reviewed extensively in chapter 8, and the reader is referred there for a more thoroughgoing review.

Finally, it is necessary to show that the social skills deficits that psychiatric patients have are the ones that impede functioning effectively in social exchange; that is, are the skills taught relevant for quality of life improvement (Donahoe & Driesenga, 1988)? This question has not been addressed specifically. Rather, particular skills taught have resulted from clinical experience and are assumed to be the ones that will be instrumental in improving the quality of the patient's life.

appropriate laughter), a type of learning that is more difficult for patients to accomplish; moreover, it is unclear exactly what patients were taught (e.g., recognize cues of appropriate use or inappropriate use). The exceptions are Elder, Eldelstein, and Narick (1979), who taught verbally and physically assaultive adolescents to not interrupt, and S. L. Jones, Kanfer, and Lanyon (1982), who taught alcoholics to resist the temptation to drink alcohol.

Some studies have concentrated primarily on a variety of specific "topographical features" such as appropriate speech duration, intonation, and gestures (Finch & Wallace, 1977; Monti, Curran, Corriveau, DeLancey, & Hagerman, 1980). Other studies have involved training patients to conduct appropriate verbal interactions, such as expressing compliments (e.g., Bellack, Turner, Hersen, & Luber, 1984). Not all social skills training has focused on interpersonal behavior. For example, social interaction skills have been taught within a context of community living skills and have included such areas as grooming and medication management (Wallace, Liberman, MacKain, Blackwell, & Eckman, 1992), finance, nutrition, and time management (Brown & Munford, 1983; Wallace & Liberman, 1985). Skills like grooming are considered social because they influence how others respond to the "groomed" or "ungroomed" individual. A relatively new development has been the integration of problem-solving training with social skills training, either as a central focus of the group (e.g., Hansen, St. Lawrence, & Christoff, 1989) or as one part of the training (e.g., Wallace & Liberman, 1985). This variant of the behavioral model makes use of the same procedures (assessment, modeling, instructions, behavioral rehearsal, feedback, and homework) as do others but includes the problem-solving steps outlined in chapter 8 (problem identification, goal definition, generation of alternative solutions, and selection of the most effective one after weighing the consequences; e.g., Hansen et al., 1989). This variant is not discussed further given that it is reviewed in detail in chapter 8.

## Empirical Comparison Studies

Compared with the other models, the social skills variation of the behavioral model has a burgeoning empirical literature to support its efficacy in inpatient group therapy. The first set of studies we discuss compared inpatient group social skills training with some other type of inpatient group. One methodological limitation of almost all of these studies is the unequal specification of the different group treatments. That is, for the most part, the social skills group was well articulated, but the other treatment was usually less well defined, which suggests a potential bias in what was being measured resulting from differential enthusiasm and expertise of the leaders. In addition, the social skills model was often compared with models that are unlikely to be used in today's inpatient environment (e.g., sensitivity training; Monti et al., 1980). The details and findings are presented in Appendix B.

Perhaps the most well-designed study is that of Liberman et al. (1986), who studied state hospital male chronic schizophrenics who received either holistic therapy or social skills training. The social skills training incorporated a problem-solving model that taught receiving, processing, and sending skills. The holistic therapy consisted of yoga exercises, positive expectations for recovery, understanding causes of stress, art therapy, and developing positive life goals. Patients were pretested, posttested, and tested at 2-year follow-up on role-playing assessments, social adjustment ratings (by relatives), naturalistic observations, and symptom ratings. Results indicated that both groups showed improvement on psychopathology assessments and increased employment. However, on almost every measure, the social skills training group showed significantly more improvement. The social skills group also showed greater ability to generalize the skills that they had learned in talking with strangers, having fewer symptom relapses, and experiencing decreased rates of rehospitalization and days in the hospital than did the holistic group. At the 2-year follow-up, the social skills group maintained significantly more of the acquired social skills than did the holistic group. Thus, this study provides evidence for the acquisition, generalization, and maintenance of social skills through use of a specialized program to teach these skills. In addition, it provides evidence that social skills training aids in decreasing both symptoms and relapse rates for state hospital schizophrenics.

Bellack et al. (1984) also used a chronic schizophrenic patient population from a partial hospitalization program to compare social skills training with some form of a task-oriented discussion group. Although both groups had decreased symptoms, those subjects who received the social skills training (conversational skills, expressing compliments, and making complaints) improved their social skills significantly more from pretest to posttest in self-reports and on role-play assessments than did the other group. The social skills group continued to maintain and even improve their social skills at 6-month follow-up; in contrast, the other group maintained or lost their skills. However, almost 50% of the members of both groups were rehospitalized within a year, with no difference between the groups. Thus, despite the improvement in social skills, social skills training was not sufficient to prevent hospitalization.

Another study using a similar chronic schizophrenic inpatient population compared social skills training (using role playing, instruction, modeling, and feedback to teach verbal and nonverbal skills) with remedial drama (role playing without instruction) and with nondirective group discussion (Spencer, Gillespie, & Ekisa, 1983). They found that the social skills training group performed better on the role-play test than did the remedial drama group or the discussion group. The social skills group's improvement was maintained at a 2-month follow-up. However, an in vivo sampling and nursing reports of unit behavior showed only a marginal difference between patients in the social skills training group and those in other groups, suggesting that the social skills learned did not generalize even to the hospital setting.

A fourth study also used chronic male inpatients to compare five different group conditions: role playing with feedback, a monetary incentive for appropriate ward behavior, the combination of role playing and money, no treatment, and a nonspecific group using lecture, transactional analysis, and conflict analysis (Doty, 1975). Assessment before and after treatment of behavior on the unit and in a discussion group with the group therapist indicated that only the incentive condition had a positive effect on social skills. Because the assessment occurred only on the unit, it is unclear whether the skills would generalize to behavior outside the unit, and the lack of follow-up makes it unclear whether these behaviors would be maintained.

Gutride, Goldstein, and Hunter (1973) compared both acute and chronic inpatients in a structured learning program (including modeling, social reinforcement, behavioral rehearsal, and feedback) and in nondescriptive individual or group psychotherapy. The patients could receive any one of the three therapies alone or in combination or no treatment at all. Results indicated that the skills training was effective for both chronic and acute patients. Psychotherapy (individual or group) was more effective than was no psychotherapy. Structured learning therapy enhanced the effects of psychotherapy. However, when both psychotherapy and structured learning therapy were combined, effectiveness was inhibited, particularly for the chronic patients. One of the problems with this study is that the specific skills taught in the structured learning program were not specified (i.e., although the program specified 36 skills, it is unlikely that all 36 could have been covered in the short period of time). Generalization to unit behavior was assessed, but no follow-up was done.

Another study, which used a veteran inpatient population suffering from social anxiety, compared assertion training with insight-oriented group therapy (Lomont, Gilner, Spector, & Skinner, 1969). The insight-oriented group focused on catharsis and group transference, with an emphasis on understanding past and present behaviors in the context of recapitulation of a punitive conflict. The assertion training used Wolpe's (1958) model of reciprocal inhibition; the relation of assertiveness to anxiety was discussed, followed by role playing using scripts. The researchers found that patients in the assertion training group showed significant decrease in their Minnesota Multiphasic Personality Inventory (Hathaway & McKinley, 1967) clinical scales measuring paranoia, schizophrenia, and psychopathic deviation and significant increase in the dominance–submission dimension of the Learly Interpersonal Checklist compared with the insight-oriented group. No actual behavioral measures were taken nor was there any follow-up.

With a similar population, Monti et al. (1980) compared a social skills training program with a sensitivity training group.

The social skills group was conducted in accordance with Monti's manual and included teaching skills such as starting a conversation and giving and receiving compliments and criticisms. The sensitivity training was conducted according to the Planned Experiences for Effective Relating program (Berzon, Reisel, & Davis, 1969) in which the group listened to an audiotape, discussed it, participated in the exercise, and was then given intensive feedback. Self-reports and role-play measures were collected before and after treatment. Both self-report and role-play measures indicated that the social skills group members were less anxious and had better social skills than did the sensitivity training group members at both the end of treatment and 6-month follow-up. This study provides strong support for acquisition and maintenance of social skills; the only flaw of this study is that there was no measure of generalization.

E.J. Jones and McColl (1991) studied adult male offenders in an inpatient setting. They compared a life skills program with an interactional agenda model. The life skills program was designed to decrease antisocial behaviors by increasing prosocial behaviors through didactic presentation, modeling, role playing, and feedback. Self-report pretests and posttests were given to both groups. The researchers found that both groups expressed increased desire to participate in social groups. However, the life skills group better helped members to be able to take a greater range of roles than did the interpersonal group, particularly those roles that the members valued. A problem with this study is that assessments were all self-reports and not based on behavioral change. This group of patients, in particular, may have been motivated by legal reasons to present themselves in a more socially desirable manner without actually changing their behavior. Behavioral assessment for generalization and follow-up would have aided in answering this criticism.

The next three studies that we discuss involve hospitalized alcoholics and compare social skills training with other treatments such as cognitive restructuring (Jackson & Oei, 1978; Oei & Jackson, 1982) and supportive group psychotherapy (Oei & Jackson, 1980, 1982). Each condition used a 24-session (12-week) program. At the end of treatment, social skills training was in all cases superior to traditional supportive psychotherapy as measured by social skills ratings and nurses' ratings (Jackson & Oei, 1978; Oei & Jackson, 1980, 1982). Moreover, group social skills training was superior to individual social skills training (Oei & Jackson, 1980). When social skills training was compared with cognitive restructuring, an interesting pattern emerged across the studies. At posttreatment, social skills training was superior to the cognitive restructuring in the skills acquired (Jackson & Oei, 1978) but was equal to the combination of social skills training and cognitive restructuring (Oei & Jackson, 1982). However, at follow-up (varying from 3 months to 12 months depending on the study) cognitive restructuring was superior to social skills training, and the cognitive restructuring–social skills combination was superior to social skills training alone in reducing alcohol consumption and improving social skills (Jackson & Oei, 1978; Oei & Jackson, 1982). In contrast to the Oei and Jackson studies, S. L. Jones et al. (1982) found no difference between a social skills training group that attempted to teach skills to deal with anger and frustration, negative mood states, interpersonal pressure, and intrapersonal temptation and a discussion group that attempted to deal with the emotional nature of alcoholism ("Why and what keeps you an alcoholic?"). All groups, including a control group (no treatment), improved on a self-report measure and on a behavioral role play of social skills during their hospital stays. At 11- to 14-month follow-up, there was a trend for the social skills training group and the discussion group toward greater sobriety and better social skills than for the control group.

The comparative studies just discussed used a population of adults under age 65. The only comparative inpatient group study with adolescents compared assertiveness training with a nondescript "traditional" process-oriented group (Fiedler, Orenstein, Chiles, Fritz, & Breitt, 1979). The assertiveness training group, which used role-playing feedback and discussion, was more globally assertive in a role-play assessment than was the traditional therapy group. Generalization and follow-up were not assessed.

One study already discussed in the interpersonal model chapter (Beutler, Frank, Schieber, Calvert, & Gaines, 1984) reported somewhat negative comparative results. These researchers compared an expressive experiential group (which encouraged exaggerated negative emotions and increased affective levels by role playing uncomfortable emotions), an interactive group (which used the interpersonal model), a behavioral group (which defined target behaviors, established reinforcement contingencies, and developed individualized programs for each patient in the group, as well as incorporating relaxation training, anxiety management, and exercise), and a no-treatment group. Groups were open-ended, and the unit was a short-term acute one. This study is uniquely characterized by continuous monitoring of the group sessions by expert supervisors using the Group Environment Scale. Patients completed questionnaires, and nurses and therapists completed assessments and evaluations. Patients attended group twice a week for an average total of three sessions. This study failed to discover an interaction between treatment and diagnosis. The results suggest that the expressive experiential group experienced increased symptoms (as assessed by self-reports and nurse checklist), whereas the behavioral group and no-treatment group experienced no effects. The interactive group showed the best results (as assessed by self-reports and nursing reports of ward behavior). There were no significant differences between the groups in doctor ratings of patients. Similar results were found at 13-month follow-up.

Taken together, these studies suggest that socials skills training is more successful in improving social skills and even social adjustment than is no treatment at all. The lack of generalization testing and follow-up data limit the conclusions that can be drawn concerning its effectiveness in improving social adjustment.

## Social Skills Training in a Diagnostically Mixed Inpatient Population

There is overwhelming evidence that social skills training can be accomplished in a diagnostically mixed group in an acute care facility (see Appendix C). Although some of the studies used a no-treatment comparison group (e.g., unit therapy or standard hospital treatment) and random assignment of individuals (e.g., Katz, 1986; Powell, Illovsky, O'Leary, & Gazda, 1988; van Dam-

Baggen & Kraaimaat, 1986), most studies compared patients before and after treatments, using a no-control condition or randomization method (e.g., Douglas & Mueser, 1990; Fromme & Smallwood, 1983; Mueser, Levine, Bellack, Douglas, & Brady, 1990; Zappe & Epstein, 1987). To date, only one study has explored the relation of symptoms to the rate of social skill acquisition. Mueser, Bellack, Douglas, and Wade (1991) found that for schizophrenic and affective-disordered patients, baseline symptoms were not predictive of improvement of social skills with training. For schizophrenics, memory impairment is associated with both greater social skills deficits and a slower rate of social skills acquisition. Once the skill is acquired, however, memory deficits do not seem to impair the maintenance of a skill. For affective disorders, there appears to be no relation between memory and the acquisition rate of social skills.

Quite a range of skills can be effectively taught (see Appendixes A and C). Assertion training seems to be the most commonly researched. It has been taught as a single complete skill (Katz, 1986; Zappe & Epstein, 1987) as an aspect of another skill; for example, the expression of negative feelings (Douglas & Mueser, 1990; Mueser, Levine et al., 1990) or positive self-assertion (van Dam-Baggen & Kraaimaat, 1986). Other skills that have been successfully taught with a diagnostically mixed population are compromise and negotiation (Douglas & Mueser, 1990; Mueser et al., 1991; Mueser, Levine et al., 1990); empathic listening and self-disclosure (Fromme & Smallwood, 1983); vocational skills (Powell et al., 1988); starting, maintaining, and ending a conversation; giving and receiving feedback; and problem solving and self-management (van Dam-Baggen & Kraaimaat, 1986).

In terms of group structure, there is no research that examines the structural elements of the group as independent variables. Reviewing studies with positive findings of social skills acquisition reveals that social skills can be effectively taught in a closed-ended group (Powell et al., 1988; van Dam-Baggen & Kraaimaat, 1986; Zappe & Epstein, 1987) or an open-ended one (Douglas & Mueser, 1990; Katz, 1986; Mueser, Levine et al., 1990). These groups are usually conducted for an hour, but some run as long as an hour and a half (Powell et al., 1988; van Dam-

Baggen & Kraaimaat, 1986). The number of sessions required ranges from a minimum of 2 (Douglas & Mueser, 1990; Mueser, Levine et al., 1990) to a maximum of 20 (Powell et al., 1988).

There are a few problems with the research on diagnostically mixed groups. First, most of the outcome measures are self-reports. Although self-ratings are important, individuals are often not good judges of their own performance, although as a group, patients in many of the studies reported are probably more accurate in these assessments than would be patients from a chronically ill population. Only Mueser and his colleagues used therapist ratings and role play as methods of assessment (Douglas & Mueser, 1990; Mueser et al., 1991; Mueser, Levine et al., 1990). Second, none of the studies included measures of generalization, and only three presented follow-up assessment at 1 month (Mueser et al., 1991), 3 months (van Dam-Baggen & Kraaimaat, 1986), and 1 year (Powell et al., 1988). Powell et al. (1988) were able to show that his program (30 hours of training) resulted in fewer hospitalizations and greater employment than did a no-treatment control condition. Taken together, although the studies are flawed, they provide consistent evidence for the efficacy of social skills training (particularly assertiveness training) in a short-term acute care facility with a diagnostically mixed group.

## Social Skills Training With a Chronic Population

One of the most impressive aspects of this model is the preliminary findings of the improvement in the quality of life for the chronically mentally ill (see Appendix D). Most published studies have used the patient as his or her own control and have thus measured success by the patient's ability to improve on skills from baseline performance (for exceptions, see Booraem & Flowers, 1972; Field & Test, 1975; Finch & Wallace, 1977). There is accumulating evidence that suggests that social skills training groups in either a day-hospital program (Holmes, Hansen, & St. Lawrence, 1984; Kelly, Laughlin, Claiborne, & Patterson, 1979; Kelly, Urey, & Patterson, 1980; Williams, Turner, Watts, Bellack, & Hersen, 1977) or a state hospital setting can help chronically mentally ill individuals improve their social skills (Brown & Munford, 1983; Fecteau & Duffy, 1986; Liberman et al., 1984;

Magaro & West, 1983; Mueser, Kosmidis, & Sayers, in press; Wallace et al., 1992; Williams et al., 1977).

The specific skills that have been successfully taught vary among studies to include assertion training (Booraem & Flowers, 1972; Field & Test, 1975; Williams et al., 1977), verbal and non-verbal conversational elements (Fecteau & Duffy, 1986; Finch & Wallace, 1977; Liberman et al., 1984; Williams et al., 1977; Wong et al., in press), independence (Goldstein et al., 1973), appropriate self-disclosure (Foxx, McMorrow, Bittle, & Fenlon, 1985; Holmes et al., 1984; Kelly et al., 1980), expressing negative feelings and compromise and negotiation (Mueser et al., in press), listening (Fecteau & Duffy, 1986), asking questions and expressing interest (Holmes et al., 1984), using compliments (Kelly et al., 1980), and such life skills as medication management, recreation, and grooming (Wallace et al., 1992), and health, nutrition, finance, and time management (Brown & Munford, 1983; see Appendixes A and D for more details).

For severely mentally ill patients who have been unresponsive to traditional social skills training, a special attention-focusing and prompting procedure has been developed (Massel et al., 1991; Wong et al., in press). In this procedure, patients are seen in small groups (two to three patients). They are given short, discrete trials of training with prompting and additional prompts in vivo if necessary. They are reinforced with primary reinforcers (e.g., food) and continual social reinforcement, which is then phased out after the skill is acquired. This procedure is effective in enabling severely mentally ill individuals to acquire social skills and has been found to generalize to ward behavior. Another interesting variation of the skills training used a format from a commercially available game (Sorry) and a technique known as "stacking the deck" to facilitate feedback, self-monitoring, individualized reinforcers, and individualized performance criteria (Foxx et al., 1985).

Although none of the studies used the structural parameters of the group as independent variables, they offer some information about successful procedures. For example, most groups with this population run about 1 hour (e.g., Williams et al., 1977), but some operate as long as 4 hours in 1 day (Brown & Munford, 1983). Successful acquisition of social skills for this state hospital population has occurred in as few as 12 hours (Field & Test, 1975; Finch & Wallace, 1977) and as many as 140 hours (Brown & Munford, 1983) or 160 hours (Liberman et al., 1984). For this population, skills training needs to occur at least twice a week (Fecteau, & Duffy, 1986; Field & Test, 1975; Wallace et al., 1992); patients have benefited from meetings as frequent as 6 days a week (Liberman et al., 1984). Only day-hospital programs were successful with sessions once a week (Kelly et al., 1980). The more limited the time frame, the more modest the goals must be. For the chronic population, group size is generally smaller than in the acute care facility with a diagnostically mixed population. Although there have been reports of successful treatment with up to eight group members (Wallace et al., 1992), it is not uncommon to have successful treatments in groups with three patients and two therapists (Fecteau & Duffy, 1986; Liberman et al., 1984). Small size is particularly necessary in the attention-focusing procedure (Massel et al., 1991; Wong et al., in press).

Researchers designing studies for the chronic population have been particularly sensitive to issues of generalization and maintenance. More than half the studies in this group attempted to assess whether generalization of the skill had occurred. Attempts included nurses' assessments of ward behavior (Liberman et al., 1984; Massel et al., 1991), a simulated job interview with a real interviewer (Kelly et al., 1979), and conversation with an unfamiliar partner or staff member (Fecteau & Duffy, 1986; Kelly et al., 1980). Almost all efforts at generalization reported positive results; patients were able to generalize the skills to some extent.

Researchers with this population also appear to have been more conscious of the importance of follow-up data; more than half the studies attempted to assess the skill at some interval after training. Most included follow-up at 3 months (Finch & Wallace, 1977; Holmes et al., 1984; Liberman et al., 1984; Wong et al., in press), but one study assessed follow-up at 1 year (Wallace et al., 1992). Follow-up data, when reported, were consistently positive; skills were maintained. The one exception to this is the study by Mueser et al. (in press). In their analysis, they divided their schizophrenic and schizoaffective population into those with and without an enduring thought disorder throughout

treatment. They found that although patients showed no difference in acquisition of the skills, those with the enduring thought
disorder did not retain their newly acquired skills and within a
month returned to baseline.

## Social Skills Training by Age

When the research on social skills training is viewed with respect
to age as a variable, some interesting findings emerge. Most studies have used the standard adult population (see preceding discussion). However, a few studies have attempted skills training
with other age cohorts (see Appendix E). The one study that
used 9- to 11-year-olds suggests that social skills training with
children is a very encouraging area. Matson et al. (1980) found
that a small group of children could be taught skills such as
giving help and compliments, appropriate affect, eye contact, and
body posture. These behaviors were generalized to the ward
setting and were maintained even 15 weeks after training was
completed. Matson et al. (1980) added two interesting features.
First, they added two booster sessions a couple of weeks after
training was completed, although there was no measure of the
necessity of this procedure. Second, they had two children observe two other children learning the skill. They tracked the
children during both their observation time and practice time
and discovered that observing the model and other children
learning the skills was not sufficient for them to acquire the skill.
It was only after the children were themselves able to role play
the skills that they acquired them.

Preliminary studies with adolescents are also promising. Hospitalized adolescents have been successfully taught assertion
training (Fiedler et al., 1979); modification of interruption behavior, requests for behavioral change, and responses to negative
communication (Elder et al., 1979); and self-disclosure, asking
questions, speech acknowledging, and use of high-interest topics
(Hansen et al., 1989). Skills have been taught in as few as 4
sessions for assertion training (e.g., Fiedler et al., 1979) and as
many as 14 sessions for training verbally and physically assaultive adolescents to decrease interruptions and modify their
responses to negative communication and requests for behav-

ioral change (Elder et al., 1979). Assessment of learning was predominantly through role-play assessments. When generalization was measured, it was shown to occur in ward behavior and with peer and nonpsychiatric individuals. When follow-up was reported, skills were maintained; 9 months was the longest follow-up (e.g., Elder et al., 1979).

Because most of the studies presented in the previous section were done with adults less than 65 years of age, they are not be reviewed again. One interesting finding in the Zappe and Epstein (1987) study with acute care patients was their assessment of acquisition of social skills broken down by age. Their youngest grouping ranged from 22 to 26 years of age. Their oldest grouping were those over 65. They found that the most significant changes occurred in the age group of 47 to 55 years and that this change was not due to initial differences.

Although there is significant evidence for successful use of social skills with the elderly in the community or outpatient setting (Gambrill, 1985), the evidence for the efficacy of skills training with an inpatient geriatric population is somewhat mixed. Patterson, Smith, Godale, and Miller (1978) had elderly residential and day-program patients participate in either a conversation maintenance group or a social skills training group. At a posttreatment assessment with an outsider on the ward, social skills training participants had significantly superior social skills. In contrast to this study, Lopez and her colleagues used structured learning therapy with geriatric patients in a state hospital and found that although the skills were initially acquired, they did not generalize well to behavior on the ward even when a monetary incentive was used (Lopez, 1980; Lopez, Hoyer, Goldstein, Gershaw, & Sprafkin, 1980).

In summary, the research to date suggests that social skills training has been shown to be effective with a wide range of diagnostic groups (e.g., in short-term care facilities, 28-day alcohol programs, day-hospital settings, long-term state hospital settings). Although most of the studies have used an adult population, there is some promising work with children and adolescents. The results of studies with geriatric patients are somewhat mixed, but it is still too early to make any definitive statements about this group.

# Critique of the Model

## Strengths

Social skills training accomplishes the goals that the model sets forth—namely to teach or modify interpersonal skills. This model is unique in its emphatic concern for identifying and specifying concrete and measurable goals (i.e., behavior), whether they be in the realm of communication skills (receiving, processing, or sending) or personal skills (e.g., self-care, job interviewing). This model also stresses the importance of monitoring progress quantitatively throughout treatment. Significant interpersonal behavioral change has been demonstrated in a wide range of ages from children to geriatric adults. Because the emphasis is on changing behaviors rather than cognitions or affects, it requires of members fewer linguistic skills than do other models and can thus be used effectively with patients who are less verbal. It has been shown to be effective with individuals who have significant intellectual deficits. Although the behavioral model traditionally has been used with a higher functioning patient group (e.g., college students with relatively minor psychopathology—test anxiety or dating difficulties), it has been demonstrated to be effective even with chronic and severely impaired psychiatric patients when some technique modifications are made. These changes have been found to be maintained at 1-year follow-up.

This model explicitly attempts to provide a method to improve interpersonal functioning. There is a vast array of interpersonal skills that can be chosen for change. The particular skills focused on can be taught to the entire group, or skills can be customized for each individual within the group. In addition, symptomatic and self-esteem changes occur as well, despite the lack of emphasis on or training of them.

The kinds of behaviors that this model seeks to alter are those that may be troublesome to unit staff (e.g., pestering, threatening, and intrusive behavior). Hence, staff members are likely to be enthusiastic when goals involve any amelioration in these targeted interpersonal behaviors. Members' success in modifying these unacceptable behaviors will further nurture a pro-group climate. Additionally, the fact that the model breaks the members' problems into such small steps helps to ensure that the group therapist, the members, and the unit staff will see some progress. The therapist's awareness of positive changes will maintain his or her motivation relative to those models that define the members' progress in broad terms. The members' recognition of positive changes is likely to further enhance their enthusiasm for attendance.

Technically, this model is extraordinarily well developed. That is, screening, assessment, preparation, format of sessions, and articulation of method and technique are extremely detailed. More than any model, proponents of this model offer myriad illustrations that enable the therapist to replicate the details of this treatment. There are also video demonstrations and in-service training guides available (Liberman et. al, 1989). In addition, the model is highly programmatic; for example, in contrast to the educative model, which assumes a background in group dynamics, this model assumes no other knowledge base than what is articulated in the literature. The aphorism "What you see is what you get" aptly applies. Because it gives the therapist a more limited scope of operation, it relies less on inference making, and hence the therapist is less likely to make mistakes stemming from incorrect inferences. For example, it is much easier for a therapist to correctly identify whether a patient maintains appropriate interpersonal distance than whether the group is dealing with issues of trust or authority. Thus, social skills training can be added to the existing repertoire of any clinician. In fact, many of the behavioral procedures are carried out in other types of clinical practice but are not labeled as such. That is, it has been said that most therapists use assertion training and attempt to aid the patient in making change in small steps. Behavioral therapy, and in particular social skills training, spells out in inordinate detail the other changes that other models leave unspecified.

Social skills training does not require the therapist to embrace a particular philosophy of human behavior or theory of treatment. Given the limited assumptions that the model places on the background of the therapist, it is more likely to be applicable to a wider range of settings than are some of the more theoretically demanding models. Social skills training has been successfully implemented by psychiatric technicians, occupational therapists, nurses, and vocational counselors as well as social workers, psychiatrists, and psychologists. In fact, it has been demonstrated that nonprofessionals (those not specifically trained in the mental health field but with minimal education of a high school degree) can be trained (24 hours of classes) to successfully implement a social skills program (Thompson, Gallagher, Nies, & Epstein, 1983). Additional flexibility of the model is provided by its capacity to be used with rotating therapists. Whereas some models such as the developmental model demand therapist consistency, the application of this model can actually benefit from a change in therapists. However, it is essential that the new therapist have an awareness of the assessment and treatment plan for each member. Because the model requires that therapists routinely record this information, it is a relatively easy demand to fulfill.

This model has mechanisms for creating motivation for the members' group involvement. Unlike, for example, the interpersonal model, which requires that members be motivated to alter their social behaviors, this model makes no such demands. It has its own mechanisms for instilling motivation. This provision is crucial given the types of patients with whom this model is often used who may not be psychologically sophisticated enough to appreciate the connection between interpersonal difficulties and sense of well-being. In addition, these individuals often have difficulties in proceeding through the sequence of cognitive operations that would enable them to recognize how present changes will be connected to long-term goals such as having their own residence.

## Weaknesses

Our discussion focuses on three areas of weakness in social skills training: patient characteristics and their motivation for the training, the patient–therapist relationship, and the usefulness of the particular skills taught. The first area involves types of patients who may not be entirely well served by this model. Specifically, although higher functioning or psychologically sophisticated patients may show positive behavioral changes related to their deficits in interpersonal skills, it is possible that they will not find the model to be sufficiently challenging and engaging. Some patients with significant narcissistic qualities may perceive the role-playing and practice aspect to be demeaning and infantilizing. Such reactions are likely to dampen their interest in posthospital therapeutic involvement in this and any other form of treatment. This is an important concern because it has been repeatedly noted that the ability of hospitalized patients to remain in the community is dependent on their involvement in continued outpatient treatment (Yalom, 1983).

This model provides incentives for the overtly uncooperative patient in the form of tokens and rewards for participation when the group as a whole is likely to benefit from this incentive; although lack of patient cooperation is often a problem in residential treatment facilities and state hospitals, in a short-term acute care facility, individuals are generally cooperative. However, this model does not distinguish between noncompliance and resistance in the way other models presented in this text do. That is, this model provides little guidance for working with those patients who appear to be cooperative but who in subtle ways sabotage treatment. Except for cajoling, verbally encouraging, and providing positive reinforcement for their participation, there is little within the model to decrease more generalized noncompliance or resistance. For example, individuals with passive–aggressive tendencies may be able to complete an assignment but may do so only perfunctorily. It is possible that the efficacy of the model could be augmented if there were techniques available to address powerful characterological styles, such as the passive–aggressive one, rather than ignoring them.

Related to issues of cooperation are problems concerning the necessity of establishing the appropriate motivational set for group participation. Therapists may experience difficulty in convincing some members of the usefulness of this model. Like the interpersonal model, this model focuses on the social interactional aspect of members' difficulties. The lack of obvious connection for members between their lack of social skills and their symptoms or current predicaments may diminish their motivation to work within the group. Also related to motivation is the fact that although social skills training is empirically based in its assessment and measure of success of the training, it defines target behaviors for training by what the therapist believes contributes to the social skill. That is, the skills taught—assertion training, conversational skills, personal self-care, and job interviewing skills—are largely derived from the intuitions and values of therapists and researchers (Christoff & Kelly, 1985). The model provides no means of ensuring that the skills on which the therapy focuses are those are skills about which group members care.

A second set of problems pertains to the therapist–patient relationship. There may be a certain artificiality in the way that the model requires that the therapist interact with patients. The therapist could readily feel as if he or she is patronizing the patients and sometimes functioning more like a cheerleader than the traditionally defined therapist, particularly with the amount of verbal positive reinforcement that is heaped on the patients. The therapist who is most successful with these patients and with using this model is highly charismatic and enjoys showmanship. The therapist lacking in these qualities may be disadvantaged.

This model focuses on the method and technique of treatment and has very little to offer therapists who have personal reactions to either patients or the method of treatment. In relation to the latter, compared with other models presented in this book, there is quicker mastery of the method of treatment. However, concomitant with mastery is a possibility that therapist boredom may occur earlier in this model than in others. Although there is some acknowledgment of the value of a positive therapeutic relationship and the importance of empathy, these elements are given considerably less attention than the specification of the techniques and method. In our opinion, attention to the therapeutic relationship is insufficient.

A final set of problems concerns the usefulness of the social skills training. Social skills training, for the most part, is a "component analysis" approach (i.e., it teaches and builds on specific components); it is utilitarian in that it allows the assessment and teaching of target behaviors in a very specific manner. Most programs attempt to judge adequacy on whether and to what extent the individual displays the competent skill. However, it has been argued that social skills training, in its specific and concrete approach to behavior, takes a simplistic view of complex and often ambiguous social exchanges by ignoring the more difficult-to-define aspects of social interaction; in isolating only discrete, small units of observable behavior, behavioral therapy and social skills training may be incapable of addressing the complexity of social interaction. For example, although teaching improved eye contact is a reasonable task, developing the ability to recognize inconsistencies between what is verbally articulated and body language may be an overwhelming goal. Even if this skill can be successfully taught, the issue of generalization is far more problematic. Akin to the complexity issue is the lack of research and clinical formulation within this model about certain personality disorders. For example, social skills training has no easy way of addressing the patient whose psychopathology has a strong masochistic component, narcissistic features, or passive-aggressive tendencies.

Finally, although there are many studies that demonstrate that social skills can be acquired in a simulated or role-play situation, few have shown that patients can use these skills during in vivo social interactions outside the treatment environment or that changes in these skills in fact confer on patients better social judgment (Christoff & Kelly, 1985).

# Demands of the Model

## Clinical Mission

This model, a version of behavioral group therapy, proposes to improve social competence, which is viewed as the individual's repertoire of social skills. Thus, the model is compatible with any clinical setting that sees these skills as important and permits them to be taught or modified. Social skills training is in principle compatible with a biological or pharmacological approach; in fact, one of the modules of many of the programs teaches medication management. This model is likely to have more difficulty thriving in a purely psychoanalytic setting wherein underlying motivation and the affects and impulses that sustain behavior are considered the sine qua non of treatment. Social skills training explicitly does not attend to *why* questions or emotional underpinnings of behavior.

Although often not specifically addressed in the literature, the attitude of the unit staff toward the treatment is important. It is particularly important in long-term settings with chronic patients; the model is optimally applied when staff are enthusiastic participants, willing to reinforce, prompt, and rehearse the target skills with the patient outside the group setting (K. T. Mueser, personal communication, July 8, 1992).

## Context of the Group

The quality and efficacy of the group is unaffected by whether the group is conducted on the unit in which patients reside or is a compilation of patients from various units. The therapists can be part of the unit staff or can be outside consultants so long as there is an avenue for staff to know members' homework assignments and for staff members to be attuned to the goals of social skills training. It is the feeling of some that the effectiveness of the training rests largely on the shoulders of a cooperative and enthusiastic staff.

## Temporal Variables

This model can be structured to be successful in a closed-ended or open-ended group. In some ways, a closed-ended group is easier on the therapist because each skill can be taught to all the members together. If the group is open-ended, two options are available: Either single skills can be taught continuously, such as how to start a conversation, or in a longer term setting, each individual can be uniquely assessed and goals can be designed to teach the specific social skills in which an individual might be deficient. Specific skills then can be introduced and taught when patients are ready to acquire those particular target behaviors.

An advantage of this model is the degree to which the therapist can tailor the structure and specific skills taught to the number of sessions in which the average member participates. For example, Goldstein et al. (1976) developed a program to teach 36 skills, whereas Douglas and Mueser (1990) reported teaching only two skills. In general, the greater the number of sessions that the patient can attend, the more likely he or she is to acquire, generalize, and maintain a particular skill. Moreover, longer participation enables the patient to acquire multiple skills, which is important given that most inpatients with social skills deficits are deficient in more than a single skill. In addition, with social skills training, the intersession interval is important because smaller intervals are more conducive to skill acquisition. This is particularly true for the more severely mentally ill. In a meta-analysis of 27 studies looking at social skills training for schizophrenics (only some of which were group format), Benton and Schroeder (1990) found that 41% of the studies used 10 hours of training or less but that some used more than 100 hours; the amount of training appeared to have no relation to outcome. There is no study or technique paper that suggests a single session is beneficial (Benton & Schroeder, 1990). Training in most studies continued until acquisition of the skill had occurred. The number of trials required varied depending on the skill being taught and the level of patient functioning (Donahoe & Driesenga, 1988).

## Size

This model has considerable flexibility in terms of numbers of patients attending the group, particularly with higher functioning patients. The recommended number of group members is between 4 and 16. For more chronic patients, a smaller group, sometimes with as few as two members and 2 therapists but no more than 4 or 5 members, is recommended.

## Composition

**Diagnostic grouping.** Social skills training has a wide range of utility in terms of diagnostic composition. This model has been found to be effective with affective disorders, chronic and acute schizophrenics, arsonists, alcoholics, anxiety disorders, impulsive disorders, and aggressive behavior in acute care settings, day hospitals, and the longer term state hospital programs. The optimal arrangement for groups appears to be that in which there is a homogeneous level of functioning and the social skills deficits have some commonality. Successful treatments have been developed with heterogenous populations, although care must be taken to teach a skill on which all members can improve. Perhaps one of the most difficult arrangements is that wherein chronic schizophrenics with acute exacerbations are in the same group with patients who primarily have personality disorders; in these cases, the higher functioning personality-disordered patients often become uninterested with the more chronic patients, and the chronic patients have little to offer the personality-disordered patients.

It appears that patients who exhibit continuous psychotic symptoms throughout training may not be entirely well served by this model if it entails only a finite inpatient program; although it appears these patients can acquire skills, they are unable to retain them on follow-up (Mueser et al., in press). For this group, ongoing training or booster sessions may need to be built into their programs when they leave the hospital. For schizophrenics who have memory deficits, the rate of acquisition of social skills is slower than if the memory deficit is not present. However, once the skill is acquired, patients with these deficits are as able to maintain them on follow-up as are those without memory difficulties.

**Age and gender.** Most of the programs have been used with adults from ages 18 to 65. There is some promising work with children, adolescents, and even geriatric patients that should come to fruition in the next decade. Almost all the work that has been reported has used homogeneous age groupings. It is not clear whether this is by design or because of population availability and unit groupings. There appears to be no outstanding evidence for gender differences, with the exception of training of compromise and negotiation and expression of negative feelings; males appeared to be better able to acquire the skills than were females (Douglas & Mueser, 1990; Mueser, Levine et al., 1990).

## Therapist Variables

Therapists can come from a broad spectrum of professional disciplines—psychology, psychiatry, nursing, social work, occupational therapy, vocational counseling, and other human service occupations. Neophyte group therapists who have a methodological behaviorist orientation would be at ease with this model. However, it is not actually necessary for a therapist to be a behaviorist to be able to successfully and enthusiastically use this model. It is essential that the therapist view the alteration of social behaviors as beneficial either in its own right or because it produces some secondary benefit such as increase in self-esteem. Additionally, the therapist must not be uncomfortable with the high level of activity required of a therapist in this model. A flare for the dramatic is also helpful but not essential. The therapist also needs a minimum amount of social skill and comfort with other people.

In terms of technical expertise, this model is one of the few that does not require an extensive training background, the acquisition of advanced degrees, or previous exposure to the model through a mentor. Use of this model has been taught with positive results in a 12-hour course to interested people who have at least a high school education; there was no difference in the outcome for patients who were taught by a "professional" and those who were taught by a "nonprofessional" (Thompson et al., 1983). For those with a background in the mental health field, there are available a multitude of training manuals that are usually generously offered by their authors. These manuals spell out in great detail and assessible language the procedures that the therapist follows.

For technical reasons, co-therapy is perhaps more important for this model than for any of the others presented in this book. The co-therapy team is a very active one—therapists physically move about more than most. Co-therapy is often very important in the role play, particularly with chronic patients. While the therapist is busily directing the format and flow of the session, the co-therapist assists in watching the other members, writing homework assignments, keeping track of goals, and participating in role plays.

## Summary

The behavioral model is a relative newcomer to the inpatient group therapy scene. Although there are many variations of the

model, most of them have at their core a methodologically behavioral theoretical foundation. At the nexus of the model is an
empirical foundation that focuses primarily on measurable behavior and current environmental antecedents and consequences
in an action-oriented therapeutic setting. The central goal of therapy is to change behavior.

Because the range of technical considerations and research to
date for all the variants of this model are so vast, we chose social
skills training as a representative variant of the behavioral model
to explore in more detail. Social skills training focuses on the
acquisition or modification of interpersonal behavior. Technically, this model is extraordinarily well developed, with a multitude of manuals available for the neophyte therapist. The therapist is very active in structuring the session, which provides
instruction, discussion, and modeling of the particular skill to be
learned. Participants then role play, receive and give feedback,
and complete homework.

There is extensive research on the efficacious use of group
social skills in acute inpatient settings, day hospitals, and state
hospital programs with patients who have a variety of diagnoses.
This model uniquely offers a procedure to train schizophrenics.
There is promising new work on its use with children, adolescents, and geriatric patients. Perhaps the most notable flaw in
the research is in demonstrating that the skills acquired generalize to the natural environment. This problem is twofold, involving whether patients are capable of discriminating the particular cues that call for the use of the skill and whether there
are conditions under which certain skills are not retained. More
work certainly can be done in these areas.

In addition to its applicability to a wide range of hospitalized
patients, social skills training has the advantage of being able to
be tailored to the length of hospital stay. However, it is not a
one-session model. The model's application is limited by the
requirement of a co-therapy team. However, the composition of
the team need not be stable from session to session provided
the therapists are apprised of the prior session's homework assignments. The model can be used in any setting in which the
philosophy incorporates the notion that social skills are important to patients' overall adjustment. Yet, the model is effective

when the milieu actively supports not only the model but also its methods. Such active support takes the form of staff members facilitating the execution of homework assignments and prompting the in vivo practice of skills and rewarding their use.

# References

Allyon, T., & Azrin, N. H. (1968). *The token economy: A motivational system for therapy and rehabilitation.* New York: Appleton-Century-Crofts.

American Psychiatric Association. (1987). *Diagnostic and statistical manual of mental disorders* (3rd ed., rev.). Washington, DC: Author.

Andrasik, F., & Matson, J. L. (1985). Social skills training for the mentally retarded. In L. L'Abate & M.A. Milan (Eds.), *Handbook of social skills training and research* (pp. 418–454). New York: Wiley.

Arkowitz, H., & Hannah, M. T. (1989). Cognitive, behavioral, and psychodynamic therapies: Converging or diverging pathways to change? In A. Freeman, K. Simon, L. Beutler, & H. Arkowitz (Ed.), *Comprehensive handbook of cognitive therapies* (pp. 143–168). New York: Plenum Press.

Austin, N. K., Liberman, R. P., King, L. W., & DeRisi, W. J. (1976). A comparative evaluation of two day hospitals: Goal attainment scaling of behavior therapy vs. milieu therapy. *Journal of Nervous and Mental Disease, 163,* 253–262.

Baker, B. L., Brightman, A. J., Heifetz, L. J., & Murphy, D. M. (1978). *Steps to independence.* Champaign, IL: Research Press.

Bandura, A. (1969). *Principles of behavioral modification.* New York: Holt, Rinehart & Winston.

Bandura, A. (1974). Behavior therapy and the models of man. *American Psychologist, 12,* 859–869.

Bandura, A. (1977a). Self-effacy: Toward a unifying theory of behavioral change. *Psychological Review, 84,* 191–215.

Bandura, A. (1977b). *Social learning theory.* Englewood Cliffs, NJ: Prentice-Hall.

Bandura, A. (1978). The self system in reciprocal determinism. *American Psychologist, 33,* 344–358.

Bandura, A., Adams, N. E., Hardy, A. B., & Howells, G. N. (1980) Tests of the generality of self-efficacy theory. *Cognitive Therapy and Research, 4*(1), 39–66.

Becker, R. (1990). Social skills training. In A. S. Bellack & M. Hersen (Eds.), *Handbook of comparative treatments for adult disorders* (pp. 88–104). New York: Wiley.

Becker, R. E., Heimberg, R. G., & Bellack, A. S. (1987). *Social skills training treatment for depression.* New York: Pergamon Press.

Beidel, D. C., Bellack, A. S., Turner, S. M., Hersen, M., & Luber, R. F. (1981). *Social skills training for chronic psychiatric patients: A treatment manual.* Unpublished manuscript, University of Pittsburgh.

Bellack, A. S., Morrison, R. L., & Mueser, K. T. (1989). Social problem solving in schizophrenia. *Schizophrenia Bulletin, 15,* 101–116.

Bellack, A. S., Morrison, R. L., Wixted, J. T., & Mueser, K. T. (1990). An analysis of social competence in schizophrenia. *British Journal of Psychiatry, 156,* 809–818.

Bellack, A. S., Turner, S. M., Hersen, M., & Luber, R. F. (1984). An examination of the efficacy of social skills training for chronic psychiatric patients. *Hospital and Community Psychiatry, 35,* 1023–1028.

Benton, M. K., & Schroeder, H. E. (1990). Social skills training with schizophrenics: A meta-analytic evaluation. *Journal of Consulting and Clinical Psychology, 58*(6), 1–7.

Berzon, B., Reisel, J., & Davis, D. P. (1969). PEER: An audiotape program for self-directed small groups. *Journal of Humanistic Psychology, 9,* 71–86.

Beutler, L. E., Frank, M., Schieber, S. C., Calvert, S., & Gaines, J. (1984). Comparative effects of group psychotherapies in a short-term inpatient setting: An experience with deterioration effects. *Psychiatry, 47,* 66–76.

Booraem, C. D., & Flowers, J. V. (1972). Reduction of anxiety and personal space as a function of assertion training with severely disturbed neuropsychiatric inpatients. *Psychological Reports, 30,* 923–929.

Bornstein, M., Bellack, A., & Hersen, M. (1980). Social skills training for highly aggressive children: Treatment in an inpatient psychiatric setting. *Behavior Modification, 4,* 173–186.

Breckenridge, J, Thompson, L. W., Breckenridge, J. N., & Gallagher, D. E. (1985). Behavioral group therapy with the elderly: A psychoeducational approach. In D. Upper & S. M. Ross (Eds.), *Handbook of behavioral group therapy* (pp. 275–302). New York: Plenum Press.

Brown, M. A., & Munford, A. M. (1983). Life skills training for chronic schizophrenics. *Journal of Nervous and Mental Disease, 171,* 466–470.

Chiodo, J. (1990). Behavior therapy. In A. S. Bellack & M. Hersen (Eds.), *Handbook of comparative treatments for adult disorders* (pp. 355–370). New York: Wiley.

Christoff, K. A., & Kelly, J. A. (1985). A behavioral approach to social skills training with psychiatric patients. In L. L'Abate & M. A. Milan (Eds.), *Handbook of social skills training and research* (pp. 361–387). New York: Wiley.

Cohn, N. B., & Mayerson, N. H. (1985). Preparing clients for behavioral group therapy. In D. Upper & S. M. Ross (Eds.), *Handbook of behavioral group therapy* (pp. 63–118). New York: Plenum Press.

Curran, J. P., Wallander, J. L., & Farrell, A. D. (1985). Heterosocial skills training. In L. L. L'Abate & M. A. Milan (Eds.), *Handbook of social skills training and research* (pp. 136–169). New York: Wiley.

Donahoe, C. P., & Driesenga, S. A. (1988). A review of social skills training with chronic mental patients. In M. Hersen, R. Eisler, & P. M. Miller (Eds.), *Papers in behavior modification* (pp. 131–164). Newbury Park, CA: Sage.

Doty, D. W. (1975). Role playing and incentives in the modification of the social interaction of chronic psychiatric patients. *Journal of Consulting and Clinical Psychology, 43*(5), 676–682.

Douglas, M. S., & Mueser, K. T. (1990). Teaching conflict resolution skills to the chronically mentally ill. *Behavior Modification, 14*(4), 519–547.

Eisler, R. M., Blanchard, E. B., Fitts, H., & Williams, J. G. (1978). Social skill training with and without modeling for schizophrenic and non-psychotic hospitalized psychiatric patients. *Behavior Modification, 2*(2), 147–171.

Elder, J. P., Edelstein, B. A., & Narick, M. M. (1979). Adolescent psychiatric patients: Modifying aggressive behavior with social skills training. *Behavior Modification, 3*(2), 161–178.

Ellis, A. (1990). Rational–emotive therapy. In I. L. Kutash & A. Wolf (Eds.), *The group psychotherapist's handbook* (pp. 289–315). New York: Columbia University Press.

Ellis, A., & Grieger, R. M. (1977). *Handbook of rational emotive therapy* (Vol. 1 & 2). New York: Springer.

Emmelkamp, P. M. G. (1986). Behavioral therapy with adults. In S. L. Garfield & A. E. Bergin (Eds.), *Handbook of psychotherapy and behavioral change* (pp. 385–442). New York: Wiley.

Eriksen, L., Bjornstad, S., & Gotestam, G. (1986). Social skills training in groups for alcoholics: One-year treatment outcome for groups and individuals. *Addictive Behaviors, 11,* 309–329.

Eysenck, H. J. (1959). Learning theory and behaviour therapy. *Journal of Mental Science, 105,* 61–75.

Falloon, I. R. (1981). Interpersonal variables in behavioral group therapy. *British Journal of Medical Psychology, 54,* 133–141.

Falloon, I. R. H., Lindley, P., McDonald, R., & Marks, I. M. (1977). Social skills training of out-patient groups. *British Journal of Psychiatry, 131,* 599–609.

Fecteau, G. W., & Duffy, M. (1986). Social and conversational skills training with long-term psychiatric inpatients. *Psychological Reports, 59,* 1327–1331.

Ferguson, J. M. (1976). A clinical program for the behavioral control of obesity. In B. J. Williams, S. Martin, & J. P. Foreyt (Eds.), *Obesity: Behavioral approaches to dietary management* (pp. 153–167). New York: Brunner/Mazel.

Field, G. D., & Test, M. A. (1975). Group assertive training for severely disturbed patients. *Journal of Behavioral Therapy and Experience in Psychiatry, 6,* 129–134.

Fiedler, P. E., Orenstein, H., Chiles, J., Fritz, G., & Breitt, S. (1979). Effects of assertive training on hospitalized adolescents and young adults. *Adolescence, 14*(5), 523–528.

Finch, B. E., & Wallace, C. J. (1977). Successful interpersonal skills training with schizophrenic inpatients. *Journal of Consulting and Clinical Psychology, 45*(5), 885–890.

Flowers, J. V. (1979). Behavioral analysis of group therapy and a model for behavioral group therapy. In D. Upper & S. M. Ross (Eds.), *Behavioral group therapy 1979: An annual review* (pp. 5–37). Champaign, IL: Research Press.

Flowers, J. V., & Booraem, C. D. (1990). The effects of different types of interpretation on outcome in group psychotherapy. *Group, 14*(2), 81–88.

Flowers, J. V., & Schwartz, B. (1985). Behavioral group therapy with hetero-geneous clients. In D. Upper & S.M. Ross (Eds.), *Handbook of behavioral group therapy* (pp. 145–170). New York: Plenum Press.

Foy, D. W., Resnick, H. S., Carroll, E. M., & Osato, S. S. (1990). In A. S. Bellack & M. Hersen (Eds.), *Handbook of comparative treatments for adult disorders* (pp. 302–315). New York: Wiley.

Foxx, R. M., McMorrow, J., Bittle, R. G., & Fenlon, S. J. (1985). Teaching social skills to psychiatric inpatients. *Behavioral Research Therapy, 23*(5), 531–537.

Franks, C. M., & Barbrack, C. R. (1983). Behavior therapy with adults: An integrative perspective. In M. Hersen, A. E. Kazdin, & A. S. Bellack (Eds.), *The clinical psychology handbook* (pp. 507–564). New York: Pergamon Press.

Fromme, D. K., & Smallwood, R. E. (1983). Group modification of affective verbalizations in a psychiatric population. *British Journal of Clinical Psychology, 22,* 251–256.

Gallagher, D. (1981). Behavioral group therapy with elderly depressives: An experimental study. In D. Upper & S. Ross (Eds.), *Behavioral group therapy, 1981: An annual review* (pp. 187–224). Champaign, IL: Research Press.

Gambrill, E. (1985). Social skills training with the elderly. In L. L'Abate & M. Milan (Eds.), *Handbook of social skills training and research* (pp. 326–357). New York: Wiley.

Gambrill, E., & Barth, R. (1982). *Social situations of concern to elderly community residents.* Unpublished manuscript, University of California, Berkeley.

Gazda, G. M., & Brooks, D. K. (1985). Life skills training. In L. L'Abate & M. A. Milan (Eds.), *Handbook of social skills training and research* (pp. 77–100). New York: Wiley.

Goldstein, A. P., Gershaw, N. J., & Sprafkin, R. P. (1985). Structured learning: Research and practice in psychological skills training. In L. L'Abate & M. A. Milan (Eds.), *Handbook of social skills training and research* (pp. 284–302). New York: Wiley.

Goldstein, A. P., Martens, J., Hubben, J., van Belle, H. A., Schaaf, W., Wiersma, H., & Goedhart, A. (1973). The use of modeling to increase independent behavior. *Behavior Research and Therapy, 11,* 31–42.

Goldstein, A. P., Sprafkin, R. P., & Gershaw, N. J. (1976). *Skill training for community living: Applying structured learning therapy.* New York: Pergamon Press.

Gordon, R. E., & Gordon, K. K. (1985). A program of modular psychoeduca-tional skills training for chronic mental patients. In L. L'Abate & M. A. Milan (Eds.), *Handbook of social skills training and research* (pp. 388–417). New York: Wiley.

Gutride, M. E., Goldstein, A. R., & Hunter, G. F. (1973). The use of modeling and role playing to increase social interaction among asocial psychiatric patients. *Journal of Consulting and Clinical Psychology, 40*(3), 408–415.

Halford, W. K., & Hayes, R. (1991). Psychological rehabilitation of chronic schizophrenic patients: Recent findings on social skills training and family psychoeducation. *Clinical Psychology Review, 11,* 23–44.

Hansen, D. J., St. Lawrence, J. S., & Christoff, K. A. (1989). Group conversational-skills training with inpatient children and adolescents. *Behavior Modification, 13*(1), 4–31.

Hathaway, S. R., & McKinley, J. C. (1967). *Minnesota Multiphasic Personality Inventory: Manual for administration and scoring.* New York: Psychological Corporation.

Hayes, S. C. (1987). A contextual approach to therapeutic change. In N. S. Jacobson (Ed.), *Psychotherapists in clinical practice* (pp. 327–388). New York: Guilford Press.

Hayes, S. C., & Hayes, L. J. (1992). Some clinical implications of contextualistic behaviorism: The example of cognition. *Behavior Therapy, 23,* 225–249.

Hersen, A. E., Bellack, A. S., Turner, S. M., Williams, M. T., Harper, & Watts, J. G. (1979). Psychometric properties of the Wolpe–Lazarus assertiveness scale. *Behavioral Research and Therapy, 17,* 63–70.

Hollander, M., & Kazaoka, K. (1988). Behavioral therapy groups. In S. Long (Ed.), *Six group therapies* (pp. 257–338). New York: Plenum Press.

Holmes, M. R., Hansen, D. J., & St. Lawrence, J. S. (1984). Conversational skills training with aftercare patients in the community: Social validation and generalization. *Behavior Therapy, 15,* 84–100.

Jackson, P., & Oei, T. P. (1978). Social skills training and cognitive restructuring with alcoholics. *Drug and Alcohol Dependence, 3*(5), 369–374.

Jaffe, P. C., & Carlson, P. M. (1976). Relative efficacy of modeling and instructions in eliciting social behavioral from chronic psychiatric patients. *Journal of Consulting and Clinical Psychology, 44*(2), 200–207.

Jones, E. J., & McColl, M. A. (1991). Development and evaluation of an interactional life skills group for offenders. *Occupational Therapy Journal of Research, 11*(2), 81–90.

Jones, S. L., Kanfer, R., & Lanyon, R. I. (1982). Skill training with alcoholics: A clinical extension. *Addictive Behaviors, 7*(3), 285–290.

Kanfer, R. H., & Phillips, J. S. (1970). *Learning foundations of behavior therapy.* New York: Wiley.

Katz, G. (1986). Group assertive training with psychiatric inpatients. *Psychiatric Journal of the University of Ottawa, 11*(2), 62–67.

Kelly, J. A., Laughlin, C., Claiborne, M., & Patterson, J. (1979). A group procedure for teaching job interviewing skills to formerly hospitalized psychiatric patients. *Behavior Therapy, 10,* 299–310.

Kelly, J. A., Urey, J. R., & Patterson, J. (1980). Improving heterosocial conversational skills of male psychiatric patients through a small group training procedure. *Behavior Therapy, 11,* 179–188.

Koegel, R. L., & Rincover, A. (1977). Research on the difference between generalization and maintenance in extra-therapy responding. *Journal of Applied Behavior Analysis, 10,* 1–12.

Kolko, D. J., Dorsett, P. G., & Milan, M. A. (1981). A total-assessment approach to the evaluation of social skills training: The effectiveness of an anger control program for adolescent psychiatric patients. *Behavioral Assessment, 3,* 383–402.

L'Abate, L., & Milan, M. A. (1985). *Handbook of social skills training and research.* New York: Wiley.

Ladd, G. W., & Asher, S. R. (1985). Social skill training and children's peer relations. In L. L'Abate & M. A. Milan (Eds.), *Handbook of social skills training and research* (pp. 219–244). New York: Wiley.

Lange, A. J., & Jakubowski, P. (1976). *Responsible assertive behavior: Cognitive/behavioral procedures for trainers.* Champaign, IL: Research Press.

Lazarus, A. A. (1958). New methods of psychotherapy: A case study. *South African Medical Journal, 32,* 660–663.

Lazarus, A. A. (1961). Group therapy of phobic disorders by systematic desensitization. *Journal of Abnormal and Social Psychology, 63*(3), 504–510.

Lazarus, A. A. (1976). *Multimodal behavior therapy.* New York: Springer.

Ledwidge, B. (1979). Cognitive behavior modification: A step in the wrong direction? *Psychological Modification, 85,* 353–375.

Liberman, R. (1970). A behavioral approach to group dynamics. *Behavior Therapy, 1,* 141–175.

Liberman, R. P., DeRisi, W. J., & Mueser, K. T. (1989). *Social skills training for psychiatric patients.* New York: Pergamon Press.

Liberman, R. P., Lillie, F., Falloon, I. R. H., Harpin, R. E., Hutchinson, W., & Stoute, B. (1984). Social skills training with relapsing schizophrenics: An experimental analysis. *Behavior Modification, 8*(2), 155–179.

Liberman, R. P., Massel, H. K., Mosk, M. D., & Wong, S. E. (1985). Social skills training for chronic mental patients. *Hospital and Community Psychiatry, 36*(4), 396–403.

Liberman, R. P., Mueser, K. T., & Wallace, C. J. (1986). Social skills training for schizophrenics at risk for relapse. *American Journal of Psychiatry, 143,* 523–526.

Lindsley, O. R., Skinner, B. F., & Solomon, H. C. (1953). *Studies in behavior therapy: Status report I.* Waltham, MA: Metropolitan State Hospital.

Lomont, J. F., Gilner, F. J., Spector, N. H., & Skinner, K. K. (1969). Group assertion training and group insight therapies. *Psychological Reports, 25,* 463–470.

Lopez, M. A. (1980). Social-skills training with institutionalized elderly: Effects of precounseling structuring and overlearning on skill acquisition and transfer. *Journal of Counseling Psychology, 27*(3), 286–293.

Lopez, M. A., Hoyer, W. T., Goldstein, A. P., Gershaw, N. J., & Sprafkin, R. P. (1980). Effects of overlearning and incentive on the acquisition and transfer of interpersonal skills with institutionalized elderly. *Journal of Gerontology, 35,* 403–408.

Lovaas, I. O. (1987). Behavioral treatment and normal educational and intellectual functioning in young autistic children. *Journal of Consulting and Clinical Psychology, 55*(1), 3–9.

Lovaas, I. O., Berberich, J. P., Perloff, B. F., & Schaeffer, B. (1991). Acquisition of imitative speech by schizophrenic children. *Focus on Autistic Behavior, 6,* 1–5.

Mahoney, M. J., & Kazdin, A. E. (1979). Cognitive behavior modification: Misconceptions and premature evaluation. *Psychological Bulletin, 86,* 1044–1049.

Magaro, P. A., & West, A. N. (1983). Structured learning therapy: A study with chronic psychiatric patients and level of pathology. *Behavior Modification, 7*(1), 29–40.

Massel, H. K., Corrigan, P. W., Liberman, R. P., & Milan, M. A. (1991). Conversation skills training of thought-disordered schizophrenic patients through attention focusing. *Psychiatry Research, 38,* 51–61.

Masters, J. C., Burish, T. G., Hollon, S. D., & Rimm, D. C. (1987). *Behavior therapy: Techniques and empirical findings* (3rd ed.). San Diego, CA: Harcourt Brace Jovanovich.

Matson, J. L., Esveldt-Dawson, K., Andrasik, F., Ollendick, T. H., Petti, T., & Hersen, M. (1980). Direct, observational, and generalization effects of social skills training with emotionally disturbed children. *Behavior Therapy, 11,* 522–531.

McFall, R. M., & Twentyman, C. T. (1973). Four experiments on the relative contributions of rehearsal, modeling and coaching to assertion training. *Journal of Abnormal Psychology, 81,* 199–218.

Milan, M. A., & Kolko, D. J. (1985). Social skills training and complementary strategies in anger control and the treatment of aggressive behavior. In L. L'Abate & M. Milan (Eds.), *Handbook of social skills training and research* (pp. 101–135). New York: Wiley.

Monti, P. M., Curran, J. P., Corriveau, D., DeLancey, A. L., & Hagerman, S. M. (1980). Effects of social skills training groups and sensitivity training groups with psychiatric patients. *Journal of Consulting and Clinical Psychology, 48*(2), 241–248.

Monti, P. M., Fink, E., Norman, W., Curran, J., Hayes, S., & Caldwell, A. (1979). Effect of social skills training groups and social skills bibliotherapy with psychiatric patients. *Journal of Consulting and Clinical Psychology, 47*(1), 189–191.

Monti, P. M., & Kolko, D. J. (1985). A review and programmatic model of group social skills training for psychiatric patients. In D. Upper & S. M. Ross (Eds.), *Handbook of behavioral group therapy* (pp. 25–61). New York: Plenum Press.

Morris, R. J., & Suckerman, K. R. (1974). Therapist warmth as a factor in automated systematic desensitization. *Journal of Consulting and Clinical Psychology, 42,* 244–250.

Mueser, K. T., Bellack, A. S., Douglas, M. S., & Wade, J. H. (1991). Prediction of social skill acquisition in schizophrenic and major affective disorder patients from memory and symptomatology. *Psychiatry Research, 37,* 281–296.

Mueser, K. T., Bellack, A. S., Morrison, R. L., & Wixted, J. (1990). Social competence in schizophrenia: Premorbid adjustment, social skill, and domains of functioning. *Journal of Psychiatry Research, 24,* 51–63.

Mueser, K. T., Levine, S., Bellack, A. S., Douglas, M. S., & Brady, E. U. (1990). Social skills training for acute psychiatric inpatients. *Hospital and Community Psychiatry, 41*(11), 1249–1251.

Mueser, K. T., Kosmidis, M. H., & Sayers, M. S. (in press). Symptomatology and the prediction of social skills: Acquisition in schizophrenia. *Schizophrenia Research.*

Oei, T. P., & Jackson, P. (1980). Long-term effects of group and individual social skills training with alcoholics. *Addictive Behaviors, 5*(2), 129–136.

Oei, T. P., & Jackson, P. R. (1982). Social skills and cognitive behavioral approaches to the treatment of problem drinking. *Journal of Studies on Alcohol, 43*(5), 532–547.

Patterson, R. L., Eberly, D. A., Harrell, T. L., & Penner, L. A. (1983). Behavioral assessment of intellectual competence, communication skills, and personal hygiene skills of elderly persons. *Behavioral Assessment, 5*(3), 207–218.

Patterson, R. L., Smith, G., Godale, M., & Miller, C. (1978). *Improving communication skills of psycho-geriatric clients.* Paper presented at the meeting of the Southwest Psychological Association, Atlanta, GA.

Pillay, M., & Crisp, A. H. (1981). The impact of social skills training within an established in-patient treatment programme for anxorexia nervosa. *British Journal of Psychiatry, 139*, 533–539.

Powell, M., Illovsky, M., O'Leary, W., & Gazda, G. M. (1988). Life-skills training with hospitalized psychiatric patients. *International Journal of Group Psychotherapy, 38*(1), 109–117.

Rathus, S. A. (1972). An experimental investigation of assertive training in a group setting. *Journal of Behavior Therapy & Experimental Psychiatry, 3*, 81–86.

Rice, M. E., & Chaplin, T. C. (1979). Social skills training for hospitalized male arsonists. *Journal of Behavior, Therapy and Experimental Psychiatry, 10*, 105–108.

Rimm, D. C., & Masters, J. C. (1979). *Behavior therapy.* San Diego, CA: Academic Press.

Rose, S. D. (1977). *Group therapy: A behavioral approach.* Englewood Cliffs, NJ: Prentice-Hall.

Rose, S. D. (1989). *Working with adults in groups: Integrating cognitive–behavioral and small group strategies.* San Francisco: Jossey-Bass.

Rose, S. D., & LeCroy, C. W. (1985). Improving children's social competence. In D. Upper & S. M. Ross (Eds.), *Handbook of behavioral group therapy* (pp. 173–202). New York: Plenum Press.

Schwartz, R. M. (1982). Cognitive–behavior modification: A conceptual review. *Clinical Psychology Review, 2*, 267–283.

Shaffer, J., & Galinsky, M. D. (1989). *Models of group therapy.* Englewood Cliffs, NJ: Prentice-Hall.

Skinner, B. F. (1938). *The behavior of organisms: An experimental analysis.* New York: Appleton.

Skinner, B. F. (1974). *About behaviorism.* New York: Vintage.

Spencer, P. G., Gillespie, C. R., & Ekisa, E. G. (1983). A controlled comparison of the effects of social skills training and remedial drama on the conversational skills of chronic schizophrenic inpatients. *British Journal of Psychiatry, 143*, 165–172.

Spiegler, M. D., & Agigian, H. (1977). *The community training center.* New York: Brunner/Mazel.

Sundel, M., & Sundel, S. S. (1985). Behavior modification in groups: A time limited model for assessment, planning, intervention and evaluation. In D. Upper & S. M. Ross (Eds.), *Handbook of behavioral group therapy* (pp. 3–24). New York: Plenum Press.

Thompson, L. W., Gallagher, D., Nies, G., & Epstein, D. (1983). Evaluating effectiveness of professionals and nonprofessional as instructors of "coping with depression" classes for elders. *Gerontologist, 23*, 390–396.

Upper, D., & Ross, S. M. (Eds.). (1979). *Behavioral group therapy.* Champaign, IL: Research Press.

van Dam-Baggen, R., & Kraaimaat, F. (1986). A group social skills training program with psychiatric patients: Outcome, drop-out rate and prediction. *Behavioral Research and Therapy, 24*(2), 161–169.

Wallace, C. J., Boone, S. E., Foy, D. W., & Donahoe, C. P. (1985). The chronically mentally disabled: Independent living skills training. In D. H. Barlow (Ed.), *Clinical handbook of psychological disorders* (pp. 462–501). New York: Guilford Press.

Wallace, C. J., & Liberman, R. P. (1985). Social skills training for patients with schizophrenia: A controlled clinical trial. *Psychiatry Research, 15*, 239–247.

Wallace, C. J., Liberman, R. P., MacKain, S. J., Blackwell, G., & Eckman, T. A. (1992). Effectiveness and replicability of modules for teaching social and instrumental skills to the severely mentally ill. *American Journal of Psychiatry, 149*(5), 654–658.

Watson, J. B. (1920). Is thinking merely the action of language mechanisms? *British Journal of Psychology, 11*, 87–104.

Watson, J. B. (1924). *Behaviorism.* New York: Norton.

Wessler, R. L., & Hankin-Wessler, S. (1989). Cognitive group therapy. In A. Freeman, K. Simon, L. Beutler, & H. Arkowitz (Eds.), *Comprehensive handbook of cognitive therapy* (pp. 559–582). New York: Plenum Press.

Williams, M. T., Turner, S. M., Watts, J. G., Bellack, A. S., & Hersen, M. (1977). Group social skills training for chronic psychiatric patients. *European Journal of Behavior Analysis Modification, 4*(4), 223–229.

Wixted, J. T., Bellack, A. S., & Hersen, M. (1990). Behavior therapy. In A. S. Bellack & M. Hersen (Eds.), *Handbook of comparative treatments for adult disorders* (pp. 17–33). New York: Wiley.

Wolpe, J. (1958). *Psychotherapy by reciprocal inhibition.* Stanford, CA: Stanford University Press.

Wolpe, J., & Lazarus, A. A. (1969). *Behavior therapy techniques.* New York: Peragmon Press.

Wong, S. E., Martinez-Diaz, J. A., Massel, H. K., Edelstein, B. A., Wiegand, W., Bowen, L., & Liberman, R. P. (in press). Conversational skills training with schizophrenic inpatients: A study of generalization across settings and conversants. *Behavior Therapy*.

Wong, S. E., & Woosley, J. E. (1989). Re-establishing conversational skills in overtly psychotic, chronic schizophrenic patients: Discrete trials training on the psychiatric ward. *Behavior Modification, 13*, 431–447.

Yalom, I. (1983). *Inpatient group psychotherapy*. New York: Basic Books.

Zappe, C., & Epstein, D. (1987). Assertive training. *Journal of Psychosocial Nursing, 25*(8), 23–26.

Zubin, J., & Spring, B. (1977). Vulnerability: A new view of schizophrenia. *Journal of Abnormal Psychology, 86*, 103–126.

Zuriff, G. E. (1985). *Behaviorism: A conceptual reconstruction*. New York: Columbia University Press.

# Appendix A
## Specific Social Skills Successfully Taught to Inpatients

| Social Skills | Population | Study |
|---|---|---|
| Assertiveness (or component parts) | Nonpsychotic adolescents | Fiedler, Orenstein, Chiles, Fritz, & Breitt (1979) |
| | Nonpsychotic adults | Lomont, Gilner, Spector, & Skinner (1969) |
| | Mixed acute adults | Katz (1986); Monti, Curran, Corriveau, DeLancey, & Hagerman (1980); Monti, Fink, Norman, Curran, Hayes, & Caldwell (1979); Zappe & Epstein (1987) |
| | Day hospital | Bellack, Turner, Hersen, & Luber (1984); Williams, Turner, Watts, Bellack, & Hersen (1977) |
| | Chronic schizophrenics | Field & Test (1975) |
| | Male psychotics | Booraem & Flowers (1972) |
| | Acute and chronic schizophrenics | Foxx, McMorrow, Bittle, & Fenlon (1985) |
| | Male, chronic, nonassertive | Finch & Wallace (1977) |
| | Nonpsychotic alcoholics | Eriksen, Bjornstad, & Gotestam (1986) |
| | Alcoholics | Jackson & Oei (1978) |
| | Male arsonists | Rice & Chaplin (1979) |

| | | |
|---|---|---|
| | State hospital adolescents | Elder, Edelstein, & Narick (1979) |
| Initiating and ending conversation | Nonpsychotic | Katz (1986) |
| | Mixed diagnosis, acute adult | Gutride, Goldstein, & Hunter (1973); Monti et al. (1979, 1980) |
| | Alcoholics | Oei & Jackson (1980, 1982) |
| | Day hospital | Bellack et al. (1984) |
| | Male, chronic schizophrenics | Liberman, Mueser, & Wallace (1986); Wallace & Liberman (1985) |
| | State hospital | Wallace, Liberman, MacKain, Blackwell, & Eckman (1992) |
| | Geriatric, state hospital | Lopez, Hoyer, Goldstein, Gershaw, & Sprafkin (1980) |
| Expressing and receiving compliments | Nonpsychotic | Katz (1986) |
| | Acute, mixed diagnosis | Katz (1986); Monti et al. (1979, 1980); van Dam-Baggen & Kraaimaat (1986) |
| | Day hospital | Bellack et al. (1984) |
| | Male, day hospital | Holmes, Hansen, & St. Lawrence (1984); Massel, Corrigan, Liberman, & Milan (1991) |
| | Male schizophrenics, day hospital | Kelly, Urey, & Patterson (1980) |
| | Chronic psychotics | Magaro & West (1983); Wong et al. (in press) |
| | Chronic schizophrenics | Foxx et al.(1985) |
| | Alcoholics | Oei & Jackson (1980, 1982) |

*(Appendix A continues on next page)*

| Social Skills | Population | Study |
|---|---|---|
| | Aggressive 9–11 year olds | Matson, Esveldt-Dawson, Andrasik, Ollendick, Petti, & Hersen (1980) |
| | Adolescents | Hansen, St. Lawrence, & Christoff (1989) |
| | Geriatric state hospital | Lopez (1980); Lopez et al. (1980) |
| Expressing complaints or negative feelings | Adult, acute, mixed diagnosis | Bellack, Douglas, & Brady (1990); Monti et al. (1979, 1980); Mueser, Bellack, Douglas, & Wade (1991); Mueser, Kosmidis, & Sayers (in press); Mueser, Levine, Douglas & Mueser (1990) |
| | Chronic, day hospital | Bellack et al.(1984) |
| | Chronic schizophrenics | Foxx et al. (1985) |
| | Male, chronic | Wong et al. (in press); Massell et al. (1991) |
| | Geriatric, chronic | Lopez (1980) |
| Compromise and negotiation | Acute, mixed diagnosis | Douglas & Mueser (1990); Mueser, Levine et al. (1990); Mueser et al. (1991, in press) |
| | Chronic schizophrenics | Foxx et al. (1985) |
| | Chronic, verbally assaultive adolescents | Elder et al. (1979) |

| | | |
|---|---|---|
| Refusing unreasonable requests | Nonpsychotic adults | Katz (1986) |
| | Day hospital | Bellack et al. (1984) |
| | Alcoholics | Oei & Jackson (1980, 1982) |
| Topic selection | Male, chronic | Doty (1975); Lopez et al. (1980) |
| | Day hospital | Holmes et al. (1984) |
| Asking questions | Mixed diagnosis, adult | van Dam-Baggen & Kraaimaat (1986) |
| | Chronic schizophrenics | Foxx et al. (1985) |
| | Male, day hospital | Kelly et al. (1980); Massel et al. (1991) |
| | Day hospital | Holmes et al. (1984) |
| | Adult male, chronic | Doty (1975); Wong et al. (in press) |
| | Children, 11–16 years | Hansen et al. (1989) |
| Improving listening, social perception | Mixed diagnosis, nonpsychotic | Fromme & Smallwood (1983) |
| | Mixed diagnosis, acute | van Dam-Baggen & Kraaimaat (1986) |
| | Day hospital | Bellack et al. (1984) |
| | Female, chronic | Fecteau & Duffy (1986) |
| | Male, chronic | Liberman et al. (1986); Wallace & Liberman (1985) |
| Expressing positive feelings or emotion | Mixed diagnosis, nonpsychotic | Fromme & Smallwood (1983) |
| | Day hospital | Bellack et al. (1984) |
| | Adult male, chronic | Doty (1975) |

*(Appendix A continues on next page)*

| Social Skills | Population | Study |
| --- | --- | --- |
| Giving feedback | Mixed diagnosis, nonpsychotic | Fromme & Smallwood (1983) |
| Expressing empathy | Acute, nonpsychotic | Fromme & Smallwood (1983) |
| Self-disclosure | Day hospital | Holmes et al. (1984) |
| | Male, day hospital | Kelly et al. (1980) |
| | Male, chronic | Massell et al. (1991); Wong et al. (in press) |
| | Children, 11–16 years | Hansen et al. (1989) |
| | Nonpsychotic male offenders | E. J. Jones & McColl (1991) |
| Pro-social behavior (honesty, cooperation) | Nonpsychotic male offenders | E. J. Jones & McColl (1991) |
| Acknowledgements | Male, chronic | Wong et al. (in press) |
| Medication management | Chronic | Wallace et al. (1992) |
| Increased independence | Chronic schizophrenics | Goldstein, Martens, Hubben, van Belle, Schaaf, Wiersma, & Goedhart (1973) |
| Grooming | Chronic | Wallace et al. (1992) |
| Dating | Day hospital | Bellack et al. (1984) |
| Recreation | Chronic | Wallace et al. (1992) |
| Job interviewing, vocational skills | Day hospital | Bellack et al. (1984) |
| | Day hospital, chronic schizophrenics | Kelly, Laughlin, Claiborne, & Patterson (1979) |

|  | Male, mixed diagnosis | Powell, Illovsky, O'Leary, & Gazda (1988) |
|---|---|---|
| Resource management | Chronic | Wallace et al. (1992) |
| Nutrition | Chronic | Brown & Munford (1983) |
| Health | Chronic | Brown & Munford (1983) |
| Finance | Chronic | Brown & Munford (1983) |
| Time management | Chronic | Brown & Munford (1983) |
| Responses to negative communication | State hospital assaultive adolescents | Elder et al. (1979) |
| Making requests | State hospital assaultive adolescents | Elder et al. (1979) |
|  | Alcoholics | Oei & Jackson (1980, 1982) |
| Resisting temptation | Nonpsychotic alcoholics | S. L. Jones, Kanfer, & Lanyon (1982) |
| Individualized programs for patients | Short term, acute | Beutler, Frank, Schieber, Calvert, & Gaines (1984) |
| Eye contact | Male, chronic | Doty (1975); Liberman et al. (1985); Wallace & Liberman (1985) |
|  | Day hospital | Williams et al. (1977) |
|  | Alcoholics | Oei & Jackson (1980, 1982) |
|  | Aggressive children | Matson et al. (1980) |
|  | Children, 11–16 years | Hansen et al. (1989) |

*(Appendix A continues on next page)*

| Social Skills | Population | Study |
| --- | --- | --- |
| Voice volume | Male, chronic | Liberman et al. (1986); Wallace & Liberman (1985) |
| | Female, chronic | Fecteau & Duffy (1986) |
| Fluency | Male, chronic | Liberman et al. (1986) |
| Gestures | Day hospital | Williams et al. (1977) |
| Posture | Male, chronic | Liberman et al. (1986) |
| | Female, chronic | Fecteau & Duffy (1986) |
| | Aggressive children | Matson et al. (1980) |
| Facial expression | Male, chronic | Liberman et al. (1986) |
| Intonation | Day hospital | Williams et al. (1977) |

# Appendix B
## Inpatient Research Studies Comparing
## Social Skills Training Group With Another Model

| Study | Subjects | Group | Design/Skills taught | Outcome | Generalization | Follow-up |
|---|---|---|---|---|---|---|
| Bellack, Turner, Hersen, & Luber (1984) | $N = 64$ Adult day hospital chronic patients. | 12 wk, 3x/wk. | Social skills training (SST; instruction, modeling role play, feedback, homework) vs. discussion group (D): Initiating, maintaining ending conversation; expressing compliments and complaints; social perception. | Both groups improved. SST showed greater improvement on social skills; groups equal on symptoms. | Not assessed (NA) | 6 month: SST > D on social skills. 12 month: 50% rehospitalized, no difference among groups. |
| Beutler, Frank, Schieber, Calvert, & Gaines (1984) | $N = 176$ Short term, mixed diagnosis. | Short term, open ended. 2x/wk. Average number of sessions attended = 3. | Behavioral therapy (BT; individualized goals) vs. expressive experiential (EE; role play of intense negative emotions) vs. interpersonal (I) vs. no group (NG). | I showed improvement; BT and NG showed no change, EE showed deterioration in symptoms (self-report). | Most for I, none for BT and NG, deterioration for EE according to nurse ratings of ward behavior. | 13 month: Same as post-treatment. |

(Appendix B continues on next page)

| Study | Subjects | Group | Design/Skills taught | Outcome | Generalization | Follow-up |
|---|---|---|---|---|---|---|
| Doty (1975) | $N = 56$ Chronic male inpatients. | 4 patients per group. 4 sessions. | Role play (RP) vs. incentives (I) vs. role play & incentive vs. no treatment vs. NG. Ward social interaction including topic selection, eye contact, voice volume, expressing feelings, asking questions. | RP + I showed greater improvement on ward behavior and social responsiveness in group discussion. | Some, to discussions with ward therapist and observed ward behavior. | NA |
| Fiedler, Orenstein, Chiles, Fritz, & Breitt (1979) | $N = 25$ No acutely psychotic, age 13–24 years. | 2 wk, 2x/wk. | Assertiveness training (AT; distinguish between assertiveness and aggressiveness, respond to criticism) vs. process training (PT; promoting interaction and insight). | More improvement for AT than for PT on measures of global assertiveness and self-control. | NA | NA |
| Gutride, Goldstein, & Hunter (1973) | $N = 87$ (30 acute, 57 chronic) 75% schizophrenic. | 5–8 patients per group. 4 wk SST: 3x/wk. Individual or group psychotherapy: 2x/wk. | SST vs. individual psychotherapy (IP) vs. group psychotherapy (GP) vs. SST + IP vs. SST + GP. Structured learning therapy skills. | More improvement for SST and either IP or GP; more improvement for SST than for no SST. More improvement with IP and GP than without only for acute patients. | Some, to ward. | NA |

| Study | Sample | Duration | Treatment | Results | Generalization | Follow-up |
|---|---|---|---|---|---|---|
| S. L. Jones, Kanfer, & Lanyon (1982) | N = 74 Alcoholic, nonpsychotic. | 5 patients per group. 4 wk, 2x/wk for 90 minutes. | SST vs. discussion control (DC; emotional nature of problem) vs. NG. Resisting interpersonal pressure and temptation; handling anger, frustration, and negative mood states. | No differences among groups as measure by pre- and post-assessment, self report of alcohol use, and Adaptive Skill Battery. | NA | 11–14 month: SST and DC > NG as measured by self-report. |
| E. J. Jones & McColl (1991) | N = 24 Adult male offender, nonpsychotic. | Short term, open ended. | SST vs. interactional agenda model. Prosocial behaviors. | No differences on observation of desire to participate in groups. SST expressed greater desire and ability to take on new roles in groups. | NA | NA |
| Liberman, Mueser, & Wallace (1986); Wallace & Liberman (1985) | N = 28 Male chronic schizophrenics with 2 or more previous hospitalizations. | 9 wk, 5x/wk for 2 hr. | SST vs. holistic therapy (HT; yoga, discussion, positive expectations, stress). Sending, receiving, processing skills. | SST showed greater improvement on psychopathology, social skills, and symptoms. | To conversations with strangers, more for SST. | 9 month, 24 month: Less psychopathology for both groups. SST > HT on social skills, hospitalization. |
| Lomont, Gilner, Spector, & Skinner (1969) | N = 12 Social anxiety; no thought disorder. | 6 wk, 5x/wk for 1.5 hr. | Insight training (I) vs. SST. Group assertion training. | SST showed greater improvement on MMPI scales Pd, PA, Sc and on McLeary Scale for dominance/submission. | NA | NA |

(Appendix B continues on next page)

| Study | Subjects | Group | Design/Skills taught | Outcome | Generalization | Follow-up |
|---|---|---|---|---|---|---|
| Monti, Curran, Corriveau, DeLancey, & Hagerman (1980) | $N = 46$ No thought disorder. | 5 wk, 4x/wk. | SST vs. sensitivity training (PEER; intensive feedback, discussion). Giving and receiving compliments, criticism, starting conversations, business assertion. | SST showed less anxiety as measured by pre- and postassessment, self-reports, and role play. | NA | 6 month: SST > PEER as measured by role play and self-report. |
| Monti, Fink, Norman, Curran, Hayes, & Caldwell (1979) | $N = 30$ Inpatient and day hospital, psychotic and neurotic. | 10 patient per group. 2 wk, 5x/wk for 1 hr. | SST vs. bibliotherapy (B) vs. NG. Giving and receiving compliments and criticism, starting conversations. | SST showed greater improvement on Rathus Assertiveness Scale and on simulated interaction. | Not significant in vivo. To untrained role play, greater improvement for SST. | 10 month: Greater improvement for SST. |
| Spencer, Gillespie, & Ekisa (1983) | $N = 33$ Chronic schizophrenics. | 8 patients per group. 8 wk, 2x/wk for 1 hr. | SST vs. remedial drama (RD; role play without instructions, modeling, or feedback) vs. group discussion (nondescriptive discussion). Nonverbal and verbal targets. | SST showed greater improvement on role play assessment. | Nurses reported improvement for SST and RD. With in vivo sampling, more for SST. | 2 month: SST retained skills. |

# Appendix C
## Group Social Skills Training in a Diagnostically Mixed Inpatient Population (Short-Term Stay)

| Study | Subjects | Group | Design/Skills taught | Outcome | Generalization | Follow-up |
|---|---|---|---|---|---|---|
| Eriksen, Bjornstad, & Gotestam (1986) | N = 24 Alcoholics, nonpsychotics. | 6 patients per group. 8 wk, 1x/wk for 90 minutes, closed ended. | Social skills training (SST; instruction, modeling, role play, feedback, homework) vs. control discussion group (D). Skills assertiveness, social skills. | Postassessment, self-report, significant others' report assessed in following year (see Follow-Up). | Not assessed (NA) | 1 year: Fewer hospitalized days, consumed less alcohol, more working days for SST. |
| Fromme & Smallwood (1983) | N = 24 No overt psychosis, mixed population. | 4 patients per group. 2 wk, 2x/wk. | Feedback, reinforcement. Empathy, perception of another. No control group. | Pre- and posttreatment self-disclosure. Empathy increased over time. | 1 wk later, able to disclose and be empathic. | 1 week: Skills maintained. |
| Katz (1986) | N = 53 No active psychosis. | 7 sessions, short term, open ended. | Assertiveness training (AT; relaxation, homework, peer feedback, minilecture) vs. control. Social conversation, compliments. | Pre- and posttreatment self-report, Bakker Inventory, Rathus Assertiveness Scale. AT showed greater improvement. | NA | NA |

*(Appendix C continues on next page)*

| Study | Subjects | Group | Design/Skills taught | Outcome | Generalization | Follow-up |
|---|---|---|---|---|---|---|
| Douglas & Mueser (1990); Mueser, Levine, Bellack, Douglas, & Brady (1990) | $N = 300$ Acute, mixed population. | 5–10 patients per group. 3x/wk for 1 hr, open ended. | SST. Compromise and negotiation, expressing negative feelings. No control group. | Ratings on attention, cooperation, role-play test. Skill performance and cooperation improved. More role playing led to greater improvement. Number of sessions not related to improvement. Men improved more than women, and younger more than older, regardless of symptoms. | NA | NA |
| Mueser, Bellack, Douglas, & Wade (1991) | $N = 63$ Acute exacerbation, affective disorder, schizophrenia, schizoaffective | 2 wk, 3x/wk for 1 hr, open ended. | SST. Compromise and negotiation, expressing negative feelings. No control group. | Pre and post social skills role-play assessment, BPRS. Less improvement in social skills predicted by memory impairment for schizophrenics and schizoaffective but not affective disorder. Those with memory impairment did learn skills but at a slower rate. | NA | 1 month: Gain maintained as measured by role-play assessment. |
| Mueser, Kosmidis, & Sayers (in press) | $N = 54$ Schizophrenia and schizoaffective with and without enduring thought disorder. | 5–10 patients per group. 3x/wk, open ended. | SST. Compromise and negotiation, expressing negative feelings. No control group. | Pre and post role-play assessment. Both groups acquired skills and improved global assertiveness. No difference at end between groups. | NA | 1 Month: Those without enduring thought disorder retained skills. |

| Study | Sample | Format | Design | Outcome measures/results | Follow-up (short) | Follow-up (long) |
|---|---|---|---|---|---|---|
| Powell, Illovsky, O'Leary, & Gazda (1988) | N = 89 Male Veterans Administration, mixed population, decreased communication. | 5 wk, 4x/wk for 1.5 hr. | SST (life skills) vs. control group. | Global rating, vocational development. SST showed greater improvement on vocational and communication skills. | Greater use of life skills at follow-up and higher employment for SST. | 1 year: Fewer hospitalizations for SST (50% vs. 57%). |
| Rice & Chaplin (1979) | N = 10 Male arsonists, personality disorder. | 4 wk, 4x/wk. | SST vs. control group (nondirective). Cross-over design. Assertion skills. | Role-playing assessment, questionnaire on skills. SST showed significant improvement on role playing. Questionnaire results similar. | NA | 1 year: No fire setting. |
| van Dam-Baggen & Kraaimaat (1986) | N = 131 Inpatients and outpatients, avoids social situations, biased sample. | 5-8 patients per group. 17 sessions, 1x/wk for 1.5 hr. | SST vs. control. Making and refusing requests, starting and continuing conversations, asking for information, positive self-assertion, problem solving, self-management. | Self-report, role play. SST showed decreased social anxiety and increased skills. Hospitalization or high anxiety impeded improvement in SST. | NA | 3 month: SST maintained skills. |
| Zappe & Epstein (1987) | N = 160 21-day acute stay, mixed population. | 2 wk, 2-3x/wk. | Assertion training. Labeling and responding to feelings; problem areas. No control group. | Self-report. Improvement most significant in 47-55 year age group. | NA | NA |

# Appendix D
## Group Social Skills Training in Chronic Inpatient Population

| Study | Subjects | Group | Design/Skills Taught | Outcome | Generalization | Follow-up |
|---|---|---|---|---|---|---|
| Booraem & Flowers (1972) | $N = 14$ Male psychotic inpatients, Veterans Administration. | 6 wk, 2x/wk. Closed ended. | Assertion training (AT; role play, homework, feedback) vs. no group. Positive and negative assertion. | Measurement of personal space, unobtrusive self-report. AT showed greater improvement. | Not assessed (NA) | NA |
| Brown & Munford (1983) | $N = 28$ Chronic patients with more than 4 hospitalizations. | 6–8 patients per group. 7 wk, 5x/wk for 4 hr. | Life skills training (LST; interpersonal and instrumental) vs. control (VA program). Interpersonal, nutrition, finance, time management, community network. | Life Skills Inventory, attitude and affective measures, self-report, role play. LST showed more improvement on self-report and role play. | NA | NA |
| Fecteau & Duffy (1986) | $N = 7$ Chronic female inpatients, hospitalized 20 years. | 3–4 patients per group. 7 wk, 2x/wk for 90 minutes. | SST (prompting basic orientation and attention, decrease in psychotic talk, listening, eye contact, posture, voice modulation). | Conversation with therapist. Improvement on all skills. | More eye contact and less psychotic talk with other staff member. | NA |
| Field & Test (1975) | $N = 10$ Chronic schizophrenics. | 6 wk, 2x/wk. | Assertiveness training with role play (AT) vs. AT with no role play. | AT improved more on role play; judged more assertive by therapist. | NA | 10 month: AT maintained skills. |

| Study | | Procedure | Measures | Generalization | Follow-up |
|---|---|---|---|---|---|
| Finch & Wallace (1977) | $N = 16$ Nonassertive schizophrenics in state hospital. | 4 wk, 3x/wk for 1 hr. | SST (with feedback in homework dyads) vs. control (hospital routine). | Wolpe Quaire behavioral test, questionnaire. SST improved more on behavioral skills. | SST did better on untrained situation. | 3 month: Greater number of SST patients discharged. |
| Foxx, McMorrow, Bittle, & Fenlon (1985) | $N = 6$ Acute and chronic schizophrenics deficient in social skills. | 3 patient per group. 12 sessions. | Structured game "Stacking the Deck." Compliments, politeness, criticism, social interaction and confrontation. | Assessment of correct responses during game. Program increased appropriate responding in all skill areas. | Ability to use acquired skills in office and lounge. | NA |
| Goldstein et al. (1973) | $N = 54$ Chronic schizophrenics hospitalized at least 8 yr. | Not specified. | 2 x 2 design (Modeling [M] x [I] Instructions). Increase independence. | Assessment of independence score (Likert scale based on 50 situations. $M + I = M$ only $= I$ only $>$ no M or I. | NA | NA |
| Holmes, Hansen, & St. Lawrence (1984) | $N = 10$ Partial hospitalization. | 3x/wk. for 20 minutes. | SST. Conversation skills, including self-disclosure, speech acknowledgers, high interest statements. | Assessment of conversation with other group members. Improvement on all components. | Generalized to nonpsychiatric partners. | 1, 3, and 7 month: Skills maintained. |
| Kelly, Laughlin, Claiborne, & Patterson (1979) | $N = 6$ Partially hospitalized schizophrenics. | 4 wk, 3–4x/wk for 45 minutes. | SST. Job interview skills. | Improvement on answering questions, giving positive information, showing enthusiasm. | To simulated interviews with real interviewers. | NA |

*(Appendix D continues on next page)*

| Study | Subjects | Group | Design/Skills taught | Outcome | Generalization | Follow-up |
|---|---|---|---|---|---|---|
| Kelly, Urey, & Patterson (1980) | $N = 3$ Male schizophrenics in day hospital. | 9 wk, 1x/wk. | SST. Eliciting information from another, appropriate self-disclosure, giving compliments. | Assessment of 8-minute conversation with unfamiliar female after each group. Increased frequency of target skills. | To conversation with unfamiliar female. | 10 wk: Skills maintained with unfamiliar partner. |
| Liberman et al. (1984) | $N = 3$ Schizophrenics. | 8 wk, 6x/wk for 2.5 hr. Return after discharge for 5 wk. of outpatient therapy. | SST (personal effectiveness training). Communication skills. | Behavioral Assessment Test (BAT), Interpersonal Situations Inventory (self-report), role play test, Personal Adjustment Role Scale. Improvement on BAT. | To assignments on ward, interaction with family and in community. | 3 months: Gain sustained in 2 out of 3 patients. |
| Magaro & West (1983) | $N = 38$ Psychotics hospitalized average of 802 weeks. | 4–6 patients per group. 6 months, 4x/wk. | Structured learning therapy. 20 skills, including conversation skills, expressing self, responding to others, alternatives to aggression. | Social skills survey, social participation survey. Improvement on both. Patients highest in projection and psychotic disorganization improved the most. | NA | 3 months: Follow-up gains maintained. |
| Massel, Corrigan, Liberman, & Milan (1991) | $N = 3$ Chronic schizophrenics. | 3 patients per group. 5x/wk. | SST vs. SST + attention-focusing procedure (AFP; 3 levels of prompts to facilitate mastery, reinforcement continual then faded). Conversation skills. | AFP showed more improvement. | To ward for some patients. | NA |

| Study | Subjects | Intervention | Outcome | Generalization | Follow-up |
|---|---|---|---|---|---|
| Wallace, Liberman, MacKain, Blackwell, & Eckman (1992) | N = 108 Chronic patients (91% schizophrenic or schizoaffective) in state hospital. | SST. Solving resource management and outcome problems; medication management, grooming, recreation. | Questions and role play. Patients learned 3 modules and showed significant improvement. | NA | 1 year: No decline in social skills. |
| Williams, Turner, Watts, Bellack, & Hersen (1977) | N = 6 Day hospital chronic schizophrenics. | SST. Eye contact, number of words spoken, intonation, gestures, overall assertion. | Role play. Improvement in all targeted behaviors. | To 8 different role-play scenes. | NA |
| Wong et al. (in press) | N = 3 Chronic male schizophrenics. | SST (in vivo training, prompts, shaping and fading, homework with intermittent prompts). Conversational skills (verbal and nonverbal). | Significant improvement in social skills in group and on ward. | In response to prompt in ward setting. | 3 month: verbal skills maintained |

# Appendix E
## Empirical Studies of Group Social Skills Training Listed by Age
## (Inpatient Population)

| Study | Subjects | Group | Design/Skills Taught | Outcome | Generalization | Follow-up |
|---|---|---|---|---|---|---|
| Matson et al. (1980) | $N = 4$ Ages 9–11, aggressive children. | 4 patients per group. 15 sessions + 2 booster sessions 2.5 wk later. | 2 children learned, 2 observed, then switched. Giving help and compliments, appropriate affect, eye contact, posture. | Assessment after each session with role play by unknowing staff. Improved skills with training. | To ward environment. | 15 wk: Retained skills. |
| Hansen, St. Lawrence, & Christoff (1989) | $N = 9$ Ages 11–16. | 4–5 patients per group. 2x/wk for 30 minutes. | When able to perform one skill, went on to next. Asking questions, self-disclosure, speech acknowledgers and reinforcers, high interest topics. | Preassessment Likert scale, assessment after each session with other group members. Improvement. | To nonpsychiatric patients and nonpatient peers; to hospital cafeteria. | 1, 3 month: Skills maintained. |
| Elder, Edelstein, & Narick (1979) | $N = 4$ State hospital verbally and physically assaultive adolescents. | 14 sessions, 4x/wk for 45 minutes. | Resisting interrupting, responses to negative communication, responding to request for behavior change. | Assessment in group and generalized scenes showed improvement in interrupting. Standard ratings showed improvement in other skills. | To lunch room and day room. | 3, 9 month: 3 of 4 patients successfully discharged to community. |

| Study | Sample | Sessions | Treatment | Results | Transfer | |
|---|---|---|---|---|---|---|
| Fielder, Orenstein, Chiles, Fritz, & Breitt (1979) | N = 25. Ages 13–24, acute but not psychotic patients. | 2 wk, 2x/wk. | Assertion training (AT; distinguish between assertiveness and aggressiveness, respond to criticism) vs. process training (PT; promoting interaction and insight). Assertiveness; responding to criticism. | More improvement for AT than for PT on measures of global assertiveness and self-concept. | NA | NA |
| Zappe & Epstein (1987) | N = 160. Ages 22–65, acute stay, mixed population adults. | 2 wk, 2–3x/ wk for 1 hr. | Assertion training. Labeling and responding to feelings, assertive technique, problem areas. | Self-reports of conflict resolution. Improvement in all, most in age group 47–55. | NA | NA |
| Lopez (1980) | N = 66. Average age = 65, state hospital. | 5 patients per group. 40-minute sessions, 4 (low), 6 (medium), or 8 (high) over-learning sessions. | Low required to complete role play correctly 1x, medium 2x, high 3x. Control group discussed neutral topics. Expressing appreciation. | Behavioral test. All skills acquired. | Only medium group able to transfer skills to interactions with aids, high showed decreased transfer ability. | NA |
| Lopez, Hoyer, Goldstein, Gershaw, & Sprafkin (1980) | N = 56. Average age = 66, hospitalized average of 20 years. | 5 patients per group. 40-minute sessions, 4 (low), 6 (medium), or 8 (high) over-learning sessions. | Monetary incentive for half of patients when skill learned. Greeting, making small talk. | Behavioral test. No significant effects of monetary incentive or overlearning; improved social skills. | Only medium group able to transfer skills to ward. | NA |

# III

## Integration

# 10

# The Seven Models: A Comparative Analysis

T his final chapter is designed to provide a comparative exploration of the seven models discussed in this book. Our comparative analysis of the models is followed by an examination of the relations of the models to different potential features of the treatment environment. We consider what environmental characteristics strengthen or diminish the effectiveness of each model. As in chapter 2, we define the treatment environment in terms of broad institutional variables, immediate contextual variables, and variables pertaining to the therapeutic frame, the patient population, and the therapist as an individual. We close this chapter by providing examples of several treatment environments and by walking the reader through the process of model selection.

## Commonalities Among Models

Commonalities among models are important because they are likely to reveal the essential characteristics of any efficacious inpatient model. That is, if all inpatient model builders have seen fit to include some particular feature as part of their models, it may be because that feature has broad utility. There appear to be five features that the models presented in this text share. One such feature is a high level of specificity in terms of goals of treatment, characterization of the change processes, and methods of intervention. At first, this point may appear to be tautological given that we selected these models partly for their specificity. However, it is noteworthy that less than 15 years ago, the selection criteria used in this text would have been unrealistic: Highly delineated approaches to inpatient groups simply did not exist. It would seem that greater specificity in goals, methods, and the like is not a gratuitous phenomenon but rather is one mandated by the clinical circumstances in which groups take place. The models, of course, differ on which of their aspects are best developed. For example, relative to other models, the object relations/systems model provides a refined exposition of the assumptions made about psychopathology in relation to the change processes in the group. The interactional agenda version of the interpersonal model involves an especially programmatic description of the methods used in the group. The educative model offers a very elaborate description of the orientation and pretraining process. We found that all models in this text could profit from further refinement in some area.

A second shared feature pertains to how the models handle the relation between affect and cognition in the group. Relative to earlier approaches, current approaches appear to offer group members a much more substantial cognitive framework for organizing and understanding their affective life. This provision derives from a now common recognition of the disorganizing effects of uncontained affective expression (Beutler, Frank, Schieber, Calbert, & Gaines, 1984; Kanas, Rogers, Kreth, Patterson, & Campbell, 1980; Pattison, Brissenden, & Wohl, 1967). The models vary in how they provide this cognitive framework. For example, consider the following excerpt from a session:

> Max, a patient with an anxiety disorder (among other problems), storms into group and says he is going off his medication because it was revealed to him the previous night that he had been mistakenly given another patient's medication. Other members immediately categorized this event as being a "one-in-a-million" occurrence and suggested that he was worrying about it needlessly. Max responded by pulling his chair back several inches, staring out the window, and nervously fidgeting with a paper cup.

All models have some mechanism for helping Max and the group to organize the affect that he brought to the group and that he stimulated in other members (despite their appearance of non-responsivity). The therapist implementing the problem-solving model would help the group identify the alternatives available to Max (and, by implication, to others) besides taking the medication compliantly or rejecting it altogether. The awareness of a diversity of options as well as Max's recognition of his power to choose among them would be expected to serve as an antidote to his and others' anxiety. The object relations/systems model would immediately accept the reasonableness of Max's fright in relation to this rather egregious error. The acknowledgment of the reality of the event would itself lead to a bridling of Max's anxiety because the definition of the event limits its scope and, hence, its effect. Moreover, in this model, through clarifications, the therapist would help members accept an identification with Max's fright. In assisting members in tolerating their identification with Max's discomfort, the therapist would interrupt a sequence of escalating projective identifications. Within the cognitive–behavioral model, the cognitive distortion overgeneralization that perhaps interfered with Max's ability to recognize alternate solutions would be identified. Although the mechanisms of the models differ, the intended effect of all of them is to help members circumscribe their disturbing affective experience.

A third common feature is the posture of the leader. No model in this text advocates that the leader assume a Tavistockian position of passivity and inscrutability. Rather, the generally recommended attributes of the inpatient group leader are ones of warmth, responsivity, and a moderate level of transparency. Within all models, the leader is extremely active in pursuing goals and establishing and supporting norms that are compatible with the group's goals. These features are consistent with what has emerged from a considerable body of research on what constitutes effective leadership in short-term groups (see Dies, 1983, for a review of this literature).

A fourth shared attribute is the insistence on the maintenance of consistent and clear internal and external boundaries. Again, the models differ on how boundary stability is to be achieved.

For example, one respect in which the interactional agenda version of the interpersonal model creates a stable boundary is through the therapist's meticulous attendance to the precise beginning of the group, as is seen, for example, in the therapist's refusal to allow late members entrance into the group. Within the educative and cognitive–behavioral models, the boundary is created by the requirement that no member can be accepted into the group unless he or she can remain in the group for several sessions. Despite this variability in methods of boundary setting, models are in accord in seeing stability of boundaries as a prerequisite of the group's accomplishing its goals.

A fifth characteristic is a strong emphasis on the domain of experience tapped for the group's focus, namely, the here-and-now as opposed to the there-and-then. The *here* refers in a geographic way to the immediate social context of the group. Within the inpatient setting, the *here* extends beyond the group to the treatment environment or unit on which the group is held. It is distinguished from *there*, which pertains to experiences that a given member may have outside the group to which other members are not directly privy. For example, an event that occurred at a member's home when the member was away on a pass would be considered there rather than here. The *now* in the here-and-now is a temporal concept that refers to the patient's recent (but not necessarily present) experience in the setting. For example, now may include an altercation between two group members on the unit in the evening prior to a session. By way of contrast, an event in a member's childhood would belong to then.

All of the models in this text have some here-and-now aspect, an inclusion based on the presumption that the here-and-now provides more accurate data and more potential for engaging members in the group (Ferencik, 1991). Each of the models highlights a slightly different aspect of the here-and-now. The object relations/systems model focuses on the affects and impulses stimulated by the group. The problem-solving model delves into members' here-and-now interpersonal information processing. It also gives priority to the examination of interpersonal problems that emerge among group members. The interpersonal model considers the present social interactions among members. The behavioral model analyzes the microscopic features of members' social behaviors. In our estimation, the model placing the least intensive emphasis on the here-and-now is the cognitive–behavioral model. However, even this model contains here-and-now elements. For example, members' reports on their homework experiences on the unit tap the extended here-and-now. More significantly, the discussion of all events, inside or outside the group, enables the recognition of each member's automatic thoughts and cognitive schemes, which are assumed to be in continuous operation. Although many of these models permit members to make excursions into the there-and-then, they are used to provide a segue to the here-and-now or to enable the group to discern what present elements are most worthy of the group's consideration. For example, the educative model requires members to disclose the circumstances that led to their hospitalizations so that the group can know what aspects of members' behavior should be given careful attention within the group.

In summary, then, from the aforementioned areas of commonality, it may be inferred that any adequate approach to inpatient group psychotherapy must involve (a) well-articulated goals and methods, (b) containment of affect through the incorporation of a cognitive framework by which affect can be organized, (c) a leader who is highly active and emotionally available, (d) consistent internal and external boundaries that serve as the framework of the group, and (e) a focus on the here-and-now.

# Differences Among Models

Differences among models are important because they highlight critical areas of controversy, many of which can be addressed empirically. The identification of differences also leads to the delineation of important setting and population variables that must be considered in selecting a model for a given setting. Many frameworks for comparing models of group psychotherapy have been proposed (e.g., Bascue, 1978; Klein, 1983; Long, 1988). Our categories of comparison overlap to varying degrees with all of the aforementioned conceptual schemes. However, they also differ from all of them because we have used those categories that, in our view, discriminate best the particular models we have included in this text.

We consider differences among models in four areas: (a) the philosophical underpinnings of the models, (b) the goals of the group, (c) the model's perspective on the group–unit relation, and (d) the role of the leader.

## Philosophical Underpinnings

The most basic area of differences among the models is the set of assumptions that they make about psychopathology. One heuristic distinction for capturing philosophical differences among the models is whether a model sees psychopathology as deficit based or conflict based (Kibel, 1987a). The deficit models see psychopathology as a result of a developmental arrest or loss that deprives the person of the necessary structures, processes, or repertoires of behaviors essential for maintaining a stable sense of well-being. In contrast, the conflict models seek modification in already-present structures and processes. They assume that psychological problems are rooted in the individual's difficulty in managing the presence of opposite-poled cognitions, affects, and impulses.

Among the models in this book, those most clearly falling into the conflict framework are the object relations/systems model, the developmental model, and the unstructured version of the interpersonal model. The object relations/systems and developmental models explicitly define themselves as conflict models. The unstructured version of the interpersonal model seems to have a conflict foundation given that its application frequently entails members' gaining awareness of how their warded-off affects and impulses control maladaptive social behaviors.

The clearest examples of a deficit model are those models that entail members' acquisitions of a skill in the group. The problem-solving model, which regards members' psychopathologies as fundamental to their lack of effective decision-making processes, is a good example of a deficit model. Other models that appear to be most accurately classified as having a deficit rather than conflict orientation are the social skills version of the behavioral model, the educative model, the focus group and interactional agenda versions of the interpersonal model, and Meichenbaum's stress inoculation and self-instruction training versions of the cognitive–behavioral model (Meichenbaum, 1977; Meichenbaum & Goodman, 1971). As Kibel (1987b) pointed out, although these models do not clearly declare their assumptions about psychopathology, they hold that individuals in need of hospitalization lack a particular psychological commodity essential to the achievement of a sense of well-being: a lack of basic skills in relating to others and a lack of knowledge of others' reactions to their behaviors. The interventions associated with these models are "designed to promote some sort of ego growth" (Kibel, 1987a, p. 114).

Although the deficit/conflict distinction is useful in that it enables an understanding of other differences among models, it does not provide a perfect framework for comparison because the notions of conflict and deficit do not represent endpoints of a univariate continuum. It is possible for models to have both conflict and deficit elements. Even the object relations/systems model, which is a prime example of a conflict model, has deficit components, namely members' lack of tolerance for their negative affects and their inability (at the time of admission) to engage in splitting.

Despite these deficit components, the object relations/systems model clearly emphasizes the conflict over the deficit aspect. There are other models wherein the emphasis is less obvious, particularly those models that have been influenced by widely diverging theoretical orientations. Beck's (1976, 1991) version of the cognitive model, with its complex theoretical foundations, is one such model. Reflecting its psychoanalytic roots, the model seeks to alter preexisting structures, namely, the cognitive schemes, responsible for the individual's disturbing affects. Like the conflict models, the model assumes (without embracing the notion of defense, however) that these schemes are not entirely within conscious awareness and that part of the therapeutic task is to make them so. In consonance with both the behavioral roots of the model and a deficit perspective, the model emphasizes the acquisition of adaptive skills such as the ability to correct distorted thoughts. Although we see the deficit aspect as being the more conspicuous in the model, others may disagree.

Particularly for those models that are easily classified using the deficit/conflict distinction, this philosophical difference concerning defining psychopathology sets the stage for other differences on how psychopathology is best treated. An important difference is the therapist's response to the emergence of affect in the group. It was suggested earlier that although all models help members organize affect, especially hostility, models vary on the extent to which negative feelings are allowed entrance in the sessions. Some models (e.g., interactional agenda) actively discourage aggression in the group in anything but the most muted form; others (e.g., educative) support its emergence only if it is related to the members' reasons for hospitalization; still others create such a high level of cognitive structuring of experience (e.g., cognitive–behavioral, problem solving) that although hostility is not being explicitly discouraged, it is given little room to surface.

All of these approaches have in common the implicit position that hostility is a problem that need not be dealt with directly in the patient's treatment. It is seen as secondary to a more fundamental problem: the absence of some psychological commodity, the acquisition of which would lead to the hostility's spontaneous dissipation. For example, within the interactional agenda model, it is assumed that hostility can be dealt with adequately if the individual learns appropriate behavioral responses to "young anger" (i.e., mild irritation that could develop into more intense hostility). As Kibel (1987a, 1987b) noted, this view toward hostility is consonant with Kohut's (1971) perspective on the role of aggression in psychopathology wherein aggression results from the arrested development of a cohesive sense of self. If an individual is provided with the appropriate growth opportunities leading to the emergence of a cohesive sense of self, the individual's aggression diminishes naturally.

Other models of inpatient group psychotherapy, such as the object relations/systems model and the developmental model, see the exploration of members' hostility as critical to their progress. The object relations/systems approach helps members recognize how their hostility is linked to commonly experienced tensions within the milieu. The developmental model focuses on the hostility that members share resulting from frustration with the authority figures in the group. Both models aim to help members modulate their aggression through the awareness that it is both a shared and a coherent response to reality. The effort of each model to assist members in harnessing aggression is compatible with the conflict view of psychopathology. Within this view, aggression is not a mere by-product of a more fundamental problem; the individual's inability to contain aggression and to integrate it with more positively toned affects is itself the problem, or at least a major dimension of it. Given the central role of aggression within a conflict view of psychopathology, the group format is developed to assist members in achieving a more effective intrapsychic organization of aggressively related representations through a safe experience of expressing hostility within the group.

Another feature of models that is related to the conflict/deficit distinction is whether the model accepts members' communications on a manifest level or whether it seeks to unlock latent or hidden meanings in the members' communications. Whereas the deficit models may focus on either the latent or manifest aspects, the conflict models invariably require the therapist to search for latent content. According to conflict-based models, the individual's intolerance of some (or any) polarity in experience necessitates defensive activity to render experience more consistent. Defended-against contents emerge symbolically rather than directly. The therapist who is interested in helping the member to be more tolerant of polar cognitions, feelings, or impulses can assist the member in identifying (and eventually accepting) unwanted psychological elements by listening to the member's communications as metaphors, symbols, or derivatives. For example, within the developmental model, the therapist listens to the members' comments about events outside the group to discern parallel affects and impulses that may be stimulated by the group process. Within the object relations/systems model, the therapist listens to material with an ear to how it may reflect reactions to events on the unit. Although attendance to the covert level of communication is certainly compatible with the unstructured version of the interpersonal model, it seems to be less of an emphasis in the interactional and focus group versions.

Deficit models in no way preclude the therapist's search for latent meanings because the notion of individuals protecting themselves from psychological discomfort is wholly compatible with at least some of these models. For example, an individual could speak in metaphorical terms about the deficit itself when the full and direct acknowledgment of its existence would be intolerable. However, the deficit perspective does not require attendance to latent meaning: There are some deficit models (e.g., behavioral, educative) that take members' comments entirely at face value.

## Goals of the Group

Related to, but separable from, the philosophical underpinnings of the model are the goals of the group. Models vary from one another in what area they establish as being the primary target of change. As Erickson (1984) noted, a taxonomy of goals has yet to be established for group psychotherapy. However, one distinction that can be made among different approaches is in whether the type of change they seek is intrapsychic, experiential, behavioral, or administrative. These goals are not mutually exclusive. For example, a model could embrace intrapsychic and experiential goals.

Models that target intrapsychic or dynamic change seek to alter the balance of psychological forces within the psyche. These forces may or may not be conscious. All conflict-based models fall into this category. By design, both the developmental and the object relations/systems models assist individuals in returning to their premorbid levels of defensive functioning, which entails a reorganization in their representations of self and other. The unstructured version of the interpersonal model also may allow for some degree of intrapsychic change. Compatible with models in this category are interventions formulated to help individuals gain access to the preconscious affects and impulses that control their maladaptive social behaviors.

In the second category are those models that assume that the member's phenomenology or conscious experience can be altered through group participation. Models that seek experiential change can be divided into those that emphasize affective versus cognitive aspects of experience. In the former category are the educative, interpersonal, developmental, and object relations/ systems models. For example, the educative model seeks to cultivate in members a more pervasively hopeful outlook. The interpersonal model attempts to increase the member's openness to interactions with others. The developmental and object relations/systems models aim to effect a diminution in the member's hostility toward self and others.

Models that seek a more cognitive type of experiential change are the problem-solving and cognitive–behavioral models. The experiential changes sought by the problem-solving model are in the individual's achievement of greater clarity in relation to any problem at hand, greater awareness of a diversity of solutions to a problem, and greater confidence in choosing among them. These changes are accompanied by an enhanced sense of control and competence in facing life's tasks. The cognitive-behavioral model seeks a change in both the cognitions that induce painful affect and the painful affects themselves.

Many of the models in this text claim to produce behavioral change. The type of change and level of specificity is highly variable from model to model, and some models expect to produce either general or specific changes. On a very general level, the developmental, educative, interpersonal, and object relations/systems models all expect that members' group participation will awaken in them a desire for relationships. Members should exhibit a greater frequency of engagement behaviors as a result of group involvement.

Seeking even more specific behavioral changes than a general increase in interpersonal involvement are the developmental and object relations/systems models, both of which assume that group participation results in a lessened use of projective identification, especially in relation to aggression. Projective identification has a definite behavioral component: the individual's coercion of others into the containment of his or her rejected parts. Although this type of behavior is subtle and, hence, difficult to measure, it should be manifested in the reduction of the frequency and intensity of hostile exchanges with others.

Models that predict highly individualized changes anticipate even more specific behavioral changes. If the goals of the unstructured version of the interpersonal model are fulfilled, the individual should show a diminished proclivity to engage in whatever particular behaviors alienated him or her from others. The monopolizer should monopolize less. The interrupter should interrupt less. The educative model also seeks fairly specific changes. The individual should show more effective coping responses in relation to the specific symptoms that afflict him or her. For example, the individual with a schizophrenic diagnosis should have a well-defined repertoire of coping responses in relation to the reemergence of hallucinations and delusions. Application of the cognitive–behavioral model should diminish the frequency and intensity of whatever behaviors were associated with the individual's negative cognitions and affects. For example, depressed individuals who benefit from this approach might show less avoidance of interpersonal contacts and a greater frequency of positive statements.

Probably at the endpoint of the continuum of specificity is the behavioral model, which demands very concrete, measurable changes in a member's communication behaviors before the model can be deemed successfully applied. For example, a particular group member may be expected to show better voice modulation as a function of group involvement.

All of the aforementioned types of goals concern changes in the individual. As Erickson (1984) pointed out, certain models seek more systemic changes as a consequence of successful application. He referred to goals that pertain either to the broader context in which the group takes place or to the individuals' behaviors in that context as *administrative goals*. Certain of the models featured in this text very explicitly posit administrative goals. The object relations/systems model sees the group as a place in which tensions on the unit can be diminished. The interactional agenda and focus group versions of the interpersonal model, the object relations/systems model, and the developmental model assume that successful group participation leads to patients' increased receptivity to other modalities.

## The Models' Perspectives of the Group Within the System

Models vary in how they conceptualize the relation between the group and the treatment context in which the group is embedded. Although most models seem to recognize that the group exists within a hierarchy of systems, the point of difference is whether the model views the group as capable of becoming a system in its own right. On one end of the continuum is the perception of the group as so completely open to the influence of the unit that the group is unable to achieve its own integrity as a system. It remains forever a subsystem. Within this perspective, because the group is unable to have a life of its own (i.e., its own dynamic process and its own structural features), then the group therapist must necessarily focus on group–unit relations. This view leads inexorably to the notion that no event in the group can be adequately understood simply in relation to the group itself. Group events are elucidated by referral to life on the unit. Representing this position is the object relations/systems model. The system of meaning proposed by this model is one wherein the group events are seen as reflecting unit dynamics. The most critical or mutative interventions associated with this model are designed to help members recognize the connection between group and unit events.

On the other end of the continuum is the position that the psychotherapy group, even in the inpatient setting, can potentially achieve the status of a bona fide system with sufficiently limited boundary permeability to permit the group to develop its own dynamic concerns, goals, norms, and so on. The developmental model is an example of an approach that takes such a position. This model directs the therapist to focus simply on the events of the group itself and the history of the group as it is contained within the present so as to decipher the meaning of the events. References outside the group are regarded at once as being resistance to and derivative expressions of group tensions. Another example of this view of the group–unit relation is the problem-solving model, which teaches members a method of thinking that is assumed to have value independently of the particular problems with which members are struggling, including problems emerging on the unit. The behavioral and cognitive–behavioral models are additional examples of models that treat the group as autonomous from the unit.

Those models that might be positioned more centrally on this continuum of group–unit separateness are ones that see the group as having a high level of boundary permeability but not so much that the group is unable to pursue its own goals independently of the unit. These models tend to view the external environment as a resource to the group and vice versa. For example, the interactional agenda model looks to members' interactions with one another as a source of material for the establishment of agendas. It also sees the group as a place in which unit-level problems can be productively addressed, thereby leading to a diminishment of tension on the unit. Both the interpersonal and educative models see members' interactions outside the group as laying the foundation for the establishment of a higher level of cohesiveness than if the group were freestanding.

The degree of potential autonomy that a given model attributes to the inpatient group vis-à-vis the broader treatment context is not independent of the conditions under which the model was developed. Those models that see the inpatient group as being able to become a system in its own right are ones that were constructed generally in a setting in which treatment took place off of residential units and in which groups were composed of members from different units. Consequently, the only larger system encompassing all patients and staff was the organization of the hospital itself. Although in this circumstance the dynamics of the hospital do affect the group, a focus on their elucidation (i.e., the ways in which the group reflects hospital dynamics) would give the group an abstract character and would have little emotional resonance for members. For example, suppose that members complain that they are anxious about whether the group can help them during their brief stay. It has little meaning to them to be shown that they may be containing staff's frustration with the pressure that they feel from managed health care systems. A model emphasizing the group's internal dynamics is also often used in a setting wherein the group can achieve some membership stability over time, enabling the crystallization of issues, role patterns, and so on.

In contrast, models that emphasize group–unit relations generally occur with groups that take place on a unit. In this arrangement, the social system that comprehends the group (i.e., the unit) is immediate to the group—spatially, temporally, and organizationally. While the group is in progress, members can constantly feel the presence of the unit. The membership instability that these models assume to exist also contributes to the openness of the group to the unit. The entrance and departure of members frequently takes the group back to the earliest stage of development when the boundary separating the group from the unit is tenuously drawn. Moreover, the group simply lacks the time to develop its own structure and functional features.

## The Role of the Leader

Although there are certain attributes that all of the models see as characterizing the effective leader, there are important differences among the models in the leader's role.

**Emphasis on techniques versus the patient–therapist relationship.** Some models see the relationship between the therapist and group member as a focus of the group's work and an instrument in members' progress. For example, both the developmental and object relations/systems models assume that the therapist is likely to evoke the reactions that members have toward authority figures. These models further assume that the exploration of these reactions is extremely useful in nurturing members' self-acceptance.

Other models that are more technique oriented see the patient–therapist relationship as having a more collateral effect on the treatment. A positive therapist–patient relationship is useful in that it renders the group members more receptive to the techniques the therapist presents. However, it is the techniques and not the relationship from which members directly benefit. Probably the best example of a technique-oriented model is the social skills version of the behavioral model. Within this approach, the therapist is primarily a technician. The quality of the relationship is important but only in that it affects members' responsivity to the therapist's techniques.

The problem-solving model places a more moderate level of emphasis on the relationship. Because the therapist in this model takes a fairly autocratic role (Coché & Flick, 1975), the members must have sufficiently positive regard for the leader to accept his or her direction. Beyond this factor, however, the model has a proviso that problems that arise within the sessions have priority over those that emerge outside the group. Hence, if a member were to experience himself or herself as having a problem with the leader (or any group member for that matter), that problem would be given priority in relation to problems external to the group. The educative model takes a somewhat similar position as the problem-solving model in that preference is given to the exploration of relationships in the group. However, problems with the leader are not given prolonged attention unless the members' presenting complaints include difficulties with authority figures.

**Level of conceptualization.** Another dimension of difference is level of conceptualization. There are three levels at which the therapist might conceptualize: group-as-a-whole (and subgroup), interpersonal, and individual. We discuss each level in turn.

Some models assume that dynamics exist pertaining to the group as a social system apart from the issues that surface for any individual member. They further hold that there is therapeutic utility in the therapist's attendance to these group-as-a-whole phenomena. Examples of models in this category are the object relations/systems and developmental models. It might be noted that the group-as-a-whole perspective does not mandate the exclusive or even predominant use of group-as-a-whole interpretations. Models involving this level of conceptualization also require the use of interventions at the individual, interpersonal, and subgroup levels.[1]

---

[1] Interventions at levels other than the group-as-a-whole occur for two reasons. A first reason is based on the general principle of systems theory that a change in part of the system affects in some fashion the group-as-a-whole. That is, if the therapist is seeking to effect a change in the group-as-a-whole, one means of doing so is to alter some subsystem of the group. In fact, within

Another set of models featured in this text involves the therapist's conceptualization of occurrences in the group on an interpersonal or dyadic level. Specific member–member or leader–member interactions are the primary unit of analysis. Examples of models that place emphasis on the interpersonal level of conceptualization are all versions of the interpersonal model and the educative model. Once again, although this level of analysis represents the emphasis of these models, it is by no means the exclusive focus. For example, both the interpersonal model and the educative model emphasize the importance of building cohesiveness within the group, which implies an aspect of the group that exists apart from the feelings that any two members have toward one another. Also, these models specifically stress the importance of the therapist's intervening on the individual level to deal with particularly withdrawn or anxious members or to respond to emergencies that might develop with any given member, as when a member attempts to leave the group.

A third category of models emphasizes a conceptualization of problems at the individual level. Examples of approaches within this category are the cognitive–behavioral, problem-solving, and

---

some systems perspectives (e.g., Agazarian, 1992), interventions at the group-as-a-whole level are not seen as providing members with the same level of protection and, hence, the same tolerance of discomfort as are interventions at the subgroup level. That is, when members can clearly see themselves as joining together in relation to some specific commonality (that clearly distinguishes them from others), they can use that sense of unity to brave the consideration of less ego-syntonic, more threatening aspects of themselves.

A second reason is that an individual's membership in the group requires that his or her boundaries are sufficiently permeable to receive and transmit information. Although a therapist may place a patient in a group with other patients, that placement in and of itself is not sufficient for group membership in the absence of some permeability of boundaries on the part of the individual member. Models that emphasize the importance of a group-level conceptualization also see value in interventions at the individual level to foster each member's openness to the group experience. Although models that rely on a group-as-a-whole level of conceptualization support the use of interventions at all levels, those interventions that are deemed to be most powerful in advancing the goals of the group are ones formulated at the subgroup and group-as-a-whole levels. Other levels of intervention may be seen as developing members' receptivities to an eventual group-as-a-whole interpretation.

behavioral models. Generally, these models involve not only conceptualization but also intervention at the individual level. Although some proponents of these models talk about the necessity of developing a certain emotional atmosphere in the group that is propitious for individual work (Coché, 1987; Rose, 1989), group-level factors are less of a focus in the cognitive–behavioral model than they are in the other two models. Also, something resembling interpersonal interventions are used occasionally within this model, as when members participating in a cognitive–behavioral group test out dysfunctional beliefs using feedback from other group members. However, unlike their use in the interpersonal model, these interventions are designed to benefit only one person rather than both members of the dyad.

**Directive versus reactive.** Another set of variables that distinguishes each model is the extent to which the therapist assumes a directive versus a reactive posture in relation to the content and the process of the session. As we illustrate, the therapist's levels of directiveness in regard to the content and process aspects of the session are potentially separable.

Models vary in the freedom that they accord members in determining the content of the session. Here, the term *content* refers to what the group talks about (in contrast to how it talks about it). For example, if in a segment of a session, members talk about their relationships with their psychiatrists, that topic is the content of the segment. In some models, the therapist intervenes in such a way as to guarantee the emergence of very specifically defined material and to support the submergence of other topics. Such models require a highly directive posture on the part of the therapist, who predetermines about what the group will talk. Contrasting with this posture is one in which the therapist is primarily reactive to whatever is spontaneously produced in the group. Although the therapist may guide the group to some broad realm of exploration such as the here-and-now rather than the there-and-then, the group is nonetheless accorded considerable latitude in the particular concerns it addresses. Models that require a reactive posture in relation to content frequently emphasize the importance of the therapist's accurate discernment of the concerns (explicit or implicit) occupying the group's attention. That is, reactive models highlight the therapist's diagnostic activity vis-à-vis group, subgroup, interpersonal, or individual dynamics. Such models generally provide the therapist with various types of information that can be used to make an assessment of the group, such as the observation of verbal and nonverbal behaviors, the analysis of countertransference responses, and so forth.

An example of a model that is directive vis-à-vis the content of the session is a behaviorally oriented assertiveness-training group. To enhance members' engagement in appropriate assertive behaviors, the therapist might ask them to recount situations in which they had either failed or succeeded in exhibiting assertive behaviors. Other material is either categorized by the therapist as "irrelevant" or used as a segue to discussing assertiveness-related situations. Another example of a model that requires the therapist's adoption of a directive posture toward the content of the session is the educative model. In this model, members are supported by the therapist in talking about only those particular here-and-now experiences that relate to the dysfunctional behaviors that precipitated their hospitalization.

Examples of models that are on the reactive end of the continuum are the unstructured version of the interpersonal model and the object relations/systems model. Although both of these models guide members in focusing on certain domains of experience (i.e., the here-and-now), members' communications within the group are for the most part spontaneous and free-flowing. Provided that members remain within the designated realm of exploration (i.e., the here-and-now), there is little on which the members might focus that would be regarded by the therapist as irrelevant to the aims of the group.

The interactional agenda version of the interpersonal model represents an intermediate point on the continuum of degree of therapist control over the session's content. Members are free to bring up any agenda item they wish provided that the agenda has certain characteristics such as concreteness, an interpersonal orientation, and a feasibility of being addressed in the group. However, once agendas have been set, the therapist constrains the members to their continued examination and fulfillment. Little leeway is given for the surfacing of new concerns within a particular session.

Therapists may be relatively directive or reactive in the processes that are deployed in group. Process is to be distinguished from content in that process refers to how the group pursues its work. In the former example in which members were talking about their psychiatrists, the process of the group might refer to a format that evolved in the group wherein each member made a comment and waited for the therapist to respond. Some models specify in a highly detailed and programmatic way how problems or issues are to be addressed. Usually, these models require that sessions be highly formatted. Other models provide only general guidelines that can be observed in various ways both by the group members and by the therapist.

Two examples of models that require a high level of therapist directiveness in regard to the group process are the cognitive–behavioral and problem-solving models. Within each, the sessions have a highly articulated format, and the patient–therapist and member–member interactions are clearly proscribed by the model. In contrast, such models as the educative and object relations/systems models provide the therapist with a set of goals and a range of interventions that may be helpful in pursuing group goals. However, what interventions should be deployed at any moment of the group's life is largely left to the judgment of the therapist.

The reader may notice that whether the therapist is reactive or directive in relation to content does not determine his or her stance in regard to process. In other words, these dimensions are independent. For example, the educative therapist is directive with respect to content but is reactive with respect to process. The problem-solving therapist is reactive with respect to content but is directive with respect to process. The cognitive–behavioral therapist is directive with respect to both content and process. The object relations/systems therapist is reactive with respect to both content and process.

A model's stance on the deficit/conflict issue has a bearing on the therapist's levels of reactivity and directiveness on both the content and process dimensions. Generally, the conflict models assume that what creates a problem for patients is not what is missing but what is present. They assume that if members are provided with the conditions to speak openly about their experience, the therapist will have the necessary material for the work of the group. The therapist then reacts to the emergence of such material with interventions designed to foster its organization. Hence, conflict therapists are inclined to assume a primarily reactive posture with respect to both process and content. However, some directive elements may be present such as when the therapist fosters a process of members giving feedback to one another.

The deficit models see as problematic what is missing or deficiently present in the patient. The therapist must create the necessary experiences within the group so that some structure, process, or repertoire of behaviors can either be acquired or strengthened. Hence, deficit models tend to place the therapist in a position of being directive. To the extent that the model sees the deficit as being one of process, the therapist is likely to be directive with respect to the process of the group. An example of this is the problem-solving model, which sees patients as lacking effective means to solve problems. Within this model, the therapist is highly directive with respect to the group process and is less directive with respect to its content. Conversely, models that see the deficit as residing not in broad psychological processes but in specific responses tend to require the therapist's directiveness vis-à-vis the content of the group. An example of this type of model is the educative model, in which the therapist is directive in getting members to focus on target complaints.

## Dimensions of the Setting

In the preceding comparative analysis, we discussed the models in isolation of the context in which they are applied. Our analysis would certainly be incomplete if we did not return to the treatment settings themselves and consider how the features of different settings either potentiate or inhibit the effectiveness of each of the models. In this section, we revisit the dimensions of the setting described in chapter 2. We show how a setting's position on each of the variables associated with the dimension determines what models are viable and useful in the setting.

## Clinical Mission of the Care Setting

**Philosophy, values, and goals.** In chapter 2, we pointed out that there are a number of variables at the level of the institution as a whole and its relation to the broader community that affect what types of group psychotherapy are most feasible with that institution. It is beyond the scope of this text to offer a typology of institutions in terms of their highly varied philosophical and value structures. Our interest, rather, is merely to encourage the practitioner to look beyond the most immediate context in which the group takes place to the whole hierarchy of systems in which the group resides, including the system of the institution itself.

For example, in chapter 2, we contrasted settings that define change in a holistic versus a focal way. Institutions that seek holistic change regard the person as a concatenation of systems (e.g., biological, interpersonal, spiritual), all of which affect one another as well as the overall well-being of the person. In holistically oriented institutions, the treatment package addresses all systems that define a person. Those institutions that are more focally oriented in the nature of the change sought embrace intervention strategies that are directly linked to the patient's complaints, that is, the symptoms or problems that brought the patient into the hospital.

The models that require a holistic treatment philosophy on the part of both the institution and the immediate context of treatment are the interpersonal, object relations/systems, developmental, and problem-solving models. The goals of these models would be deemed irrelevant by an institution seeking direct connections between interventions and target complaints. Although the other models are compatible with a holistic orientation, they do not require one.

There are other models that are compatible with the mission of institutions seeking more focal change. Inevitably, the focal change that such institutions target pertains to the symptoms that precipitated the patient's hospitalization. Models that directly operate on target complaints are the educative, cognitive–behavioral, and some forms of the behavioral model.

**Theoretical orientation.** Not only do institutions sometimes embrace particular theoretical orientations but they also, at times, adopt a stance against a specific orientation. That is, whereas some institutions are adamantly psychoanalytic, others are adamantly nonpsychoanalytic. Among the models we have reviewed, there are those models that are clearly allied with a traditional school of psychotherapy. Probably most notable among these are the object relations/systems and behavioral models. The application of these models would be compromised if the institution were to define itself in terms of an alternate model or the repudiation of that model.

Some models we have presented are more indeterminant than the aforementioned models in that they have complex historical links with various schools of thought. Any of these links can be emphasized in developing a pro-group climate for that model. For example, connections can be validly drawn between the interpersonal model and psychoanalysis and between the interpersonal model and social learning theory. The cognitive–behavioral model provides another example of the abilities of these models to have shifting emphases and to be translated into diverging conceptual frameworks. These features give them a protean quality in that they are potentially appealing to a wide range of psychotherapeutic palates.

## Context of the Group

**The locus of the group in the system.** In chapter 2, we contrasted the unit-based group with the mixed-unit group. The reader will recall that the essential feature of the unit-based group is not where the group is physically held but who is in the group. In the same-unit group, all members of the group are drawn from one particular unit. In the mixed-unit group, the group is composed of members from two or more units.

The boundary arrangements of same-unit and mixed-unit groups differ considerably. In the same-unit group, the boundaries of the unit comprehend the group entirely. The nesting of the group within the unit makes the group open to all aspects of unit life: the emotional atmosphere, the norms, the goals, and so on. It is therefore impossible to conceptualize the group independently of the unit. Hence, events within the group would be incoherent to all members including the therapist if there were no effort to relate them to events in and the climate of the unit. As Ghuman and Sarles (1989) found, in the unit-based group, members spontaneously talk about occurrences and conflicts on the unit. If a model has a means by which to address group–unit relations, that model is better able to illuminate the phenomena that are likely to emerge than are models that place less emphasis on such relations.

Among the models we have considered, the object relations/ systems model stands out as offering the most developed conceptual structure and technical tools to respond to the presence of the unit within the group. There are a number of other models that use the context of the unit (a) to achieve a higher level of cohesiveness than if members were involved with one another outside of group and (b) to garner information about the group member and his or her behavior on the unit that can be used in the group. The interpersonal and educative models use the group's presence on the unit in both of these ways.

In the type of group that combines members from different units, the boundaries of the group overlap with many treatment units but are not comprehended by any one unit. As demonstrated by Karterud (1988), different units can have very different emotional climates. Although each of the units from which members are drawn continuously affects the group, it is more difficult relative to the unit-based group to disentangle the influence of the units on the group from the influence of other subsystems of the hospital. Moreover, because mixed-unit groups have a greater capacity to develop their own structural characteristics, some of what emerges in the group belongs to the group itself and is not directly derivative of any related system. Hence, the mixed-unit group is not particularly conducive to the exploration of group–unit relations. Furthermore, members appear less inclined in a mixed-unit group to introduce spontaneously aspects of their life on the unit than they are when in a same-unit group (Ghuman & Sarles, 1989). Models that make use of this intragroup focus (e.g., the developmental model) or that, at the very least, do not require the use of a great deal of information about unit life (e.g., problem-solving models) would be particularly appropriate for the mixed-unit group.

**The system perception of the group.** All models in this text profit from the presence of a pro-group environment and are hindered by an interpersonal environment that either devalues group psychotherapy or harbors misconceptions about the purpose and method of the group. For some models, however, the endorsement of the group by other staff is of the utmost importance. We have identified three features that a model may possess that make it vulnerable in predictable ways to the absence of a pro-group climate. The negative impact of all of these features is likely to be exacerbated if the staff who run the group are not regular members of the treatment team.

A first feature is when the therapist requires information from members' lives on the unit either to formulate goals for individual group members (e.g., the interactional agenda version of the interpersonal model) or to interpret events in the group (e.g., the object relations/systems model). In circumstances in which a pro-group environment is lacking, the group therapist may be hindered in obtaining the information needed to run the group effectively, as when the therapist enters the group without having been informed of the elopement of a well-known patient on the unit.

A second feature is when the model explicitly focuses on group–unit relations (e.g., the object relations/systems model). When the model involves the therapist specifically talking about the unit within the group, the staff must be sufficiently cognizant and accepting of the group's way of working to tolerate the group's exploration of events or aspects of unit life in which they may have been involved. Otherwise, the staff can readily establish a projective identificatory relationship with the group wherein the group is seen as a threatening and hostile force to the maintenance of their personal and professional well-being on the unit.

A third feature is when the therapist is dependent on extra-group staff to reinforce learning from the group or to oversee the execution of homework assignments. The cognitive–behavioral model and the social skills training version of the behavioral model provide examples of this type of group–unit relation. In the absence of a pro-group climate, staff can readily give members the message that group-related activities between group sessions are unimportant.

## Temporal Variables

**Duration of participation in the group.** The models are highly varied in the length of participation in the group that they require. We attempt to classify the models into those that involve extremely brief participation (e.g., one session), those that require participation over several sessions, and those that require a more protracted tenure in the group (e.g., four or more sessions). As we classify models, we attempt to analyze the features of the model that place it in one temporal demand category or another.

The models that we have reviewed in this text that seem to be able to tolerate the briefest durations of participation are the interactional agenda version of the interpersonal model and the object relations/systems model. Members can make significant progress in achieving the goals of the group through attendance of a single session. Moreover, these models have technical maneuvers to ensure that each member is engaged in the group's work so that every member can potentially benefit from every session. The interactional agenda model involves a go-around in which each member formulates a goal. If the member does nothing else but to develop an agenda in here-and-now, interpersonal, and concrete terms, the member has fulfilled two major objectives of the group: to spot problems and to recognize that psychological difficulties have an important interpersonal aspect. The object relations/systems model ensures each member's participation through individually oriented interventions that help members to identify with other members. Through group-as-a-whole clarificatory statements, members learn to recognize their participation in a group theme.

Models that require a slightly longer tenure include the educative model and the unstructured version of the interpersonal model as well as some forms of the behavioral model such as social skills training. Maxmen (1978) specifically indicated that members should be in the group for three or four sessions so that they feel reasonably comfortable in exploring the details surrounding their hospitalization. The unstructured version of the interpersonal model requires that members have an opportunity to exhibit their difficulties in the group. Although some of these members may reveal their characteristic problems in a single session (particularly if their difficulties happen to be in the area of trust or the withdrawal from relationships), other members may require more time to exhibit their problematic social behaviors within the group. For example, if members have difficulty specifically in their relations with authority, these difficulties are unlikely to show themselves when members first enter the group. There are some members for whom a much longer duration of membership would be necessary for them to show their dysfunctional social behaviors.

The demands that models make on members' tenures in the group depend to some extent on what is perceived by the model as helpful within the group. For example, within the interactional agenda version of the interpersonal model, what is helpful is the member's exposure to the process of getting feedback rather than the specific feedback itself. With the unstructured version of the interpersonal model, it is not just the process but the content of the feedback itself that is important. That is, if patients receive accurate feedback, they are able to make significant changes in their interpersonal functioning. Whereas a subject can participate in the process if they attend only one session, the reception of accurate feedback will take some time as members get to know one another better. Hence, when it is not only the process but the content of information that is important, greater demands are made on the members' tenures in the group. Some models establish as a goal members' acquisitions of new skills or processes, whereas other models simply presume that members' exposures to a process in the group will be beneficial in some regard. The expectation of the acquisition of, rather than exposure to, a process places greater demands on members' tenures in the group. For example, the problem-solving model assumes that members acquire problem-solving skills. Although members can be exposed to the steps of problem-solving in a single session, it takes several sessions for them to incorporate this process (i.e., to be able to use it spontaneously as new problems emerge).

Models that require members to be present for more than a handful of sessions are the cognitive–behavioral, problem-solving, and developmental models. The cognitive–behavioral and developmental models have in common a reliance on a set of stages that define the learning process. For the cognitive–behavioral group, the stages are prescribed by the treatment itself. For the developmental model, the stages are those that are seen as naturally emerging in the course of group process. The problem-solving model requires multiple sessions because the steps associated with this model are sufficiently complex and challenging to require repetition over time.

As discussed in chapter 2, there do exist settings in which patients remain in the hospital for an extended period. Some of the models described in this text are more adaptable than are others to a long-term time frame. There seem to be two factors that affect the extent to which a model is suitable for long-term use. The first is the degree to which the content and process of the model are predetermined. The more open-ended the content and process, the more suitable the model is for long-term use. The second is whether the model has the potential for the development of a set of goals that is different from those embraced for the model's short-term application.

An example of a model that may not be suitable for use over an extremely long period of time (e.g., 6 months) is the problem-solving model. Although this model is variable in terms of content, the process is entirely predetermined. Moreover, the goal of the model, to help members acquire the steps of the problem-solving process, is static. Certainly, with more sessions, members could establish the steps as more permanent parts of their ego organizations. However, at some point, the repetitive aspect of the model would be likely to diminish their engagement in the sessions.

In contrast, the object relations/systems model is flexible both from the standpoint of content and process. Members are able to talk about whatever comes to mind, although certainly there is a bias in the direction of the extended here-and-now (i.e., immediate events in the group or within the broader treatment environment). Although this model establishes as a short-term goal the reacquisition of the defense of splitting, if members were in a stable group over a long period of time, the group could move into working on the integration of opposite-poled self and object images. Moreover, as Kibel (1986) pointed out, longer term involvement would enable a more intensive focus on group (as opposed to unit) dynamics, leading to clearer identification of the defensive patterns of individual group members.

**Closed-ended versus open-ended groups.** Within the group psychotherapy literature, it is generally assumed that a closed-ended group is capable of achieving a higher level of cohesiveness than is an open-ended group. Because group cohesion has been found to benefit groups with a variety of different formats (Lieberman, Yalom, & Miles, 1973), the closed-ended structure may be a felicitous feature for any model described in this text. However, there are certain models that are likely to be more beneficially affected by the closed-ended feature than other models. Those models that require members to transfer from session-to-session learning information or knowledge about prior group proceedings are facilitated by a closed-ended format. Examples of such models are the developmental and problem-solving models. The developmental model also acquires a specific benefit from the closed-ended format in that the longer the membership of a group remains constant, the more likely it is that a group gets beyond the earliest stage of development (Schopler & Galinsky, 1990).

**Number of sessions per week.** The number of sessions per week is also likely to affect cohesiveness. With frequent meetings, members are not only provided with more abundant opportunities to bond but also to perceive the group as a psychological staple, a dependable resource in their lives within the hospital. Insofar as all models are abetted by a high level of cohesiveness, more frequent sessions enhance the operation of each model. In the previous section, a number of models were identified as being especially dependent on either the achievement of a high level of cohesiveness or members' access to material from prior sessions. These are the same models that may particularly profit from more frequent sessions.

There are some models, however, that can be used when the group meets as minimally as once a week. Examples are the interactional agenda version of the interpersonal model and the content-oriented educational version of the cognitive–behavioral model (Sank & Shaffer, 1984).

## Size of the Group

Although many of the models featured in this text claim to be able to accommodate from 4 to 12 members, 8 to 10 is commonly cited as being the optimal range. Those models that seem to be most compromised by an increase in the number of members beyond the specified limits are the highly directive and structured models such as the cognitive–behavioral model, the problem-solving model, the social skills version of the behavioral model, and to a somewhat lesser extent, the interactional agenda version of the interpersonal model. All of these models emphasize individual intervention in at least one part of the session. With an increase in the number of members beyond a certain limit, the therapist is handicapped in giving each individual the attention needed to fulfill the goals of the model. The cognitive–behavioral model is likely to be most affected by group size in that most of the session consists of individual interventions. In contrast, the interactional agenda model involves individually centered interventions only in the initial portion of the session. However, as Froberg and Slife (1987) pointed out, the more that the group is occupied with agenda setting, the less time they will have for the more interactive process of agenda fulfilling.

Models may also be adversely affected by too few group members, particularly those models that capitalize on differences among members. Some models such as the interpersonal model, the educative model, and the developmental model rely on differences in members' interpersonal styles. Other models require variability in members' areas of difficulty. For example, in the problem-solving model, when members do not have a significant number of examples of problems to consider, they tend to focus on the content of problems rather than on the principles of problem solving. Hence, when deciding whether a model is likely to be unduly compromised by a small number of members, the therapist must assess whether the members are sufficiently variable on the dimensions most critical to the model.

One model impresses us as particularly adaptable to groups of different sizes is the object relations/systems model. This adaptability derives from the range of levels of intervention available to the therapist. The group therapist can easily move from the individual level when membership diminishes to a relatively greater emphasis on group-as-a-whole interventions when membership is increased. The model's flexibility would make it potentially useful in circumstances in which group size is likely to change radically over time. Although the developmental model also uses individual, interpersonal, and group-as-a-whole lines of interpretation, it places more emphasis on the interpretation of subgroup patterns than does the object relations/systems model. When membership falls below five, there is a tendency for subgroups of one to form. This circumstance is detrimental both to the solitary individual who feels isolated and rejected and to the rest of the group whose fears of the destructive effects of their own affects and impulses are reinforced.

## Group Composition

**Level of functioning.** In chapter 2, we discussed the fact that one of the better researched variables in the treatment setting is the level of ego functioning of the group members. As a consequence of the empirical work done in the field, we now recognize that there are at least four elements that characterize effective work with the lower functioning inpatient such as the highly disorganized, acutely psychotic patient or the chronic patient showing a paucity of resources for working in treatment. These elements are (a) a highly supportive emotional climate, (b) the absence of anxiety-promoting interventions such as confrontation, (c) the curtailment of potentially regression-promoting group processes such as a high level of self-disclosure or the intensive exploration of experience, and (d) highly structured sessions wherein members can anticipate the flow of events.

There are several models that have most if not all of these features. The social skills version of the behavioral model requires a very warm and supportive leadership style and directs the therapist to provide continuous verbal reinforcement of members' efforts. Members are never confronted on their deficiencies, nor are they required to engage in the kinds of processes that frequently evoke anxiety (e.g., self-disclosure).

The focus group version of the interpersonal model was developed specifically for a low-functioning population and not surprisingly has all of the features that characterize an effective group for this patient population. As indicated in chapter 4 on the interpersonal model, Yalom (1983), probably more than any other writer on inpatient populations, provided a detailed analysis of how the therapist builds support into an inpatient group. Yalom was also explicit in his exclusion of interventions and processes that can precipitate further decompensation. His focus group entails a session with a prescribed sequence of steps and has built-in mechanisms (such as an orientation and wrap-up) that make the session's organization evident to members.

The cognitive–behavioral and problem-solving models have some of the features associated with positive outcomes in lower functioning populations. However, these models' procedures require a level of ability in synthesizing information that is often not present in this population. As such, the procedures of both models require some fairly substantial modification to allow for the slower acquisition of information and the greater need for repetition in this population. For example, Edelstein, Couture, Cray, Dickens, and Lusebrink (1980) altered the method of the problem-solving model in such a way that one skill could be taught at a time so that it could be used with a highly regressed patient population. Similarly, Greenwood (1987) developed a methodology wherein the steps of the cognitive–behavioral approach could be taught more slowly to a more regressed patient population; Massel, Corrigan, Liberman, and Milan (1991) did the same for the behavioral model.

Relative to lower functioning patients, higher functioning patients have been observed to better tolerate the anxiety that might be stimulated by more exploratory (rather than supportive) processes. Examples of processes that evoke anxiety are the giving and receiving of feedback, the analysis of preconscious impulses and affects that may be associated with interpersonal difficulties, self-disclosure, and the expression of affect. Although these processes are likely to be more useful to higher functioning inpatients than to lower functioning inpatients, they should, even with the former group, be used in moderation. Moreover, they should be combined with a higher dose of support than is needed by some outpatient groups. Among the models that involve these processes are the cognitive–behavioral, developmental, and object relations/systems models as well as the interactional agenda version of the interpersonal model.

In some inpatient circumstances, clinical exigencies demand that patients of very diverse levels of functioning be placed in a group together (Erickson, 1986). There are some models that are particularly suited to a group that is heterogeneous in level of functioning. In chapter 3, we showed how the therapist applying the educative model is able to treat, within the same group, extremely disorganized psychotic patients and borderline patients. We showed that the model allows for the titration of self-exploration based on the therapist's knowledge of the members' degrees and acutenesses of pathology and levels of anxiety. The object relations/systems model has the same capability of adaptation to the level of functioning of the member. The major exploratory efforts occur on a group-as-a-whole level. The group's affects are connected to the unit events that precipitated them. The nonindividual character of the exploratory statements that the members make limits their power to evoke anxiety. Yet, within the model, one could help a particular person see that his or her unique way of responding to a group tension may have adverse interpersonal or intrapsychic consequences. However, these individually directed comments would be reserved for members who are relatively high functioning, have been long-term participants in the group, and have achieved a considerable level of comfort in the group. The effect of these more probing comments on others in the group must also be considered. Although both the educative and object relations/systems models permit a titration in the depth of the interventions directed at individuals, some extremely regressed members may find the lack of structure that characterizes sessions run according to these models threatening and, hence, disorganizing.

**Diagnosis.** In the literature, there is a belief commonly expressed that diagnostically heterogeneous groups work better for the treatment of interpersonal problems, whereas homogeneous groups work better for the treatment of focal problems and symptom constellations (e.g., see Beutler & Clarkin, 1990; Yalom, 1985). For reasons delineated in chapter 2, this formulation has a great deal of intuitive appeal. However, the empirical and anecdotal evidence that we have reviewed suggests that heterogeneity or homogeneity of diagnosis is not a seriously limiting factor. For example, there are numerous examples of the literature of interpersonally oriented groups composed of members who share a diagnosis (e.g., Kaplan, Kerr, & Maddocks, 1992; Weiner, 1987; Yehoshua, Kellerman, Calev, & Dasberg, 1985). Although it is not clear that these groups would be as effective as groups composed of diagnostically heterogeneous members, it is nonetheless the case that the authors describing these groups perceive the groups as working effectively and, in some cases, present data to support their perceptions. Although this variable needs to be studied empirically, for the present, it would seem that if the practitioner has already chosen a model and has the option to create a diagnostically heterogeneous or homogeneous group, then he or she might follow the common wisdom of basing this decision on whether the type of change sought is interpersonal or symptomatic. However, if diagnostic composition is a given, then there is no strong basis for seeing it as constraining model selection in any particular direction.[2]

**Psychological sophistication.** Different models make different demands on members' abilities to think in a psychological way. Probably the least demanding models on this dimension are the behavioral, educative, and problem-solving models in that order. For the most part, these models direct the member's focus to the outside world and the stimuli that evoke symptoms.

Somewhat more demanding are the cognitive–behavioral and interpersonal models. Cognitive–behavioral therapy requires that the individual recognize that thoughts that are quickly passing and barely accessible influence affect. Interpersonal models require that individuals have some acceptance of the notion that often underlying symptoms are difficulties in relationships. This

---

[2] For a given diagnostic population, homogeneity may be preferable across models. For example, Barr (1986) described the multiple advantages of treating acutely psychotic schizophrenics in homogeneous groups. We are not taking a position on the relative merits of homogeneity versus heterogeneity in general or for any specific group. Rather, our intent is to consider how each of these arrangements may or may not create constraints in model selection.

awareness is not so important in terms of a member's ability to participate in the group as is his or her motivation to be in the group. A woman who enters the hospital with a severe depression is not likely to be interested in talking about her passivity in relationships unless she perceives that it relates to her depression.

Those models that place the greatest demands on members establish as a goal internal, intrapsychic conflict resolution. This goal entails that the individual gain access to material against which there has been some significant level of resistance. The developmental model is an example of a model that makes such demands. The group member successfully participating in such treatment must be willing to accept a certain worldview that events (i.e., psychological experience or behavior) are not always as they seem and that one's behavior is often motivated by factors outside of one's awareness.

Although this variable has received little empirical attention, we believe that the modal level of psychological sophistication of the members should be considered in the selection of a model. Certain patients by virtue of their defensive structure will not see as meaningful the kinds of explorations that certain models entail. For example, all of the interpersonally oriented models require that members recognize the value of a focus on their social difficulties. It is true that the recognition that interpersonal difficulties underlie symptoms can be cultivated and the achievement of it is, in fact, a goal of the interactional agenda model. However, the short-term time frame of most inpatient experiences does not afford the therapist an opportunity to dismantle certain major resistances. Individuals who tenaciously use somaticization, externalization, or some other maneuver that is at odds with a psychological perspective would be better served in groups whose goals accord better with their own.

**Gender.** The literature suggests that the vast majority of inpatient groups are heterogeneous with respect to gender. All of the models we have featured have been used with a mixed-gender group, and there is no suggestion that any of these models would be compromised by this arrangement.

Groups that are homogeneous for gender often occur in circumstances in which the group is homogeneous for diagnosis, as in the case of a group of female patients with eating disorders. The covariation of the two variables, gender and diagnosis, makes it impossible to disentangle the effects of each. However, as was noted previously in this chapter's section on composition, it appears that many of the models can be used with groups that are homogeneous for diagnosis. Because many of the groups were also homogeneous for gender, it would seem that this type of homogeneity does not substantially limit the practitioner's range of potential models. In view of the lack of systematic investigation of this variable, however, these comments should be regarded as speculative.

**Age.** Inpatient groups may be heterogeneous or homogeneous in terms of the ages of group members. Age heterogeneity (i.e., the inclusion of individuals from different age ranges) is compatible with all of the models featured in this text except the problem-solving model. The problem-solving model is most effectively applied with an age-homogeneous group because each application of the model is tailored to cognitive capabilities that are age related. In an age-heterogeneous group, it would be nearly impossible to maintain a pace that would be appropriate for all members.

As indicated in chapter 2, age-homogeneous groups are increasingly common. The age-homogeneous group that has received the greatest attention in the literature is the adolescent group. Among the models featured in this text that have been applied to adolescent groups are the educative (R. Gogineni, personal communication, April 11, 1992), object relations/systems (Setterberg, 1991), developmental (Bernfeld, Clark, & Parker, 1984), cognitive–behavioral (Feindler, Ecton, Kingsley, & Dubey, 1986; Grossman & Freet, 1987), and problem-solving (Spivack, Platt, & Shure, 1976) models and the social skills training version of the behavioral model (Hazel, Sherman, Schumaker, & Sheldon, 1985). Although reports across all models have tended to be quite positive for adolescent groups, these reports are based largely on clinical observations rather than experimental data. Only the cognitive–behavioral model (Feindler et al., 1986) has received experimental support for utility with this population.

There has been little consideration in the literature of the utility of the different models with geriatric groups. Some support has been obtained for the use of the cognitive–behavioral model (Zerhusen, Boyle, & Wilson, 1991) and a social skills version of the behavioral model (Lopez, 1980) with an elderly population. In general, however, the elderly in inpatient group psychotherapy has been a neglected topic (Fallon & Brabender, 1992). In chapter 2, we hypothesized that models that limit elderly patients to the here-and-now and require them to process interpersonal differences may not be maximally congruent with their developmental needs. However, there is no research support for these hypotheses. Moreover, it is likely that the high level of variability among the elderly on basic perceptual, cognitive, and social variables necessitates that subpopulations of the elderly be differentiated from one another in terms of the efficacy of different models.

## Therapist Variables

Although there are probably many therapist variables that affect the therapist's ability to effectively use a given model, we have focused on a limited set of variables in this text: the theoretical preference and level of experience of the therapist and the desirability of a single therapist versus a co-therapy team. Our rationale for selecting these variables as opposed to all of the variables we might have considered is that frequently, model builders discuss their models in relation to these therapist variables. Other variables pertaining to the therapist's personality, cognitive style, and preferred leadership posture may be equally important but have been largely unaddressed by either model builders or the empirical inpatient group psychotherapy literature.

In an earlier section, we described how the models vary with respect to the role of the leader. We outlined three areas of difference: whether the model is relationship oriented or technique oriented; whether the model requires an individual, interpersonal, or group-as-a-whole level of conceptualization; and whether the model requires that the leader take a reactive versus directive stance toward the group's process and content. An optimal model for a leader would be one in which the leader experienced a reasonably high comfort level with the model's position on these dimensions.

Models vary in the demands that they place on the therapist to accept a particular view of psychopathology. Some models place a rather stringent requirement on the therapist for a certain theoretical allegiance. Other models are more flexible and are compatible with a wide variety of theoretical orientations or even the lack of an orientation on the part of the therapist.

Examples of models that place fairly strict theoretical demands on the therapist are the object relations/systems and developmental models. Both require the therapist's acceptance of the basic postulates of a psychoanalytic view of psychopathology, including the existence of an unconscious and the principle of psychological determinism (Rutan, 1992). Additionally, the practitioners of these models must see value in the adoption of a general systems theory framework in the conceptualization of group process.

These models are to be contrasted with the educative model, which endorses no particular set of assumptions about psychopathology. Just as this model could be adopted by a wide variety of institutions, so could it be used by a therapist of virtually any theoretical persuasion including a medical model orientation. Other models are in a more intermediate position on this dimension. For example, although the interpersonal model is potentially compatible with either a psychodynamic or behavioral perspective, it is not compatible with a medical model. However, whether the practitioner is psychodynamically oriented or behaviorally oriented would make some difference in how the model is applied. The psychodynamic therapist would work to foster insight into the unconscious factors underlying maladaptive interpersonal behaviors, whereas the behavioral therapist would emphasize mechanisms that are common to a social behavioral framework such as imitation, modeling, and so on.

Another set of variables on which models differ is the degree and type of experience needed for the therapist to use the model. Models that we see as highly demanding of the therapist's background are the developmental model, the educative model, and the unstructured version of the interpersonal model. The developmental and interpersonal models require the therapist to integrate different conceptual frameworks in theory and technique. The educative model is demanding in its lack of clear and detailed guidelines for intervention, thus necessitating the therapist to access a knowledge base about group process that is not provided by the model itself.

Placing somewhat less stringent demands on the therapist's background are the object relations/systems and cognitive–behavioral models as well as the focus group and interactional agenda versions of the interpersonal model. Although like the developmental model, the object relations/systems model entails an integration of different conceptual frameworks, a therapist could use the model on a rudimentary level by grasping and applying the notion that the group reflects unit events and issues. However, an understanding of the complexities of object relations theory would be a great asset to the therapist. The therapist with little formal training in group therapy could use the interactional agenda and focus group models because of the specificity of these models' goals and methods. On the other hand, an analysis of the Yalom videotapes (Yalom, 1990) makes it very apparent that a more senior therapist can use this model in a different fashion than can the junior therapist. The former can subtly interpret for members the defensive aspects of their behavior and still operate within the confines of the model. Many of Yalom's interventions on the videotapes would be inaccessible to the therapist lacking psychodynamic understanding. The focus group allows the therapist great latitude in pitching the interventions at the appropriate level given members' levels of anxiety and functioning. This latitude is a burden to the neophyte therapist who has not accumulated the kind of experience from which comes such sensitivity. The cognitive–behavioral model requires the therapist's grasp of a fairly well-elaborated theoretical base and a set of techniques consistent with this base.

The models that are most accessible to the inexperienced group therapist are the problem-solving model and the social skills version of the behavioral model. These models tap a fairly circumscribed theoretical base and provide a well-defined set of interventions. The fact that these models do not require a knowledge of group process or dynamics makes them more accessible to the new practitioner. Although such knowledge would be helpful to the therapist, it is not essential because it is not formally incorporated into these models.[3] However, we predict, on the basis of trends in the literature, that the development of these models will lead to their greater use of systems theory as it applies to the understanding of the characteristics of the group as an entity. Consequently, the present models may actually become less amenable to practitioners who perceive groups as an assembly of individuals.

Another important variable is the leadership format. Is it more optimal to have a single therapist or a co-therapy team? Some writers (e.g., Rutan & Stone, 1984) have argued that a co-therapy arrangement diminishes the uncomfortable affects that the therapist is likely to experience in the session. Co-therapy thereby reduces the information that such disturbing affects might provide in the therapist's understanding of the group. This argument seems to have little resonance for writers on inpatient group therapy, including those who emphasize the use of countertransference to elucidate group dynamics. As has been widely noted, the inpatient group is an affective cauldron capable of stimulating extremely intense feelings in the therapist (e.g., Brabender, 1987; Hannah, 1984; Kibel, 1992). However, such strong feelings are evoked whether or not a co-therapy team is present. The co-therapy feature frequently brings each inpatient group therapist's anxiety and other uncomfortable feelings within tolerable limits wherein they can be used even more effectively to understand the group. The co-therapist relationship also provides an opportunity for the therapists to confirm the validity of their own perceptions of the group, which are sometimes skewed because of the successful projective identifications of group members. Moreover, the disparity in the co-therapists' perceptions provide diagnostic information about group-level defenses (Greene, Rosenkrantz, & Muth, 1986). Finally, the co-therapy structure per-

---

[3] There are a few writers, such as Flowers (1979), who have emphasized the importance of the therapist's understanding of the group-level phenomena as well ability to make groupwide interventions. However, these writers are still the exception.

mits a sharing of the sometimes numerous leader tasks. For these reasons, the major proponents of the models we present advocate co-therapy as the more optimal leadership structure.

Despite the preferability of co-therapy for all models, there are some models for which co-therapy is more crucial. The application of the developmental and object relations/systems models may be rendered less effective by the lack of a co-therapy team because these models rely heavily on the exploration of members' negative reactions to the leader. Rutan and Stone (1984) believed that these reactions are more difficult to acknowledge when there is a co-therapy team because such an arrangement makes the leadership appear more intimidating. However, Greene (1988) discussed how members frequently direct aggression toward one therapist while preserving the other therapist as a positive figure. The availability of only a single therapist augments members' fears of the negative consequences of directing aggression toward authority (e.g., retaliation, loss of nurturance).

A common circumstance in inpatient settings is the change in group leadership due to therapist vacation, resignations, transfers, new staff patterns, and so on. Some models are better able to tolerate changes in leadership than are others. For example, the problem-solving model is likely to withstand leadership turnover with few adverse consequences. In this model, the leader requires little or no information from prior sessions and does not demand the kind of high cohesiveness that stable leadership fosters. In fact, a problem-solving group whose repetitive aspect may weary higher functioning members may be invigorated by a change in leadership. On the other hand, the cognitive–behavioral model and the social skills version of the behavioral model require the therapist's understanding of each member's homework assignment and how it fits in with the member's overall program of involvement in the group. At the very least, this requirement would necessitate a high level of communication between the new and old therapists. The developmental, educative, and interpersonal models place an even greater demand for leader continuity because unlike the aforementioned models, they are heavily reliant on the group's achievement of a high level of cohesiveness.

# Case Examples

To demonstrate the process of model selection, we consider three case examples.

## Case 1

**Description.** A group psychotherapist had recently joined the treatment team of an acute-care psychiatric unit of a general hospital that had a longstanding reputation as a training institution. The ambience of the unit was one of respect among the professionals, which was in part due to their endorsement of a holistic view of treatment. However, in the past several years, the staff had been feeling a growing frustration with their sense that nothing of substance could be accomplished given patients' ever-diminishing lengths of stays. The average length of stay was 6 days, although some patients stayed for only 2 to 3 days.

The unit was mixed in terms of level of functioning and diagnosis. About half of the unit consisted of members with some kind of psychotic diagnosis. The other half had character pathologies of various types. A psychotherapy group that had met on the unit for several years was led by a psychodynamically oriented therapist who claimed to use an eclectic approach. Staff reported that he attempted to have members change inappropriate social behaviors by gaining insight into childhood roots of present problematic behaviors. Staff reported having had difficulty getting members to attend the group and expressed some puzzlement as to whether members' resistances were due to the inherently threatening nature of group therapy or to the particular methods of the therapist. When the new therapist had interviewed for the position, the unit administrator had expressed a wish that he would run a group that patients would "like better." The previous group met four times weekly for hour-long sessions. This time frame was also available for the new therapist's group. The group was open-ended, and membership changed on an almost daily basis. Generally, members entered the group immediately after admission to the unit.

The orientation of the new therapist was broadly psychodynamic.

**Analysis.** In this circumstance, the selection of an appropriate model would benefit not only the members of the group but also the unit at large. The therapist's demonstration of the value of a delimitation and concretization of goals would serve as an antidote to staff frustration and possibly provide an example for other modalities.

In selecting a model, the therapist can make a systematic decision by "walking through" the classes of variables that we have presented.[4] A good beginning point is the fixed features of the setting because these features are maximally constraining to the therapist. Although these fixed features are often global aspects of the setting, this is not invariably the case. For example, member tenure in the group is a highly specific setting feature and is frequently not under the therapist's control given that it is linked to length of hospitalization. In our analysis, we begin with the more global variables such as the philosophy of the institution, recognizing that some alternative order may be useful in other practitioners' settings.

In this example, because the practitioner's unit and possibly the institution embraced a holistic perspective, the therapist was minimally constrained in model selection philosophically. The caveat to this evaluation is that staff's escalating frustration and sense of helplessness in relation to the demand to operate within a strict temporal frame may precipitate their adoption of a radically different perspective. Hence, the therapist must recognize that the frustration of the staff creates an unstable climate that must be taken into account in both selecting the model and planning its presentation to the treatment team.

For this group, the embeddedness of the group on the unit was a major force in the group dynamics. In any setting, a group on a unit will be greatly affected by unit dynamics, events, issues and so on. In such a circumstance, the therapist must anticipate the likelihood that staff's shared dissatisfaction will probably be a particularly powerful presence in the group. The therapist must find a way to use this dissatisfaction to further members' well-

---

[4] Of course, the reader should also consider any additional variables that may be relevant to his or her setting.

being. As we have mentioned repeatedly, there are some models (e.g., the developmental and problem-solving models) that provide little opportunity for the group to deal with unit-level issues. Simply on the basis of the variables that have been considered, these models would not seem to be a good match for the practitioner's setting.

The temporal variables might be reviewed next. Because staff were responding strenuously to one particular temporal feature, the average length of stay, one could anticipate that this feature would play a major role in the selection of an appropriate model. Within this setting, members' tenures in the group were fairly brief. Of even greater import was the rather considerable segment of the admitted population that remained in the hospital for no more than two sessions. This brevity required that a single session be viewed as the length of the group. In other words, the therapist should not anticipate that members are able to transfer information from session to session. Moreover, the group should be designed so that each member can derive some benefit from each session. These considerations would raise questions about the feasibility of the cognitive–behavioral (with the exception of Freeman's theme-based cognitive–behavioral model), developmental, educative, and problem-solving models, all of which require that a member's tenure be at least several sessions.

Compositional variables are always important in model selection. Patients on this unit were fairly heterogenous in functioning. The therapist could deal with this heterogeneity in at least two ways. He could select a model such as the educative model that is conducive to the inclusion of members of radically different levels of functioning, or he could establish admission criteria for the group that would create greater homogeneity in functioning (e.g., the presence of a particular social skills deficit). These alternatives are not mutually exclusive. In a setting of this nature, a certain percentage of members probably would be so acutely disturbed that they would be unable to participate in any sort of group. The issue, then, is what degree of homogeneity of functioning is sought. One consideration in this regard is what other groups are present on the unit. For example, if there are activity therapy groups that have the earlier-cited characteristics of an effective group for low-functioning patients, then the therapist may wish to design a group serving the special needs of the higher functioning patients. The great diagnostic variability may render the use of the cognitive–behavioral model difficult, particularly in view of patients' typically brief hospitalizations.

From this analysis, three models emerge as being reasonably congruent with the features of the setting: the object relations/systems model and the interactional agenda and focus group versions of the interpersonal model. The interactional agenda group would be a possibility especially if the needs of the lower functioning members could be served by either a focus group or, as suggested earlier, an activities therapy group. However, an advantage of the object relations/systems model over the interactional agenda group is its ability to focus systematically on unit dynamics. In this case, staff's high level of frustration makes unit dynamics particularly important. As indicated in chapter 4, although the interactional agenda model can address individual member's idiosyncratic and maladaptive reactions to the unit, it has no mechanism to work with the reactions as the group-as-a-whole. The interactional agenda format could, of course, be modified to address group-as-a-whole phenomena, and there are some indications in the literature that some clinicians are making such modifications (Duncan & Kennedy, 1992).

The object relations/systems model would also be likely to have a salubrious effect on the unit as a system. Because the model operates on the group in its status as a subsystem of the unit, any change in organizational features or affective tone of the group is likely to permeate through the broader community. The object relations/systems model would also be compatible with this particular therapist's theoretical orientation.

In summary, in this example, we see some advantage in the object relations/systems model over the interactional agenda group primarily because of the emotional tenor of the unit. However, we see the interactional agenda approach as having a strength that the object relations/systems model lacks: face validity from a staff standpoint. In most institutions, the goals and methods of any interpersonal model are likely to be coherent to the staff. In contrast, the goals of the object relations/systems model are sometimes seen by staff as either elusive or counter-intuitive. The goals of this model are at odds with the common assumption of the staff that their efforts should be to help members overcome their proclivity for splitting. In view of the perceived (if not real) failure of the previous group and the biases in the staff that this failure created, if the therapist adopts an object relations/systems model, he must put great effort into staff education and the active nurturance of a pro-group climate.

## Case 2

**Description.** A private nonprofit psychiatric hospital had recently established a 16-bed geropsychiatry unit. The average length of stay was 26 days, although there were generally a few patients on the unit who remained for several months. Approximately 80% of the patients on the unit had a depressive diagnosis, whereas 20% were diagnosed as having some organic disorder. Members varied greatly in their levels of functioning, with some being quite verbal and insightful and others being unable to maintain orientation of person, place, and time.

On the unit, a medical model prevailed. The staff saw the patients' medication regimes as being the primary interventions. Other interventions were viewed as merely adjunctive. There were a variety of activities therapy and rehabilitation groups available to patients on the unit. However, staff felt that there were a handful of patients who appeared to have a capacity for, and interest in, discussing issues pertaining to family issues, aging, and death. Staff had some trepidation about the potential of group psychotherapy to stimulate the members' anxiety in an unproductive way. They sought a group format that would take into account both members' needs and limitations.

The designated therapist was a psychiatric resident with an uncertain theoretical orientation and no prior experience in conducting psychotherapy groups.

**Analysis.** This setting deviated in a variety of ways from that of the prior example. Although, as in the first case, the group was to take place on the unit, the ethos of the unit differed greatly in that a sense of therapeutic community had not been established. A consequence of this absence is that a model that emphasizes the exploration of unit dynamics (e.g., the object relations/systems model) would probably not fare well. At best, staff would see the group's focus on the interconnections between the group and the unit as irrelevant to members' needs. At worst, staff could find the orientation of the group as well as specific explorations (e.g., to staff behaviors that angered members) threatening to their sense of professional efficacy.

Another contextual difference between the first and second example is that in the second case, staff had a clearer view of what subpopulation of the unit they wanted the group to serve and what goals they saw as being appropriate for the group. The importance of the group therapist taking into account staff's expectations of the group has been noted repeatedly in this text and elsewhere (e.g., Leszcz, 1986). Consequently, assuming that the therapist perceived some value in staff's wishes for the group, he or she should incorporate these wishes into the model selection process. In the second example, the specific agenda of the treatment team was to provide members with a forum in which they could discuss age-related issues. In fact, the literature cited in chapter 2 supports this emphasis with the elderly. Approaches such as the developmental or interactional agenda may give the members too little latitude in exploring issues and relationships that they consider important. The social skills version of the behavioral model, with its emphasis on behavioral rather than experiential change, would also be at odds with staff's vision for the group. The focus group would be geared for a patient population other than the one staff wanted the group to serve.

The cognitive–behavioral, educative, and problem-solving models would enable members to focus on the issues that the staff saw as important and as unaddressed elsewhere. They also would use the group's potential to become a cohesively functioning unit. Each of these models has a specific profile of strengths and weaknesses in the setting. The high percentage of individuals with depression provided the opportunity for creating a symptomatically homogeneous group. This selection procedure would allow for the efficient application of a cognitive–behavioral model. However, such selection criteria may lead to the rejection of certain nondepressed patients whom the staff saw as appropriate for a psychotherapy group. More important, however, given their adherence to a medical model, there might be some resistance from staff to the notion that symptoms can be treated through psychological means.

The problem-solving group would necessitate the use of selection criteria guaranteeing that the members would be relatively homogeneous with respect to cognitive functioning. However, the variability in cognitive resources of patients may be so great that this demand may not be satisfied. The problem-solving model and to some extent the cognitive–behavioral model also have the potential limitation that their high level of structure may not give members sufficient opportunity to express and explore the affects associated with painful life issues.

The educative model would seem to have a number of advantages for this setting and population. By design, this model is eminently compatible with a medical model orientation because it seeks to treat not the symptoms but the sequelae of the symptoms. The educative model provides for a great deal of flexibility with respect to the focus of the group. A here-and-now focus could be titrated to the extent that members tolerate it and see it as relevant to their needs. It is adaptable to a wide variety of levels of functioning. Moreover, the highly supportive group atmosphere as well as insistence on respectful interactions among members would help to contain the anxiety that staff feared members would experience in being in a group. The only respect in which the model is not compatible with the features of the setting is the inexperience of the therapist.

## Case 3

**Description.** Seven state hospital patients had been identified as having, relative to many of the other patients, a high level of potential for community living. The targeted patients lived in five different units of the hospital, and most did not know one another. They were scheduled to be transferred to a home in the community where they would have a much lower level of supervision and a much greater opportunity to assume responsibility for their lives. For example, once in the group home, they would be expected to take public transportation daily to a sheltered workshop.

To ready them for this transition, a predischarge program was being designed. The program included a variety of activities geared toward helping these patients master the activities of daily living such as housekeeping, grocery shopping, and taking public transportation. Group therapy was also included in the program. The staff person assigned to lead the group had been given little direction on its expected goals or format. She was merely told to design an experience that would help members to remain in the community.

Although relative to the hospital population, these seven individuals functioned well, relative to the members of the community outside the hospital, they functioned poorly. All of them had difficulties with both activities for daily living and social relations. Some had not lived outside of an institution environment for 40 years. Others (typically the younger patients) had been in the hospital only several months. They were also relatively homogeneous from the standpoint of diagnosis: All of them had been diagnosed as having some chronic psychotic condition. They ranged in age from 28 to 70 years.

The psychotherapy group, like all of the other groups in the program, was scheduled to meet daily for 45-minute sessions.

The co-leaders for the group were a psychiatric nurse and a social worker, both of whom defined themselves as having an interpersonal orientation. Both leaders were experienced in running interpersonally oriented groups.

**Analysis.** In the model-selection process for this case, the compositional variables have an especially constraining role. The level of functioning of the members would preclude the use of a number of the models, especially the cognitive–behavioral, developmental, and interactional agenda models, which are designed for higher functioning members.

The context of the group would be incompatible with the use of the object relations/systems model because members were combined from many different units. Also, it could be questioned whether the conflict view of psychopathology on which this model is based is most appropriate for a group of individuals who have failed to evolve a defensive structure that would permit residency in the community for more than brief periods.

The educative, problem-solving, and social skills model have all been successfully applied with state hospital patients. However, these models must be evaluated from the perspective of their relative utility in preparing members for life in the community. Although the educative model can be applied with a low-functioning population, it is better suited for members who have experienced acute episodes and have some premorbid living skills to access. Only to a limited extent does it provide the necessary experience for the acquisition of these skills.

The problem-solving model would probably have much to offer this group of patients. Whereas other groups may prepare these patients for particular situations, the problem-solving model would equip them with the necessary cognitive processes to negotiate more effectively any social circumstance. Moreover, the fact that this group can meet essentially as a closed-ended group would further enhance application of this model. A potential obstacle to the use of this model would be the circumstance of a high level of heterogeneity in cognitive functioning among the members. A high level of variability on this dimension is certainly possible given the wide age and length of institutionalization ranges.

Another model that may have some utility for this group is the social skills version of the behavioral model. Unlike the problem-solving model, this model makes no demands on members for relative homogeneity in cognitive functioning. If fulfilled, the goal of the social skills model, to assist individuals in becoming more interpersonally competent, would certainly contribute to their survival in the community. The fact that the group could meet daily over a 3-week period would be an asset to the implementation of this model because a continuously meeting, stable group is necessary for creating a progressively more difficult series of tasks both inside and outside the group. However, the 3-week tenure of the group may not be sufficient to give members an opportunity to address the complex tasks that they are likely to encounter in the community. Yet, a group of this nature could be continued once members were placed in the group home. An advantage of this model is that the staff involved with the group home, even if they had little prior experience in conducting psychotherapy groups, could be taught the techniques of a behavioral group in a relatively brief period of time.

However, the social skill model also has an important constraint: All members must be reasonably homogeneous in their social functioning. For example, if five of the members have a great deal of trouble even initiating contact and two members can do so with ease, the latter two may find the group's necessarily protracted focus on offering salutations and practicing introductory questions somewhat tedious and potentially quite alienating.

The reader may recognize that the compositional constraints of both the problem-solving and social skills models may preclude both of them because it is likely that there is some connection between members' cognitive and social resources. For instance, the most cognitively limited individuals in the group would tend to be among the most socially inept. This does not mean that these models need to be eliminated from consideration. Rather, it requires that the therapist make some creative use of the variability to satisfy all members' needs. For example, to prevent the more cognitively or socially sophisticated members from becoming disenchanted with the group experience, the therapist might give them distinctive roles in the group that may even prepare them for performing valuable leadership functions within the home.

# A Final Note

It is an exciting time to practice inpatient group psychotherapy because the field has begun to embrace the realities of contemporary psychiatric inpatient practice. Many practitioners have come to accept the presence of certain features of inpatient hospitalization that once were seen as precluding any effective treatment. There is greater acceptance that cost containment and brief periods of hospitalization will continue to be with us and will crucially inform the work that we do. Also recognized is the probability that as the criteria for admission become more stringent and as other alternatives to hospitalization emerge, hospital clinicians will be confronted with more distressed and disturbed populations of patients. The seven models we have described and compared are the offspring of this acceptance. Because all of these models have features that take into account the realities and complexities of inpatient settings, they all offer the promise of effective application.

It is also an interesting time to practice inpatient group psychotherapy because of the changing attitude of the broader mental health community toward theoretical and methodological pluralism. Clinicians in all modalities are converging on a recognition that different approaches are a necessity given the diversity of problems that we face. As Lazarus, Beutler, and Norcross (1992) observed, "many clinicians have realized that one true path to formulating and treating problems does not exist—no single orientation has all the answers" (p. 11). This realization has replaced the contentious debates so common to a field in its infancy. In the past, this pluralism has been reflected in systems such as differential therapeutics (Frances, Clarkin, & Perry, 1984) and technical eclecticism (Beutler & Clarkin, 1990; Lazarus et al., 1992), which seek to provide guidelines for matching patients with specific treatments. Current attitudes toward pluralism give the inpatient group therapist the freedom to make an active decision about which model is best for the situation in which he or she practices. Although, as we have stressed, practitioners must be cognizant of the theoretical orientation of the other staff in the setting, inpatient group psychotherapists are no longer in the paradigmatic vise that they once were. Because the staff of most institutions have been affected by the very trend herein described, there exists more tolerance for and even excitement concerning new ideas and methods.

It is an auspicious time to practice inpatient group psychotherapy because there is an accumulating knowledge base to assist the therapists in making informed and systematic choices. We have observed a burgeoning of research on some of the classes of variables reviewed in this book. The current standard in the literature requiring proponents of a model to detail the goals and methods of their models in manuals that enable the comparative evaluation has contributed to the research effort to understand what works, with whom, and when (Dies, 1992).

All of these trends bode well for the future of inpatient group psychotherapy. In this book, we have attempted to augment even further the usefulness of inpatient group psychotherapy models by emphasizing the importance of considering the total system in which the psychotherapy group resides. We have argued that an effective model for an inpatient group is one that is compatible with rather than imposed on the surrounding setting. None of the models presented in this text is likely to be successfully applied in all inpatient settings; all of them depend on the presence of particular resources within a setting to activate their strengths. Certainly, there is still much to be learned about the interactions of different group treatments with different inpatient environments. It is our intention that this text serve as a catalyst to this line of investigation.

Indeed, with the theoretical developments of the past 15 years, the inpatient group psychotherapist is in a better position than ever to conduct groups that staff and patients alike will see as having an important role in the overall treatment package. Although the selection of an appropriate model will enable the therapist to work with a greater sense of efficacy, the real benefactor is the inpatient group member himself or herself. Given the level of distress and the enormity of stressors afflicting hospitalized patients, there is no clinical population more in need of competent treatment. It is our expectation and hope that this text will contribute to this effort.

# References

Agazarian, Y. (1992). Contemporary theories of group psychotherapy: A systems approach to the group-as-a-whole. *International Journal of Group Psychotherapy, 42,* 177–203.

Barr, M. A. (1986). Homogeneous groups with acutely psychotic schizophrenics. *Group, 10*(1), 7–12.

Bascue, L. (1978). Conceptual model for group therapy training. *International Journal of Group Psychotherapy, 28,* 445–452.

Beck, A. T. (1976). *Cognitive theory and the emotional disorder.* Madison, CT: International Universities Press.

Beck, A. T. (1991). Cognitive therapy: A 30-year retrospective. *American Psychologist, 46*(4), 368–375.

Bernfeld, G., Clark, L., & Parker, G. (1984). The process of adolescent group psychotherapy. *International Journal of Group Psychotherapy, 34*(1), 111–126.

Beutler, L. E., & Clarkin, J. R. (1990). *Systematic treatment selection: Toward targeted therapeutic interventions.* New York: Brunner/Mazel.

Beutler, L. E., Frank, M., Schieber, S. C., Calbert, S., & Gaines, J. (1984). Comparative effects of group psychotherapies in a short-term inpatient setting: An experience with deteriorating effects. *Psychiatry, 47,* 66–76.

Brabender, V. (1987). Vicissitudes of countertransference in inpatient group psychotherapy. *International Journal of Group Psychotherapy, 37*(4), 549–567.

Coché, E. (1987). Problem-solving training: A cognitive group therapy modality. In A. Freeman & V. Greenwood (Eds.), *Cognitive therapy: Applications in psychiatric and medical settings* (pp. 83–102). New York: Human Sciences Press.

Coché, E., & Flick, A. (1975). Problem-solving training groups for hospitalized psychiatric patients. *Journal of Psychology, 91,* 19–29.

Dies, R. R. (1983). Leadership in short-term groups. In R. R. Dies & K. R. MacKenzie (Eds.), *Advances in group psychotherapy: Integration research and practice* (pp. 27–78). Madison, CT: International Universities Press.

Dies, R. (1992). *The future of group therapy.* Psychotherapy, 29(1), 58–64.

Duncan J., & Kennedy, S. H. (1992). Inpatient group treatment. In H. Harper-Giuffre & R. R. MacKenzie (Eds.), *Group therapy for eating disorders* (pp. 149–160) Washington, DC: American Psychiatric Press.

Edelstein, B. A., Couture, E., Cray, M., Dickens, P., & Lusebrink, N. (1980). Group training of problem solving with psychiatric patients. In D. Upper & S. M. Ross (Eds.), *Behavioral group therapy: An annual review* (pp. 85–102). Champaign, IL: Research Press.

Erickson, R. C. (1984). *Inpatient group psychotherapy: A pragmatic approach.* Springfield, IL: Charles C Thomas.

Erickson, R. C. (1986). Heterogeneous groups: A legitimate alternative. *Group, 10*(1), 21–26.

Fallon, A., & Brabender, V. (1992). *Trends in articles on inpatient group psychotherapy over twenty years.* Manuscript in preparation.

Feindler, E. L., Ecton, R. B., Kingsley, D., & Dubey, D. R. (1986). Group anger control training for institutionalized psychiatric male adolescents. *Behavior Therapy, 17,* 109–123.

Ferencik, B. M. (1991). A typology of the here-and-now: Issues in group therapy. *International Journal of Group Psychotherapy, 41*(2), 169–183.

Flowers, J. V. (1979). Behavioral analysis of group therapy and a model for behavioral group therapy. In D. Upper & S. M. Ross (Eds.), *Behavioral group therapy 1979: An annual review* (pp. 5–37). Champaign, IL: Research Press.

Frances, A., Clarkin, J., & Perry, S. (1984). *Differential therapeutics in psychiatry.* New York: Brunner/Mazel.

Froberg, W., & Slife, B. D. (1987). Overcoming obstacles to the implementation of Yalom's model of inpatient group psychotherapy. *International Journal of Group Psychotherapy, 37*(3), 371–388.

Ghuman, H. S., & Sarles, R. M. (1989). Three group psychotherapy settings with long-term adolescent inpatients: Advantages and disadvantages. *Psychiatric Hospital, 19*(4), 161–164.

Greene, L. R. (1988). Implications of object relations theory for research on group psychotherapy of borderline patients. In N. Slavinska-Holy (Ed.), *Borderline and narcissistic patients in therapy* (pp. 499–519). Madison, CT: International Universities Press.

Greene, L. R., Rosenkrantz, J., & Muth, D. Y. (1986). Borderline defenses and countertransference: Research findings and implications. *Psychiatry, 49*(3), 253–264.

Greenwood, V. B. (1987). Cognitive therapy with the young adult chronic patient. In A. Freeman & V. Greenwood (Eds.), *Cognitive therapy: Applications in psychiatric and medical settings* (pp. 103–110). New York: Human Sciences Press.

Grossman, R., & Freet, B. (1987). Cognitive approach to group with hospitalizatized adolescents. In A. Freeman & V. Greenwood (Eds.), *Cognitive therapy: Applications in psychiatric and medical settings* (pp. 132–151). New York: Human Sciences Press.

Hannah, S. (1984). Countertransference in in-patient group psychotherapy: Implications for technique. *International Journal of Group Psychotherapy, 34*(2), 257–272.

Hazel, J. S., Sherman, J. A., Schumaker, J. B., & Sheldon, J. (1985). Group skills training with adolescents: A critical review. In D. Upper & S. M. Ross (Eds.), *Handbook of behavioral group therapy* (pp. 203–246). New York: Plenum Press.

Kanas, N., Rogers, M., Kreth, E., Patterson, L., & Campbell, R. (1980). The effectiveness of group psychotherapy during the first three weeks of hospitalization: A controlled study. *Journal of Nervous and Mental Disease, 168*(8), 487–492.

Kaplan, A. S., Kerr, A., & Maddocks, S. E. (1992). Day hospital group treatment. In H. Harper-Giuffre & K. R. MacKenzie (Eds.), *Group psychotherapy for eating disorders* (pp. 161–179). Washington, DC: American Psychiatric Press.

Karterud, S. (1988). The influence of task definition, leadership and therapeutic style on inpatient group cultures. *International Journal of Therapeutic Communities, 9*(4), 231–247.

Kibel, H. D. (1986). Acute to long-term inpatient group psychotherapy. *Psychiatric Journal of the University of Ottawa, 11*(2), 58–61.

Kibel, H. D. (1987a). Contributions of the group psychotherapist to education on the psychiatric unit: Teaching through group dynamics. *International Journal of Group Psychotherapy, 37*(1), 3–29.

Kibel, H. D. (1987b). Inpatient group psychotherapy—Where treatment philosophies converge. In R. Langs (Ed.), *The yearbook of psychoanalysis and psychotherapy* (Vol. 2, pp. 94–116). New York: Gardner Press.

Kibel, H. D. (1992). Inpatient group psychotherapy. In A. Alonso & H. Swiller (Eds.), *Group therapy in clinical practice* (pp. 93–112). Washington, DC: American Psychiatric Press.

Klein, R. (1983). Group treatment approaches. In M. Hersen, A. Kazdin, & A. Bellack (Eds.), *The clinical psychology handbook* (pp. 593–610). New York: Pergamon Press.

Kohut, H. (1971). *The analysis of the self.* Madison, CT: International Universities Press.

Lazarus, A., Beutler, L. E., & Norcross, J. C. (1992). *The future of technical eclecticism. Psychotherapy, 29*(1), 11–20.

Leszcz, M. (1986). Inpatient groups. In A. J. Frances & R. E. Hales (Eds.), *American Psychiatric Press review of psychiatry* (Vol. 5, pp. 411–433). Washington, DC: American Psychiatric Press.

Lieberman, M. A., Yalom, I., & Miles, M. (1973). *Encounter groups: First facts.* New York: Basic Books.

Long, S. (1988). The six group therapies compared. In S. Long (Ed.), *Six group therapies* (pp. 327–338). New York: Plenum Press.

Lopez, M. A. (1980). Social skills training with institutionalized elderly: Effects of precounseling structuring and overlearning on skill acquisition and transfer. *Journal of Counseling Psychology, 27*(3), 286–293.

Massell, H. K., Corrigan, P. W., Liberman, R. P., & Milan, M. A. (1991). Conversation skills training of thought-disordered schizophrenic patients through attention focusing. *Psychiatric Research, 29,* 51–61.

Maxmen, J. S. (1978). An educative model for inpatient group therapy. *International Journal of Group Psychotherapy, 28,* 321–337.

Meichenbaum, D. (1977). *Cognitive behavior modification: An integrated approach.* New York: Plenum Press.

Meichenbaum, D., & Goodman, J. (1971). Training impulsive children to talk to themselves: A means of developing self-control. *Journal of Abnormal Psychology, 77,* 115–126.

Pattison, E. M., Brissenden, E., & Wohl, T. (1967). Assessing special effects of inpatient group psychotherapy. *International Journal of Group Psychotherapy, 17,* 283–297.

Rose, S. D. (1989). Working with adults in groups: Integrating cognitive–behavioral and small group strategies. San Francisco: Jossey-Bass.

Rutan, J. S. (1992). Psychodynamic group psychotherapy. *International Journal of Group Psychotherapy, 42*(1), 19–35.

Rutan, J. S., & Stone, W. N. (1984). *Psychodynamic group psychotherapy.* Lexington, MA: Heath.

Sank, L. I., & Shaffer, C. F. (1984). *A therapist's manual for cognitive behavior therapy in groups.* New York: Plenum Press.

Schopler, J. H., & Galinksy, M. J. (1990). Can open-ended groups move beyond beginnings? *Small Group Research, 21*(4), 435–449.

Setterberg, S. R. (1991). Inpatient child and adolescent therapy groups: Boundary maintenance and group function. *Group, 15*(2), 89–94.

Spivack, G., Platt, J. J., & Shure, M. B. (1976). *The problem-solving approach to adjustment.* San Francisco: Jossey-Bass.

Weiner, H. D. (1987). An innovative short-term group therapy model for inpatient addiction treatment. *Employee Assistance Quarterly, 2*(4), 27–30.

Yalom, I. D. (1983). *Inpatient group psychotherapy.* New York: Basic Books.

Yalom, I. D. (1985). *The theory and practice of group psychotherapy.* New York: Basic Books.

Yalom, I. D. (1990). *Understanding group psychotherapy: Process and practice* [Film]. Pacific Grove, CA: Brooks/Cole.

Yehoshua, R., Kellerman, P. F., Calev, A., & Dasberg, H. (1985). Group psychotherapy with inpatient chronic schizophrenics. *Israeli Journal of Psychiatry and Related Sciences, 22*(3), 185–190.

Zerhusen, J. D., Boyle, K., & Wilson, W. (1991). Out of the darkness: Group psychotherapy for depressed elderly. *Journal of Psychosocial Nursing, 29,* 16–21.

# Index

Acceptance, 341
Action orientation, 509
Active disputing, 416
Active listening, 351n.7
Activity levels, 87–88
Activity scheduling, 413
Addictions, 384, 385n.8
*See also* Alcohol abuse;
Substance abuse
Adolescents
cognitive–behavioral model
and, 339, 344–345, 352,
354, 356–357, 386, 391
developmental model and, 302
educative model and, 103
interpersonal model and, 169
model selection and, 45–48
object relations/systems
model and, 202, 234–235
problem-solving model and,
477
problem-solving skills and,
422n.3, 425
social skills training and, 577–
578, 583–584
Advice giving
developmental model and, 256
educative model and, 84, 90–
91, 99
Affect
behavioral model and, 516
developmental model and,
273, 277
educative model and, 59, 85
interpersonal model and, 124
models and, 630–631, 633,
636
object relations/systems
model and, 199, 631
use of term, 85
*See also* Negative affect

Affective disorders, 579
Affective expression
behavioral model and, 516
developmental model and,
273, 277
interpersonal model and, 159
models and, 630–631
object relations/systems
model and, 199
Affiliative skills, 528
Agazarian, Y., 266, 274
quoted, 251, 262
Age
cognitive–behavioral model
and, 344, 385n.8, 391
developmental model and, 313
educative model and, 103, 108
group composition and, 664–
665
interpersonal model and, 169
model selection and, 45–48
object relations/systems
model and, 234–235
problem-solving model and,
432, 475–476, 479–480
social skills training and, 530,
583–584, 593–594, 595
Agenda
cognitive–behavioral model
and, 350–351
interpersonal model and, 133–
134, 158–160
Agenda go-around, 133–134,
158–159
Aggression
developmental model and,
264–267, 274–275, 280–281
educative model and, 97, 100
models and, 676
object relations/systems
model and, 200, 206, 224–
226, 236

687

*Coping With Substance Abuse*
(Beck & Emery), 348, 359
Corrigan, P. W., 681
Corsini, R., 84, 152
Cost containment, 680
Co-therapy
cognitive–behavioral model
and, 342, 363, 365, 367,
370, 390, 394–398
developmental model and,
295, 313–314
educative model and, 104
interpersonal model and, 170
models and, 665, 668–669
model selection and, 49
object relations/systems
model and, 207–208, 226,
235–236
problem-solving model and,
437–438, 482, 490
social skills training and, 523–
524, 543, 555–557, 560,
565, 594–596
Countertransference
developmental model and,
273–274
object relations/systems
model and, 198, 207–208,
226
Couture, E., 660
Covert conditioning, 323
Covi, L., 342
Cray, M., 680
Critiques
of cognitive–behavioral model,
390–395, 399
of developmental model, 307–
309, 314–315
of interpersonal model, 160–
166
of object relations/systems
model, 227–230, 236–237
of problem-solving model,
481–486
of social skills training, 585–
590, 595–596

Crouch, E., 152
Crystallization, 279, 285, 298
Cultural background, 21–22
Cureton, E. E., 93

Dacey, C., 29
Dartmouth–Hitchcock Medical
Center, 58
Dasberg, H., 150
Davison, G., 430
Death, fear of, 47
De-catastrophizing, 417
Decision making, problem-
solving model and, 448–449
*Decoding*, use of term, 206n.8
Decompensation, 184
Defense mechanisms
object relations/systems
model and, 195–198
object relations theory and,
181–182
Deficit models, 634–638, 648–
649
DeJong, R., 386
Dependency–power orientation,
246
Depression
cognitive–behavioral model
and, 325, 332, 337, 343–
345, 384, 387
educative model and, 67
interpersonal model and, 155
model selection and, 39
object relations/systems
model and, 233
problem-solving model and,
431, 472–473
Deri, J., 304
DeRisi, W. J., 513n.4
Desmond, R. E., 95
Developmental approach,
interpersonal model and,
164
Developmental model, 14
clinical mission and, 309–310
clinical vignette of, 287–299

# About the Authors

VIRGINIA BRABENDER, PhD, is director of Internship Training at the Institute for Graduate Clinical Psychology of Widener University and directs a concentration in group psychotherapy. She was formerly a senior staff psychologist at Friends Hospital. She holds a diplomate in clinical psychology (ABPP). Her scholarly interests include group psychotherapy, personality assessment, and graduate training in clinical psychology.

APRIL FALLON, PhD, is associate director of Outpatient Services and director of the Group Therapy Training Program in the Department of Psychiatry at the Medical College of Pennsylvania. Previously, she was director of the psychological testing services. Her scholarly interests include group psychotherapy, personality assessment, and eating disorders.

(665)

cf. p 648-9 and my edn Sacral Xoy paper